Data Structures Featuring C++:
A Programmer's Perspective

Data Structures Featuring C++:
A Programmer's Perspective

SRIDHAR RADHAKRISHNAN
University of Oklahoma

LEE WISE
MSCI, Inc.

CHANDRA N. SEKHARAN
Loyola University at Chicago

PUBLISHER	SRR, LLC
EDITORIAL ASSISTANT	Sridhar Radhakrishnan and Lee Wise
SENIOR PRODUCTION EDITOR	Sundar
COVER DESIGNER	Jack E. Bailey (bailey.jack.e@gmail.com)
TEXT DESIGNED	Medlar Publishing Solutions, INDIA

This book was set in Bembo 11/14 by the author using word document and then converted to Adobe InDesign. It is printed and bound by createspace, an Amazon company, USA.

ISBN: 978-0-9890959-0-7

Printed in the United States of America

10 9 8 7 6 5 4 3 2 1

To my father S. R. Radhakrishnan and mother Dr. Kamala Radhakrishnan
Sridhar Radhakrishnan

To James, Rosemary, and Verena Wise
Lee Wise

To my wife Mathangi and my dedicated collaborator Sridhar Radhakrishnan
Chandra N. Sekharan

Contents

Preface

Welcome to the first edition of *Data Structures Featuring C++: A Programmer's Perspective*. In contemporary undergraduate computer science curricula, the study of data structures is usually introduced in the second course for the majors. The study forms the core knowledge upon which several subsequent courses are built. The field of data structures has its origins in the early days of the field of computing and closely tied to the design, and development of algorithms for various problems.

Data structures, as the name suggests, relates to organizing information in a structured way. Structured data offers many advantages over unstructured data, the most important of which, is the ability to access with ease select portions of the data. Enormous amounts of data are collected everyday for personal and commercial uses. Commercial data have grown to truly astronomical sizes, due mainly to the explosion in the Web. Several search engines host data in tera-byte sizes; banks, insurance companies, large e-commerce enterprises, and airlines are no exception. Weather modeling and satellite imagery take the storage needs up to petabytes and more. The need for structuring data in these application contexts is especially critical owing to performance issues. There are essentially two performance benchmarks of data, size of storage needed and time taken to access data. The price of storage has fallen dramatically and hence size of storage needed is less of an issue when compared to cost of accessing. In fact, it can be argued that inexpensive storage has caused a meteoric rise in usage and hence has precipitated in an even greater need to improve efficiency of access. This motivates the necessity to cover data structures from both perspectives. Besides the benchmarks, the development of data structures needs to be done in conformance with standard practices in software development for ease of maintenance. Certainly, object-oriented framework is central to software development. Hence this book is written with the troika of conceptual ideas, namely, storage size, access time, and object-orientation.

Both ACM and IEEE curricula in computer science have advocated freshman courses in college to consist of principles of programming and data structures. Commonly referred to as CS1, and CS2, the first course CS1, introduces programming and the second CS2, data structures. Although, data structures can be taught without adhering to any specific programming language syntax, the common practice of using programming languages and associated tools, in vogue, is well justified. Objected-oriented design has become the paradigm of choice in software engineering and complex data structures, their implementation, and access algorithms are best elucidated in the object-oriented framework.

About the Book

This is a book for students and instructors who love programming in object-oriented style. The authors understand how to write object-oriented code and how to explain it to students. The strength of the book comes from the single-minded focus that we have had throughout the writing of it, on explaining the code thoroughly and consistently. Normally, books on data structures and software in general, do an excellent job explaining the algorithm but somehow fail to follow up the rigor of the algorithm with the clarity of the code resulting from it. It is almost as if the designers wave a wand and utter the magic words "abracadabra" and the code jumps out. We have consciously made an effort to connect the linkages that exist naturally between different phases of data structures design, and implementation. The second, perhaps more important, development is the use of STL or Standard Template Library in some texts. Experience professors who teach data structures are pretty evenly split between teaching data structures by designing them ground up and teaching data structures using STL. Each approach has its merits and demerits. Our book, while adhering to designing most data structures from the scratch also employs STL for those who want to follow this approach. We believe this balance is much needed.

Complex data structures are best explained in object-oriented style. Object-oriented design is language independent but its implementation benefits from a language that is designed as object-oriented from the scratch. The popular object-oriented languages that are in vogue today include C++, Java, C#, and Smalltalk. Although many books do use C++ or Java as the programming language of implementation, in our opinion, they do not fully take advantage of the object-oriented features available in the languages but instead simply translate the code from C or Pascal. The techniques we have used have been explained thoroughly and used consistently in the textbook.

To facilitate an understanding of our approach to implementing data structures, we have used a pattern containing the following salient characteristics:

- Defining a data structure as an **abstract data type**;

- Providing type information about data that will be stored in the structure; we have used **templates** for all data that is stored in the data structures,

- determine what errors will require **exceptions** to be thrown and write the exception class hierarchy;

- write an **abstract base class** for the data structure so that we could implement it more than one way, if necessary;

- determine the fields required in the C++ class and write the **constructors** to initialize those fields and **destructors** to dispose of them;

- write **accessor** methods to allow the user to examine the fields;

- write **insertion** and **deletion** methods (and other methods if necessary);

- design an **Enumeration** class for the data structure;

- write an **ostream** << method;

- write a **test method** for the class, which can be called from a *main()* function.

In addition, the text provides a suite of STL methods to illustrate a complementary approach.

Complete coverage of many data structures with complete implementation

We have designed and implemented many data structures. We also employ STL for the sake of completeness and broader coverage. We have developed the implementation of each data structure systematically and explained the development of code consistently. One can consider this book to be even alternatively titled as "*Data Structures Featuring C++: Code Explained.*" In our teaching experience (a combined 45 years), students are better learners of programming when provided with code for reading and testing. Many current textbooks on data structures fall short of this goal.

Professional Code Designed and Tested

The code that is explained in the textbook has been written to professional standards and tested thoroughly. It has been used at the authors' host institutions for 20 consecutive terms. The textual material has been honed to professional grade based on reviews and comments from hundreds of students. Copies of the code can be obtained by sending a email with appropriate return address and date of book purchase to *dataplusplus@gmail.com*.

Object-Oriented Programming

Apart from learning data structures, algorithmic issues related to data structures and construction of data structures in an object-oriented manner, we believe that students will gain knowledge in object oriented design and programming. Many advanced C++ features have been introduced in a simple and lucid manner in our textbook. We believe that readers will gain significant knowledge in object-oriented programming.

Teaching Supplements

Complete Microsoft PowerPoint slides are available for all the chapters. These PowerPoint slides are in color with animation to show the actions of various data structures. The slides are linked to the C++ source code for the instructor to click and show the execution of the actual code. This book has the benefit of feedback from many of the over 1000 students at the authors' institutions who have used the contents of the text.

Programming Projects

For course instructors we will make available 8 semesters of programming projects descriptions. Each semester we have provided 5 projects with increasing complexity of programming. These are provided as a set because in some semesters a project may involve building additional functionality based on a previous project.

Suggestions

We would forever grateful for your suggestions and bug reports. For all improvements and bug reports please send your correspondence to profsradhakrishnan@gmail.com.

Acknowledgements

Countless number of individuals have contributed to make this textbook a reality. To our students we are very appreciative for their patience especially during the initial development stages. Over 40 university professors have reviewed this textbook and I would like to thank everyone of them for their detailed comments, corrections, and suggestions.

About the Authors

Sridhar Radhakrishnan is a Professor in the School of Computer Science at The University of Oklahoma, Norman, Oklahoma since the Fall of 1990. Prior to joining The University of Oklahoma, he completed his PhD degree in Computer Science from Louisiana State University, Baton Rouge, Louisiana. He has been teaching the Sophomore level course in Data Structures for many years that resulted in the creation of this textbook. He has published widely and his publications appear in numerous IEEE publications and other professional conferences and journals.

Lee Wise has been a software architect and analytics developer for MSCI, Inc., and a predecessor company, RiskMetrics Group, Inc., since 1998. Her particular project, written in C++, has grown from the work of a single programmer to the work of dozens spread across the planet, and from a monolithic program running on a single box to distributed applications running on thousands of cores, handling terabytes of data and processing millions of complex queries per day.

Chandra N. Sekharan is a Professor in the Department of Computer Science, Loyola University Chicago. Prior to joining Loyola University Chicago in 1993, he was with the Center for Parallel Computation, Department of Computer Science at University of Central Florida, Orlando. He completed his PhD degree in Mathematical Sciences at Clemson University under the supervision of Stephen Hedetniemi. Professor Sekharan has taught many courses in computer science at both undergraduate and graduate levels. His recent focus in teaching has been on introducing concepts of parallel computing in the CS2 course at Loyola. He has published in IEEE and ACM conferences extensively in the areas of parallel computation, graph algorithms and mobile networking.

1 Introduction to Object-Oriented Programming in C++

COMPUTER HARDWARE IS getting more complex with every passing year and yet it has become, and remains, highly reliable. A modern desktop computer is several thousand times as powerful (in terms of processing speed) as the first computer, ENIAC, yet it is considerably more reliable, requiring little repair or maintenance. A serious error in widely used hardware, such as the Pentium bug, is so remarkable as to be a cause for national headlines.

Computer software is also getting more complex with every passing year, but it has never been, and is not now, as reliable as hardware. The fact that a major software package is buggy may make the news, but the specific bugs do not make the news, for the simple reason that there are too many bugs to describe. Users of major software packages are forced to tolerate bugs, lockups, and crashes, which may occur even after the package has been in use, and repeatedly patched and upgraded, for years. Why is a major software package so much less reliable than the hardware on which it runs?

The problem is that a major software package is extraordinarily complex; indeed, it is claimed, "Software applications, for their size, are the most complex entities that humans build" [Riel 96]. Major software packages are not merely so complex as to be *difficult* for any single human being to understand in full; many of them are so complex as to be *impossible* for any single human being to understand. They require the joint efforts of a team of programmers, even though no single human being can fully understand the program to be coordinated. Worse yet, while a hardware design like a memory chip can often be used in many devices, so that extensive work on testing and perfecting the design is cost-effective, a software design often seems so specialized as to defy reuse anywhere else, tempting programmers to skimp on the extensive work which may be required to make the design truly reliable and, of course, the complexity of the design may make it difficult even to determine what needs to be tested.

Various styles of programming and language constructs have been developed to make the writing of software less complex, and therefore the software itself more reliable, so that it might at least approach the reliability of the hardware on which it runs. Structured programming which was one of these programming styles, and which the reader may already have encountered works well for many "medium-sized" projects. Unfortunately, with structured programming it is the responsibility of the programmer to keep track of every variable, and to see to it that there are no unfortunate interactions among variables. Keeping track of a large number of details in mind is like juggling a large number of balls in the air. A good juggler can keep several balls in the air at one time; a great juggler can keep even more. But, no matter how good the juggler, if more and more balls are added, eventually the juggler will start dropping balls.

Computers have grown ever more powerful and users have demanded ever more "user-friendly" software, so there are ever more details to keep in mind. Like overloaded jugglers, programmers begin dropping details and unreliable software results. Structured programming is not sufficient for more complex projects. Object-oriented programming is one of the tools developed to combat the complexity of projects too large for structured programming. In the object-oriented programming style, some of the details are "off-loaded" to specialized code (objects) which can be relied upon to keep them straight, as if the overloaded juggler were allowed to toss some of the extra balls into baskets, or perhaps toss them to another juggler, thereby keeping them off the floor.

1.1   Object-Oriented Programming

Object-oriented programming is based on "objects". The fundamental idea of object-oriented programming is that one should model software systems as collections of cooperating objects. [Booch 94] Each object belongs to a class of similar objects. The term "class" refers to the type of object, while the term "object" refers to an instance (that is, a particular case) of that class. All instances of a particular class will exhibit the same behavior, because their class defines that behavior.

The idea of a system composed of collections of cooperating objects is, in a sense, quite natural, for we live in the midst of such systems. When we wish to converse with someone across the country, for instance, we pick up a telephone, which is an object belonging to the class "telephone," all instances of which can be relied upon to exhibit certain behavior such as giving a dial tone, allowing entry of a number, transmitting a voice, responding to an attempted call, and so on. When the telephone is dialed, it sends the requested number to a telephone company, which is an instance of the class of "telephone company," all of which exhibit the same behavior of trying to locate and contact the requested number, giving an error message or busy signal in case of failure to connect. The telephone and the telephone company cooperate in attempting to put through the call.

In programming terms, an object is a conceptual package that contains data and code relating to that data, or, put another way, an object represents data bundled together in a syntactic unit with the code that operates on the data. Programs written in the object-oriented programming style are organized around the interactions of objects, which maintain their own data, rather than around functions that operate on data, as is the case in non-object-oriented programs. Because objects are self-contained, that is, they take responsibility for their own data and do not allow changes to that data except according to a specified interface; the programmer can disregard the details of a well-designed object and simply rely on it to work properly. This reduces the number of details, which the programmer must juggle at any given time, and therefore improves the chance of producing reliable software.

Object-oriented programming has a vocabulary that differs somewhat from the non-object-oriented programming vocabulary. Each object belongs to a class. The object has fields or members (corresponding to variables) that hold its data and methods defined by the class, which specify its behavior. Methods are canned snippets code that can be executed by appropriate invocation (called by various names in various languages, such as "functions" in C++ and C, or "functions" and "procedures" in Pascal, and "subroutines" in FORTRAN). A method is part of a class whereas subroutines exist outside of classes. Each object is referred to as an "instance" of its class. Instances of the same class may differ in the data which they contain, and may act differently because of the differences in data, but they share the underlying behavior relating to their data since that behavior is specified by the class to which they belong.

The development of a software system using the object-oriented programming style, therefore, involves identifying the objects that occur in the system, determining the data that they must maintain, modeling their behavior, and then modeling their cooperation. This is in opposition, in some ways, to the structured programming style of developing a software system by identifying a series of tasks to be carried out, then breaking them down into smaller and smaller subtasks until the smallest subtasks can be directly implemented in code.

Structured programming does still have its place in object-oriented programming; the behavior of the object is modeled using code, which may be developed using structured programming techniques. However, the overall focus of object-oriented programming is on the objects rather than on the tasks and subtasks.

Some of the goals of object-oriented programming are to isolate sections of code from one another as much as possible, so that errors and bugs can be (relatively) easily located and so that errors and bugs in one section will not propagate to others; to allow and encourage reuse of code, so that it is worthwhile to invest the time necessary to fully test and debug the code; and to simplify the programmer's task and reduce the memory load, or the burden of remembering all the various details of different parts of the program. To achieve these goals, object-oriented programming uses the following concepts:

Encapsulation

Inheritance

Polymorphism

These three important concepts are described below. All of them can be used, with varying degrees of difficulty, in non-object-oriented programming languages. The difference between object-oriented and non-object-oriented languages is that object-oriented languages make their use easy and natural by providing compiler support for their use.

1.1.1   Encapsulation

One of the main concepts of object-oriented programming is encapsulation (also called information hiding): information relating to an object is kept within it and accessed only by specific methods written for that purpose. That is, the data is *encapsulated* within the object and, as much as possible, communication among objects is restricted to a well-defined interface that is separate from, and independent of, the implementation. It is important to note that information hiding does *not* mean that information is literally kept secret from others; it merely means that others cannot write code that relies on the "hidden" information, even if it is freely accessible for their perusal and even if the "other" is, in fact, the original writer of the "hidden" information.

The intent of encapsulation, or information hiding, is to allow others to access the data in an object by a specified and unchanging interface, not by knowledge of the (current) implementation. This allows the class to which the object belongs to change its implementation quite radically, if necessary, without disrupting those who use it.

Encapsulation is important even in "real life": an automobile, for instance, has a specified and unchanging interface. There is always a steering wheel, turning the steering wheel counterclockwise turns the automobile to the left, and turning the wheel clockwise turns the automobile to the right. There are always an accelerator and a brake, which have the same meaning in every automobile. It is not necessary for the driver to know anything about the actual "implementation" of an automobile in order to use it. The interface is the same for an automobile with the engine in front or in back, for an automobile with front wheel, rear wheel, or four-wheel drive, for an automobile with an internal combustion engine or an electric engine. Even a driver who knows the "implementation" of any automobile cannot use this information in order to bypass the "interface" so as to, for instance, cause the automobile to maneuver without the use of the steering wheel.

In the programming context, suppose that, in designing a program without using the object-oriented style, the programmer initially decides to keep certain values in an array, and writes reams of code which access these values through the array. Later, the programmer decides that these values could be more efficiently provided through a function that computes each value based on what was the index into the array. Now the programmer must go through all those reams of code and replace all references to the array with references to the function. 333Using the object-oriented style, on the other hand, the programmer could have encapsulated the values into an object and allowed access to the values *only* through a method of the object. In the initial design, the object could have stored the values in an array and the method could have returned a value from the array based on the index it was given. All of those reams of code would have called the method instead of accessing the array. When the programmer later decided to use a function to provide the values, the method within the object would change and not one line of code would have changed outside that object. Because the values were encapsulated within the object and all access was constrained to pass through the method (the interface of the object), the programmer could not use knowledge of the initial implementation anywhere else in the program, and therefore, when the implementation changed, no other part of the program had to change.

There are further advantages to encapsulation. If all accesses to certain data must pass through a specified interface, improper accesses (such as setting fields to illegal values, or setting only one of two fields which need to be coordinated) can be prevented. It is only necessary for the *object itself* to check each access; it is not necessary for every section of code that accesses the data to check that its actions are correct, and that all changes are made in a coordinated fashion.

The language C++ provides several flexible schemes to implement information hiding. Class members (fields and methods) can be defined to be *public*, *private*, or *protected*. Members defined as public are visible (that is, can be accessed) to everyone that operates the object; members declared private are truly encapsulated and hence not visible to the outside; and members declared protected are visible only to methods defined in the class and to methods in its subclasses. Also in C++ , a notion of *friend* is available, wherein an external class or method that is made a friend in a given class has access to all the private members of the class. This notion is not available in all object-oriented languages, and it is frowned upon in some circles as a violation of the notion of encapsulation. If an external class or method is declared as a friend of the class, then that friend has access to *every* member function or variable of every instance of the class, even if it was expected to need access to only one private function.

1.1.2   Inheritance

A second major concept of object-oriented programming is inheritance, which is a mechanism for allowing code reuse in a controlled and efficient manner.

Code reuse has always been recognized as desirable, but each new programming problem always seems to have its own particular quirks, which make prior code unusable as is and require tedious and error-prone modification of code. At the same time, there are commonalities among even the most disparate programs; the same sorting and searching algorithms keep reappearing, for instance.

Object-oriented programming attacks this problem by allowing the extension of classes: a class can be written to solve a generic problem, and then extended by a subclass to handle the quirks of a particular problem without changing the original code. Inheritance defines a "kind of" relationship between the class and the subclass, that is, any instance of the subclass is a "kind of" instance of the class.

We can see examples of inheritance in "real life." We have the class of automobile (See Figure 1.1), but there are numerous subclasses of automobiles, such as vans, sports car, pickup trucks, sedan, and so on. Each of these subclasses has the basic automobile interface, such as a steering wheel, accelerator, and brake, but they are used for different problems: sedans are a kind of automobile used for the problem of hauling up to about six people, station wagons are a kind of automobile used for the problem of hauling numerous people and property, and sports cars are a kind of automobile used for the problem of accumulating large numbers of speeding tickets.

It is also important to point out that a subclass can have more than one parent class. For example, today there are several cross-over automobiles that combine features from multiple traditional models such as sedan and pickup trucks. Such automobiles belong to the class that inherits properties of both a sedan and a pickup. This example illustrates the concept of *multiple inheritance*.

A subclass (also called a descendant class, derived class, or child class) inherits all the behavior of the class (also called a base class or parent class, or the superclass of the subclass), except those parts that it must modify to handle its particular problem. All of the methods of the base class are available to the derived class, and yet the derived class can add new behavior, which extends the parent's behavior. If the base class was properly implemented and thoroughly tested, so that it is known to be reliable, in theory only the (relatively few) modifications must be tested in order to ensure that the subclass is also reliable.

The base class and its subclasses form a hierarchy with the class at the top and the subclasses below. Furthermore, each of the subclasses may, themselves, be base classes for their own subclasses, and so on, to form as deep a hierarchy as may be necessary for a particular application.

It is important to distinguish between classes that inherit and the ones that use objects belonging to other classes. For example, in the world of geometry, the primitive structure is a Point that has two values in two dimensions and multiple values for higher dimensions. A Circle, Interval, or Polygon (see Figure 1.2) all contains Point objects. A Circle contains a Point object and a radius and can be thought of being a subclass of the class Point. A Cylinder class can now inherit from the Circle class and it contains the field height. A Point with a color attribute associated with it can inherit from the class Point and appropriately named as ColorPoint. This is illustrated in Figure 1.3. The Interval or Polygon object does not inherit from the Point class but rather uses it. Polygons which are more general than Interval objects contain a set of Point or Interval objects.

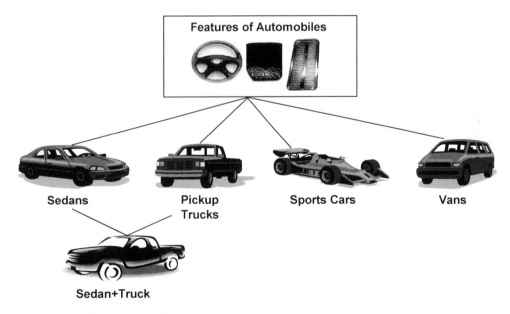

Figure 1.1: Illustration of inheritance and multiple inheritance.

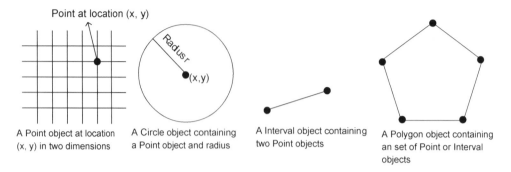

A Point object at location (x, y) in two dimensions

A Circle object containing a Point object and radius

A Interval object containing two Point objects

A Polygon object containing an set of Point or Interval objects

Figure 1.2: Point object and geometric structures that uses them

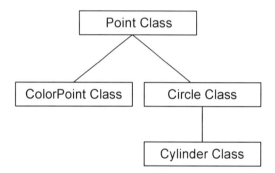

Figure 1.3: The Point class hierarchy

One may visualize another hierarchy as shown in Figure 1.4 where Shape is the base class (or parent class) and all the other geometric objects derive from the base class. As described above, all geometric objects can be thought of using Point class objects. The Point objects that form the geometric objects can be stored in the base class in an array data structure. For the Circle object, this array will contain one object, for the Interval object it will contain two Point objects, and so on. The Shape class can provide a common interface named *area* which is a method that determines the area of the geometric object. Of course, each geometric object will implement its own *area* method.

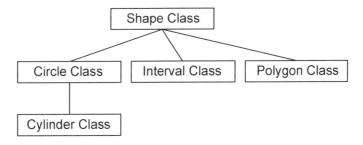

Figure 1.4: The Shape class hierarchy

1.1.3 Polymorphism

The term "polymorphism" literally means "capable of assuming many forms or shapes". In the context of programming languages, this means something similar. For example, consider the class "automobiles" and subclasses "sports car" and "station wagon." A driver behind the wheel of any automobile can depress the accelerator (invoking the "method" of accelerating) and expect the automobile to accelerate. If the automobile happens to be a sports car, it will accelerate very rapidly; if it happens to be a station wagon, it will do so more slowly. The different subclasses (sports car and station wagon) respond to the same method invocation differently.

Polymorphism is not, in fact, a new concept. In most programming languages, the programmer may write a function which calls for a floating point number as an argument, but the compiler will permit the function to be called with an integer as an argument instead, and will handle the argument properly even though it is an integer, because the compiler is aware that the integers are, in a sense, a subclass of the floating point numbers. This is polymorphism.

It is also possible in many languages for the programmer to write a function which accepts a pointer as an argument, identifies the type of the data pointed to, and then (using a *switch* statement in C, other statements in other languages) takes different action depending on the type of data pointed to. This, too, is polymorphism, but it obviously takes some careful programming and is "fragile," that is, if another type of data is needed, every such function must be individually modified to accommodate the new type.

The language C++ supports polymorphism in three ways: it allows the programmer more than one method with the same name but with different parameter lists; it allows methods to be specified for operators to provide semantic meaning for them; and it allows the programmer to specify *templates* for class members, class methods as well as for non-class functions. For example, if there is a need for two or more functions with identical behavior but differ only in their formal argument data type definition, then in C++ one can write a *function template*. A function template will tell the compiler how to generate an actual function by looking at the name of the function and the argument list of an invocation.

What is new in object-oriented programming languages is the ability of the programmer to create a hierarchy of classes which respond to method invocations in a polymorphic way, and the ability of the compiler to take responsibility for identifying the class of object involved in a method call and invoking the proper method for that class.

1.2   Encapsulation in C++

The *class* structure in C++ is the mechanism to provide encapsulation. Within a class in C++ fields or variables and class methods can be defined. The fields capture the state of the instantiated object, while the behavior is characterized by the methods defined in the class. As noted earlier, "information hiding" is provided in C++ by use of three different visibility characters of fields and methods, namely *private*, *protected*, and *public*.

Consider the following Point class:

```cpp
#include <iostream>
using namespace std;

class Point
{
private:
    double _x;
    double _y;
public:
    Point ();
    Point (double x, double y);
    void setX (double x);
    void setY (double y);
    double getX();
    double getY();
    void display ();
};
```

The fields _x and _y are not visible (that is, not accessible) outside of the class Point. For example, if myPoint is an object of the class Point, then myPoint._x = 10 is not a legal statement outside of methods of Point itself. In order to access the private fields, we have to have accessors and modifier methods that are visible. In the above class Point, the two methods Point () and Point (double _x, double _y) are the modifiers and the method display () is the accessor. These method definitions are provided below along with a main program that operates on these methods.

```
Point::Point ()
{
    _x = 0;
    _y = 0;
}
// ------------------------------------------------------------
Point::Point (double x, double y)
{
    _x = x;
    _y = y;
}
// ------------------------------------------------------------
void Point:: setX (double x)
{
    _x = x;
}
// ------------------------------------------------------------
void Point:: setY (double y)
{
    _y = y;
}
// ------------------------------------------------------------
double Point:: getX ()
{
    return _x;
}
// ------------------------------------------------------------
```

```
double Point:: getY ()
{
    return _Y;
}
// ------------------------------------------------------------
void Point::display ()
{
    cout << "x = " << _x << " y = " << _y << endl;
}
void main ()
{
    Point p1; // constructor with no arguments
    Point p2 (5, 10);
    p1.display ();
    p2.display ();
}
```

The output of the above main program is given below.

```
(5.5,6.6,3)
ColorPoint destructor. . .Destructor called on Point
```

The methods Point() and Point (double _x, double _y) are called *constructors*.

We have seen so far that a single class in C++ can be defined to hide information from external methods and also provide access to information through controlled methods as in the display() method. There are many instances wherein two or more cooperating objects need to access the private fields and methods of each other. This is made possible in C++ with help of a *friend* function or class.

A "friend function" of a class is a function which is entitled to access the non-public parts of the class as freely as the class itself. A friend of a class is, therefore, a very trusted friend, a friend who has been given the keys to the front door and invited to make it at home. Just as you do not freely hand out your front door keys, you should not freely give friend status to functions that use a class you are developing. Further, the friend functions, like any friends, should refrain from making themselves obnoxious; they should use the non-public parts of the class only when they must. Often friend functions will restrict themselves to using the values of non-public fields, and will refrain from altering them.

How do we declare that a function is a friend of another class? We place the function prototype inside the class declaration, preceded by the word "friend".

In the following code, we have included a method mycout() that prints the contents of _x and _y. Note that the mycout() method has access to all the fields and methods (including those defined as private) defined in the Point class.

```
#include <iostream>
using namespace std;

class Point
{
friend void mycout(Point myPoint);
private:
    double _x;
    double _y;
public:
    Point ();
    Point (double x, double y);
    void setX (double x);
    void setY (double y);
    double getX();
    double getY();
    void display ();
};
void mycout(Point myPoint)
{
    cout << "The values are _x = "<< myPoint._x << " _y = "
        << myPoint._y;
}
```

Similar to keeping a method as a friend in a class, C++ allows a class to be friend in another class. In this case, all the methods in the friend class have access to all the fields and methods of the class in which it is defined. As a friend of a class clearly has access to parts of the class that are intended to be encapsulated, creation of a friend is a violation of the principle of information hiding. In considering whether to make a function or class a friend of your class, you should first consider whether there is another way to accomplish your goals by asking the following questions. Does the information it needs to access truly need to be hidden, or could it be moved to the public section? Could you add a public method that supplies the needed information?

1.3   Inheritance in C++

The discussion so far has described how to define classes and we have seen, at least roughly, how to encapsulate data and behavior in objects in C++ . But encapsulation is only one of the concepts important to object-oriented programming. We will look closely at the second concept: inheritance.

To gain the benefits of inheritance, we need to declare subclasses. Unlike some languages, C++ does not presume a base class, the ultimate ancestor of all classes in the language. This is in some ways a disadvantage, and it forces us to take pains to add desired behavior to all classes we create. Of course, we are in no way prevented from deriving all of our own classes from a single class that we have created.

To declare that a class is a subclass of some class, we simply follow the class identifier with a colon, the word "public"[1], and the identifier for the superclass:

```
class ColorPoint : public Point
{
friend ostream& operator << (ostream& s, ColorPoint& p);
protected:
    int _color;
public:
    virtual ~ColorPoint ();
    void setColor (int color);
    int getColor();
    void display(ostream& s);
};
ColorPoint::~ColorPoint ()
{
    cout << "ColorPoint destructor. . .";
}
```

---

1 If we have to specify the word "public", it does not seem unlikely that we might have specified instead the word "protected" or "private". Indeed we could have, and the behavior of our class would have been a bit different. However, we are still resisting the impulse to complicate this introduction, so we will defer discussion of protected and private inheritance.

```
void ColorPoint:: setColor (int color)
{
    _color = color;
}
// -----------------------------------------------------
int ColorPoint:: getColor ()
{
    return _color;
}
// -----------------------------------------------------
ostream& operator << (ostream& s, ColorPoint& p)
{
    p.display(s);
    return s;
}
// -----------------------------------------------------
void ColorPoint::display(ostream& s)
{
    s << "(" << p.getX()<< ","<< p.getY()<< "," << p._color
      << ")";
}
// -----------------------------------------------------
void main ()
{
    ColorPoint colorPoint;
    colorPoint.setX (5.5);
    colorPoint.setY (6.6);
    colorPoint.setColor (3);
    cout << colorPoint << endl;

}
```

Here is the output from the program, which may be a bit surprising:

```
(5.5,6.6,3)
ColorPoint destructor. . .Destructor called on Point
```

There are several points to be noted about the ColorPoint subclass above, and the output when the program is compiled and run. First, ColorPoint is unable to directly access _x and _y because they are private fields of its superclass. Second, ColorPoint has its own field, _color, and methods. Third, not only was the colorPoint local variable destroyed and the destructor called (see Appendix A on destructors), but the parent class' destructor was *also* called automatically even though the ColorPoint destructor made no reference whatsoever to the Point destructor. C++ will, in fact, work its way all the way up the class hierarchy, calling the destructors every step of the way.

Every ColorPoint object is also a Point object. If we assign the ColorPoint object to a Point object (*upcasting*) then, only the values _x and _y from the ColorPoint object will be copied. This is known as *object slicing*.

In C++ "information hiding" is facilitated with the use of *protected* declaration of a field or method in a class. Fields and methods that are declared as being protected (say, in a class Point) are not visible to objects outside of the class Point and these are very similar to the ones defined as being private. The fundamental difference between private and protected then is that subclasses do not have access to the fields and methods defined as private in the parent class and the ones declared as protected are accessible in the subclasses. For example, in the class Point variables _x and _y are not accessible in the class colorPoint as they are declared as private. If they are declared as proteced, the colorPoint class can directly modify them.

The ostream operator has been declared as a friend of ColorPoint. This allows it to access the variable _color without the use of getColor() method. The display method has permission to access the variable _color since it is a member of the Color-Point class.

1.3.1   Constructors for Subclasses

The alert reader may have noticed that neither ColorPoint nor SubClass had a constructor. The writing of constructors for subclasses is a little trickier than that for stand-alone classes, but not drastically so. The constructor of the subclass must call the parent's constructor before it, itself, takes any action at all.

The "superclass parameters" are those required by the chosen superclass constructor.

For a specific example, let us give ColorPoint its own constructor, without making any other changes to either Point or ColorPoint:

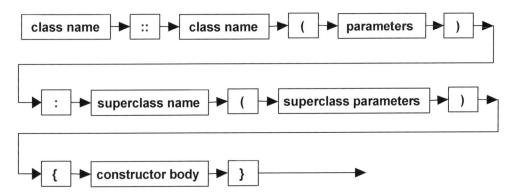

Figure 1.5:   Syntax for class constructor method definition that includes calls to the
                  superclass' constructor methods.

```
class ColorPoint : public Point
{
friend ostream& operator << (ostream& s, ColorPoint& p);
protected:
    int _color;
public:
    ColorPoint ();
    ColorPoint (double x, double y, int color);
    virtual ~ColorPoint ();
    int getColor ();
    void setColor (int color);
    void display(ostream& s);
};
// ---------------------------------------------------------
ColorPoint::ColorPoint () : Point ()
{
    _color = 0;
}
// ---------------------------------------------------------
ColorPoint::ColorPoint (double x, double y, int color) :
Point (x, y)
{
    _color = color;
}
```

```
// ----------------------------------------------------------
// other methods of class ColorPoint appear here, unchanged
// ----------------------------------------------------------
void main ()
{
    ColorPoint colorPoint (5.5, 6.6, 3);
    cout << colorPoint << endl;
}
```

The output from this program is shown below. At this point the reader should have little trouble explaining how the program actually functions:

```
(5.5,6.6,3)
ColorPoint destructor. . .Destructor called on Point
```

1.3.2   Abstract Classes

An abstract class is a class that can serve only as a parent class for other classes. No instance of the class can be created. To make a class abstract, we need only flag at least one method as "pure virtual". To accomplish this, we use a special syntax, adding "= NULL" to the declaration of a virtual method[2] and providing no implementation for that method:

```
class AbstractAutomobileClass
{
    virtual Brake() = NULL;
}
```

The class AbstractAutomobileClass is now abstract, no matter what other methods or fields it may contain, and any subclass of AbstractClass is also abstract unless the subclass overrides the *Brake()* method. The *Brake()* method is called "pure virtual" since it is nothing but a virtual method; it has no behavior at all. We will see, in the discussion of multiple inheritance, how useful abstract classes can be.

---

2 Often "= 0" is added instead. However, 0 is clearly an integer number, whereas NULL is related to pointers and methods. Thus, we prefer the "= NULL" usage instead. The two are identical to the compiler.

1.3.3 Multiple Inheritance

Inheritance ensures that a method which expects an argument which is a reference to class A will accept, and properly handle, an argument which is a reference to class A1, where A1 is a subclass of class A. But we might have a class B which is clearly separate and distinct from A, and cannot be either a superclass or a subclass of A. We also might want class B to have some behavior in common with A and also wish to have a method which will accept references to class A or class B or subclasses of either, but to no other class.

For a real-world example consider the relationship between cars and pickup trucks. Both cars and pickup trucks are vehicles. There are both diesel-powered and gasoline-powered cars, and both diesel-powered and gasoline-powered pickup trucks. Certainly diesel-powered cars are a special case of cars, and similarly diesel-powered pickup trucks are a special case of pickup trucks. So we can imagine a hierarchy of vehicles:

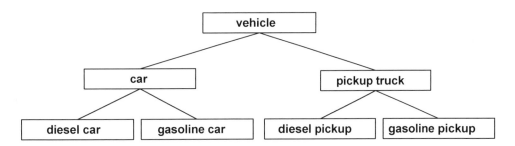

Figure 1.6: A vehicle hierarchy.

Diesel-powered cars and diesel-powered pickup trucks have particular requirements for fuel which they do not share with gasoline-powered vehicles. Although diesel-powered pickup trucks cannot possibly be considered either a subclass or a superclass of diesel-powered cars, nonetheless there are circumstances (such as a diesel pump at a gas station) where we would accept an instance of either of them, but not a gasoline-powered car.

How can we indicate that two distinct classes can be treated as related for some purposes, as the diesel-powered cars and trucks are related for purposes of refueling, but not for other purposes? In C++ , we can accomplish this by multiple inheritance: we have classes Car, PickupTruck, GasolinePowered, and DieselPowered. The class DieselPoweredCar is a subclass of both Car and DieselPowered:

```
class DieselPoweredCar : public Car, DieselPowered
{
}
```

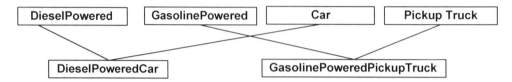

Figure 1.7:   Example of multiple inheritance in the automobile industry.

1.3.4   Diamond Inheritance

Suppose we have four classes, related in the following way: ClassA is the superclass of ClassB and ClassC. ClassD is a subclass of both Class B and Class C, using multiple inheritance. The situation is diagrammed below, showing the reason this situation is referred to as diamond inheritance.

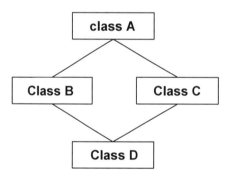

Figure 1.8:   Example for diamond inheritance.

An example of this inheritance is presented in Figure 1.1 where a sedan + truck (such as an El Camino) inherits both a sedan and a pickup truck and both of these have generic properties of automobiles such as a steering wheel, brake and accelerator. Further, suppose that we have a virtual method $m1()$ declared in ClassA and overridden (differently) in ClassB and ClassC. Now, if d is an instance ClassD, what behavior will $d.m1()$ exhibit, ClassB's version or ClassC's version?

The answer is that the compiler will be unable to decide resulting in a compile-time error requiring us to disambiguate the method call by indicating which we want. This makes multiple inheritance clearly different from single inheritance, where we need not know exactly where a method is implemented, in the subclass or the super-class.

In addition to the need to disambiguate method calls, diamond inheritance can cause problems with fields in the base class. If ClassA has a field named $f1$, then an instance of ClassB would have the same field, inherited from ClassA, as would an instance of ClassC. But what about an instance of ClassD? Does it have two instances of the field, one inherited from each parent? In fact it will, unless we take steps to avoid this result. Where any class is derived from an abstract class or classes, we can flag the derivation by placing the word "virtual" immediately before the word "public" that indicates the mode of inheritance – this flag indicates to the compiler that, in case of a diamond inheritance pattern, as above, ClassD will be considered as a descendant of ClassA. Our declarations of the class above might then look like this:

```
class ClassA
{
    int f1;
};
class ClassB : virtual public ClassA
{
};
class ClassC : virtual public ClassA
{
};
class ClassD : public ClassB, public ClassC
{
};
```

To avoid the diamond inheritance problem and others which result when the multiple parent classes of a given class have the same field or method names, we will greatly restrict the kind of class that we allow in multiple inheritance in this text. In particular, we will be interested in abstract classes and virtual inheritance.

1.3.5   Abstract Classes and Virtual Inheritance

An abstract class, as previously mentioned, is a class with at least one pure virtual function. We will require in this text that, in case of multiple inheritance:

♦   At most one of the parent classes will be non-abstract;

♦   Abstract classes will be "pure" abstract classes – they will have no fields or non-abstract methods, whether in their own code or in that of an ancestor class;

♦   Where any class is derived from an abstract class or classes, the derivation will be flagged by placing the word "virtual" immediately before the word "public" that indicates the mode of inheritance.

Thus the problem described above (ClassB and ClassC override ClassA's method differently) will not arise in this text since we allow neither two non-abstract classes in multiple inheritance nor any overridden methods in an abstract class.

We shall see throughout this text that this limited form of multiple inheritance actually allows us great flexibility in writing data structures.

1.4   Polymorphism in C++

We mentioned earlier that one of the mechanisms by which C++ provides polymorphism is through operator overloading. The simplest example of this can be found in the cout statement with the ostream "<<" operator. The operator can take strings as well as other system defined data types such as integers or expressions that result in system defined data types. We can say that the "<<" operator is overloaded or polymorphically applied. In the program below, the operator "<<" can take the string "Data Structures is" as well as an integer variable *i*.

```
#include <iostream>
using namespace std;

void main ()
{
    int i = 100;
    cout << "Data Structures is " << i << "% great!" << endl;
}
```

The output of the above programming segment is given below.

▨ `Data Structures is 100% great!`

In this subsection, we will discuss various approaches that C++ provides to implement polymorphism including operator and function overloading, polymorphism through pointers, and polymorphism using templates.

1.4.1 Overloaded Operators

Let us consider the Point class again. It would be nice to be able to add two instances of the Point class. For the time being, we will make _x and _y, the two fields, public again to simplify this discussion, but we will not change any other part of the class implementation previously presented:

```cpp
#include <iostream>
using namespace std;

class Point
{
friend ostream& operator << (ostream& s, Point& p);
public:
    double _x;
    double _y;
    Point ();
    Point (double x, double y);
    void display (ostream& s);
};
```

Now we will make a first cut at a function to add two Points. If for some reason we were writing a function to add two ints, we might produce a function that looked something like this:

```cpp
int add (int a, int b)
{
    int c;
    c = a + b;
    return c;
}
```

Using the above as a model, we will write a function which takes two Point instances as parameters, and returns a Point result:

```
Point add (Point a, Point b)
{
    Point c;
    c._x = a._x + b._x;
    c._y = a._y + b._y;
    return c;
}
```

For now, we will ask the reader to take it for granted that we *can* have Point as a return type, and that we can return c just as we could have returned an int variable. We test this function with a *main()* function:

```
void main ()
{
    Point p1 (1,2);
    Point p2 (3,4);
    Point p3;

    p3 = add (p1, p2);
    cout << p3 << endl;
}
```

The output from this function shows that p3 did receive the right value:

```
x = 4 y = 6
```

Our *add()* function did work correctly, but it is not really aesthetically pleasing. Wouldn't we really rather replace the *add(p1, p2)* call with the expression *p1 + p2*?

In many languages, our aesthetic displeasure would be irrelevant, since the + operator does not apply to the Point class and that is the end of the story. But in C++ we can overload the + operator just as we can overload a function name. Let us begin by simply renaming our function:

```
Point operator+ (Point a, Point b)
{
    Point c;
    c._x = a._x + b._x;
    c._y = a._y + b._y;
    return c;
```

```
    }
void main ()
{
    Point p1 (1,2);
    Point p2 (3,4);
    Point p3;
    p3 = operator+ (p1, p2);
    cout << p3 << endl;
}
```

Here we can see that "operator + " is a function name – a funny-looking name, to be sure, but a function name. The reader will probably object at this point that, even if the above compiles, runs, and produces the same output as the previous program with the *add()* function (which it does), it is even less aesthetically pleasing. That is a worthy objection, but operators are special. The compiler *knows* that we prefer to see a binary operator between its operands rather than before them as above, and so it will permit us to place the operator between the operands. We can now rewrite *main()* exactly as we desire:

```
void main ()
{
    Point p1 (1,2);
    Point p2 (3,4);
    Point p3;
    p3 = p1 + p2;
    cout << p3 << endl;
}
```

We have taken a step – a small step perhaps, but a definite step – toward making our Point class act like a primitive type. We could, in the same way, overload the –, $\star$, and / operators, and even the relational operators like <. However, we can do more: we can place the operator overloading inside of the class, so that it is not necessary to make _x and _y public.

All instance methods have the invisible parameter "*this*". Imagine that we simply change the name of the first parameter of our overloaded operator, producing the following code:

```
Point operator+ (Point this, Point b)
{
    Point c;
    c._x = this._x + b._x;
    c._y = this._y + b._y;
    return c;
}
```

Obviously a different name for the first parameter would not change the essence of this function, but the code above strongly suggests the correct way of writing our overloaded operator as a method: remove the first parameter and consider it to be replaced by the invisible *this*[3] parameter. Then our method looks like this:

```
Point Point::operator+ (Point b)
{
    Point c;
    c._x = _x + b._x;
    c._y = _y + b._y;
    return c;
}
```

We can now modify our Point class accordingly. Note that the method ~Point() is called a *destructor* and the role of a destructor will be discussed in the Appendix A. In the following code segment note that the variables _x and _y are declared as being protected instead of private as previously defined.

```
#include <iostream>
using namespace std;

class Point
{
friend ostream& operator << (ostream& s, Point& p);
protected:
    double _x;
    double _y;
```

---

3 The *this* operator is a pointer to the object itself. For example, in the code for operator + we could have replaced the statement c._x = _x + b._x; with c._x = (*this)._x + b._x;

```
public:
    Point ();
    Point (double x, double y);
    ~Point ();
    void display (ostream& s);
    Point operator+ (Point b);
};
```

However, the compiler still knows that we like our operators between the operands, and our *main()* function, above, will still work correctly.

Now, let us clean up our method a little. There is no particular reason to use pass-by-copy on *b*, and we can speed matters up somewhat by using pass-by-reference instead (this would be an important consideration if the Point class had more fields). So we can use this signature instead:

```
Point operator+ (const Point& b);
```

We must change the actual definition of the method as well, since the definition of the method and the declaration of the method in the class must agree in every detail. Next, we can make use of the constructor to set the fields of *c*:

```
Point Point::operator+ (const Point& b)
{
    Point c (_x + b._x, _y + b._y);
    return c;
}
```

Now, what use is *c*? We do not really need it, and could just use this code instead:

```
Point Point::operator+ (const Point& b)
{
    return Point (_x + b._x, _y + b._y);
}
```

The writing of other overloaded operators such as minus and multiplication by a constant for Point are left as an exercise for the reader. We will find overloaded operators extremely useful in implementing some of our data structures.

Left Shift << and cout

From the above discussion, we can now explain clearly the meaning of the statements we have been using involving *cout*:

```
cout << "Result: ";
```

The left shift << operator has been overloaded so that in this case, where the left operand is an ostream instance like *cout* and the right operand is a string of characters (we will explain strings more fully in Chapter 3), the string will be output by the ostream instance.

Now, let us consider this section of code:

```
int result = 10;
cout << "Result: " << result;
```

The << operator is a binary operator. What is the left operand of the << operator before "result"? The answer is that the left operand is the entire expression *cout << "Result: "*. The expression must have a type and, given that *result* is output, the expression must be of type ostream, just like *cout*. In fact, since *result* is output to the screen just like "Result: ", the value of the expression must be *cout* itself.

We can conclude, therefore, that the function which overloads << to output an instance of a given type must look something like this (we shall see below the meaning of a return type which is a reference to an instance of a type):

```
ostream& operator<< (ostream& s, type& var)
{
    s << var.anyField; (or you can call display(var) method)
    return s; // return the ostream we were given, for next <<
}
```

Let us try out our knowledge on our favorite class, Point:

```
ostream& operator << (ostream& s, Point& p)
{
    p.display(s);
    return s; // return the ostream we were given, for next <<
}
void display (ostream& s)
{
    s << "(" << _x << "," << _y << ")";
}
```

In the example above, we can modify our Point class to allow our overloaded <<
operator to access the non-public fields of the class:

```
class Point
{
friend ostream& operator << (ostream& s, Point& p);
protected:
    double _x;
    double _y;
public:
    Point ();
    Point (double x, double y);
    ~Point ();
    void display (ostream& s);
    Point operator+ (Point b);
};
```

It does not really matter where we put the friend declaration (even in the protected or public sections) since access modifiers in Point have no effect on a function
outside of Point. Thus, we can simply collect friend declarations together in one place,
and we have chosen to put them at the top.

Let us test our new function:

```
void main ()
{
 Point p (1, 2);
 cout << "The point is " << p << "." << endl;
}
```

The resulting output shows that our function works correctly:

```
The point is (1,2).
```

Writing a "friendly left-shift" method like this for a class allows us to treat it like
a primitive type by incorporating it into *cout* statements, and is highly recommended.

Assignment '=' operator

We clearly know that the assignment operator assigns the value in the right hand side
to the variable in the left hand side of the assignment statement. For example if x is an
integer in the statement $x = 2$, then the value of 2 is placed in the memory location

corresponding to the variable x. On the other hand, in the statement $x = y$, where y is an integer, the value in memory location corresponding to y is copied into the memory location that corresponds to x. We say this to be a "bit-by-bit" copy or sometimes refered to as a "shallow" copy.

Let us consider the following main program that uses the Point class.

```
void main ()
{
    Point p (1, 2);
    Point q (2, 3);

    cout << "The point p is " << p << "." << endl;
    cout << "The point q is " << q << "." << endl;

    q = p;
    cout << "The point q after bit-by-bit copy is " << q
        << "." << endl;
}
```

The output of the above main program is as follows:

```
The point p is (1,2).
The point q is (2,3).
The point q after bit-by-bit copy is (1,2).
```

In the above program, the assignment statement q = p performs a bit-by-it copy thereby resulting in the value of _x in q to be equal to 1 and the value of _y to be equal to 2. If we overload the assignment operator in the Point class, then during the execution of the assignment statement q = p, the overloaded operator method in the Point class would be invoked. The copying method that is done using an overloaded assignment operator is named as "deep" copy.

Consider again the assignment statement q = p, where q and p are point class objects. In order to implement the deep copy, we need to take the value of _x and _y in object p and copy them into the corresponding variables in the point object q. That is _x and _y of q should be equal to p._x and p._y, respectively. Unfortunately, we cannot apply the "." operator on _x and _y as they are protected fields. Let us assume that there are two public accessor methods getX() and getY() in the point class that return _x and _y, respectively. Now the code segement for the overloaded assignment operator in the point class will be as follows:

```
Point Point::operator= (const Point& b)
{
    _x = b.getX();
    _y = b.getY();
}
```

For the above Point class example, the shallow and deep copy has the same effect. Then why do we need a deep copy? To answer this we have to take a close look at how the field's _x and _y are defined. In the point class these fields are defined to have double data type. Assume that instead of defining them as double we define them to be a pointer to a double (like double★ _x, and double★ _y) and now both _x and _y will contain an address where the actual values are stored. Of course the constructors and all the methods of the point class have to be changed to take this into account. Now if we use a shallow copy, then the _x and _y values of the point object q will contain the addresses stored in _x and _y of p. This is depicted in Figure 1.4 and 1.5.

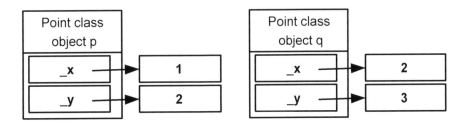

Figure 1.9:   Assuming that _x and _y values in the point class are defined as double★ (pointer to double), the above figure shows where the _x and _y are pointing to initially in objects p and q.

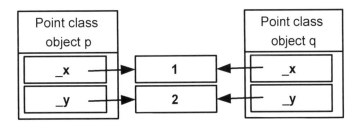

Figure 1.10:   After the shallow copy q's _x and _y point to the same location pointed by _x and _y, respectively of point object p.

After the shallow copy if object p changes the value of _x or _y, then consequently, the values of _x and _y for q will also be changed. Clearly, this is not the
desired effect and a deep copy is required. Consider that getX() and getY() return _x
and _y, respectively. Note that we have assumed for the purpose of illustrating the deep
copy that both _x and _y are defined as double★ (pointer to a double). Now the code
for the overloaded = operator is as follows:

```
Point Point::operator= (const Point& b)
{
    _x = new int(*(b.getX()));
    _y = new int(*(b.getX()));
}
```

In the above code ★(b.getX()) is the integer value stored at the pointer location
_x of point object b. The statement _x = new int(★(b.getX())) creates a new memory
location of type integer, initializes that with the value ★(b.getX()), and returns the
address of the new memory location which is stored in _x. This operation is called as
the deep copy. The location that pointed by _x before the assignment statement stays
in memory as garbarge which must be removed by using the delete operation discussed
appendix A.10.5. Code that takes into account garbage collection is presented below.

```
Point Point::operator= (const Point& b)
{
// assume that _x and _y are initialized to NULL in the
// default constructor
    If (_x != NULL) delete _x; _
    x = new int(*(b.getX()));
    if (_y!= NULL) delete _y;
    _y = new int(*(b.getX()));
}
```

1.4.2 Overloaded Functions

C++ identifies functions not merely by their names (identifiers) but also by their
parameters. That is, C++ regards these two functions as distinct and different, even if
they appear in the same file:

```
#include <iostream>
using namespace std;

void doSomething ()
{
    cout << "doSomething()" << endl;
}
// ------------------------------------------------------------
void doSomething (int withThis)
{
    cout << "doSomething(" << withThis << ")" << endl;
}
// ------------------------------------------------------------
void main ()
{
    doSomething(5);
    doSomething();
    doSomething(10);
}
```

The output for the above program segment is:

```
doSomething(5)
doSomething()
doSomething(10)
```

The reader may wish to experiment with the ordering of the functions in the above program to confirm that the *main()* function *must* appear last. The reason for this requirement of ordering is that, in effect, the compiler must know what "doSomething" means before it can use that word in its compilation. We shall see later how to relax this requirement, but for now we shall simply accept it.

When this program is compiled and run, we can see that the first *doSomething()* is called when there is nothing between the parentheses in the function call in the *main()* function, and the second is called when there is something between the parentheses.

So how does C++ know which *doSomething()* is invoked by a function call? It examines the parameter list of the call. If it can find a matching parameter list for a function by that name, it chooses that function. Otherwise, it fails and produces a compiler error. Thus, to make a function call, we give the name of the function and then a list of parameters which exactly matches, in order, number, and type, those in the function declaration.

Functions that have the same name but different parameter lists and belong to the same program are called as "overloaded" functions. The name and the parameter list together are called the "signature" of the function. Function overloading is usesful if a program has two or more functions with the same name and the actions of those functions are logically related.

1.4.3   Polymorphism Through Casting

A cast is an explicit type conversion which orders C++ to treat a variable of one type as being a variable of another type. There are several types of casts available. The simplest, most powerful, and most dangerous cast, the C-style cast, is written:

```
(target-type) variable
```

So if we want to treat an instance of ColorPoint (described above) as an instance of Point, and thus access Point's methods, we could cast it as follows:

```
ColorPoint myColorPoint;
((Point) myColorPoint).display();
```

As we can see in the example above, it is necessary to put the whole cast in parentheses in order to call methods of the target type, because of the precedence relations of the dot operator and the cast operator. If the variable is not, in fact, of the target type, or a subclass of the target type, C++ will probably cause a run-time error.

A safer way to cast in C++ is to use a dynamic_cast, which orders the compiler to check that the casting is safe during run time. The dynamic_cast is used for downcasting and is written as follows:

```
ColorPoint* myColorPtr = dynamic_cast<const ColorPoint* >
                            (myPointPtr);
if (myColorPtr == NULL)
    cout << "Invalid Casting" << endl;
else
    (*myColorPtr).display();
```

In the above program segement, if myPointPtr is an instance of ColorPoint, then the downcasting will not result in a NULL value; otherwise myColorPtr will be set to NULL. To determine the datatype of a variable or object belonging to a class, we can use the *typeid* function which is provided in the ANSI C++ specification. The following program segement illustrates this feature:

```
#include <iostream>
#include <typeinfo>
using namespace std;

//definitions of classes Point and ColorPoint go here

void main()
{
    ColorPoint* myColorPtr;
    Point myPoint;

    const char* dataType;

    dataType = typeid(myColorPtr).name();
    cout << dataType << endl;

    dataType = typeid(myPoint).name();
    cout << dataType << endl;
}
```

The output of the above program is given below:

```
class ColorPoint *
class Point
```

From the first line of the output we can see that myColorPtr is a pointer to ColorPoint.

1.4.4 Templates

One of our goals in writing data structures is to make them universally useful; we would not want data structures usable only with one specific type of data. But we have a little problem: normally we need to inform the compiler what type of local variables, parameters, and return values we intend to use for our methods and functions.

Parameterized Functions

For instance, a *swap()* function like this:

```
void swap (int& a, int& b)
{
    int temp;
    temp = a;
    a = b;
    b = temp;
}
```

The above method will swap the values of variables of type int, but it most certainly will not swap the values of instances of type Point, or even of variables of type double.

We don't really want to write a *swap()* function for each and every class we write and for each and every primitive type, especially since all of the *swap()* functions will be exactly the same except for the types of the two parameters and the local variable. Fortunately, the C++ language has a solution: allow the programmer to give the compiler a template (a pattern) for a *swap()* function, including type tokens for the types which need to be replaced, and enable the compiler to generate the correct swap function for each type of variable as needed. Giving the template for a function is very simple: precede the function with the reserved word *template* and a list of the type tokens to be used for the types, and then use the type tokens instead of the type names. In this case, we need only one type token, since there is only one type:

```
template <class Data>
void swap (Data& a, Data& b)
{
    Data temp;
    temp = a;
    a = b;
    b = temp;
}
```

The word "class" is simply required before the name of a type token in the template statement; it does not indicate that the type in question is in fact a class type rather than a primitive type. Most compilers would allow one to replace the word "class" in the template with "typename." We have chosen to use the word class since it indicates that we can use complex data types as well. With the above function, we can swap integers, doubles, or Points with equal ease:

```
void main ()
{
    int i = 1;
    int j = 2;
    double x = 10.0;
    double y = 20.0;
    Point p (2,4);
    Point q (3,6);
    swap (i, j);
    cout << "i = " << i << ", j = " << j << endl;
    swap (x, y);
    cout << "x = " << x << ", y = " << y << endl;
    swap (p,q);
    cout << "p = " << p << ", q = " << q << endl;
}
```

It should be noted that the compiler really does generate three separate *swap()* functions for the three different variable types. It should also be noted that no *swap()* function at all exists unless the compiler sees the need to generate one because of a function call like those above. Therefore, a function with a template (a parameterized function) should *not* be separately compiled (what is there to compile?) and should be placed in a header file. Furthermore, since some compilers have difficulty properly matching up prototype and implementation for a parameterized function, the prototype belongs in the same file with the function itself (which rather defeats the purpose of the prototype, in some ways). Our swap function therefore goes in a file named swap.h, which looks like this:

```
#ifndef __SWAP__H
#define __SWAP__H

template <class Data>
void swap (Data& a, Data& b);

template <class Data>
void swap (Data& a, Data& b)
{
    Data temp;
    temp = a;
    a = b;
    b = temp;
}

#endif
```

Statements that begin with a "#" sign are called compiler directives and will be covered later in Section 1.5.2. Assume that a user defined class, say Point is used as parameter to a templated method such as the swap method above. The "=" operator is applied on the parameter and this operator should in general be defined (overloaded) in the Point class. In general all operators applied on the parameters in the templated method should be overloaded in the class corresponding to the parameter.

Parameterized Classes

We can parameterize a class just as we can a function. For instance, suppose we wanted to allow the possibility of attaching some data to each Point instance, but did not know exactly what kind of data we wanted to attach in any given program (perhaps sometimes a string, other times a string of values like height, color, etc.). Then we could parameterize Point as follows:

```
template <class DataType>
class Point{
protected:
    double _x;
    double _y;
    DataType _data;
public:
    Point (double x, double y, const DataType& data);
// etc.
    DataType& data();
    friend ostream& operator<< <DataType>(ostream& s,
                                           const Point& p);
};
```

Now, every single method implementation must also be parameterized, since otherwise the compiler will not be able match up the template above with the implementations. The implementations look like this:

```
template <class DataType>
Point<DataType>::Point (double x, double y,
                        const DataType& data)
{
    _x = x;
    _y = y;
    _data = data;
}
// ----------------------------------------------------------
template <class DataType>
DataType& Point<DataType>::data()
{
    return _data;
}
// ----------------------------------------------------------
template <class DataType>
ostream& operator<< <DataType>(ostream& s,
                               const Point<DataType>& p) {
    s << "(" << p._x << "," << p._y << "," << p._data << ")";
    return s;
}
```

Note here that the "template <class DataType>" line precedes every method implementation and every friend function; also observe that every single use of the class name has "<DataType>" attached to it. The use of "<DataType>" informs the compiler as to which item is actually parameterized (the Point, not the ostream, in the operator<< implementation, for instance).

Each instance of the Point class must also be parameterized to show the type to which Data corresponds. Thus, if we want to attach a single int to each point, we might have a *main()* function like this:

```
void main ()
{
    Point<int> p (5.0, 10.0, 7);
    cout << p << endl;
}
```

Here the reader should note that the "<Data>" term in the class implementation is matched by the "<int>" term in the variable declaration. We could, of course, have parameterized Point with a much more complicated class. Parameterized classes will be used extensively in this text.

1.5 Exceptions

As previously noted, the reliability of programs is a great concern. One aspect of such reliability is that a program should not behave incorrectly or fail unexpectedly in response to an error. Errors, in this context, refer not only to hardware problems (missing drives), but also to software errors (dividing by zero) and input errors (the user inputs "rt" when asked to input a number). Achieving this aspect of reliability requires four conditions: (1) every error must be detected; (2) every error must be appropriately handled; (3) the "main line" of the program (followed when no error occurs) should not be completely obscured by error handling code; (4) vital actions (such as releasing system resources) must carried out even in the face of errors.

Ensuring that every error is detected is not as easy as one might suppose. Imagine, for instance, a subroutine that opens a file, reads in four characters from a specified position in the file, treats these four characters as a representation of an integer (e.g., "0010" is 10), and returns the integer. The "main line" of the subroutine is as follows:

```
1.  Open file by name.
2.  Seek to specified position.
3.  Read four characters into buffer.
4.  Parse buffer to get integer.
5.  Return integer.
```

Any of the first four steps might fail. If we add in all the error checking, the steps might look more like this:

```
1.   Try to open file by name.
2.   if fail to open file
3.   Give notice of missing file.
4.   else
5.       Try to seek to specified position.
6.       if fail to find position
7.           Give notice of error.
8.       else
9.           Try to read four characters into buffer.
10.          if fail to find four characters
11.              Give notice of error.
12.          else
13.              Try to parse buffer to get integer.
14.              if fail to parse buffer
15.              Give notice of bad format.
16.              else
17.              Return integer.
18.              endif
19.          endif
20.      endif
21. endif
```

Note that the steps that we expect to follow in the "normal" case are obscured by the error handling code, even though we have not specified what the error handling code will actually do. How should this function give notice of errors? It cannot give a valid result if the file is missing, or the four characters do not represent an integer; what should it return in these cases? Perhaps it returns an illegal value, such as a negative integer, but this requires the caller to test the returned value and, if the programmer forgets to test, the error will not be detected. Perhaps the function can set a flag indicating an error, but again this requires that the caller test the flag and, again, if the programmer forgets to test, the error will be missed.

Ensuring that an error is appropriately handled is another problem. What part of the program is responsible for the handling? Should it be the subroutine where the problem arose, or the caller of the subroutine, or the caller of the caller? Perhaps, in different parts of the program, the answer will differ, and, perhaps, different program-mers will have different opinions, with the result that the error is never handled at all. A language should have the flexibility to allow errors to be passed back up to a caller, if that is desirable, while still ensuring that every error is, in fact, handled by some part of the program and not overlooked by the programmer of the caller's caller's caller.

For purposes of maintenance and extension of code, it is important not to make a program difficult to read and understand (and therefore difficult to maintain) by inserting large sections devoted to error handling in the middle of the normal flow of execution that will be followed in the absence of errors.

Finally, there are actions that must be carried out even if an error has occurred. If system resources are seized, they must be released no matter what problems the program may have had.

C++ meets the problems of error handling by using exceptions. Briefly speaking, the occurrence of an error causes the program to "throw an exception." This exception must be handled (the program must "catch" the exception) somewhere before the main line of execution can be resumed. If the exception is not caught in the method where it occurs, that method will terminate and control will return to the caller. If the caller does not catch the exception, the caller too will terminate, and control will return to the caller's caller. This process repeats until the exception is caught or until the original main method terminates in which case the runtime environment itself catches the exception and handles it by printing a message and halting. Thus, an exception cannot be silently ignored, as in the example of an integer-valued function that returns a negative number in the event of error. On the other hand, exception handling can be separated, to some extent, from the code that gives rise to the exception, so that the normal flow of control is not obscured by error-handling code. Furthermore, the programmer can provide for some portions of code to be carried out even while an uncaught exception is pending.

An example of a program that has an error is the following:

```cpp
void main ()
{
    int i = 0;
    cout << "Before error" << endl;
    cout << (5/i) << endl;
    cout << "After error" << endl;
}
```

Not surprisingly, when this program is compiled and run, it causes an error and simply dies without outputting either the quotient or the "After error" message.

The statement to output the quotient was not executed, since the error caused the program to halt before execution of that statement. But all we have so far is a program that halts with an error, which we could have accomplished in almost any language. We will now modify our program so as to throw an exception and then catch it:

```
class ExceptionDivideByZero { };
// -----------------------------------------------------------
void main ()
{
    int i = 0;
    cout << "Before error" << endl;
    try
    {
        if (i == 0) throw ExceptionDivideByZero();
        cout << (5/i) << endl;
    }
    catch (ExceptionDivideByZero myException)
    //myException is an object belonging to
    //ExceptionDivideByZero class that was created when the
    //exception was thrown using the throw statement above.
    {
        cout << "Catch divide by zero" << endl;
    }
    cout << "After error" << endl;
}
```

When we compile and run this program, the output is:

```
Before error
Catch divide by zero
After error
```

This time the program did not halt when the error occurred; the code in the catch block was executed, and the final print statement was reached. Let's see what output we get if we change the value of *i* from 0 to 1:

```
Before error
5
After error
```

This time, the words "Catch section" were not output. The program skipped right over the catch block and went to the code which follows it. What is going on here? Why did we need the ExceptionDivideByZero class – especially since it has no fields or methods?

In C++ , any code may be placed inside a try block, followed by one or more catch blocks. Execution can flow through the block normally, as it did when we set *i* to 1. If we wish, however, we can throw an exception, using the reserved word throw, at which point control will leave the try block (regardless of how many statements remain to be executed in the try block), and falls immediately into the first catch block. The reserved word "catch" is followed by what amounts to a parameter list containing a single parameter. If the exception that was thrown matches the type of the parameter (or is a subclass of that type), then the catch block is entered and the code is executed; when the catch block terminates, control continues with the following statement. However, if the exception that was thrown does *not* match the type of the parameter, the catch block is not entered and the next catch block is checked.

Multiple catch blocks, each of which catches a different class of exceptions, may follow a try block. Thus, a whole section of code, where multiple exceptions may occur, can be enclosed in a single try block with multiple catch blocks, at most one of which will be executed (the first one which catches exceptions of a class which matches or is a superclass of the exception).

Thus, the syntax of a try block looks like this:

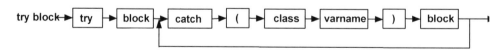

Figure 1.11: Syntax for try block for handling exceptions.

As noted above, catch blocks catch exceptions of the specified class or subclasses of the specified class. In fact, in C++ , a catch block can catch exceptions of any type, even primitive types, but in this text we will require exceptions to belong to a class. We can therefore see the purpose of the ExceptionDivideByZero class: it gives us a type for the throw statement. It has no methods or fields because it needs none; it exists only to match the parameter of a catch statement.

If an exception is not caught in the method where it occurs, the method returns to its caller, and execution proceeds as if the exception had been thrown in the caller. If it is not caught there, the caller also returns to its own caller and execution continues there until some catch block is able to catch the exception, or until the *main*() function returns in this way and the program dies.

(The reader may have reached the conclusion at this point that a programmer who fails to catch possible exceptions is rather remiss, perhaps even irresponsible. This is not always the case; sometimes there is no reasonable way for a method to handle an error except to let the caller deal with it. For instance, a method which opens a disk file for the caller certainly cannot decide whether, if the file is missing, the program should halt, prompt the user to insert a disk, try an alternate file, or any of a number of other possible actions.)

1.5.1   The Exception Class and Its Subclasses

We will create a very simple Exception class from which all exception classes in this text will be derived. The entire description of this class is as follows:

```
class Exception { };
```

In order to use this class in any program, we must inform the compiler of its existence, that is, we must include the above declaration in the program. We could then save this class in a file named Exception.h, which we can include in other files which have need of exceptions. Creating a new exception class is as simple as this:

```
#include "Exception.h"
class ExceptionDivideByZero : public Exception { };
```

We can save this class in a file called ExDiv0.h. But now we have a little problem: What if a single program includes *both* Exception.h and ExDiv0.h? Consider this program:

```
#include "Exception.h"
#include "ExDiv0.h"
void main ()
{
}
```

This program will not compile because it has a multiple declaration of the Exception class: from the point of view of the compiler, the class is declared once when Exception.h is included in the main file and again when Exception.h is included in ExDiv0.h, which is then included in the main file. Of course, we can avoid this problem by removing the

■   `#include "Exception.h"`

line, but we would prefer to persuade the compiler to handle the problem by itself. This brings us to a brief discussion of the pre-processor.

1.5.2   Pre-Processor Commands

A C++ compiler actually has two parts: the C++ compiler itself and the pre-processor. The C++ compiler does not actually operate on the source files as we have written them. Instead, it operates on a kind of "virtual" source file. The pre-processor reads special commands which start with the # sign and uses them to shape the virtual source file. It may remove parts of the source file, add other parts, and so on.

Since the command

■   `#include <iostream>`

starts with the # sign, one might guess that it is a pre-processor command, and one would be right. This command instructs the pre-processor to incorporate the entire text of iostream.h in the virtual source file exactly where the #include command appears.

In the case of Exception.h, we wish to include the text only once, no matter how many times the

■   `#include "Exception.h"`

command appears. To accomplish this, we will create a flag for the pre-processor in the Exception.h file. Creating a flag is simple; we need only give it a name satisfying the ordinary C++ rules for identifiers, like __EXCEPTION__H, and then define it as follows:

```
#define __EXCEPTION__H
class Exception { };
```

Before the #define line is encountered, the __EXCEPTION__H flag does not even exist. After the #define line is encountered, the flag does exist. So what we want is a way to test whether the flag exists, and exclude the above two statements if the flag already exists. The pre-processor has two commands to handle this task: #ifndef and #endif. The following command

```
#ifndef __EXCEPTION__H
```

tells the pre-processor, "if the __EXCEPTION__H flag is not defined (does not exist), include in the virtual source file everything from here to the next #endif command, otherwise exclude everything from here to the next #endif command."

So, finally, our Exception.h file will read as follows:

```
#ifndef __EXCEPTION__H
#define __EXCEPTION__H
class Exception { };
#endif
```

The reader should make the indicated changes to Exception.h and compile this program to verify that the problem has been solved:

```
#include "Exception.h"
#include "ExDiv0.h"
void main ()
{
}
```

The above discussion about setting a flag to avoid multiple inclusion of a header file applies to every header file without exception. Thus, we should similarly modify ExDiv0.h:

```
#ifndef __EXDIV0__H
#define __EXDIV0__H

#include "Exception.h"
class ExceptionDivideByZero : public Exception { };

#endif
```

We now see the reason for the rather odd name we chose for the flag: we need to ensure that each header file will have its own unique flag, so we derive the name of the flag from the name of the file. The reader should similarly modify the Point.h file previously created; using a flag called __POINT__H, and should modify any other header files the reader may have written.

1.5.3   Throwing an Exception

An exception can be thrown by simply throwing a given type:

```
#include <iostream>
using namespace std;

#include "ExDiv0.h"
void main ()
{
    try
    {
        throw ExceptionDivideByZero();
        cout << "This line is never reached" << endl;
    }
    catch (ExceptionDivideByZero myException)
    {
        cout << "Threw an exception" << endl;
    }
    cout << "After exception" << endl;
}
```

When this program is compiled, the output is:

```
Threw an exception
After exception
```

We will have much more experience with exceptions in the course of this text.

1.6   Standard Methods for Classes

There are certain methods and friend functions which should be considered when designing any class in C++:

At least one constructor. Every single field must be initialized; it is extremely unsafe to rely on the user to properly call set-up methods. If there are a number of fields and several constructors, then the programmer should consider writing a protected helper method for the constructors. Each constructor would pass the same set of parameters to the helper method, getting some of them from its own parameters and computing or using defaults for others.

A copy constructor and an overloaded assignment operator if a deep copy is desired. Usually a pointer field will indicate the need for such methods, although not always.

A destructor (always virtual if the class is derived or may become a base class for other classes), even if the class does not allocate any memory on the free store. Later evolution of the class may change the current situation, and in the meantime, the destructor can display debugging information (as does our Point class' destructor).

An overloaded == operator. This is usually necessary bitwise comparison will probably be incorrect It might also be necessary if a partial match is acceptable. For instance, in the parameterized Point class, we might take the position that two Points are equal if they have the same coordinates, even if the _data field is different; to accomplish this result we must overload the = operator.

A *display*() method and an ostream << function. It is helpful to have a quick and convenient way of outputting an instance of the class even if, in fact, we would not want to display it that way in a real application. It is easier to debug a program if we can output the fields of an instance with a simple *cout* << statement, instead of working through a list of fields. Also, in order to output the fields from our *main*() function or other functions outside the class, we must either make them public or use accessor methods – which may themselves be in need of debugging - to obtain the values. However, to produce polymorphic output, it is not enough to have an ostream << function. To accomplish polymorphic output, the ostream << function must call some virtual method of the class. Therefore, we will have a very simple ostream << method:

```
ostream& operator<< (ostream& s, MyClass& m)
{
    m.display(s);
    return s;
}
```

The *display()* method is *always* virtual because any class can have subclasses and the *display()* method in each of the the subclasses should be able to override parent method. So for the Point class, it might be something like this:

```
virtual void display (ostream& s)
{
    s << "(" << _x << "," << _y << ")";
}
```

1.7   Guidelines for Writing Object-Oriented Programs

Numerous books have been written both about object-oriented design and about the pitfalls of object-oriented design. This section can only touch on this large topic.

1.7.1   Model the Problem With Objects

The basic idea of object-oriented programming is to model the problem to be solved in terms of cooperating objects, each responsible for maintaining its own state. Correctly identifying the high-level objects involved in the problem is of great importance. One simple way to do this is to describe the problem at a high level (e.g., "the program will keep track of students enrolled in the university, including the courses they take and the grades they receive"); every noun which appears in the description (in this case, students, university, courses, grades) can be tentatively considered an object. Of course, natural languages are not precise, so this simple method can overlook necessary objects and include unnecessary objects.

Further analysis is then made as to the fields of the proposed objects and the actions which the objects engage in, which will be modeled as methods. In this process, some objects (like grades) may be found to have so few fields and so little behavior that no class needs to be created for them, and new objects may appear to be necessary. In the example above, how is the relationship between a student and a course represented? Perhaps a student object keeps a list of courses taken and grades achieved in each course. Then the program requires a class, the instances of which represent a course taken by the student, and another class, the instances of which are capable of holding a list of objects of the student_course class.

The methods of the classes are then developed in a top-down fashion. Initially, each method is described in terms of top level tasks, which are then broken down into subtasks, which are further refined until they are simple enough to translate directly into C++ code which performs simple, well-defined actions. Other necessary methods and unanticipated fields, may be discovered in the process of top-down design. In the example above, students (instances of the student class) should be able to report their GPA. Thus, the student class should have a method for returning a GPA. At the top level, such a method might be described as follows:

Get the total hours completed

Get the total grade points earned

Divide the total grade points by the total hours to get the GPA

The first two tasks might themselves be reasonable methods for the student class; for instance, the total hours completed might be of interest since a certain number of completed hours might be required for graduation. In any event, the first two tasks themselves need to be broken down into subtasks, but this requires that certain issues be resolved. How does the student object know its total hours completed? One possible implementation is for the student object to store the number as a field, changing it as courses are taken, and simply reporting the number when queried for total hours. Another possible implementation would be for each student_course object to keep the hours completed in a single course, so that the student object must query each student_course object in its list and return the total when queried for total hours.

This issue obviously must be resolved in order to write the *total_hours_completed*() method and to establish the fields required for the student object. However, it is not actually relevant to either the *GPA*() method or to any callers of the *total_hours_completed*(). Therefore, the *GPA*() method can simply call the *total_hours_completed*() method without worrying about how it works. Similar considerations apply to *total_grade_points*(). Thus, the *GPA*() method reduces to just division using the results of two method calls, and the two new methods need to be analyzed in a similar top-down fashion.

The goal of programming, whether in the object–oriented style or not, is always to create a reliable, maintainable program. Here are some important guidelines which can help you achieve this goal.

1.7.2   Constants

Literal constant numbers appearing in code are generally not a good idea. No matter how stable a constraint may seem initially, it has a tendency to change over the lifetime of a program. We can declare constants quite easily in C++ :

■
```
const double GPA = 4.0;
```

This statement might be placed at the beginning of a header file, where it will be easy to see and modify.

1.7.3   Simple syntax

C++ allows quite cryptic syntax, like these examples:

```
z = x + +  + --y;
if ((x + + > 3) && (y-- < 7) || ((z = x * y) > 20)) { }
```

These examples are syntactically correct but incomprehensible without analysis. The second one is particularly hard to understand since it mixes the operations of testing values and changing values, so that it has side-effects in addition to selecting code for execution. Side effects are undesirable because it is easy to lose track of them. Each operation should appear in a separate statement for ease of understanding and maintainability of code over its lifecycle.

1.7.4   Classes

The watchword for the designer of a class is *independence*. The class should not depend on the internal workings of any other class, except possibly its ancestors, nor should any other class except possibly its descendants depend on its internal workings. Classes should interact solely through their public interfaces. This independence ensures that each class can be implemented and modified as appropriate without breaking code in other classes.

The public interface of a class should be designed in advance, as much as possible, based on the purpose of the class. It may evolve somewhat over the course of development, but if it is well designed, it should evolve by adding functionality, not by radically modifying the existing functionality. The public interface should not slavishly reflect the underlying implementation, but should present the functions of the class in a clear and useful manner.

Each class should be well designed and carefully tested to ensure that it does perform the functions advertised in its public interface reliably. A class may make use of, or have fields that are instances of, another class, and it must be tested in conjunction with that class, but it should be tested independent of any hypothetical class that may make use of it. Every class can have a "main" method, and test code can be placed in that method.

Often, a single "primary" class, which is made public and available to others, will need "helper" classes, classes which handle aspects of the primary class' duties in an efficient way, but which are not used by, or relevant to, any other classes. A helper class may be placed in the same file with its primary class, provided that this does not make the primary class long and confusing.

1.7.4.1   Fields

Most classes are likely to have member fields. Fields should not be public except under special conditions; and they should generally be private or protected. If a field is public, the programmer should add a comment indicating why that field is public. Fields and local variables should be explicitly initialized in constructors.

Most classes have expectations about the state of their fields (for instance, that a field is never negative, or that it never takes certain values, or that it bears a certain relationship with another field). These are the invariants of the class. Access to the fields must be carefully controlled, and every method must ensure that under no circumstances can the fields assume illegal states, violating the class invariants.

1.7.4.2   Constructors

Every instance of a class must be constructed, and it is not in general safe to rely on the default constructor provided by the compiler. Constructors must set the fields to proper values so as to maintain the class invariants. Every class should have a default constructor (without any parameters) if there is any meaningful way of setting the fields to default values. The default constructor should set all variables to the most commonly needed values. If, in use of the class, instances are often created with a different specific set of values, then another constructor may need to be created.

1.7.4.3   Destructors

If a class allocates memory from the free store or seizes resources, it should be very careful to release the memory or resources in its destructor. Even if it does not have an obvious need for a destructor, it should contain one to accommodate future changes. As noted previously, all destructors should be flagged as virtual if the class will or may later participate in a class hierarchy.

1.7.5   Subclasses

A class should be made a subclass of another class only if these two classes share some code. If the subclass overrides virtually all the code in the parent class, or if the subclass makes no use at all of the parent class' fields but instead declares its own, then perhaps the two should be sibling classes, with an abstract parent class which implements what little code they have in common.

1.7.6   Methods

Besides constructors and destructors public class methods fall basically into three types. These are accessor methods, which report aspects of the state of the class, mutator methods, which change the state of the class, and the application specific class methods that manipulate information. It should be noted that these methods need not (indeed should not) reflect the internal structure of the class; an accessor method may report the value of a field, but it may also report a function computed from the fields defined in the class, and similarly a mutator method 1.7.4.5 provides value which is obtained by processing the fields defined in the class.

1.7.6.1   Names

An accessor method of a class should be named in a way that indicates that it reports a state or property of an instance. For instance, it might begin with "is" or "has," or might be an adjective such as "*full()*" or "*empty()*." If an accessor method reflects a single field, one convention is that the method has almost the same name as the field, but the field name begins with an underscore and the method does not. It should not be obvious to the user of a class that certain methods do reflect underlying fields and others do not (after all, the implementation might change).

A mutator method should have a name which is an active verb, like "*add()*" or "*close()*," or it might be one of a small number of names like "*next()*" and "*prev()*" which are not verbs but are so often used that the user of the class will expect them to change the state of the object and will not find them confusing. If a mutator method changes a single field, it may be named "set" plus the name of the field (without the underscore). A mutator method that changes more than a single field is also named "set" plus another word or words, which describe (from the user's view) what is changed.

In general, method names should not contain redundant information. Unless the class handles different types of parameters differently, *and* those differences are important to the user, identifiers for types of parameters should not appear in method names.

1.7.6.2 Operations

In general, any public method of a class should perform only one function. If it performs many functions, its internal complexity may be great so it is likely to have many bugs; it is also likely to require more preconditions, so there may be many circumstances in which it will not be useful where a simple function would be; and it may also require many arguments to perform its various functions, which makes it harder for the user to call it correctly.

The one-method-one-function rule is somewhat less rigid for private methods, where the class designer has an opportunity to control completely access, set up parameters, check preconditions, and so forth. Often it does make sense to consolidate a number of different methods with a single block of code, execution of which is controlled by arguments. Still, greater complexity means greater chance of bugs.

An aspect of the one-method-one-function rule is that accessor methods should *never* change the state of the object in a way detectable to the user. Sometimes mutator methods can return a value, if the value is a meaningful result of the change in internal state (meaningful to the user of the class, that is), and is clearly documented by the name of the method.

In the *Iterator* abstract class described below, for instance, there is an accessor method, *hasMoreElements*(), and a mutator method, *nextElement*(), which changes the internal state by moving to the next value. The method *nextElement*() does return a value, but that value is the result of the change and is clearly documented in the name: the user would not be surprised if *nextElement*() returned an element, but would probably be very surprised if *hasMoreElements*() were to do the same.

1.7.6.3   Return Values

If a method normally returns a given type of value, it should always return that type of value. It should not return a different type of value to indicate a failure. For instance, if the method returns a count of items in a file, it should not return a –1 value to indicate that the file was missing or in the wrong format. When the value of count is 0 it could indicate one of two things: the number of items in the file is 0 or the file does not exist. It is advisable to not to mix two different semantics using a single return value and for the case for missing file an exception can be thrown. This discourages the user from trying to use a result that is incorrect, triggering an even worse exception or just undetected erroneous results, neither of which is desirable.

In particular, an accessor method returns a value, which reflects the state of the object. If the above guidelines are followed, then that state should always be valid. If, through some chance, the state is not valid, the accessor method should throw an exception rather than reporting a state, which is not useful because the object is corrupted.

If a mutator method fails, this generally indicates that something is very wrong — a resource failure or a programmer error. Therefore, the method should throw an exception rather than returning, for instance, a boolean value indicating success or failure. Besides ensuring that the error will be noticed and, with luck, handled, this allows the user of the class to handle the problem in a try block rather than including tests in several places.

The one partial exception to this rule is that mutator methods that find the next (or previous) object in a series and return it may return null if no next (or previous) object is found. The user of the class would not be surprised to run eventually out of next (or previous) objects, and running out is neither a resource failure nor a programmer failure. Further, it is so common to use code like:

```
while (x.Next() != NULL)
{
 // do something
}
```

that returning a NULL instead of throwing an exception may be permitted. However, if a mutator method is used in a conditional statement, as above, it should not appear in a compound conditional statement, so as to avoid confusion as to whether the mutator was actually called and actually changed the state of the object.

1.7.6.4   Convenience methods

Sometimes several methods of a class will always be called in the same sequence, over and over again every time the class is used. In this case, there is a strong temptation to combine the whole sequence into a single, convenient method, even though that method performs several functions.

If a combined function really is a conceptual unit (getting an integer value from a file in a specified format, for instance) then a method may be created for it. However, it is important not to have so many "convenience" methods that the user is overwhelmed by the public complexity of the class.

1.7.7   Exceptions

In the course of performing its methods, a class may run into exceptional difficulties. Hard drives, modems, or printers may fail, and in a multiuser or multitasking environment, files can disappear even when the hardware is functioning perfectly. A class should check every single resource allocation, hardware usage, or other operation that is capable of failing, and take what action it can to mitigate the damage. This may be as little as setting a flag for it to indicate that it cannot perform its duties, and then throwing an exception.

The one thing a class should not do is allow its methods to terminate prematurely with unnoticed exceptions (as opposed to catching an exception, taking action, and then re-raising the exception to terminate the method), since a method, which terminates prematurely with an *unnoticed* exception may not maintain the invariants of the class.

1.8   Designing Object-Oriented Data Structures

A data structure is a programming language construct that stores a collection of data. Data structures, such as those presented in this book, have no reason for existence other than reuse in programs, and for that reason their design should have several special characteristics: they should be designed with as few presumptions as possible about the programs in which they may be used or even the type of data they may be required to store; they should have as few interconnections with other data structures as possible, so that they can be used independently; and they should be as simple as possible for the programmer to "plug in" and use, so that it is not necessary for the programmer to understand thoroughly the implementation of a given data structure in order to use it in a program.

Data structures are, therefore, prime candidates for object-oriented programming. Since the best way to learn something is to see it done and then try to do it yourself, this book will demonstrate object-oriented programming in the context of developing object-oriented data structures.

General guidelines for structuring object-oriented data structures reflect the goals of independence from other data structures, ease of use in many different programs and, of course, reliability.

1.8.1   Abstract data type

An abstract data type is a conceptual description of a data type together with the operations defined on that type. An abstract data type describes the behavior of the type; it does not include any of the implementation details. It is written in more or less natural language, not in C++ or in any other programming language. The term suggests an analogy between abstract data types and well-known data types such as integers.

Integers are defined by their behavior (addition, multiplication, additive inverse). They are not defined by their limits — integers as a type are of infinite extent. The limits of integers in computer languages are an implementation detail, not part of the type. Similarly, an abstract data type should be defined by its behavior, that is, the operations which it is capable of performing, not by any limits or compromises forced on us by the language in which we implement the abstract data type or the physical machines, which will carry out its operations.

Each data structure class is (or at least should be intended to be) an implementation of an abstract data type. The abstract data type should be described first, setting out the behavior expected. This behavior is then modeled through the public methods of the data structure class. This pattern will be illustrated throughout the text.

1.8.2   Abstract Base Classes

Many data structures are designed to accomplish the same task, for instance, to allow rapid retrieval of data given a key. Therefore, an abstract base class should be created that reflects the methods necessary to accomplish that task, and that the various data structure classes will implement. This allows a programmer to design a program that uses the abstract base class, but not the concrete class, except for the constructor that creates the instance. Then, by simply changing the constructor, the programmer can rapidly switch to another data structure class that performs the same task, even if the second class is radically different in its workings.

1.8.3   Data Classes

A data structure works with data stored in units called nodes, which it places in some relationships, one with another. It should not have presumptions about the type of data that it is to store. We would not write a data structure for the sole purpose of storing String instances or ints, for we might later wish to use it to store some other type of object.

There is a problem here, however, since the data structure class may be required, for instance, to sort its data in order. How can it do this if it does not even know what kind of data it has?

The answer is to allow the data structure class to require that its data satisfy a minimal interface, one that provides only and exactly the functionality which the data structure requires for proper action. In general, we can categorize a data structure's requirements in one of three ways: no requirements, requirement of a test for equality, requirement of a three-way comparison. There are other possibilities for more complex data structures, but the data structures addressed in this book will generally require nothing more than a three-way comparison.

1.8.3.1 No Requirements

Some data structures, such as the Stack or the Queue, which we will meet in Chapter 5, do not require anything of their data. They simply place the data in a particular place in the structure and then return it when it moves to the front of the structure. We can therefore use a template class for the implementation of the data structure without regard to the class of the data.

1.8.3.2 Requirement of a Test for Equality

Some other data structures, such as the linked list or the array, which we will meet in chapters 3 and 4, allow the user to test whether a given node is present in the data structure or not. In order to do so, the data structure must be able to compare its nodes with others for equality. Fortunately, C++ is able to test for equality in many cases using the == operator. However, the default test for equality seeks bitwise equality; if the data structure contains a pointer field, the default test will report inequality unless the pointer fields in the two instances point to the same area of memory. As we have seen, we normally do not want the pointer fields to point to the same area of memory, even if we consider the two instances identical (for instance, when one is a copy of the other, produced by a copy constructor). In such cases, we can overload the == operator to produce a correct test. Therefore, our data structure may be a template class and need only document the fact that the test for equality is required of the data class.

1.8.3.3   Requirement of a Three-Way Comparison

Many data structures, such as the binary search trees, sort their data. Since the data structure is required to make as few assumptions as possible about the data inserted into it, any comparison "hard-wired" into the data structure is unlikely to be satisfactory. Therefore, in order to accomplish the feat of sorting the data, such data structures must require that their nodes be able to make a three-way comparison, reporting whether the result of the comparison is greater than, less than, or equal.

The C++ language is not able to perform three-way tests on non-primitive types; it does not even have a default test. Thus, if you wish to make a three-way test on a class, you must overload the following operators:

    ==   !=   <   >   <=   >=

The implementations of some of these operators may be written using the other operators (as <= may be written using < and =), but the compiler will not assume that any of these operators use the others. You must write each of the six explicitly.

If the data structure requires a three-way comparison of the data class, we must document that fact and be careful not to use it with any data class that does not support the comparison.

1.8.4   The Enumeration Abstract Class

In general, each data structure should be capable of reporting all of the data stored in the structure. Even if this capability is not used in production — even if there is no conceivable reason for a caller to use it — the capability should still be there for testing purposes.

It is helpful to provide this capability in a standard way. The standard way in this book is to create a helper class; if the data structure class is called "dsClass," this helper class is called "dsClassEnumerator." The helper class derives from a virtual base class, *Enumeration*, and we provide a method, *elements ()*, in the data structure class which returns an instance of the helper class. The helper class is not independent of the data structure class, since it must know how to access the elements, but it is independent of the caller. The *Enumeration* class is very simple, consisting of only two methods:

```
template <class DataType>
class Enumeration
{
// boolean method which determines whether there are any
// more elements in the data structure being Enumerated
    virtual int hasMoreElements() = NULL;
    virtual DataType& nextElement() = NULL;
// returns the object which is the next element
};
```

Now, we must consider what happens if *nextElement ()* is called and there is no element to return (in other words, when *hasMoreElements ()* is false). In that case, there is simply no valid return value for the method, and the only reasonable response is to throw an exception. Thus, we will create one exception for the *Iterator* class. The entire `Iterator.h` file is, therefore, as follows:

```
#ifndef __ITERATOR_H
#define __ITERATOR_H

#include "Exception.h"

class EnumerationException : public Exception { };

template <class DataType>
class Enumeration
{
public:
// boolean method which determines whether there are any
// more elements in the data structure being Enumerated
    virtual bool hasMoreElements() = NULL;
    virtual DataType& nextElement() = NULL;
// returns the object which is the next element
};


#endif
```

There will be many examples of using *Enumeration* subclasses in the course of this text. One *Enumeration* subclass for a data structure will be enough for testing purposes, but there may even be several such helper classes, each returning the elements in a different order, or perhaps returning a different subset of them.

1.8.5   Exceptions

A single data structure may have the potential to produce multiple errors. Along with the data structure, the designer should design a tree of exceptions: the root of the tree is an exception class called "dsClassException," which is a subclass of Exception assuming that the data structure is called "dsClass". Every possible exception thrown by the data structure is then declared as a subclass of this root. None of these classes need have any behavior at all; their mere existence is sufficient.

This hierarchy of exceptions allows the caller to catch all exceptions in a simple fashion (by catching dsClassException) or to catch each type of exception individually, depending on the needs of the program.

1.8.6   Reliability

Every data structure class should be tested with extreme thoroughness and its code should be carefully and critically reviewed. It should have a *main*() method which performs a "self test" function, exercising every aspect of the data structure.

1.8.7   Presentation of Data Structures in This Book

We shall follow the same pattern in each data structure that we implement in this book:

♦   describe the operations of the data structure and define the abstract data type;

♦   determine what type of data will be stored in the structure when it is implemented in C++ ;

♦   determine what errors will require that exceptions be thrown and write the exception class hierarchy;

♦   write an abstract base class for the data structure so that we could implement it more than one way, if necessary;

◆   determine the fields required in the C++ class and write the constructors to ini-
    tialize those fields and destructors to dispose of them;

◆   write accessor methods to allow the user to examine the fields;

◆   write insertion and deletion methods (and other methods if necessary);

◆   design an Enumeration class for the data structure;

◆   write an ostream << method;

◆   write a test method for the class, which can be called from a *main()* function.

Nearly all parts of the data structure will be presented as working C++ code.

1.9   The Limits of Information Hiding

We have stressed the importance of information hiding and encapsulation, pointing
out the benefits of writing code that does not depend on the underlying implementation of a class. Nevertheless, at *some* point we must choose to use one implementation over any other possible implementations. On what basis do we make that
choice?

The choice to use one implementation over others must be based on factors such
as efficiency of operation, ease of implementation, maintainability, and suitability for
the particular problem we wish to attack. In the case of data structures, it is possible
that different implementations of the same data structure may be preferred in different
parts of the same program.

For example, as we shall see, the Set abstract data type may be implemented with
a tree-based implementation. Such an implementation is capable of supporting a very
large universe of elements, but taking the union of two sets takes time proportional to
$NlogN$, where N is the number of elements in the union. On the other hand, the Set
abstract data type may be implemented with a bitset implementation. Such an implementation is limited to a small universe of elements, but taking the union of two such
sets is a constant-time operation and the data structure consumes less memory than a
tree-based structure. Which is better? It depends on the problem, and in a single large
program it may be that one set must be implemented using a tree while another can
properly be implemented using a bitset.

Code that *uses* an instance of a particular data structure class should make no
assumptions about the implementation. However, code that *creates* an instance of a

particular data structure class should, indeed must, decide which implementation to use. For example, the following function *uses* an instance of a Set class, so it should make no assumptions about the implementation:

```
template<class DataType>
void useSet (AbstractSet<DataType>& intset)
{
...
}
```

However, the following code *creates* an instance for use:

```
void main ( )
{
    TreeSet<int> mySet;
    useSet(mySet);
}
```

The programmer of this function must choose a specific concrete subclass of AbstractSet to instantiate an instance. If more than one concrete subclass is available, the programmer can use knowledge of the exact problem to be solved and the exact implementations that are available to determine which subclass to use. In this case, if it is found that the bitset implementation can be used instead, with greater efficiency, then *main()* can be changed as follows without any changes to *useSet()*:

```
void main ( )
{
    BitSet mySet;
    useSet(mySet);
}
```

For these reasons, although implementation details should normally be hidden, in the case of alternate concrete subclasses of an abstract data type class, we consider it appropriate to indicate the implementation in the name of the subclass, so that the choice of subclass can be made more easily. Note that in general code that *uses* instances of the class cannot make use of knowledge about the implementation since the underlying data representation is not part of the interface.

1.10   Exercises

1.1.   What constitutes the "behavior of a class"?

1.2.   Consider a software system that keeps track of information pertaining to individual movies. This information is to be used by individuals to select movies to be rented. Develop a set of class objects that are relevant to this system.

1.3.   Discuss how polymorphism would be useful in the software system mentioned in problem 1.2.

1.4.   In a graphical system we have windows. Basic figures like line, circles, and triangle can be drawn. Figures can be grouped. Window, groups, and figures can be resized, copied, and deleted. Develop a set of class objects and the inheritance structure for the graphical system.

1.5.   Determine the individual fields for each of all the class objects in the graphical system in problem 1.4.

1.6.   Discuss how polymorphism is useful in developing the graphical system in problem 1.4.

1.7.   An airplane class can be described containing the following information:

- the carrier name that owns it
- current flight number
- the manufacturer and date of manufacture
- capacity in terms of number of seats
- last FAA inspection date

One can obtain information about an airplane in addition to the above information it stores:

- the age of the airplane
- when the next inspection is due, assuming that the FAA inspection is to be carried out every 60 days.

Construct a class structure for the airplane class along with appropriate methods including constructor methods.

1.8.   A publicly traded stock can be described as containing the following information:

- stock symbol

- exchange that trades it

- current ask price

- current bid price

- yesterday's closing price

- total number of shares traded today

- total number of shares traded yesterday

Apart from the basic a) to g) information, one can obtain the following information:

- percentage of increase or decrease in today's stock price compared to yesterday's.

- how much money is required to buy x number of shares at the asking price.

- amount of money that will be obtained if one sells x shares at the bid price.

- buying shares.

- selling shares.

Construct a class structure for the publicly traded stock class along with appropriate methods including constructor methods.

1.9.   Develop a class *Interval* which is represented by a left end point and a right end point. For example [-3, 4] presents an interval with left end point of -3 and a right end point of 4. Arithmetic operations on two intervals A=[As, Ae] and B=[Bs, Be] are defined as follows:

- A + B = [As + Bs, Ae + Be]

- A – B = [As – Be, Ae – Bs]

- A★B = [min (As★Bs, As★Be, Ae★Bs, Ae★Be), max (As★Bs, As★Be, Ae★Bs, Ae★Be)]

- Write the class structure of the class interval.

- Write constructor methods.

- Write methods to perform the arithmetic operations.

- Write overloaded operator methods to perform the above arithmetic operations.

- Write an ostream<< function to print an interval.

1.10. A *complex number* is of the form $a + bi$ where a is the real part and b is the imaginary part. The complex number is represented as (a,b). The arithmetic operations on complex numbers are defined as follows:

- (a,b) + (c,d) = (a + c, b + d)

- (a,b) − (c,d) = (a − c, b − d)

- (a,b) ★ (c,d) = (a★c − b★d, a★d + b★c)

- (a,b) / (c,d) = ((a★c + b★d)/(c² + d²), ((b★c − a★d)/(c² + d²))

- In order to compare two complex numbers, we need to compare the real parts and the imaginary parts separately. For a complex number (a, b) to be less than (c, d) we should have a < c and b < d. If we store a real or integer value in a complex number, then the real part of the complex number will get the value to be stored and its imaginary part will be set to 0.0. The complex conjugate of a complex number (a, b) is (a, −b). The absolute value of a complex number is   (a, b) ★ (a, −b) which is a² + b², a real number.

- Write the class structure of the class ComplexNumber.

- Write constructor methods that set the real and imaginary parts of the complex number.

- Write overloaded operators to implement the operations on complex number, including operations such as computing the product of a real and a complex number.

- Write overloaded operators that will allow all the relational operations on complex numbers.

- Write an ostream<< function to print complex numbers.

1.11. Both complex number class and the interval class have two data points to deal with. Given this, both the classes can be derived from an abstract Point class. Write this abstract Point class and appropriately change the class structure for interval and complex number classes. Also show how the methods for arithmetic operations (+ , -, and ★) can be developed polymorphically.

1.12. A *circle* class can be derived from the point class discussed in this chapter. The _x and _y values would correspond to the coordinates of the center of the circle in the derived class. In addition a data member named *radius* has to be included in the class circle. Design the circle class along with the following methods:

- constructor methods

- a method that, when passed a circle object, determines if the given circle intersects with the circle specified in the passed object.

- a method that determines and returns the area of the circle

- a method that translates the circle to a new position, that is modifies, the _x and _y values.

1.13. Consider the class movie which contains two data fields: the name of the movie and the date on which it is released. A movie falls in three categories: drama, comedy, and fiction. A drama can be end in a happy note or in a tragedy. A comedy can be slapstick or filled with one liner jokes. A fiction can be scientific or historical. Action movies are a drama, comedy and fiction. Romance movies are a drama and comedy. Thriller movies are a drama and a fiction. For the problem above discuss the set of classes and the hierarchy required. Set up the classes along with appropriate fields. Write the constructor classes for each of the classes that you build.

1.14. Consider the class Performer that contains two fields: Name and Salary. Actor and Musician are subclasses of the Performer class with appropriate fields. A Troupe is a subclass of both Actor and Musician classes. Construct the class hierarchy in C++ with appropriate fields, constructors, and methods.

1.15. Assume that a Point class exists. Given the following program determine the number of times the destructor will be invoked after the following function completes its execution. Explain why each invocation of the destructor occurs.

```
Point add (Point a, Point b)
{
    Point c;
    c._x = a._x + b._x;
    c._y = a._y + b._y;
    return c;
}
```

1.16. The Point class discussed in the text assumes that the _x and _y values stored are of data type double. Rewrite the point class with the help of templates such that it takes either double or integer as data types for _x and _y.

1.17. Why is a destructor declared to be virtual? What is the connection between virtual functions and polymorphism?

1.11   References for Further Reading

Aho, A. V., Hopcroft, J. E., and Ullman, J. D., *Data Structures and Algorithms*, Reading, MA: Addison-Wesley, 1983.

Bergin, J., *Data Abstraction, The Object-Oriented Approach Using C++* , McGraw-Hill, New York, 1994.

Booch, G., *Object-Oriented Analysis and Design*, 2nd ed., Benjamin-Cummings, Redwood City, Calif., 1994.

Budd, T. A., *Classic Data Structures in C++* , Addison-Wesley, Reading, Mass., 1994.

Carrano, F. M., *Data Abstraction and Problem Solving with C++* , Walls and Mirrors, Benjamin-Cummings, Redwood City, Calif., 1995.

Headington, M.R. and Riley, D.R., *Data Abstraction and Structures Using C++* , Reading, MA: D.C. Health and Company, 1994.

Horowitz, E., Sahni, S., Mehta, D. and Freeman, E., *Fundamentals of Data Structures in C++* , NY: 1994.

Itai, A., "Optimal Alphabetic Trees", *SIAM J. Comput.*, vol. 5, no. 1, Mar. 1976.

Johnsonbaugh, R., and Kalin, M., *Object-Oriented Programming in C++* , Prentice Hall, Englewood Cliffs, N.J., 1995.

Kruse, R. L. and Ryba, A. J., *Data Structures and Program Design in C++* , Prentice-Hall, NJ: 1999.

Pohl, I., *C + + for C Programmers*, 2nd ed., Benjamin-Cummings, Redwood City, Calif., 1994.

Riel, A. J., *Object-Oriented Design Heuristics*. Addison-Wesley, Reading, MA, 1996.

Sengupta, S., and Korobkin, C.P., *C++ Object-Oriented Data Structures*, Springer-Verlag, New York, 1994.

Stroustrup, B., *The C++ Programming Language*, 3rd edition, Addison-Wesley, Reading, MA: 1997.

Wood, D., *Data Structures, Algorithms and Performance*, Addison-Wesley, Reading, MA: 1993, 594 pages.

2   Algorithms and Recursion

THE NOTION OF an *algorithm* is very basic to computer science. An algorithm specifies a computational method to perform a task of interest. The specification should be rigorous and clear. Traditionally, an algorithm can be thought of as consisting of a set of finite number of steps satisfying the following conditions:

1. Input: The number and type of input values must be made clear.
2. Precise specification of each step: Each step or instruction of an algorithm must be feasible and unambiguously defined.
3. Finiteness: For all input possibilities, the algorithm must terminate in finite time.
4. Result: It must be clear what the algorithm is intended to accomplish. There may be an output that spells out the outcome of the execution of the algorithm.

The condition (2) makes the algorithm *deterministic*. If that condition is dropped then you have a different class of algorithms called the *non-deterministic* algorithms. The class of non-deterministic algorithms is beyond the scope of this book. In some cases, property 3) may not be satisfied. Typically, such algorithms constantly wait for user input or input from another algorithm to move forward. These are non-terminating by design and form an important part of the world of algorithms. Such algorithms are classified as belonging to *reactive systems*. A computer operating system is an Example of a reactive system. Sometimes they are also called *procedures* to distinguish them from algorithms that always terminate in a finite time. The term *program* is generally used to denote an implementation of an algorithm, although when there is no confusion, it is sometimes used to denote an algorithm as well. The algorithms we will study in this text fall into the category of deterministic, non-reactive algorithms.

2.1   Pseudo-Language

An algorithm expressed in a high-level language such as C + + can often present syntactic distractions that may make its formal performance analysis difficult. This is primarily due to the many and complicated features available in a programming language. Hence it is often the case that a form of a pseudo-programming language is used to describe the algorithm. The pseudo-language combines some features of a high-level language with some natural language extensions that help describe the algorithm in a concise and informative manner. In the following several Example program segments our principal focus is on analyzing steps rather than aesthetically composing programs using structured programming constructs. Hence programming language constructs for unconditional jumps such as GOTO, while discouraged, are used in the Examples, without any restriction.

Example 2.1

To illustrate this, let us consider the problem of sorting an array A of n integers in ascending order. The pseudo-language description of a simple sorting algorithm for this problem is shown below. The idea behind the sorting algorithm is quite simple. Let us use the notation $A[i:n - 1]$ to denote the set of array elements $A[i], A[i + 1],...,A[n-1]$. We first find the minimum integer in the array $A[0:n - 1]$ and swap it with the number in $A[0]$. Then we find the minimum in the array $A[1:n - 1]$ and swap it with the number in $A[1]$ and so on. To write the pseudo − language description of the algorithm, we will use iterative loop called the "FOR" loop. All statements within the FOR and ENDFOR statements will be executed a number of times specified in the FOR statement. For Example, The FOR statement in the algorithm below is executed $n - 1$ times and statements labeled 2 and 3 are also executed $n - 1$ times.

```
ALGORITHM SIMPLESORT (A, n )
Input: An array A of n integers.
Output: A sorted array A in ascending order of the numbers it holds.

1.   For i←0 to (n-2) Do
2.          Find the minimum integer in the array A[i:n]:
                 Let j be such that A[j] = min A[i:n]
3.          Swap A[i] with A[j]
4.   ENDFOR
```

The following Example shows the workings of the algorithm SIMPLESORT. Consider an array A of size 5 indexed from 0 through 4. During the first iteration of the For loop the value of i is 0 and the smallest value is 30 at the index position j = 2.

0	1	2	3	4
80	90	30	60	50
		j		

The contents of A[j] and A[i] that is A[2] and A[0] will be swapped resulting in the following.

0	1	2	3	4
30	90	80	60	50
		j		

During the second iteration the value of i will be 1 and the smallest value in the array in index positions 1 through 4 will be 50 at index position 4, that is j = 4.

0	1	2	3	4
30	90	80	60	50
		j		J

After swapping A[j] and A[i] that this swapping A[4] and A[1] we will get the following.

0	1	2	3	4
30	50	80	60	90
				j

The next iteration of the For loop will have value for i = 2 and the smallest value in array positions A[2]..A[4] will be at position 3 that is j = 3 with A[3] = 60.

0	1	2	3	4
30	50	80	60	90
			j	

After swapping A[j] and A[i] that this swapping A[3] and A[2] we will get the following.

0	1	2	3	4
30	50	60	80	90
			j	

The final iteration will have a value for i as 3 and the smallest value in the array positions A[3]..A[4] will be at position 3 that is j = 3 with A[3] = 80. Since i and j are the same we do not need to swap, but this is not reflected in the algorithm. Even when we perform this swapping the value 80 will remain in position 3.

It is clear that the pseudo-language description of the algorithm SIMPLESORT is intuitive, and it achieves a high degree of conciseness by reusing code by encapsulating the "minimum-finding" method. What makes it especially appealing is the ease with which one can analyze such a pseudo-language description of the algorithm, as we will see soon. In later chapters we will use such pseudo-language features for describing an algorithm whenever we think they are needed.

2.2   Resources of a Computer Algorithm

There are two resources that are generally attributed to a computer algorithm, one being *space* and the other *running time*. These are used as measures to describe the complexity of an algorithm in terms of its performance. Roughly speaking, *space complexity* refers to the amount of memory required and *time complexity* refers to the amount of time required to complete the execution of the algorithm.

Complexity is, in general, represented by mathematical expressions that rigorously describe the performance of an algorithm with respect to some parameters. The parameters are usually the sizes of the input variables. For instance, if we are sorting n integers, the size of the input can be represented by n. It then makes sense to express the running time of a sorting algorithm in terms of n. In a similar vein, it makes sense to express the space requirements of a sorting algorithm in terms of n.

The size of the input is usually a simplified measure of the size of the actual storage (in terms of bits) in a computer. Instead of expressing running time or space complexity by a mathematical expression involving input parameters we can present the performance of an algorithm using a chart or a graph. For Example, if we empirically observe that a certain algorithm took t units of time on an input of size of n, we can represent this data point by (n, t) in a two-dimensional plot. Such a graph may look like as shown in Figure 2.1.

In general, the actual running time of a program depends on the hardware (processor speed, memory, clock frequency etc.) and on the software (operating system, compiler etc.). It also varies for distinct inputs of the same size. It is quite conceivable for a program to run in t_1 time units for an input size of n_1 and to run in t_2 units of time for an input of size of n_2, where $n_2 > n_1$ and $t_2 < t_1$. However, there will always be a certain specific input of size n_2 that exceeds the running time of any input of size n_1. This fact helps in understanding the important statement that the running time increases as the input size is increased. The notion of input size is to be contrasted with the notion of input magnitude. For instance, in sorting a thousand numbers the input size is 1000 whereas the input magnitude might indicate the largest number in the input as, say, 10^9.

For a given problem, identifying the size of input has to be done with care, otherwise inconsistent or erroneous estimates of the running time will result. Furthermore, there can be more than one input size for a problem. Let us consider for Example, a matrix of integers of size $n \times n$. There are a total of n^2 entries. Hence while you can take the input size to be either n or n^2, most matrix algorithms have their run-time estimates done using the input size n.

Although estimating the space requirements of an algorithm is just as important as estimating time requirements, it is often the case that obtaining time-complexity estimates is more crucial. There are circumstances as the one of embedded hardware specially used for sensing and communication wherein space becomes a vital resource and hence space-complexity has to be addressed. We will also see later that while recursive algorithms are elegant to specify they sometimes consume enormous time and space at the same time. In what follows, unless otherwise mentioned, we will be primarily interested in the time-complexity of an algorithm.

2.3 General Approach for Performance Analysis

An empirical approach to understanding the performance of an algorithm is very useful but it does suffer from some limitations.

One limitation is that the algorithm has to be actually implemented. This implies that we have to select specific hardware and software environments to run the algorithm. Comparison of different algorithms for the same problem has to be done in exactly the same computer environments.

Another limitation is that empirical data can be obtained only for a limited set of inputs, as it may be quite time-consuming to try all possible inputs. This may skew any conclusion one might make on the behavior of an algorithm.

Hence it is important to use a quantitative methodology for performance analysis of an algorithm that is free of the above limitations. We will soon see that such analysis can be achieved by associating a function $f(n)$ with the running time of the algorithm where n is the size of the input. We will then be able to say that the running time (in specific time units, say seconds) of the algorithm cannot exceed $c \times f(n)$ time units, where c is a constant independent of n. We will also be able to say that an algorithm A is better than algorithm B by comparing the functions $f(n)$ and $g(n)$ that describe their running times, respectively. For Example, if $f(n)$ and $g(n)$ are $c \times n \log n$ and $c \times n^2$, respectively, then clearly $g(n)$ is larger than $f(n)$. In the next section we will see how an algorithm can be empirically evaluated in term of time it takes to complete its execution. Later we will present approaches to formally evaluate the performance of algorithms.

2.4   Measuring Program Execution Time

Before we begin to describe the methodology with which algorithms are evaluated in terms of mathematical functions, we will describe the tools available to measure execution time of programs. In general the template for measuring the time it takes to execute a program goes some this like this.

Start a timer
Run the program
End the timer

We can use the wall clock to determine the time it takes for the program to run. If the programs runs for a very long time then the mechanism will work as long as we are not interested in determining time with a high-level of precision. Wall clock will work when the desired precision is in seconds. But to measure using wall clock we need to be looking at the clock and checking the computer screen to determine if the program completed its execution. Certainly this process is error-prone. One way to alleviate this is to use embeded statements within the program that is being measured to help find the running program. Such a program will look like this.

1.   start = clock();
2.   // Code for program that is being measured
3.   end = clock();
4.   CPUTimeUsedByProgam = (end - start);

In the above, the function clock() is available as part of all C compiler library in the header file time.h. But unfortunately, the clock gives a measurement that is inaccurate in the following sense. Let us say that the CPU executes the program above and after step 1 is executed the operating system interrupts your program and executes another program P. Further assume that your program is again executed by the CPU starting at step 2. The clock time determined in step 3 will also include time consumed to execute steps in program P. If we are trying to determine the amount of CPU time consumed by your program the clock() function is useless.

In Unix systems there is a function getrusage() can be used to determine the time spent on your program. This function is not available in Windows operating systems. In the following, we show how this function can be used.

```
#include < sys/time.h >
#inlcude < sys/resource.h >

void main()
{
    struct timeval start;
    struct timeval end;
    struct rusage ru;
    double CPUTimeUsedByProgram;

    // Start timer
    getrusage(RUSAGE_SELF, &ru);
    start = ru.ru_utime;

    // Code for the program that is being measured.

    // Stop timer
    getrusage(RUSAGE_SELF, &ru);
    end = ru.ru_utime;

    // Calculate time in microseconds
    double startMicroSec = start.tv_sec*1000000 + (start.tv_usec);
    double endMicroSec = end.tv_sec*1000000 + (end.tv_usec);
    CPUTimeUsedByProgram = endMicroSec - startMicroSec
}
```

Note that the getrusage() function provides additional details about the program that you are evaluating and is quite useful. Consult your Unix man pages or the web for additional information on how to use getrusage() function.

The following program segment can be used on Windows operating system to measure with high granularity the time take for the program to execute.

```
#include < windows.h >

void main( void )
{
    LARGE_INTEGER start, stop, frequency;
    double CPUTimeUsed;

 // Find out the number of ticks per second
    QueryPerformanceFrequency(&frequency);

    QueryPerformanceCounter(&start);//start the tick counter

// Code for the program that is being measured.

    QueryPerformanceCounter(&stop);//end the tick counter

    CPUTimeUsed = (stop.QuadPart - start.QuadPart)/
                  (frequency.QuadPart/1000);
}
```

To empirically evaluate an algorithm the following steps need to be adopted.

1. Code the algorithm in a choice of programming language.
2. Include the timing logic as discussed above.
3. Supply various sets of input; some of which can be obtained as benchmarks, if one exits.
4. For each input, determine the CPUTimeUsed and run statistics on all the data collected.

Be aware that the timing calculations are elapsed times. When the CPU executes your program it can be interrupted and other programs may get their turn to be executed by the CPU. The elapsed time measurement does not give you the amount of time the CPU spends on your program. There are mechanisms that will allow one to determine this time and they are all quite involved. As long as we limit the number of programs that are executing in the system and calculate the time often, the elapsed time calculation is a good approximation.

2.5   Analysis of Algorithms

The basic premise in any analysis of an algorithm is that the mathematical estimates should closely reflect experimental results to the extent possible. But we know that experimental results depend on specific hardware and software environments. The real question is, therefore, how can we abstract away such environment specific details and still obtain mathematical estimates that would be corroborated by experiments?

The key to this question lies in controlling the dependence of running times on high-level language description by getting somewhat closer to architectural details of the underlying machine. In some sense, this would be equivalent to translating the high-level language description of the algorithm to the assembly language of the machine and then analyzing the assembly code. The intriguing aspect of this approach is that the analysis can be achieved without actually going through the translation itself.

This approach is as follows: Any code that describes an algorithm in great detail or a pseudo-language that describes an algorithm concisely can be thought of as consisting of a certain number of primitive operations or instructions. The collection of such primitive operations is derived from an understanding of generic computer architecture and the features of a generic assembly language.

2.5.1   Primitive operations

It is of paramount importance to choose the right kind of primitive operations for the purpose of analysis, as otherwise mathematical estimates would not be supported by experimental results. Although, in reality, several hardware architectures exist (Intel's x86, Sun's Sparc, Silicon Graphics' MIPS, Motorola's PowerPC, Digital's Alpha etc.) the assumption of a primitive computational operation as an invariant across these architectures is reasonably justifiable. Of course, radically new computer architectures such as those based on molecular computing and optics would have to be modeled differently. For the purposes of this text primitive operations include:

◆   Assignment of a value to a variable.
◆   Comparing two numbers.
◆   Arithmetic operations such as addition, subtraction, multiplication etc. between two numbers.

♦ Invoking a function or a method and returning from a function or method. Note that this does not include the number of operations required to complete the execution of the function or method. For Example, if we call log(x), invoking the log function will take constant time, but it will take more primitive operations to actually determine log of x.

♦ Indexing into an array.

♦ Unconditional jumps from one step of the code to another.

The execution times of these operations depend on the architecture and the data types of the operands but are constant otherwise. Hence instead of timing the operations we can count the number of such primitive operations to estimate the actual running time of the algorithm.

Example 2.2

We will illustrate this way of analyzing an algorithm for the following problem. The problem is to find the sum of n integers in an array A. The pseudo-code for this problem is given in the below.

```
ALGORITHM SUM(A,N)
Input: An array A storing n integers.
Output: Sum of the integers in the array, i.e., A[0] + A[2] +
... + A[n-1].

1.   sum ← 0
2.   i ← 0
3.   if i > n-1 then go to step 7
4.   sum ← sum + A[i]
5.   i ← i + 1
6.   go to step 3
7.   return sum
```

We could have written the above algorithm using a FOR loop instead of using the GOTO statement along with a conditional statement. Every FOR loop is coded in the assembly language with an assignment, conditional test and branching, and increment and unconditional branching statements. The algorithm is shown above with the

GOTO statement in order to accurately determine the number of primitive operations. Later we will show the number of primitive operations for a FOR loop and use them in our algorithms.

Analysis of SUM

Steps 1 and 2 above account for one primitive operation each (assignment) for a total of 2 operations. Step 3 accounts for one primitive operation (comparison operation) whenever $i \leq n$ and two otherwise (a comparison and a jump). Step 4 accounts for three operations (array indexing, sum and an assignment). Step 5 takes two operations (a sum and an assignment) and steps 6 and 7 account for one operation each. Whenever $i \leq n$, steps 3,4,5 and 6 are executed exactly n times, costing 7 operations in each pass for a total of $7n$ operations. When $i > n$, step 3 costs 2 operations and step 7 costs 1 operation for a total of 3 operations. Hence the total number of operations is equal to $2 + 7n + 3 = 7n + 5$. We can also say that the running time is proportional to $7n + 5$.

One notable feature of Algorithm SUM(A,n) is that the running time for a fixed value of n is independent of the actual values stored in the array. In other words, the running time is independent of the input itself for fixed n. However, in many algorithms the running time does depend on the nature of the input even for a fixed value of the input size.

Example 2.3

Let us consider the problem of finding the minimum value in an array A of n integers. The solution is simple. We start with the first element of the array as the initial minimum denoted by $minA$. We then continue to compare the current minimum with each number in the array. If we find a number N smaller than the current candidate minimum $minA$ then we set $minA \leftarrow n$. The pseudo-language description of the algorithm is given in the figure below.

Analysis of FINDMIN

We will now obtain the operation count for Algorithm FINDMIN.

```
ALGORITHM FINDMIN(A,n)
Input: An array A storing n integers.
Output: The minimum value minA among all numbers in A.

1.  minA ← A[0]
2.  i ← 1
3.  if i > n-1 then go to step 7
4.  if A[i] < minA then minA ← A[i]
5.  i ← i + 1
6.  go to step 3
7.  return minA
```

First, we would like to point the tremendous similarity in the code given for SUM and FINDMIN. Step 4 is where they differ mainly, by way of a comparison operation. Steps 1 and 2 contribute three operations. Step 3 accounts for one operation if $i \leq n - 1$, two otherwise. Step 4 accounts for four operations if the comparison is successful and two otherwise. Steps 5 and 6 account for three operations in each pass for a total of $3(n - 1)$ operations and step 7 accounts for one operation. Hence when the comparison in step 4 is successful for each of the $(n - 1)$ passes, we get the maximum number of operations performed, which is equal to $3 + n - 1 + 1 + 4(n - 1) + 3(n - 1) + 1 = 8n - 3$. When the comparison operation fails in step 4 in each of the $(n - 1)$ passes, we get the minimum number of operations performed, which is equal to $3 + n + 2(n - 1) + 3(n - 1) + 1 = 6n - 1$.

A little thought reveals that the comparison operation in step 4 is successful in every pass if the input numbers are in descending order. This is the worst-case input scenario. If the minimum number in the array were already in location $A[0]$ then the comparison operation would fail in every pass, which represents the best-case input. Hence we now know even for the same input size n we could get different running times depending on the nature of the input. It must be mentioned, however, that in reality such differences may not be noticeable until we get to input sizes in excess of several million. This is because modern day processors perform several hundreds of million primitive operations a second.

2.5.2   Asymptotic Notation

As we saw in the analysis of the algorithm FINDMIN above, the running time of an algorithm varies with the nature of the input as it does with its size. There are inputs that can tax an algorithm to the maximum and there are inputs that do not, and there are others somewhere in between. Hence the intriguing question in the analysis is how to capture the performance in a meaningful way.

There is no single, perfect answer to this question. We can analyze an algorithm in one of three ways: (a) with best-case inputs, (b) worst-case inputs, and (c) average-case inputs. It turns out that analyses based on both the best and worst-case inputs are usually straightforward to obtain. The average-case analysis depends on the input distribution and is usually difficult to produce. The best-case analysis yields a lower bound on the running time of an algorithm and the worst-case, an upper bound. If we do not know anything about the nature of the input (we do not know whether, for instance, the numbers to be sorted are almost always nearly sorted already), then the worst-case estimate has been found to be a better tool to compare the performance of algorithms than the best-case estimate. It is important to keep this in mind, as we will revisit it shortly.

2.5.3   Simpler Analysis

Although it was straightforward to count the number of primitive operations in the case of Algorithm FINDMIN, counting is very cumbersome in many algorithms. Furthermore, we would like to analyze an algorithm without having to convert it into a pseudo-assembly language code, and we do not need the amount of detail obtainable in such an analysis. Hence an easier approach to analysis is called for.

This type of analysis is made possible by "bunching up" a convenient number of constant-time primitive operations and counting them as one (large) constant-time step of the algorithm. For Example, if there is an assignment statement like $x \leftarrow 5 + 4 \times x + y / 10$, then we treat this as just one step. It is typically fairly easy to spot the constant-time steps by a casual observation of the code, though sometimes a more careful inspection of the code is required. By constant-time step we mean any number of operations whose execution time is independent of the input parameter(s). Sometimes we will use «time» and «step» interchangeably.

Let us revisit the code for FINDMIN in Figure 2.4. The constant-time steps are: (1) the assignment step $minA \leftarrow A[i]$, (2) the comparison step, IF $A[i] < minA$ THEN $minA \leftarrow A[i]$, and (3) the RETURN $minA$ step. We can count both (1) and (3) together as one constant-time step represented by c_1 time units. The comparison step represented by c_2 time units, is executed $(n - 1)$ times. Hence the total execution time is $(n - 1)c_2 + c_1 = nc_2 + c_1 - c_2$ time units $= nc_2 + c_3$ time units.

As one can readily see, the simplified analysis is relatively easy to perform but seems to hide the exact values of the constants. In reality, the constants depend on the hardware and software environment in which the code is executed, and hence the simplified step-count is just as useful as the operation-count.

As the input size n becomes larger and larger for FINDMIN, we will be justified in saying that the running time is "of the order of n". We will formalize this notion in the next section. Before we do that, let us quickly perform a simplified analysis of algorithm SIMPLESORT previously presented.

We know that step 1 of the algorithm can be done in $nc_1 + c_2$ steps using the FINDMIN algorithm and step 2 would take c_3 steps, where $c_1, c_2,$ and c_3 are constants independent of n. Both steps are performed for a total of $(n-1)$ times. Hence the total number of steps in the FOR loop is $(n-1)(c_1 n + c_2 + c_3)$ which is representative of the time taken by the entire algorithm. Therefore the running time of the algorithm can be expressed as $c_1 n^2 + n(c_2 + c_3 - c_1) - (c_2 + c_3)$ time units.

2.6   The "Big-Oh" Notation

Usually, instead of expressing the running time by means of an algebraic expression as in the above Examples, a simpler method is used. This is based on the premises that (i) we are only interested in the worst-case performance of the algorithm, and (ii) the performance of the algorithm for large input sizes and not on small input sizes. This method allows the analysis to be quick and at the same time captures the idea that the performance of the algorithm for small input sizes is mostly irrelevant for real-life application scenarios that are computationally time-intensive. To make the last point clearer, let us consider the implementation I of an algorithm A for a problem P that runs in time bounded by 50 seconds for all inputs of size up to one million, and runs in time bounded by seven hours for all inputs of size up to 1 billion. For the same problem P it is possible to have either a different implementation of the same algorithm or an implementation of a different algorithm. For the point we are about to make it does not really matter which one it is. Hence, let us consider an implementation I' of a different algorithm A' that runs in time bounded by 100 seconds for all inputs of size up to 1 million and runs in time bounded by five hours for all inputs of size up to 1 billion. Let us also say that beyond inputs of size 1 billion algorithm A' performs worse than A in terms of the running time. Then we say that algorithm A is better than algorithm A' *asymptotically*. In fact, the formal setting in which algorithms are analyzed follow this idea closely as we will see below.

In formal analysis, we would like to use functions to describe the running-time or storage that are dependent on the input size n. It is possible the input size may be described by more than one parameter but for all practical purposes there is no loss of generality in assuming that there is only one parameter. The functions describing complexity of algorithms should be simple and capture the asymptotic notion. To achieve the first objective, we will generally not use constants and for the second we will specify an input size beyond which the behavior of the algorithm does not change very much.

Definition: Formally, let $f(n)$ and $g(n)$ be functions mapping nonnegative integers to real numbers. We say that $f(n) \in O(g(n))$ (read as "$f(n)$ is of order $g(n)$" or as "$f(n)$ is big-oh of $g(n)$") if there is a real number $c > 0$ and a fixed integer $n_0 \geq 1$ such that $f(n) \leq cg(n)$ for every integer $n \geq n_0$.

Intuitively, the function $g(n)$ describes the function $f(n)$ without any frills and makes it look simple while satisfying our objectives. For instance, if you had a complicated function $f(n) = 5.6n^2 + \sqrt{n} + 100n$, then the behavior of this function for large values of n is determined by the n^2 part rather than the other parts of the expression. For small values of n the behavior of the function is determined by $100n$ and hence the graph looks to be linear for small values of n. The function ends up being parabolic because of the n^2 factor. Therefore, we could describe the asymptotic behavior of $f(n)$ by $g(n) = n^2$. In the spirit of the above definition, we can now say that $f(n) \in g(n)$. We will more Examples of this as we proceed further.

The following functions illustrate the big-oh notation.

♦ $f(n) = \log n + n$. Then $f(n) \in O(n)$. This is because $\log n + n \leq n + n = 2n$.
♦ $f(n) = n^2 + n \log n$. Then $f(n) = O(n^2)$. This is because $n^2 + n \log n \leq n^2 + n^2 \leq 2n^2$.
♦ $f(n) = \log^k n$, $k > 1$. Then $f(n) = O((\log n)^k)$.
♦ $f(n) = 2^n + n^{100}$. Then $f(n) = O(2^n)$. First note that n^{100} is $O(2^n)$. Here is the reason $\dfrac{n100}{2n}$ tends to 0 as n goes to infinity. To see this more clearly, take the logarithm. We get $\dfrac{100 \log n}{n \log 2}$. Now assuming that all logarithms are to the base 2 we obtain $\dfrac{100 \log n}{n \log 2}$ and this clearly indicates that this value goes to 0 as n goes to infinity. Now we have $f(n) = 2^n + O(2^n)$ and from the facts about big-oh we have $f(n) = O(2^n)$.

The following Examples demonstrate the additional proof methodology.

Example 2.4

$f(n) = c_1 n + c_2 = O(n)$. To prove this we can take $n_0 = c_2/c_1$. Then we can verify that $c_1 n + c_2 \leq 2c_1 n$ for all $n \geq c_2/c_1$. We can now say that the FINDMIN algorithm's running time is $O(n)$.

The big-oh notation is asymptotic in the sense that it only addresses the behavior of a function for "sufficiently" large values of the input size (those larger than n_0). It captures the running time of the algorithm for arbitrarily large values of the input by means of a function. Its usefulness is supported by the fact that performance estimates for small values of the input do not make much of a difference in the execution time.

Example 2.5

Extending the Example above, we can also say that any polynomial function $f(n) = c_k n^k + c_{k-1} n^{k-1} + \dots + c_1 n + c_0 \in O(n^k)$, and prove the assertion in the following manner. Let C be the maximum of the absolute values of the coefficients c_i of $f(n)$ then

$$f(n) \le \sum_{i=0}^{k} |c_i| \le \sum_{i=0}^{k} |c_i| n^k \le x \times (k+1) n^k \text{ and hence } f(n) = O(n^k).$$

Using this result we can see that the SIMPLESORT algorithm given above is of time-complexity $O(n^2)$.

We will now see how we can find out the time-complexities of simple program segments. These segments do not accomplish much in terms of an end goal but help illustrate the science of estimating time-complexity of algorithms.

Item	Program Segment	Time-Complexity

1.	FOR $i \leftarrow 1$ TO n DO
	    FOR $j \leftarrow 1$ TO I DO
	    some constant-time
	    operation
	    ENDFOR
	ENDFOR
		The constant-time operation is performed 1 time ($i = 1$), 2 times ($i = 2$), 3 times ($i = 3$) and so on. Hence the running-time is proportional to $1 + 2 + 3 + \dots + n = n(n + 1)/2$. The time-complexity is $O(n^2)$.

2.	WHILE ($i >= 1$) DO
	    $i \leftarrow n/2$
	ENDWHILE
		Let us assume the division operation is a constant-time operation. Then for a given value of n, the while loop repeatedly halves the value of n until the value becomes less than 1. If n is a power of 2, the reader can easily verify that the number of times the WHILE loop iterates is $\log_2 n$. If n is not a power of 2, then the WHILE loop could only go for at most one extra iteration (corresponding to the next-immediate power of 2). As an example, let us say that $n = 2^{20} + 1$. Clearly, n is not a power of 2. The number of times the WHILE loop iterates is 21. Hence, in either case the time-complexity is $O(\log_2 n)$.

3.	FOR $j \leftarrow 1$ TO n DO
	WHILE ($i >= 1$) DO
	......$i \leftarrow n/2$
	    ENDWHILE
	ENDFOR
		It is straightforward to see that the inner-loop iterates $O(\log_2 n)$. The outer-loop goes for n times. Hence, the total number of iterations or the time-complexity is $O(n \log_2 n)$.

The definition of the big-oh notation and the usage of it may be slightly confusing. Some books will use the notation "$f(n) = O(g(n))$", but the " $=$ " is to be read as "is big-oh" and it should not be interpreted as an "equality" symbol. In particular, the two sides of the apparent equation can never be reversed, i.e., it is never correct to say "$O(g(n)) = f(n)$." The usage herein, "$f(n) \in O(g(n))$", should suggest that there is a set of functions which are all $O(g(n))$, and that $f(n)$ is one of that set.

We write $O(1)$ for constant running-time, $O(n)$ for linear-time, $O(n^2)$ for quadratic-time, and $O(2^n)$ for exponential time. Using these functions we can describe different algorithms for the same problem as being slower or faster. For instance, we can say that an algorithm with time-complexity $O(\log n)$ is faster than an algorithm whose time-complexity is $O(n)$.

The big-oh notation is also somewhat loose in the following sense. Given a function $f(n) = n$, it is true that $f(n) \in O(n)$, $f(n) \in O(n \log n)$, $f(n) \in O(n^2)$, and $f(n) \in O(2^n)$. Hence the big-oh notation provides an upper bound but not necessarily a tight one. When we analyze an algorithm using the big-oh notation, we should try to state the time or space-complexities as tightly as possible. For instance, if we had an algorithm with step-count $c_1 n^2 + c_2 n + c_3$, we should avoid saying that the running time is $O(n^3)$, although it is technically correct to say it.

The following Examples demonstrate the additional proof methodology.

Example 2.6

We can show that n^3 is not $O(n^3)$ by contradiction. Assume that there exists a constant $c > 0$ such that $n^3 \le c \times n^2$ for all $n \ge 0$. Let a be a constant that is greater than n_0 and c. Now letting $n = a$, we get $a^3 \le c \times a^2$ and this results in $a \le c$ and a contradiction. Hence n^3 is not $O(n^3)$.

The following facts can be proved from the definition of big-oh and should be borne in mind when analyzing resource complexities of an algorithm.

FACTS: Let $f(n), g(n)$, and $h(n)$ be functions mapping nonnegative integers to real numbers. Then the following statements hold:

$f(n) + g(n) \in O(\max\{f(n), g(n)\})$.

If $f(n) \in O(g(n))$ and $g(n) \in O(h(n))$ then $f(n) \in O(h(n))$.

If $f(n) \in O(g(n))$, then $f(n)h(n) \in O(g(n)h(n))$.

Some points are worth noting. The complexity analysis of algorithms can sometimes be simplified even more. For a complexity theorist, it may be sufficient to show that a certain a problem can be solved in polynomial time or in exponential time. Often in such cases, the precise bound may never be stated explicitly; that the algorithm runs in polynomial-time or takes an exponential time is all that may be brought out.

Although the big-oh notation helps express the resource complexities of an algorithm in a simple manner, it does suffer from one major drawback — huge, hidden constants. These hidden constants drag the performance down in actual problem instances for most input sizes. A good Example of this is the linear-programming problem.

Example 2.7

A linear program is set of linear inequalities that need to be optimized with respective to a linear objective function. The classical algorithm, the *simplex method*, which has an exponential time complexity, is the most used algorithm in practice and is more practical than theoretically elegant, polynomial algorithms that were discovered recently, but which perform poorly in practice due to high, hidden constants.

We will now see how we can find out the time-complexities of simple program segments. These segments do not accomplish much in terms of an end goal but merely illustrate the science of estimating time-complexity. It is important to keep the problem of huge hidden constants in mind when comparing algorithms. Fortunately, algorithms with smaller asymptotic running-time functions oftentimes also perform better in practice.

The difference in running times for algorithms with different time complexities can be enormous. Suppose, for instance, that we had access to a supercomputer capable of executing one primitive operation per nanosecond (10^{-9} second), and we wish to perform algorithms with varying complexities and inputs of various sizes.

Input size	log n	n	n log n	n2	n3	2n
10	3.322 ns	10 ns	33 ns	100 ns	1 μs	1 μs
20	4.322 ns	20 ns	86 ns	400 ns	8 μs	1 ms
30	4.907 ns	30 ns	147 ns	900 ns	27 μs	1 sec
40	5.322 ns	40 ns	213 ns	2 μs	64 μs	18.3 min
50	5.644 ns	50 ns	282 ns	3 μs	125 μs	13.0 days
100	6.644 ns	100 ns	664 ns	10 μs	1 ms	40,197 aeons
1000	10 ns	1 μs	10 μs	1 ms	1 sec	
10,000	13 ns	10 μs	133 μs	100 ms	16.7 min	
100,000	17 ns	100 μs	2 ms	10 sec	11.6 days	
1,000,000	20 ns	1 ms	20 ms	16.7 min	31.7 years	

Figure 2.1:   Time required for various time complexities.

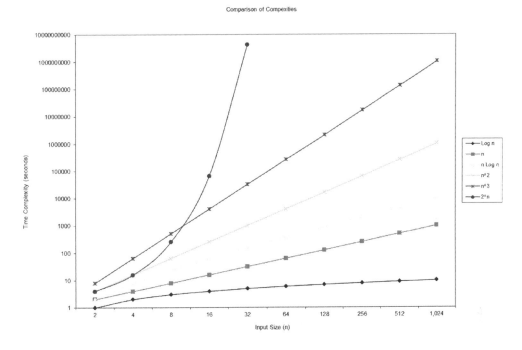

Figure 2.2:   Plot of various algorithmic complexities.

The following Figure 1.1 depicts the actual time required on this exceedingly fast computer. Note that 1 μs is a microsecond, or 10^{-6} seconds, 1 ms is a millisecond, or 10^{-3} seconds, and an aeon is a billion years.

Figure 2.2, above, is a logarithmic graph of the time complexity curves for the functions given above. The reader should note that even with a logarithmic graph, the curve for 2^n rapidly runs off the page. Exponential time complexity indicates an algorithm which is hopelessly infeasible for any but "toy" problems.

2.6.1   Notions Related to the Big-Oh

The big-oh notation captures the notion of a function being "less than or equal to" another function in an asymptotic sense.

The "big-Omega" notation captures the notion "greater than or equal to". Formally, we say that a function $f(n) \in \Omega(g(n))$ if there is a constant $c > 0$ and an integer $n_0 \geq 1$ such that $f(n) \geq cg(n)$, for all $n \geq n_0$. In this case, $g(n)$ is a lower bound of $f(n)$.

Analogously, the "big-Theta" function captures the notion of "exact order". Formally, $f(n) \in \Theta(g(n))$ if $f(n) \in O(g(n))$ and $f(n) \in \Omega(g(n))$. For Example, $f(n) = \log n + n \in \Omega(n)$ and $g(n) = n^2 + n + \log n \in \Theta(n^2)$.

2.6.2   Lower Bound for a Problem

In general, the bounds on time that we obtain apply to a specific algorithm for a certain problem. This enables us to compare algorithms in terms of their performance. The techniques for analyzing algorithms are useful, but they always leave one wondering if there may be better algorithms.

We may be able to say that a certain algorithm has a better time-complexity than all other existing algorithms so far, but could we say there can be no better algorithm? This is one of the greatest challenges in computer science: to prove *lower bounds* on general models of computation.

The lower bound defines the best possible efficiency of any algorithm that solves the problem, including any algorithms that may be discovered in the future. Oftentimes, trivial lower bounds can be obtained. For instance, we can always say that any problem with an input of size n that requires the input to be scanned at least once will have a lower bound $W(n)$. Examples include: adding n numbers, finding the minimum of n numbers etc. Such bounds are called trivial because they can be obtained without any effort. We have also seen algorithms for these problems with running time $O(n)$, which are upper bounds. Such algorithms are called *optimal* when their running times match the lower bounds.

An often ignored fact when analysis of algorithms is performed is the *model of computation*. The most popular and standard model is the Random Access Memory model where integer operations ($+$, $-$, $\star$, $/$) are assumed to take unit time irrespective of the size of the numbers and unit cost memory access time. In fact, all of our analyses thus far and in the upcoming Chapters assume this general model, unless specified. This RAM model is especially useful in obtaining worst-case time or space complexities. But when it comes to obtaining non-trivial lower bounds, the RAM model is too strong and general. Hence, most researchers assume simpler models than RAM and try to obtain lower bounds under such restricted models. Such studies are intrinsic to mathematics where a sub problem is solved if the more general problem is difficult to solve. This is done in an attempt to make incremental progress towards solving the larger goal. Note that a hard disk with spinning platters constitutes the Direct Access Memory (DAM) model. In the DAM model in order to access a location on a disk the read/write head has to move to the right track and wait for the sector containing data to come to under the read/write head to complete the reading/writing.

Example 2.8: The Sorting Problem

Let us consider the problem of sorting n numbers. We know that any algorithm for sorting n numbers will have to read the input at least once and hence the problem has a trivial lower bound $W(n)$. We saw that algorithm SIMPLESORT has a running time of $O(n^2)$. Therefore a natural question arises: are there faster algorithms for sorting?

It turns out there are faster sorting algorithms with $O(n \log n)$ time-complexities as we will see in later chapters. We will also see that, in a limited computational model where only comparisons are allowed, the problem of sorting has a lower bound $W(n \log n)$ running time. This lower bound is obtained by nontrivial arguments involving binary decision trees. This lower bound shows us that the $O(n \log n)$ sorting algorithms are, in fact, the best we can hope for in this context. We cannot improve on the complexity, and can only hope to improve the hidden constants.

Obtaining lower bounds for a problem remains one of the hardest challenges in computer science, especially in general computational settings.

2.7   Recurrence Equations

A *recurrence relation* or an equation is a mathematical equation in which a quantity is expressed in terms of itself. Sometimes a recurrence relation is referred to as a recursive function. This may be somewhat counter-intuitive at first blush. However, we will see soon that the notion of a recurrence relation is well-founded and can be understood relatively easily. A recurrence relation is sometimes also known as a *difference equation* that is closely related to the notion of a *generating function* and is akin to differential equations in the world of calculus.

A recurrence equation is specified by one or more two self-defined equations in one or more variables with a set of initial conditions. Let us look at a few Examples.

Example 2.9

$F(n) = F(n-1) + 1$, $n > 1$. The initial condition is $F(1) = 1$. Using this we can compute $F(2) = F(1) + 1 = 1 + 1 = 2$. And we can compute $F(3) = F(2) + 1 = 2 + 1 = 3$. By extending this calculation along similar lines we get the positive integer series $\{1,2,3,4,5,\ldots\}$. The initial value determines where the series starts. Notice that the series does not terminate but can be expressed, succinctly, in *closed-form* as $F(n) = n$, for all integers $n > 0$. The closed-form expression is called the *solution* to the recurrence equation.

Example 2.10

$F(n) = 2F(n - 1)$, $n > 1$ and initial condition is $f(1) = 2$. We can compute that $F(2) = 2 \times F(1) = 4$, and $F(3) = 2 \times F(2) = 8$ and $F(4) = 16$, and so on. This expresses the familiar power series of 2, namely, $\{2, 4, 8, 16, 32, 64, ...\}$. The closed-form solution of this recurrence relation is $F(n) = 2^n$, for all integers $n > 0$.

Example 2.11

Let us ask a different type of question. How do you generate the set of even integers $\{2, 4, 6, 8, 10, 12, 14, ...\}$ using a recurrence equation? We can see that the initial condition would be $F(1) = 2$. The next number $F(2)$ can be expressed as $F(2) = F(1) + 2$, and $F(3) = F(2) + 2$, and so on. A little reflection will reveal that these ideas can be generalized to result in the needed recurrence equation $F(n) = F(n-1) + 2$, $n > 1$ with the initial condition $F(1) = 2$. The closed-form solution is $F(n) = 2n$, for $n > 0$. It is an interesting exercise to verify that the set of odd integers can be generated by the same recurrence equation $F(n) = F(n - 1) + 2$, $n > 1$ however, with a different initial condition $F(1) = 1$. The closed-form solution is $F(n) = 2n-1$, for $n > 0$.

Example 2.12

A slightly more complicated Example is the famous Fibonacci series. It is said that the Fibonacci series was designed to capture the rate at which rabbits reproduce. As a recurrence equation it can be expressed as

$F(0) = 0$, $F(1) = 1$, as the initial conditions and
$F(n) = F(n - 1) + F(n - 2)$, for $n > 1$.

The first several numbers generated by the Fibonacci recurrence are 0, 1, 1, 2, 3, 5, 8, 13, 21, 34, 55, ... This series starts out slow but the numbers get fairly big rapidly. Unlike the previous Examples, computing the closed-form expression requires tools that are beyond the scope of the text. However, we will see the closed-form solution of the Fibonacci recurrence later in the Chapter without the details of how it was obtained.

There are systematic ways in which certain types of recurrence equations can be solved to get closed-form expressions. But most of the recurrences used in this text can be solved by using guesswork, intuition, and recognizing patterns. After arriving at a plausible closed-form expression, a formal proof needs to be given to indeed make sure that the guess is correct. The next section deals with the computational side of recurrence equations in the form of recursive algorithms.

2.8   Recursive Algorithms

Recursion is an extremely powerful problem-solving technique that in many cases can yield short and efficient algorithms. Problems that at first appear to be quite difficult often have simple recursive solutions. A function or a program unit, in general, when invoked, executes, and returns control to the place from which it was called. A *recursive function* is a function that makes a call to itself. A function may call itself before it finishes execution, producing what is called *direct recursion*, and two functions may call each other, producing what is called *indirect recursion*. For recursion to be successful the recursive call must be on a problem smaller than the original. In this section, we will concern ourselves with only direct recursion.

Any recursive program consists of two parts: a *base case*, where the terminating condition is specified, and a *recursive part*, where the algorithm makes a call to itself with the problem size reduced from the original. Recursion is a powerful method by which algorithms can be expressed in a succinct manner. The analysis of recursive algorithms is much more complicated than that of non-recursive algorithms. In certain cases, the analysis can be carried out by fully exploding the recursive steps by appropriate expressions that reflect their running times.

A simple Example of recursion is a function to calculate the sum of N (N is a positive number) consecutive integers from 1 to N. For instance, *Sum*(5) should be return the value of $5 + 4 + 3 + 2 + 1 = 15$. This problem can be solved using an *iterative* solution.

ALGORITHM SUM(*N*)
Input: The positive integer value N.
Output: Sum of the integers from 1 through N.

```
1.   sum ← 0
2.   if N < 1 then go to step 6
3.   sum ← sum + N
4.   N ← N-1
5.   go to step 2
6.   return sum
```

An equivalent *recursive* solution is also possible for the same problem.

Algorithm SUM(*N*)
Input: The positive integer value *N*.
Output: Sum of the integers from 1 through *N*.

1. if *N* = 1 then return 1
2. else return SUM(*N*-1) + *N*

Notice that the in the recursive solution, the function *SUM(N)* is defined in terms of itself. The code for the else statement is a *recursive* call to the function itself, which is:

$$SUM(N-1) + N$$

This statement implies that one can define *SUM(N)* in terms of *SUM(N − 1)* and *N*. Unlike the familiar iterative solution with a loop, recursive functions need to be scrutinized more carefully to understand how they work. Let us try to analyze how the recursive solution actually works. The above algorithm will generate a series of calls with *N* being decremented at each call as follows:

$SUM(5) = SUM(4) + 5$
$SUM(4) = SUM(3) + 4$
$SUM(3) = SUM(2) + 3$
$SUM(2) = SUM(1) + 1$
$SUM(1) = 1$

Each of these calls is placed on a stack since they cannot be evaluated completely until the function stops calling itself. When *SUM*(1) is reached then the function explicitly states that the result returned is one. This is the *base case* of the recursion and the function stops calling itself when it reaches this case. Once the base case is reached, then each of the calls placed on the stack will be calculated in the reverse order in which they were called (which is the characteristic of evaluating stack-calls, viz., in a first-in-last-out manner).

Each of the recursive calls on the stack evaluating can be given as follows:

$SUM(2) = SUM(1) + 2$ would evaluate to $1 + 2 = 3$
$SUM(3) = SUM(2) + 3$ would evaluate to $3 + 3 = 6$

$SUM(4) = SUM(3) + 4$ would evaluate to $6 + 4 = 10$
$SUM(5) = SUM(4) + 5$ would evaluate to $10 + 5 = 15$
$SUM(1) = 1$

Recursive definitions of problems are similar to Mathematical Induction and the correctness of recursive functions is often proved using induction. Notice that without a base case this recursive function would call itself indefinitely and cause a stack overflow. Every recursive function needs to follow roughly four basic criteria:

1. The function needs to call itself.
2. At each recursive call the value determining the recursion needs to be decremented.
3. The function needs to handle the base case differently from other recursive calls.
4. The function must be guaranteed to reach the base case, to prevent infinite recursion.

We will look at two more simple Examples that illustrate this approach.

2.8.1 Computing the Factorial

The problem of finding a factorial is as follows:

$Factorial(N) = N \times (N-1) \times (N-2) \times \ldots \times 1$ for any integer $n > 0$

For Example, $Factorial(5) = 5 \times 4 \times 3 \times 2 \times 1 = 120$. The first step in recursively defining $Factorial(N)$ is to define $Factorial(N)$ in terms of the factorial of a smaller number. Notice that the factorial of N is equal to the factorial of $(N-1)$ multiplied by N. That is,

$Factorial(N) = N \times Factorial(N-1)$

Next a base case needs to be found which is simply that $Factorial(0) = 1$. The complete recursive definition of the Factorial function is:

$$Factorial\ (N) = \begin{cases} 1 & if\ N = 0 \\ N \times Factorial\ (N-1) & if\ N > 0 \end{cases}$$

Once the recursive definition is established the code can be written as follows:

```
ALGORITHM FACTORIAL(N)
Input: The positive integer value N.
Output: The factorial of N

1.  if N = 0 then return 1
2.  else return N*FACTORIAL(N-1)
```

Walking through how the recursive factorial function would be executed on the computer will clarify the correctness of the code. Consider the Example of *Factorial*(5). The recursive calls placed on the stack will be as follows:

$Factorial(5) = 5 \times Factorial(4)$
$Factorial(4) = 4 \times Factorial(3)$
$Factorial(3) = 3 \times Factorial(2)$
$Factorial(2) = 2 \times Factorial(1)$
$Factorial(1) = 1 \times Factorial(0)$

At this stage the Factorial(0) statement would be the base case which would return the value 1. The calls on the stack will now be executed as follows:

$Factorial(0) = 1$, hence $Factorial(1) = 1 \times 1 = 1$
$Factorial(1) = 1$, hence $Factorial(2) = 2 \times 1 = 2$
$Factorial(2) = 2$, hence $Factorial(3) = 3 \times 2 = 6$
$Factorial(3) = 6$, hence $Factorial(4) = 4 \times 6 = 24$
$Factorial(4) = 24$, hence $Factorial(5) = 5 \times 24 = 120$

Analysis of Factorial

For the first time, we will show how to analyze the complexity of a recursive program using the Factorial algorithm. The analysis is simple. Each time the recursive call is made; there are two comparison operations and one multiplication, all of which may be regarded as a single constant-time operation. The value of n decreases by one for every recursive call, in the sequence n, n-1, $n - 2$, ... 1. Hence there are exactly $(n - 1)$ constant time operations performed if $n \geq 2$. Hence the time–complexity is $O(n)$.

2.8.2   Exponentiation

The Exponent of an integer can be computed using either of the following methods.

Exponent(N, x) = N^x for any integer $N > 0$
Exponent(N, x) = $N \times N \times N \times \ldots \times N$ for x number of times.

For Example, *Exponent*(2,5) = 2^5 = $2 \times 2 \times 2 \times 2 \times 2$ = 32. The first step in recursively defining *Exponent*(N) is to define *Exponent*(N) in terms of the exponent of a smaller number. This can be done by noticing that the exponent of N is equal to N multiplied by *Exponent*(N,x-1). That is,

Exponent(N, x) = $N \times$ *Exponent*(N, x − 1)

Next a base case needs to be found which is simply that *Exponent*(N, 0) = 1. The complete recursive definition of the Exponent function is therefore:

$$Exponent\ (N,x) = \begin{cases} 1 & if\ x = 0 \\ N \times Exponent\ (N, x-1) & if\ x > 0 \end{cases}$$

As the reader would have observed by now the structure of the above definition looks identical to both *Factorial* and *SUM* functions described earlier. Once the recursive definition is established the code can be written as follows:

```
ALGORITHM EXPONENT (N, x)
Input: The positive integer value N and x.
Output: The factorial of N

1.  if x = 0 then return 1
2.  else return N*EXPONENT (N, x-1)
```

The reader is urged to construct the series of calls leading to the computation of the exponent by following the previous two Examples.

2.8.3   Writing a String Backwards

We have so far seen some recursive methods for algebraic functions. However, finding a recursive solution to nonnumeric or non – algebraic problems has to be approached differently. We will illustrate one such Example in the context of writing a string backwards. Given a string of characters, writing it backwards would be to print it in the reverse order of the occurrence of the characters that make up the string. For Example, the string "smart" should be written out as "trams". We will develop a recursive algorithm that computes the function WriteBackward. The function will produce the reverse string of an input string. For instance,

WriteBackward("Example") = "elpmaxe"

The first step in recursively defining WriteBackward(S) is to define WriteBackward(S) in terms of the same function on a smaller string S. Notice that writing string S backward is equivalent to writing the last character and then writing the string S decreased by the last character in reverse.

WriteBackward(S) = output the last character and WriteBackward(S - last char)

The base case of the WriteBackward algorithm is when the string has no more characters and in this case WriteBackwards will simply not do anything and return to the previous call. The complete recursive definition of the WriteBackwards function is:

```
ALGORITHM WRITEBACKWARD (S)
Input: The string S with length S.length.
Output: The reverse of the string S.

1. if S.length > 0 then
2.        OUTPUT (S.CharAT (S.length-1);
3.        WriteBackward(S.SubString(0,S.length-1))
4. endif
```

The function SubString (*beginIndex*, *endIndex*) is a built in function, which will create a substring with the specified indices. Likewise, CharAt(*index*) function returns the character at the specified index. The S.length-1 is needed to specify the last index because the string is indexed from zero to (length-1).

It is helpful to illustrate how the recursive WriteBackwards function would be executed on a computer. Let us consider how the code will execute on the input string "hello", WriteBackwards("hello"). The recursive calls placed on the stack and the corresponding output are as follows:

WriteBackwards("hello") = output "o" then call WriteBackwards("hell")
WriteBackwards("hell") = output "l" then call WriteBackwards("hel")

WriteBackwards("hel") = output "l" then call WriteBackwards("he")
WriteBackwards("he") = output "e" then call WriteBackwards("h")
WriteBackwards("h") = output "h" then call WriteBackwards("")

At this stage the WriteBackwards ("") statement is the base case and will not display anything. This function when an empty string is passed with WriteBackwards will terminate. Upon the return of this function the function WriteBackwards("h") will terminate and son on until WriteBackwards("hell") terminates.

2.8.4   Fibonacci numbers

Let us consider the slightly more complicated problem of computing the numbers in a Fibonacci sequence. Recall that a Fibonacci sequence f_n is defined by the following equations:

$$f_0 = 0, f_1 = 1$$
$$f_n = f_{n-1} + f_{n-2} \text{ for } n > 1$$

The first several numbers of the Fibonacci sequence are 0, 1, 1, 2, 3, 5, 8, 13, 21, 34, 55, 89. Although the numbers in the sequence start out small, they get very big fairly quickly. This recursive definition lends itself to a natural recursive algorithm, REC_Fibonacci, as shown below.

```
ALGORITHM REC_FIBONACCI (N)
Input: The positive integer value N.
Output: The Nth Fibonacci number.

1.  if N ≤ 2 then return 1
2.  else return REC_Fibonacci(N-1) + REC_Fibonacci(N-2)
```

Notice that there will be two sets of recursive calls generated by this function at each invocation of the recursive function. This can be better understood by looking at the following diagram that illustrates the generated calls for REC_FIBONACCI(5), abbreviated as Fib(5).

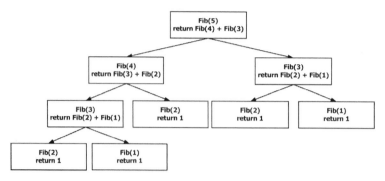

Figure 2.3: Recursive calls generated for REC_FIBONACCI(5).

Analysis of REC_Fibonacci

Each recursive call consists of constant time arithmetic operations. Let $t(n)$ represent the number of times the recursive calls are made. This represents the time required for the algorithm. Clearly, $t(0) = t(1) = 0$ and $t(n) = t(n-1) + t(n-2) + 2$ for $n > 2$, with $t(2) = 0$. If we solve for $t(n)$ using standard techniques for solving recurrences (recursive functions) then we get $t(n) = \left(\phi^n - \hat{\phi}^n\right)/\sqrt{5}$ where $\phi = \left(1 + \sqrt{5}\right)/2$ also known as the *golden ratio*, and $\hat{\phi} = \left(1 - \sqrt{5}\right)/2$. It can be seen therefore that the running time of the algorithm is exponential. For Example when $n = 16$ $t(n) = 987$ and when $n = 32$ we have $t(n) = 2,178,309$. For techniques on solving recurrence equations the reader is advised to consult texts on discrete mathematics.

Some recursive algorithms such as REC_Fibonacci are very inefficient because they calculate the same values over and over again possibly leading to exponential running time. By avoiding such repetitive calculations, we can obtain the following iterative algorithm for calculating the Fibonacci sequence that is vastly more efficient.

```
ALGORITHM ITER_FIBONACCI (N)
Input: A nonnegative integer n.
Output: The Nth Fibonacci number.

1.  if n < 2 then return n
2.  i ←1
3.  j ←0
4.  for k ←1 to n do
5.      j ← i + j
6.      i ← j-i
7.  endfor
8.  return j
```

With just a for loop that iterates a total of n times and constant time operations on each iteration, the time-complexity of this algorithm is clearly $O(n)$. In reality, of course, the numbers i and j get very big as the value of n is increased, causing an integer overflow. Hence we assume, for linearity of the algorithm, that the primitive arithmetic operations take a constant time regardless of the size of the numbers involved. This is not a new assumption, as it was implicitly assumed of the REC_Fibonacci algorithm as well and hence comparisons between the algorithms are fair. Arithmetic operations involving arbitrarily large numbers can be performed in conventional computers that hold only fixed size integers (16, 32 or 64 bits) in one "word" using algorithms that take an additional $O(p)$ time where p is the number of bits required to represent n.

Hence the iterative algorithm is substantially faster than the recursive algorithm. There is yet another algorithm for computing f_n with running time $O(\log n)$ which is even faster than the iterative algorithm [Reference 11].

2.8.5 More Advanced Recursive Solutions to Problems

Finding the Largest Item

Finding the largest item among a list of items is an important task that occurs frequently in various problems. Searching through an array of integers for instance to locate the largest one can be done by simply considering each item of the array sequentially. This is an iterative approach to the problem. The recursive solution can be done by a divide-and-conquer method. The array is divided into approximately two equal halves and each of the halves is then searched recursively. This process continues until the divided or partitioned half of the array is equal to just one item. The recursive FindLargest algorithm is presented below. The variables L and R are left and right indices of the array A which have initial values of 0 and $N - 1$, where N is the size of the array A. This recursive solution takes $O(N \log N)$ time and is substantially slower than the optimal solution of $O(N)$ time.

```
ALGORITHM FINDLARGEST (A, L, R)
Input: The array A containing integers and L and R are left
and right indices, respectively.
Output: The largest integer stored in Array positions L through R.

1. if L = R then return A[L]
2. MID = (L + R)/2 // integer division operation
3. return MAXIMUM (FindLargest(A,L,MID),
                   FindLargest(A,MID + 1,R))
```

Towers of Hanoi

The problem of the "Towers of Hanoi" is said to have been devised by an ancient Emperor in the city of Hanoi in Vietnam. The puzzle of consists of an arbitrary number of N disks and three poles. The pole A (the source), the pole B (the spare) and C (the destination). The disks were of different sizes and had holes in the middle so they could fit on the poles, but because of their weights disks could only be placed on top of larger disks. Initially all the disks were on pole A and the puzzle was to move the disks one by one from pole A to pole C. Pole B could be used in the course of transferring the disks but a disk could be placed only on top of a disk that is larger.

This problem has an elegant recursive solution. It can be described in three steps:

1. Ignore the largest disk at the bottom and move the top $N-1$ disks from A to B. (using C as a spare pole)
2. Move the largest disk from A to C.
3. Now move the $N-1$ disks from B to C using A as the spare.

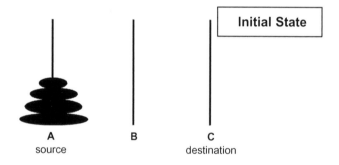

Figure 2.4:   Initial state for Towers of Hanoi Problem.

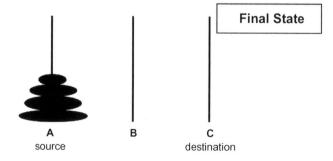

Figure 2.5:   Final state for Towers of Hanoi problem.

These three steps can be used recursively to solve the problem for any arbitrary number of disks. The algorithm for the problem is given below:

```
ALGORITHM SOLVETOWERS (COUNT, SOURCE, DESTINATION, SPARE)
Input: Count is the number of disks and three pegs.
Output: Move all disks from source peg to destination peg
following the rules and using the spare peg.

1. if (COUNT = 1) then
2. Move a disk directly from source to destination
3. else
4.      SolveTowers (Count-1, Source, Spare, Destination)
5.      SolveTowers (1, Source, Destination, Spare)
6.      SolveTowers (Count-1, Spare, Destination, Source)
7. endif
```

Eight Queens Problem

This problem involves a chessboard containing 64 squares that form 8 rows and 8 columns. The most powerful piece in a chess game is the queen since it can attack any other piece within its row, within its column, or along its diagonal. The eight queens problem is to figure out how to place eight queens on the chessboard so that no queen can attack any other queen. The following diagram shows the field of influence of the queen at a few positions on the chessboard, who may not know the rules of the chess game.

The obvious solution would be to attempt all possible positions. But observing that no queen can reside in a row or column that contains another queen simplifies the

Figure 2.6: Field of influence of the queen on a chessboard

problem. Now the problem is only to check for possible attacks along the diagonals. This is has an elegant recursive solution which also involves some backtracking.

The algorithm should place a queen in a column, provided that the queens have been placed correctly on the previous columns. If there are no more columns to consider, this is the base case. Otherwise, once a queen is placed correctly on the current column the next column needs to be considered. The problem starts with 8 columns and recursively breaks down to a problem with fewer columns.

However there is one extra complication. Sometimes a queen cannot be placed correctly on a particular column. Here the algorithm needs to backtrack to the previous column and place the previous queen differently. For Example if considering column 6 and the queen may not be placed on any of column 6's rows, the algorithm will backtrack to column 5 and change the position of column 5's queen.

The algorithm for the recursive solution of the problem is as follows:

```
ALGORITHM PLACEQUEENS (COLUMN)
Input: Column is an integer that is initially 1 where the
queen will be placed.
Output: Place the Queens in such way that they do not attack
each other.

1.  if (Column > 8) then
2.     The problem is solved
3.  else
4.     while (unconsidered squares exist in Column and
             the problem is unsolved)
5.        Determine the next square in the Column that is not
          under attack by a queen in the earlier column
6.        if (such a square exists) then
7.           Place queen in that square
8.           PlaceQueens (Column + 1) // try next column
9.           if (queen cannot be placed in Column + 1) then
10.             Remove queen from Column and consider the next
                square in that column
11.          endif
12.       endif
13.    endwhile
14. endif
```

2.8.6   Use of the Stack in Implementation of Recursive Algorithms

Before we explain how a stack is used in recursion let us first see briefly how memory is organized for an executable program. The layout for memory for an executable program looks like the one shown in the following figure.

In the code section the executable binary will reside along with statically allocated variables say for Example integers and doubles that are declared in the program. All dynamically allocated data is stored on the heap and it grows upwards. For Example, all objects creates using the new statement will be stored on the heap. The stack as you see in the figure grows in the opposite direction (counter intuitive to how you put items on the top of the stack) and stores the activation records that is discussed below for the factorial function.

Stack is a data structure (described in Chapter 5) that plays a crucial role in the implementation of recursive algorithms on computers. On a stack data structure

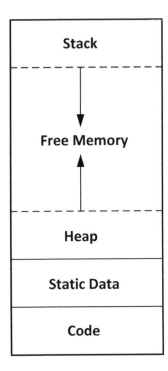

Figure 2.1:   Memory Organization for a typical executable code.

the operations or performed on the top of the stack or push (for insert) and pop (for remove). If the stack is implemented using an array, a variable *top* keeps track of the index position of the array were the most recently pushed element is placed. New elements are pushed in the position *top* + 1 and an element stored at position *top* is popped and the *top* value is decremented by one. We will illustrate the use of the stack with a detailed Example using a recursive implementation of the factorial function.

2.8.6.1   Example: A Recursive Implementation of the Factorial Function

Consider the following short program:

```
#include < iostream >
using namespace std;

int factorial (int n)
{
    int f;
    if (n < 1) return 1;
    f = factorial (n-1);
//  fact() return address
    return n * f;
}

void main ()
{
    cout < < factorial (4) < < " = 4!" < < endl;
}
```

Let us consider what happens when the execution of this program reaches this line:

```
cout < < factorial (4) < < " = 4!" < < endl;
```

Obviously, we must make a function call to *factorial()*, and when we finish the execution of *factorial()*, we must output the result along with additional characters. The output with *cout* << requires another function call, but we will not worry about that here.

If we are to make a function call to *factorial()* and then take some other action, we must be able to find our way back to the location in the executable code which follows the call to *factorial()*. (It should be noted that in the machine language translation of this program every line you see will be translated as multiple lines, so in the above program we want to return to the middle of the line and continue with *cout < <* , but in the machine language translation we will be returning to the beginning of an instruction.) The location that follows a function call is called the *return address*, and it is stored in the stack. Also, parameters passed to the function must be stored in the stack, and the local variables that the function declares are stored in the stack. As each item is stored in the stack, the stack pointer changes value. So, for Example, in the above program, the call to *factorial*(4) changes the stack as follows. For simplicity, we have assumed that the address is the same size as an *int* variable.

Initially	
	stack contents
stackptr→	

Parameter			Return address			Local variable	
	stack contents			*stack contents*			*stack contents*
n	4		n	4		n	4
stackptr →				main()rtnadrs			main () rtnadrs
			stackptr →			f	???
						stackptr →	

Figure 2.2: This figure shows the changes to the stack as the function is invoked.

The entire package – arguments, return address, and local variables, is called an *activation* record. Note that we have put names beside the items placed on the stack. These are the names with which this activation of *factorial()* will refer to the memory. Also note that the initial value of *f* is unknown. Now, what happens when *factorial()* executes the recursive call in the line $f = factorial\ (n - 1)$? This call is handled exactly the same way, by putting the arguments, return address, and local variables on the stack:

Parameter	
	stack contents
	4
	main() rtnadrs
	???
n	3
stackptr→	

Return address	
	stack contents
	4
	main() rtnadrs
	???
n	3
	fact() rtnadrs
stackptr→	

Local variable	
	stack contents
	4
	main () rtnadrs
	???
n	3
	fact() rtnadrs
f	???
stackptr→	

Figure 2.3:   This is a continuation of Figure 2.8 showing the contents of the stack.

Note that we have moved the label for *n* and *f*. This is because every activation of a function identifies its parameters and local variables as being in a particular position *relative to the stack pointer*. Thus, the second activation of *factorial()* will never think that its *n* has the value 4, because that value is in the wrong position in the stack. Now, let's show another call, this time to *factorial*(2):

Parameter	
	stack contents
	4
	main() rtnadrs
	???
	3
	fact() rtnadrs
	???
n	2
stackptr→	

Return address	
	stack contents
	4
	main() rtnadrs
	???
	3
	fact() rtnadrs
	???
n	2
	fact() rtnadrs
stackptr→	

Local variable	
	stack contents
	4
	main () rtnadrs
	???
	3
	fact() rtnadrs
	???
n	2
	fact() rtnadrs
f	???
stackptr→	

Figure 2.4:   Continuation of Figure 2.9 after few more recursive calls.

Note here that the two return addresses in *factorial()* have the same value: the position that we want to return to in the executable code is the same in both cases. Now we have one more call to make, this time to *factorial*(1):

Parameter		Return address		Local variable	
	stack contents		*stack contents*		*stack contents*
	4		4		4
	main() rtnadrs		main() rtnadrs		main () rtnadrs
	???		???		???
	3		3		3
	fact() rtnadrs		fact() rtnadrs		fact() rtnadrs
	???		???		???
	2		2		2
	fact() rtnadrs		fact() rtnadrs		fact() rtnadrs
	???		???		???
n	1	n	1	N	1
stackptr→			fact() rtnadrs		fact() rtnadrs
		stackptr→		F	???
				stackptr→	

Figure 2.5:   Contents of the stack after the maximum number of recursive calls.

Note that we now have three copies of the return address in *factorial()* on the stack. Again, they are all the same address.

At long last, we have reached a base case and can return a result. The result is passed in a register, which you may think of as a "scratch pad". The register contains the value only briefly, just long enough for it to be used by being stored in a variable or used in a computation or another function call. So the return value does not appear in the stack[1]. When we return from a function call, the entire activation record is removed from the stack, in the sense that the stack pointer is moved above them. However, the values themselves remain unchanged and this is why the initial value of f is unknown; its value is derived from whatever happened to be at that location in the stack on some previous function call. When we return from the function call, we return to the most recent return address on the stack. In this case, it is the return address in *factorial()*.

---

1 Sometimes the return value *is* on the stack, but not in this case and there's no need to make this more complicated.

On the return from the *factorial*(1) call, the return value of 1 is in a register, and the relevant portion of the stack looks like that on the left below, and after storing the return value of 1 in *f*, it looks like that on the right below. Note that this invocation of *factorial*() has a different *n, f* pair from the previous invocation, but that they are still at the same locations relative to the stack pointer.

	stack contents			stack contents
	4			4
	main () rtnadrs			main () rtnadrs
	???			???
	3			3
	fact() rtnadrs			fact() rtnadrs
	???			???
n	2		n	2
	fact() rtnadrs			fact() rtnadrs
f	???		f	1
stackptr→	1		stackptr→	1

Figure 2.6:   Change in the stack after the return statement has been executed.

Now we calculate 2*1 and return that result in a register. We return to the last return address on the stack, which is again the return address in *factorial*(), and we get the stack on the left below. After putting the value 2 into *f*, we get the stack on the right below.

	stack contents			stack contents
	4			4
	main() rtnadrs			main () rtnadrs
	???			???
n	3		n	3
	fact() rtnadrs			fact() rtnadrs
f	???		f	2
stackptr→	2		stackptr→	2

Figure 2.7:   Continuation of Figure 2.12 after one more execution of the return statement.

Now we calculate $3\star2$ and return that result in a register. We return to the last return address on the stack, which is again the return address in *factorial*(), and we get the stack on the left below. After putting the value 6 into *f*, we get the stack on the right below.

	stack contents			stack contents
n	4		n	4
	main() rtnadrs			main () rtnadrs
f	???		f	6
stackptr→	3		stackptr→	3

Figure 2.8: Content of the stack before the execution of the last return statement.

Finally, we calculate $4\star6$ and return that result in a register. We return to the last return address on the stack, which is that in *main*(). Now we can go on to printing the output.

2.8.6.2 Recursive Functions and Large Local Variables

As we saw with the recursive version of *factorial*(), every time a recursive function calls itself, another activation record is created. If the recursion continues too long, activation records can in time overfill the stack, and the program will crash. This is, in fact, the normal fate of programs whose recursive procedures have no base cases. Even in the absence of recursion, the stack can be overfilled by excessively large local variables. If you seem to be having stack problems and you are not using a recursive function, the culprit is probably local variables, particularly very large arrays.

2.9 Strategies for Algorithms

There are many types of algorithms which have been developed and which remain to be developed. Some algorithms are quite straightforward, like that for sequential search of a list, but sometimes a straightforward algorithm is simply too slow for practical use. In such cases, we must be cleverer in constructing our algorithms. Some such clever algorithms are called greedy algorithms, divide-and-conquer algorithms, dynamic programming algorithms, backtracking algorithms, and branch-and-bound algorithms.

In general, we know that a problem can be solved using many approaches. Not all approaches, however, may solve the problem optimally or be as efficient as any other. This idea needs to be borne in mind especially in optimization problems. An optimization problem is one that tries to find the "maximum" or "minimum" of a certain function on variables of interest in the problem. Typically, not only would we want to find out the maximum or minimum value of such a function but also the assignment of values to variables of the function that produces the extreme value. There are many tens, if not hundreds, of real world problems that do fall under the category of optimization problems. The field of Operations Research is devoted to solving business and scientific optimization problems. Problems in airline scheduling, crew management, networking, databases, and others are a rich source of optimization problems that have been studied in the literature.

We will now describe briefly the various algorithmic strategies that are commonly used to solve many optimization problems. A more detailed use of these strategies are described and illustrated in later chapters of this book. For illustration of these algorithmic strategies we will use the Knapsack problem. The Knapsack problem is described as follows. You are given n items with each item i having a weight of w_i and value of v_i. You have a sack that can accommodate a subset of items who total weight does not exceed W (weight constraint). The Knapsack problem is to determine the subset of items that can be placed in the sack so that the weight constraint can be satisfied and the sum of the values of the items are maximized.

Let us consider 7 items as below and a sack with weight constraint of 15 (that is $W = 15$).

Items	A	B	C	D	E	F	G
Value	7	9	5	12	14	6	12
Weight	3	4	2	6	7	3	5

A brute-force strategy would be to find all combinations of items and then we have to find the combination with a maximum total value that also satisfies the weight constraint. This brute-force strategy will require $O(2^n)$ time-complexity. The optimum combination of items is {A, B, F, G} with a total value of 34 and weight of 15.

2.9.1   Greedy Algorithms

Greedy algorithms are used for solving optimization problems, in general. A greedy algorithm works by making the decision that seems most promising at any given time;

it never reconsiders or reverses this decision. Although a greedy algorithm is used for optimization problems, it may not be guaranteed always to yield an optimal solution. In some cases, a greedy strategy results in near-optimal or approximate solutions that may be good enough for all practical purposes.

Let us see the application of a greedy strategy to the Knapsack problem. Our strategy should be to select items one at time in an increasing order of their value. Each item we select an item we need to make sure that the item weight along with the weights of the items selected so far does not exceed the constraint weight W. If the item chosen exceeds the weight W, then we process the next item with the highest value and so on until no more items can be added or all items have been processed.

First let us sort the items in the increasing order of their values. This will result in the following table.

Items	E	D	G	B	A	F	C
Value	14	12	12	9	7	6	5
Weight	7	6	5	4	3	3	2

First we will select item E giving us a value of 14 and total current weight in the sack as 7. Next item D will be selected and the value and weight in the sack now will be 26 and 13, respectively. Next, C will be the only item selected (for otherwise the total sack weight will be over 15) giving us a total sack weight of 15 and value of 31. Thus for the above sorted list the items that will be selected are {E, D, C}. We have sorted differently by swapping D and G in the above table, then we would have selected items {E, G, A} giving us a total value of 33. Note that the greedy algorithm is very simple and given us close to the optimal result.

2.9.2 Dynamic Programming

Dynamic programming is a *bottom-up* technique. We start by obtaining solutions to the smallest sub-instances and repeatedly combine the solutions to get solutions for larger instances until finally we arrive at the solution of the original instance. One of the recurring themes in dynamic programming technique is using tables to store results calculated so far and avoiding wasteful, duplicate calculations. By using partial solutions in the tables, the strategy never backtracks.

Consider the following recurrence equations for computing the Fibonacci numbers that we studied earlier

$f_0 = 0, f_1 = 1$

$f_n = f_{n-1} + f_{n-2}$ for $n > 1$

In the tree tracing the recursion for the above computation, several duplicate calculations were performed. These duplicate computations can be avoided by using the dynamic programming approach. An array can be used to store the values that are computed.

The dynamic programming strategy can be very nicely adopted to find an optimum solution for the knapsack problem, however the time-complexity of the algorithm is $O(nW)$ where n is the number of items and W is the weight constraint. For large values of W clearly this algorithm can be potentially exponential time complexity. As illustrated above for the case of Fibonacci sequence, our goal is to compute solutions for smaller sets of items and use this information to compute the solutions for larger sets of item. That is, we need to find solutions to smaller subproblems and use them to find solution to larger problems. The trick here is to define those subproblems.

Let us again consider $W = 15$ and the items along with their values and weights as previously. Let us try to break the problem into subproblems based on the items. For Example, when we solve the problem for the items A through F we will select the items $\{A, B, C, D\}$ with a total value of 33. Now including the item G the solution is $\{A, B, F, G\}$ with a total value of 34. The solution to the larger problem (that is, one with more items) does not contain the solution to the smaller problem. Hence, the formation of the subproblems has to be done more cleverly.

Let $V[k, r]$ represent the maximum value that can be achieved when considering items numbered 0 through $k - 1$ items with the weight constraint $W = r$. For the items specified earlier, we need to find out $V[6, 15]$. Note that for items A through G specified earlier we will number them 0 through 7, respectively. The subproblems are to determine $V[i, j]$ for $0 \le i \le k - 1$ and $0 \le j \le W$ and can be recursively defined as follows:

$$V[k, r] = \begin{cases} V[k-1, r], & if \ w[k] > r \\ \max\{V[k-1, r], V[k-1, r - w_k] + v[k]\}, & otherwise \end{cases}$$

Note that $v[k]$ and $w[k]$ above is the value and weight of item numbered k. Imagine V to be a two dimensional array where you have k rows one for each item and $W + 1$ columns for weights 0 through W. This two dimensional array is filled row by row. In order to compute the values of the second row the values in the first row are required and so on. Once again, this is the essence of dynamic programming to use table look up for determining solutions to larger subproblems. The following algorithm solves the Knapsack problem in that it determines the maximum value that can be achieved without violating the weight constraint. The modification of the algorithm to determine the actual items to be included is left as an exercise to the reader.

ALGORITHM KNAPSACK (ITEMS T, KNAPSACKWEIGHT W)
Input: The items T contains for each item i its value v[i] and weight w[i]
Output: Determine maximum value of items that can be placed in the Knapsack with total weight less than W.

```
1.   for i = 0 to W do V[0,i] = 0
2.   for j = 1 to n do B[j,0] = 0
3.   for k = 1 to n do
4.     for r = 0 to W
5.        if w[k] < = r then
6.             if (v[k] + V[k-1, r-w[k]]) > V[k-1,r] then
7.                 V[k,r] = v[k] + V[k-1, r-w[k]]
8.             else
9.                 V[k,r] = V[k-1,r]
10.            endif
11.       else
12.            V[k,r] = V[k-1,r]
13.       endif
14.  endfor
15. endfor
16. output V[number of items, W]
```

2.9.3 Backtracking

Backtracking is a top-down approach that typically uses a depth-first search algorithm in its basic form. Examples of problems amenable to a backtracking strategy include: finding winning moves in games like chess and decision-tree problems, and many optimization problems. The algorithm to the eight queens problem is a classical Example of a backtracking strategy.

Backtracking works on a graph problem. Even some problems that are not graph problems can be formulated in terms of exploring an *implicit graph*. Such a graph may be either infinite or extraordinarily large. In such cases it may be impractical or wasteful of storage, respectively, to try to construct the implicit graph all at once and look for solutions. Using rules based on the problem at hand, the vertices and edges of the implicit graph can be built as the search progresses. In this way computing time is saved whenever the search succeeds before the entire graph has been built. Furthermore such an approach makes efficient use of storage because vertices that have already been searched can be discarded, making room for subsequent vertices to be explored. Sometimes the graph is also called the search space.

Given a starting vertex, the goal of the backtracking technique is to determine a destination vertex in the graph that contains the optimal solution. We will say that if v is a current vertex in the graph, then exploring u, a neighbor of v is *promising* if visiting u could lead to the possibility of determining the solution (or reaching the destination node). Otherwise, the vertex u is a *non-promising* vertex.

The depth first search strategy that the backtracking technique uses starts the search from a given vertex in the graph and explores a neighboring vertex. If this vertex is a promising one, then the strategy explores one of its neighbors, otherwise it goes back to the parent vertex and chooses another neighbor. Because of this "going-back" feature, the technique is dubbed backtracking.

We can apply the backtracking strategy to solve the Knapsack problem. Note that the time required to solve the Knapsack problem using backtracking strategy is proportional to the size of the input graph. We will see that the size of this graph for the Knapsack problem is exponential and hence the time complexity using the backtracking strategy is exponential. Recall that if we have n items we can use a brute-force strategy to solve the Knapsack problem by looking at 2^n combinations of items and choosing one with that maximum total value that satisfies the weight constraint. These combinations can be thought of as a graph which is a rooted tree. We will start with the first item A and for this item we have two choices: selected and not selected. If the item is selected on the basis that it does not violate the weight constraint, we move left (left branch) and process the next item. If the item is not selected, we move the right (right branch) and process the next item. For the items with values and weights given earlier we will have the following tree to be explored.

As we explore the graph in Figure 2.9, the backtracking can begin as soon as the current weight of the is greater-than or equal to the weight constraint W. For Example, as soon as we select item D (going left of node B and left of node C to reach node D) giving us the pair (33; 15) we can begin the backtracking as we have reached the weight constraint of 15. Of course we have to assume all items have a weight greater than 0, otherwise we need to explore further. Similar arguments can be made for nodes

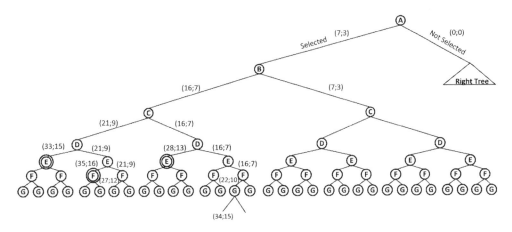

Figure 2.9:   The figure shows a partial graph that needs to be explored as part of the backtracking strategy. To indicate where the backtracking begins, we have marked some of the nodes in double circles.

F (when D is not selected) and E (when C is not selected and D is selected) marked in double circles in Figure 2.9. The size of this graph as in Figure 2.9 is exponential and hence it takes exponential time to find the items set with maximum value that satisfies the weight constraint.

2.9.4   Branch-and-Bound Algorithms

Branch-and-Bound is similar to the backtracking technique but differs in the mechanism used to select and explore vertices in the graph. Branch-and-Bound algorithms are used to solve many optimization problems such as finding the next best move in a game of chess or the knapsack problem.

The branch-and-bound algorithm determines a value called the *bound* at a vertex to determine whether it is promising. This number is the bound on the value of the solution (that is, the maximum value) that could be obtained by expanding this vertex and vertices from it. If this value at the vertex is no better than the best value found so far, then it is called non-promising, otherwise it is called promising. Unlike the backtracking technique, the branch-and-bound algorithms may visit several promising vertices at a given step. For Example, in the case of the knapsack problem, we will say that a node is promising if we get a pair (x; y) after its selection and the value of x is greater than a desired value and the value of y is bounded by another value. In the case of the knapsack problem we would want x to be larger in relation to a small value of y. For Example after B is selected in Figure 2.9 by going left of A and left of B. We can explore two nodes resulting from when C selected and when C is not selected giving us the pairs (21; 9) and (16; 7). The branch-and-bound selection criteria can choose one or more nodes to explore simultaneously.

2.9.5   Divide-and-Conquer Algorithms

Divide-and-conquer is a top-down technique for designing algorithms that first decomposes an instance of a problem into a number of smaller sub-instances of the same problem, solving independently each of these sub-instances and then merging the solutions to obtain the solution of the original instance. One of the fundamental issues in a divide-and-conquer approach is to use a simple algorithm when the instance is small (called the *base* instance) but decomposes the instance when the instance is fairly large. The intriguing aspect of this strategy is to figure out of the size of the base instance, which is usually a constant. Merging or combining the solutions of the sub-instances is a non-trivial task. Clever techniques have to be used which do not cause large increases in time complexity.

The algorithm we developed to determine the maximum is an Example of the divide-and-conquer algorithm. The running times of many divide-and-conquer algorithms are described by a recursive function called a *recurrence* relation of the form

$$
T(n) = \begin{cases} \Theta(1) & \text{if } n \le n_0 \\ aT(n/b) + \Theta(n^k), & \text{if } n \le n_0 \end{cases}
$$

where n is a positive integer and $a \ge 1$, $b > 1$, and $k \le 0$, and $n_0 \ge 0$ are constants. Note that in our Example of finding the largest item $a = b = 2$ and $k = 1$. That is, in general a is the number of times the algorithm is called from a given call the algorithm or the number of subproblems and n/b is the size of the subproblem. The quantity $\Theta(n^k)$ is the amount of time required to divide the problem into subproblems and to combine the solutions to the subproblems. In the largest item problem computing the MID value is and computing the maximum of two items are the problem of dividing into subproblems and combining the solution. These computations take constant time for each of the subproblems. If the input size is small enough, that is if $n \le n_0$, then the recurrence equation indicates that the problem can be solved in $\Theta(1)$ time.

The above recurrence relation can be bounded as follows

$$
T(n) = \begin{cases}
\Theta(n^k), & \text{if } a < b^k \\
\Theta(n^k \log n), & \text{if } a = b^k \\
\Theta(n^{\log_b a}), & \text{if } a > b^k
\end{cases}
$$

Based on the above equations and the values of a, b, and k discussed earlier, the largest item problem has a $T(n)$ equal to $\Theta(n\log_2 n)$. There are powerful sorting techniques such as merge sort and quick sort that adopt the divide and conquer strategy.

The Knapsack problem is not amenable to the divide and conquers strategy as illustrated below. If we take an ordering of the items we must decide what the value of b should be and then determine how the solutions to the subproblems be combined. Let us say that solution to any subset of items given us an optimal solution for those items. Now we have to combine the results of these optimal solutions. This is impossible unless we investigate all the items in both the subproblems and this is the problem we originally started with. Hence divide and conquer strategy is useful when the solutions for the subproblems can be combined using a simple strategy.

2.10 Exercises

2.1. Determine the number of primitive operations and the big-oh notation for the following segments of code:

(a) 1. for i = 1 to n do
    2.   A = B ⋆ C + i
    3. endfor

(b) 1. for i = 1 to n do
    2.   for j = 1 to n do
    3.   if A[i] > A[j] then
    4.   SWAP (A[i], A[j])
    5. endif
    6. endfor
    7. endfor

(c) 1. for i = 1 to n do
    2.   for j = 1 to n – i do
    3.   if A[i] > A[j] then
    4.   SWAP (A[i], A[j])
    5. endif
    6. endfor
    7. endfor

(d) Function WhatisIt (n)
    1. if n = 1 then
    2.   return 1
    3. else
    4.   RESULT = 0
    5.   for i = 2 to n do
    6.   RESULT = RESULT + WhatisIt (n – 1)
    7.   endfor
    8. endif

(e) Function Deeper (LeftIndex, RightIndex)'
    1. if LeftIndex < RightIndex then
    2.   Middle = (LeftIndex + RightIndex) / 2
    3.   Deeper (LeftIndex, Middle)
    4.   Deeper (Middle + 1, RightIndex)
    5. endif

2.2.   Write an algorithm for the following problems and determine give their time-complexity in terms of the big-oh notation.

(a) Given n Boolean variables x_1, x_2, …, x_n, print all possible combinations of truth values they can have. When $n = 2$ the truth value combinations are (true, true), (true, false), (false, true), and (false, false)

(b) Given a polynomial $A(x) = a_n x^n + a_{n-1} x^{n-1} + \ldots + a_1 + a_0$ one can evaluate the polynomial for a at a given value of x say x_0 using a minimum number of multiplications. Such a method is called the Horner's rule. Using this rule the polynomial can be written as $A(x_0) = (\ldots((a_n x_0 + a_{n-1})x_0 + \ldots + a_1)x_0 + a_0)$

(c) Given a set of n items determine the kth largest element.

(d) If x is a positive integer and not a prime number, then it can be written as a product of prime numbers. This is called the prime factorization of the given number.

(e) Given a set with $n \geq 1$ items, one can print out all the $n!$ permutations of this set. The permutations of the set $\{a, b, c\}$ are $\{(a, b, c), (a, c, b), (b, a, c), (b, c, a), (c, a, b), (c, b, a)\}$

(f) A *powerset* of a given set S is the set of all subsets of the set including the null set. Write an algorithm to compute the powerset of a given set S.

2.3. Show that the following statements are correct.

a) $3n + 2 \in O(n)$

b) $100n + 6 \in O(n)$

c) $10n^2 + 4n + 2 \in O(n^2)$

d) $n! \in O(n^n)$

e) $3n + 3 \in Q(n)$

f) $\sum_{i=0}^{n} i^2 \in \Theta(n^3)$

g) $\sum_{n}^{n} i^3 \in \Theta(n^4)$

h) $\sum_{i=0}^{n} i^k \in O(n^{k+1})$

2.4. Write recursive algorithms for the following recurrence relations:

(a) The binomial coefficient given integers n and m is given by:

$$\binom{n}{m} = \frac{n!}{m!(n-m)!} = \binom{n-1}{m} + \binom{n-1}{m-1}$$

(b) Ackerman's function $A(m, n)$ is defined as:

$$A(m,n) = \begin{cases} n+1, & \text{if } m = 1 \\ A(m-1,1), & \text{if } n = 0 \\ A(m-1, A(m,n-1)), & \text{otherwise} \end{cases}$$

(c) The time-complexity of an algorithm is given as:

$$T(n) = \begin{cases} T(n/2)+1, & \text{if } n \text{ is even} \\ 2T((n-1)/2) & \text{if } n \text{ is odd} \end{cases} \text{ and } T(1) = 1.$$

(d) The recursive function for evaluating the higher-order *Bessel* function of order n that is used for evaluating an integral with variable x is

$$J_n(x) = 2(n-1)/xJ_{n-1}(x) - J_{n-2}(x), n \geq 2,$$

where J_0 and J_1 are defined as j0 (double) and j1 (double) in the math.h library.

(e) The greatest common divisor (GCD) of two positive integers m and n is given by the following recurrence equation:

$$GCD(m,n) = \begin{cases} m & \text{if } n = 0 \\ n & \text{if } m \bmod n = 0 \\ GCD(n, m \bmod n) & \text{if } n \neq 0 \end{cases}$$

2.5. Consider the algorithm for computing Ackerman's function designed in Exercise 2.4. Draw the call tree for the algorithm with m = 10 and n = 5, as was done for the Fibonacci function in the text.

2.6. Consider the GCD algorithm designed in Exercise 2.4. Write a C + + implementation of the algorithm. Then, draw a schematic diagram for the stack contents during execution of the C + + function with m = 84 and n = 14, as was done for the factorial function in the text.

2.7. Given that there are 5 disks in the Tower of Hanoi problem and moving a disk from one peg to another is one primitive operation, how many primitive operations are required to move all the disks to the destination peg. For n disks calculate the number of primitive operations.

2.8. Rewrite the algorithm for the Eight Queens problems such that the first queen can be placed anywhere in the chessboard.

2.9. There are n gifts of a same variety that needs to be placed in boxes for shipping. There are three kinds of boxes each store up to 10, 5 and 3 gifts, respectively. When placing the gifts in the boxes two rules apply 1) the boxes should be stored to its capacity and 2) a minimum number of boxes should be used to pack all the n gifts. Write a greedy algorithm to pack the n gifts and argue that your algorithm is optimal.

2.10. Write a divide-and-conquer algorithm to determine the first largest and the second largest item given a set of n items. Derive the time-complexity of your algorithm.

2.11   References for Further Reading

Aho, A.V, Hopcroft, J. E., and Ullman, J. D., *Data Structures and Algorithms*, Reading, MA: Addison-Wesley, 1983.

Aho, A.V, Hopcroft, J. E., and Ullman, J. D., *The Design and Analysis of Computer Algorithms*, Reading, MA: Addison-Wesley, 1974.

Augenstein, M., and Tenenbaum, A. "A Lesson in Recursion and Structured Programming", SIGCSE Bull., vol. 8, no. 1, pp.17-23, Feb. 1976.

Augenstein, M., and Tenenbaum, A. "Program Efficiency and Data Structures", SIGCSE Bull., vol. 9, no.3, pp. 21-37, Aug. 1977.

Baase, S, *Computer Algorithms – Introduction to Design and Analysis*, Reading, MA: Addison-Wesley, 1988.

Barron, D.W., *Recursive Techniques in Programming*, New York: Elsevier, 1968.

Bellman, R.E., *Dynamic Programming*, Princeton, NJ: Princeton University Press, 1957.

Bird, R.S. "Improving Programs by the Introduction of Recursion", *Communications of the ACM* vol. 20, no.11, Nov. 1977.

Bird, R.S., "Notes on recursion elimination", *Communications of the ACM* vol. 20, pp. 434-439, 1977.

Bitner, J.R., "Heuristics that dynamically organize data structures", *SIAM Journal of Computing* vol.8, pp. 82-110, 1979.

Brassard, G. and Brately P. "Fundamentals of Algorithmics", Simon and Schuster, 1995.

Cormen, T., Leiserson, C. and Rivest, R., *Introduction to Algorithms*, McGraw-Hill, NY: 1992.

Dijkstra, E.W., "Recursive Programming", *Numerische Mathematik* vol.2, pp. 312-318, 1960.

Eric, S.R., *Thinking Recursively*, John Wiley & Sons, NY: 1986, 179 pages.

Fillmore, J.P., and Williamson, S.G., "On Backtracking: A Combinatorial Description of the Algorithm", *SIAM Journal of Computing* vol. 3, no.1, Mar. 1974.

Hartmanis, J. and Hopcroft, J.E., "An overview of the theory of computational complexity", *Journal of the ACM* vol.18, pp. 444-475, 1971.

Knuth, D.E., *The Art of Computer Programming*, Addison-Wesley, Reading, MA.

Knuth, D.E., "Big omicron and big omega and big theta", *SIGACT News*, vol. 8, pp. 18-24, April-June 1976.

Leuker, G.S., "Some techniques for Solving Recurrences", *Computing Surveys* vol.12, no. 4, pp. 419-436, December, 1980.

Manber, U., *Introduction to Algorithms: A Creative Approach*, Reading, MA: Addison-Wesley, 1989.

Mehlhorn, K., *Data Structures and Algorithms, Vol I : Sorting and Searching*, Berlin: Springer, 1984.

Rivin, I., Vardi, I., and Zimmermann, P., "The n-Queens Problem", *The American Mathematical Monthly* vol.101, no.7, pp. 629-639, 1994.

Tanner, M.R., "Minimean merging and sorting: An algorithm", *SIAM Journal of Computing* vol. 7, pp. 18-38, 1978.

Wood, D., "The Towers of Brahma and Hanoi revisited", *Journal of Recreational Math* vol.14, pp.17-24, 1981-82.

Wood, D., *Data Structures, Algorithms and Performance*, Addison-Wesley, Reading, MA: 1993, 594 pages.

CHAPTER

3

Arrays, Strings, Matrices, and Vectors

ARRAYS ARE BUILDING blocks of many data structures. This primitive data structure is used to store sets of elements, and represents sets of consecutive logical memory locations. Arrays are referred to as "static" data structures, that is, once an array with a specified size is created, it cannot grow or shrink in size. Strings store a sequence of characters and are often implemented using arrays. In this chapter we will study several interesting algorithms to manipulate strings.

Vectors are array data structures that are "dynamic" in the sense that new memory space can be created for additional storage and this additional storage can be added to the existing storage. In this chapter, we will study these data structures along with several interesting applications in which they play important roles.

3.1 Arrays

An array data structure is a basic building block for many important data structures. Any homogeneous set of objects can be stored in an array. For example, a list of members, a list of students, a deck of cards, and a collection of movies directed by Steven Spielberg are all objects that can be stored in an array. An object of an array is called an element or component of that array. Components of the array are logically stored[1] contiguously and can be accessed through integer indices.

---

1 By logical storage we imply that from the user's perception, elements of the array are stored next to each other, but in reality the elements of the array in main memory need not be contiguously stored.

3.1.1   Abstract Data Type: Array

We shall specify an abstract data type for arrays, which contains only the primitive operations that an array must be able to perform. Using these primitive operations we can build more complex operations as necessary for our programs.

For example, if A is an array storing integers, we may write an operation that will determine the index position of A that contains the largest integer. The primitive operations required include finding the number of objects (call it n) in an array, setting index position i to be 0, getting the object at index position i, performing a comparison and making assignments based on the comparison, and incrementing the index position i by 1 until i reaches $n - 1$. These primitive array operations (finding the number of objects in the array and getting the object at a particular index position) are therefore part of the abstract data type. A specification of an abstract data type for arrays is given below:

```
create (n)
    // create an array of size n
putObject (newObject, k)
    // place an object newObject at index position k
getObject (k)
    // get the object at index position k
size ( )
    // find the number of elements which can be accommodated
    // in the array
```

Note that if you add data sequentially to a data structure, you may regard it as having two related operations, size() and capacity(), where size() reports the number of elements added so far and capacity() reports the number of elements that would fit in the data structure. However, piecemeal addition to an array is a use of the array, not part of the array abstract data type itself. Thus, size() in the abstract data type for arrays refers to the number of elements which can be accommodated, not to the number currently in use by the application.

The array type, partially implementing the above abstract data type, is built into the C++ language. The array type in C++ does not fully implement the abstract data type as it does not support the size() operation. We will now examine how each of the primitive operations of the array abstract data type is implemented in C++ .

3.1.2   Creation of Array of Objects

The array type is built into the C++ language. We can create an array of some type by a variable declaration, which includes brackets and the number of elements in the array. The type in question could be any type, including a class developed by the reader. Below, we create an array of ten ints:

```
void main ()
{
    int aiSample [10];
}
```

This declaration creates space for ten ints. The size of the array aiSample is fixed at creation and cannot be altered. If we wish to change the size of an array, or simply to create the space in the free store instead, we must use a different (and perhaps surprising) syntax:

```
void main ()
{
    int* paiSample = new int [10];
}
```

The use of int* as the type of paiSample, above, points up the very close connection between pointers and arrays in C++ (ref. 14 in Chapter 1)

3.1.2.1   Relationship Between Pointers and Arrays in C++

Let us look again at the following code:

```
void main ()
{
    int aiSample [10];
}
```

The compiler treats the variable aiSample as a fixed pointer to an int. For example in Figure 3.1 the value of aiSample is 00A1. That is, we cannot change the value of the pointer – it always points to the first int in the array – but we can change the value of the int to which it points.

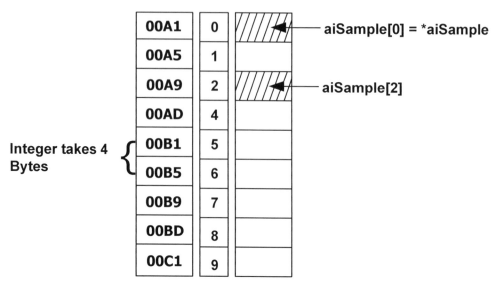

Figure 3.1: Figure illustrating the relationship between arrays, pointers, and array addresses.

To illustrate the close link between pointers and array variables, the following code assigns the pointer value from aiSample to an int* variable:

```
void main ()
{
    int aiSample [10];
    int* paiSample = aiSample;
}
```

It is not necessary to place the address of aiSample in paiSample; in fact it is an error to do so, since aiSample itself is of type int[10] and not of type int. The value of paiSample from Figure 3.1 is 00A1.

With the above in mind, we can understand the following code:

```
void main ()
{
    int* paiSample = new int [10];
}
```

Here, paiSample is a variable which holds a pointer to int, while "new int [10]" returns a pointer to int, just as aiSample was, in fact, a pointer to int in the example above. Thus, the assignment is compatible.

As we well know, memory created by the programmer using "new" must be destroyed using "delete". The syntax is slightly different where the pointer in question points to an array:

```
void main ()
{
    int* paiSample = new int [10];
    delete[] paiSample;
}
```

The brackets after "delete" indicate to the compiler that paiSample actually points to an array. If they are omitted, this particular program will compile and run without an error or even a warning. In fact it will delete the first location of the array since paiSample contains the address of the first location of the array. Additionally, if[] is not used after the delete operation and if paiSample had pointed to an array of instances of a class, the destructors would not be called on the instances unless the "delete[]" syntax was used rather than the "delete" syntax. To avoid problems, the reader should always use the "delete[]" syntax with arrays. It is important, however, never to use the "delete[]" syntax with non-arrays!

3.1.3 Accessing an element in an array

There are actually two ways of accessing the elements in an array, because of the relationship between pointers and arrays, noted above. If we choose to use array notation, we can use indices in brackets to refer to a particular element or object of an array. All arrays in C++ are zero-based, so the first element in an array is at index 0, and the last element of an array of size n is at index $n - 1$. Thus, we can make use of an array of ints as follows:

```cpp
#include <iostream>
using namespace std;

void main ()
{
    int aiSample [10];
    for (int i = 0; i < 10; i++)
    {
        aiSample[i] = i*2;
    }
    for (int i = 0; i < 10; i++)
    {
        cout << aiSample[i] << ",";
    }
    cout << endl;
}
```

The above program outputs the numbers from 0 through 18, by twos as shown below:

```
0,2,4,6,8,10,12,14,16,18,
```

If we choose to use pointer notation and pointer arithmetic, we can refer to the first element of an array *a* as $*a$, the next as $*(a + 1)$, etc. For example, the following program has precisely the same effect as the preceding program:

```cpp
#include <iostream>
using namespace std;
void main ()
{
    int aiSample [10];
    for (int i = 0; i < 10; i++)
    {
        *(aiSample+i) = i*2;
    }
    for (int i = 0; i < 10; i++)
    {
        cout << *(aiSample+i) << ",";
    }
    cout << endl;
}
```

3.1.4 Overrunning the bounds of an array

What happens if we overrun the end of an array? For instance, in the example above, suppose we used 11 instead of 10 as our terminating value:

```cpp
#include <iostream>
using namespace std;

void main ()
{
    int aiSample [10];
    for (int i = 0; i < 11; i++)
    {
        aiSample[i] = i*2;
    }
    for (int i = 0; i < 11; i++)
    {
        cout << aiSample[i] << ",";
    }
    cout << endl;
}
```

This program produces no errors and no warnings, and **may**[2] run without a hitch, outputting the values from 0 through 20, by twos. Where did it get the extra space for aiSample[10]? The answer is that it used the space in the memory that follows aiSample. Probably this space is unused and it causes no problems. The output of the above program is as follows:

```
0,2,4,6,8,10,12,14,16,18,20,
```

---

2 Some compilers after execution will produce a runtime error as we observed in the Visual Studio.Net environment.

Now consider this program:

```
#include <iostream>
using namespace std;

void main ()
{
    int i;
    int aiBefore [10];
    int aiSample [10];
    int aiAfter [10];
    for (i = 0; i < 10; i++)
    {
        aiBefore[i] = i;
        aiSample[i] = i;
        aiAfter[i] = i;
    }
// At this point, all three arrays are alike
    cout << "aiBefore[0] = " << aiBefore[0] << endl;
    cout << "aiAfter[0] = " << aiAfter[0] << endl;
    for (i = 0; i < 20; i++)
    {
        aiSample[i] = i*2;
    }
// At this point, aiSample has changed, but so has aiBefore
// or aiAfter!
    cout << "aiBefore[0] = " << aiBefore[0] << endl;
    cout << "aiAfter[0] = " << aiAfter[0] << endl;
}
```

Depending on the compiler, this code may produce a run-time error, or it will change either aiBefore or aiAfter, without any hint to the programmer that such results may occur. The reader may experiment with negative indices as well. The output of the above program is as follows:

```
aiBefore[0] = 0
aiAfter[0] = 0
aiBefore[0] = 24
aiAfter[0] = 0
```

The above program demonstrates that C++ does not check the bounds on array indices, and it is the responsibility of the programmer to be careful with them.[3]

3.1.5 Initializing the objects in an array

C++ does not initialize the objects in an array to any particular value. We can initialize an array by proceeding through a loop and making an assignment within the loop, as illustrated above.

We can also initialize the values at the time of creation. The following statement both creates an integer array containing 10 objects and initializes the array elements:

```
int aiSample[] = {1,2,3,4,5,6,7,8,9,10};
```

Note that here it is not necessary to give the number of elements in the array, although we can do so if we wish. For example, consider the following example.

```
int aiSample[10] = {99};
```

In the above example the first location of the array aiSample that is aiSample[0] will be initialized to 99 and all others locations will be initialized to 0's.

Here are additional examples to illustrate how array objects can be created and initialized.

```
char Vowels[] = {'a','e','i','o','u'};
int Fibonacci[] = {0,1,1,2,3,5,8,13,21};
```

If we do actually specify the number of elements in the array, but the number of elements in our list is less than the specified number, then the remaining elements are initialized. Thus, in the program below, the last two elements of the Vowels array are initialized to a single blank space.

---

3 Why doesn't C++ check the bounds on array indices? C++ can be used for system programming, in which we might want to treat some part of memory (like video RAM or the ROM) as an array. In this case, our program never allocated the memory in the first place, so if C++ checked the bounds, it would disallow access.

```cpp
#include <iostream>
using namespace std;

void main ()
{
    char Vowels[7] = {'a','e','i','o','u'};
    for (int i = 0; i < 7; i++)
    {
        cout << "'" << Vowels[i] << "'" << " ";
    }
    cout << endl;
}
```

The output of the above program segment is given below.

```
'a' 'e' 'i' 'o' 'u' ' ' ' '
```

It is an error to give more elements in the list than the size of the array.

3.1.6   Using Arrays as Function Parameters

Suppose we write the following program:

```cpp
#include <iostream>
Using namespace std;

void output (int a[5])
{
    for (int i = 0; i < 5; i++)
    {
        cout << a[i] << " ";
    }
    cout << endl;
}
void main ()
{
    int aiSeven [7] = {701,702,703,704,705,706,707};
    int aiThree [3] = {301,302,303};
    output (aiSeven);
    output (aiThree);
}
```

The above program has the following output:

```
701 702 703 704 705
301 302 303 -858993460 -858993460
```

The negative numbers are printed when aiThree is passed and the array a in the formal parameter is of size 5. Thus the program will compile and run without any errors even though both aiSeven and aiThree appear to be of a different type from the parameter which output() expects. However, output() expects a pointer to int, which is what both aiSeven and aiThree are; since C++ does not do any bounds checking on arrays, the size of the array parameter is essentially ignored.[4] The size can be omitted:

```
void output (int a[])
{
    for (int i = 0; i < 5; i++)
    {
        cout << a[i] << " ";
    }
    cout << endl;
}
```

Unfortunately, the C++ array does not fulfill our array abstract data type, as it is impossible to obtain the size of the array, so if we want to print the whole array, we have to pass the size to the function:

```
void output (int a[], int size)
{
    for (int i = 0; i < size; i++)
    {
        cout << a[i] << " ";
    }
    cout << endl;
}
```

---

4 To illustrate again the close kinship between pointers and array variables, the signature of the *output()* function could be altered to the following without changing the function or the rest of the program at all: void output (int* a)

3.1.6.1 Constant parameters

One of the side effects of the close relationship between pointers and array variables is that arrays seem to be passed by reference, not by value. In truth, the pointer value *is* passed by value, but that gives the function a pointer to the actual array, so that it can alter the array. If we want to prevent the function for altering the array, we can flag it as constant:

```
void output (const int a[], int size)
{
    for (int i = 0; i < size; i++)
    {
        cout << a[i] << " ";
    }
    cout << endl;
}
```

As noted in Chapter 1, any parameter can be flagged as constant by preceding it with the word "const". If the parameter is a reference or pointer, as *a* effectively is above, then the object it refers to or points to cannot be changed.

3.1.7 Arrays Storing Heterogeneous Objects

A C++ array can hold only one type of item. An array of *Point*, for instance, cannot hold ColorPoint items as well as *Point* items. However, an array of pointers to *Point* can hold pointers to *Point* or ColorPoint, because ColorPoint is a subclass of *Point* and therefore a pointer to a ColorPoint instance is in fact a pointer to a *Point* instance as well. So for instance, the following program will compile correctly:

```
#include "ColorPoint.h"
void main ()
{
    Point* paPoint [3]; // an array of three pointers to Point
    paPoint[0] = new Point (1,2);
    paPoint[1] = new ColorPoint (5, 4, 3);
    paPoint[2] = new Point (6,7);
}
```

3.1.8 Implementation of the Array Abstract Data Type

We shall now design our first class implementing an abstract data type: the ArrayClass class, which implements the array abstract data type previously described. The array type built into the C++ language does not implement this abstract data type, but it provides us a good foundation.

3.1.8.1 Element data type

The array abstract data type described previously involves no comparisons of elements stored in the array. Our class will ultimately be parameterized, and each element of the array will of type 'DataType'.

3.1.8.2 Exceptions

There are basically two errors that can occur with respect to an array: it may not fit into the available memory, or we may have tried to access an element outside the range of the array. We will declare a small family of exceptions:

```
class ArrayException : public Exception { };
class ArrayMemoryException : public ArrayException { };
class ArrayBoundsException : public ArrayException { };
```

3.1.8.3 Abstract Base Class

We can declare an abstract base class for the ArrayClass, since we might wish to implement it some other way at a later date. To declare such a class, we must decide on the methods to be included. Clearly one method is *size ()*; this is the one missing from the C++ array.

We could implement a putObject() method and a getObject() method, corresponding precisely to the operations in the abstract data type. If we did this, the method signatures in our class would be as follows.

```
int size ();
void putObject (DataType newObject, int k);
DataType getObject (int k);
```

However, we can also take advantage of the ability to overload operators. If we overloaded the array operator[], then a call like "myArray.putObject(data, k)" could be written instead as "myArray[k] = data", while a call like "cout << myArray.getObject (k)" could be written instead as "cout << myArray[k]". This is more consistent with the syntax for a C++ array.

What is the return type of the overloaded array operator? It must be DataType&, for otherwise the expression myArray[k] could not appear on the left side of an assignment. Thus, the method signatures will be as follows:

```
int size ();
DataType& operator[] (int k);
```

Now we can write our abstract base class. It is parameterized, so it must appear in a header file, as previously explained. We will give the full file contents:

```
#ifndef __ABSTRACTARRAY__H
#define __ABSTRACTARRAY__H

#include <iostream>
using namespace std;
#include "Exception.h"
class ArrayException : public Exception { };
class ArrayMemoryException : public ArrayException { };
class ArrayBoundsException : public ArrayException { };

template <class DataType>
class AbstractArrayClass
{
public:
    virtual int size () const = NULL;
    virtual DataType& operator[] (int k) = NULL;
};

#endif
```

The reader should particularly note the word *const* which follows the (empty) parameter list for the *size ()* method. This word indicates to the compiler that the instance on which *size ()* is called is unchanged by the method. Thus, the method can be called even on instances of the class that are declared as constant.

3.1.8.4   Class definition

With the abstract base class and the exception classes in hand, we can define a class *ArrayClass* which will use the built-in array type but add the *size()* method we desire. First, we must consider the protected fields and the constructor and destructor that act on them.

Fields, Constructors, and Destructor

If different *ArrayClass* instances are to have different sizes of arrays, each *Array-Class* instance must create its array in the free store, which means that (a) there might be an out-of-memory error in creation and (b) the *ArrayClass* instance must destroy its own array. Further, if we are to be able to report the size of the array belonging to an instance, we must store the size in an instance field. Thus, we can conclude that the class, with its fields, is initially as follows:

```
template <class DataType>
class ArrayClass : virtual public AbstractArrayClass<DataType>
{
protected:
    DataType* paObject;
    int _size;
};
```

An instance of the ArrayClass is pictorially depicted in Figure 3.2. Each object of the class ArrayClass has a pointer and an integer variable. The variables are initialized appropriately in the constructors that will be discussed. The circle in Figure 3.2 depicts the memory space and fields contained in the object belonging to the ArrayClass. The paObject is not initialized in Figure 3.2 (a) and Figure 3.2 (b) shows this after initialization. The array pointed by paObject resides outside the space allocated for an instance of the ArrayClass.

In order to create an array, we must know the size of the array. Thus, our constructor must accept an integer parameter giving the size. We will also throw an exception if the allocation fails. If an allocation using *new* fails, the return value is NULL, so we can test for this special value.

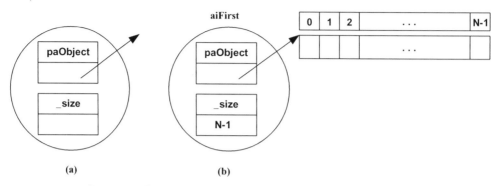

Figure 3.2: The ArrayClass instance with and without initialization of field variables.

```
template <class DataType>
class ArrayClass : virtual public AbstractArrayClass<DataType>
{
protected:
    DataType* paObject;
    int _size;
public:
    ArrayClass (int n);
};
// -------------------------------------------------------
template <class DataType>
ArrayClass<DataType>::ArrayClass (int n)
{
    _size = 0; // default in case allocation fails
    paObject = new DataType[n];
    if (paObject == NULL) throw ArrayMemoryException();
    _size = n;
}
```

We have above repeated the class definition with the method prototype added, but for the sake of efficiency we shall omit this step for the rest of the discussion. The complete class definition will be given when all methods have been written, though the reader should practice by inserting the method prototypes in the class definition as they are discussed.

If we create an array in the free store, we must also delete it when we finish with it, but we must be sure not to delete it if it was not properly allocated:

```
template <class DataType>
ArrayClass<DataType>::~ArrayClass ()
{
    if (paObject != NULL) delete[] paObject;
    paObject = NULL;
    _size = 0;
}
```

In the above program segment for the destructor the variable paObject is not deleted after the delete[] statement. Recall that if we use the statement delete paObject then it would delete only the first element of the array pointed by paObject. Actually, the paObject is a pointer to the first element of the array. Our constructor/destructor pair is now complete. For convenience, we can add two more constructors, one of which accepts an initial value for all elements of the array:

```
template <class DataType>
ArrayClass<DataType>::ArrayClass (int n, const DataType& val)
{
    _size = 0; // default in case allocation fails
    paObject = new DataType[n];
    if (paObject == NULL) throw ArrayMemoryException();
    _size = n;
    for (int i = 0; i < n; i++)
        paObject[i] = val;
}
```

The other constructor will be a default constructor. What is a reasonable size for an array for which no size is specified? We will give it a default size of 1, but use a named constant so we can easily change it later:

```
const int ARRAY_CLASS_DEFAULT_SIZE = 1;

template <class DataType>
ArrayClass<DataType>::ArrayClass ()
{
    _size = 0; // default in case allocation fails
    paObject = new DataType[ARRAY_CLASS_DEFAULT_SIZE];
    if (paObject == NULL)  throw ArrayMemoryException();
    _size = ARRAY_CLASS_DEFAULT_SIZE;
}
```

Copy Constructor and Assignment Operator

Our new class has a pointer instance variable. This indicates that we need a copy constructor and an assignment operator. Consider what happens when the compiler finds an assignment like this:

```
ArrayClass<int> aiFirst;
...
ArrayClass<int> aiSecond;

aiSecond = aiFirst;
```

The variables aiFirst and aiSecond have already been created. Now we wish to set aiSecond equal to aiFirst. In the absence of other instructions, the compiler will do a bitwise copy of the fields of aiFirst to the fields of aiSecond. In other words, it will do the following and pictorially depicted in Figure 3.3.

```
aiSecond.paObject = aiFirst.paObject;
aiSecond._size = aiFirst._size;
```

Now we have a problem: aiFirst and aiSecond *both* have pointers to aiFirst.paObject. Whichever instance is destroyed first will delete aiFirst.paObject and return its memory to the free store for reuse by other objects. However, the surviving instance will still have a pointer to aiFirst.paObject and may write to it, thereby corrupting the use by another object. But then when the surviving instance is itself destroyed, it will try to delete aiFirst.paObject again, corrupting the free store as well. Clearly we cannot allow the compiler to do a bitwise copy of an instance of ArrayClass.

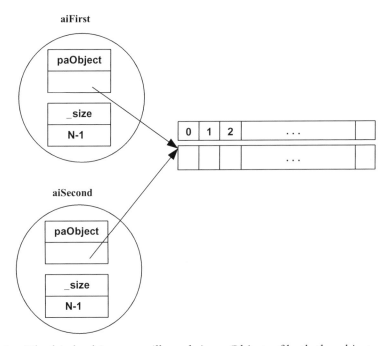

Figure 3.3: The bit-by-bit copy will result in paObject of both the objects pointing to the same array.

The same problem arises if we try to construct aiSecond from aiFirst:

```
ArrayClass<int> aiFirst;
...
ArrayClass<int> aiSecond (aiFirst);
```

Once again, in the absence of instructions, the compiler will do a bitwise copy of aiFirst.

The solution to these problems is to give the compiler explicit instructions on how to implement an assignment or construction with a copy. We do this by overloading the assignment operator and writing a copy constructor.

A copy constructor is simply a constructor with only one parameter, which is a reference to an instance of the class. The copy constructors are called whenever we create objects and we need to use old instances of objects to initialize the newly created object. Also, the copy constructor will be called whenever we pass by value or return by value. In this case, the copy constructor simply involves copying the _size_ field of the initializing instance, creating an array of the appropriate size, and copying over the values:

```
template <class DataType>
ArrayClass<DataType>::ArrayClass (const ArrayClass<DataType>& ac)
{
    if (&ac != this) //disallow copying the object on to itself
    {
        _size = 0; // default in case allocation fails
        paObject = new DataType[ac._size];
        if (paObject == NULL) throw ArrayMemoryException();
        _size = ac._size;
        for (int i = 0; i < _size; i++)
        {
            paObject[i] = ac.paObject[i];
        }
    }
}
```

The assignment operator will do exactly the same thing, first deleting the
already existing array. The assignment operator is used whenever we need to assign
the object with another one that is compatible with it. This suggests that we should
create a protected method copy() to do the actual copying, replace the copy constructor above with the much simpler one below, and write a very simple assignment
operator:

```
template <class DataType>
void ArrayClass<DataType>::copy (const ArrayClass<DataType>& ac)
{
    _size = 0; // default in case allocation fails
    paObject = new DataType[ac._size];
    if (paObject == NULL) throw ArrayMemoryException();
    _size = ac._size;
    for (int i = 0; i < _size; i++)
    {
        paObject[i] = ac.paObject[i];
    }
}
// ------------------------------------------------------------
```

```
template <class DataType>
ArrayClass<DataType>::ArrayClass (const ArrayClass<DataType>& ac)
{
    if (&ac != this) //disallow copying the object on to itself
        copy (ac);
}
// ---------------------------------------------------------
template <class DataType>
void ArrayClass<DataType>::operator=
(const ArrayClass<DataType>& ac)
{
    if (&ac != this) //disallow copying the object on to itself
    {
        if (paObject != NULL) delete[] paObject;
        copy (ac);
    }
}
```

Accessor and Mutator Methods

Now we have two methods to implement: *size ()* and the overloaded array operator[]. The *size ()* method is relatively simple, though the reader should note that a *const* method must be flagged as *const* in both the class definition and the implementation of the method.

```
template <class DataType>
int ArrayClass<DataType>::size () const
{
    return _size;
}
```

The overloaded array operator is slightly more complicated, as we must check for a valid index and throw an exception if the index is invalid:

```
template <class DataType>
DataType& ArrayClass<DataType>::operator[] (int k)
{
    if ((k < 0) || (k >= size())) throw ArrayBoundsException();
    return paObject[k];
}
```

The ostream << function

Normally, at this point in developing a data structure, we would write an Iterator class for the data structure. However, access to the *ArrayClass* is so extremely simple that we will leave that development as an exercise. We can, however, write an *ostream* << function to simplify the process of outputting *ArrayClass* instances. Since we can use the virtual methods from *AbstractArrayClass* in our function, we need not refer specifically to *ArrayClass* in the function and our function will work for any subclass of *AbstractArrayClass*. Therefore, this code should be placed in the AbstractArray.h file. We will enhance our output by putting commas between the elements and brackets around the entire array:

```
template <class DataType>
ostream& operator << <DataType>(ostream& s,
                     AbstractArrayClass<DataType>& ac)
{
    s << "[";
    for (int i = 0; i < ac.size (); i++)
    {
        if (i > 0)
        {
            s << ',';
        }
        s << ac [i];
    }
    s << "]";
    return s;
}
```

The class header file

Putting the above methods and function together, we have the following header file for the *ArrayClass* class[5]:

---

5 Your compiler, such as Visual C++ may require you to add an *ostream* << method for *Array-Class* itself in addition to the one in *AbstractArrayClass*. However, you can just copy the existing one and change the type of the second operand.

```
#ifndef __ARRAYCLASS__H
#define __ARRAYCLASS__H

#include "AbstractArray.h"

const int ARRAY_CLASS_DEFAULT_SIZE = 1;

template <class DataType>
class ArrayClass : virtual public AbstractArrayClass<DataType>
{
protected:
    DataType* paObject;
    int _size;
    void copy (const ArrayClass<DataType>& ac);
public:
    ArrayClass ();
    ArrayClass (int n);
    ArrayClass (int n, const DataType& val);
    ArrayClass (const ArrayClass<DataType>& ac);
    virtual ~ArrayClass ();
    virtual int size () const;
    virtual DataType& operator[] (int k);
    void operator= (const ArrayClass<DataType>& ac);
};

// All the methods previously presented go here

#endif
```

The main() function

Finally, we test our class with a simple main() function:

```
#include "ArrayClass.h"
void main ()
{
    ArrayClass<int> ai(5, 4);
    ArrayClass<int> ai2 = ai;
    ArrayClass<int> ai3 (10);

    cout << ai << endl;
    cout << ai2 << endl;
    cout << ai3 << endl; // output varies as ai3 is uninitialized
    cout << endl;
    for (int i = 0; i < ai.size (); i++)
    {
        ai[i] = i*2;
    }
    try      // demonstrate exception handling
    {
        ai[5] = 10; // this line outside of try will end program
    }
    catch (ArrayBoundsException e)
    {
        cout << "Index out of bounds" << endl;
    }
    cout << endl;
    ai3 = ai;
    cout << ai << endl;
    cout << ai2 << endl;
    cout << ai3 << endl;
}
```

The output of this class demonstrates that the class works correctly:

```
[4,4,4,4,4]
[4,4,4,4,4]
[96,18195,21575,0,0,0,0,0,0,0]

Index out of bounds

[0,2,4,6,8]
[4,4,4,4,4]
[0,2,4,6,8]
```

3.1.9   Applications

In this section, we will present two applications that use arrays of integers. These applications show how arrays can be used to solve practical applications in an elegant manner.

3.1.9.1   A simple bucket sorting program

Statement of the problem: given M integers whose values are in the range from *0* to *N-1*, sort the M integers in $O(N + M)$ time. The algorithm we will use is Bucket-Sort, and is described as follows:

```
Algorithm Bucket-Sort (A,B)
Input: An array A is the array of M integers
Output: Array B containing sorted integers from A.
1. B ← createNewArray (N)  //Create a new array of size N
2. i ← 0                   //Initialize all positions in B to 0
3. while (i < N)
4.    B[i] ← 0
5.    i ← i+1
6. endwhile
7. i ← 0                   //For each integer x in the input
8. while (i < N)           //place 1 in position x of B
9.    B[A[i]] ← 1
10   i ← i+1
11. endwhile
```

After the M integers have been sorted using bucket-sort, we can go through the loop starting from the smallest index 0 to the largest index of N-1 and print the index value j, if at position j there is a 1. The resulting output is a sorted list of the M integers. To initialize the array will take $O(N)$ units of time, to process the M integers will take $O(M)$ units of time, and to output the sorted M integers will take $O(N)$ time. Hence the total time required is $O(N + M)$.

In the following figures, we provide an example of the workings of this algorithm. Figure 3.4 shows the numbers to be sorted, which are initially out of order.

$$15, 3, 2, 0, 1, 4, 7$$

Figure 3.4:   Numbers to be sorted by bucket sorting.

In Figure 3.5, we see the array for sorting, initialized to 0's. The reader will note that although we have just seven numbers to sort, we must have an array for the range from 0 to 15, that is, for the range of the values.

0	1	2	3	4	5	6	7	8	9	10	11	12	13	14	15
0	0	0	0	0	0	0	0	0	0	0	0	0	0	0	0

Figure 3.5:   Array B initialized to 0's.

In Figure 3.6, below, we see that each element of the original set to be sorted is represented by a "1" in the array B.

0	1	2	3	4	5	6	7	8	9	10	11	12	13	14	15
1	1	1	1	1	0	0	1	0	0	0	0	0	0	0	1

Figure 3.6:   Array B with positions given in Figure (a) equal to a 1.

We can now simply scan across the array, outputting the index of each slot in the array that is non-zero. Figure 3.7, below, shows the output.

$$0, 1, 2, 3, 4, 7, 15$$

Figure 3.7:   Output when array B is scanned from index positions 0 through 15.

You will see in later Chapters the existence of sorting algorithms that can sort M integers in $O(M \log M)$ time. As noted above the simple bucket sorting algorithm has a complexity of $O(n + M)$. Clearly, $O(n + M) < O(M \log M)$ as long as $O(n) < O(M \log M)$. That is, the largest integer in the set to be sorted with simple bucket sort, should be less than $O(M \log M)$.

In the following, we present a program to perform the above steps.

```cpp
#include "ArrayClass.h"

ArrayClass<int> bucketSort (ArrayClass<int>& ac, int max)
{
    ArrayClass<int> bucket(max+1);
    int i;
    for (i = 0; i < max+1; i++) { bucket[i] = 0; }
    for (i = 0; i < ac.size(); i++) { bucket[ac[i]] = 1; }
    return bucket;
}
// ----------------------------------------------------------
void main ()
{
    int ints[] = {8, 11, 4, 30, 22, 10, 15, 3, 7, 29};
    ArrayClass<int> aInts (10);

    cout << "The initial sample values are " << endl;
    cout << "8, 11, 4, 30, 22, 10, 15, 3, 7, 29 "<<endl;

    for (int i = 0; i < 10; i++)
    {
        aInts[i] = ints[i];
    }

    ArrayClass<int> bucket = bucketSort (aInts, 30);

    cout<<"The initial sample values are " << endl;
    for (int I = 0; i< 31; i++)
    {
        if (bucket[i] > 0) cout << i << ", ";
    }
    cout << endl;
}
```

The output of the above program is given below:

```
The initial samples values are
8, 11, 4, 30, 22, 10, 15, 3, 7, 29
3, 4, 7, 8, 10, 11, 15, 22, 29, 30,
```

The above main() function suggests that we might desire another constructor for the *ArrayClass* type: one which accepts an array of ints and a number of elements. The writing of such a constructor is left as an exercise for the reader.

3.1.9.2   Merging two sorted arrays

Statement of the problem: given two sorted arrays of integers A and B of size n and m, respectively, create a sorted array C of size $n + m$ containing elements from both A and B. A simple algorithm to do this would be to store elements from both A and B into C, and use a sorting algorithm to sort C, without taking advantage of the fact that A and B are already sorted. Since C contains $n + m$ elements, the minimum sorting time is $O((n + m)log(n + m))$ as discussed in the first chapter. In this section, we will present an algorithm to produce a sorted array C in $O(n + m)$ time by using the fact that A and B are already sorted.

Informally, the algorithm proceeds by moving through the three arrays in order. At each step, the current element of A is compared with the current element of B, and the smaller of the two is copied to the current position in C. The current position in C advances by one at every step, while the current position in A or B advances only after an element is copied from the array to C. Eventually, either A or B will have been fully copied, and then all remaining elements of the other will be copied over to C.

Clearly, after each comparison, exactly one element is copied to C, and since C contains no more than N + M elements, the complexity of the above technique is $O(n + m)$. The algorithm may be more formally described as follows:

```
Algorithm Merge (A,B,C)
Input: Arrays A and B of sorted integers
Output: Sorted Array C containing elements from Arrays A and B.

1.   C ← createNewArray (A.size + B.size)
2.   i ← 0    //i will index on A (the array is 0-based)
```

```
3.    j ← 0      //j will index on B
4.    k ← 0      //k will index on C
5.    while (i < A.size) and (j < B.size)
      //repeatuntil one array has been fully copied
6.      if A[i] < B[j]
7.        C[k] ← A[i]
8.        i ← i + 1
9.      else
10.       C[k] ← B[j]
11.       j ← j + 1
12.     endif
13.     k ← k + 1
        // at the end of the while loop, either A or B has been
        // fully copied.
14.   endwhile

15.   while (i < A. size)
      //if A has not been fully copied, copy the rest of A
16.     C[k] ← A[i]
17.     i ← i + 1
19.     k ← k + 1
19.   endwhile
20.   while (i < B. size)
      //Otherwise B has not been fully copied, so copy the rest.
21.     C[k] ← B[j]
22.     j ← j + 1
23.     k ← k + 1
24.   endwhile
```

We provide an example below of the workings of this algorithm. We have two arrays, which need not be of the same size. In this case, one is of size 7 and the other of size 5. The result will be an array of size 12.

0	1	2	3	4	5	6
3	19	27	36	42	55	70

Array A

0	1	2	3	4
2	4	5	6	26

Array B

Figure 3.8: Two sorted arrays A and B.

The variables i, j, and k, all begin at value 0. Since B[0] is less than A[0], the value from B[0] is copied into C[0], and j and k are both incremented. The variable i is unchanged.

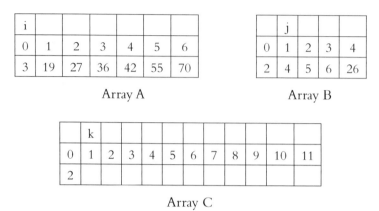

Array A

Array B

Array C

Figure 3.9: The content of C[0] is 2 after a single comparison. Also, note that the index position of i remains the same while the index positions of k and j have moved by one.

For the next step, we will find that $A[i] = 3$ and $B[j] = 4$. Thus, $A[i]$ will be copied to $C[k]$, and i and k will be incremented, leaving j untouched.

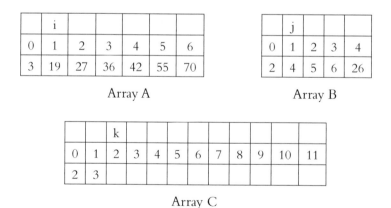

Array A

Array B

Array C

Figure 3.10: Results after two comparisons.

From now on, j will be incremented until it reaches index position 4 where 26 is stored, since all the numbers from index position 1 to 3 in B are less than 19. Then

A[1] will be copied and *i* incremented, producing the result below:

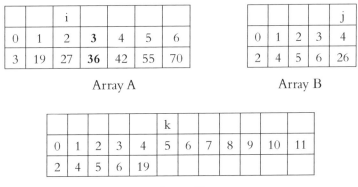

Array A

Array B

Array C

Figure 3.11: Results after six comparisons.

On the next step, we will copy the last value from array B and increment *j* and *k*, after which we will copy all of the remaining values from array A. The final result is:

0	1	2	3	4	5	6	7	8	9	10	11
2	3	4	5	6	19	26	27	36	42	55	70

Array C

Figure 3.12: The sorted array C after the execution of the merge algorithm.

In the following, we will present a program to implement and test the above algorithm. We assume below that the reader has implemented a constructor for Array-Class, which accepts an array of elements and a size.

```
#include "ArrayClass.h"

template <class DataType>
ArrayClass<DataType> merge
    (ArrayClass<DataType>& arrayA, ArrayClass<DataType>& arrayB)
{
    ArrayClass<DataType> arrayC (arrayA.size() + arrayB.size());
    int i = 0, j = 0, k = 0;
    while ((i < arrayA.size()) && (j < arrayB.size()))
```

```
    {
            if (arrayA[i] <= arrayB[j])
                arrayC[k++] = arrayA[i++];
            else
                arrayC[k++] = arrayB[j++];
    }
    while (i < arrayA.size())
    {
            arrayC[k++] = arrayA[i++];
    }
    while (j < arrayB.size())
    {
            arrayC[k++] = arrayB[j++];
    }
    return arrayC;
}
// ------------------------------------------------------
void main ()
{
    int intsA[] = {2, 7, 8, 12, 25, 30, 80};
    int intsB[] = {10, 15, 20, 35, 100};
    ArrayClass<int> arrayA (intsA, 7);
    ArrayClass<int> arrayB (intsB, 5);
    for (i=0; i < 7; i++) arrayA[i] = intsA[i];
    for (i=0; i < 5; i++) arrayB[i] = intsB[i];

    cout << "arrayA = " << arrayA << endl;
    cout << "arrayB = " << arrayB << endl;
    ArrayClass<int> merged = merge (arrayA, arrayB);
    cout << "merged = " << merged << endl;
}
```

When the above program is run, the output is as follows:

```
arrayA = [2,7,8,12,25,30,80]
arrayB = [10,15,20,35,100]
merged = [2,7,8,10,12,15,20,25,30,35,80,100]
```

Although the Merge algorithm could be useful in itself, in some circumstances, it is normally used by a larger algorithm, called MergeSort, which sorts an array using the technique known as divide–and–conquer. The MergeSort algorithm is discussed in Chapter 9.

DIVIDE-AND-CONQUER ALGORITHMS

Divide-and-conquer is a top-down technique for designing algorithms that first decomposes an instance of a problem into a number of smaller sub-instances of the same problem, solving independently each of these sub-instances and then merging the solutions to obtain the solution of the original instance. One of the fundamental issues in a divide-and-conquer approach is to use a simple algorithm when the instance is small (called the *base* instance) but decompose the instance when the instance is fairly large. The important aspect of this strategy is determining the size of the base instance, which is usually a constant.

EXAMPLE OF A DIVIDE-AND-CONQUER ALGORITHM

Let us illustrate the divide-and-conquer method by a concrete example.

The problem is to sort n numbers. To solve this problem by the Divide-and-Conquer approach, we first divide an instance into two equal sized lists, recursively, until we get to instances of sufficiently small size. For sorting the small instances we can use a simple sorting algorithm, such as the *insertion sort*.

In the recursive process of combining the solutions, the idea is to *merge* two sorted lists into one larger list. We have already presented an efficient algorithm for merging two sorted lists which only takes $O(n + m)$ time where n and m are the sizes of the respective sorted lists. In this problem the number of sub-instances is two.

CHARACTERISTICS OF A DIVIDE-AND-CONQUER ALGORITHM

For the divide-and-conquer algorithm to be effective there are three primary ingredients:

- Equal sized sub-instances.
- Existence of efficient algorithms for merging solutions to sub-instances.
- Appropriate invocation of the base algorithm.

TEMPLATE FOR A DIVIDE-AND-CONQUER ALGORITHM

Consider an arbitrary problem, and let *base* be the algorithm for solving the small sub-instances. The general template for a divide-and-conquer algorithm is as given in the figure below.

```
Algorithm Divide-and-Conquer(I)
Input: A problem instance I
Output: A solution to the instance I

if I is small or simple then return base(I)
decompose I into sub-instances I_1,I_2,I_3,...,I_k
for j ← 1 to k do
    S_j ← Divide-and-Conquer(I_j)
endfor
Merge S_j's to obtain the solution for I
```

3.2 Strings

A string is a sequence of characters. There are many applications that require storage and processing of strings. The String Abstract Data Type's minimal specification is given below. Although C++ does not have a built-in data type called the string, it does have numerous methods that handle arrays of characters in order to provide the string operations.

3.2.1 Abstract Data Type

```
createString (n)
    // create a string of size n
getChar (index)
    // get the character stored at position index in the
    // string
putChar (newCharacter, index)
    // replace the character at position index with
    // newCharacter
insertChar (newCharacter, index)
    // insert newCharacter after the character at position
    // index in the string
deleteChar (index)
    // delete the character at position index and
    // reconstruct a new string without that character.
concat enate (s)
    // attach a copy of s to the end of the string
length ()
    //  get the length of the string
equals (s)
    // returns true if the string is exactly equal to string s,
    // otherwise false
comparesTo (s)
    // returns an indicator for whether the string is less than,
    // equal to, or greater than s
substring (left, length)
    // returns a substring of length length, starting at position
    // left.
index (c, start)
    // returns the index of the first position of character c
    // at or after index start in the string, or else −1,
lastIndex(c, end)
    // returns the index of the last position of character c
    // at or after index start in the string,or else −1
```

Given the above primitive operations as a basis, we can create more complex and useful operations including searching for a string in a given string.

3.2.2   Arrays of Characters

We will give a few examples of the use of the built-in functions for dealing with arrays of characters (i.e., "strings") in C++. It is easy to place a string in a C++ program and then print it:

```
#include <iostream.h>
void main ()
{
    char hello[] = "Hello, world";
    cout << hello << endl;
}
```

In the above code, the reader should note that *hello* is of type *char[]*, meaning that it points to an array of type *char*. The literal string "Hello, world" is equivalent to an array initializer, with special syntax for the convenience of mere humans. The *hello* variable could have been declared as follows, with the rest of the program remaining unchanged:

```
char hello[]={'H', 'e', 'l', 'l', 'o', ',',
    ' ', 'w', 'o', 'r', 'l', 'd', '\0'};
```

But what is the '\0' doing at the end of this array? The answer is that the built-in string routines in C++, including the overloaded << operator for *ostream*, used above, all expect that strings will be null-terminated. That is, these routines expect that the last character in the array will always be a null, or '\0'. If we had not terminated the string with a null, *cout* would have blithely continued to print characters after the end of "Hello, world" until it happened to hit a memory address which contained a null. The reader should experiment by removing the terminal null, or by placing a null earlier in the array.

The C++ string manipulation routines are provided as part of the standard libraries, so to access them you must include the appropriate header file, string.h. The reader must bear in mind once again that these routines operate on arrays of characters, and *do not know* how much space has been allocated for a given array. Thus, they can readily run off the end of an array, potentially trashing the stack or other variables in the free store.

Consider first the function *strcpy()*. The name stands for "string copy" and that is exactly what the function does. It copies each character from the source string to the corresponding position in the destination string, stopping after it copies the terminating null. Thus, the destination string will be properly null-terminated. The signature of *strcpy()* is as follows:

▦   `char *strcpy(char* dest, const char* src);`

Since an array variable name is really a pointer to the underlying type, we can call this function with two arrays as well as with pointers. Now, let us consider this program:

```
#include <iostream.h>
#include <string.h>
void main ()
{
    char hello[] = "Hello, world";
    char newHello[13]; // "Hello, world" is 12 chars, plus null
    cout << hello << endl;
    strcpy (newHello, hello);
    cout << newHello << endl;
}
```

The output is quite boring: just "Hello, world" printed twice. But the reader should note the array size of *newHello*: it is big enough to hold all of the characters of *hello*. What if it weren't? Let us reduce its array size somewhat:

```
#include <iostream.h>
#include <string.h>
void main ()
{
    char hello[] = "Hello, world";
    char newHello[6]; // now newHello has insufficient space
    cout << hello << endl;
    strcpy (newHello, hello);
    cout << newHello << endl;
    cout << hello << endl;
}
```

The result varies by compiler. When it was tried on one[6], it produced no error as written, but when hello was initialized to "Hello, world and universe", it produced a memory error which halted the program. This behavior indicates that the compiler was

---

6 Microsoft Visual C++ Studio 2010.

aligning the variables on 16-byte boundaries, and further that overrunning the end of newHello trashed an important part of memory.

On two other compilers[7], the program did not crash, but it produced an output (displayed below) that indicates that part of the hello variable was copied on top of the *hello* variable itself, in the course of copying it to newHello. The output also shows that newHello, though declared as size 6, was actually allocated 8 bytes, indicating that the variables are aligned on 4-byte boundaries.

```
Hello, world
Hello, world
world
```

The reader may wish to experiment on other compilers; the results are unlikely to be encouraging. It would be nice if we could restrict the copying to no more than the available space, and we can, using *strncpy()*. The signature is almost the same, except that we add an additional argument that gives the maximum length to be copied:

```
char *strncpy(char *dest, const char *src, int maxlen);
```

We must be careful not to overrun the end of the destination array, as *maxlen* does *not* include the terminating null (worse, the terminating null may not be added if the source string is longer than *maxlen*). Thus, we could rewrite our *main()* function as follows:

```cpp
#include <iostream.h>
void main ()
{
    char hello[] = "Hello, world";
    char newHello[6]; // now newHello has insufficient space
    cout << hello << endl;
    strncpy (newHello, hello,5);
    cout << newHello << endl;
    cout << hello << endl;
}
```

The output shows that this time there is no overlap:

```
Hello, world
Hello
Hello, world
```

---

7 Borland C++ 5.01, and g +-+ running on Red Hat 5.1 Linux

Of course, we have to know how many characters *newHello* can accommodate, which makes *strncpy()* inconvenient to use. There is a function *strlen()*, which will return the length of an array of characters, but this is only the length of the string to the terminating null, *not* the size of the array. Given the intricacies of dealing with the string handling functions, we will write our own String class using them so that we will not have to deal with the intricacies in our programs, only in the class.

3.2.3   String Handling Functions

Some of the useful string handling functions that are defined in C++ are listed in the following table. We will make use of them below.

```
int strcmp (const char* s1, const char* s2);
// compares two strings, halting when it reaches null of
//.either string. Result is <0 if s1 < s2; >0 if s1 > s2;
// and 0 if s1 = s2. This comparison is case-sensitive.
int stricmp (const char* s1, const char* s2);
// strcmp, but case-insensitive (hence the i) in stricmp()
int strncmp (const char* s1, const char* s2, int maxlen);
// strcmp, but compares no more than maxlen characters
int strlen (const char* s);
// returns the number of characters before the null
char* strcat (char* dest, const char* src);
// appends a copy of src to the end of dest, changing dest in
// the process. The dest array must be large enough to
// accommodatethe resulting string!
char* strchr (const char* str, char c);
// returns a pointer to the first occurrence of c in str,
// or null if c is not present
char* strrchr (const char* str, char c);
// returns a pointer to the last occurrence of c in str,
// or null if c is not present
```

3.2.4   The String Class

We will now create a *String* class that implements the String abstract data type using the string handling functions from C++. Our intention is to make strings easier to use, without requiring the user to check for string lengths or do other tedious manipulations. As an added bonus, because our *String* objects are *objects*, not just arrays of characters, we can overload the comparison operators so that our programs do not have to compare using *strcmp()*.

Just as C++ uses arrays of characters to represent strings, we will use our *ArrayClass* class to implement our *String* class. *ArrayClass* already has methods to access the elements of the underlying array directly, and to return the size. We will add methods to implement the operations of the String abstract data type. Since we already know the types of our elements (they are of type *char*), the *String* class will not be parameterized, but will be a subclass of *ArrayClass <char >* .

3.2.4.1   Exceptions

The same two errors which occur with arrays also occur with strings: out-of-memory and out-of-bounds errors. Additionally, we might try to concatenate two strings, or insert a character or characters into a string, but find that we have exceeded the size of the string. We will throw another exception in this case. Since *String* is a subclass of *ArrayClass <char>*, it is reasonable to make its exception part of the *Array-Exception* family:

```
class StringSizeException : public ArrayException { };
```

3.2.4.2   Class definition

With the base class chose and the new exception class in hand, we can define a class *String* which will use the built-in array from ArrayClass and the string handling functions from string.h. First, we must consider the protected fields and the constructor and destructor which act on them.

Fields, Constructors, and Destructor

We can always obtain the length of the string using *strlen()*. If we prevented the user from accessing the individual characters of the string, we could store this value in an instance variable. However, if we allow the user free access, then our instance variable can't be guaranteed to be accurate. To make our *String* class compatible with the normal C++ "string", we will allow free access. So it appears that the only instance variables required are those which already exist in *ArrayClass*. The shell of our class is therefore as follows:

```
class String : virtual public ArrayClass<char>
{
};
```

Now, what about constructors? We might want to create a String instance with an allocated size, but initially empty, and we might also want a default constructor to produce an empty string of minimum size. We could accomplish both by constructing the parent ArrayClass with a size and an initial value:

```
class String : virtual public ArrayClass<char>
{
    String ();
    String (int n);
};
String::String () : ArrayClass<char> (1, '\0') { }
String::String (int n) : ArrayClass<char> (n+1, '\0') { }
```

The reader should note several points about this constructor. First, we have no need to do any initialization ourselves as *ArrayClass* can handle the problem, so the body of the constructor is empty. Second, we don't expect the user to remember to leave space for the null character, so we add one to the number of characters allocated. Third, the parent class constructor does *not* have to match the subclass' constructor in the number of parameters. Finally, we showed both the class definition and the method implementation, but hereafter, for the sake of efficiency, we will show only the method implementations and expect the reader to fill in the class definition.

Now let us consider another constructor. What if we wanted to initialize a *String* instance with a literal string like this:

```
String s = "Hello, world";
```

As noted in Chapter 1, we can always use = followed by a value when the constructor we wish to use takes only a single parameter. So the above statement will compile if the *String* class has a constructor which accepts a single parameter, which is a *char** variable. To initialize a *String* instance with a literal string, we need to allocate enough space, then copy over the string. These operations are readily implemented using the string handling functions:

```
String::String (char* s) : ArrayClass<char> (strlen(s)+1)
{
    strcpy (paObject, s);
}
```

The destructor need do nothing, since the *String* class itself did not allocate any memory from the free store (*ArrayClass* did, but it will deallocate that in its own destructor). So our destructor is mercifully brief, though the reader must remember to tag it as "virtual" in the class definition:

```
String::~String() { }
```

Copy Constructors and Assignment Operator

In this case, we have a pointer instance variable in the superclass, so we need a copy constructor and an assignment operator. Fortunately, the superclass has a copy constructor already, and we need add nothing to its operation:

```
String::String (const String& str) : ArrayClass<char> (str) { }
```

The assignment operator is a little different, as we would like to copy the text (if it fits) but not change the allocated array size, so we will throw an exception if the string passed to us is larger than we can accommodate (remembering to place a terminating null). If this exception is caught but ignored, the effect will be to truncate the string. However, there is one complication: a *String* created by the default constructor has size 1, and we would not like such *String*s to be permanently empty. Thus, if we see a *String* instance of size 1, we will cause this to expand to match the *String* instance passed as a parameter. This allows us to declare a *String* instance with no pre-determined size, and then set its size by assigning a value to the instance.

```
void String::operator= (const String& str)
{
    if (size() == 0)// constructed by default
    {
        ArrayClass<char>::operator= (str);
                    // call parent operator
        return;
    }
    int max = str.length();// not constructed by default
    bool overflow = false;
    if (_size-1 < max)
    {
        overflow = true;
        max = _size-1;
                // note, we should replace _size-1 with
                // size() as soon as we implement size()
    }
    strncpy (paObject, str.paObject, max);
    paObject[max] = '\0';// always null terminate!
    if (overflow) throw StringSizeException();
}
```

At this point, given a *String* object *s1*, we can write the statement *s2="Hello"*, which compiles and runs even though we have no assignment operator for *String* with a *char** parameter! The reason is that we have a constructor with a *char** parameter, so the compiler inserts code along these lines for the statement:

```
String temp = "Hello";
s2 = temp;
```

Accessor and Mutator Methods

As a subclass of *ArrayClass*, the *String* class already has an overloaded index operator which has the effect of implementing the required getChar() and putChar() operations. It also has a *size()* method which returns the number of characters it can store. However, this is not quite correct, as we have to leave room for the terminating null.

Thus, we want to override the inherited *size ()* method and return a value one less. The reader may wish to review the implementation of the overloaded index operator to observe that this has the effect of making it impossible for the user to overwrite the terminating null.

```
int String::size () const
{
    return ArrayClass<char>::size()-1;
}
```

We would also like to provide the length of a string, and this is quite simple:

```
int String::length() const
{
    return strlen (paObject);
}
```

The equals() and comparesTo() operations required by the String array data type can be implemented using overloaded operators and the *strcmp ()* function. We implement two of the possibilities, and leave the rest as exercises for the reader.

```
bool String::operator== (const String& str) const
{
    return (strcmp(paObject, str.paObject) == 0);
}
// ------------------------------------------------------------
bool String::operator< (const String& str) const
{
    return (strcmp(paObject, str.paObject) < 0);
}
```

In addition to the exact equality required by the == operator, we may want to test for equality without case sensitivity. As mentioned previously, we can use stricmp() to perform this operation:

```
bool String::equalsIgnoreCase (const String& str)
{
    return (stricmp(paObject, str.paObject));
}
```

By this time, it should be obvious how we will implement the required *concatenate()* method:

```
void String::concatenate (const String& str)
{
    int len = length(); // store length() for efficiency's sake
    int max = str.length();
    bool overflow = false;
    if (size() < max+len)
    {
        overflow = true;
        max = size()-len;
    }
    strncpy (paObject+len, str.paObject, max);
    paObject[max+len] = '\0'; // always null terminate!
    if (overflow) throw StringSizeException();
}
```

With *concatenate()*, we can readily overload the + operator to allow statements like *s1 = s2 + s3*, where *s1*, *s2*, and *s3* are *String*s:

```
String String::operator+ (const String& str)
{
    String temp (length() + str.length());
    temp = (*this);
    temp.concatenate (str);
    return temp;
}
```

We leave the *insertChar()* and *deleteChar()* methods for the reader to implement. Both require simple array manipulations, but both are capable of throwing exceptions.

The *index()* and *lastIndex()* methods are a little tricky to implement, if we use the library functions *strchr()* and *strrchr()*, previously described. These functions deal with *char** values, whereas we wish to return index positions. Fortunately, C++ allows us to use pointer arithmetic to find the index relative to *paObject*, based on the pointer position:

```
int String::index (char c, int start) const
{
// if start is past the end, obviously c isn't present
    if (start >= length()) return -1;
    char* pc = strchr(paObject + start, c);
    if (pc==NULL) return -1;
    return (pc-paObject);
}
```

The implementation of *lastIndex* () is obvious, and is left as an exercise. For convenience, we may also overload the methods to accept a single *char* parameter, since we usually do want to search the whole string:

```
int String::index (char c) const
{
    return index (c, 0);
}
```

Finally, the *substring* () method requires us to produce a new *String* object which will contain the desired substring of our original *String* object. We will return the object itself, not a pointer because we don't want to produce garbage if the user fails to delete the object. The actual creation of the substring object is simple, but we do have to do some checking:

```
String String::substring (int left, int len) const
{
// a negative index is illegal
    if (left < 0) throw ArrayBoundsException();
// no need to throw exception if left is at least
// legal, if not actually in bounds
    String sub(len);
    if (left > length()) return sub;
    int max = len;
    if (max+left > length()) max = length() - left;
    strncpy (sub.paObject, &paObject[left], max);
    sub.paObject[max] = '\0'; // always null terminate!
    return sub;
}
```

The ostream << function

And now, the method we have all been waiting for: a method to actually print out a
String object, so we can observe the class in action:

```
ostream& operator<< (ostream& s, const String& str)
{
    s << str.paObject;
    return s;
}
```

The class header file

Putting the above methods and function together, we have the following header file
for the *String* class:

```
#ifndef __STRING__H
#define __STRING__H
#include "ArrayClass.h"
class StringSizeException : public ArrayException { };
class String : virtual public ArrayClass<char>
{
friend ostream& operator<< (ostream& s, const String& str);
public:
    String ();
    String (int n);
    String (const String& str);
    String (char* s);
    virtual ~String ();
    void operator= (const String& str);
    virtual int length() const;
    virtual int size () const;
    bool operator== (const String& str) const;
    bool operator< (const String& str) const;
    void concatenate (const String& str);
    int index (char c, int start) const;
    int index (char c) const;
    int lastIndex (char c, int start) const;
    int lastIndex (char c) const;
    String substring (int left, int len) const;
    String operator+ (const String& str);
    bool equalsIgnoreCase (const String& str);
#endif
```

The methods go in a separate file called String.cpp.

The main() function

Finally, we test our class with a simple *main()* function:

```
#include "String.h"
void main ()
{
    String s1 = "String1";
    String s2 = s1;
    s2[6] = '2';
    String s3(20);
    s3 = s1;
    s3.concatenate(" + ");
    s3.concatenate(s2);
    cout << s1 << ", " << s2 << ", " << s3 << endl;
};
```

The output of this class demonstrates that the class works correctly:

```
String1, String2, String1 + String2
```

3.2.5   Applications

In the following we will present three applications that use strings, together with a novel algorithm due to Knuth, Morris, and Pratt for string matching.

3.2.5.1   A simple name formatting program

Statement of the problem: given N names stored in an array of $String$ objects with each name in the format "FirstName LastName", convert the names into the format "LastName,FirstName", and store them in another array of $String$ objects. To solve this problem, for each $String$ object we will perform the following operations: first, extract the LastName and the FirstName by locating the character ',' with the *index()* method, then use the *concatenate()* method to concatenate the first and last name in the desired order and form a new string. In implementing this function, we will use the $ArrayClass$ to hold the $String$ instances in which we are interested.

```
#include "String.h"

const int MAX_STRING = 100;// maximum length for strings
ArrayClass<String> formatNames (ArrayClass<String>& asSource)
{
    int spacePos;
    String FirstName (MAX_STRING);
    String LastName (MAX_STRING);

    ArrayClass<String> asResult(asSource.size());
    for (int i=0; i<asSource.size(); i++)
    {
        spacePos = asSource[i].index (' ');
        FirstName = asSource[i].substring(0,spacePos);
        LastName =
            asSource[i].substring(spacePos+1,asSource[i].length());
        asResult[i] = LastName + "," + FirstName;
    }
    return asResult;
}
// ------------------------------------------------------------------
void main ()
{
    ArrayClass<String> asNames(3);
        // note that all strings in asNames are default, length 1
    asNames[0] = "Steven Spielberg";
        // changes the size of asNames[0]
    asNames[1] = "George Lucas";
    asNames[2] = "David Lynch";
    cout << asNames << endl;
    cout << formatNames (asNames) << endl;
}
```

3.2.5.2   Counting letters in a string

Statement of the problem: given a string containing only ASCII characters, find the number of occurrences of each letter in the alphabet.

```
ArrayClass<int> countLtrs (String& myString)
{
    ArrayClass<int> counters(256,0);

    for (int i=0; i < myString.length(); i++)
        counters [myString[i]]++;
    return counters;
}
```

In the above code segment the reader will observe that character indices are used. C++ automatically converts and gives the integer equivalent of the character in the context where it is being used.

Statement of the problem: given a line of text T and a pattern P, both stored as array of characters, determine whether the pattern P is found in the text T. Assume that the length of the pattern P is less than the length of the text T.

A straightforward algorithm for this task follows.

```
STRING-MATCH (T, P)          // T and P are arrays of
  i ← 0                      // characters and T is the text
  while (i < T.length −      // and P is the pattern
  P.length + 1)              // i will index on T (the array
    if T.substring           // is 0-based)
    (i, P.length) = P        // stop searching when the
      return true            // remaining string is shorter
    else                     // than P.length
      i ← i + 1
  return false
```

In Figure 3.13, we see a sequence of comparisons between the text "xyxxyxyxyyxyxyxyyyxyxyxx" and the pattern "xyxyyxyxyxx". After each comparison, which produces a mismatch, we shift the pattern right by one and try again.

Position	00	01	02	03	04	05	06	07	08	09	10	11	12	13	14	15	16	17	18	19	20	21	22	23	
Text	x	y	x	x	y	x	y	x	y	y	x	y	x	y	x	y	y	y	x	y	x	y	x	x	
Pattern	x	y	x	y	y	x	y	x	y	x	x						Mismatch at index position 3 of pattern								
			x	.	.	.	.										Mismatch at position 0								
				x	y	.	.	.									Mismatch at position 1								
				x	y	x	y	y	.	.	.						Mismatch at position 4								
					x	.	.	.	.								Mismatch at position 0								
					x	y	x	y	y	x	y	x	y	x	x		Mismatch at position 10								

Figure 3.13:   A partial sequence of comparisons performed by the straightforward string matching algorithm.

The comparison of a substring with P takes P.length comparisons of pairs of characters. The total number of comparisons made by the above approach is therefore (P.length)(T.length–P.length + 1), which is the complexity of the straightforward string matching technique.

The above algorithm can be readily translated into C++ :

```cpp
bool stringMatch (String& T, String& P)
{
    int i = 0;
    while (i < T.length() - P.length() + 1)
    {
        if (P.equalsIgnoreCase(T.substring(i, i +
            P.length())))
            return true;
    else
        i++;
    }
  return false;
}
```

3.2.5.3   A fast string matching technique - KMP algorithm

Statement of the problem: given a line of text T and a pattern P, both stored as array of characters, determine whether the pattern P is found in the text T. Assume that the length of the pattern P is less than the length of the text T. We will now describe the technique of Knuth, Morris, and Pratt for the string matching problem.

The complexity of this algorithm is $O(T.length + P.length)$, hence it is much superior to the straightforward string matching algorithm given above.

The basic idea of the KMP algorithm is to reduce the number of comparisons required when the pattern has repetitive substrings. Consider, for instance, the text "aaaaab" and the pattern "aaab". Aligning the two initially, we find a mismatch at index 3 of the pattern:

	0	1	2	3	4	5
Text	a	a	a	a	a	b
Pattern	a	a	a	b		

With the naïve string-matching algorithm, we would shift the pattern over by one and try again. However, this would require us to compare the first two *a*'s of the pattern with the characters at indices 1 and 2 of the text.

	0	1	2	3	4	5
Text	a	a	a	a	a	b
Pattern		a	a	a	b	

If we were somehow able to observe that the pattern started with three *a*'s, we would know that shifting the pattern over by one would produce a match at the first two characters, so that we could start comparing at index 3 in the text – the same position where we had a mismatch before. Further, once we find a mismatch at index 3 in the pattern (which does not match index 4 of the text), we can shift the pattern over by one and, again, we could start our comparison process at index 4 of the text, not at index 2.

	0	1	2	3	4	5
Text	a	a	a	a	a	b
Pattern			a	a	a	b

Now, let us try another text and pattern:

	0	1	2	3	4	5	6	7	8
Text	a	b	a	b	a	b	a	b	b
Pattern	a	b	a	b	b				

This time, we find a mismatch at index 4 in the pattern. It is clearly pointless to shift the pattern right by just one; since the characters at indices 0 and 1 of the pattern are different, the initial character clearly will not match after such a shift:

	0	1	2	3	4	5	6	7	8
Text	a	b	a	b	a	b	a	b	b
Pattern		a	b	a	b	b			

Instead, we need to shift by two:

	0	1	2	3	4	5	6	7	8
Text	a	b	a	b	a	b	a	b	b
Pattern			a	b	a	b	b		

And here, again, we see that our comparisons need only start at index 4 in the text, the position where the mismatch occurred before. This time, there is a mismatch at index 4 of the pattern, which does not match the character at index 6 of the text. Once again, we can shift by two and start out comparisons at index 6 of the text, and this time we have a match.

	0	1	2	3	4	5	6	7	8
Text	a	b	a	b	a	b	a	b	b
Pattern					a	b	a	b	b

This is the basic idea of the KMP algorithm: to observe repetitions in the pattern and make use of the repetitions to decide how far to shift after each mismatch, so that we can begin our comparisons at the index in the *text* of the last mismatch. The question that we ask ourselves is, what is the index in the *pattern* where we must begin our comparisons.

Preliminaries

A string w is a prefix of a string x if $x = wy$, where y is a string, possibly empty. If y is not empty then w is a proper prefix of x. Also, if y is not empty, then y is a suffix of the string x. The string y is a proper suffix if w is not empty.

Consider this string: "*aba*". Note that the proper prefix of length one is the string "*a*" and is the same as the proper suffix of length one, the string "*a*". The following table gives examples of strings and the length of the proper prefix that is also the same as the proper suffix of the same string.

String	Length of the proper prefix that is the same as the proper suffix	Proper prefix
a	0	empty
ab	0	empty
aba	1	a
abab	2	ab
ababa	3	aba
ababaaabab	4	abab
aaabb	0	empty

Now, suppose that (1) we have matched k characters of the pattern to the text, (2) there is a mismatch at position $k + 1$, and (3) in the first k characters of the pattern there is a proper prefix w that matches a proper suffix y. This means that we can shift the pattern to the right so that its first character matches the first character of the suffix y. We are then guaranteed that all of the proper prefix w matches the text up to the point of the mismatch. We can then start comparing at that point.

We will now state the following subproblem which is a part of the KMP algorithm.

Subproblem statement

Given a string P of length n, for each i, $0 \leq i < n$, determine the length of the proper prefix of the string P[0 .. i] that is also a proper suffix of the string P[0 .. i]. Let next[i] be this length. Formally, next[i] is the maximum j ($0 \leq j < i$) such that P[$i - j + 1$ .. i] is equal to P[0 .. $j - 1$], and -1, if no j exists between 0 and i.

Solution Methodology

Clearly next[0] = 0, since a string of length 1 has no proper prefix or suffix The following example illustrates how the next[] values are computed for the pattern P = "xyxyyxyxyxx".

i	0	1	2	3	4	5	6	7	8	9	10
P	x	y	x	y	y	x	y	x	y	x	x
Next	0	0	1	2	0	1	2	3	4	3	1

Let us assume that the values of next[] for $0, 1, 2, ..., i - 1$ have been computed. We now will show how to compute next[i]. Assuming that $\text{next}[i - 1] \neq 0$, we know that $P[0..\text{next}[i-1]-1] = P[(i-1)\text{-next}[i-1]+1..i-1]$. For simplicity, let us call next[i − 1] by the name q. We have two possibilities.

♦ If $P[q]$ is in fact equal to $P[i]$, then both the proper prefix and the proper suffix can be extended by one and they will still match; in this case, $\text{next}[i] = \text{next}[i-1] + 1$.

♦ But suppose the two characters *don't* match. If $P[q] \neq P[i]$, we need to find the longest proper prefix of $P[0..q-1]$ which matches a suffix of $P[i-q..i-1]$, and then checking whether it is followed by a character matching $P[i]$. However, because we already know that $P[0..q-1]$ and $P[i-q..i-1]$ are equal, finding the longest matching prefix and suffix as described amounts to finding the longest proper prefix of $P[0..q-1]$ which matches a proper suffix of $P[0..q-1]$. But we know what *that* is: it is next[q − 1]. We therefore compare $P[\text{next}[q-1]]$ with $P[i]$. If they match, we have found next[i] to be next[q − 1] + 1. If not, we let $q = \text{next}[q-1]$, and try again. When we find $q = 0$ and there is no match, we know there is no proper prefix matching a proper suffix.

The reader should note that the computation of next[] depends solely on the pattern, not on the text at all. We present the C++ code for computing next[] below:

```
ArrayClass<int> computeNext (String& pattern)
{
    int p;
    int q;
    ArrayClass<int> next(pattern.length(),0);
    for (p = 2; p < pattern.length(); p++) // p is position of right end
```

```
    {
        q = next[p-1]; // q is presumed value of next[p]-1
        do
        {
            if (q >= 0)
            {
                if (pattern[q] == pattern[p])
                {
                next[p] = q + 1;
                break;
                }
                else
                {
                if (q == 0)
                        break;
                else
                        q = next[q-1];
                }
            }
        } while (q >= 0);
        cout << "finally p = " << p << " next = " << next << endl;
    }
    return next;
}
```

Main Algorithm

Given that next[] has been computed for the pattern, we are now ready to describe the
KMP algorithm. The straightforward string matching algorithm increments the shift
one at a time until a match occurs or no match is found. The KMP algorithm, on the
other hand, tries to increase the value of the shift by more than one without missing
any matching patterns in the text, using the following idea. Consider the following
example, where the Text (T) is matched with the pattern (P) starting from the text
position T[5].

	0	1	2	3	4	5	6	7	8	9	10	11	12	13	14	15	16	17	18	19	20	21	22
T	x	y	x	x	y	x	y	x	y	y	x	y	x	y	x	y	y	x	y	x	y	x	x
P						x	y	x	y	y	x	y	x	y	x	x							
						0	1	2	3	4	5	6	7	8	9	10							

Note that P[10] did not match with T[15]. Our naive algorithm would have a shift of one and will start by comparing P[0] with T[6] and so on. Clearly, P[0] ≠T[6]. Also T[5..14] = P[0..9]. The largest proper suffix of P[0..9] that is also the proper prefix of P[0..9] is the string xyx with a length of 3. In other words, we have a mismatch at the text position T[15], the largest substring of T[5..14] that will match the prefix of P is of length 3. This implies that we can start comparing T[15] with P[3] and skip three comparisons. Let us now abstract out the basic tenet of the algorithm.

If a mismatch occurs at position P[j] with the text position T[i], then let k be the length of the largest proper prefix of P[0..j-1] that is also a proper suffix. The next comparisons will start from text position T[i] with pattern position P[k + 1]. In order to find the k value defined above for every $1 \leq j \leq |P|$, we need to preprocess P and compute the next function as described previously. We are now ready to present the KMP string matching algorithm written in C++ .

```
int KMPStringMatch (String& T, String& P)
// returns index of start of P in T or -1 if P is not a substring
{
    if (P.length() == 0)
        return 0; // 0-length string is always substring
    if (T.length() == 0)
        return -1; // 0-length string has no substrings

    ArrayClass<int> next = computeNext (P);
    int pPos = 0;
    int tPos = 0;
```

```
while (tPos < T.length())
{
    if (P[pPos] == T[tPos]) // the two are matched so far
    {
        pPos++;
        tPos++;
    }
    else // we just found a mismatch
    {
        if (next[pPos] <= 0)
        {
            tPos++;
            pPos = 0;
        }
        else
        {
            pPos = next[pPos-1];
        }
    }
    if (pPos == P.length())
    {  // we've matched all of the pattern, so we just find
       // starting position and return it
        return (tPos - P.length());
    }
}
return -1; // string was not found
}
```

3.3 Multidimensional Arrays of Objects

Arrays with more than one dimension are useful in many ways. Arrays with two
dimensions are referred to as matrices. Matrices arise in many application areas including image processing, solutions of simultaneous equations and graph algorithms. A
three dimensional matrix can be used to store information that is at most a 4-tuple. For
example, courses taken by a student during each semester of each year could be stored
in a three dimensional array. The primitive operations that can be applied to single
dimensional arrays can also be applied to multidimensional ones.

3.3.1   Abstract Data Type: Matrix

Specification of an Abstract Data Type for a two dimensional array is given below. Extension to more than two dimensions is obvious.

```
create (n, m)
  //size n and m of first and second dimension, respectively.
putObject (newObject, i, j)
  //place an object newObject at row position i and column j.
getObject (i, j)
  //get the object at row position i and column position j
size (d)
  //find the size of the dth dimension of the array
```

C++ implements a two-dimensional array as an array of arrays. Therefore, although C++ has no specific data structure for a two-dimensional array, all of the operations required by the abstract data type can be carried out using built-in language structures. Again, however, C++ does not check bounds on arrays and will not report the dimensions of an array. Therefore, we shall design a C++ matrix class.

3.3.2   Implementation of the Matrix Abstract Data Type

As in the case of the *ArrayClass*, we shall implement a parameterized *Matrix*. In fact, since a matrix can be regarded as an array of rows (or columns), we shall make *Matrix* a descendant of the *ArrayClass*. It shares the element type and the exceptions used by the *ArrayClass*.

3.3.2.1   Exceptions

However, we will add one more exception, used when requested matrix manipulations (such as multiplication) are impossible because the matrices involved are of incompatible dimensions. As usual, this exception is simple:

```
class MatrixIncompatibleException : public ArrayException { };
```

3.3.2.2 Class definition

As indicated, *Matrix* will be a descendant of *ArrayClass*. But if *m* is an instance of *Matrix*, what is the type of *m[0]*? As indicated, we regard a matrix as an array of rows, so that *m[0]* must be a row, that is, it must itself be an instance of *Array-Class*. Then what is the type of *m[0][0]*? It must be of the type indicated by the type token *Object*, for it is an element of the matrix. It appears initially that we need to use nested templates:

```
template <class DataType>
class Matrix : public ArrayClass < ArrayClass<DataType> >
{
};
```

An instance of the matrix class using the above definition is shown in Figure 3.14. The pointer variable in the instance of the Matrix class points to an array and it is an array of ArrayClass objects shown as small circles in Figure 3.14. This should be thought of as rows of the matrix. Each ArrayClass objects actually stores the values in the array pointed its paObject and it is the columns of the matrix.

Fields, Constructors, and Destructor

Now we must consider the constructors. As usual, we need a default constructor that creates a minimum-size matrix (1 × 1). We would also like to have a constructor to create an $n \times m$ matrix (*n* rows and *m* columns). Finally, we would like to have a constructor, which creates an $n \times m$ matrix and also initializes its elements.

But now we have a problem. When an array of instances of a class is created, all of the instances are created using the default constructor. That is, if *Matrix* is an *Array-Class* whose elements are of type *ArrayClass*, although we can create a matrix of *n* rows, every row will be of size 1. This is not a desirable outcome. Since there is no method to resize the rows[8], we can only ensure that they are of the right size to begin with. Therefore, we must create them in the *Matrix* constructor. But then we must create them using *new*, so the rows of the Matrix must actually be pointers to Array-Class objects (shown in Figure 3.15 where each element in the array location points to an ArrayClass object). Worse, the type of *m[0]* must be different from the type of the rows, so that the caller will not need to dereference *m[0]*. We seem to be at an impasse.

---

8 Why not just add one? Because the ability to resize is not part of the array abstract data type and produces a different sort of structure, more like the Vector described later.

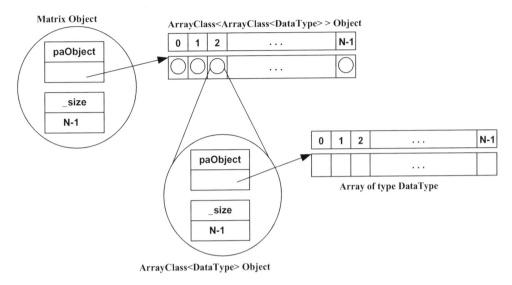

Figure 3.14:   The Matrix class implemented using ArrayClass of ArrayClass objects.

However, all is not lost. We can derive *Matrix* not from *ArrayClass*, but from *AbstractArrayClass*. We can then place a pointer to an instance of *ArrayClass* as an instance field within *Matrix*, and then conceal all the complications from the user:

```
template <class DataType>
class Matrix : public AbstractArrayClass < ArrayClass <DataType > >
{
protected:
    ArrayClass < ArrayClass<DataType>* >* theRows;
}
```

The An instance of the Matrix class object using the above definition is shown in Figure 3.15. The default constructor must create a row with one element, and then initialize that one element. In the code below, the use of *(*theRows)[0]* should be noted: the index operator has higher precedence than the deference, so we must dereference *theRows* before using the index operator.

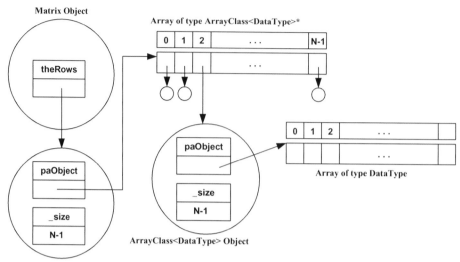

Figure 3.15: An instance of the matrix class where each array element points to an ArrayClass object.

```
template <class DataType>
Matrix<DataType>::Matrix ()
{
    theRows = new ArrayClass < ArrayClass <DataType>* > (1, NULL);
    if (theRows == NULL)
    {
        throw ArrayMemoryException();
    }
    (*theRows)[0] = new ArrayClass <DataType> ();
    if ((*theRows)[0] == NULL)
    {
        throw ArrayMemoryException();
    }
}
```

The first *n* × *m* constructor creates an array of instances of *ArrayClass*, theRows, and then initializes all of its elements:

```
template <class DataType>
Matrix<DataType>::Matrix (int n, int m)
{
    theRows = new ArrayClass <ArrayClass <DataType>* > (n, NULL);
    if (theRows == NULL)
    {
        throw ArrayMemoryException();
    }
    for (int i = 0; i < n; i++)
    {
        (*theRows)[i] = new ArrayClass <DataType> (m);
        if ((*theRows)[i] == NULL)
        {
            throw ArrayMemoryException();
        }
    }
}
```

Our last constructor obviously takes the same action as the previous constructor, but also initializes the elements:

```
template <class DataType>
Matrix<DataType>::Matrix (int n, int m, DataType v)
{
    theRows = new ArrayClass <ArrayClass <DataType>* > (n,NULL);
    if (theRows == NULL)
    {
        throw ArrayMemoryException();
    }
    for (int i = 0; i < n; i++)
    {
        (*theRows)[i] = new ArrayClass <DataType> (m, v);
        if ((*theRows)[i] == NULL)
        {
            throw ArrayMemoryException();
        }
    }
}
```

Since *Matrix* has a pointer field, and all of the rows have been allocated on the free store, we must have a destructor to delete all allocated space if necessary, but not otherwise. However, we will similarly wish to delete all allocated space in the course of copying a Matrix, so we will place the deletion code in a separate, protected method:

```
template <class DataType>
Matrix<DataType>::~Matrix ()
{
    deleteRows();
}
// ------------------------------------------------------------
template <class DataType>
void Matrix<DataType>::deleteRows ()
{
    if (theRows != NULL)
    {
        for (int i = 0; i < theRows->size(); i++)
        {
            if ((*theRows)[i] != NULL) delete (*theRows)[i];
            (*theRows)[i] = NULL;
        }
        delete theRows;
    }
    theRows = NULL;
}
```

Copy Constructor and Assignment Operator

The copy constructor and assignment operator are modeled on those of *Array-Class*, and the assignment operator has the same effect of changing the size of the matrix, if necessary:

```
template <class DataType>
void Matrix<DataType>::copy (Matrix<DataType>& m)
{
    deleteRows();
    theRows = new ArrayClass <ArrayClass <DataType>* >
    (m.size(), NULL);
    if (theRows == NULL) throw ArrayMemoryException();
    for (int i = 0; i < m.size(); i++)
    {
        (*theRows)[i] = new ArrayClass <DataType> (m[i]);
        if ((*theRows)[i] == NULL) throw ArrayMemoryException();
    }
}
// -----------------------------------------------------------
template <class DataType>
Matrix<DataType>::Matrix (Matrix<DataType>& m)
{
    theRows = NULL;
 copy (m);
}
// -----------------------------------------------------------
template <class DataType>
void Matrix<DataType>::operator= (Matrix<DataType>& m)
{
    copy (m);
}
```

Accessor and Mutator Methods and the ostream << function

Now we need to allow the caller to access the rows of *Matrix* *m* using an expression like *m[i]*. Since the caller is not interested in the intricacies of our implementation, we must return an instance of *ArrayClass*, not a pointer to *ArrayClass*. Therefore, we have the method below. The reader should note that *(*theRows)* is of type *ArrayClass* but *(*theRows)[index]* is of type *ArrayClass**. Therefore, we have to dereference it before returning it.

```
template <class DataType>
ArrayClass<DataType>& Matrix<DataType>::operator[] (int index)
{
    return (*(*theRows)[index]);
}
```

Now the caller can use *m[i]* just as the caller would use as any other instance of *ArrayClass*. In particular, the expression *m[i][j]* will return a reference to the *j*th element of *m[i]*, or in other words, the element in the *i*th row and *j*th column of *m*.

We must override the *size()* method of *AbstractArrayClass*; this method will report the number of rows, for consistency with other arrays. We will add a *rows()* method which reports the number of rows, and a *columns()* method which reports the number of columns (the two together correspond to the size() operation of the multidimensional array abstract data type). It should be noted with respect to all three of these methods that, rather than store the dimensions in the *Matrix* instance, we rely on *theRows* and *(*theRows)[0]* to report the size of the rows.

```
template <class DataType>
int Matrix<DataType>::rows()
{
    return theRows->size();
}
// ------------------------------------------------------------
template <class DataType>
int Matrix<DataType>::columns()
{
    return (*this)[0].size();
}
// ------------------------------------------------------------
template <class DataType>
int Matrix<DataType>::size() const
{
    return theRows->size();
}
```

The ostream << function for *AbstractArrayClass* is acceptable for a *Matrix* and no new function is provided.

The class header file

Putting all of the above together, we have the following header file:

```
#ifndef __MATRIX__H
#define __MATRIX__H
#include "ArrayClass.h"

class MatrixIncompatibleException : public ArrayException { };

template <class DataType>
class Matrix : public AbstractArrayClass<ArrayClass <DataType> >
{
protected:
    ArrayClass < ArrayClass<DataType>* >* theRows;
    void copy (Matrix<DataType>& m);
    void deleteRows ();
public:
    Matrix ();
    Matrix (int n, int m);
    Matrix (int n, int m, DataType v);
    Matrix (Matrix& m);
    virtual ~Matrix();
    void operator= (Matrix& m);
    void operator= (const DataType* list);
    virtual int size() const;
    int columns();
    int rows();
    virtual ArrayClass<DataType>& operator[] (int index);
};

// methods previously presented go here

#endif
```

The main() function

For illustration, we will now overload *operator** to perform matrix multiplication, and then multiply some matrices. We have implemented this function solely for matrices of *double*s and have not added it to the class, for if we implemented it for the template class *Matrix*, the only element types allowed in a *Matrix* would be those which support both addition and multiplication[9]. The other algebraic operations such as addition, subtraction, and (a little harder) scalar multiplication, are all left for the reader.

```cpp
#include "Matrix.h"
Matrix<double> operator* (Matrix<double>& matA,
Matrix<double>& matB)
{
    if (matA.columns() != matB.rows())
        throw MatrixIncompatibleException();
    Matrix<double> matC(matA.rows(),matB.columns(),0);

    for (int i=0; i < matA.rows(); i++)
        for (int j=0; j < matB.columns(); j++)
        {
            for (int k=0; k < matA.columns(); k++)
                            matC[i][j] = matC[i][j] +
                            matA[i][k]*matB[k][j];
        }

    return matC;
}
// --------------------------------------------------------
void main ()
{
    Matrix<double> m2x3 (2, 3, 0);
    Matrix<double> m3x2 (3, 2, 0);
    Matrix<double> m2x2;
    Matrix<double> m3x3;
    m2x3[0][0] = 1; m2x3[0][1] = 2; m2x3[0][2] = 1;
    m2x3[1][0] = 0; m2x3[1][1] = 1; m2x3[1][2] = 3;

    m3x2[0][0] = 1; m3x2[0][1] = 1;
    m3x2[1][0] = 0; m3x2[1][1] = 1;
    m3x2[2][0] = 1; m3x2[2][1] = 1;

    m2x2 = m2x3 * m3x2;
    cout << m2x3 << " * " << m3x2 << " = " << m2x2 << endl;
    m3x3 = m3x2 * m2x3;
    cout << m3x2 << " * " << m2x3 << " = " << m3x3 << endl;
}
```

---

9 The reader may notice that this function is not a friend of Matrix (if it were, it would affect the possible element types just as if it were a method of the class). In general, a function must be a friend of a class if (a) it uses protected or private members of the class; or (b) the class that it uses is a template class such as Matrix<DataType>. Here, the function uses the class Matrix<double>, which is not a template class itself, but an instantiated class.

The two multiplications correspond to:

$$
\begin{vmatrix} 1 & 2 & 1 \\ 0 & 1 & 3 \end{vmatrix}
\begin{vmatrix} 1 & 1 \\ 0 & 1 \\ 1 & 1 \end{vmatrix}
=
\begin{vmatrix} 2 & 4 \\ 3 & 4 \end{vmatrix}
\qquad
\begin{vmatrix} 1 & 1 \\ 0 & 1 \\ 1 & 1 \end{vmatrix}
\begin{vmatrix} 1 & 2 & 1 \\ 0 & 1 & 3 \end{vmatrix}
=
\begin{vmatrix} 1 & 3 & 4 \\ 0 & 1 & 3 \\ 1 & 3 & 4 \end{vmatrix}
$$

The output shows that the multiplication was correctly performed:

```
[[1,2,1],[0,1,3]] * [[1,1],[0,1],[1,1]] = [[2,4],[3,4]]
[[1,1],[0,1],[1,1]] * [[1,2,1],[0,1,3]] =
[[1,3,4],[0,1,3],[1,3,4]]
```

Concluding Remarks

The reader should note above that the implementation of *Matrix* is concealed from the user. Pointer manipulations are completely invisible. All bounds are properly checked (though we wrote no code in *Matrix* to check them). Our concerns about ensuring that any memory allocated is ultimately deallocated are met, despite the nesting in the test program above of *double* array pointer within *ArrayClass* pointer within *ArrayClass* pointer within *Matrix* instance.

An *ArrayClass* which holds pointers, and correctly deletes all the pointers it holds when it is destroyed, is useful in itself, since it avoids the problem of default initialization of the elements. A *PointerArray* class can be extracted from *Matrix*, making *Matrix* merely a specialized subclass of *PointerArray*.

The implementation of *Matrix* also indicates a logical method for implementing a three-dimensional array: just as a *Matrix* instance holds a pointer to an array of one-dimensional arrays, a three-dimensional array instance should hold a pointer to an array of matrices. The implementation of three-dimensional and higher-dimensional arrays is left as an exercise for the reader. As a particularly challenging exercise, is it possible to write a class of which different instances have different dimensionality? For instance, one instance might be two-dimensional and another four-dimensional.

3.3.3   Applications

We now present two applications in which multidimensional arrays play useful roles. Solving systems of simultaneous equations is a traditional use of matrices, and the first application demonstrates such solution using Gaussian elimination. In image processing, the image data is stored as a matrix; the second application demonstrates the use of matrices in such processing.

3.3.3.1   Solving a system of Linear Equations

The discussion and examples for this section are based on the information presented in the text book titled "FORTRAN with Engineering Applications" authored by Koffman and Friedman", Addison Wesley, 1993.

$$\text{Let } A = \begin{bmatrix} 1 & 1 & 1 \\ 2 & 3 & 1 \\ 2 & -1 & -1 \end{bmatrix} \text{ and } X = \begin{bmatrix} 1 \\ 2 \\ 1 \end{bmatrix} \text{ be two matrices. The product A} \times \text{X is the}$$

$$\text{matrix } Y = \begin{bmatrix} 4 \\ 9 \\ -1 \end{bmatrix}. \text{ Now given the matrix A and the vector Y, we want to determine}$$

the vector X. In order to do this we have to solve the following equations:

$$\begin{bmatrix} 1 & 1 & 1 \\ 2 & 3 & 1 \\ 2 & -1 & -1 \end{bmatrix} \times \begin{bmatrix} X[0] \\ X[1] \\ X[2] \end{bmatrix} = \begin{bmatrix} 4 \\ 9 \\ -1 \end{bmatrix}$$

Written as a set of simultaneous equations we have three equations and three unknowns as given below.

X[0] + X[1] + X[2] = 4

2X[0] + 3X[1] + X[2] = 9

2X[0] − X[1] − X[2] = −1

We can now solve these equations using Gaussian elimination. Gaussian elimination process will convert a system of n linear equations into its *upper triangular form*. A matrix is in its triangular form if all the diagonal elements are 1 and elements below the diagonal are all 0. Once we have a matrix that is in its triangular form we can solve for the unknowns using a method called *back substitution*.

In constructing the triangular matrix, we start with a matrix of coefficients of the terms in the n linear equations with n unknowns. For the set of equations specified above, the matrix of coefficients is the matrix A given previously. From the coefficient matrix we construct the augmented matrix by adding the vector Y as the $(N + 1)^{th}$ column of the coefficient matrix A. For example, if A[i][j] represents the coefficient of the jth term in the ith equation then the general form of the augmented matrix and the augmented matrix in our example are given below. Let us call the augmented matrix AUG

$$\begin{bmatrix} 1 & 1 & 1 & 4 \\ 2 & 3 & 1 & 9 \\ 2 & -1 & -1 & -1 \end{bmatrix} \quad \begin{bmatrix} A[0][0] & A[0][1] & A[0][2] & Y[0] \\ A[1][0] & A[1][1] & A[1][2] & Y[1] \\ A[2][0] & A[2][1] & A[2][2] & Y[2] \end{bmatrix}$$

Example   **General Form**

Gaussian elimination process first involves triangulating the augmented matrix. Of course one can notice that the augmented matrix is not a square matrix (the number of rows and the number of columns are not the same). So triangulating the augmented matrix means that we need to make the elements AUG[i][i] for $0 \le i \le N - 1$ to be equal to 1 and all elements below this diagonal should be a 0.

In order to perform the triangulation process we have to execute operations on the augmented matrix. The operations that are allowed to be executed on the augmented matrix are:

♦ Multiply any row by a nonzero number.
♦ Add the values of any row a multiple of any other row.
♦ Swap any two rows.

The triangulation process proceeds by processing elements along the diagonal of the augmented matrix starting from the diagonal element AUG[0][0]. The diagonal element chosen for processing will be called the *pivot*. Thus, initially AUG[0][0] is the pivot element. If AUG[i][i] is the current pivot element, then the row i will be called the *pivot row*. Given a pivot element AUG[i][i] we have to change its value to 1 by *normalizing* the pivot row. The normalizing process is performed by multiplying the elements in row i by 1/AUG[i][i]. After the normalization process all coefficients in the column below the pivot is set to zero. That is, all the elements in AUG[i + 1,i], ..., AUG[N − 1, i] should have the value of 0. We can perform this operation by multiplying the pivot row i by −AUG[j][i] and then adding the result to row j. Note that we need to start the addition from column i + 1 since all the elements in columns 0 through i of the pivot row are all 0.

It is recommended that the largest value in the column be used as the pivot value. To find this element we need to search all the elements in the column below the position of the pivot element. Let the largest element be in row k. Now, swap rows i and k. This process of performing the after choosing the largest element is called *pivoting*. Note that if the largest coefficient is a 0, then the system of equations does not have a unique solution. Based on the above discussion, the algorithm for performing triangulation process using Gaussian elimination is given below.

```
Algorithm Triangulate

Input: A: The augmented matrix
Output: The triangulated matrix if there is a unique solution

1. Solution = true  //assume that there exists a unique solution
2. i = 0  //pivot position is i
3. while (Solution and (i < N))
   //Perform the pivoting operation
4.        Starting from row i find the row k which contains
          the largest absolute value in column i.
5.        if the largest absolute value is a 0
6.             Solution = false;
7.        else
8.             Swap rows i and row k
9.             Normalize the pivot row
10.            Eliminate the coefficients beneath the pivot row
11.            i ← i + 1
12.       endif
13. endwhile
14. if (Solution) then Normalize row N-1;
```

For the AUG matrix in our example, the triangulated augmented matrix is presented below.

$$\begin{bmatrix} 1 & 1 & 1 & 4 \\ 0 & 1 & -1 & 1 \\ 0 & 0 & 1 & 1 \end{bmatrix}$$

3.3.3.2 Image Processing Applications

Image processing research and development deal with the capture, storage, manipulation, and recognition of images. Every digital image has an associated size given as the number of rows and columns. Each element of a image I, given as I[i,j], is called a pixel. Pixel values are integer values representing gray values or intensity. Several standard operations can be performed to improve the quality of an image. We will describe them in the following and present algorithms to manipulate them. For all our discussion

Figure 3.16: Lena's image is used as an input for demonstrating image processing applications.

below we will use the famous picture of Lena[10] that is most often used for demonstrating image processing algorithms.

Thresholding

Thresholding is a method by which the gray scale image is converted into a binary image. A binary image is an image in which pixel values are either 0 or 1. The thresholding operation removes noise (extraneous values) to a certain level by setting lighter intensity pixels to 0 and the dark intensity pixels to 1. Thus, this process "cleans up" the image.

The following code segment converts gray image into a binary image using a *threshold* value of T.

```
for (i=0; i < n; i++)
    for (j=0; j < n; j++)
        if (i [i][j] < T)
            i [i][j] = 0;
        else
            i [i][j] = 1;
```

10 Excerpts from www.lena.org: "'lena' or 'lenna' is a digitized Playboy centerfold, from November 1972. (Lenna is the spelling in Playboy, Lena is the Swedish spelling of the name.) Lena Soderberg (ne Sjööblom) was last reported living in her native Sweden, happily married with three kids and a job with the state liquor monopoly. In 1988, she was interviewed by some Swedish computer related publication, and she was pleasantly amused by what had happened to her picture. That was the first she knew of the use of that picture in the computer business."

Histogram Analysis

Another way to remove noise from an image is to remove pixels whose gray values occur infrequently in the image. Histogram analysis determines the number of times each pixel value appears in an image. Using the histogram analysis we can create a binary image by substituting a zero in pixel positions that have a gray value whose frequency count is less than some threshold count and placing a 1 in all other positions. At the end of the following code segment, the count array contains the number of occurrences of each gray level in the image I, assuming 256 gray levels.

```
ArrayClass<int> count (256, 0);
for (int i=0; i < n; i++)
    for (int j=0; j < n; j++)
        count[ I [i] [j] ]++;
```

The following code segment creates a binary image using the histogram analysis.

```
for (int i=0; i < n; i++)
    for (int j=0; j < n; j++)
        if (count[ I [i] [j] ] < thresholdCount)
            I [i] [j] = 0;
        else
            I [i] [j] = 1;
```

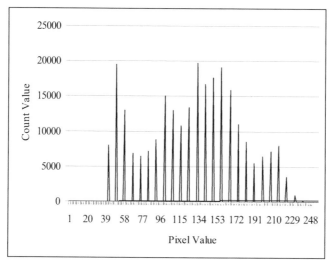

Figure 3.17: Graph plot of the histogram analysis of the original Lena picture

Figure 3.18:   Image of Lena after applying the threshold value of 127 and converted
to a binary image.

The average pixel value is 127 for the original Lena image. Applying the threshold-
Count of 127 to the original image the binary image we obtained is given in Figure 3.18

Connected Components

Given a binary image I, a single pixel I[i,j] is connected to another pixel I[m,n], if the
values of m and n are among the following:

- $m = i + 1, n = j + 1$;
- $m = i + 1, n = j - 1$;
- $m = i-1, n = j + 1$;
- $m = i - 1, n = j - 1$;
- $m = i + 1, n = j$;
- $m = i - 1, n = j$;
- $m = i, n = j + 1$;
- $m = i, n = j - 1$.

That is, the pixels I[i,j] and I[m,n] are connected if they are both 1 pixels and
I[m,n] is one of the eight pixels surrounding I[i,j] in the grid. A set of pixels in which,
for each 1 pixel in the set, there exists at least one other pixel to which it is connected,
is called a connected component.

Finding connected components is an important operation in image processing.
After finding connected components we can determine for each connected component the number of pixels forming the connected component. Using this number
we can delete connected components that contain a number of pixels less than some
threshold value. Thus finding connected components can also be useful to remove
noise from images.

The following recursive algorithm assigns a unique label to all pixels in the same component.

```
Algorithm ConnectedComponents
//Main algorithm
Input: An Image
Output: The connected components of the input image obtained
        by labeling

1.       componentNum ← 0
2.       comp ← createArray (Image.length(1), Image.length(2))
         //comp is created with
         //same dimensions
3.     repeat
4.          Scan the image to find an unlabeled 1 pixel (i,j)
5.          if no unlabeled pixel found then return
6.          recursiveLabel (image, comp, i, j, componentNum)
7.          componentNum ← componentNum + 1
8.     until (no unlabeled pixel found)

//recursive procedure used by the main algorithm
Algorithm recursiveLabel (image, Comp, i, j, num)
1. if (i is out of bounds) or (j is out of bounds) then return
2. if (Image[i,j] = 0) or (Comp[I,j] > 0) then return
3. Component [i, j] ← num
4. recursiveLabel (Image, comp, i-1, j-1, num)
5. recursiveLabel (Image, comp, i-1, j, num)
6. recursiveLabel (Image, comp, i-1, j+1, num)
7. recursiveLabel (Image, comp, i, j-1, num)
8. recursiveLabel (Image, comp, i, j+1, num)
9. recursiveLabel (Image, comp, i+1, j-1, num)
10. recursiveLabel (Image, comp, i+1, j, num)
11. recursiveLabel (Image, comp, i+1, j+1, num)
```

We are now ready to present the C++ code for the above algorithm.

```cpp
void recursiveLabel (Matrix<int>& Image, Matrix<int>& comp,
    int i, int j, int numComponent)
{
    if ((i < 0) || (i >= Image.columns()) ||
        (j < 0) || (j >= Image.rows()) || (Image[i][j] == 0) ||
            comp[i][j] > 0)
        return;

    comp[i][j] = numComponent;

    recursiveLabel (Image, comp, i-1, j-1, numComponent);
    recursiveLabel (Image, comp, i-1, j, numComponent);
    recursiveLabel (Image, comp, i-1, j+1, numComponent);
    recursiveLabel (Image, comp, i, j-1, numComponent);
    recursiveLabel (Image, comp, i, j+1, numComponent);
    recursiveLabel (Image, comp, i+1, j-1, numComponent);
    recursiveLabel (Image, comp, i+1, j+1, numComponent);
    recursiveLabel (Image, comp, i+1, j+1, numComponent);
}
// ------------------------------------------------------------
Matrix<int> connectedComponents (Matrix<int>& Image)
{
    int i, j, numComponents = 0;
    Matrix<int> comp (Image.rows(), Image.columns(), 0);

    for (i=0; i < Image.columns(); i++)
        for (j=0; j < Image.rows(); j++)
          if ((Image[i][j] == 1) && (comp[i][j] ==0))
          {
            numComponents = numComponents + 1;
            recursiveLabel (Image, comp, i, j, numComponents);
          }
    return comp;
}
```

3.4   Vectors

Let us imagine several students who share an apartment and attempt to put together a complete shopping list. They begin with a single piece of paper and (because they do want to be neat) they put one item on each line, moving to the next line for the next item. Over the course of a day, they notice additional items they lack, and they add each as soon as they see it. Soon they find that the piece of paper with which they started has become full. But one of the few things they do not lack is paper, so they add another piece of paper and continue the list.

The analogous operations in a computer program are more difficult, given only the data structures we have now. A programmer may create an array to hold the shopping list, but, as we have seen, this array has a fixed size. How does the programmer do the equivalent of adding another piece of paper to hold the rest of the list? This can be accomplished only by creating a larger array, copying the values from the old array into it, deleting the old array, and then using the larger array instead. Further, the procedure of filling in the array one item at a time requires that the programmer maintain a count of the items added so far so that the next item will be placed in the right place. These operations can be readily programmed, but since this sort of problem is likely to arise again, we would like to write a data structure that will support them automatically.

A list of values is called a vector and an array can be used to represent a vector. A vector is unlike an array in that the size of a vector can grow and shrink as items are added and deleted. Thus in addition to the operations that can be performed on an array, add and delete operations can also be performed on a vector.

3.4.1   Abstract Data Type

A specification of an Abstract Data Type for a vector class is given below:

```
create (n)
    //create a vector of size n.
putObject (newObject, i)
    //place an object newObject at position i.
getObject (i)
    //get the object at position i.
```

```
insertObject (newObject, i)
    // insert a new object at position i in the vector.
    // The size of the vector increases by one.
removeObject (i)
        // remove the object at position i of the vector.
        // The size of the vector decreases by one.
addObject (newObject)
        // adds newObject at the end of the Vector
        // The size of the vector increases by one.
size ()
        // returns the (current) size of the vector
```

3.4.1.1   Example of Using a Vector

Using the vector abstract data class, we can provide a pseudo code program to help the students write their shopping list (they discovered that they lack paper also and are forced to use the computer to record the list):

```
MakeStudentShoppingList

1. shoppingList ← CreateVector (20)  //get the list
2. while (not done)  //however long it takes
3.       item ← input from user
4.       shoppingList.addObject(item)
5. endwhile

6. i ← 0  //print it out on the one remaining
7. while i < shoppingList.size  //piece of paper so the students
8.       item ← shoppingList.getObject ( i )
         //don't have to take the computer
9.       display item  //to the mall
10.      i ← i + 1
11. endwhile
```

3.4.2   Implementation of Vector

We can now proceed with the implementation of the vector abstract data type in C++. The most obvious way to implement this type is by deriving our *Vector* class from the existing *ArrayClass* and adding methods to add, delete, and insert elements. However, this is not the only way to implement it. Therefore, we will write an *AbstractVector* class from which our *Vector* class will be derived, and which will act as the parent class for other vector implementations we may later write.

The derivation of *Vector* from *ArrayClass* is highly appealing and will simplify our implementation substantially, so we are not willing to give it up. The *Vector* class will be our first example of multiple inheritance.

3.4.2.1   Exceptions

The *Vector* class will not throw any exceptions other than those already declared for the *ArrayClass*.

3.4.2.2   Abstract Base Class

Given the specification of the abstract data type for a vector, we can prepare an abstract base class for the class that we will write. The class is given below.

```
template <class DataType>
class AbstractVector : virtual public
AbstractArrayClass<DataType>
{
public:
    virtual void insert (const DataType& item, int index) = NULL;
        //insert a new object at position index in the vector.
    virtual void remove (int index) = NULL;
        //remove the object at position index of the vector.
    virtual void add (const DataType& item) = NULL;
        //adds item at the end of the Vector
};
```

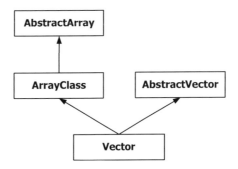

Figure 3.19:   The vector class that is uses multiple inheritance.

3.4.2.3   Class Definition

As noted, our *Vector* class will be a descendant of both *ArrayClass* and *AbstractVector*. The reader will note that *Vector* has one concrete parent (*ArrayClass*) and one pure abstract class (*AbstractVector*). Furthermore, the two classes have no common methods other than those inherited from their common parent. This hierarchy is presented in Figure 3.18.

Fields, Constructors, and Destructors

Since the *Vector* class is a descendant of *ArrayClass*, it has a pointer to an array of elements. We can increase or decrease the size of the vector by creating a new array, copying the data, and then deleting the old array. The abstract data type indicates that the size of the vector increases by just one for every object inserted or added. However, efficiency considerations indicate that we must increase the vector by some larger amount and then "grow into" the new array. This implies that we need a field to hold the current size of the vector (not the number of objects the underlying array can hold), and the increment factor (the amount by which the vector grows, when it grows). Our *Vector* class therefore has this shell:

```
template <class DataType>
class Vector : virtual public ArrayClass<DataType>,
        virtual public AbstractVector<DataType>
{
    int _currSize;
    int _incFactor;
}
```

The constructors required for a *Vector* are the same as those required for an *ArrayClass*: a default constructor, one to create a *Vector* with a specified size, and one to create a *Vector* with a specified size and then initialize the elements. In each case, *_currSize* is initially 0, since no objects have been added:

```
template <class DataType>
Vector<DataType>::Vector ()
    : ArrayClass<DataType>()
{
    _currSize = 0;
    _incFactor = 5;
}
// ---------------------------------------------------------
template <class DataType>
Vector<DataType>::Vector (int n)
    : ArrayClass<DataType>(n)
{
    _currSize = 0;
    _incFactor = (n+1)/2; //This is arbitrary and one can use a
                          //different increment
}
// ---------------------------------------------------------
template <class DataType>
Vector<DataType>::Vector (int n, DataType& val)
    : ArrayClass<DataType>(n, val)
{
    _currSize = 0;
    _incFactor = n/2; //This is arbitrary and one can use a
                      //different increment
}
```

Since *Vector* does not have any pointer variables other that those contained in *ArrayClass*, the destructor is trivial (just empty braces) and will not be presented.

Copy Constructor and Assignment Operator

The copy constructor and assignment operators can simply rely on the *ArrayClass* operations for copying the data from the underlying array, and then update the *_currSize* and *_incFactor* fields. It also seems reasonable to write a constructor (nearly a copy constructor) and an assignment operator to allow an instance of *ArrayClass* to be assigned to a *Vector*.

```
template <class DataType>
Vector<DataType>::Vector (const Vector<DataType>& v)
    : ArrayClass<DataType> (v)
{
    _currSize = v._currSize;
    _incFactor = v.incFactor();
}
// ------------------------------------------------------------
template <class DataType>
Vector<DataType>::Vector (const ArrayClass<DataType>& ac)
    : ArrayClass<DataType> (ac)
{
    _currSize = ac.size();
    _incFactor = (_currSize+1)/2;
}
// ------------------------------------------------------------
template <class DataType>
void Vector<DataType>::operator= (const Vector<DataType>& v)
{
    ArrayClass<DataType>::copy (v);
    _currSize = v._currSize;
    _incFactor = v.incFactor();
}
// ------------------------------------------------------------
template <class DataType>
void Vector<DataType>::operator= (const ArrayClass<DataType>& ac)
{
    ArrayClass<DataType>::copy (ac);
    _currSize = ac.size();
    _incFactor = (_currSize+1)/2;
}
```

Accessor and Mutator Methods and the ostream<< function

In order to behave as a proper *ArrayClass* instance, print out correctly, and so on, a Vector must report the number of objects currently stored in its list as its size, not the number it could hold. This forces us to override the *size()* method to return *_currSize* instead of *_size*, and provide a different method, *capacity()*, to report the number of elements in the underlying array. We will also report the increment factor. All of these methods are simple:

```
template <class DataType>
int Vector<DataType>::size() const
{
    return _currSize;
}
// ------------------------------------------------------------
template <class DataType>
int Vector<DataType>::capacity() const
{
    return _size;
}
// ------------------------------------------------------------
template <class DataType>
int Vector<DataType>::incFactor() const
{
    return _incFactor;
}
```

We can also provide methods to set the capacity (i.e., change the size of the underlying array) and the increment factor. Negative increment factors are silently ignored. Changing the capacity involves (as explained in the student shopping list example) creating a new array, copying over the items, and deleting the old array. Setting the capacity to less than *_currSize* truncates the array and discards the items beyond the capacity.

```cpp
template <class DataType>
void Vector<DataType>::setIncFactor(int f)
{
    if (f >= 0) _incFactor = f;
}
// -----------------------------------------------------------
template <class DataType>
void Vector<DataType>::setCapacity(int c)
{
    int len = _currSize;
    if (len > c) len = c;
    DataType* paNew = new DataType[c];
    if (paNew == NULL)
    {
        throw ArrayMemoryException();
    }
    for (int i = 0; i < len; i++)
    {
        paNew[i] = paObject[i];
    }
    if (paObject != NULL)
    {
        delete[] paObject;
    }
    paObject = paNew;
    _size = c;
    if (_currSize > len)
    {
        _currSize = len;
    }
}
```

How should we handle the index operator? In particular, what if the caller attempts to access an element past the last actual element? Should we expand the capacity to make the access legal? Although the Vector grows as needed, we cannot allow it to grow in this situation, for we would not have valid objects between the last actual element and the newly accessed element. Therefore, in this situation, we should throw an exception. This is the *ArrayClass* behavior, so we will not override the inherited index operator.

The basic steps for inserting into a *Vector* are as follows:

1. Check whether the index (place to insert) is legal: is it 0 or more? Is it within the array or just after the end, i.e., less than or equal to *_currSize*? Throw an exception if it is illegal.
2. Check whether there is enough space, i.e., if *_currSize + 1* is less than *_size*.
3. Expand the capacity if necessary, by adding *_incFactor* to *_size*. Move elements to the right by one position starting from the highest index position down to the position where the element has to be inserted.
4. Place the new element in a desired location.

At some point we must increase *_currSize*, as there is now one more element in the *Vector*. When should we do this? If we use the index operator in our loop to move the elements out of the way, we must increase *_currSize* before that step. With these considerations in mind, we can write the *insert ()* method:

```
template <class DataType>
void Vector<DataType>::insert (const DataType& item, int
index)
{
    if ((index < 0) || (index > _currSize))
    {
        throw ArrayBoundsException();
    }
    if (_currSize+1 == _size)
    {
        setCapacity (_size + _incFactor);
    }
    _currSize++;
    for (int i = _currSize-1; i > index; i--)
    {
        (*this)[i] = (*this)[i-1];
    }
    (*this)[index] = item;
}
```

The `add()` method is simple to implement, since it consists of inserting just after the current end of the *Vector*, i.e., at position `_currSize`:

```
template <class DataType>
void Vector<DataType>::add (const DataType& item)
{
    insert (item, _currSize);
}
```

The *remove()* method is almost the reverse of the *insert()* method, although we shrink the array only when the difference between the allocated size of the array and the number of elements actually held exceeds `_incFactor`, and of course we move elements starting with the lowest index:

```
template <class DataType>
void Vector<DataType>::remove (int index)
{
    if ((index < 0) || (index >= _currSize))
    {
        throw ArrayBoundsException();
    }
    if (_currSize <= _size-_incFactor)
    {
        setCapacity (_size - _incFactor);
    }
    for (int i = index; i < _currSize-1; i++)
    {
        (*this)[i] = (*this)[i+1];
    }
    _currSize--;
}
```

The *ostream* `<<` method inherited from *AbstractArrayClass* is adequate for the *Vector* class, and we shall not revise it.

The class header file

Putting all of the above together, we have the following header file for the *Vector* class:

```
#ifndef __VECTOR__H
#define __VECTOR__H

#include "ArrayClass.h"
#include "AbstractVector.h"

template <class DataType>
class Vector
    : virtual public ArrayClass<DataType>,
          virtual public AbstractVector<DataType>
{
protected:
    int _currSize;
    int _incFactor;
public:
    Vector ();
    Vector (int n);
    Vector (int n, DataType& val);
    Vector (const Vector<DataType>& v);
    Vector (const ArrayClass<DataType>& ac);
    virtual ~Vector();
    void operator= (const Vector<DataType>& v);
    void operator= (const ArrayClass<DataType>& ac);
    virtual void insert (const DataType& item, int index);
    virtual void remove (int index);
    virtual void add (const DataType& item);
    virtual int size() const;
    virtual int capacity() const;
    virtual int incFactor() const;
    virtual void setIncFactor(int f);
    void setCapacity(int c);
};

// previously described functions go here

#endif
```

The main() function

To demonstrate the *Vector* class, we will create a *Vector*, add five items to it, add five more, interleaving them with the others, remove the latter five, and then remove the first five, leaving the *Vector* empty:

```
void main()
{
   Vector<int> v;
   cout << v << ",cap " << v.capacity() << endl;
   for (int i = 0; i < 5; i++)
 {
    v.add (5*i);
       cout << v << ",cap " << v.capacity() << endl;
 }
 for (int i = 0; i < 5; i++)
 {
    v.insert (-5*i, 2*i);
       cout << v << ",cap " << v.capacity() << endl;
 }
   for (int i = 4; i >= 0; i--)
 {
    v.remove (i*2);
       cout << v << ",cap " << v.capacity() << endl;
 }
 for (int i = 4; i >= 0; i--)
 {
    v.remove (i);
       cout << v << ",cap " << v.capacity() << endl;
 }
 }
```

The output demonstrates the correct operation of the *Vector* class:

```
[],cap 1
[0],cap 6
[0,5],cap 6
[0,5,10],cap 6
[0,5,10,15],cap 6
[0,5,10,15,20],cap 6
[0,0,5,10,15,20],cap 11
[0,0,-5,5,10,15,20],cap 11
[0,0,-5,5,-10,10,15,20],cap 11
[0,0,-5,5,-10,10,-15,15,20],cap 11
[0,0,-5,5,-10,10,-15,15,-20,20],cap 11
[0,0,-5,5,-10,10,-15,15,20],cap 11
[0,0,-5,5,-10,10,15,20],cap 11
[0,0,-5,5,10,15,20],cap 11
[0,0,5,10,15,20],cap 11
[0,5,10,15,20],cap 6
[0,5,10,15],cap 6
[0,5,10],cap 6
[0,5],cap 6
[0],cap 6
[],cap 1
```

3.4.3   Vectors the STL Way

STL is part of the C++ language definition and can be used implement many data structures. The three main components of the STL are *containers* which are the templated data structures, *iterators* that allow one to enumerate the contents of the data structures, and *algorithms* that can be applied on the data structures.

The Vector class we developed previously resembles the *vector* container discussed in STL. In the *vector* container, the element access methods such as *front()* and *back()*, return the first and last element in the vector, respectively. The method *push_back*(Object) allows the Object to be inserted as the last element of the vector. Instead of the *remove*(int Pos) method that we have developed for our Vector class in this chapter, the STL provides a *erase* method. The *erase* method when provided with an iterator (similar to a pointer) to the element to be deleted will remove the element from the vector.

The iterators allow programmers to examine or output elements in a logical sequence that are stored in a container. For example, in a vector the logical sequence is the index positions 0, 1, 2, and so on. The containers in STL overload the "++" operator on the iterator to move through the logical sequence (just as pointer increments[11]). Just as in the case of a pointer variable, the "*" operator on iterator variable is used to obtain the associated element. Assuming that a vector (in STL) stores a set of integers, the declaration statement to create an iterator is given below.

`vector<int>::iterator myIterator;`

Two methods belonging to the vector container that returns a iterator are *begin()* and *end()*. The *begin()* method returns the iterator positioned at the first element of the vector and the *end()* method returns the iterator position at the element immediately after the last element of the vector. Once we have an iterator, then using the "*" operator we have access to the element positioned at the iterator. This element can be modified if required. If we have set of items that cannot be modified (the ones defined using a *const*) then we can use a constant iterator which is defined using the keyword *const_iterator* instead of the *iterator* keyword. Now consider the following program segment.

```
#include <iostream> // for i/o functions
#include <vector> // for vector
using namespace std;

void main ()
{
    vector<int> v;
    vector<int>::iterator i;

    v.push_back(100);//first element of the vector
    v.push_back(200);//current last elemen of vector
    v.push_back(50);//last element of vector
    cout << "Printing the contents of the vector" << endl;
    for (i = v.begin(); i != v.end(); i++)
        cout << *i << endl;//print the element at iterator
}
```

---

11 The operator "--" is allowed only on the container *list* which is doubly linked list and is discussed in Chapter 4.

vector < DataType > ()	Default constructor
vector < DataType > (*intn*)	Construct a vector of initial size *n*
vector < DataType > (int n, const DataType& value)	Construct a vector of initial size *n* and each element is set to be equal to *value*.
vector < DataType > (const vector < DataType > & vector)	The copy constructor
~*vector* < DataType > ()	Destructor
=	vector < DataType > & operator=(const *vector* < DataType > & *rhsVector*) Overloaded assignment operator. The contents of the vector on the left hand side are replaced with the contents of the vector on the right hand side of the assignment operator.
==	bool operator==(const vector < DataType > & rhsVector) Return true if both the vectors contain the same items in the same order, false otherwise.
<	bool operator < (const *vector* < DataType > & *rhsVector*) Return true if first vector is lexicographically less than the second vector, false otherwise.
[](int index)	DataType& operator[](int index) Return a reference to the *index*[th] element.
DataType& front()	Return a reference to the first element.
DataType& back()	Return a reference to the last element.
iterator begin()	Return the iterator positioned at the first element.
iterator end()	Return the iterator positioned immediately after the last element.
iterator insert(iterator pos, *const* DataType& *value*)	Insert *value* at *pos* and return an iterator pointing to the new element's position.
void erase(iterator pos)	Erase the element at *pos*.
void push_back(const DataType& value)	Add *value* to the end of the vector.
void pop_back()	Erase the last element of the vector.
int capacity()	Return the number of elements that the vector can store without having to allocate more memory.
int size()	Return the number of elements stored in the vector.
bool empty()	Return true if the vector does not contain any elements, false otherwise.

Figure 3.20:   Methods of the STL vector container.

The above program segment when executed gives the following output.

```
Printing the contents of the vector
100
200
50
```

In the above program the "!=" operator compares the iterator given by i with the past-the-end value (v.end()). The *insert* and *remove* methods described in the vector class developed in this textbook require an index position whereas in the STL implementation it requires the iterator position. In the above example we can print the element using the output stream operator " << " since the elements are integers (the standard data types). For other objects that are stored in the vector, we have to overload the " << " operator in their respective class definition of the objects. For a complete description of the vector container in STL the readers are encouraged to refer to the book by Glass and Schuchert. In Figure 3.11 a set of methods of the vector container of the STL is provided.

Exceptions in STL

The exceptions in STL are a subset of the exception classes defined in < stdexcept.h > . Figure 3.12 gives a hierarchical representation of the various exceptions that are thrown by STL.

Allocators in STL

The *new*() and *delete*() operations allow data structures to be created and deleted from memory which is generally the heap that is supports the C++ implementation. In STL memory allocation and deallocation are performed automatically using special objects called allocators. The type of allocator is specified to each container (and adapters that

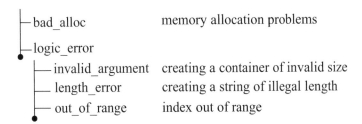

Figure 3.21: A hierarchy of exceptions in STL along with brief descriptions.

use the containers) at the time of creation. For example, in the main program above, we could have created the same vector using the following statement.

```
vector<int, allocator> v;
```

The keyword allocator in the template above the default allocator and can be omitted in the declaration. One can use specialized allocators using a user defined allocator class that allocated and deallocates memory. The user defined allocator class (call it *myAllocator*) should support two standard methods which are given below with their interfaces.

```
// create a contiguous array containing n objects of type
Object and //return the pointer to the array.
DataType* allocate (size_t n);


// deallocate the storage that was previously
// allocated at the location ptr.
void deallocate (DataType* ptr);
```

Using the *myAllocator* class the vector can be created using the following statement.

```
vector<int, myAllocator> v;
```

The implementation of allocate and deallocate methods are beyond of the scope of this textbook.

3.4.4   Application - Binary Search and Insertion

We will now explain a simple and fast searching mechanism called the binary search. Using a vector as the data structure, we will show how we can insert elements into the vector using binary search.

Binary Search

Consider the following common programming problem: given an array A having n elements, which are known to be sorted on some key, and further given an element

q, determine whether q exists in A, and if so, where in A it appears. Nothing more is known about A or q, except that elements of A can be compared with q. In particular, the probability that q, if present, appears at any given position in A is assumed to be $1/n$.

One obvious way to determine whether q is present in A is to compare q with $A[1]$ (the first element of A); if $q = A[1]$ then the search is done, but otherwise compare q with $A[2]$, and so on, until either k is reached such that $q = A[k]$, or the end of A is reached, in which case q is not present in A. If q is not present in A, this procedure will take n comparisons, but if q is present, it will have a $1/n$ probability of taking one comparison, a $1/n$ probability of taking two comparisons, and so on up to a $1/n$ probability of taking n comparisons. Thus, if q is in fact present, the expected number (E) of comparisons will be:

$$E = \sum_{i=1}^{n} \frac{i}{n} = \frac{1}{n} \sum_{i=1}^{n} i = \frac{1}{n} \frac{n(n+1)}{2} = \frac{(n+1)}{2}$$

This would not be a very efficient way to search a list of one million words!

The sequential search described above makes no use of the fact that the elements of A are ordered, and therefore that we could compare q with, say, $A[i]$, and, based on the result of the comparison, rule out all elements left of $A[i]$ (because $A[i]$ is less than q so all elements left of $A[i]$ are also less than q), or rule out all elements right of $A[i]$. The question is what rules should we use to pick i so as to make the minimum number of comparisons before finding a match with q or determining that no such match exists?

Suppose we pick i so that the number of elements left of $A[i]$ is pn and the number right of $A[i]$ is $(1-p)n - 1$. When we compare q with $A[i]$, the chance of a match is $1/n$; the chance that q lies left of $A[i]$ is p, and the chance that q lies right of $A[i]$ is $(1-p)-1/n$. An equation for $f(p)$, the expected number of elements remaining to be compared given p, is:

$$f(p) = 0/n + p(pn) + (1 - p - 1/n)(n - pn - 1)$$
$$= p^2 n + n - pn - 1 - pn + p^2 n + p - 1 + p + 1/n$$
$$= 2p^2 n - 2pn + 2p + n - 2 + 1/n$$

This is a function $f(p)$ which we would like to minimize. Taking the first derivative, we have:

$$f'(p) = 4pn + 2 - 2n$$

Setting this equal to 0, we have:

$0 = 4pn - 2n + 2$

$0 = 4p - 2 + 2/n$

As n grows toward infinity, $2/n$ approaches zero, so it has negligible impact when n is large. We find that $4p2 = 0$ when $p = \frac{1}{2}$. But is $f(\frac{1}{2})$ a minimum or a maximum? Taking the second derivative, we find that:

$f''(\frac{1}{2}) = 4$

so we have, indeed, found a minimum. Now, $f(\frac{1}{2}) = n/2 - 1 + 1/n$. Considering the extremes, we have $0 \leq p \leq 1$; $f(0) = n - 2 + 1/n$ and $f(1) = n + 1/n$. Since $f(\frac{1}{2}) < f(0) < f(1)$ for all $n > 2$, we can conclude that the absolute minimum occurs at $p=\frac{1}{2}$. Comparing q with the middle element of A, and similarly searching the left half or right half of A based on the result of that comparison, is the search algorithm which requires the minimum number of comparisons. This search algorithm reduces the problem to be solved by half at every step: on the first step, there are n elements in the portion to be searched; on the second there are $n/2$; and in general, on the k-th step there are $n/2^{k-1}$.

An example of the operations of the binary search algorithm is shown below. We begin with twelve items, already in order, and we seek value 41.

0	1	2	3	4	5	6	7	8	9	10	11
2	3	4	5	6	19	26	27	36	42	55	70

Figure 3.22: The initial sorted array A for performing binary search.

Iteration Number	left	right	mid	A[mid]	Comment
1	0	11	5	19	19 < 41; Go right of mid
2	6	11	8	36	36 < 41; Go right of mid
3	9	11	10	55	55 > 41; Go left of mid
4	9	9	9	42	42 > 41; Go left of mid
5	9	8	–	–	Exits from the while loop

Figure 3.23: Sequence of comparisons done by binary search to locate the value of 41.

Not surprisingly, this particular search algorithm has a name; it is called binary search. Pseudo code for the algorithm is as follows:

```
Algorithm Binary-Search (q, A, left, right)
1.  left ← 0                        //Array is 0-based
2.  right ← Size(A)-1
3.  while (left ≤ right)
4.        mid ← (left+right)/2
5.        if (A[mid] = q)
6.              return mid          //return position of q in A
7.        else if (A[mid] < q)
8.              left ← mid + 1      //search only right half
9.        else
10.             right ← mid - 1     //search only left half
11.       endif
12. endwhile
```

The expected number of comparisons required by the binary search algorithm if q is present can be computed: the chance that q is found in one comparison (it is the middle element of A) is $1/n$. The chance that it is found in two comparisons (it is the middle element of the left half or the right half) is $2/n$. In general, the chance that it is found in k comparisons is $2^{k-1}/n$. If q is present, it must be found at the latest when the number of elements in the portion to be searched is one. This occurs when $k = \lceil \log_2 n \rceil$.

So the expected number of comparisons, if q is in fact present, is

$$\sum_{i=1}^{\lceil \log_2 n \rceil} i 2^{i-1} \bigg/ n = \frac{1}{n} \sum_{i=1}^{\lceil \log_2 n \rceil} i 2^{i-1}$$

$$= \frac{1}{n} \left(1 + (\lceil \log_2 n \rceil - 1) 2^{\lceil \log_2 n \rceil} \right) \leq \frac{1}{n} + \frac{1}{n} \left(\log_2 n \right) 2^{\log_2 n + 1}$$

$$= \frac{1}{n} + \frac{1}{n} 2n \log_2 n = \frac{1}{n} + 2 \log_2 n \in O(\log_2 n)$$

On the other hand, if q is not in fact present, this fact cannot be determined until the number of elements in the portion to be searched is one, and that one is found not to be equal to q. Therefore, the expected number of comparisons if q is not present is $\lceil \log_2 n \rceil + 1 \in O(\log_2 n)$.

The expected number of comparisons is, therefore, $O(\log_2 n)$. To find q in a list of a million words by binary search would take approximately 20 comparisons, whether

q is present or not, as opposed to the expected half million comparisons required by sequential search.

According to the above discussion, the binary search is the most efficient search algorithm based on comparison where all elements are equally likely, and the expected number of comparisons using binary search is $O(\log_2 n)$. Therefore, the lower bound on searching algorithms based on comparison where all elements are equally likely is $\log_2 n$.

Below, we present a program that will insert an integer x into the *Vector* A in such as way that A maintains a sorted list of integers. This is accomplished as follows: first search the *Vector* A, for a position where x can be inserted, and then insert it at that position. A binary search is performed to locate this position since A is a sorted list. A recursive implementation of binary search for our *Vectors*, and the insertion program, are presented below. The reader should note that the binary search functions are implemented for *String*s, only. If they were generalized for all *Vectors*, all element types used with *Vectors* would have to support == and <.

```
int binarySearch(Vector<String>& A, String& x, int first, int last)
{
    int mid;
    String midval;

    if (first < last)
    {
        mid = (first+last)/2;
        midval = A[mid];
        if (x == midval) return mid+1;
        else if (midval < x)
                    return binarySearch (A, x, mid+1, last);
        else return binarySearch (A, x, first, mid);
    }
    else
    {
        if ((first == last) && (A[first] < x))
            result = first+1;
        else
            result = first;
    }
    return result;
}
// ----------------------------------------------------------------
```

```
    void insertInto (Vector<String>& A, String x)
    {
        int position;
        position = binarySearch (A, x, 0, A.size()-1);
        A.insert (x, position);
    }// ------------------------------------------------------

    void main ()
    {
        Vector<String> vs;

        insertInto (vs, "One");
        insertInto (vs, "Two");
        insertInto (vs, "Three");
        insertInto (vs, "Four");
        insertInto (vs, "Five");
        insertInto (vs, "Six");
        insertInto (vs, "Seven");
        insertInto (vs, "Eight");
        insertInto (vs, "Nine");
        insertInto (vs, "Ten");
        cout << vs << endl;
    }
```

The output shows that the Strings were correctly sorted in a lexicographic order:

```
[Eight, Five, Four, Nine, One, Seven, Six, Ten, Three, Two]
```

3.5 Exercises

3.1. Create an array of objects belonging to the class MovieDirector containing fields directorName, numMoviesDirected, and numOscarAwards. Use a constructor method to initialize the appropriate fields.

3.2. Assuming that there are no more than 50 add and delete operations, create an array of objects belonging to the class MovieDirector specified above. Also provide methods to perform the following operations:

- addMovieDirector() method that inserts a new movieDirector object in the array of objects; it keeps track of the number of objects in the array using a variable num-MovieDirectors which is incremented after each insertion and decremented after each deletion.
- deleteMovieDirector() method that deletes a MovieDirector object from the array given the name of the movieDirector.
- findMovieDirector() method that given a name of the director prints all the fields in the object containing the input director name.

3.3. Write a constructor for ArrayClass that accepts an array of elements with the signature ArrayClass (int n, int count, DataType★ list), where n is the size of the array to be created and count is the number of elements in the array list. If n ≥ count, then all the elements in list are copied onto the new array that is created, otherwise up to n elements from the array list are copied into the newly created array.

3.4. Given a set of elements that are integers, write a method to eliminate duplicates from the set. (Hint: use the simple bucket sorting program with modifications)

3.5. Modify the class Merge given in section 2.1.8.2 such that it can be invoked as merge (X, p, q, r, s). The two arrays A and B specified in the class Merge in section 2.1.8.2 are in X, where elements in positions p to q correspond to array A and elements in positions r to s correspond to the array B.

3.6. Provide a C++ implementation of the merge sort algorithm. The merge sort algorithm given below sorts an array of elements and is invoked as mergeSort (A, 0, N-1), where N is the number of elements stored in the array A.

```
Algorithm mergeSort (A, left, right)
int mid;
Begin
  if (left < right)
     mid = (left+right)/2;
     mergeSort (A, left, mid);
     mergeSort (A, mid+1, right);
     merge (A, left, mid, mid+1, right);
  endif
End.
```

3.7. One way to improve the performance of the merge sort algorithm is to not call the recursion if the sub array is already sorted. Write a method to test if an array is already sorted and use this method to conditionally invoke the recursive call to merge sort.

3.8.   Another way to improve the performance of the merge sort algorithm is to divide the array into k sub arrays, sort each of the $k = 2^p$ for some $p > 0$ subarrays, and merge them. Use the method developed in exercise 3.8 to check if each of the k subarrays are sorted and if not recursively call the merge algorithm.

3.9.   One can write an iterative version of the merge sort. In this version, the algorithm proceeds in phases. In the first phase, the input array containing n elements is considered to be an array containing n sorted lists, each of length 1. Adjacent lists are merged to get n/2 sorted lists of size 2 and a list of size 1 if n is odd. In the second phase, the adjacent lists of size 2 are merged to form n/4 sorted lists of size 4 each and a list of remaining elements. Write a C++ method to implement the iterative merge sort.

3.10.   Write a complete matrix class A with the implementation of the following methods.
- Multiplying a given matrix by another matrix of a scalar.
- Multiplying a row of a matrix by a scalar.
- Adding two matrices or adding each matrix element to a scalar.
- Adding a row of a matrix to a scalar or another row.
- Swapping two rows of a matrix.
- Creating a transpose of a given matrix.

3.11.   A two dimensional matrix A is stored in a *row major order* if after storing the elements of the first row consecutively, the elements of the second row are stored consecutively following them and similarly the third row elements follow the second row elements and so on. Let X be the single dimension array that stores the elements of A in the row major order. Assuming that the matrix A contains n rows and m columns the A[i][j] element is stored in position $i \times m + j$.

3.12.   If a three dimensional array A of size $n \times m \times p$ is stored in row major order in a single dimensional array determine the position of the element A[i][j][k] in the single dimension array.

3.13.   Given an array B of size $n \times m$ containing integer values, write a function that creates a two-dimensional array with n rows and m columns and contains the integer values stored in B.

3.14.   Create a matrix class in which the elements are stored in a single dimension array using row major presentation. Write methods to access elements of the matrix.

3.15.   A matrix with n rows and m columns can be implemented using vectors by creating an array of n vectors. Using this vector implementation, construct the matrix class along with appropriate methods.

3.16. A matrix X is said to be *sparse* if there are many zero entries compared to non-zero entries. A sparse matrix can be represented using an array-of-objects representation, where each object stores the row index, column index and the value X[rowindex] [columnindex] of the matrix X. Given sparse matrix representations of matrices write methods to perform the following functions and produces a sparse matrix representation as an output.

- Multiply two matrices.
- Find the transpose of the given sparse matrix keeping the rows indices in sorted order. Device a technique to obtain the sorted order without having to use sorting techniques.

3.17. Rewrite the Gaussian Elimination program assuming that the matrix of coefficients is stored using the sparse matrix representation.

3.18. Write a program which, given a sparse matrix representation of a matrix A, checks if the matrix A is an upper triangular matrix by processing its sparse matrix representation.

3.19. A polynomial is a sum of terms, where each term is of the form cx^e, where c is the coefficient, x is a variable, and e is the exponent. The largest exponent in a polynomial is called the degree of the polynomial. For example, $A(x) = 2x^6 + 10x^3 - 2x + 4$ is a polynomial containing four terms with non-zero coefficients and the degree of the polynomial is 6. This polynomial can be represented using a vector A of size 4. The addition of two polynomial $A(x) = \sum a_i x_i$ and $B(x) = \sum b_i x_i$ is defined as $A(x) + B(x) = \sum (a_i + b_i) x_i$. The multiplication of the polynomials $A(x)$ and $B(x)$ is defined as $A(x).B(x) = \sum (a_i x^i \times \sum (b_j x^j))$.

- evaluatePoly (x) – Given a value for x evaluate the polynomial and print the result.
- addTerm (coefficient, exponent) – add a term to the polynomial and make sure that the polynomial is kept in sorted order of the exponent. Overload the ' + ' operator.
- deleteTerm (exponent) – delete the term, that is set the coefficient to be zero for the term containing the exponent specified as the parameter.
- addPolynomial (polynomial) – Perform polynomial addition with the polynomial specified in the parameter and create a new polynomial.
- multiplyPolynomial (polynomial) – Perform polynomial multiplication with the polynomial specified in the parameter and create a new polynomial. Overload the '★' operator.
- printPolynomial () – Print the polynomial in a suitable form such that polynomial can be read. Also, write an ostream function which uses printPolynomial().

3.20. As this text will repeatedly stress, ensuring that all allocated memory is deallocated is an endless problem. We might use the ArrayClass template to create an array of pointers to instances of another class, but the instances pointed to would not be deleted when the ArrayClass instance was deleted. Write an ArrayOfPtr class template which

- has a constructor which requires declaration of the number of pointers to be stored;
- allows a pointer to be placed in a particular position in the array, with the previous pointer in that position (if not NULL) being deleted;
- allows a pointer in a particular position in the array to be *replaced* by another, with the previous pointer in that position being returned to the caller for deletion or other use;
- automatically deletes all non-NULL pointers in the array when the array itself is deleted.

3.21. Do you see any problems that might arise in the use of this class, or any precautions that must be followed by the user?

3.22. Write a function that reads a string of no more than length n from a specified *istream*, returning a String instance containing that string.

3.23. Write a function which takes a filename and an instance of Vector < String >, opens the file (which must be a text file), and reads the entire file line-by-line into the instance of Vector < String > .

3.24. Write an iterator class for the vector class defined in the textbook. The iterator class should perform the functions of an iterator defined in the STL. The iterator object for the vector class is created at the time of vector creation (in its constructors).

3.6   References for Further Reading

Al-Suwaiyel, M. and Horowitz, E., "Algorithms for trie compaction", *ACM Transactions on Database Systems* vol. 9, pp. 243-263, 1984.

Baeza-Yates, R.A., "Improved String Searching. Software – Practice and Experience", *Acta Informatica*, vol. 19, pp. 257-271, 1989.

Boyer, R.S. and Moore, J.S., *A Computational Logic*, New York, NY: Academic Press, 1979.

Dvorak, S., and Durian B., "Unstable linear time O(1) space merging", *The Computer Journal* vol. 31, pp. 279-283, 1988.

Glass G. and Schuchert B., *The STL < PRIMER >*, Prentice Hall PTR, 1996.

Huang, B.C. and Langston, M.A., "Practical in-place merging", *Communications of the ACM* vol. 31, pp. 348-352, 1988.

Lesuisse, R., "Some lessons drawn from the history of the binary search algorithm", *The Computer Journal* vol. 26, pp. 154-163, 1983.

Meyers, S., *Effective C++*, second ed., Addison-Wesley, Reading, Mass., 1997.

Pooch, U. W., and Nieder A. "A Survey of Indexing Techniques for Sparse Matrices", *Comput. Surveys*, vol. 15, pp. 109, 1973.

Reynolds, J. C. "Reasoning about Arrays," *Communications of the ACM* vol. 22, no. 5, May 1979.

Rosenberg, A.L., "Allocating storage for extendible arrays", *Journal of the ACM* vol. 21 pp. 652-670, 1974.

Tompa, F.W., "A practical example of specification of abstract data types", *Acta Informatica* vol.13, pp. 205-224, 1980.

Wagner, R.A., and Fischer, M.J., "The string-to-string correction problem", *Journal of the ACM* vol. 21, pp. 168-173, 1974.

Weiner, P., "Linear pattern matching algorithms", In Conference Record of the IEEE 14th Annual Symposium on Switching and Automata Theory, pp.1-11, 1973.

Wood, D., *Data Structures, Algorithms and Performance*, Addison-Wesley, Reading, MA: 1993, 594 pages.

4 Linked List Structures

A S WE HAVE seen, both arrays and Vectors provide access to every element by index, a very convenient feature in many applications. However, each of these two data structures has its limitations. An array cannot be expanded, and so must be created with enough capacity for the maximum intended use. Thus, if an application using an array is normally expected to handle just a hundred items, but is occasionally called upon to handle up to a hundred thousand items; its array must be large enough to accommodate a hundred thousand items, a gross waste of space in the average case.

A Vector, on the other hand, can indeed be expanded, but produces fragmentation of memory. We have taken pains to ensure that the memory is properly deallocated, but such deallocation takes processor time that could be used more productively.

Any element in an array can be accessed in constant time, as it is only necessary to calculate the memory offset from the first element in order to find the element's data. If constant time access to elements by index is not required, and sequential access suffices, a different data structure, the linked list, can be used, avoiding the problems of both the array and the Vector.

4.1 Linked Lists

A linked list might be thought of as resembling an anchor chain: one end is in our hands and the link at that end is immediately accessible to us, while each link of the chain other than the first can be reached only by following the preceding links, so that the very last link (where the anchor would be in this analogy) can be reached only after every preceding link has been passed. In a linked list, every link has its own data that is of interest to the user, so the analogy is not perfect. On the other hand, the analogy is precise in one way: in both an anchor chain and a linked list, it is impossible to tell, just by looking at the end in our hand, how long the chain is. We can know the length only by external records (keeping track as the anchor chain is paid out, or as links are added to the linked list) or by counting the links all the way to the end.

With this in mind, we shall begin our discussion of the linked list data structure with a concrete example.

4.1.1   Example

To understand linked lists, we must first think in terms of pointers or references. Let us consider a simple class called "Student" with just two fields (for simplicity of explanation, they will be public). The class *Student* is as follows:

```
class Student
{
public:
    String name;
    String major;
};
```

We would like the *name* and *major* fields to be of fixed size, but that cannot be accomplished by allowing them to be constructed by the default constructor. It also cannot be accomplished by constructing them in the body of a constructor, as they are already constructed when the body of the constructor is entered. We seem to be at an impasse. However, just as we can call the parent class' constructor before entering the body of the constructor, we can also call the constructors of the fields themselves. This new usage is relatively clear, as we can simply add a default constructor like this:

```
Student::Student (): name(50), major(50) { }
```

An object belonging to the class *Student* can now be created using the following statement.

```
Student* student1 = new Student ();
```

When the above statement is executed, memory space is allocated for the object and it is accessed by means of the symbol *student1*. The symbol *student1* can also be called a reference, or pointer, to the memory location containing two pieces of information, which are the *name* and *major*. We say two pointers, or references, are compatible if they point to the same object type. The following statement creates a *Student* pointer with a symbolic name of *student2*.

■   `Student* student2;`

The above statement does not create any memory space for the Student object, but creates a pointer variable of type *Student*. The following statement initializes this pointer.

■   `student2 = student1;`

Now, the pointer *student2* points to the same memory location as *student1*. Thus in general, the statement on the right hand side of an assignment statement, *new DataTypeClass(P)*, allocates memory space for an object instance of *ObjectClass* and returns a pointer to the memory location. Now clearly, a pointer is a logical memory address. A NULL is a special pointer that has an address value of 0. A pointer variable that has a value of NULL is considered to point to an empty location that is a memory location that is not part of the memory space of this program. When a pointer is first declared, where it is pointing to is undefined and hence it is a good idea to initialize it with the NULL value. This is called the null pointer. Derefencing a pointer variable is retrieving the value or object that the pointer variable is pointing to. A pointer variable that has the NULL value may not be derefenced.

We can define objects that have object pointers as fields. For example, in the class *Student* we could create a pointer to *Student* called *nextStudent*. A subclass of the class *Student*, with the added field, is given below.

```
classLinkedStudent : public Student
{
public:
    LinkedStudent* nextStudent;
    LinkedStudent ();
};
LinkedStudent::LinkedStudent () : Student(), nextStudent(NULL)
{
}
```

Note that in the *LinkedStudent* class we have initialized *nextStudent* before the body of the constructor, instead of in its body. Either method is permissible for a pointer field like this[1].

The following statements create two objects belonging to the class *LinkedStudent*.

```
LinkedStudent* firstStudent = new LinkedStudent ();
LinkedStudent* secondStudent = new LinkedStudent ();
```

In the above statements one can see that we can dynamically allocate a series of record locations and tie them together with pointer fields. Such series of objects, tied together with pointer fields, is called a linked structure. For example, the *firstStudent* object is linked to the *secondStudent* object as follows.

```
(*firstStudent).nextStudent = secondStudent;
```

The result of the above statements is illustrated pictorially below.

In C (and hence in C++) the operator "−>" (minus sign immediately followed by a greater than sign) is used to access the fields of a object (resp. struct as in the case of C) using a pointer to that object (resp. struct). For example, the statement (*firstStudent). nextStudent is same as firstStudent −> nextStudent.

We have now created a very short chain of two objects. Notice that *firstStudent* is the "head" end of the chain; we don't really need the variable *secondStudent*, because we can find the object to which it points by following the *nextStudent* pointer of *firstStudent*. We must keep a pointer to *firstStudent*, however, since there is no way to find the object to which it points, given only *secondStudent*. Using only the *firstStudent* object pointer we can change the *name* field of the *secondStudent* now by the following:

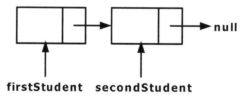

firstStudent secondStudent

Figure 4.1: Example of a linked structure.

---

1 The reader may have noticed that the destructor is missing, even though we have a pointer field. It is omitted because a proper destructor would complicate this example. We will discuss the destructor, copy constructors, and assignment operator, when we discuss the LinkedList class.

■ `firstStudent->nextStudent->name = "Robert Frost";`

The following statements create a chain of ten *LinkedStudent* objects with unini-
tialized name and major fields.

```
LinkedStudent* temp;
LinkedStudent* current;
int i;

firstStudent = new LinkedStudent ();
current = firstStudent;
for (i=0; i < 9; i++) {
    temp = new LinkedStudent ();
    current->nextStudent = temp;
    current = temp;
}
```

Using Figures 4.2-4.4 we will show how the linked list objects are created.

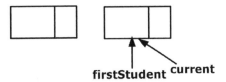

Figure 4.2: Both firstStudent and current point to the same LinkedStudent during
the execution of the first two statements.

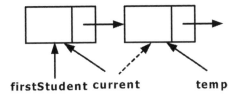

Figure 4.3: When the value of i = 0, a new LinkedStudent object pointed by temp
is created. The first LinkedStudent object pointed by current is linked to
the new LinkedStudent. The value of the current pointer is moved to the
new LinkedStudent shown by dotted line.

Figure 4.4:   At the end of the loop, there are a total of 10 LinkedStudent objects that were created and the current pointer points to the last LinkedStudent object in the linked list. The nextStudent pointer of the last LinkedStudent object points to NULL.

The reader should note that *firstStudent* is the head end of the list and its value must be held in a variable. On the other hand, none of the other objects in the list even have variable names; and can be accessed only by tracing the pointers, starting at *firstStudent*. The reader should also note that new objects are being added to the "tail" of the list, that is, the end away from the head.

Several primitive operations can be executed on the linked list data structure, including the following.

```
traverse a linked list: go through each node of the linked list
search for an object in the linked list
insert an object into a linked list
delete a object from a linked list
get an object at a particular position in the linked list
```

We shall illustrate these primitive operations using a concrete example. Traversing a linked list is an important utility. The following programming segment traverses the linked list.

```
LinkedStudent* current = firstStudent;
while (current != NULL)
{
    /* Process the current node or object */
    current = current->nextStudent;
}
```

Other important operations on a linked list are insertion and deletion. Suppose that we would like to insert an object *newStudent* in the beginning of a list. We perform the following operations.

```
LinkedStudent* newStudent = new LinkedStudent();
newStudent->nextStudent = firstStudent;
firstStudent = newStudent;
```

Recall that *firstStudent* is the head end of the list, the end which we keep "in hand", and where we start each traversal of the list. Here, we are adding at the head end of the list, so the object currently pointed to by *firstStudent* must be displaced to the second position in the list, and we must put a pointer to the new head into the *firstStudent* variable. The above steps must be done in the order given, for if *first-Student = newStudent* were executed before *newStudent –> nextSudent = firstStudent*, we would have lost our only pointer to the head end of the list, and the whole list would be lost, just as if we had dropped overboard the one end of the anchor chain which we held.

Suppose that we would like to insert a new *Student* with *name* initialized to "Peter" after an object with *name* field "Smith." Then we must first find the *Student* object with *name* field "Smith" in the linked list by traversing the linked list from the beginning. The following code traverses the linked list and returns a pointer pointing to the object with *name* field *newName* if it exists in the linked list, and otherwise returns a NULL.

```
LinkedStudent* lookFor (LinkedStudent* firstStudent, String& newName)
{
    LinkedStudent* current;
    current = firstStudent;
    while ((current != NULL) && (current->name != newName))
    // note that we are using the overloaded != operator for string
    // comparison.
    {
        current = current->nextStudent;
    }
    return current;
}
```

The following code segment does the remaining job in the insertion process.

```
LinkedStudent* temp = lookFor (firstStudent, "Smith");
if (temp != NULL)
{
    newStudent->nextStudent = temp->nextStudent;
    temp->nextStudent = newStudent;
}
```

The reader should note again the importance of retaining pointers; if *temp.nextStudent = newStudent* is done before *newStudent = temp.nextStudent*, the pointer to the object following the student named 'Smith' would be lost, so that the list would be terminated at that point and all subsequent objects lost, as if we had cut one of the links in our anchor chain.

Deletion of an object from the linked list is simple. For example, to delete the first element of the linked list we can use the following:

firstStudent = firstStudent->nextStudent;

Now, since no symbolic name is associated with the previous *firstStudent* object, we will lose the memory allocated to it. Thus, we must be careful to save that pointer and delete it after we obtain *firstStudent −> nextStudent* from it.

In order to delete an arbitrary object, say an object containing the name "Smith", we have to perform the following steps. First, we need to traverse the linked list one object at a time until either we find an object with the *name* field equal to "Smith" or we have reached the end of the linked list without finding such an object. If we don't find such an object, we do not change the list. Otherwise, we have found a node, which we shall call *current*, which contains the *name* "Smith." If node *current* happens to be the first node, then we can delete it using the statement above. If node *current* is any other node, then we need to make sure that the node which immediately precedes *current*, and has a *nextStudent* pointer that points to *current*, will be given a *nextStudent* pointer that points to *current −> nextStudent*, the next node in the linked list. We will thus have "spliced" the chain to leave out *temp*, so when we traverse the linked list, we will skip the node *current* altogether. It has therefore been deleted from the linked list.

To find and delete a node, we will need to keep moving two pointers during traversal. One, which we shall call *current*, will point ultimately to the node to be deleted. The other, which we shall call *previous*, will point to the node immediately before current, that is, we want *previous −> nextStudent* to be equal to *current*. Initially, the pointer *previous* points to the first, or head, element of the linked list. At any point of the traversal, the *current* pointer will point to the node being examined, and the *previous* pointer will point to the node that precedes the current node. If we find the necessary node, we can splice it out, but we cannot simply lose the pointer to the deleted node; what do we do with it? We have two choices: delete the node immediately, or pass the pointer back to the caller so that the caller can choose whether to delete it. We have chosen below to pass the pointer back to the caller.

The following code performs deletion from a linked list.

```
LinkedStudent* deleteStudent
    (LinkedStudent firstStudent, String& deleteName)
{
    LinkedStudent* previous, current;

    if (firstStudent->name == deleteName)
    {
        current = firstStudent;
        firstStudent = firstStudent->nextStudent;
        current->nextStudent = NULL;
        return current;
    }
    else
    {
        previous = firstStudent;
        current = previous->nextStudent;

        while ( (current != NULL) &&
             (current->name != deleteName))
        {
            previous = current;
            current = current->nextStudent;
        }
        if (current != NULL)
        {
            previous->nextStudent = current->nextStudent;
            current->nextStudent = NULL;
            return current;
        }
    }
    return NULL;
}
```

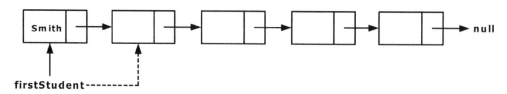

Figure 4.5:   Deletion operation in the case where Smith is contained in the first node.

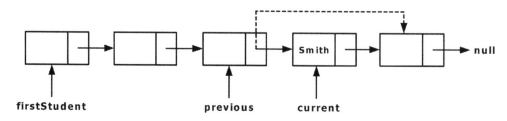

Figure 4.6:   Deletion operation in the case where Smith is not contained in the first node.

The deletion operation is shown pictorially above.

After deletion, the *firstStudent* pointer will point to the node given by the dotted arrow if "Smith" is contained in the first node.

Otherwise, after deletion, the *nextStudent* pointer corresponding to the previous node will point to the node pointed by *current* –> *nextStudent* and is shown by a dotted arrow.

An interesting question is whether we can write a deletion procedure using a single pointer. The answer is of course yes and is done as follows. Let *current* point to the node that is to be deleted. Replace the contents of node *current* with the contents of node current –> nextStudent. Now, there are two nodes in the linked list that have exactly the same contents. But during the traversal process, the old current –> nextStudent node will be skipped entirely. Care must be taken when we perform the replace step if current –> nextStudent is NULL. The following figure shows that the node containing 'John' is the one that follows the node pointed by *current*. The replace operation replaces "Smith" with "John" and the new pointer assignment is shown with a dotted arrow, in Figure 4.7.

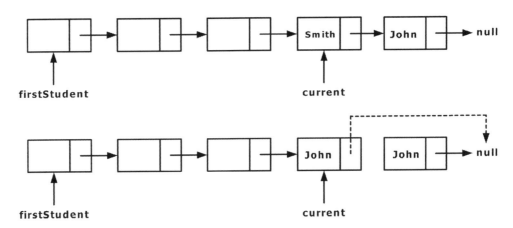

Figure 4.7:   Deletion operation using a single pointer. Note that the contents of the
node that stores the name John is copied onto the node that stores the
name Smith. This node copy process copies the next pointer also and
hence the dotted line corresponding to the next pointer of the node
containing Smith points to NULL.

4.1.2   Abstract Data Type

The essential operations on a linked list are as follows:

```
create()
    // creates an empty linked list
isEmpty()
    // returns true if the list is empty, but otherwise
    // returns false
size()
    // returns the number of nodes in the list
add (object)
    // adds object to the beginning of the list
info ()
    // returns the data from the head node, or NULL if the
    // list is empty
next ()
    // returns the linked list pointed by this linked list
setNext ()
    // attaches a linked list following the head node. The
    // linked list previously
    // following that head node is returned.
delete ()
    // deletes the first node of the linked list
```

4.1.3   Implementation of the Linked List

The linked list will be recursively defined. A linked list either is empty, or consists of a node linked to another linked list, the next linked list in the chain. From the point of view of the linked list itself, therefore, it is always the head of its own list. We shall see that a recursive implementation in C++ requires some special care in insertion and deletion, so that the user is able to hold onto the head of the linked list. But first we must deal with some preliminary considerations.

4.1.3.1   Node Data Type

The linked list abstract data type described above involves no comparisons of nodes, neither equality tests nor three-way comparisons. Therefore, we need not make any requirements of the objects to be stored in the nodes. However, in order to make the linked list more useful, we will assume that an equality test is defined on the node data type.

4.1.3.2   Exceptions

The principal problem that can arise in use of a linked list is the possibility of running out of memory. It is also possible that the user might attempt to access a node by number, when that node is out of range given the size of the list, or the user might attempt to find a node that is not present in the list. Also, as we shall allow the user to attach one list to another, and we must throw an error if the user attempts to attach a list to an empty list. As is our practice, we shall declare a family of exceptions.

```
class LinkedListException      : public Exception { };
class LinkedListMemory         : public LinkedListException { };
class LinkedListBounds         : public LinkedListException { };
class LinkedListNotFound       : public LinkedListException { };
class LinkedListAttachToEmpty  : public LinkedListException { };
```

4.1.3.3   Abstract Base Class

With the exception classes in hand, we can prepare an abstract base class based on the abstract data type. Although we shall principally discuss the pointer implementation of linked lists, there are other implementations, such as arrays. It will be useful to have an abstract base class which each of these implementations can extend, so that they can be used interchangeably in the same programs.

In addition to those operations required by the abstract data type, we shall include operations for accessing objects by index number. These operations can be easily implemented, though they are not as efficient with linked lists as with arrays and Vectors and they are not part of the abstract data type. The last two methods in the abstract base type are designed to allow for proper display of linked lists. They will be discussed in the following subsection.

```cpp
#include <iostream.h>
#include "Enumeration.h"

template <class DataType>
class AbstractLinkedList
{
public:
  virtual DataType& info () = NULL;
    //  returns the object in the head of the linked list,
    //  or throws a bounds error if the list is empty
  virtual AbstractLinkedList<DataType>* next () = NULL;
    //  returns the LinkedList pointed by this LinkedList
  virtual bool isEmpty()= NULL;
    //  returns true if the list is empty,
    //  but otherwise returns false
  virtual void add (const DataType& object) = NULL;
    //  adds object to the beginning of the list
  virtual AbstractLinkedList<DataType>* setNext
    (AbstractLinkedList<DataType>* next) = NULL;
    //  attaches next as _next field of list;
    //  returns old _next field.
    //  if current list is empty throws exception.
  virtual void insertAt (const DataType& newObj, int position) =
                      NULL;
    //  inserts newObj so that it will be at node number position
    //  (counting the head node as 0)
  virtual DataType& infoAt (int position) = NULL;
    //  return the object in the linked list at the location
    //  specified by position, or throws exception if position
    //  is beyond the end of the linked list
```

```
virtual DataType& find (const DataType& key) = NULL;
    //  returns a node matching key or
    //  throws exception if none matches
virtual Object remove () = NULL;
    //  deletes the first node of the linked list, if any, and
    //  returns it
virtual Object removeAt (int position) = NULL;
    //  deletes the node matching key, if any,
    //  and returns it.
virtual Object remove (const DataType& key) = NULL;
    //  deletes the node matching key, if any,
    //  and returns it
virtual int size()= NULL;
    //  returns the number of nodes in the list
virtual Enumeration<DataType>* enumerator ();
    //  returns an enumeration of the data contained in the list
virtual void display (ostream& s);
    // display the nodes of the linked list
};
```

Enumeration of Nodes

As mentioned in the first chapter, the *Enumeration* abstract class provides methods for enumerating a list of objects so that they can be printed, summed, or otherwise manipulated. The intent of the *Enumeration* abstract class is to provide a standardized way of enumerating the contents of data structures. If each data structure provides a method which returns an *Enumeration* object, a programmer faced with a new data structure need only determine that method and use standard code to access the elements of the data structure, rather than designing a new program segment to enumerate the elements. This is an example of "off-loading" complexity; the designer of the data structure knows its interconnections and can write good enumeration code; the programmers who merely use the data structure can rely on the designer.

A subclass of the *Enumeration* class keeps track of progress in the enumeration of a data structure; specifically, it has internal fields which allow it to determine which element comes next in the enumeration. An object of an enumeration class is expected to (1) initialize itself so that the first element, if any, will be next in the enumeration; (2) report whether any elements remain to be enumerated; and (3) return the next element to be enumerated. The two methods of the *Enumeration* class are *hasMoreElements*(), which reports whether there are any more elements to be enumerated, and *nextElement*(), which returns the next element to be enumerated. It should be noted that the order in which elements are returned is entirely up to the designer of the enumeration class; the user has no control over it.

The implementation of an enumeration method for the linked list is quite simple: it simply creates and returns an object of the appropriate class, initialized with a pointer to itself:

```
// part of the implementation of the class AbstractLinkedList
template <class DataType>
Enumeration<DataType>* AbstractLinkedList<DataType>::
          enumerator ()
// Returns an enumeration of the data contained in the list
{
    return new LLEnumerator < Object > (this);
}
```

The enumeration class itself is presented below. It has exactly three methods, corresponding to the three tasks that it is required to perform. In this case, the enumeration object retains a single pointer to a linked list. Initially, that linked list is the one passed to it by the *enumerator*() method. Every time *nextElement*() is called, the result from *info*() method from the linked list is returned to the caller, while the linked list pointer is advanced to the result of the *next*() method. This produces the effect of stepping through the linked list.

The reader should note that it is impossible to backtrack through this enumeration; it moves strictly forward, as required by the *Enumeration* abstract class. The reader should also note that there is no reason for a user to create an instance of this class except for the purpose of enumerating a linked list, and the *enumerator*() method in the *AbstractLinkedList* class itself can be used to create an instance for that purpose.

```
template <class DataType>
class LLEnumerator : public Enumeration<DataType>
{
friend AbstractLinkedList<DataType>;
protected:
    AbstractLinkedList<DataType>* _LL;
public:
    LLEnumerator ();
    LLEnumerator (AbstractLinkedList<DataType>* LL);
    virtual bool hasMoreElements ();
    virtual DataType& nextElement ();
};
// -----------------------------------------------------------
```

```
template <class DataType>
LLEnumerator<DataType>::LLEnumerator ()
{
    _LL = NULL;
}
// ----------------------------------------------------------
template <class DataType>
LLEnumerator<DataType>::LLEnumerator
                (AbstractLinkedList<DataType>* LL)
{
    _LL = LL;
}
// ----------------------------------------------------------
template <class DataType>
bool LLEnumerator<DataType>::hasMoreElements ()
{
    return ((_LL != NULL) && (!_LL->isEmpty()));
}
// ----------------------------------------------------------
template <class DataType>
DataType& LLEnumerator<DataType>::nextElement ()
{
    if ((_LL == NULL) || (_LL->isEmpty()))
                        throw LinkedListBounds();
    AbstractLinkedList<DataType>* curr = _LL;
    _LL = _LL->next();
    return curr->info();
}
```

The display() method

With our enumeration class written, we can readily write a *display()* method for use with the *ostream* class, so as to produce a meaningful representation of the *Abstract-LinkedList* instance.

```
template <class DataType>
void AbstractLinkedList<DataType>::display (ostream& s)
{
    bool first = true;
    Enumeration<DataType>* e = enumerator();
    s << "[";
    while (e->hasMoreElements())
    {
        if (!first) s << ", ";
        else first = false;
        s << e->nextElement();
    }
    s << "]";
    delete e;
}
```

Finally, we can write an ostream << operator function which uses display(). This function must be a friend of the *AbstractLinkedList* class.

```
template <class DataType>
ostream& operator << (ostream& s,
                      AbstractLinkedList<DataType>& LL)
{
    LL.display(s);
    return s;
}
```

STL Style Iterator for Linked Lists

We will write STL style of iterator of the class AbstractLinkedList. The class LLEnumerator will be expanded to accommodate the overloaded operators such as "*", "++" (pre and post increments) and "!=". Assume that i and j are iterators. The operation ++i advances one element in the linked list and returns a reference to i and the operation i++ advances one element in the linked list and returns i's previous value. The operation *i returns a reference to the element at i's current position. The statement i ! = j returns true if i and j are positioned at different elements. The following method prototypes are to be added to the class LLEnumerator.

```
virtual DataType& operator* (void);
virtual LLEnumerator<DataType>& operator++ (void); //Pre inc
virtual LLEnumerator<DataType>& operator++ (int);
virtual bool operator!= (LLEnumerator<DataType> rhs); //Post inc
```

Note that in the above definition in the post increment definition an int is passed. This is actually required in C++ to distinguish itself from the pre increment operation and hence no int value or variable is passed at the time of invocation. Since the results of the "++" operations on iterators are iterators, the return type for the overloaded "++" operators is LLEnumerator<DataType>. The method definitions for each of the above operators are given below.

```
template <class DataType>
DataType& LLEnumerator<DataType>::operator*(void)
{
    if ((_LL == NULL) || (_LL->isEmpty()))
        throw LinkedListBounds();
    return _LL->info();
}
// -------------------Pre Increment-------------------------
template<class DataType>
LLEnumerator<DataType>& LLEnumerator<DataType>::
                                    operator++(void)
{
    if ((_LL == NULL) || (_LL->isEmpty()))
    throw LinkedListBounds();
    _LL = _LL->next();
    return *this;
}
//-------------------Post Increment------------------------
template <class DataType>
LLEnumerator<DataType>& LLEnumerator<DataType>::
                    operator++(int)
{
    if ((_LL == NULL) || (_LL->isEmpty()))
        throw LinkedListBounds();
    LLEnumerator<DataType>* temp = new LLEnumerator<DataType>
                                        (_LL);
    _LL = _LL->next();
```

```
        return *temp;
}
// -----------------------------------------------------
template <class DataType>
bool LLEnumerator<DataType>::operator!=
                        (LLEnumerator<DataType> rhs)
{
    return (_LL != rhs.getLLptr());
}
```

We have added a accessor method getLLptr() to the class LLEnumerator which returns the pointer value of the protected field _LL. This method is used in the implementation of the overloaded "!=" operator.

We will next define a data type named iterator in the class AbstractLinkedList with a data type of LLEnumerator. The following statement is placed at the beginning of the AbstractLinkedList class.

```
        typedef LLEnumerator<DataType> iterator;
```

The methods begin() and end() will complete the STL iterator style definitions on the class AbstractLinkedList developed here. The begin() method returns the first element of the linked list and the end() method returns NULL for the case of the class AbstractLinkedList to specify the end of the linked list.

```
template <class DataType>
LLEnumerator <DataType> AbstractLinkedList<DataType>::
                                    begin()
{
    return *(new LLEnumerator<DataType> (this));
}
// -----------------------------------------------------
template <class DataType>
LLEnumerator <DataType> AbstractLinkedList<DataType>::end()
{
    return NULL;
}
```

We can see the use of the iterator in the main method we have provided after the class definition below.

4.1.3.4   Class Definition

With an understanding of how linked lists work, and an interface, let us now define a class *LinkedList* and present several methods that manipulate the linked list. As part of our class definition, we will treat a single node as a linked list. Then every linked list is made up of other linked lists.

Fields and Constructors

A node contains two fields:

♦   an *_info* field of type DataType*, that is, pointer to Object.
♦   a *_next* field which points to another linked list.

By storing pointers to Object in nodes of the linked list we can identify an empty list because the *_info* field will be *NULL* if, and only if, the list is empty.

We need constructor methods to initialize the node that is created when a new linked list is created. The fields and the constructor methods are presented below.

```
#include "AbstractLinkedList.h"

template <class DataType>
class LinkedList : public AbstractLinkedList<DataType>
{
protected:
    DataType* _info;
    LinkedList<DataType>* _next;
public:
    LinkedList ();
    LinkedList (const DataType& info);
    LinkedList (const DataType& info, LinkedList<DataType>*
                next);
};
// -----------------------------------------------------------
```

```
template <class DataType>
LinkedList<DataType>::LinkedList ()
{
    _info = NULL;
    _next = NULL;
}
// -----------------------------------------------------------
template <class DataType>
LinkedList<DataType>::LinkedList (const DataType& info)
{
    _info = new DataType(info);
    if (_info == NULL) throw LinkedListMemory();
    _next = NULL;
}
// -----------------------------------------------------------
template <class DataType>
LinkedList<DataType>::LinkedList
    (const DataType& info, LinkedList<DataType>* next)
{
    _info = new DataType(info);
    if (_info == NULL) throw LinkedListMemory();
    _next = next;
}
```

Destructor

Since the *LinkedList* class has instance pointer fields, we expect that we need a non-trivial destructor. Since the constructor creates the object pointed to by _info, the destructor should delete it. An important question is, what should we do about _next? There is an argument for leaving the list pointed to by _next as it is, since the caller might still have a pointer to it and would be using deallocated memory if the destructor deletes it. On the other hand, if the caller doesn't have a pointer to it, and the destructor does not delete it, the program would have a memory leak.

We have chosen to delete the list pointed to by _next to avoid memory leaks. This decision implies that, if the caller desires to retain a pointer to that list, the caller must detach the list by getting a pointer to it and setting _next to NULL before deleting the original list. This means that we must have a method to perform that operation, and we will keep that requirement in mind in writing the other methods of the class.

The destructor for *LinkedList* is, therefore:

```
template <class DataType>
LinkedList<DataType>::~LinkedList()
{
    if (_info != NULL)
    {
        delete _info;
        _info = NULL;
    }
    if (_next != NULL)
    {
        delete _next; // this produces recursive call to destructor
        _next = NULL;
    }
}
```

Copy Constructor and Assignment Operator

Since our new class has pointer instance variables, we need a copy constructor and an assignment operator. The copy constructor must copy the object pointed to by _info, and also must copy the entire linked list pointed to by _next.

```
template <class DataType>
LinkedList<DataType>::LinkedList (
            const LinkedList<DataType>& ll)
{
    if (ll._info == NULL) info = NULL;
    else
    {
        _info = new DataType (*(ll._info));
        if (_info == NULL) throw LinkedListMemory();
    }
    if (ll._next == NULL)
    {
        _next = NULL;
    }
    else
    {
        _next = new LinkedList<DataType> (*(ll._next));
        if (_next == NULL) throw LinkedListMemory();
    }
}
```

The assignment operator does exactly the same thing, first deleting the already existing objects (if any) pointed to by _info_ and _next_. This suggests that we should have a protected method copy() to do the actual copying:

```
template <class DataType>
void LinkedList<DataType>::copy (
                            const LinkedList<DataType>& ll)
{
    if (ll._info == NULL) _info = NULL;
    else
    {
        _info = new DataType (*(ll._info));
        if (_info == NULL) throw LinkedListMemory();
    }
    if (ll._next == NULL) _next = NULL;
    else
    {
        _next = new LinkedList<DataType> (*(ll._next));
        if (_next == NULL) throw LinkedListMemory();
    }
}
// ------------------------------------------------------------
template <class DataType>
LinkedList<DataType>::LinkedList
                            (const LinkedList<DataType>& ll)
{
    copy (ll);
}
// ------------------------------------------------------------
template <class DataType>
void LinkedList<DataType>::operator=
                            (const LinkedList<DataType>& ll)
{
    if (_info != NULL) delete _info;
    if (_next != NULL) delete _next;
    copy (ll);
}
```

Accessor methods

The basic accessor methods are *info()*, *next()*, and *isEmpty()*. Since we have decided that NULL_*info* indicates an empty list, these methods are quite simple.

```
template <class DataType>
bool LinkedList<DataType>::isEmpty ()
{
    return (_info == NULL);
}
// ------------------------------------------------------------
template <class DataType>
DataType LinkedList<DataType>::info ()
{
    if (isEmpty()) throw LinkedListBounds();
    return *_info;
}
// ------------------------------------------------------------
template <class DataType>
AbstractLinkedList<DataType>* LinkedList<DataType>::next ()
{
    return _next;
}
```

Now let us consider the problem of the size of a linked list. A given linked list has only a single value (which may be *NULL*) and a reference to the next linked list (which may also be *NULL*). Clearly, the length of the given linked list must be one more than that of the next linked list, assuming neither _*info* nor _*next* is *NULL*. In other words, we can implement the *size()* method recursively:

```
template <class DataType>
int LinkedList<DataType>::size ()
{
    if (_next == NULL)
    {
        if (_info == NULL) return 0;
        else return 1;
    }
    else return 1 + _next->size();
}
```

The reader will note that it is not necessary to test whether _info is *NULL* unless _next is already known to be *NULL*. We will not allow the insertion of *NULL* data, and will ensure that _info is never *NULL* when _next is not *NULL*.

The reasoning behind the implementation of *find()* is similar to that of *size()*: if the data sought is present in the linked list at all, it is present in the head's own *_info* field, or else it is present in the next linked list. Thus, we will have a recursive implementation with the recursion ending when *_info* or *_next* is *NULL*.

```
template <class DataType>
DataType& LinkedList<DataType>::find (const DataType& key)
{
    if (isEmpty()) throw LinkedListNotFound();
    if (key == *_info) { return *_info; }
    if (_next == NULL) throw LinkedListBounds();
    return _next->find (key);
}
```

The last of the accessor methods is *infoAt()*. The reasoning here is similar to that in *find()*, though somewhat more complicated since we have to contend with the *position* variable.

The value at position 0 must be the value in the head of the linked list on which *infoAt()* is called. Therefore, the value at position 1 must be the value in the head of the linked list pointed to by *_next*. That is, if *L* is a linked list, the value to be returned from *L.infoAt*(1) is the same as that to be returned from *L._next.infoAt*(0). Similarly, the value to be returned from *L.infoAt*(2) is the same as that to be returned from *L._next.infoAt*(1) or *L._next._next.infoAt*(0). Thus, it is logical to implement *infoAt()* recursively, by calling it on the *_next* linked list with the *position* variable reduced by one. The recursion ends when *position* is 0 or *_next* is *NULL*.

```
template <class DataType>
DataType& LinkedList<DataType>::infoAt (int position)
{
    if (isEmpty()) throw LinkedListBounds();
    if (position == 0) { return *_info; }
    if (_next == NULL) throw LinkedListBounds();
    return _next->infoAt (position - 1);
}
```

Methods for Inserting Data

Now we can access the data in the linked list, so we have to be able to add data to access. The method *add()* is the basic method for adding to linked lists. It adds a new node to the beginning of a list, and is essentially implemented as follows: we create a new node first and copy the contents of the first node of the linked list to the new node. The copying is performed by calling the constructor that initializes the fields *_info* and *_next* of the new node. At this point, both the head of the list and the new node contain the same information and point to the same next node. The *_info* field of the first node is then replaced with *object* and the *_next* field is made to point to the newly created node. This technique is used unless the *_info* field of the first node was originally *NULL*, which occurs either if the list is newly created with no data or if the list has become empty through deletion of all data; if the *_info* field was *NULL*, we simply replace it with *object*. This process is diagrammed below:

The result of this operation is that a new head node has been added to the front of the list. Any existing reference to the head of the list still points to the head, but the head now has different data. Some copying is necessary, but only references are copied, which takes little processor time.

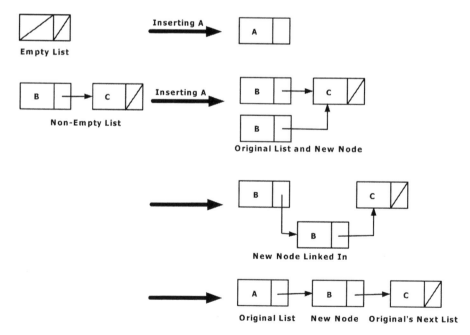

Figure 4.8:   Various steps in an insertion operation using the add method.

The *add()* method is therefore as follows:

```
template <class DataType>
void LinkedList<DataType>::add (const DataType& object)
{
    if (_info == NULL)  { _info = new DataType(object); }
    else
    {
        LinkedList<DataType>* newList =
            new LinkedList<DataType> (*_info, _next);
        if (newList == NULL) throw LinkedListMemory ();
        *_info = object;
        _next = newList;
    }
}
```

The *insertAt()* method is a little more complicated. If position 0 is specified, it can simply call add(). If a position is specified that is greater than the number of elements in the linked list, then the new object is simply added as the last element of the linked list. For all other positions the algorithm is same as for the first element and hence a recursive call is made to *insertAt()* with position one less than the previous call to *insertAt()*. The implementation of the *insertAt()* method is therefore as follows:

```
template <class DataType>
void LinkedList<DataType>::insertAt (const DataType& newObj,
                                     int position)
{
    if (position == 0) add (newObj);
    else
    {
        if (_next == NULL)
        {
            _next = new LinkedList (newObj);
            if (_next == NULL) throw LinkedListMemory ();
        }
        else
        {
            _next->insertAt (newObj, position - 1);
        }
    }
}
```

Attaching Another Linked List

Sometimes we may have an existing linked list that we would like to attach as the next linked list. That is, we want to retain the head node's value, but change the *_next* field. We can readily accomplish this, although we must be careful not to allow a list to be attached to an empty list, as this would have the effect of inserting null data at the beginning of the list, so we must throw an exception. We must not lose the prior *_next* field, so we will return it to the user.

Finally, it should be noted that placing *setNext()* in the abstract base class requires us to accept *AbstractLinkedList* objects, when in fact we want *LinkedList* objects only to be attached. The type cast below to class *LinkedList* will produce an error if the user tries to attach the wrong type of object. Avoiding this exception would require another exception class and two *setNext()* methods, and is left as an exercise for the reader.

```
template<class DataType>
AbstractLinkedList<DataType>* LinkedList<DataType>::setNext
                              (AbstractLinkedList<DataType>*
next)
{
    if (isEmpty()) throw LinkedListAttachToEmpty();
    AbstractLinkedList<DataType>* temp = _next;
    _next = (LinkedList<DataType>*) next;
    return temp;
}
```

The reader will recall that, in connection with the destructor, we discussed the decision to delete the linked list pointed to by *_next*. If the user needed to hold onto a pointer to the linked list pointed to by *_next*, we must have a way to obtain the value of the *_next* pointer and then set the *_next* pointer to *NULL*. It should be apparent that *setNext()* can be used for that purpose.

Methods for Deleting Data

The *remove()* method, which removes the first node of a list, is fairly simple to implement: copy the data from the second node into the first node, thereby "splicing" the chain of links. One complication of this method is that we cannot remove the only node of a list, since the object representing the head node of the list is, in fact, the list itself. Therefore, to remove the only node, we remove the associated data, i.e., we set *info* to *NULL*. If the list was already empty, obviously, there is no value to remove or return, so we throw an exception.

A complication of this method is that the second node might, itself, have NULL_*info*. We would not want to have a string of nodes with NULL_*info*. However, as was previously observed (in connection with the *add*() method), the only ways in which a node with NULL_*info* can be introduced into a list are: (1) by the creation of an empty list; or (2) by removal of every node in the list. In either case, the _*next* pointer of a node with NULL_*info* will itself be *NULL*. Therefore, if the second node has NULL_*info*, copying the second node into the first node will set the first node's _*next* pointer to *NULL* as well.

```
template <class DataType>
DataType LinkedList<DataType>::remove ()
{
    if (isEmpty()) throw LinkedListBounds();
    DataType temp = *_info;
    delete _info;
    if (_next == NULL) { _info = NULL; }
    else
    {
        LinkedList<DataType>* oldnext = _next;
        _info = _next->_info;
        _next = _next->_next;
        // the purpose of these two lines is to remove any
        // stray pointers into the linked list
        oldnext->_info = NULL;
        oldnext->_next = NULL;
        delete oldnext;
    }
    return temp;
}
```

A method to remove a node at a given position is presented below. The *removeAt*() method returns the object at the node that is removed. If an invalid position is specified, say a position that is greater than the number of elements in the linked list, then an error is thrown and nothing is deleted. The recursive implementation given below uses a single pointer to traverse the linked list and, when the node at *position* is located, calls *remove*() for the actual deletion.

```
template <class DataType>
DataType LinkedList<DataType>::removeAt (int position)
{
    if (isEmpty()) throw LinkedListBounds();
    if (position == 0) { return remove(); }
    if (_next == NULL) throw LinkedListBounds();
    return _next->removeAt (position - 1);
}
```

The highly similar recursive implementation of the remove(key) method set out in the *AbstractLinkedList* class is left as an exercise for the reader.

4.1.3.5   Testing the Class

A test function for the LinkedList class that shows the workings of the various methods associated with the linked list data structure is presented below. This "self-test" method inserts a number of elements and prints the list (to show the order); then it deletes one by number and prints the list again to show that the correct element was deleted; then it attempts to delete more elements than actually exist in the list, demonstrating that an exception occurs and is caught.

```
void main ()
{
    String movies[] = {"'2001'", "'Tron'", "'Wargames'",
    "'Robocop'", "'Outland'", "'Colossus'", "'Alien'"};
    LinkedList<String> L;
    try {
            for (int i = 0; i < 7; i++)
            {
                    L.insertAt (movies[i], i);
            }
    }
    catch (LinkedListException e) {
            cout << "This couldn't happen" << endl;
    }
```

```
LinkedList<String>::iterator t;
bool first = true;
cout << "[";
for (t = L.begin(); t != L.end(); t++)
{
        if (!first) cout << ", ";
        first = false;
        cout << *t;
}
cout << "]" << endl;;

L.removeAt (4);
cout << L << endl;

try {
        while (!L.isEmpty()) { L.remove (); }
}
catch (LinkedListBounds e) {
        cout << "This couldn't happen" << endl;
}
try {
        L.remove ();
}
catch (LinkedListBounds e) {
        cout << "Tried to delete non-existent node"
        << endl;
}
cout << L << endl;
}
```

The output of this function is as follows:

```
['2001', 'Tron', 'Wargames', 'Robocop', 'Outland', 'Colossus', 'Alien']
['2001', 'Tron', 'Wargames', 'Robocop', 'Colossus', 'Alien']
Tried to delete non-existent node
[]
```

4.2   Other Forms of Linked Lists

There are other forms of linked lists including doubly linked lists, circularly linked lists, and generalized linked lists. We will now examine each of these structures. Implementation of these structures is left as an exercise.

4.2.1   Doubly Linked Lists and STL list container

In a linked list we add another pointer, _previous, which points to the previous element of the linked list. This modified linked list is called a doubly linked list. This is pictorially depicted below.

The doubly linked list can be traversed backwards and forwards from any node of the linked list using _previous and _next pointers, respectively.

Doubly linked lists are implemented in the standard template library and they are referred as the list container. Unlike the iterator for the vector container, the iterator for the list container is a bidirectional in the sense that it can move forward and backward. If i is of type list iterator, then the operation ++i moves the iterator to the next element and the operation --i moves the iterator to the previous element. The add method provided in this chapter for linked lists is equivalent to the push_front method of the list container in STL. The STL provides a push_back method to insert elements at the end of the linked list. Similarly, the remove[2] method in our implementation of the linked list is equivalent to the erase method provided for the list container. The methods insert and erase for the list container require that the iterator be passed to it. For example, if you have to remove the 5th element in the linked list we have to move the iterator to the 5th position by using ++ operator 4 times on an iterator say x and then execute the erase function by passing the iterator x.

The following code demonstrates the use of a list container.

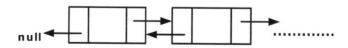

Figure 4.9:   Example of a doubly linked list structure.

---

2 The remove method in list container of STL requires a value to be passed as a parameter. This method then removes all nodes in the linked list that contains the value that is passed.

```
#include <iostream> // for i/o functions
#include <list>

using namespace std;

void main ()
{
    list<int> listInts;
    for (int i = 0; i < 10; ++i)
            listInts.push_back(i);

    cout << "List with 10 values using iterator" << endl;
    list<int>::iterator pLInt = listInts.begin();
    const list<int>::iterator pLIntEnd = listInts.end();
    for (   ; pLIntEnd != pLInt; ++pLInt )
    {
        cout << *pLInt << ", ";
    }
    cout << endl;

    cout << "Removing the 5th element of the linked list." << endl;
    pLInt = listInts.begin();
    for (i = 0; i < 5; i++) ++pLInt;
    listInts.erase(pLInt);

    pLInt = listInts.begin();
    for (   ; pLIntEnd != pLInt; ++pLInt )
    {
        cout << *pLInt << ", ";
    }
    cout << endl;
}
```

The output of the above program is given below.

```
List with 10 values using iterator
0, 1, 2, 3, 4, 5, 6, 7, 8, 9,
Removing the 5th element of the linked list.
0, 1, 2, 3, 4, 6, 7, 8, 9,
```

Figure 4.10 provides a set of methods that are part of the list container in the standard template library.

list<DataType>()	Default constructor
list<DataType> (int n)	Construct a list of initial size n
list<DataType> (int n, const DataType& value)	Construct a list of initial size n and each element is set to be equal to value.
list<DataType>(const list<DataType>& list)	The copy constructor
~list<DataType>()	Destructor
=	list<DataType>& operator=(const list<DataType>& rhsList) Overloaded assignment operator. The contents of the list on the left hand side are replaced with the contents of the list on the right hand side of the assignment operator.
==	bool operator==(const list<DataType>& rhsList) Return true if both the lists contain the same items in the same order, false otherwise.
<	bool operator<(const list<DataType>& rhsList) Return true if first list is lexicographically less than the second list, false otherwise.
DataType& front()	Return a reference to the first element.
DataType& back()	Return a reference to the last element.
iterator begin()	Return the iterator positioned at the first element.
iterator end()	Return the iterator positioned immediately after the last element.
iterator insert(iterator pos, const DataType& value)	Insert value at pos and return an iterator pointing to the new element's position.
void erase(iterator pos)	Erase the element at pos.
void push_back(const DataType& value)	Add value to the end of the list.
void push_front(const DataType& value)	Add value in front of the first element.
void pop_back()	Erase the last element of the list.
void pop_front()	Erase the first element of the list.
int size()	Return the number of elements stored in the list.
bool empty()	Return true if the list does not contain any elements, false otherwise.
splice(iterator pos, list<DataType>& _list)	Remove all of the elements in the _list and insert them at position _pos.

Figure 4.10:   The methods of the list container in the STL

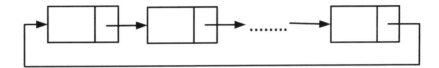

Figure 4.11:   Example of a circularly linked list structure.

4.2.2   Circularly Linked Lists

In a linked list, if we make the last node of the linked list point to the first node of the linked list, then we have a circularly linked list. This is pictorially depicted above.

Circularly linked lists are useful whenever we need to process elements in a round robin fashion. For example each node in a circularly linked list could correspond to a process (a program in execution) that is waiting for CPU time. In a time-sharing system each of the process is given equal time quantum and processed in a round-robin manner until it terminates. A round-robin is a scheme in which each process is processed on at a time starting from the first process and after the last process is processed, we start all over again with the first process. Another variation of the circularly linked list is the circularly linked doubly linked list. Here the _previous pointer of the first element points to the last element of the doubly linked list and the _next pointer of the last element points to the first element.

Certain methods of the linked list interface, such as find() and insertAt() are a bit more tricky to implement in a circularly linked list than in a linked list. Also, the *LLEnumerator* previously described will definitely not work correctly on a circularly linked list!

4.2.3   Generalized Lists

In the class definition of the linked list, we will add another field of data type linked list called _sublist. Given this definition we can see that each node of the linked list points to two linked lists: one using the _next pointer and another using the _sublist pointer. Pictorially it appears as given below.

We can represent the generalized list in Figure 4.12 in the parenthesis form. For example, if a, b, c, … are objects in Figure 4.12, the parenthesis form of the above-generalized list is (a (d e (i)) b c (f g h)). We say that a, b, and c are first level elements, (d e) and (f g h) are second level elements belonging to a and c, respectively, and the element (i) is the third level element whose first level element is a and second level element is e.

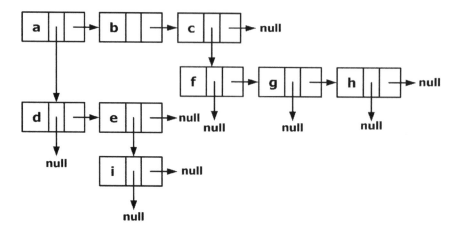

Figure 4.12: Example of a generalized list structure.

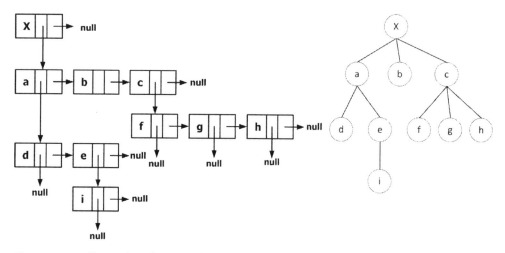

Figure 4.13: Example of a generalized list structure used to store a tree data structure.

The generalized list can also be used to present a rooted tree. Note that a tree is a data structure where each of the nodes stores some information and each node has a single parent and a set of children. For example, a genealogy is represented by a tree. A tree and the corresponding generalized list are shown above.

In the tree in Figure 4.13, x is the parent node also called the 'root' of the tree since it does not have a parent. Nodes marked a, b, and c are siblings are children of the node x. Node a has two children d and e. Nodes f, g, and h are siblings of each other and are the children of node c.

4.2.4   Other Implementations of Linked Lists

We have presented a recursive implementation of the linked list because the definition of the data type is strongly recursive. However, this is not the only way to implement it. Two other possibilities are presented briefly here. In these cases, the requirement that we be able to return a linked list corresponding to the _next pointer is not satisfied, so our abstract data type cannot be perfectly implemented. However, they are useful in their own right.

4.2.4.1   Non-Recursive Implementation

We can distinguish between the head of a linked list and all other nodes of the list by declaring a LinkedNode class consisting of data and a pointer to another node (only a partial implementation is shown):

```
template<class DataType>
class LinkedNode<DataType>
{
protected:
    DataType* _data;
    LinkedNode<DataType>* _next;
public:
    LinkedNode<DataType>* next ();
    DataType& data ();
};
// ------------------------------------------------------------
LinkedNode<DataType>* LinkedNode<DataType>::next ()
{
    return _next;
}
// ------------------------------------------------------------
template<class DataType>
DataType& LinkedNode<DataType>::DataType& data ()
{
    return *_data;
}
```

Our LinkedList class can then consist of a pointer to one LinkedNode instance, that representing the head of the list:

```
template<class DataType>
class LinkedList
{
protected:
    LinkedNode<DataType>* _head;
};
```

We can identify an empty list as one where the _head field is NULL. Instead of accessing nodes recursively, we can loop over the LinkedNodes. Thus, the find() method could be implemented as follows:

```
template <class DataType>
DataType& LinkedList<DataType>::find (const DataType& key)
{
    if (_head == NULL) throw LinkedListNotFound();

    LinkedNode<DataType>* pNode = _head;

    while (pNode ->data() != key)
    {
        if (pNode->next == NULL) throw LinkedListBounds();
        pNode = pNode->next;
    }

    return pNode->data();
}
```

Implementation of a non-recursive LinkedList class is left as an exercise for the reader.

4.2.4.2 Vector and Array Implementation

As noted earlier a *Vector* class allows objects to be inserted at any position and deleted from any position. It grows and shrinks in size as items are added and deleted from it. Thus a *Vector* class implements a linked list very naturally. (Conversely, we could implement a *Vector* using a linked list.) Yet another implementation of a linked list that does

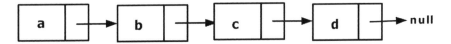

Figure 4.14:   Linked list with a, b, c and d as objects in the _info field.

	_info	_next
0	NULL	-1
1	a	3
2	c	5
3	b	2
4	NULL	-1
5	d	-1
6	NULL	-1

Figure 4.15:   Table of values for array implementation of linked list structure.

not use pointers is the array implementation of the linked list, where the nodes are elements of an array rather than in memory that is individually allocated. Since an array is limited in size, an array implementation of the linked list does not allow the linked list to grow indefinitely as the abstract data type indicates it can. This is a limitation of the particular implementation, just as the representation of an integer by four bytes in the computer's memory limits the possible values even though an integer may properly take on any of an infinite number of values (countably infinite, of course).

The array implementation is pictorially depicted below. Consider the linked list with a, b, c, and d as objects in the _info field.

In the array implementation of the linked list, the _next field will be an integer that will have the index value in the array that contains the object next to the current object in the linked list. This is shown above.

The first element is in position 1 of the array and the next element is at position 3 given by the _next integer value corresponding to object at position 1. Thus using the _next index position we can traverse the linked list. The _next of the last element d is set to −1 to indicate that it is the last element and is similar in semantics to NULL. As with the dynamic implementation of the linked list we need to store the location of the first element of the linked list. Another important question we need to address is how to find space in the array for new nodes that will add to the linked list? First note that in the above figure, the length of the array is 7 and the linked list represented by this array cannot be more than 7 elements. In order to place a new element in the linked list we need to find a free slot in the array. A free slot in the array could be recognized by the presence of a NULL object in the _info field. This can be detected by searching the array sequentially. One way to avoid the sequential searching to find the empty free slot is to link the empty free slots so that it forms a linked list. This can be accomplished by having a third field names _freeNext which is of type integer and a variable called firstFree which will give the index position of the first free slot. For the example in Figure 4.15 firstFree will be equal to 0. The freeNext corresponding to index position 0 will be 4, the freeNext corresponding to position 4 will be 6, and the freeNext corresponding to index position 6 will be a −1 indicting the last element of the linked list that contains index positions that are free. A free slot is determined by looking at the variable firstFree. When a node is removed, the index position is simply added to the beginning of the freeList and firstFree now will contain the index position that is just removed.

The reader may wonder what use a linked list in an array might have, particularly since it is inefficient to reuse space after a deletion. Uses for such an implementation are unusual, but they do exist.

Consider this specific example: we have a number of Items to be partitioned among a number of Cells. There is a function we can apply to each Item to determine the Cell to which it will be assigned. We do not know how many Items will be assigned to any given Cell, and we know that the Items are not in order. Thus, the first Item might be assigned to Cell 50, the next to Cell 3, and the third to Cell 85. We also know that we will never remove an Item from any Cell once it is assigned. How can we perform this assignment?

One possibility is to create a linked list of Items for each Cell. We loop over the Items and determine the Cell for each Item. As we determine the Cell for an Item, we add the Item to that Cell's linked list. This operation will require the allocation of one linked list for each Item. If the number of Items is small, that is acceptable. If the number of Items is large, say twelve million, the cost of individual allocations becomes prohibitive.

A second possibility is to loop over the Items twice. On the first pass, we determine the Cell for each Item but merely increment a counter for that Cell. After the first loop, we have a count of the number of Items for each Cell. We then allocate an array of the correct size for each Cell, and loop over the Items a second time. This time, as we determine the Cell for each Item, we copy it into the array for that Cell. This reduces the number of individual allocations to the number of Cells. However, if the cost of determining the Cell for each Item is very high, this operation will be prohibitively expensive in time.

A third possibility is to create an implementation of a linked list within an array. We know the total length of all the linked lists required for all the Cells, even though we do not know in advance the length of the list for any given Cell, since the Items are partitioned among the Cells. We can therefore allocate an array large enough to hold all the linked lists required for all the Cells. Initially, every Cell has an empty linked list in the array, and all the other lists are unused. We keep an index of the first unused list. As we loop over the Items and identify the Cell for each Item, we can obtain the first empty, unused list from the array, set its data to the Item, and attach it to the Cell's own list. After the loop, the lists for the various Cells are intricately entangled within the array, but we can start with the list for one Cell and enumerate or act on it, without concerning ourselves with the layout of the array. This operation reduces the number of allocations to a minimum (one) and requires only one pass through the Items.

Implementation of the array implementation is left as an exercise for the reader.

4.2.4.3   Performance Comparisons

We have seen that the linked list data structure can be implemented using the either a recursive definition of the linked list or a non-recursive definition where there exists a special node called first that indicates the first node of the linked list. The linked list can also be implemented using the vector data structure (call it vectorLinkedList) or the array data structure (call it arrayLinkedList) as seen previously. To add a new node in the arrayLinkedList, first a empty slot has to be determined by going through the entire array and this will take $O(n)$, where n is the size of the arrayLinkedList. Another way to find the free locations is to use an array data structure (call this a freeLocations) that keeps track of the free locations (index positions) in arrayLinkedList. Initially, freeLocations will contain a list of all index positions in arrayLinkedList. For each addition of a node in arrayLinkedList the index position stored in the last position of freeLocations is used and the size of freeLocations is decremented by one. This operation will take $O(1)$ time. When a node is deleted from the arrayLinkedList, the index position of the node is added to the end freeLocations and its size is incremented by one. This operation will also take $O(1)$ time. The operations of additions and deletions from last location of the data freeLocations correspond to operations on a Stack data structure that is discussed in Chapter 5. The following table (Figure 4.14) lists the time-complexity for the various linked list operations on all the representations.

The qualitative assessment of the various structures used to represent a linked list is presented in Figure 4.14.

Linked List Implementations Worst-case Time Complexity Comparisons				
Operation	Recursive	Non-Recursive	vectorLinkedList	arrayLinkedList
Create()	$O(1)$	$O(1)$	$O(n)$	$O(n)$
isEmpty()	$O(1)$	$O(1)$	$O(1)$	$O(1)$
Size()	$O(n)$	$O(1)$	$O(1)$	$O(1)$
Add(element)	$O(1)$	$O(1)$	$O(1)$	$O(1)$
RemoveAt(pos)	$O(n)$	$O(n)$	$O(n)$	$O(n)$
lookFor(element)	$O(n)$	$O(n)$	$O(n)$	$O(n)$
destructor	$O(n)$	$O(n)$	$O(n)$	$O(n)$

Figure 4.16: Comparison of worst-case execution times of Linked List operations on different representations. The variable n is the initial size of the vector that represents the linked list.

Linked List Implementations Qualitative Assessment	
Implementation	Assessment
Recursive	Follows the recursive definition of the linked list. The size of the linked list can grow and is limited only to the size of memory. It takes $O(n)$ time to determine the size of the linked list containing n elements.
Non-Recursive	In the non-recursive implementation an extra pointer is needed to keep track of the first element of the linked list. A single size variable can be used to keep track of the number of elements in the linked list.
vectorLinkedList	The implementation is similar to the one for non-recursive implementation. Needs to keep track of free index locations of the vector in a separate array as described previously. The vector's size can be incremented or decremented.
arrayLinkedList	Similar to the comments for vectorLinkedList.

Figure 4.17: Qualitative assessment of various Linked List implementations.

4.3   Application of Linked Lists

We will present an application of the linked list, a technique that uses linked lists for storage allocation in main memory management.

4.3.1   Main Memory Management

The main memory is divided into two partitions: one to accommodate the operating system and the other to the user processes. In a multiprogramming environment it is desirable to allow several user processes to remain in main memory. With respect to the main memory management we make the following assumptions:

Each user process (job) requests a particular size of memory that must be available contiguously (one block). If there is a contiguous block of memory that is large enough to fit the new job, then the new job is loaded into memory.

When a job terminates, its allocated block of memory becomes free space or hole.

Initially the user's space is one large chunk of free space or hole. As jobs are added to the main memory, the hole gets smaller and smaller. Jobs terminate arbitrarily leaving more than one hole, which may or may not be contiguous in memory. The figure below shows a memory scheme in which the user's space is free.

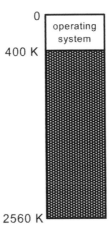

Figure 4.18:   An example of a memory scheme. The operating system occupies 400K of memory and the shaded area represents free memory space available for programs.

Consider the following sequence of operations on this memory:

a. allocate P_1 600k
b. allocate P_2 1000k
c. allocate P_3 300k
d. terminate P_2
e. allocate P_4 700k
f. terminate P_1
g. allocate P_5 400k

The memory dynamics after each of the above operations is shown below.

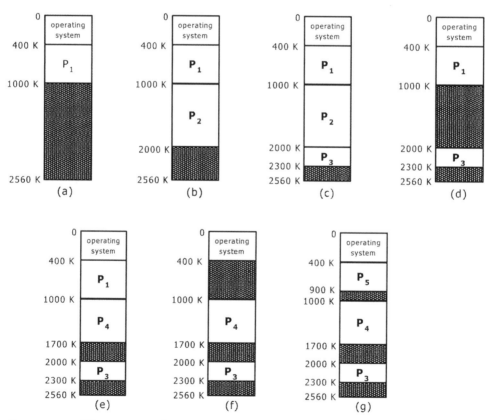

Figure 4.19: The memory dynamics after each of the allocation and termination operations.

A singly linked list representation of the space in memory will allow us to implement each of the above operations. First let us define a partition class with fields to indicate the partition's beginning address, end address, free or taken status, and process identifier of the process using the partition if it is taken.

```
class Partition
{
    int beginAddress;    // beginning address of the partition
    int endAddress;      // end address of the partition
    boolean hole;        // hole is false if it is occupied
                         // by a process, true otherwise
    int processID;       // if hole is false, it contains
                         // the process identifier of the
                         // process using the partition,
                         // otherwise -1.

}
```

Each node of the linked list stores a partition object. Initially, there exists a single node with the object whose fields are initialized as given below.

```
beginAddress = 400;
endAddress = 2560;
hole = true;
processID = -1;
```

The above initialization to the fields of the object that is contained in the node is shown pictorially below.

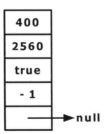

Figure 4.20:   Alternate representation of initial state for memory management scheme.

Now in order to execute the instruction allocate P1600k, we need to search the linked list and find a node with hole set to true and (endAddress–beginAddress) >= 600.

After we find such a node, we need to split the node into two nodes. As shown pictorially below, the first node contains a partition object for P1 and the second node is a node that contains a partition object for the free space.

The following figures show how the linked list appears after the execution of each of the instructions described previously.

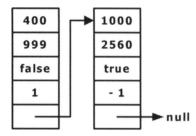

Figure 4.21: Memory dynamics after allocation of 600K for P1.

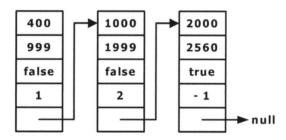

Figure 4.22: Memory dynamics after allocation of 1000K for P2.

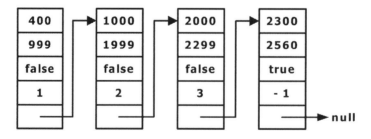

Figure 4.23: Memory dynamics after allocation of 300K for P3.

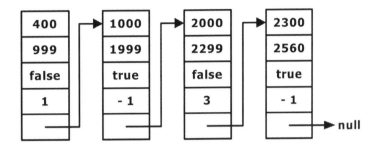

Figure 4.24: Memory dynamics after termination of P2.

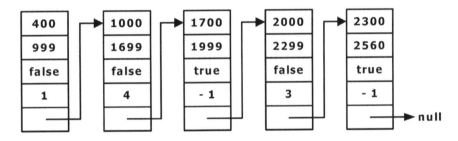

Figure 4.25: Memory dynamics after allocation of 700 K for P4.

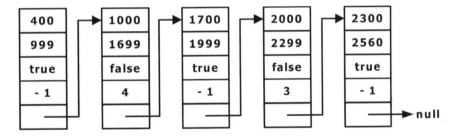

Figure 4.26: Memory dynamics after termination of P1.

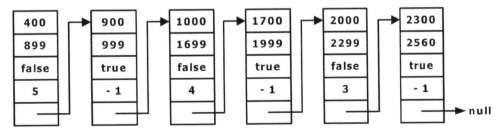

Figure 4.27: Memory dynamics after allocation of 500K for P5.

4.4   Skip Lists

The skip list is a linked–list–based data structure that is used to organize data for efficient searching. We saw earlier that in order to perform binary search, the data elements have to be stored in a sorted order in an array so that rapid random access to any data element in the array is possible. Accessing a data element in the linked list involves traversal of the linked list, and is not rapid.

Insertion and deletion of data items from an array is an expensive operation even after the position to be inserted or deleted is known, because data items have to be moved to the right or left. In the worst case this will require O(n) operations, where n is the number of elements stored in the array. In the case of the linked list, insertion or deletion is a simple operation involving pointer adjustments, once the location to insert at or to be deleted is known.

The skip list data structure is an alternate way to arrange data items in a linked list with additional pointers, such that search, insert and delete operations can be performed in an efficient manner. Consider the first linked list shown below. Search for a data item will require at most n comparisons. In the second linked list below, every other node has two pointers, one pointing to the next node in the linked list and the other pointing to the node pointed by the next's next pointer, i.e., the node two ahead in the linked list. These pointers are called forward pointers and nodes having two forward pointers are called level 2 nodes. Thus the numbers of forward pointers determine the level of the node. In a simple linked list all nodes are of level 1 and is shown in the figure below.

The middle list above also shows a dummy head node containing an array of forward pointers. The dummy node is a level 2 node that does not contain any data item.

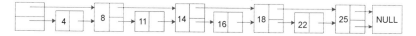

Figure 4.28:   A linked list with elements stored in sorted order. All nodes are of level 1.

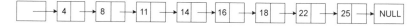

Figure 4.29:   A dummy head with two forward pointers and nodes with values 6, 14, 18 and 25 are level 2 nodes.

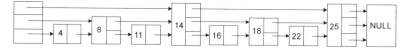

Figure 4.30:   A dummy head with three forward pointers and nodes with values 14 and 25 are level 3 nodes.

The linked list pointed by forward[0] of the dummy node connects all nodes at level 0, and forward[1] of the dummy node connects all nodes at level 2. The third list below shows a dummy head node of level 3.

In order to search for a data item in the linked list in Figure 4.28 above, we first start from the dummy node and traverse the linked list pointed by forward[1]. If we locate the search data item then we are done, otherwise; we determine two nodes, p and q, of level 2, which bracket the range in which the search data item falls. Now, starting from p we traverse the linked list pointed by p $-$> forward[0] visiting level 0 nodes until we reach q. This method of search requires, in total, at most $\lceil n/2 \rceil + 1$ comparisons.

Let us extend this idea and allow every fourth node to have a pointer to every fourth node in the linked list. Now the search will start from the head $->$ forward[2] and visit level 3 nodes, followed by nodes with level of 2 if necessary and nodes that are in level 1 if necessary. This search will require at most $\lceil n/4 \rceil + 2$ comparisons. In general if every (2i)th node has a pointer to 2i nodes that are ahead in the linked list, then the maximum number of comparisons needed to search for a data element is $\lceil \log 2n \rceil$.

The skip list data structure is described as follows. There exists a dummy header node that contains an array of pointers called forward such that forward[i] is the head of a linked list that connects all nodes that have a level of i + 1. Associated with each node is a place for the data element (referred as the key) and an array of forward pointers whose size is equal to the level of the node. A variable called level is associated with each node and contains the level of the node. The variable maxlevel is used to keep track of the maximum of all levels of the nodes of the skip list. The search algorithm is presented below.

```
Algorithm search (list, searchKey)
1.  x ← list.header        // The dummy header
2.  for i ← list.level-1 downto 0
3.        while (x.forward[i] is not NULL) and
                        (x.forward[i].key < searchKey)
4.              x ← x.forward[i]
5.        if (x.forward[i] is NULL) return FALSE
6.  x ← x.forward[0]
7.  if (x.key=searchKey)
8.        return TRUE
9.  else
10.       return FALSE
```

4.4.1   Insertion and Deletion

The description above, where every odd-numbered node is of level 1 and every even-numbered node is of level 2 or more is, in fact, an idealization. We could not readily create such a list unless (1) we knew how many nodes there were, so that we knew the necessary maximum level; and (2) we received the nodes in order, so that we could determine whether a node was odd-numbered or even-numbered at the time of insertion and be certain that it would not change. Clearly, if we had that sort of information to start with, we could simply create an array to hold the data, and would not need a skip list at all!

If we intend to support insertion and deletion efficiently in a skip list, we need to choose the level of an inserted node without counting the number of nodes preceding the inserted node or altering the levels of any nodes in the course of deletion. If we do not know how many nodes actually precede the inserted node, we really have no basis on which to determine the level of the node. In other words, we will simply have to guess.

4.4.1.1   Insertion

Insertion of an element e is done in two steps. In the first step, we will apply the search algorithm and find the node y such that the new node containing e will be inserted to its right. In the second step, a new node x will be created to store the element e and a random number will be generated to assign a level to this node (that is, we guess at the correct level). Let us call this random number newLevel.

An array of forward pointers of size newLevel is created and nodes at appropriate levels to the left of the new node x are made to point to x and the forward pointers of x are made to point to appropriate nodes to the right of the node x. This amounts to splicing x into a series of linked lists.

We can keep track of the nodes at appropriate levels to the left of the new node x during the process of search. We will call the array of nodes links and links[i] will contain a pointer to the rightmost node of level i or higher that is to the left of the new node x. The insert algorithm is presented below.

```
Algorithm Insert (list, newElement)
1.  x ← list.header
2.  for i ← list.level-1 downto 0
3.        while x.forward[i].key < newElement
4.              x ←x.forward[i]
5.        links[i] ← x
6.  x ← x.forward[0]
7.  if x.key ≠ newElement
8.        newLevel ← randomLevel ()
9.        if newLevel > list.level
10.             for i ← list.level to newLevel
11.                   links[i] ← list.header
12.        list.level ← newLevel
13.        x ← makeNode (newLevel, newElement)
14.        for i ← 0 to list.level-1
15.              x.forward[i] ← links[i].forward[i]
16.              links[i].forward[i] ← x
```

When a level is chosen at random for the new node its value can be very large. Pugh presents the following random level generation algorithm which guarantees that the probability that the maximum level in a list of n elements is significantly larger than L(n) is very small, where L(n) = log(1/p)n and p is the fraction of the nodes with level i pointers also have level i + 1 pointers. The value of p is usually chosen to be ½. The randomLevel algorithm uses a variable called MaximumLevel which is set to L(n). If theMaximumLevel is set to 16 and p = 1/2 then the number of elements that can be stored in the skip list is 2^{16}.

```
Algorithm randomLevel (p, MaximumLevel)
1.  level ← 1    • random () returns a number x with 0 < x < 1.
2.  while random() < p and level < MaximumLevel
3.        level ← level + 1
4.  return level
```

4.4.1.2   Deletion

Deletion is similar to deletion in a linked list, in that we remove a node and splice together the remaining list. The only detail of concern is the fact that the node to be deleted will be part of a number of linked lists, the number being equal to its level. The deletion algorithm is presented below.

```
Algorithm Delete (list, searchKey)
1.  x ← list.header;
2.  for i ← list.level-1 downto 0
3.        while (x.forward[i] ≠ NULL) and
                (x.forward[i].key < searchKey) x ← x.forward[i]
4.        links[i] ← x
5.  x ← x.forward[0]
6.  if x.key = searchKey
7.        for i ← 0 to list.level-1
8.            if links[i].forward[i] ≠ x RETURN
9.                links[i].forward[i] ← x.forward[i]
10.       while (list.level > 1) and
                (list.header.forward[list.level-1] = NULL)
11.           list.level = list.level-1
```

4.4.1.3   Complexity of Insertion and Deletion

A probabilistic analysis beyond the scope of this book reveals that the number of operations to perform insertion and deletion has a worst case expected number of comparisons of O(log n).

4.4.2   Abstract Data Type

The essential operations on a skip list are as follows:

```
create() // creates an empty skip list
isEmpty() // returns true if the list is empty, but otherwise
          //returns false
size() // returns the number of nodes in the list
maxLevel() // returns the maximum level of all nodes in the list
insert (object) // inserts object in its correct position in
                // the sorted list
delete (key) // deletes the object matching key from the
             // list, if it is present
find (key) // returns the object matching key from the list,
           // if it present, otherwise NULL
```

4.4.3   Implementation of the Skip List

The skip list described above can be implemented in C++ using a linked-list-like structure.

4.4.3.1   Node Data Type

Since the nodes of a skip list are maintained in order, it is evident that we must be able to compare them. Therefore, the nodes must implement the three-way comparison operators described in the first chapter.

4.4.3.2   Exceptions

A skip list has the same family of exceptions as a linked list, and we shall simply use the linked list exception family.

4.4.3.3   Abstract Base Class

The abstract base class for the skip list is readily derived from the abstract data type given above:

```
template <class DataType>
class AbstractSkipList
{
friend ostream& operator<< (ostream& s,
AbstractSkipList<DataType>& SL);
public:
    virtual boolisEmpty() = NULL;
    // returns true if the list is empty, but otherwise
    // returns false
    virtual int size()= NULL;
    // returns the number of nodes in the list
    virtual intmaxLevel()= NULL;
    // returns the maximum level of all nodes in the list
    virtual void insert (DataType& object) = NULL;
    // inserts object in its correct position in the sorted list
    virtual void remove (DataType& key) = NULL;
    // removes the object matching key from the list, if it
    // is present
```

```
        virtual Object find (DataType& key) = NULL;
        // finds and returns the object matching key from the list,
        // if it is present, or else throws error
        virtual Enumeration<DataType>* enumerator ()= NULL;
        // returns an Enumeration object which lists all elements
        virtual void display (ostream& s);
};
```

The *enumerator()* method makes the *display()* method quite simple, and the *display()* method, in turn, makes the ostream << function simple:

```
template <class DataType>
void AbstractSkipList<DataType>::display (ostream& s)
{
    bool first = true;
    Enumeration<DataType>* e = enumerator();
    s << "[";
    while (e->hasMoreElements())
    {
      if (!first) s << ", ";
      first = false;
      s << e->nextElement();
    }
    s << "]";
    delete e;
}
// --------------------------------------------------------
template <class DataType>
ostream& operator << (ostream& s,
                    AbstractSkipList<DataType>& SL)
{
    SL.display(s);
    return s;
}
```

4.4.3.4   Class Definition

With our node data type, exceptions, and interface in hand, we can begin the implementation of the *SkipList* class. It is evident, however, that we will need a supporting class: the multilevel links that make up the various linked lists.

SkipListLink Class

The *SkipListLink* class, then, must store data and a variable number of links to other instances of the *SkipListLink* class. Since we will use this class only as a supporting class for the *SkipList*, we will protect its constructor and fields. This ensures that only a friend class can construct an instance, but such a friend can directly access the fields so as to reduce the amount of code we must present. The class itself is quite simple:

```
template<class DataType>
class SkipListLink
{
friend SkipList<DataType>;
protected:
    SkipListLink (int level);
    DataType* _object;
    SkipListLink<DataType>** _links;
// i.e., _links is a pointer to an array of pointers
    int _level;
public:
    virtual ~SkipListLink();
};
// -------------------------------------------------------
template<class DataType>
SkipListLink<DataType>::SkipListLink (int level)
{
    _object = NULL;
    _links = new SkipListLink<DataType>* [level+1];
    if (_links == NULL) throw LinkedListMemory();
    _level = level+1;
    for (int i = 0; i <= level; i++)
      _links[i] = NULL;
}
```

The only sticking point is the destructor. We saw in the *LinkedList* class a destructor which destroyed all linked objects. Should the *SkipListLink* destructor do the same? This is a specific instance of a more general problem: assigning responsibility of deallocating memory among cooperating objects and their users. In this case, a *SkipListLink* object takes no responsibility for the elements of its _links field. A *SkipListLink* object exists only to serve as a container used by its owner, and it is therefore the owner's responsibility to deal with the allocated memory. The *SkipListLink* destructor will delete only the memory pointed to by _object and the array pointed to by _links (but not any of the memory pointed to by the elements of _links):

```
template<class DataType>
SkipListLink<DataType>::~SkipListLink ()
{
    if (_object != NULL) delete _object;
    _object = NULL;
    if (_links != NULL) delete _links;
    _links = NULL;
}
```

Fields and Constructors

From the description of the skip list given above, it is evident that we must have a header field, which will be a *SkipListLink* with no data. In the algorithm, this header starts with only one level and then increases in level over time. The maximum number of levels is relatively small, however, as it is only log2n, where n is the maximum number of nodes, so we will simplify our code and accept the small inefficiency of creating a header with the maximum number of levels initially. For consistency with the description of levels given previously, we will use levels 1 through *maxLevel* and disregard level 0.

We need a field to hold the maximum level and also a field to hold the number of nodes in the skip list.

What is the maximum level of a skip list? We will allow the creator of the skip list to make that decision via the constructor.

Thus, our *SkipList* class will initially appear as follows:

```
template<class DataType>
class SkipList : public AbstractSkipList<DataType>
{
protected:
    SkipListLink<DataType> _header;
    int _maxLevel;
    int _size;
public:
    SkipList (intmaxLevel);
};
// ---------------------------------------------------------
template<class DataType>
SkipList<DataType>::SkipList (intmaxLevel):_header(maxLevel+1)
{
    _maxLevel = maxLevel;
    _size = 0;
}
```

But now we have a problem: *SkipList* uses *SkipListLink*, and vice versa. Which should appear first in the source code? This is the same sort of problem we had with functions which called each other, and the solution is the same: in effect, we give a "prototype" for one of the classes:

```
template<class DataType> class SkipListLink;// the prototype
// ---------------------------------------------------------
template<class DataType>
class SkipList : public AbstractSkipList<DataType>
{// as above }
// ---------------------------------------------------------
template<class DataType>
class SkipListLink
{
friend SkipList<DataType>;
    // as above
};
```

Destructor

As noted previously, the *SkipListLink* destructor does not delete other *SkipListLink* objects which may be linked to an instance being deleted. It is therefore the responsibility of the user of a *SkipListLink* object, in this case an instance of *SkipList*, to delete the linked objects. Although such deletion could be done recursively, in this case we shall do it iteratively. Since all of the objects in the skip list are linked together by level 1 pointers, we will follow the level 1 pointers to find objects which need to be deleted.

```
template<class DataType>
SkipList<DataType>::~SkipList ()
{
    SkipListLink<DataType>* curr = _header._links[1];
    SkipListLink<DataType>* next;
    while (curr != NULL)
    {
        next = curr->_links[1];
        delete curr;
        curr = next;
    }
}
```

Accessor Methods

The accessor methods other than *find()* are obvious:

```
template<class DataType>
boolSkipList<DataType>::isEmpty()
{
    return (_size == 0);
}
// ------------------------------------------------------------
template<class DataType>
intSkipList<DataType>::size()
{
    return _size;
}
// ------------------------------------------------------------
```

```
template<class DataType>
int SkipList<DataType>::maxLevel()
{
    return _maxLevel;
}
```

Now let us consider the *find()* method. From the description of the skip list, above, we can make a first cut by simply moving through the linked lists, starting with the top level and working our way down until we find the desired key or determine that it is not present.

```
template<class DataType>
DataType SkipList<DataType>::find (DataType& key)
    // finds and returns the object matching key from the list,
    // if it is present, or else throws error
{
    SkipListLink<DataType>** links =
        new SkipListLink<DataType>* [_maxLevel+1];
    for (int i = 0; i <= _maxLevel; i++) links[i] = NULL;
    links[_maxLevel] = &_header;
    for (int level = _maxLevel; level > 0; )
    {
    // we are through with this level when we reach the end of the
    // list or we reach a node which equals or exceeds the key
        if   ((links[level]->_links[level] == NULL) ||
             (*links[level]->_links[level]->_object >= key))
        {
        // in either case, we need to drop down a level
            level--;
        // and start where the search left off on the level above
            links[level] = links[level+1];
        }
        else
        {
        // otherwise, we need to keep looking in this level
            links[level] = links[level]->_links[level];
        }
    }
```

```
// at the end of this loop, either links[1]->_links[1] is NULL (the
// key is greater than any in the skip list, or links[1]
// points to an existing node.  We need only compare that
// node with the key.
    if    ((links[1]->_links[1] != NULL) &&
              (*links[1]->_links[1]->_object == key))
    {
         Object found = *links[1]->_links[1]->_object;
         delete[] links;
         return found;
    }
    delete[] links;
    throw LinkedListNotFound();
}
```

Let us reconsider the *find()* method, however, in light of the fact that our insertion and deletion algorithms are required to identify the predecessors of the desired node in each of the linked lists. Those predecessors are precisely the nodes given in the links array, above. Rather than duplicate the above code for the insertion and deletion algorithms, we can move most of the code into a protected method which creates and returns the *links* array. The actual *find()* method can then simply do the test which it already does as its final step:

```
template<class DataType>
SkipListLink<DataType>** SkipList<DataType>::_find (DataType&
key)
// finds the predecessor of key at each level
{
    SkipListLink<DataType>** links =
         new SkipListLink<DataType>* [_maxLevel+1];
    for (int i = 0; i <= _maxLevel; i++) links[i] = NULL;
    links[_maxLevel] = &_header;
    for (int level = _maxLevel; level > 0; )
    {
    // we are through with this level when we reach the end of the
    // list or we reach a node which equals or exceeds the key
        if    ((links[level]->_links[level] == NULL) ||
              (*links[level]->_links[level]->_object >= key))
```

```
                {
                // in either case, we need to drop down a level
                    level--;
                // and start where the search left off on the level above
                    links[level] = links[level+1];
                }
                else
                {
                // otherwise, we need to keep looking in this level
                    links[level] = links[level]->_links[level];
                }
        }
        return links;
}
// ---------------------------------------------------------
template <class DataType>
Object SkipList<DataType>::find (DataType& key)
//  finds and returns the object matching key from the list,
    //   if it is present, or else throws error
{
    SkipListLink<DataType>** links = _find(key);
// at the end of this call, either links[1]->_links[1] is NULL (the
// key is greater than any in the skip list, or links[1]
// points to an existing node.  We need only compare that
// node with the key.
    if ((links[1]->_links[1] != NULL) &&
            (*links[1]->_links[1]->_object == key))
    {
        Object found = *links[1]->_links[1]->_object;
        delete[] links;
        return found;
    }
    delete[] links;
    throw LinkedListNotFound();
}
```

The insert() method

With the _find() method in hand, the complexity of insert() is greatly reduced. If the key is not already present, we need only find the predecessors at all levels through _find(), generate a node of the appropriate (randomly-determined) height, and splice the new node in.

Generating random numbers in C++ requires the use of the rand() function, the prototype of which appears in the stdlib.h header file. This function returns an integer from 0 to MAXINT (a value which varies according to implementation). To obtain an integer in a specific range, we use the % operator (modulo operator). Now we can write the randomLevel() method corresponding to the randomLevel algorithm given above:

```
template<class DataType>
intSkipList<DataType>::randomLevel ()
{
    int level = 1;
    while ((rand()%2 < 1) && (level < _maxLevel))
    {
        level++;
    }
    return level;
}
```

We have "hardwired" the value of p as ½. The reader may wish to experiment with a SkipList class which allows the value of p to be specified.

At last we are ready to write the insert() method itself:

```
template <class DataType>
void SkipList<DataType>::insert (DataType& object)
{
    SkipListLink<DataType>** links = _find(object);
// if there is a matching node, replace it
    if ((links[1]->_links[1] != NULL) &&
            (*links[1]->_links[1]->_object==object))
    {
        delete links[1]->_links[1]->_object;
        links[1]->_links[1]->_object = new DataType (object);
    }
```

```
// otherwise, create a new node and splice it in
    else
    {
        SkipListLink<DataType>* link =
            new SkipListLink<DataType> randomLevel()+1);
        link->_object = new DataType(object);
        for (int level = 1; level < link->_level; level++)
        {
            link->_links[level] = links[level]->_links[level];
            links[level]->_links[level] = link;
        }
    }
        delete[] links;
}
```

The remove() Method

Removal is even simpler than insertion; we need only find the predecessors and splice the node out:

```
template<class DataType>
void SkipList<DataType>::remove (DataType& key)
{
    SkipListLink<DataType>** links = _find (key);

// if there is a matching node, splice it out and return the
// prior value
    SkipListLink<DataType>* deleted = links[1]->_links[1];
    if ((deleted != NULL) && (*deleted->_object == key))
    {
        for (int level = 1; level < deleted->_level; level++)
        {
            links[level]->_links[level] = deleted->_links[level];
        }
        delete deleted;
    }
// otherwise, the node is not present
    delete[] links;
}
```

Enumeration of Nodes

Finally, we must provide for the enumeration of nodes. The implementation of the skip list given so far is inadequate to allow enumeration as specified by the Enumeration interface. We must therefore modify our class somewhat.

The modifications we shall make allow for simple enumeration. It is most efficient when a skip list is enumerated by one enumerator at a time, and no insertion or deletion is done. It does, however, allow enumeration in other cases as well, though less efficiently. In effect, we shall add a method called next(), which can find the node which follows a given value, and provide a pointer to the last node accessed by next(). If a single enumerator is working its way through the skip list, it will access the nodes in order. In other cases, we will have to locate the last position before we can execute next(). The *next()* method is not part of the skip list abstract data type, and further allows direct access to the objects in the list, since it returns a pointer to the most recent node. We do not wish to allow the user to directly access the nodes, since the list is sorted, and uncontrolled modification of nodes could destroy the sorting property. Thus, we will make *next()* a protected method, and make our enumerator subclass a friend.

```
template<class DataType>
class SkipList : public AbstractSkipList <DataType>
{
friend SkipListEnumerator<DataType>;
protected:
    SkipListLink<DataType>* lastAccess;
        // initialize to NULL in constructor
    DataType* next (DataType* prev);
// as previously presented
public:
// as previously presented
}
// -------------------------------------------------------
```

```
template<class DataType>
DataType* SkipList<DataType>::next (DataType* prev)
{
    if (prev == NULL) // this is the first access
    {
        lastAccess = &_header;
    }
    else if ((lastAccess == NULL) ||
            (*lastAccess->_object != *prev))
    {
        SkipListLink<DataType>** links = _find(*prev);
        lastAccess = links[1];
        delete [] links;
    }
    lastAccess = lastAccess->_links[1];
    if (lastAccess == NULL)
    {
        return NULL;
    }
    return lastAccess->_object;
}
```

We can now write an *Enumeration* subclass:

```
template<class DataType>
class SkipListEnumerator : public Enumeration<DataType>
{
protected:
    SkipList<DataType>* _SL;
    DataType* lastValue; // last value returned, for next()
    DataType* toReturn;  // next value to return
    boolnoMore;          // flag for detecting no more
public:
    SkipListEnumerator (SkipList<DataType>* SL);
    boolhasMoreElements ();
    DataType&nextElement ();
};
// ------------------------------------------------------------
```

```
template <class DataType>
SkipListEnumerator<DataType>::SkipListEnumerator
(SkipList<DataType>* SL)
{
    _SL = SL;
    lastValue = NULL;
    toReturn = NULL;
    noMore = false;
}
// ------------------------------------------------------------
template <class DataType>
boolSkipListEnumerator<DataType>::hasMoreElements()
{
    if (_SL == NULL) { return false; }
// if list is invalid, no more
    if (noMore) { return false; }
// if we've already checked...
// if we got a value by checking for more, and haven't used it,
// there is clearly at least one more
    if (toReturn != NULL) return true;

// get the next value and hold onto it for return by nextElement()
    toReturn = _SL->next (lastValue);
    if (toReturn == NULL)
    {
        noMore = true;
        return false;
    }
    lastValue = toReturn;
    return true;
}
// ------------------------------------------------------------
```

```
template<class DataType>
DataType&SkipListEnumerator<DataType>::nextElement ()
{
    if (!hasMoreElements()) throw LinkedListBounds();
// set toReturn to NULL to indicate that the value has been used
    DataType* temp = toReturn;
    toReturn = NULL;
    return *temp;
}
```

Our enumerator method is quite simple:

```
template<class DataType>
Enumeration<DataType>* SkipList<DataType>::enumerator ()
{
    return new SkipListEnumerator<DataType> (this);
}
```

4.4.3.5   Testing the Class

We will demonstrate this class by adding some values, in different orders, and then deleting some values:

```
void main ()
{
try
{
    SkipList<int>sl (5);
    int i;

// insert in order
        for (i = 21; i < 30; i++)
        {
                cout << "+" << i << ":   ";
                sl.insert (i);
                cout << sl << endl;
        }
```

```
    // insert in reverse order
        for (i = 9; i > 0; i--)
        {
            cout << "++" << i << ":   ";
            sl.insert (i);
            cout << sl << endl;
        }

    // delete two that exist and two that don't
        for (i = 8; i < 12; i++)
        {
            cout << "--" << i << ":   ";
            sl.remove (i);
            cout << sl << endl;
        }

    // delete the first
        cout << "--1:   ";
        sl.remove (1);
        cout << sl << endl;

    // delete the last
        cout << "-29:   ";
        sl.remove (29);
        cout << sl << endl;

    // delete a node after the last
        cout << "-29:   ";
        sl.remove (29);
        cout << sl << endl;

    // insert in the position where last deletion occurred
        cout << "+30:   ";
        sl.insert (30);
        cout << sl << endl;
    }
catch (Exception e)  { }
}
```

The output from this method indicates that the skip list is working correctly:

```
+21:   [21]
+22:   [21, 22]
+23:   [21, 22, 23]
+24:   [21, 22, 23, 24]
+25:   [21, 22, 23, 24, 25]
+26:   [21, 22, 23, 24, 25, 26]
+27:   [21, 22, 23, 24, 25, 26, 27]
+28:   [21, 22, 23, 24, 25, 26, 27, 28]
+29:   [21, 22, 23, 24, 25, 26, 27, 28, 29]
++9:   [9, 21, 22, 23, 24, 25, 26, 27, 28, 29]
++8:   [8, 9, 21, 22, 23, 24, 25, 26, 27, 28, 29]
++7:   [7, 8, 9, 21, 22, 23, 24, 25, 26, 27, 28, 29]
++6:   [6, 7, 8, 9, 21, 22, 23, 24, 25, 26, 27, 28, 29]
++5:   [5, 6, 7, 8, 9, 21, 22, 23, 24, 25, 26, 27, 28, 29]
++4:   [4, 5, 6, 7, 8, 9, 21, 22, 23, 24, 25, 26, 27, 28, 29]
++3:   [3, 4, 5, 6, 7, 8, 9, 21, 22, 23, 24, 25, 26, 27, 28, 29]
++2:   [2, 3, 4, 5, 6, 7, 8, 9, 21, 22, 23, 24, 25, 26, 27, 28, 29]
++1:   [1, 2, 3, 4, 5, 6, 7, 8, 9, 21, 22, 23, 24, 25, 26, 27, 28, 29]
--8:   [1, 2, 3, 4, 5, 6, 7, 9, 21, 22, 23, 24, 25, 26, 27, 28, 29]
--9:   [1, 2, 3, 4, 5, 6, 7, 21, 22, 23, 24, 25, 26, 27, 28, 29]
--10:  [1, 2, 3, 4, 5, 6, 7, 21, 22, 23, 24, 25, 26, 27, 28, 29]
--11:  [1, 2, 3, 4, 5, 6, 7, 21, 22, 23, 24, 25, 26, 27, 28, 29]
--1:   [2, 3, 4, 5, 6, 7, 21, 22, 23, 24, 25, 26, 27, 28, 29]
-29:   [2, 3, 4, 5, 6, 7, 21, 22, 23, 24, 25, 26, 27, 28]
-29:   [2, 3, 4, 5, 6, 7, 21, 22, 23, 24, 25, 26, 27, 28]
+30:   [2, 3, 4, 5, 6, 7, 21, 22, 23, 24, 25, 26, 27, 28, 30]
```

Whether the skip list is, in fact, more efficient than other data structures can only be determined by an empirical comparison. As the reader progresses through this text and learns of other sorted data structures, it may be instructive to run comparisons among them.

4.5   Exercises

4.1.   Using the linked list class developed in this chapter implement the following methods to insert nodes into the linked list.

   a) insertBefore (DataType& target, DataType& newObject) inserts a node containing newObject after the node that contains the object target.

   b) insertAfter (DataType& target, DataType& newObject) inserts a node containing newObject before the node that contains the object target.

4.2.   Using the linked list class developed in this chapter implement the following methods that remove nodes from the linked list:

   a) remove (DataType& target) removes the node that contains the target object.

   b) clip (intstartposition, intendposition) removes nodes from the linked list starting from the startposition to the endposition of the linked list.

   c) clipAndSave (intstartposition, intendposition) same as clip except it creates a new linked list containing nodes in position startposition to endposition.

4.3.   Write a recursive method called reverse () that modifies the original linked list such that each node in the linked list points to its predecessor. Now the last node in the linked list will become the first node in the linked list.

4.4.   Write a method randomwalk (int i, int j) on a linked list, which moves a temporary pointer to the node at position i (left-to-right traversal) and moves backwards (right-to-left traversal) skipping j nodes. You are to reverse the directions of the links during the left-to-right traversal and fix them during the right-to-left traversal.

4.5.   Assume that a linked list stores a set of objects, which belong to the class of integers. Let S be a set of integers that are stored in a linked list. We say two sets are *equivalent* if they contain the same set of integers. Write a method to check if two sets stored in two linked lists are equivalent. Overload the == operator to perform this test.

4.6.   We say a set S_1 is a subset of the set S_2 if the elements in S_1 are in S_2. Assuming that the sets are stored in a linked list write a method to check if a set is a subset of the other set. Can this method be used to verify the equivalent? How should it be performed? Compare the efficiencies of the method to be derived in 4 and this approach for equivalence testing.

4.7.   A linked list is *ordered* if it stores objects at nodes in a sorted order based on some data field of the objects. Given an ordered linked list, write a binary search method to locate an object in the linked list. What is the time-complexity of your method?

4.8. Write a method moveToFront (DataType& target) that performs a sequential search to locate the node containing the object target and moves the node to the front of the linked list. If the object is not in the linked list, then the last node in the linked list is moved to the front of the link list. Create a linked list with 100 objects and perform over 1000 random searches for objects in the linked list. Keep track of the clock time required to perform a single random search. You will notice that as the number of random searches increases the time needed to search for a random item decreases.

4.9. Repeat exercises 3.1 and 3.2 assuming that the objects are stored in a linked list.

4.10. Implement the polynomial manipulation described in exercise 1.16 assuming that each node of the linked list stores objects each corresponding to a term in the polynomial. Each object stores the coefficient and exponent of the term it represents.

4.11. In exercise 3.16 an array representation of the sparse matrix was presented. Provide an implementation of the sparse matrix using linked lists and give methods for matrix transpose and matrix multiplication.

4.12. Consider the representation for sparse matrices using linked lists in which each node has fields *down, right, row, col,* and *value*. The representation consists of two linked lists. The first list formed using the *right* links is called the *row list* consists of linking nodes by rows and within rows by columns. The second list is formed by *down* links is called the *column list* and its links are by columns and within column by rows. The two lists share a common head node that stores the dimension of the matrix. Define a class definition for this representation and develop methods to perform matrix addition, multiplication and print.

4.13. Assuming that a linked list is represented using arrays, write the methods that are part of the abstract linked list class.

4.14. Rewrite the methods in the linked list class assuming that the underlying data structure is a doubly linked list.

4.15. The iterator for the *list* container in the STL allows the following operations in addition to the ones developed in this chapter. Implement all the STL operators on the doubly linked list class (exercise 4.14). Assuming that i and j are iterators here is a list of other operations on iterators along with a brief description.

$i == j$	return true if i and j are both positioned at the same element.
$--i$	go to the previous element and return i's new value.
$i--$	go to the previous element and return i's previous value.
$i += n$	advance by n locations and return a reference to i.

$i\mathrel{-}=n$ go to the previous n locations and return a reference to i.

$i+n$ return an iterator that is positioned n elements ahead of i's current position.

$i-n$ return an iterator that is positioned n elements behind i's current position.

$i[n]$ return a reference to the nth element from i's current position.

4.16.   Develop a class for generalized list that makes use of the linked list class. What are the methods that are relevant to the generalized list data structure?

4.17.   The generalized list data structure can be represented in the parenthesized form as described in this chapter. Assuming that the input is a parenthesized form and each object is of character data type, develop a method that constructs the generalized list.

4.18.   Given a generalized list, write a method to print the contents of the nodes in the parenthesized form.

4.19.   Develop a method to search for an object in the generalized list.

4.20.   Consider the memory management application presented in this chapter. Develop appropriate objects to store the memory information and develop methods to allocate and deallocate memory as defined in this chapter. Also develop a method to print the contents for each node that represents a contiguous portion of memory.

4.21.   The memory allocation scheme that is discussed in this chapter is called the first fit allocation in which the first memory block that is large enough to hold the processes is allocated. Two other schemes have been suggested and these are best fit and worst fit. In the best-fit scheme the contiguous block of memory that is small enough to hold the process is allocated to the process. The worst fit scheme searches for the largest contiguous block that can hold the processes and allocates it. Write methods to allocate using best fit and worst fit methods.

4.22.   As memory space is allocated and deallocated the number of nodes in the linked list that represent the contiguous blocks of memory increases. It is possible to have enough free space to place a job in memory, but this space may not be contiguous. This situation is called external fragmentation. One way to solve the external fragmentation problem is to perform compaction. The process of compaction is to completely rearrange memory in such a way that all the free spaces are in one contiguous block. This means that processes location is memory have to be changed. Write a method to perform compaction.

4.23.   The process of coalesce is to make adjacent free blocks into one large block. Whenever a process completes execution its memory space is deallocated. At the time of deallocation, the memory spaces represented in the neighboring nodes are checked to see if they are free. The free memory in the neighboring nodes and the deallocated memory are combined to form a new contiguous block of memory. Write a method to perform the coalesce operation.

4.6 References for Further Reading

Foster, J.M., *List Processing*, London: McDonald, 1967.

Hansen, W.J., "A predecessor algorithm for ordered lists", *Information Processing Letters*, vol. 7, pp. 137–138, 1978.

Knuth, D.E., *The Art of Computer Programming, Vol. 1: Fundamental Algorithms*, Addison-Wesley, Reading, MA.

McCarthy, J., "Recursive Functions of Symbolic Expressions and Their Computation by Machine, Part I", *Communications of the ACM* vol. 3, no. 4, pp. 184–195, 1960.

Standish, T.A., *Data Structure techniques*, Reading MA: Addison-Wesley 1980, Chs. 5, 6.

Valiveti, R.S., and Oommen, B.J., "Self-Organizing Doubly Linked Lists", *Journal of Algorithms* vol. 14, pp. 88–114, 1993.

Vitter, J. S., and Chen, W.C., "Optimum Algorithms for a Model of Direct Chaining", *SIAM Journal of Computing* vol. 14, no.2, 1985.

Wilkes, M.V., "Lists and why they are useful", *Computer Journal* vol. 7, pp. 278–281, 1965.

5   Stacks and Queues

CONSTRUCTING DATA STRUCTURES from primitive ones such as the array, linked list, or vector will be the focus of this chapter. In fact, we will see that restricting the operations that can be performed on the primitive data structures will aid in developing powerful data structures such as a stack and a queue.

When we see the word "Stack" we are reminded of phrases like "a stack of books" and "a stack of trays." On a stack of trays, the operations that can be performed are "place a tray or trays on the top of the stack" or "remove a tray or trays from the top of stack." It is important to realize in the example above, that operations are performed on the top of the stack only. Thus, a set of objects can be stored in any of the primitive data structures and if we restrict operations such as delete (pop in stack terminology) and insert (push in stack terminology) to apply only to the "top" of the data structure, then we have a stack data structure. Stacks are called the Last-in, First-out (LIFO) data structures, since the last object pushed onto the stack will be the first element to be popped.

Queues contain a set of objects that are waiting for some service. For example operating systems maintain a set of programs (or processes) to be executed in a queue named Running Queue. These are processes that are in memory and the CPU is allocated to them in the order in which they have been placed in the queue. We may stand in a queue for almost every kind of service when we go out in real life. Queues allow the service provider to deal with its customer in a fair manner. Elements in a queue are processed in the order in which they joined the queue. This immediately tells us that, on a queue of elements, the insert operation (enqueue in queue terminology) is performed on one end of the queue, which we call the rear of the queue, and the delete operation (dequeue in queue terminology) on the opposite end of the queue, called the front. Queues are called a First-in, First-out (FIFO) data structure, since the first object that is enqueued will be first object to be dequeued.

5.1   Stacks

A stack is a data structure that can be used to remember the past so that we can go back to the past whenever we need to. Let us consider a practical example of such "remembering."

Consider a program in which a method A invokes method B. The invocation of method B can be anywhere in method A. At all times, the CPU executes the instruction stored at the memory address specified in the program counter (PC). When the method A invokes method B, the address of the first instruction of method B is stored in the PC, so that the CPU executes that instruction. The PC is also incremented so that the CPU will execute the next instruction of method B. After the execution of method B is completed the CPU has to return to the calling method, which is method A, and continue executing the instruction in method A after the invocation of method B.

This means that we need to know the address of the next instruction in method A after the invocation of method B so that this address can be loaded into the PC for the CPU to execute when method B ends. This address (called the return address) must be stored somewhere while method B is executing, but where? We might have some special spot in memory for storing the return address (a register like the PC, perhaps). Unfortunately, if we had such a special storage address, we could not allow method B to invoke any other method, for if it did, its return address would be stored in that same spot in memory, obliterating method A's return address. Obviously, this is not a practical answer.

Additionally, if we wish to support recursion, we will have to store the parameters passed with each method call, so that they will still be available after return from a recursive call – we would not want parameters passed on a recursive call to overwrite the original parameters!

The return address and parameters stored when a method call is made are together called an activation record. We can conclude that we need to store activation records in some kind of data structure that can hold a fairly large number of them. Further, it is clear that such a data structure must be Last-in-First-out; if method A invokes method B, which invokes method C, the CPU must return to method B's return address, not method A's, after execution of method C. The required data structure for storing activation records is, therefore, the stack, which was described in the introduction to this chapter as a LIFO structure. When method B is invoked by method A, method B's activation record is pushed on the stack; when execution of method B is complete, its activation record is popped off the stack and the return address for method A is placed in the PC.

Now consider the scenario in which method A invokes method B, method B invokes method C, and method C invokes method D. The sequence of stack operations would then be (also shown in Figure 5.1):

```
Push the activation record of method A onto the stack (when
method A was first called)
Push the activation record of method B onto the stack
Push the activation record of method C onto the stack.
```

Now after method D completes its execution we need to continue executing method C, so we must pop its method D's activation record from the stack and load the return address into PC. Similarly, we must pop method C's activation record after it completes and method B's activation record after it completes. This sequence of operations is illustrated in the following figure. For simplicity, we have just placed the return address on the stack, so that method B's activation record consists solely of a return address from method A.

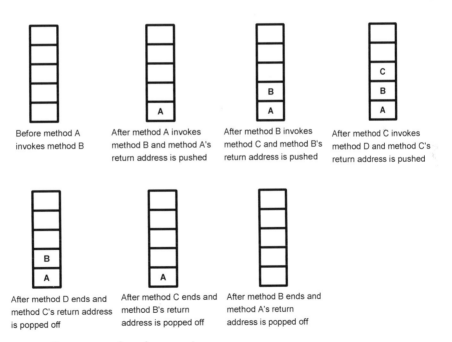

Figure 5.1:   Sequence of stack operations.

Yet another set of applications where stacks play a useful role are those involving *backtracking*. Consider the problem of traveling in a maze. The maze can be imagined as a two-dimensional matrix M. A cell M[i][j]=0 if it is a free cell, or M[i][j]=1 if it contains an obstacle, or M[i][j]=9 if it is the final destination. In this game, you must travel from one cell to the next adjacent cell that is free avoiding obstacle cells until you reach the destination cell. During the course of this travel you could end up in a dead end and in such cases you need to backtrack, that is, go back to the original place before you entered the dead end.

Here is a simple recursive algorithm that a robot could execute in order to find the destination in such a maze, returning true if the destination is found, false if it is not.

```
ALGORITHM RECURSIVE-ROBOT-NAVIGATE (MAP, POS, FOUND)
// Map is a matrix of integers
// Pos is the initial position (row, column)
// Found is a boolean flag
1.      Marks ← new matrix of booleans, of same dimensions as Map
2.      set every element of Marks to false
3.      found ← false
4.      Navigate-Recursive(Pos, found)
        // found will be set by Navigate-Recursive


PROCEDURE NAVIGATE-RECURSIVE (POS, FOUND)
1.      Marks [Pos.row][Pos.col] ← true
2.      for each neighbor NPos of Pos
3.          if (Marks [NPos.row][NPos.col] = false) and
4.                  not (Map [NPos.row][NPos.col] = obstacle)
5.              If Map[NPos.row][NPos.col] = destination
6.                  found ← true
7.                  return
8.              else
9.                  Navigate-Recursive (NPos, found)
10.         endif
11.     endif
12. endfor
```

The reader will notice that each maze location which is a neighbor of Pos is examined; if it is an obstacle, then of course it is skipped, but if not, it is visited and all of its neighbors are similarly treated. As each location is visited, it is marked as visited, so that it is never visited again. If the destination is reachable from Pos, then it must be reached by moving from Pos to a neighbor of Pos, then to a neighbor of that location, and so on until the destination is reached. Thus, the above recursive algorithm is sure to find the destination if it is reachable.

Of course, we might not wish to use a recursive algorithm (some languages do not support it). We can instead write a non-recursive algorithm which accomplishes the same thing using a stack.

```
ALGORITHM ITERATIVE-ROBOT-NAVIGATE (MAP, POS, FOUND)
// Map is a matrix of integers
// Pos is the initial position (row, column)
// Found is a boolean flag
1.   S ← createStack()
2.   Marks ← new matrix of booleans, of same dimensions as Map
3.   set every element of Marks to false
4.   found ← false
5.   Marks [Pos.row][Pos.col] ← true
6.   S.push (Pos)
7.   while (S is not empty)
8.         Pos ← S.pop()
9.         for each neighbor NPos of Pos
10.              if (Marks [NPos.row][NPos.col] = false) and
11.                  not (Map [NPos.row][NPos.col] = obstacle)
12.                 If Map[NPos.row][NPos.col] = destination
13.                     found ← true
14.                     return
15.                 else
16.                     Marks [NPos.row][NPos.col] ← true
17.                     S.push (NPos)
18.                 endif
19.             endif
20.         endfor
21. endwhile
```

Again, the above algorithm will find the destination, if there is a path connected by free cells. Every algorithm that is recursive can be implemented non-recursively using a stack and a *while* loop as illustrated above. The robot motion on the maze using stack is illustrated using the Figures 5.2–5.5. Note that stack is used to explore cells that have not been previously visited. To keep track of the path that was taken to reach the current cell, we need another stack. The details of this implementation are left to the reader.

M(0,0) 0 😊	M(0,1) 1	M(0,2) 0	M(0,3) 0	M(0,4) 0
M(1,0) 0	M(1,1) 0	M(1,2) 0	M(1,3) 1	M(1,4) 0
M(2,0) 1	M(2,0) 0	M(2,2) 1	M(2,3) 1	M(2,4) 0
M(3,0) 1	M(3,1) 0	M(3,2) 1	M(3,3) 1	M(3,4) 9

Stack: M(0,0)

M(0,0) 0 ✓	M(0,1) 1	M(0,2) 0	M(0,3) 0	M(0,4) 0
M(1,0) 0 😊	M(1,1) 0	M(1,2) 0	M(1,3) 1	M(1,4) 0
M(2,0) 1	M(2,0) 0	M(2,2) 1	M(2,3) 1	M(2,4) 0
M(3,0) 1	M(3,1) 0	M(3,2) 1	M(3,3) 1	M(3,4) 9

Stack: M(1,0)

Figure 5.2: The robot's initial position M(0,0) is pushed onto the stack. This position is popped from the stack and the robot moves to the popped position. From the robot's current position M(0,0) all free positions (marked with a 0) is pushed onto the stack. In this case it is M(1,0). Note that the robot can travel vertically or horizontally. The positions that have been visited are marked by a check mark.

M(0,0) 0 ✓	M(0,1) 1	M(0,2) 0	M(0,3) 0	M(0,4) 0
M(1,0) 0 ✓	M(1,1) 0 😊	M(1,2) 0	M(1,3) 1	M(1,4) 0
M(2,0) 1	M(2,1) 0	M(2,2) 1	M(2,3) 1	M(2,4) 0
M(3,0) 1	M(3,1) 0	M(3,2) 1	M(3,3) 1	M(3,4) 9

Stack: M(1,1)

M(0,0) 0 ✓	M(0,1) 1	M(0,2) 0	M(0,3) 0	M(0,4) 0
M(1,0) 0 ✓	M(1,1) 0 ✓	M(1,2) 0	M(1,3) 1	M(1,4) 0
M(2,0) 1	M(2,1) 0 😊	M(2,2) 1	M(2,3) 1	M(2,4) 0
M(3,0) 1	M(3,1) 0	M(3,2) 1	M(3,3) 1	M(3,4) 9

Stack: M(2,1), M(1,2)

Figure 5.3: From position M(1,0) the free position is M(1,1) and this is pushed on to the stack and once the robot moves to this position after popping M(1,1) the new free positions are M(1,2) and M(2,1).

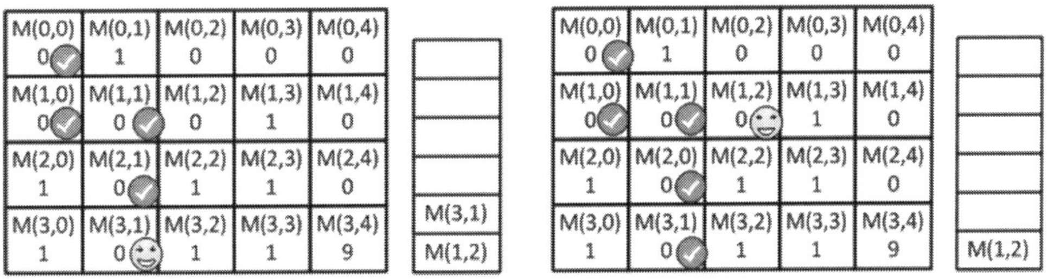

Figure 5.4: After moving to free position M(2,1) by popping from the stack, the only free position from this location is M(3,1) that is pushed onto the stack. The robot moves to this position by popping M(3,1). Once in position M(3,1) there are no new positions that the robot can move. Now the next position is popped from the stack. This position is M(1,2) and the robot moves to this position.

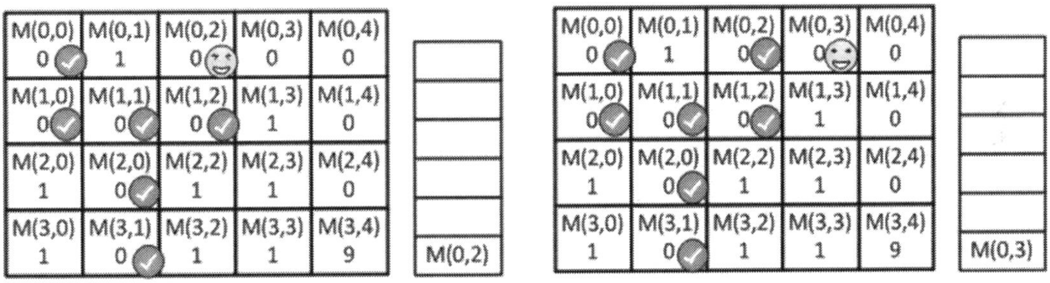

Figure 5.5: The free position from position M(1,2) is M(0,2) and this is pushed onto the stack and the robot moves to this position and pushes the next free position from M(0,2) which is M(0,3). This process continues until it reaches position M(3,4).

5.1.1 Stack Abstract Data Type

As noted in the introduction to this chapter, the essential operations on a stack are push() and pop() (in addition, of course, to create()). Another operation which is obviously necessary is empty(), which reports, as one would expect, whether the stack is empty. For convenience, another operation is added, peek(), which returns the object on top of the stack without actually popping it off (equivalent to popping it off, storing the reference to it, and then pushing it on again).

The specification of an abstract data type for a stack class is given below.

```
create ()
    // create an empty stack
empty ()
    // returns true if there are no elements in the stack,
    // otherwise false
peek()
    //get the object from the top of the stack without removing it
pop()
    //remove the object on the top of the stack
push (object)
    //insert a new object on the top of the stack.
```

5.1.2   Array implementation of Stack

We can now proceed with the implementation of the stack abstract data type in C++.

5.1.2.1   Node Data Type

The stack does nothing with its data but push it on the stack, pop it off, or return it in response to a *peek()* call. It does not expect its node data type to support equality tests or three-way comparisons. However, our implementation below does expect that the node data type supports the assignment operator, that is, that one data object can be assigned to another without error.

5.1.2.2   Exceptions

There is one obvious problem that can arise in the use of a stack: we could attempt to pop off an object when the stack is empty (this is called an underflow error). We might want to limit the number of items which can be held on the stack; if so, then we could attempt to push an object when the stack is already full (this is called an overflow error). We could also run out of memory as we add items to the stack.

Therefore, we shall create a small family of exceptions to go with our *Stack* class:

```
class StackException  : public Exception { };
class StackUnderflow   : public StackException { };
class StackOverflow    : public StackException { };
class StackMemory      : public StackException { };
```

5.1.2.3   Abstract Base Class Definition

Given the specification of the abstract data type for a stack, we can prepare an abstract base class for the stack class, or classes, which we will write. As usual, we have added an enumeration function, even though this is not actually part of the abstract data type. The interface is given below:

```
#include <iostream>
using namespace std;

#include "Exception.h"
#include "Enumeration.h"

class StackException   :   public Exception { };
class StackUnderflow   :   public StackException { };
class StackOverflow    :   public StackException { };
class StackMemory      :   public StackException { };


template <class DataType>
class AbstractStack
{
#ifndef ConcreteOut
friend ostream& operator<< <DataType> (ostream& os,
                     AbstractStack<DataType>& s);
public:
   virtual bool isEmpty() = NULL;
      // returns true if the stack is empty
      // and false if there are any DataTypes on it
   virtual DataType& peek () = NULL;
      // get the DataType that is stored in the top of the
      // stack; if the stack is empty then an empty stack
      // exception error is thrown
```

```
    virtual DataType pop () = NULL;
      // get the DataType that is stored in the top of
      // the stack and remove it from the top of the stack;
      // if the stack is empty, then an empty stack
      // exception error is thrown
    virtual void push (DataType& newDataType) = NULL;
      // add the newDataType to the top of the stack; if the
      // stack is of fixed size, then a stack overflow error
      // may be thrown
    virtual Enumeration<DataType>* enumerator () = NULL;
      // returns an EnumerationDataType for the stack
    virtual void display (ostream& os);
};
```

The reader should note that enumeration of the contents of a stack should be used for testing and debugging only. The stack abstract data structure does not allow for access to any element other than the top element, so enumeration of a stack could properly be performed only by popping elements one by one, acting on them, pushing them onto a second stack, and then when the first stack is empty, popping them off the second stack and pushing them on the first. However, programming is done in the real world, and errors do occur and need to be debugged, so enumeration of a stack should be permitted for that purpose. We can use conditional compilation using the technique discussed in Chapter 1 section 1.5.2 to compile with the display method for debugging and removing the flag (the compiler directive) after thorough testing. If you find that you do need to access the elements of a stack for purposes other than debugging, then you should reconsider your choice of data structure. Perhaps you really need an Array or Vector.

The *display()* method and *ostream* << operator for the *AbstractStack* are simple to write:

```
template <class DataType>
void AbstractStack<DataType>::display (ostream&os)
{
    bool first = true;
    Enumeration<DataType>* e = enumerator();
    os << "<";
    while (e->hasMoreElements())
```

```
        {
            if (!first) os << ", ";
            first = false;
            os << e->nextElement();
        }
        os << ">";
        delete e;
    }
    // ----------------------------------------------------------
    template <class DataType>
    ostream& operator<< (ostream& os, AbstractStack<DataType>& s)
    {
        s.display (os);
        return os;
    }
```

5.1.2.4   Class Definition

The above interface can be implemented using the built-in C++ array, or the *Array-Class*, *Vector*, or *LinkedList* classes developed in the preceding chapters, although the implementation will be different in each case. In the discussion below, the reader should note, particularly, that the stack interface is implemented by a class that uses an array or *LinkedList* or *Vector* as a field; the stack class is not itself an array, nor is it a subclass of *LinkedList* or *Vector*. If it were implemented as a subclass of *LinkedList* or *Vector*, every method available when the superclass is used would also be available to the stack class, allowing operations that are not part of the stack abstract data type.

For purposes of illustration, we shall implement a stack class using an array, which implies that the number of objects to be stored in a stack object will be limited to the size of the array when it was created.

Our array-based subclass of *AbstractStack* will be called *StackArray*, so that the implementation is revealed in the name. This is an intentional design decision as discussed in Section 1.9. If multiple concrete subclasses of *AbstractStack* are available, the programmer must decide among them based on the suitability of each implementation for the particular problem at hand, and it is easier to make that decision if the implementation is spelled out to some extent in the name of the subclass.

Fields, Constructors, and Destructor

We will make use of an integer field called _top that stores the index value of the array where a new object can be added, and another called _max that stores the size of the array. Since we do not know the size of the stack before it is created, we will need to allocate memory for the array in the constructor, which necessarily implies that we must deallocate that memory in the destructor. We will set top to 0 to indicate that the stack is empty. Thus, our *StackArray* class will be initially as follows:

```
template <class DataType>
class StackArray : virtual public AbstractStack<DataType>
{
protected:
    int _top;
    int _max;
    DataType* arr;
public:
    StackArray (int max);
    virtual ~StackArray();
};
// -------------------------------------------------------
template <class DataType>
StackArray<DataType>::StackArray (int max)
{
    _top = 0;
    _max = 0;
    arr = new DataType [max];
    if (arr == NULL) throw StackMemory();
    _max = max;
}
// -------------------------------------------------------
template <class DataType>
StackArray<DataType>::~StackArray()
{
    if (arr != NULL)
    {
        delete[] arr;
        arr = NULL;
    }
}
```

When we *push()* an element, we will store the element in the array at index *top*, then increment *top*. Thus, *top* will always point to the location where an element will be stored next.

Accessor Methods

Given that the number of objects which can be stored in the stack is limited, we need a few methods: the *max()* method, which is not in the abstract data type, to report the maximum number, the *isFull()* method, corresponding to *isEmpty()* method, which reports true if no more objects can be pushed, and size(), which reports the number of items actually in the stack and will facilitate the enumeration of a stack. Since these methods are not part of the abstract class interface, they cannot be used by code that expects to use an instance of *AbstractStack*. The *size()*, *max()*, *isFull()*, and *isEmpty()* methods are all quite simple:

```
template <class DataType>
bool StackArray<DataType>::isEmpty ()
{
    return (_top == 0);
}
// ------------------------------------------------------------
template <class DataType>
bool StackArray<DataType>::isFull ()
{
    return (_top == _max);
}
// ------------------------------------------------------------
template <class DataType>
int StackArray<DataType>::max ()
{
    return _max;
}
// ------------------------------------------------------------
template <class DataType>
int StackArray<DataType>::size ()
{
    return _top;
}
```

In the implementation of the *peek()* method, we must throw a *StackUnderflow* exception if the stack is in fact empty. If the stack does not underflow, we just return the value at index *top*-1. So the *peek()* method is implemented as follows:

```
template <class DataType>
DataType& StackArray<DataType>::peek ()
{
    if (_top == 0) throw StackUnderflow ();
    return arr[_top-1];
}
```

The push() Method

When a new object is to be added through the *push()* method, the new object is placed at the index position to which *top* now points. The field *top* is then incremented by one. During the process of pushing elements by incrementing *top*, we need to take care to avoid the possibility of overrunning the bounds of the array. In cases where a *push()* would cause such an error, we have to throw a *StackOverflow* exception. So the implementation of the *push()* method is as follows:

```
template <class DataType>
void StackArray<DataType>::push (DataType& newDataType)
{
    if (_top == _max) throw StackOverflow ();
    arr[_top] = newDataType;
    _top++;
}
```

The pop() Method

The implementation of the *pop()* method is simple. It involves decrementing *top* by 1, and returning the object at index position *top*. The operation is performed if and only if *top* is greater than 0, for otherwise, the stack is empty and a *StackUnderflow* exception must be thrown.

```
template <class DataType>
DataType StackArray<DataType>::pop ()
{
    if (_top < 1) throw StackUnderflow ();
    _top--;
    return arr[_top];
}
```

Enumeration of Nodes

The enumeration of nodes in a stack is a little difficult, since the abstract data type does not provide for access to any nodes other than the top. We can allow such access by an enumeration class by making that class a friend of *StackArray* so that it can directly access the *arr* array which stores the nodes. The *StackArray* class will contain a method to create and return an instance of an *Enumeration* subclass:

```
template <class DataType>
Enumeration<DataType>* StackArray<DataType>::enumerator ()
{
    return new StackArrayEnumerator<DataType> (this);
}
```

Now we have only to implement the *Enumeration* subclass. It is fairly simple to implement, since it need only iterate through the stack. We have chosen to iterate with the top of the stack being returned first, followed by the items lower in the stack. This is the sort of design decision that the class designer makes, not the user, when an enumeration class is written. The user of the enumeration class has no control over the order of enumeration.

Our enumeration class must keep track of the *StackArray* on which it is operating and the current position it should return, starting at the top, not the bottom. (Note that this implies that this class knows how items are stored in the *StackArray*, information which is not normally made available to the caller). So the class is initially:

```
template <class DataType>
class StackArrayEnumerator : public Enumeration<DataType>
{
protected:
    StackArray<DataType>* _stack;
    int _index;
public:
    StackArrayEnumerator (StackArray<DataType>* stack);
    bool hasMoreElements ();
    DataType& nextElement ();
};
// ----------------------------------------------------------
template <class DataType>
StackArrayEnumerator<DataType>::StackArrayEnumerator
    (StackArray<DataType>* stack)
{
    _stack = stack;
    if (_stack == NULL) { _index = 0; }
    else
    {
        _index = _stack->size();
    }
}
```

Each time we return an element, we will reduce the _index by 1 and then return the element at that position in the stack:

```
template <class DataType>
DataType& StackArrayEnumerator<DataType>::nextElement ()
{
    if (0 < _index)
    {
        _index--;
        return _stack->arr[_index];
    }
    else throw StackUnderflow();
}
```

The hasMoreElements() method just checks that _index has not reached 0 yet:

```
template <class DataType>
bool StackArrayEnumerator<DataType>::hasMoreElements ()
{
    return (0 < _index);
}
```

The reader should note that, since *StackArrayEnumerator* must be declared as a friend class of *StackArray*, and it also uses *StackArray*, we have a problem with the ordering of the class definitions. This forces us to declare the *StackArrayEnumerator* class before we define it:

```
template <class DataType> class StackArrayEnumerator;
// ----------------------------------------------------------
template <class DataType>
class StackArray : virtual public AbstractStack<DataType>
{
friend class StackArrayEnumerator <DataType>;
// method and field definitions
};
// ----------------------------------------------------------
template <class DataType>
class StackArrayEnumerator : public Enumeration<DataType>
{
// method and field definitions
};
```

Since we already wrote a *display()* method and an *ostream* << operator for AbstractStack, we are now prepared to output stacks.

5.1.2.5 Testing the Class

We shall write a very simple main() method to test the *StackArray* class. Our main() method will push five items on the stack and pop them again, showing that items come off in reverse order:

```
void main ()
{
    StackArray<int> stack (5);
    try
    {
        for (int i = 0; i < 5; i++)
        {
            stack.push(i);
            cout <<"Pushed "<<i<<" in stack"<< endl;
        }
        cout << "\nThe stack has " << stack <<
                    " as elements pushed into it"<<endl;
        for (int i = 0; i < 6; i++)
            cout << endl << "Popped out "<<stack.pop() <<
                    " from the stack"<< endl;
        cout << endl;
    }
    catch (Exception e) {cout << "Exception Thrown\n"; }
        // noexception will be thrown
}
```

The result shows the correct working of the *StackArray* class:

```
<4, 3, 2, 1, 0>
4   3   2   1   0
<>
```

5.1.3   Linked List Implementation of the Stack

Above, we chose to extend the *AbstractStack* class using an array, but we could instead have chosen to extend it using a linked list. The linked list implementation of the stack can take advantage of the operations that are provided for the linked list data structure, and allows for a potentially unlimited stack size. Below, we present such an implementation in brief. The class definition mirrors the abstract base class' definition.

```
template <class DataType>
class StackLinked : virtual public AbstractStack<DataType>
{
friend StackLinkedEnumerator<DataType>;

protected:
   LinkedList<DataType> LL;
public:
   StackLinked ();
   virtual ~StackLinked();
   virtual bool isEmpty ();
   virtual DataType& peek ();
   virtual void push (DataType& newDataType);
   virtual DataType pop ();
   virtual Enumeration<DataType>* enumerator ();
};
```

Most of the methods are simple, pushing elements by adding them to the linked list and popping them by removing them from the list, and relying on the linked list for information:

```
template <class DataType>
StackLinked<DataType>::StackLinked () : LL() { }
// --------------------------------------------------------
template <class DataType>
StackLinked<DataType>::~StackLinked() { }
// --------------------------------------------------------
template <class DataType>
bool StackLinked<DataType>::isEmpty () { return
                                        (LL.isEmpty());}
// --------------------------------------------------------
template <class DataType>
DataType& StackLinked<DataType>::peek ()
{
    if (isEmpty()) throw StackUnderflow ();
    return LL.info();
}
```

```
// -----------------------------------------------------
template <class DataType>
void StackLinked<DataType>::push (DataType& newDataType)
    { LL.add(newDataType); }
// -----------------------------------------------------
template <class DataType>
DataType StackLinked<DataType>::pop ()
{
    if (isEmpty()) throw StackUnderflow ();
    return LL.remove();
}
```

The *enumerator()* method is similar to that of the *StackArray*, but the *Enumeration* subclass itself is different. Since the *StackLinkedEnumerator* is a friend of the *StackLinked* class, it can directly access the linked list contained within an instance of *StackLinked*. Thus, it can simply move through that list in response to *nextElement()* invocations.

```
template <class DataType>
Enumeration<DataType>* StackLinked<DataType>::enumerator ()
{
    return new StackLinkedEnumerator<DataType> (this);
}
// -----------------------------------------------------
template <class DataType>
class StackLinkedEnumerator : public Enumeration<DataType>
{
protected:
    AbstractLinkedList<DataType>* LL;
public:
    StackLinkedEnumerator (StackLinked<DataType>* stack);
    bool hasMoreElements ();
    DataType& nextElement ();
};
// -----------------------------------------------------
template <class DataType>
StackLinkedEnumerator<DataType>::StackLinkedEnumerator
    (StackLinked<DataType>* stack)
```

```
{
    if (stack == NULL)
        LL = NULL;
    else
        LL = &stack->LL;
}
// ----------------------------------------------------------
template <class DataType>
DataType& StackLinkedEnumerator<DataType>::nextElement ()
{
    if (LL == NULL) throw StackOverflow();
    AbstractLinkedList<DataType>* oldLL = LL;
    LL = LL->next();
    return oldLL->info();
}
// ----------------------------------------------------------
template <class DataType>
bool StackLinkedEnumerator<DataType>::hasMoreElements ()
{
    return (LL != NULL);
}
```

The reader should confirm that this class can be directly substituted for *StackArray* in the test program and in the application program presented in section 5.1.6. Thus, from the application programmer point of view the implementation details are hidden.

5.1.4 Performance Comparisons

We have seen that the stack data structure can be implemented either using an array or a linked list data structure. The following table (Figure 5.2) lists the time-complexity for the various stack operations on both the representations. The create operation requires creating an array of size n and we are assuming that it take a unit time to create a single array element if the element is a system data type such as an integer, double, float, and others. If the elements of the stack are other complex elements then the time required is proportional to n times the time required to create a single complex object.

| Stack Implementations | | |
| Worst-case Time Complexity Comparisons | | |
Operation	Array	Linked List
Create()	$O(n)$	$O(1)$
isEmpty()	$O(1)$	$O(1)$
Peek()	$O(1)$	$O(1)$
Pop()	$O(1)$	$O(1)$
Push(*element*)	$O(1)$	$O(1)$

Figure 5.6: Comparison of worst-case execution times of stack operations on differ-ent stack representations. The variable n in the table is the initial size of the array that represents the queue.

The qualitative assessment of the various structures used to implement the stack data structure is presented in Figure 5.3.

| Stack Implementations | |
| Qualitative Assessment | |
Implementation	Assessment
Array	Does not require additional storage (next pointer in the case of linked list representation). Requires the knowledge of the maximum number of elements the stack should hold. This problem can be rectified by use of a Vector.
Linked List	Requires extra storage for the next pointer. The stack size is limited only by the size of memory.

Figure 5.7: Qualitative assessment of various stack implementations.

5.1.5   Stacks the STL Way

In the standard template library definition a stack is an adapter which uses any con-tainer (such as vector and list) that supports operations at either end of the extremi-ties. More specifically, the stack adapter allows operations such as push_back() and pop_back() to implement the first-in, last-out data structure. It is important to note that STL does not provide an iterator (enumerator as discussed in this chapter) for the stack adapter.

The operations push and pop are available in the stack adapter and they behave in similar fashion to the ones implemented in this chapter, except that the pop operation in the stack adapter does not return a value. The equivalent of the peek operation in our implementation is the top operation on the stack adapter. In general in the STL adapters are not supported by iterators and hence the stack adapter does not have any iterators. The stack operation pop (resp. push) is implemented using an inline function that calls pop_back (resp. push_back) function on the appropriate container that implements the stack.

When using the stack adapter the programmer has to specify the container that stack will be using. In the following example we are using a stack adapter that uses the list container.

```cpp
#include <iostream> // for i/o functions
#include <list>
#include <stack>

using namespace std;

void main ()
{
    stack<int, list<int>> mStack(5);

    try
    {
        for (int i = 0; i < 5; i++)
            mStack.push(i);
        for (int i = 0; i < 5; i++)
        {
            cout <<mStack.top() << " ";
            mStack.pop();
        }
    }
    catch (Exception e) { } // no exception will be thrown
}
```

The result shows the correct working of the *stack* container:

4   3   2   1   0

The methods of the stack adapter in the standard template library are given below.

stack<Object>()	Default constructor
stack<Object>(intn)	Construct a stack of initial size *n*
stack<Object>(*conststack<Object>& stack)*	The copy constructor
~stack<Object>()	Destructor
=	*stack<Object>&operator=(const* *stack<Object>& rhsStack)* Overloaded assignment operator. The contents of the stack on the left hand side are replaced with the contents of the stack on the right hand side of the assignment operator.
==	*bool operator==(const* * stack<Object>& rhsStack)* Return true if both the stacks contain the same items in the same order, false otherwise.
<	*bool operator<(const* *stack<Object>& rhsStack)* Return true if first stack is lexicographi-cally less than the second stack, false otherwise.
void pop()	Erase top element of the stack.
void push(const Object& value)	Push a copy of *value*.
Object& top()	Return a reference to the element at the top of the stack.
int size()	Return the number of elements stored in the stack.
bool empty()	Return true if the stack does not contain any elements, false otherwise.
int max_size()	Return the maximum number of items that the stack can contain.

The methods of the stack adapter in the standard template library.

5.1.6 Application

We will present an application in which the stack data structure plays a vital role, evaluating arithmetic expressions.

5.1.6.1 Expression Evaluation

Most modern calculators allow arithmetic expressions to be typed in, then evaluated when the [Enter] key is pressed. The expressions we are used to writing are called infix expressions, wherein the operator $(+, -, /, \star, \text{etc.})$ is between two operands. Consider the following equation that calculates the distance between two points (a, b) and (c,d) given their Cartesian coordinates (where $\wedge$ is the sign for exponentiation).

$$((c{-}a)\wedge 2 + (d{-}b)\wedge 2)\wedge 0.5$$

The above expression is an infix expression as the operators are between operands. In order to execute the above expression, we will convert the above expression into a postfix expression and show how the postfix expression can be evaluated by using a stack. The following table presents examples of simple infix expressions and their corresponding postfix expressions.

Infix Expression	Postfix Expression
$a + b$	$a \; b \; +$
$(a + b) \star c$	$a \; b + c \star$
$a + b \star c$	$a \; b \; c \star +$
$a \, / \, b + c \star d$	$a \; b \, / \, c \, d \star +$
$a \, /(b + c \star d)$	$a \; b \; \; c \, d \star +/$

The postfix expression for the expression given earlier to determine the distance between two points is:

$$c \; a - 2 \wedge d \; b - 2 \wedge + 0.5 \wedge$$

Before we can present an algorithm to convert an infix expression to a postfix expression, we will present an algorithm to evaluate a postfix expression, beginning with an example of such evaluation.

Consider the postfix expression a b + c ⋆ for the infix expression (a + b) ⋆ c. We will scan the postfix expression from left to right, obtaining tokens. A token is either an operand or an operator. The first token in the left to right scan is a, which is an operand, so we will push it in the stack. The second token is also an operand, b, so we will push it also in the stack. The stack will now have b, a where b is on top of the stack. The third token is an operator +. To apply this operator we need two operands and these are obtained by popping two elements from the stack: b first and a next. When we apply the operator + to these two operands, we obtain a+b that we then push on to the stack. Now the stack contains only one element that is a+b. The fourth token is c, an operand, so it is pushed on to the stack. The stack now contains c, a+b, where c is on top of the stack. The fifth token is an operator ⋆ which requires two operands. These two operands are popped from the top of the stack and the operator ⋆ is used to produce the desired result which is (a+b)⋆c. The above steps can be formally described in the algorithm below and in addition the steps are also shown in Figure 5.8.

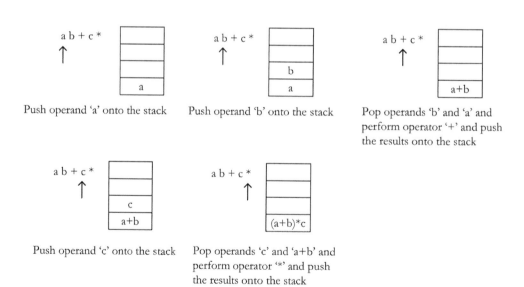

Figure 5.8:   As each token of the postfix expression is processed (indicated by the up arrow), the actions and the stack contents are shown.

```
ALGORITHM EVALUATE-POSTFIX-EXPRESSION(PE) //PE is the postfix
expression
Input: Postfix expression
Ouput: Value that is a result of evaluating the postfix expression

1.  S ← createStack()
2.  get first token T
3.  while T is a valid token
4.      if token T is an operand
5.          push T on S
6.      else
7.          pop as many operands from S as required by the operator T
8.          apply the operator T on the operands that were popped
9.          push the result on S
10.     endif
11.     get the next token T;
12. endwhile
13. pop the result from S
```

The StringTokenizer class

Implementation of the above algorithm requires the ability to "tokenize" (identify tokens in) the postfix expression. A token might be an operator, like '*' or '+', or a number, like '12' or '3.14'. We assume that there is a class called *StringTokenizer*, each instance of which is constructed to tokenize a given *String* by returning each token (substring) in turn as a *String*. The public part of the *StringTokenizer* class is defined as follows:

```
class StringTokenizer
{
public:
    StringTokenizer (String& s);
    bool hasMoreTokens ();
    String nextToken ();
};
```

Implementation of the *StringTokenizer* class is left as an exercise for the reader. The reader may wish to assume that tokens are separated by spaces, so that a string like "1.4+7.2" would have three tokens, whereas a string like "1.4+ 7.2" would have only two ("1.4+" and "7.2").

Obtaining a double value from a String

Assuming that we have read a token and believe it to be a string representation of a number, how do we go about obtaining the value from the string? Fortunately, C++ has a function *strtod()*, which has a prototype in stdlib.h. This function accepts a string to be converted and a pointer to a pointer to char, and returns a double which is the value of the string to be converted. The prototype is:

```
double strtod (const char* s, char** endptr)
```

The *strtod()* function modifies *endptr* to point to the character which terminated the conversion. If the entire string *s* constituted a valid representation of a number, then *endptr* will point to a null character. If there was an illegal character in *s*, then *endptr* will point to that character. Simply testing whether *endptr* points to a null character, therefore, tells us whether the string we tried to convert was valid.

Unfortunately, the *strtod()* function works on char arrays, not on instances of our *String* class. An instance of String has a char array inside it, but this array is protected and inaccessible to outside functions. This appears to be a problem. However, obtaining a numeric value from a string representation is not an uncommon operation, and it is reasonable to add a method for that purpose. As a bonus, such a method can hide the details of *strtod()* and simply return a flag to indicate whether conversion was successful:

```
double String::toDouble (bool& successful)
{
    char* endptr;
    double d = strtod (paObject, &endptr);
    successful = (*endptr == '\0');
    return d;
}
```

Implementation of postfix evaluation

The actual implementation of a function to evaluate a postfix expression closely follows the algorithm above, though we must deal with exceptions and possible input
errors, which are not considered in the algorithm itself. As part of the function, we
must identify the operator corresponding to a token; we will need to do the same thing
(twice) in the next function which we will approach, so we shall write a small function
to handle that particular problem. We make use of the C++ function, *pow(x,y)*, which
returns xy and has a prototype in math.h.

Note that in our implementation we have elected to use the *StackArray* class
rather than the *StackLinked* class. We do not expect to have more than fifty operands
pending at any one time, so we can limit the size of our stack. However, we could have
elected to allow an unlimited number of operands by using the linked list implementation. The evaluation code will work identically in either case, and the programmer
decides which concrete subclass of *AbstractStack* is appropriate for this problem based
on all the information available.

```cpp
const int NUM_OPERATORS = 5;
char operators[] = { '+', '-', '*', '/', '^' };
// -------------------------------------------------------
int op (String& n)
{
    if (n.length() != 1) return -1;
    for (int i = 0; i < NUM_OPERATORS; i++)
    {
        if (n[0] == operators[i]) { return i; }
    }
    return -1;
}
// -------------------------------------------------------
double evalPostfix (String& s)
{
    String next(50);          // next token
    double d;                 // temporary floating point object
    int iOper;                // operator number
    double dOp1;              // first operand
    double dOp2;              // second operand
    StringTokenizer parser    (s);
```

```
StackArray<double> stack(50);

try
{
    while (parser.hasMoreTokens ())
    {
        next = parser.nextToken();
        iOper = op (next);
        if (iOper >= 0)
        {
// Pop enough operands for the operators
            dOp2 = stack.pop();
            dOp1 = stack.pop();
// Apply the appropriate operator to the operands
            switch (iOper)
            {
                case 0:
                    d = dOp1 + dOp2;
                    break;
                case 1:
                    d = dOp1 - dOp2;
                    break;
                case 2:
                    d = dOp1 * dOp2;
                    break;
                case 3:
                    d = dOp1 / dOp2;
                    break;
                case 4:
                    d = pow (dOp1, dOp2);
                    break;
            }
// Push the result
            stack.push (d);
        }
```

```
// Push the token if it's a number (operand)
        else
        {
            bool goodNum;
            d = next.toDouble (goodNum);
            if (goodNum)
            {
                stack.push (d);
            }
            else
            {
                cout << "Bad number: " << next << endl;
            }
        }
    }
} catch (StackException e)
    { cout << "Bad token" << endl; }
// Pop off the result for return
    d = stack.pop();

// if stack is not empty now, expression was in error
    if (stack.isEmpty()) { return d; }
    else { return 0.0; }
}
```

We can test this function with a simple main() function:

```
void main ()
{
    String A = "5 3 +";
    String B = "5 7 * 3 2 + / ";
    String C = "1 4 - 2 ^ 5 1 - 2 ^ + 0.5 ^";
    cout << A << " = " << evalPostfix (A) << endl;
    cout << B << " = " << evalPostfix (B) << endl;
    cout << C << " = " << evalPostfix (C) << endl;
}
```

The output indicates that the evalPostfix() method is working correctly:

```
5 3 + = 8
5 7 * 3 2 + / = 7
1 4 - 2 ^ 5 1 - 2 ^ + 0.5 ^ = 5
```

Our next problem is to convert an infix expression into a postfix one. We will assume that the infix expression does not have any parenthesized subexpressions. The technique to obtain a postfix expression will be illustrated using the infix expression 6/3 + 4 ★ 2. As previously, we will scan the infix expression from left to right, but we shall process tokens as follows. The first token is an operand 6 and it is sent to output. The next token is an operator / which is pushed on the stack. The next token is an operand 3 and is sent to output.

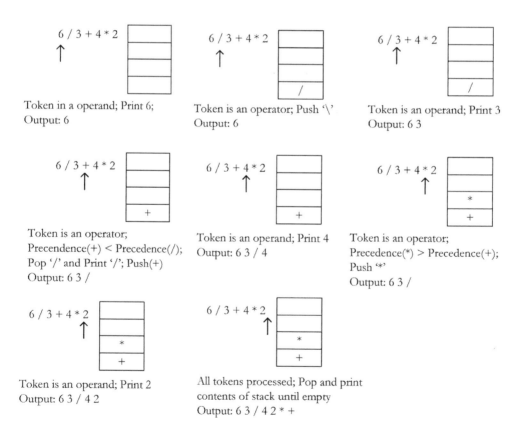

Figure 5.9:   Figure illustrating the conversion of an infix expression to a postfix expression.

The + operator is the next token. With an operator in hand and a non-empty stack, we now compare the precedence of operators between the + operator and the operator that is on top of the stack. The top of the stack contains the / operator which has higher precedence than the + operator. We therefore pop the / operator from the top of the stack and send it to output. The + operator is then pushed on the stack. If the top of the stack had had a lower precedence, we would have simply pushed the + operator.

The output so far is: 63/. We can similarly process the infix sub expression 4 ★ 2. After all the tokens are processed, the stack is emptied and its contents are sent to output. The output that will result is 63 / 42 ★ +. The above steps are explained in the figure below. We will use some of the ideas above and write the following formal algorithm.

```
ALGORITHM INFIX-TO-POSTFIX (IE)   //IE is the infix expression
Input: A infix expression
Output: A postfix expression


1.   S ← createStack()
2.   get first token T
3.   while T is a valid token
4.        if T is an operand then
5.             print T
6.        else
7.             while S not empty and (precedence(T)
                       <= precedence(element at top of S))
8.                       pop and print the element
9.             endwhile
10.            push T on the stack
11.       endif
12.       get the next token T
13. endwhile
14. while stack not empty
15.      pop and print the element
16. endwhile
```

We now present a C++ implementation of the above algorithm, which takes an infix expression in the form of a String as input and returns a postfix expression, also in the form of a String, as output. The function below belongs in the same file as *evalPostfix()*.

```
int precedences[] = {1, 1, 2, 2, 3};
// ------------------------------------------------------------
String infixToPostfix (String& s)
    {
    String post(100);           // postfix expression
    String next;                // next token
    String top;                 // token on top of stack
    double d;                   // temporary floating point object
    int iOper;                  // operator number
    int iOperStack;             // number for operator on stack
    StringTokenizer parser (s);
    StackArray<String> stack(50);

    try
    {
        while (parser.hasMoreTokens ())
        {
            next = parser.nextToken ();
            iOper = op (next);
            if (iOper >= 0)
            {
                while (!stack.isEmpty())
                {
                    iOperStack = op(stack.peek ());
                    if (precedences[iOper] <=
                            precedences[iOperStack])
                    {
                       post = post + stack.pop () + " ";
                    }
                    else break;
                }
                stack.push(next);
            }
```

```
// Output the token in the postfix expression
// if it's a number (operand)
                else
                {
                        bool goodNum;
                        d = next.toDouble (goodNum);
                        if (goodNum)
                        {
                                post = post + next + " ";
                        }
                        else
                        {
                                cout << "Bad number: " << next << endl;
                        }
                }
            }
        }
        catch (StackException e)
            { cout << "Bad token" << endl; }
// after the input tokens are exhausted, pop off the remaining
// operators
        while (!stack.isEmpty())
        {
            post = post + stack.pop() + " ";
        }
        return post;
}
```

Again, we can readily write a main() method to test this method:

```
void main ()
{
 String A = "15 / 3 + 2 * 4";
 cout << A << " = " << infixToPostfix (A) << endl;
}
```

The output demonstrates the correctness of the infixToPostfix() method:

■   15 / 3 + 2 * 4 = 15 3 / 2 4 * +

As an added bonus, we can readily write a method to evaluate infix expressions by simply combining the two methods previously given:

```
double evalInfix (String& s)
{
    return evalPostfix (infixToPostfix (s));
}
```

5.2 Queues

Queues are formed in many natural settings: buyers at a cashier in the grocery shop, cars at a tollbooth on a highway, customers in front of a bank clerk. In all these queues the customers are served in the order in which they enter the queue, for which reason queues are called first-in first-out data structures. In the world of computers, queues occur often, for instance, when processes are waiting to be executed by the CPU and when packets have to be routed to their destination by a router.

A router is a network device that receives packets containing source address, destination address, and payload. This payload contains a variety of information including user data that needs to reach the destination. When a router receives a packet checks among other things the destination address contained in the packet. Based on the destination address it determines the next outgoing link that this packet should be sent. Packets that arrive at the router are queued up for many reasons including that the rate at which the packets arrive at the router can be greater than the rate at which the router sends the packet on to the next outgoing link. The router in many instances creates several queues, all incoming packets are placed on one of many queues and packets in each queue are all processed in the first-in first-out manner. In Figure 5.9 a network is shown along with the queues of packets at routers.

The operations that can be performed on a queue are dequeue and enqueue. The dequeue operation deletes an element (packet) from the front of the queue and enqueue operation inserts an element (packet) at the rear of the queue.

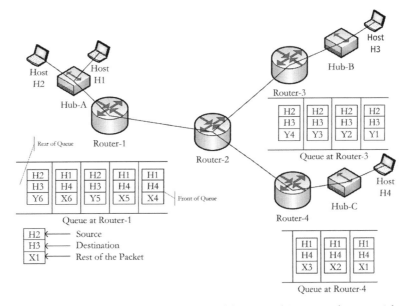

Figure 5.10: A network with routers, bus, and host machines are shown with queues on certain routers. Packets are queued up at the routers which are processed in the first-in first-out order.

5.2.1   Queue Abstract Data Type

The specification of an abstract data type for a queue class is given below.

```
create (n)
    // create a queue of size n
enqueue (object)
    // insert a new object at the rear of the queue
dequeue()
    // remove the object from the front of the queue
empty()
    // returns true if there are no elements in the queue,
    // otherwise false
front()
    // get the object from the front of the queue
size
    // determine the number of objects that the queue stores
```

5.2.2   Implementation of Queue

Again as with the stack class, we can implement a queue class using an array, a linked list, or a Vector. The array representation is used when we deal with queues with a fixed maximum size, and linked list or Vector data structures can be used for queues with no predetermined limit on size. Below, we have chosen to implement the queue using an array.

5.2.2.1   Node Data Type

Like the stack, the queue makes no assumptions about its data, so we make no requirements of the node data type.

5.2.2.2   Exceptions

The problems which can arise with a queue are identical to those which can arise with a stack: we could attempt to dequeue an object when the queue is empty, producing an underflow error. If we limit the number of items which can be held in the queue, then we could attempt to enqueue an object when the queue is already full, generating an overflow error. Finally, we could always run out of memory.

Therefore, we shall create a small family of exceptions to go with our Queue class, which we will create shortly:

```
class QueueException   :   public Exception { };
class QueueUnderflow   :   public QueueException { };
class QueueOverflow    :   public QueueException { };
class QueueMemory      :   public QueueException { };
```

5.2.2.3   Base Class Definition

Given the specification of the abstract data type for a queue, we can write the base class for queues. As usual, we have added an enumeration object.

```
template <class DataType>
class AbstractQueue
{
friend ostream& operator<< <DataType>
                        (ostream& s, AbstractQueue& q);
public:
    virtual ~AbstractQueue ();
    virtual DataType dequeue () = NULL;
// get the DataType that is stored in the front of the queue
// and remove it from the front of the queue; if the queue is
// empty then an empty queue exception error is thrown
    virtual bool isEmpty () = NULL;
// returns true if there are no elements in the queue,
// otherwise false
    virtual void enqueue (DataType& newDataType) = NULL;
// add the new object to the front of the queue; if the
// queue is of fixed size, then a queue overflow error may be
// thrown
    virtual DataType& front () = NULL;
// get the Object that is stored in the front of the queue;
// if the queue is empty then an empty queue exception
// error is thrown
    virtual int size () = NULL;
// determine the number of DataTypes that are stored in the
// queue
    virtual Enumeration<DataType>* enumerator () = NULL;
// returns an Enumeration DataType for the queue
    virtual void display (ostream& os);
};
```

The *ostream* << operator and the *display()* method are essentially identical to those for the *AbstractStack*, and are not presented here. The destructor is also trivial, and is not presented here.

5.2.2.4   Class Definition

A queue can be of fixed size, that is, with a fixed maximum size. Fixed size queues are found, for instance, in buffers allocated to a printer. Every printer has a designated fixed size buffer. The input and output device controller writes information to this buffer and the printer reads this information from its buffer and prints it. Clearly, the bytes of data that are sent to the printer buffer must be processed in a FIFO manner. Since the printer buffer is of fixed size, we have a fixed size queue.

In order to implement a queue using arrays, we must first define the maximum number of objects the queue will store. It is obvious that we cannot add items to the queue by simply putting them at ever increasing indices in the array; we will run out of locations in the array.

There are different implementations of a queue within an array (we shall discuss a circular implementation later), but a conceptually simple implementation is to simply remove elements from position 0 (the front) and add at the other end, shifting all elements forward as we remove one from the front.

Fields, Constructors, and Destructor

The following code presents an implementation of the abstract data type operations of queue using arrays, incorporating the above ideas. We will need the three fields _rear, _max, and arr, where arr is the array of *Object*, _max is the size of the array, and _rear is the current position where the next element will be enqueued (thus, initially _rear is 0 and the queue is full when _max = _rear). Thus, the class will initially be as follows:

```
template <class DataType>
class QueueArray : virtual public AbstractQueue<DataType>
{
protected:
    int _rear;
    int _max;
    DataType* arr;
public:
    QueueArray (int maximum);
    virtual ~QueueArray();
};
// -----------------------------------------------------------
template <class DataType>
QueueArray<DataType>::QueueArray (int maximum)
{
    _max = maximum+1;
```

```
        _rear = 0;
        arr = new DataType [_max];
        if (arr == NULL) throw StackMemory();
}
// ----------------------------------------------------------
template <class DataType>
QueueArray<DataType>::~QueueArray ()
{
    if (arr != NULL)
    {
        delete[] arr;
        arr = NULL;
    }
}
```

Accessor Methods

As in our array-based implementation of the stack, we have added methods isFull(), which corresponds to isEmpty(), and max(), which reports the maximum number of items which can be held in the queue. To support the enumerator() method, we have added the element() method, which returns elements by offset from the front. As noted under the stack class, this method is protected and the *Enumeration* subclass must be a friend class, since the queue abstract data type does not provide for such access.

The isEmpty() and max() methods are simple to implement:

```
template <class DataType>
bool QueueArray<DataType>::isEmpty ()
{
    return (_rear == 0);
}
// ----------------------------------------------------------
template <class DataType>
int QueueArray<DataType>::max ()
{
    return _max;
}
```

The isFull() and size() methods are simple. The front() method in the queue is similar to the *peek()* method in the stack, in that it may underflow, but otherwise returns the same value that dequeue() (or, for the stack, pop()) would return.

```
template <class DataType>
bool QueueArray<DataType>::isFull ()
{
    return _rear == _max;
}
// -----------------------------------------------------------
template <class DataType>
int QueueArray<DataType>::size ()
{
    return _rear;
}
// -----------------------------------------------------------
template <class DataType>
DataType& QueueArray<DataType>::front ()
{
    if (_rear == 0) throw QueueUnderflow ();
    return arr[0];
}
```

Finally, the element() method expects to return the element at an offset from the head of the queue:

```
template <class DataType>
DataType& QueueArray<DataType>::element (int ofs)
{
    if ((ofs < 0) || (ofs >= _rear)) throw QueueOverflow();
    return arr[ofs];
}
```

The enqueue() Method

The enqueue() method must increment the _rear field and place the new object in the slot indexed by the _rear field. However, it must be sure that this does not cause an overflow:

```
template <class DataType>
void QueueArray<DataType>::enqueue (DataType& newDataType)
{
    if (_rear == _max) throw QueueOverflow ();
    arr[_rear] = newDataType;
    ++_rear;
}
```

The dequeue() Method

The dequeue() method is more complex, as it must return the front element, but also move all elements forward and decrement the _rear field.

```
template <class DataType>
DataType QueueArray<DataType>::dequeue (){
    if (_rear == 0) throw QueueUnderflow ();
    DataType temp = arr[0];
    for (int i = 1; i < _rear; ++i)
    {
        arr[i-1] = arr[i];
    }
    --_rear;
    return temp;
}
```

Enumeration of Nodes

The *QueueArray* class will contain a method to create and return an instance of an *Enumeration* class:

```
template <class DataType>
Enumeration<DataType>* QueueArray<DataType>::enumerator ()
{
    return new QueueArrayEnumerator<DataType> (this);
}
```

Now we have only to implement the *Enumeration* subclass. It is similar to the *StackArrayEnumerator* previously implemented, except that it requests the elements in forward order, not backward order as in the *StackArrayEnumerator*. Therefore, it needs a field to keep track of the number of elements in the queue and this avoids repeated calls to the method to retrieve queue size. Because of the similarities between the two *Enumeration* subclasses, we will not explain this one in detail.

```
template <class DataType>
class QueueArrayEnumerator : virtual public
Enumeration<DataType>
{
protected:
    QueueArray<DataType>* _queue;
    int _index;
    int _size;
public:
    QueueArrayEnumerator (QueueArray<DataType>* queue);
    bool hasMoreElements ();
    DataType& nextElement ();
};
// ----------------------------------------------------------
template <class DataType>
QueueArrayEnumerator<DataType>::QueueArrayEnumerator
                  (QueueArray<DataType>* queue)
{
    _queue = queue;
    if (_queue == NULL) { _size = 0; }
    else { _size = _queue->size(); }
    _index = 0;
}
// ----------------------------------------------------------
template <class DataType>
bool QueueArrayEnumerator<DataType>::hasMoreElements ()
{
    return (_index < _size);
}
```

```
// ----------------------------------------------------------
template <class DataType>
DataType& QueueArrayEnumerator<DataType>::nextElement ()
{
    if (_index < _size)
    {
        _index++;
        return _queue->element (_index - 1);
    }
    throw QueueOverflow();
}
```

5.2.2.5   Testing the Class

The *QueueArray* class can be tested with a main() method identical to that in the *Stack-Array* class, except for appropriate changes of name. The implementation of this main() method is left as an exercise for the reader.

5.2.2.6   Related Classes: Circular Array-Based Queue

In the previous array-based implementation of a queue, we move all elements forward every time we dequeue. This makes dequeue an O(n) operation. By changing the way that we look at the array, we can reduce dequeue to a constant-time operation. We do this by treating the array as if it were circular (some refer this as a *donut array*), so that the first element of the array is adjacent to the last. Thus, when we have run out of locations at the end of the array, we can start over at the beginning again. An array and an array treated as if it were circular are illustrated below.

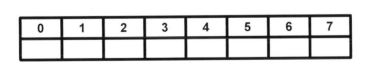
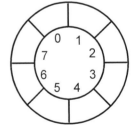

Figure 5.11:   Array implementation of a queue by considering the array as a circular array as depicted in the figure above.

Enqueuing, then, involves incrementing the rear position, wrapping around to 0 if necessary, and then placing the object in the rear position. Of course, if the array position at index 0 (or any other index) is in use, we cannot wrap around to use it again in order to enqueue an object; we must instead wait until enough objects are dequeued to make room for another object. Dequeuing must involve incrementing the front position, wrapping if necessary.

To implement the ideas above, we will make use of integer fields called front and rear. The front field holds a value one less than the position where the object in the front of the queue is stored, and the rear field holds the position of the object at the rear of the queue. Initially, when the queue is empty, front and rear are both zero. Whenever we want to insert a new object into the queue, we increment rear by one and insert the new object in that position of the array. Deletion from the queue involves returning the object at position front+1 and incrementing front. But, of course, on either increment operation, we must reduce the value obtained to the value modulo the size of the array.

To illustrate these ideas, suppose we have an array of size 8, so that valid indices are 0 through 7. Let us suppose that after a sequence of insertions and deletions, front has the value of 4 and rear has the value of 7. Then positions 0 through 4 are unused, as illustrated below.

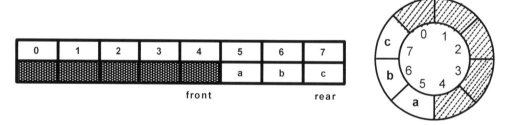

Figure 5.12:   At some instance with front being 4 and rear being 7.

Inserting a new object by incrementing rear will result in an index position of 8, which is out of the bounds of the array. Instead we set rear to the value of (rear+1) mod 8, which is 0. Now because front is equal to 4, the index position of 0 is unoccupied, so the new object can be placed, producing the result below:

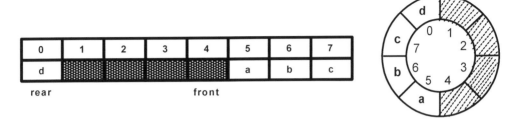

Figure 5.13: At some instance with front being 4 and rear being 0.

Now, suppose we had enqueued three more objects, without dequeuing any objects. Then front would remain at 4, while rear would have increased to 3, producing the result below:

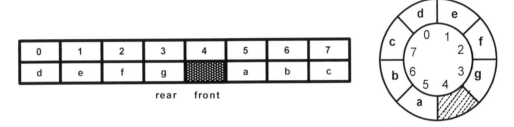

Figure 5.14: At some instance with front being 4 and rear being 3.

What happens if we now try to enqueue an object? There is certainly an empty space for it, but if we placed the object there, front would be 4 and rear would also be 4. At that point, the queue would be full, producing this result:

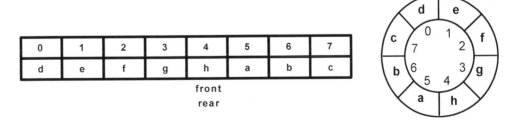

Figure 5.15: At some instance with front and rear both being 4.

Now, what if we dequeued all eight objects? The front field would go through the values 5, 6, 7, 0, 1, 2, and 3, while rear remained at 4, producing this result:

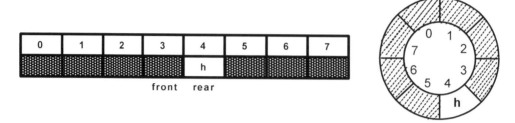

Figure 5.16:   At some instance with front being 3 and rear being 4.

If we now dequeued the last remaining element, the array would be empty, front would have the value 4 and rear would still be 4, and the result would be:

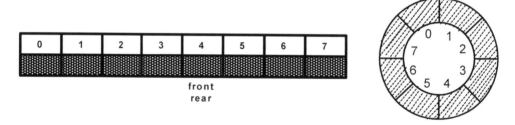

Figure 5.17:   At some instance with front and rear both being 4 once again.

But the reader will have observed the problem: front and rear are equal both when eight elements are enqueued and when the array is empty. It is difficult to distinguish the situations in the implementation without keeping a count of elements enqueued (although, if the elements were pointers, we could distinguish an empty array as one in which every element is NULL; this is not a general solution, however). If we do not keep such a count, we cannot allow front and rear to be equal except when the array is empty. Thus, we must consider the array to be full when incrementing rear would cause rear to be equal to front, and empty when rear is equal to front. Thus, if the array is of size 8, the queue can hold only 7 elements. Or, in general, if the array is of size n, the queue can hold only n–1 elements. This peculiarity of the implementation should be transparent to the user; if the user indicates a desire to have a queue capable of storing eight elements, the queue should be able to hold eight elements. Thus, the constructor will have to create an array larger by one than the user instructed, or else we must add a counter field.

Implementation of the circular array-based queue is left as an exercise for the reader. In this case, the existing implementation of the *QueueArray* class could be replaced with the new implementation, without changing the name to expose the difference in implementation. From the point of view of a client (that is, the programmer who chooses which concrete subclass is appropriate in a given case), the circular array-based queue has the same limitations as the plain array-based queue (limited size), but it is faster, so if the existing implementation is suitable for the purpose, a circular array-based implementation will be even better.

5.2.2.7   Related Classes: Linked-List-Based Queue

The above implementation uses arrays, but an implementation using linked lists is also possible. The linked list implementation of the queue can take advantage of the operations that are provided for the linked list data structure, and can grow indefinitely large. We can assign the first and last element of the list as the front and rear of the queue. Note that the first element in the linked list definition that we have used is at position 0. One way to use a linked list to implement the queue abstract data type is to implement the enqueue(newObject) method using the insertElementAt(newObject, size()) method, while dequeue() is implemented using delete(), front() using info(), and the size() method of the linked list to provide the *size*() method of the queue.

However, the *enqueue*() method implemented using *insertElementAt*() is inefficient, for it requires two complete traversals of the linked list, one to find the size, and another to insert the new item. To avoid such inefficiency, we may maintain a pointer to the last node of the linked list, so that insertion occurs in constant time. It is necessary to update this pointer upon insertion, and may be necessary to modify the pointer upon deletion. Implementation of the queue using these ideas is left as an exercise for the reader.

5.2.3   Performance Comparisons

We have seen that the queue data structure can be implemented either using an array, circular queue (that is represented as an array), or a linked list data structure. The following table (Figure 5.11) lists the time-complexity for the various queue operations on all the representations. Note that in an array representation, the dequeue() operation involves moving all the elements to the left by one. If there are n elements in the queue, this operation would take O(n) time. The enQueue() operation will add the new element at the end of the array and hence takes O(1) time.

Queue Implementations Worst-case Time Complexity Comparisons			
Operation	Array	Circular Queue	Linked List
Create()	$O(n)$	$O(n)$,	$O(1)$
isEmpty()	$O(1)$	$O(1)$	$O(1)$
enQueue(element)	$O(1)$	$O(1)$	$O(1)$
deQueue()	$O(n)$	$O(1)$	$O(1)$

Figure 5.18: Comparison of worst-case execution times of queue operations on different queue representations. The variable n in the table is the initial size of the array that represents the queue.

The qualitative assessment of the various structures used to store the set elements is presented in Figure 5.3.

Queue Implementations Qualitative Assessment	
Implementation	Assessment
Array	Does not require additional storage (next pointer in the case of linked list representation). Requires the knowledge of the maximum number of elements the stack should hold. This problem can be rectified by use of a Vector.
Linked List	Requires extra storage for the next pointer. The stack size is limited only by the size of memory.

Figure 5.19: Qualitative assessment of various queue implementations.

5.2.4   The queue Adapter in STL

The queue adapter in the standard template library uses containers that support push_back and pop_front operations. The list container supports push_back and pop_front operations while the vector container does not. Thus the queue adapter uses the list container for its implementation. If the vector container is allowed to be used for the queue adapter, then the deQueue operation which involves removing the first element of the vector will require O(n) operations for vector of size n. The pop_front operation can be implemented in O(1) time on a list container and hence it is used for implementing the queue adapter.

The STL also provides the deque container which allows efficient O(1) time insert and erase operations at both ends of the container. Consequently, the deque container supports push_back and pop_front operations. One primary advantage of using the deque container is that it allows the use of operator [] to enable random access to the elements of the container.

The operations supported by the queue adapter are front, push, and pop, where front returns the first element in the queue, and push and pop operations perform the enQueue and deQueue operations that are discussed in this chapter, respectively. Also, note that the STL does not provide iterator for the queue adapter. In the following example we are using a queue adapter that uses the deque container.

```
#include <iostream> // for i/o functions
#include <deque>
#include <queue>

using namespace std;

void main ()
{
    queue<int, deque<int>> mQueue(5);

    try
    {
        for (int i = 0; i < 5; i++)
            mQueue.push(i);
        for (int i = 0; i < 5; i++)
        {
```

```
            cout << mQueue.top() << " ";
            mQueue.pop();
        }
    }
    catch (Exception e) { } // no exception will be thrown
}
```

The result shows the correct working of the *stack* container:

    0   1   2   3   4

A complete set of methods for the queue adapter in the STL is provided below.

5.2.5   Application

The application that is to be presented uses queues in a very interesting way. The radix sort is a non-comparison based sort which relies on both arrays and queues, and is quite efficient with appropriate data.

5.2.5.1   Radix Sort

The simple bucket sort we studied in Chapter 2 is a non-comparison based technique wherein the elements to be sorted are not compared with each other. This technique can be generalized to obtain a powerful non-comparison based sorting algorithm to sort strings and numbers. We will see that the complexity of this sorting technique is dependent on the maximum length of a string or the maximum number of digits in any number of the set of strings or numbers to be sorted, respectively. That is, if the number of digits or the maximum length is kept constant, the complexity of the sorting algorithm is O(n), where n is the number of elements to be sorted. The sorting technique is called Radix Sort and it is best illustrated with the following example.

Let the set S represent the following list of numbers to be sorted: 3, 7, 70, 55, 301, 65, 4375, 20, 11, 4, 901. The element with the maximum number of digits is 4375 and we can rewrite all the numbers as: 0003, 0007, 0070, 0055, 0301, 0065, 4375, 0020, 0011, 0004, 0901. We will now initialize an array of queues A, indexed from 0 through 9, with all queues initially empty.

queue<Object>()	Default constructor
queue<Object>(intn)	Construct a queue of initial size *n*
queue<Object>(constqueue<Object>& queue)	The copy constructor
~queue<Object>()	Destructor
=	*queue<Object>&operator=(const queue<Object>& rhsQueue)* Overloaded assignment operator. The contents of the queue on the left hand side are replaced with the contents of the queue on the right hand side of the assignment operator.
==	*bool operator==(const queue<Object>& rhsQueue)* Return true if both the queues contain the same items in the same order, false otherwise.
<	*bool operator<(const queue<Object>& rhsQueue)* Return true if first queue is lexicographically less than the second queue, false otherwise.
void pop()	Erase the element in the front of the queue.
void push(const Object& value)	Add an element to the end of the queue.
Object& front()	Return a reference to the element at the front of the queue.
Object& back()	Return a reference to the element at the last element of the queue.
int size()	Return the number of elements stored in the queue.
bool empty()	Return true if the queue does not contain any elements, false otherwise.
int max_size()	Return the maximum number of items that the queue can contain.

Figure 5.20:   The methods of the queue adapter in the standard template library.

0	1	2	3	4	5	6	7	8	9
null	null	null	null	null	null	null	null	null	null

Figure 5.21: Initialization of the array of queues.

The algorithm now iterates four times, that is, a number of times equal to the maximum number of digits in any element in the given set of numbers to be sorted. During the first iteration the first digit from the right of each element is obtained. If that digit is equal to x for a given element q, then q is added to the queue A[x]. For the members of the set S above, A will appear as follows after the first iteration:

0	1	2	3	4	5	6	7	8	9
0070	0301	null	0003	0004	0055	null	0007	null	null
0020	0011				0065				
	0901				4375				

Figure 5.22: Array of queues after the first iteration.

We will next process the array of queues from index position 0 to 9 and dequeue the elements, producing the resultant set S: 0070, 0020, 0301, 0011, 0901, 0003 0004, 0055, 0065, 4375, 0007.

We will now start the second iteration, processing the set using the second number from the right. The resulting array of queues is given below:

0	1	2	3	4	5	6	7	8	9
0301	0011	0020	null	null	0055	0065	0070	null	null
0901							4375		
0003									
0004									
0007									

Figure 5.23: Array of queues after second iteration.

Once again, we dequeue the elements from the queues in the array, proceeding from index position 0 to 9, producing this resultant set S: 0301, 0901, 0003, 0004, 0007, 0011, 0020, 0055, 0065, 0070, 4375. After the third iteration, the array of queues will be as follows:

0	1	2	3	4	5	6	7	8	9
0003	null	null	0301	Null	null	null	null	null	0901
0004			4375						
0007									
0011									
0020									
0055									
0065									
0070									

Figure 5.24: Array of queues after third and final iteration.

Dequeuing now will give us the sorted set: 0003, 0004, 0007, 0011, 0020, 0055, 0065, 0070, 0301, 4375, 0901. If we perform one more iteration, then all the elements except 4375 will be queued in the position A[0], in their correct order, and dequeuing for the final time will give us the sorted list. From the above discussion we see that the complexity of the above technique is the number of iterations times maximum(number of elements, 10). The number of iterations is equal to the maximum number of digits in any element from the set of all elements to be sorted. This is not an in-place sorting algorithm, obviously, so memory will be allocated in addition to that memory which holds the elements themselves.

The algorithm for the radix sort is presented below.

```
ALGORITHM RADIX_SORT (S)
// S is the array of integers to be sorted
1.  Create an array of queues A of size 10
2.  d ← number of digits in number from the set of all numbers
        to be sorted that contains most digits
3.  k ← 1
4.  for i from 1 to d
5.      for j from 0 to S.length-1
```

```
6.                A[(S[j]/k) mod 10].enQueue(S[j]);
7.         endfor
8.         k ← k*10
9.         p ← 0
10.        for j from 0 to 9
11.            while A[j] is not empty
12.                S[p++] ← A[j].deQueue
13.            endwhile
14.        endfor
15. endfor
```

The C++ implementation of this algorithm follows the above algorithm closely. The only real difficulty not covered by the algorithm is finding the value of d. We can determine this by dividing the largest number repeatedly by 10.

```cpp
void radixSort (int S[], int count)
{
    QueueArray<int>* pqA[10];
    for (int i = 0; i < 10; i++)
    {
        pqA[i] = new QueueArray<int>(count);
    }
    // find maximum value in array S
    int max = S[0];
    for (int i = 1; i < count; i++)
    {
        if (S[i] > max) max = S[i];
    }
    // compute number of digits
    int digits = 0;
    do { max = max / 10; digits++; } while (max > 0);

    int divisor = 1;
    int index;
    try
    {
        for (int dig = 0; dig < digits; dig++)
```

```
            {
                for (index = 0; index < count; index++)
                {
                    pqA[(S[index]/divisor) %
                    10]->enqueue(S[index]);
                }
                divisor *= 10;
                index = 0;
                for (int q = 0; q <10; q++)
                {
                    while (!pqA[q]->isEmpty())
                    {
                        S[index] = pqA[q]->dequeue();
                        index++;
                    } // while queue not empty
                } // for q
            } // for dig
        } // try
        catch (Exception e)
        {
            cout << "Exception caught" << endl;
        }
    }
```

5.3 Exercises

5.1.   Write a recursive algorithm for the maze problem discussed in this chapter.

5.2.   Consider the Fibonacci sequence problem discussed in Chapter 2. Write a non-recursive method for the sequence problem that uses a stack data structure.

5.3.   Give a non-recursive method for the Ackerman's function, utilizing the stack data structure.

5.4.   Rewrite the methods in the array implementation of the stack so that it can grow in size subject only to the limitations of memory in your computer. Give appropriate exceptions whenever it is unable to grow due to memory restrictions in your computer.

5.5.   Write a method to reverse a stack without using any other data structure, even another stack.

5.6.   A given string is a *palindrome* if it reads the same both forwards and backwards. Write a method that uses the stack data structure to test if a given string is palindrome.

5.7.   A string of parentheses is said to be "valid" if and only if for every left parenthesis '('there is a right parenthesis')' to the right of it. The string '(()(()))' is valid, while '(())' ('is not valid. Write a method that uses a stack to determine whether a given string is valid. The grammar for generating a valid parenthesis string may be written as follows:

String → **(** String **)** String | <empty>

The above "production rule" indicates that a "String" may either be empty (no characters) or contain a left parenthesis, followed by another String (which is produced according to the same rule), followed by a right parenthesis, and then followed by yet another String.

5.8.   Given the following grammar:

String → **(** String **)** String | E | <empty>
E → **a** E **b** | <empty>

Write a method to verify that a given string belongs to the language specified by the above grammar, i.e., that it can be produced by the above production rules.

5.9.   In the array implementation of a linked list, in order to find a space in the array we need to search for a location in the array such that the data field is set to null (or any other marker to indicate that the array location is free). This search must be performed sequentially starting from the first position of the array. However, the index positions in the array that are free can be stored in a stack. Whenever an insert is to be performed, the free index position is that element that is popped off the stack. Whenever we perform a delete operation, the index position at which the element is deleted is pushed on to the stack. Rewrite the methods in the array implementation of the linked list data structure using a stack in this fashion.

5.10. Convert the following infix expressions to postfix expressions:
a) a + b ★ c / d / e - f
b) a - b - c / d / f / g ★ h
c) (a ★ b) + (c ★ d / e) / f
d) ((a + b) ★ (c - d / e) + f) ★ g

5.11. Convert the following postfix expressions to infix expressions:
   a) a b ⋆ c d / –
   b) a b c ⋆ d – e f ⋆ /
   c) a b c d ⋆ – e / f / /
   d) a b c / d / ⋆

5.12. Given a postfix expression, write a method to produce a fully parenthesized infix expression. In a fully parenthesized infix expression, every subexpression containing two operands and an operator is enclosed in parenthesis.

5.13. Write a method to evaluate an infix expression that may contain parenthesized subexpressions.

5.14. Write a method to evaluate an infix expression that may contain unary operators such as the unary minus.

5.15. The array of size n that is used to implement a circular queue can store only n-1 elements. How can you modify the methods belonging to the queue data structure so that it can store n elements?

5.16. Design a linked-list implementation of a queue.

5.17. A *double-ended queue* is a data structure in which enqueue and dequeue operations may be made at either end of the queue data structure. Write the complete class and appropriate methods to implement the double-ended queue.

5.18. Processes that are created in a computer system wait for their turn to be executed by the CPU. Processes have priority and the highest priority ones gets the CPU before the lower priority processes. The priority of a process can be increased or decreased from time to time. Create a class definition along with appropriate methods such that each instance has a set of queues, one for each priority level in the system. Define appropriate methods to implement such a class.

5.19. Let S be set of strings formed from the character 'A' through 'Z'. Devise a method similar to radix sort to sort the strings in S alphabetically.

5.4   References for Further Reading

Auslander, M.A., and Strong, H.R., "Systematic recursion removal", *Communications of the ACM* vol. 21, pp. 127-134, 1978.

Hamblin, C.L., "Translation to and from Polish notation", *Computer Journal* vol. 5, pp. 210-213, 1962.

Knuth, D.E., *The Art of Computer Programming*, Addison-Wesley, Reading, MA.

Reingold, E.M., "A comment on the evaluation of Polish postfix expressions", *Computer Journal* vol. 24, pp.288, 1981.

Sloyer, C., Copes, W., Sasco, W., and Starck, R., *Queues: Will this wait never end!*, Providence, RI: Janson 1987.

Stubbs, D.F., and Webre, N.W., *Data Structures with Abstract Data Types and Pascal*, Brooks/Cole Publishing Company, Monterey, Calif., 1985, 459 pages.

Ulrich, E.G., "Event Manipulation for Discrete Simulations Requiring Large Numbers of Events", *Communications of the ACM* vol. 21, no. 9, Sept. 1978.

Vaucher, J.G., and Dural, P., "A Comparison of Simulation Event List Algorithms", *Communications of the ACM* vol. 18, no.4, Apr. 1975.

Welsh, J., Elder, J., and Bustard, D., *Sequential Program Structures*, Prentice-Hall International, London, 1984, 385 pages.

6   Simple Search Trees

A COMMON PROBLEM in programming is the searching problem. That is, given a list of items, already in sorted order, find whether a particular item is present, and if so, where it is. Often the item sought is a "key" which is associated with additional data, which is the true goal of the search.

A great deal of research has gone into data structures that can store data in a way that permits rapid searching. A sorted array permits such rapid searching, as we have seen in the discussion of binary search, but it is inflexible in terms of size, so we must either know how many elements we will have in the array, or allocate as many as we could possibly need, which is inefficient. We would like a data structure that can grow as necessary but still allows rapid searching; one such data structure is the binary search tree, to be discussed in this chapter.

We will discuss single dimensional search trees, as opposed to a multidimensional search trees. A single dimensional search tree allows search on a single key for each item stored in the tree (although the single "key" could be formed by considering first one field and then, if there were a match on that field, considering a second field, and so on until the fields were exhausted or a difference were found). A multidimensional search tree would have two or more keys and might, for instance, store items that are arranged by latitude and longitude. If the same items were stored in a single dimensional search tree, we would have to use just one of the keys (latitude or longitude), or a combination of the two (using latitude for the primary comparison and longitude for the secondary comparison if two items match in latitude, for instance). In the case of the single dimensional tree, it would be difficult and inefficient to find items that fall within a box defined by both latitude and longitude, but this would be well-supported by the multidimensional tree. Multidimensional trees are more complex than binary trees, and are less common, so they will not be considered here.

6.1   The Binary Tree Data Structure

The binary tree is a finite set of nodes such that either (1) the tree is empty, i.e., the number of nodes is zero; or (2) one node is distinguished as the *root*, and the remaining nodes are partitioned into two binary trees, called the *left subtree* and the *right subtree*. The binary tree is not itself a search tree, but it is the starting point for our construction of a binary search tree.

Much of the terminology relating to binary trees has a genealogical tint to it. If node A is the root node of a binary tree T and node B is the root node of the left or right subtree of T, then A is called the *parent* of B and B is called a *child* of A. An empty subtree has no root node that could be considered a child. Therefore, a node may have zero, one, or two children, and is referred to as having a *degree* equal to the number of children (or non-empty subtrees). For example, a node with one child is of degree one. A non-empty tree always has two subtrees, though one or both may be empty. Node A is called an *ancestor* of node C if node A is the parent of node C or is an ancestor of the parent of node C. Similarly, node C is called a *descendant* of node A if node C is a child of node A or is a descendant of a child of node A. Children of the same node are referred to as *siblings*.

Returning to the botanical theme, a node that has no children (both subtrees are empty) is called a leaf node. A node that has a child or children is called an internal node.

The *level* of a node is recursively defined as follows: The root of a tree is at level one, and the children of any node at level i are at level $i+1$. It should be clear that the level of a node depends on the tree to which it is considered to belong. The *height* or *depth* of a tree is the maximum level of any node of the tree.

It should be noted that computer scientists have a somewhat unusual view of things, so binary trees grow upside down: the root is at the top and the leaves are at the bottom. Some example binary trees are as follows:

Figure 6.1 (a) is an empty binary tree, with the special box symbol instead of a node circle, so that it can be seen. In the remaining trees, the empty subtrees are not depicted as every non-empty tree is assumed to have an empty subtree or empty subtrees if necessary to bring it up to two subtrees. Figure 6.1 (b) is a binary tree containing just one node, which is the root but also a leaf, having no children and no ancestors. Figure 6.1 (c) and (d) are both two-node binary trees; in each case, node A is the root and has one child, while node B is a leaf and is at level 2.

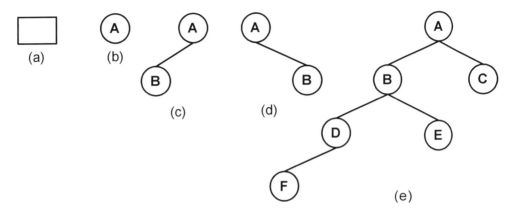

Figure 6.1:   Example of a few types of binary trees.

Finally, Figure 6.1 (e) is a six-node binary tree. All of the nodes, except node A, are descendants of node A, while nodes B and C are the only children of node A. Nodes D, E, and F are descendants of node B. Node D has just one child, node F, while node F has three ancestors, nodes D, B, and A. Node D is the parent of node F. Nodes A, B, and D are all internal, while nodes C, E, and F are the leaves. Node F is at level 4, node C is at level 2, and the height (or depth) of the tree is 4.

Certain properties may be proven about binary trees. In particular, if $n \geq 1$, the maximum number of nodes at level n in a binary tree is 2^{n-1}. This property may be proven by induction on levels of the tree. Clearly, the maximum number of nodes at level 1 is $1 = 2^{1-1}$, since the root is the only node at that level. Now, suppose that $k \geq 1$ and that the maximum number of nodes at level k in any binary tree is 2^{k-1}. Then, let T be a binary tree of height at least $k+1$. It has at most 2^{k-1} nodes at level k. Since each node at level k can have at most two children, the maximum number of nodes which T may have at level $k+1$ is $2 \times 2^{k-1} = 2^{(k+1)-1}$, so that the inductive step is proven.

Given the above property, it can be easily proven that, if $n \geq 1$, the maximum number of nodes of a binary tree of height n is $2^n - 1$. A binary tree of height n has the maximum number of nodes if every level in the tree has the maximum number of nodes for that level. But then the tree has a number of nodes equal to:

$$\sum_{i=1}^{n} 2^{i-1} = \sum_{i=0}^{n-1} 2^i = \frac{2^{n-1+1} - 1}{2 - 1} = 2^n - 1$$

A *full binary tree* of height n is a binary tree of height n with 2^n-1 nodes, i.e., a binary tree with the maximum possible nodes. Suppose that we number the nodes of a full binary tree starting at the root node, moving down level by level, and numbering the nodes of each level from left to right. Then a full binary tree of height 3 would be numbered as follows:

A binary tree with k nodes is a *complete binary tree* if and only if its nodes correspond to nodes 1 through k of a full binary tree having at least k nodes and numbered as above. Thus, in the figure below, (a) is a complete binary tree, but (b) is not.

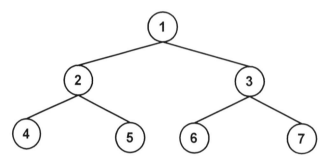

Figure 6.2:   Example of a full binary tree of height 3.

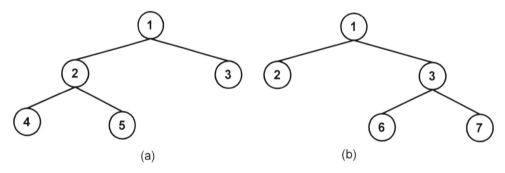

Figure 6.3:   Definition of complete binary tree: (a) is a complete binary tree but (b) is not a complete binary tree.

6.1.1   Abstract Data Type

A minimal specification of an Abstract Data Type for the binary tree is as follows:

```
createEmpty ()
    // creates an empty binary tree
createNonempty (data, left, right)
    // creates a binary tree with data in root and left and \
    // right as subtrees
isEmpty()
    // returns true if tree is empty, but otherwise false
Height ()
    // returns the height (or depth) of the tree
Size ()
    // returns the number of nodes in the tree
rootData ()
    // returns data from the root
left ()
    // returns the left subtree
right ()
    // returns the right subtree
setrootData (data)
    // places data in the root; data must not be empty
setleft (newleft)
    // sets the left subtree to newleft
setright (newright)
    // sets the right subtree to newright
```

It should be noted that the binary tree abstract data type makes no reference to ordering or searching. Indeed, the binary tree itself has no such concepts; the nodes may be arranged any way that is desirable. The binary tree, however, can be adapted to support ordering and searching. This produces the binary search tree, to be presented later in the chapter.

6.1.2   Implementation of the Binary Tree

Since the definition of the binary tree is recursive, we shall implement it recursively in C++, using pointers to binary tree objects for the left and right subtrees.

6.1.2.1   Node Data Type

The binary tree simply stores data, and makes no effort to order it. Therefore, we can use instances of any type for the nodes.

6.1.2.2   Exceptions

As a first step in implementing this abstract data type, it can be transformed into an abstract base class. We must consider the problem of the fundamental difference between an empty binary tree and all other binary trees: an empty binary tree does not have, and cannot be given, subtrees. What should happen if the user attempts to give a subtree to an empty binary tree? Obviously an error should be signaled by throwing an exception. Then what happens if the user attempts to access the (non-existent) root of an empty binary tree? Again, an exception. Finally, a binary tree is a dynamic data structure and, like any other dynamic data structure, may run out of memory. We must therefore begin by declaring a family of exceptions associated with binary trees:

```
class BinaryTreeException    :   public Exception { };
class BinaryTreeMemory       :   public BinaryTreeException {};
class BinaryTreeGaveSubtreeToEmptyTree:    public
BinaryTreeException {};
class BinaryTreeEmptyTree:        public BinaryTreeException {};
```

6.1.2.3   Abstract Base Class Definition

With these exception classes in hand, we can design our abstract base class:

```
template<class DataType>
class AbstractBinaryTree{
friend ostream& operator << (ostream& s,
    AbstractBinaryTree<DataType>& bt);
public:
    virtual ~AbstractBinaryTree ();
    virtual bool isEmpty() = NULL;
// returns true if tree is empty, but otherwise false
    virtual int Height () = NULL;
// returns the height (or depth) of the tree
    virtual int Size () = NULL;
// returns the number of nodes in the tree
    virtualDataType& rootData () = NULL;
// returns data from the root
    virtual AbstractBinaryTree<DataType>* left () = NULL;
// returns the left subtree
```

```
      virtual AbstractBinaryTree<DataType>* right () = NULL;
// returns the right subtree
      virtual void setrootData (DataType& data) = NULL;
// sets the root to a copy of data
      virtual AbstractBinaryTree<DataType>* setleft
            AbstractBinaryTree<DataType>* newleft) = NULL;
// sets the left subtree to newleft;
// return value: the former left subtree
      virtual AbstractBinaryTree<DataType>* setright
            (AbstractBinaryTree<DataType>* newright) = NULL;
// sets the right subtree to newright;
// return value: the former right subtree
      virtual void makeEmpty () = NULL;
// empties tree
      virtual Enumeration<DataType>* inOrderEnumerator ();
// Returns an inorder enumeration of the data
// from all nodes contained in the tree
      virtual Enumeration<DataType>* postOrderEnumerator ();
// Returns a postorder enumeration of the data
// from all nodes contained in the tree
      virtual Enumeration<DataType>* preOrderEnumerator ();
// Returns a preorder enumeration of the data
// from all nodes contained in the tree
      virtual void display (ostream& os);
// display tree structure
};
```

The abstract base class has no constructors, so the ADT methods *Create-Empty()* and *CreateNonempty()* must be implemented as part of a class which descend from this class. Although the ADT has no enumerator, one can easily be constructed from it, and the class includes three enumerators (to be described later) for testing purposes, along with a method for displaying the structure (*display()*, to be described). Finally, the abstract base class has a virtual destructor that is trivial, and a friend *ostream<<* function which is essentially the same as that for a *LinkedList*.

6.1.2.4   Class Definition

We shall now write a class called *BinaryTree* that is a subclass of *AbstractBinaryTree*. It uses pointers for both its data and left and right subtrees.

Fields, Constructors, and Destructor

The first step in designing this class is to decide (tentatively, at least) on the fields. It is obvious that we must have a place to store the data for the root, and that we will have to be able to find the left and right subtrees. Although there are other ways to implement a binary tree, as noted above, we will implement it recursively and we will keep pointers to the left and right subtrees in the object. We shall have a pointer to the node data, rather than holding a field of the data type within the binary tree. When is the root data NULL? According to the semantics of a binary tree, a NULL root data implies an empty tree (a tree with no data) and vice versa.[1]

It should be noted that there is no particular reason why all subtrees must belong to the same class; as long as an object is descended from *AbstractBinaryTree* it should be possible to attach that object as a subtree to a *BinaryTree*. Therefore, we will need a pointer to an DataType for the data in the root, and pointers to *AbstractBinaryTree* for the left and right subtrees.

We can begin our class as follows:

```
template<class DataType>
class BinaryTree : public AbstractBinaryTree<DataType>
{
protected:
    DataType* _rootData;
    AbstractBinaryTree<DataType>* _left;
    AbstractBinaryTree<DataType>* _right;
public:
    BinaryTree ();
};
```

---

1 We could have had a field of the data type, but then we would need a flag indicating whether the tree was empty or not. This might have simplified our code, but if the data type were very large, the tree data type would also be very large, perhaps large enough to cause stack problems.

As we did with the *LinkedList* class, we will require the constructor to create a copy of the data to be stored in the tree, and we will require the destructor to delete that data. We will need at least two constructors, corresponding to *Create(data, left, right)* and *CreateEmptyTree()* in the ADT. Initially, at least, the following constructors appear to fit the bill:

```
template<class DataType>
BinaryTree<DataType>::BinaryTree (DataType& rootData,
abstractBinaryTree<DataType>* left,
    AbstractBinaryTree<DataType>* right)
{
    _rootData = new DataType(rootData);
    if (_rootData == NULL) throw BinaryTreeMemory();
    _left = left;
    _right = right;
}
// ------------------------------------------------------------
template<class DataType>
BinaryTree<DataType>::BinaryTree ()
{
    _rootData = NULL;
    _left = NULL;
    _right = NULL;
}
```

The destructor resembles in some ways that of the *LinkedList* class: since the *BinaryTree* instance takes responsibility for creating its data, it must also delete it. Further, since the user might well forget to delete subtrees, the instance must delete its own subtrees. If the user wants to keep those subtrees, they must be detached using *setright ()* and *setleft ()* before the instance is deleted.

```
template<class DataType>
BinaryTree<DataType>::~BinaryTree ()
{
    if (_rootData != NULL)
        delete _rootData;
    _rootData = NULL;
```

```
    if (_left != NULL)
        delete _left;
    _left = NULL;
    if (_right != NULL)
        delete _right;
    _right = NULL;
}
```

Accessor Methods

The accessor methods are straightforward. Height can be defined recursively; the height of an empty binary tree is 0 and the height of any other binary tree is one more than the height of its deeper subtree. Size can be similarly defined recursively; the size of an empty binary tree is 0 and the size of any other binary tree is one more than the sum of the sizes of its subtrees. The only peril with these two is that we must be careful about left or right subtrees that are not merely empty, but non-existent (NULL).

```
template<class DataType>
bool BinaryTree<DataType>::isEmpty()
{
    return (_rootData == NULL);
}
// ----------------------------------------------------------
template<class DataType>
int BinaryTree<DataType>::Height ()
{
    int height = 0;
    int leftheight;

    if (!isEmpty())
    {
        if (_left == NULL)
            leftheight = 0;
        else
            leftheight = _left->Height();

        if (_right == NULL)
```

```
                        height = 1 + leftheight;
            else
                height = 1 + max (leftheight, _right->Height());
            // max() is in stdlib.h
    }


    returnheight;
}
// ----------------------------------------------------------
template<class DataType>
int BinaryTree<DataType>::Size ()
    // returns the number of nodes in the tree
{
    int size = 0;
    int leftsize;
    if (!isEmpty())
    {
        if (_left == NULL)
            leftsize = 0;
        else
            leftsize = _left->Size();

        if (_right == NULL)
            size = 1 + leftsize;
        else
            size = 1 + leftsize + _right->Size();
    }
    return size;
}
// ----------------------------------------------------------
template<class DataType>
DataType& BinaryTree<DataType>::rootData ()
{
    if (isEmpty()) throw BinaryTreeEmptyTree();
    return *_rootData;
```

```
}
// ---------------------------------------------------------
template<class DataType>
AbstractBinaryTree<DataType>* BinaryTree<DataType>::left ()
{
    return _left;
}
// ---------------------------------------------------------
template<class DataType>
AbstractBinaryTree<DataType>* BinaryTree<DataType>::right ()
{
    return _right;
}
```

But now we have another problem. If the user calls *bt.left().root-Data()*, and *bt* is itself empty, then *left()* will be NULL and the call will produce an error, properly so because an empty tree has no left or right subtree. But what if *bt* is not empty, but was created with the following call?

```
BinaryTree<SomeType>bt = new BinaryTree<SomeType> (data, NULL, NULL);
```

In this case, *bt* is not empty and, by definition, has two subtrees which may be empty but are certainly present, so that *bt.left()* *must* return a valid tree. We may modify *BinaryTree(data, left, right)* to throw an exception if either left or right is NULL, and provide another constructor, *BinaryTree(data)*, which will correctly create a tree with two empty subtrees; this solution, however, leaves us with a hole in the implementation since the user could create a non-empty *BinaryTree* with two empty subtrees or two non-empty subtrees, but not one non-empty subtree. Even if we added a constructor, *BinaryTree(data, child)*, this would handle only the case of a tree with a non-empty left subtree (or perhaps a right subtree, depending on the implementation). We could not have two such constructors, one for the left subtree and one for the right subtree, since they would have the same signatures.

So, let us allow the user to call *BinaryTree(data, left, right)* with *left* or *right* or both equal to NULL, but internally convert such NULL subtrees to empty trees. This has the added advantage of simplifying the code for both *Height()* and *Size()*, since a non-empty tree will never have NULL subtrees:

```
template<class DataType>
BinaryTree<DataType>::BinaryTree(DataType rootData,
                           AbstractBinaryTree<DataType>* left,
                           AbstractBinaryTree<DataType>* right){
  { _rootData = new DataType(rootData);
    if (_rootData == NULL) throw BinaryTreeMemory();
    if (left == NULL)
       _left = new BinaryTree<DataType> ();
    else
       _left = left;
    if (right == NULL)
       _right = new BinaryTree<DataType> ();
    else
       _right = right;
}
// -----------------------------------------------------------
template<class DataType>
int BinaryTree<DataType>::Height ()
{
    int result = 0;
    if (!isEmpty())
       result = 1 + max (_left->Height(), _right->Height());
    // max() is in stdlib.h
    return result;
}
// -----------------------------------------------------------
template<class DataType>
int BinaryTree<DataType>::Size ()
{
    int result = 0;
    if (!isEmpty())
        result = 1 + _left->Size() + _right->Size();
    // max() is in stdlib.h
    return result;
}
```

One design decision which has been passed over in silence is, should *left*() throw an exception, instead of returning NULL, if called on an empty tree? The decision not to throw an exception is based on the facts that (1) programmers are accustomed to testing for a NULL at the end of a linked list, so a NULL as the last subtree is not unprecedented; (2) any attempt to use the NULL pointer will produce an immediate and dramatic result, so that the problem should turn up in the first test; and (3) if *left*() threw an exception, nearly all accesses to the tree would need to be enclosed in *try* blocks, even if no attempt were made to change the tree, which seems rather excessive. Precisely the same reasoning applies to *right*(), of course.

Mutator Methods

Now we must write the mutator methods. The important consideration here is to ensure that any non-empty tree always has two valid subtrees, regardless of the user's actions, while an empty tree has no valid subtrees. Furthermore, a non-empty tree must not be inadvertently transformed into an empty tree.

```
template<class DataType>
void BinaryTree<DataType>::setrootData (DataType& data)
{
    if ( _rootData != NULL)
        delete _rootData;
    else
    {
    // if tree formerly empty, add two valid (empty) subtrees
        _left = new BinaryTree<DataType>();
        _right = new BinaryTree<DataType>();
    }
    _rootData = new DataType(data);


// -------------------------------------------------------
template<class DataType>
AbstractBinaryTree<DataType>* BinaryTree<DataType>::setleft
        (AbstractBinaryTree<DataType>* newleft)
{
    AbstractBinaryTree<DataType>* temp = _left;
    if (isEmpty()) throw BinaryTreeGaveSubtreeToEmptyTree();
//  if we reached this point, the tree isn't empty, so _left
//  isn't NULL
```

```
    //  and can't be allowed to be set to NULL
    if (newleft == NULL)
            _left = new BinaryTree<DataType> ();
        else
            _left = newleft;
        return temp;
    }
    // -----------------------------------------------------------
    template<class DataType>
    AbstractBinaryTree<DataType>* BinaryTree<DataType>::setright
            (AbstractBinaryTree<DataType>* newright)
    {
        AbstractBinaryTree<DataType>* temp = _right;
        if (isEmpty()) throw BinaryTreeGaveSubtreeToEmptyTree();
    //  if we reached this point, the tree isn't empty, so _right
    //  isn't NULL and can't be allowed to be set to NULL
        if (newright == NULL)
            _right = new BinaryTree<DataType> ();
        else
            _right = newright;
        return temp;
    }
    // -----------------------------------------------------------
    template<class DataType>
    void BinaryTree<DataType>::makeEmpty ()
        // empties tree by setting root data to
        // null and removing subtres
    {
        if (_rootData != NULL)
           delete _rootData;
        _rootData = NULL;
        if (_left != NULL)
           delete _left;
        _left = NULL;
        if (_right != NULL)
           delete _right;
        _right = NULL;
    }
```

The reader may note, above, that `makeEmpty()` uses the same code as the destructor. Removing this inefficiency is left to the reader. The reader may also notice that it is always necessary for the caller to deal with the return value from `setleft()` and `setright()`, even if the subtree returned was created solely to avoid having a NULL subtree. The reader may wish to try to devise some other way of handling this situation.

6.1.2.5 Enumeration of Nodes

Since a binary tree is recursively defined, it is natural to display binary trees in a recursive fashion (although there are other ways to display them, such as breadth-first). The data in the root must of course be displayed, and the left and right subtrees, if not empty, must also be displayed. The order of display is then the question. For people who read left-to-right, it is expected that the left subtree should be displayed before the right subtree. Should the root data be displayed before the left subtree, after the left but before the right, or after the right? The correct answer is, "all of the above." Enumeration of the root data before the left subtree is called *preorder enumeration* or *preorder traversal*, after the left but before the right is called *inorder enumeration* or *inorder traversal*, and after the right is called *postorder enumeration* or *postorder traversal*.

An example will make this discussion less abstract. In the binary tree below, a preorder enumeration would display nodes in the order A, B, D, F, E, C; an inorder enumeration in the order F, D, B, E, A, C; and a postorder enumeration in the order F, D, E, B, C, A.

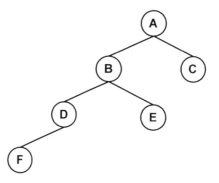

Figure 6.4: Enumeration of nodes: Example of a binary tree with nodes A, B, C, D, E and F.

Preorder Enumeration by Recursion

We can easily imagine a recursive implementation of the display of any of these enumerations. For instance, we might write our *display()* method to provide a preorder display:

```
template<class DataType>
void AbstractBinaryTree<DataType>::display (ostream& os)
{
    if (isEmpty()) return;
    os<< rootData () << " ";
    left()->display (os);
    right()->display (os);
}
```

With this function, we can finally write a *main*() function to test the class:

```
void main() {
    BinaryTree<char> abt1 ('T', new BinaryTree<char>
  ('L', NULL, NULL), new BinaryTree<char> ('R', NULL, NULL));

    cout << "Size: " << abt1.Size() << ", Height: " <<
        abt1.Height() << endl;
    cout << "<" << abt1 << ">" << endl;
}
```

When this program is run, it generates a three-node binary tree, with 'T' in the root, 'L' in the root of the left child and 'R' in the root of the right child. It produces the following output:

```
Size: 3, Height: 2
<T L R >
```

The second line of the output is precisely the preorder enumeration of the tree.

Unfortunately, although this main method demonstrates that the constructor is working correctly, this *display*() function cannot be used in the enumeration classes which we must design. The difficulty is that the *Enumeration* class, which we must derive from, has the following methods:

```
hasMoreElements ()
    // Determines whether there are any more
    // elements in the enumeration.
nextElement ()
    // Retrieves the next element in the enumeration.
```

Neither of these methods should be implemented recursively, since they will be called to return one element at a time. However, the recursive implementation gives us a hint as to the iterative implementation.

Preorder Enumeration Using the PreOrderEnumerator Class

We will write a *PreOrderEnumerator* class to support preorder enumeration of a binary tree. The fact that recursion can be used so efficiently suggests that we should implement the *PreOrderEnumerator* class using a *Stack*, which we have already developed. Having decided to use a *Stack* in our implementation, we should consider the activation records which will accumulate as the above *display()* method executes.

The first activation contains a pointer to the current instance (which we will call *bt*). This pointer is used to print the root data of *bt* and identify *bt*'s subtrees for the recursive calls. It is not used after the recursive calls to the subtrees are made. This suggests that a pointer to *bt* should be initially placed on the *Stack*, then popped off (since we will not need it again) and its subtrees (if non-empty) pushed at the same time that its data is returned to the caller in *nextElement()*. Since we are going to discard *bt*'s pointer, we cannot arrange to push the left subtree and push the right only after the left has finished, so we will let the *Stack* handle the problem by pushing the right subtree first, then the left. The subtrees are, of course, similarly pushed on and popped off again, and the *PreOrderEnumerator* will detect that there are no more elements when the *Stack* becomes empty.

Thus, in the implementation of the *PreOrderEnumerator* class, we will need a pointer to the tree being enumerated and a *Stack* field. Further, the *Stack* will need to be pre-loaded by pushing the root of the tree so that it can be popped off. Therefore, the *PreOrderEnumerator* class is initially like this:

```
template<class DataType>
class PreOrderEnumerator : public Enumeration<DataType>
{
protected:
    AbstractBinaryTree<DataType>* _tree;
    StackLinked< AbstractBinaryTree<DataType>* >* _stack;
            // since we have to return separately each node
            // found, we can't proceed recursively and
            // have to have a stack
public:
    PreOrderEnumerator (AbstractBinaryTree<DataType>* t);
};
// ------------------------------------------------------------
template<class DataType>
PreOrderEnumerator<DataType>::PreOrderEnumerator
        (AbstractBinaryTree<DataType>* t)
{
    _tree = t;
    _stack = new StackLinked< AbstractBinaryTree<DataType>* > ();
    if ((_tree != NULL) && (!_tree->isEmpty()))
        _stack->push (_tree);
}
```

In accordance with the discussion above, the enumeration will be complete when the stack is empty. Thus, the *hasMoreElements()* method is quite simple:

```
template<class DataType>
bool PreOrderEnumerator<DataType>::hasMoreElements ()
{
    return (!_stack->isEmpty());
}
```

Also in accordance with the discussion above, the *nextElement()* method should pop the last tree off the stack, then push the right subtree (if it is not empty) followed by the left subtree (if not empty), and then return the root value of the tree popped off. So the implementation is as follows:

```
template<class DataType>
DataType& PreOrderEnumerator<DataType>::nextElement ()
{
if (_stack->isEmpty() ) throw BinaryTreeEmptyTree();
    AbstractBinaryTree<DataType>* tree = _stack->pop();
if (!tree->right()->isEmpty())
      {
        _stack->push (tree->right());
      }
if (!tree->left()->isEmpty())
      {
        _stack->push (tree->left());
      }
return tree->rootData();
}
```

We can return an instance of this enumerator from the method called *preOrderEnumerator*() in the `AbstractBinaryTree` class:

```
template<class DataType>
Enumeration<DataType>* AbstractBinaryTree<DataType>::
        preOrderEnumerator () {
    return new PreOrderEnumerator<DataType> (this);
}
```

The binary tree class has a method named `preOrderEnumerator ()` and when this method is invoked on a binary tree class object (say *t*), a PreOrderEnumerator object is created. The constructor for this class stores a pointer to *t* on the top of the stack. This stack is created in the constructor of the PreOrderEnumerator. For example for the tree in Figure 6.4 when the `preOrderEnumerator ()` method is called, the pointer to the object corresponding to node A is pushed on to the stack. This is show in Figure 6.5.

Recall that the preorder enumeration for the binary tree shown in Figure 6.5 is A, B, D, F, E, and C. Given the stack contents as shown in Figure 6.5, when the *nextElement()* method is executed, it should return the top of the stack. Before it actually returns it should store the pointers to node C and node B on the stack (but in what

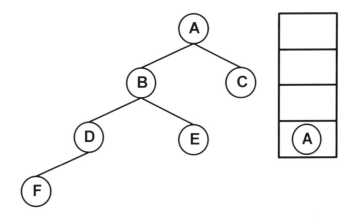

Figure 6.5:   Node A (Pointer to node A) is pushed onto the stack.

order?). A second call to *nextElement()* should return pointer to node B and hence it should be on the top of the stack. We should also keep track of the pointer to node C, since once we have enumerated the left subtree of A, we should enumerate the right subtree of A. For the reasons above, we will push pointer to node C first followed by the pushing pointer to node B. The sequences of these operations are shown in Figure 6.6.

We can then modify our previous *main ()* function to read as follows:

```
void main()
{
  BinaryTree<char> abt1 ('T', new BinaryTree<char>
    ('L', NULL, NULL), new BinaryTree<char> ('R', NULL, NULL));

    cout<< "Size: " << abt1.Size() << ", Height: " <<
    abt1.Height() << endl;

  Enumeration<char>* e = abt1.preOrderEnumerator();
  cout<< "<";
  while (e->hasMoreElements())
  cout << e->nextElement() << " " ;
  cout<< ">" << endl;
}
```

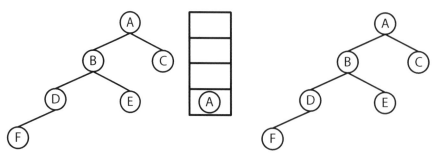

Initially A is pushed; When nextElement() is executed, A is popped and pointer to C is pushed first followed by pointer to B; push right followed by push left

When nextElement() is executed, B is popped and pointer to E is pushed first followed by pointer to D

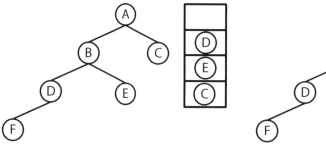

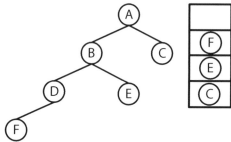

When nextElement() is executed, D is popped and pointer to F is pushed

When nextElement() is executed, F is popped and there is nothing to push

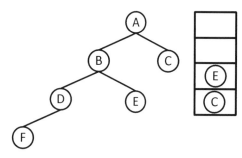

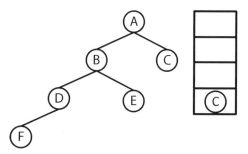

When nextElement() is executed, E is popped and there is nothing to push

When nextElement() is executed, C is popped and there is nothing to push

Figure 6.6: Figure illustrating the contents of the stack after a sequence of calls to nextElement() as part of the PreOrderEnumerator class.

As the reader can confirm, the output when the *PreOrderEnumerator* is used is the same as the output when our preorder *display*() method is used. The reader should test whether the *PreOrderEnumerator* will correctly handle the situation of an empty tree.

Inorder Enumeration by Recursion

Similarly, we can design an inorder version of *display*(), as follows:

```
template<class DataType>
void AbstractBinaryTree<DataType>::display (ostream& os)
{
    if (isEmpty()) return;
    left()->display (os);
    os<< rootData() << " ";
    right()->display (os);
}
```

The reader should note that the only difference between this and the preorder version is that two lines have been interchanged.

Inorder Enumeration Using the InOrderEnumerator Class

Now we can begin writing an *Enumeration* class for inorder enumeration. Again, the recursive implementation suggests that the *InOrderEnumerator* class should use a *Stack*, and consideration of the activation records suggests what should go on the stack.

In this case, the first activation record will hold the pointer to *bt*, however, this pointer will not be used until the left subtree is completely enumerated. Then the root data of *bt* is returned, a recursive call is made on the right subtree, and *bt* could be discarded, as it will not be used again. But if we consider the activation record containing a pointer to *bt->left()*, the same thing happens: the pointer must be kept until the left subtree is fully enumerated. It is clear that no call to *rootData*() will be made until the left subtree of some tree T is empty, at which point T's *rootData*() can be returned, T's right subtree can be pushed, and the pointer to T, formerly on the stack, can be discarded.

We can see that there is a fundamental asymmetry between left subtrees and right subtrees; a left subtree is pushed immediately after its parent, without any value being returned to the caller, while a right subtree is pushed only after its parent is popped off the stack, after which the parent's root data is returned to the caller. This implies that we need a method, which we shall call *pushToBtmLeft()*, to push left subtrees until an empty left subtree is reached, and that this method is called immediately after the original tree or any right subtree is pushed.

Given these considerations, the *InOrderEnumerator* class appears initially as follows:

```cpp
template<class DataType>
class InOrderEnumerator : public Enumeration<DataType>
{
protected:
    AbstractBinaryTree<DataType>* _tree;
    StackLinked< AbstractBinaryTree<DataType>* >* _stack;
        // since we have to separately return each node
        // found, we can't proceed recursively and
        // have to have a stack
    void pushToBtmLeft (AbstractBinaryTree<DataType>* tree);
public:
    InOrderEnumerator (AbstractBinaryTree<DataType>* t);
    virtual bool hasMoreElements ();
    virtual DataType& nextElement ();
};


// -----------------------------------------------------------
template<class DataType>
InOrderEnumerator<DataType>::InOrderEnumerator
    (AbstractBinaryTree<DataType>* t)
{
    _tree = t;
    _stack = new StackLinked<AbstractBinaryTree<DataType>*>();
    if (_tree != NULL) pushToBtmLeft (_tree);
}
// -----------------------------------------------------------
template<class DataType>
void InOrderEnumerator<DataType>::pushToBtmLeft
    (AbstractBinaryTree<DataType>* tree)
```

```
{
    do {
        if (tree->isEmpty()) return;
        _stack->push (tree);
        tree = tree->left();
    } while (true);
}
```

As in the case of the `PreOrderEnumerator`, the *hasMoreElements*() method just returns false when the stack is empty, but the `nextElement ()` method necessarily must be different. Since we have already implemented *pushToBtmLeft*(), in the *nextElement*() method we can pop off the tree on top of the stack and call *pushToBtmLeft*() on its right subtree, to set up for enumeration of that subtree, then return the node value of the tree popped off.

```
template <class DataType>
DataType& InOrderEnumerator<DataType>::nextElement ()
{
    if (_stack->isEmpty() ) throw BinaryTreeEmptyTree();
    AbstractBinaryTree<DataType>* tree = _stack->pop();
    pushToBtmLeft (tree->right());
    return tree->rootData();
}
```

The reader should write the *inOrderEnumerator*() method similar to the *preOrderEnumerator*() method previously presented and verify that the `InOrderEnumerator` produces the same output as the inorder version of *display*(), and that it will correctly handle an empty tree. The sequence of calls to nextElement() and the changes to the stack is shown in Figure 6.7.

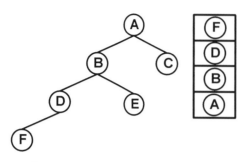

Initially A, B, D, F is pushed in that order using pushToBtmLeft() method. When nextElement() is called node F is popped and since there is nothing to the right of node F no more nodes are pushed.

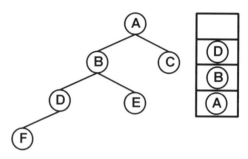

When nextElement() is called node D is popped and since there is nothing to the right of node D no more nodes are pushed.

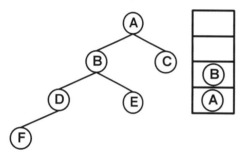

When nextElement() is called node B is popped and pushtoBtmLeft() is called on node E. This will push node E on to the stack

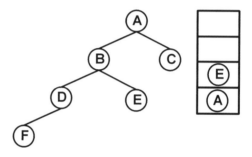

When nextElement() is executed, E is popped and there is nothing to push

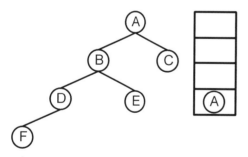

When nextElement() is executed, A is popped and pushtoBtmLeft() is called on node C. This will push node C on to the stack

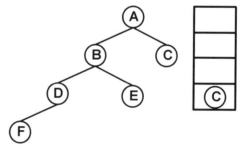

When nextElement() is executed, C is popped and there is nothing to push

Figure 6.7:   Figure illustrating the contents of the stack after a sequence of calls to nextElement() as part of the InOrderEnumerator class.

Postorder Enumeration by Recursion

Finally, we have the postorder enumeration. Like the other two, a postorder *display ()* is quite simple:

```
template<class DataType>
void AbstractBinaryTree<DataType>::display (ostream& os)
{
    if (isEmpty()) return;
    left()->display (os);
    right()->display (os);
    os<< rootData() << " ";
}
```

Postorder Enumeration Using the PostOrderEnumerator Class

Again, the *Enumeration* subclass should be implemented using a stack, and the sequence of activation records should be considered. The first activation record contains a pointer to *bt*, which must be retained until both its subtrees have been fully displayed, at which point its *rootData ()* is returned and *display ()* exits.

We can see that *bt->rootData ()* can be displayed in only three circumstances: (1) both subtrees are empty; (2) the left subtree is non-empty but has been fully displayed, while the right subtree is empty; (3) the right subtree is non-empty but has been fully displayed. We can also see that if a tree has any non-empty subtrees, the pointer to only one will appear in the activation records at any one time.

The above considerations suggest that, in the implementation of the *PostOrderEnumerator* class, the tree should be pushed on the *Stack* first, followed by its left subtree, if non-empty, or by its right subtree, if non-empty. This process should be repeated on the subtree, and so on, until a tree T with two empty subtrees is reached. T is popped off the stack and its root data returned by *nextElement ()*. Given the way trees are pushed on the *Stack*, the element just after (i.e., below) T will be its parent. The *PostOrderEnumerator*'s handling of the *Stack* will depend on whether T was a left subtree of its parent. If T was a left subtree, then its parent's right subtree, if non-empty, should be pushed on the *Stack*, followed by one of its subtrees and so on as above. But if T was a right subtree, or if the right subtree is empty, then both of the parent's subtrees have been handled, and on the next call to *nextElement ()*, T's parent should be popped off the *Stack* and its root data returned, meaning that nothing should be pushed on the *Stack* after T is popped.

Given the above discussion, the implementation of *PostOrderEnumerator* is as follows:

```
template<class DataType>
class PostOrderEnumerator : public Enumeration<DataType>
{
protected:
    AbstractBinaryTree<DataType>* _tree;
    StackLinked< AbstractBinaryTree<DataType>* >* _stack;
    // since we have to separately return each node found, we
    // can't proceed recursively and have to have a stack
    void pushToBtm (AbstractBinaryTree<DataType>* tree);
public:
    PostOrderEnumerator (AbstractBinaryTree<DataType>* t);
    virtual bool hasMoreElements ();
    virtualDataType& nextElement ();
};
// -------------------------------------------------------
template<class DataType>
PostOrderEnumerator<DataType>::PostOrderEnumerator
        (AbstractBinaryTree<DataType>* t)
{
    _tree = t;
    _stack = new StackLinked<AbstractBinaryTree<DataType>*>();
    if (_tree != NULL)
        pushToBtm (_tree);
}
// -------------------------------------------------------
template<class DataType>
void PostOrderEnumerator<DataType>::pushToBtm
        (AbstractBinaryTree<DataType>* tree)
{
    if (tree->isEmpty ()) return;
    do {
      _stack->push (tree);
    // if there is a left child, it goes first
      if (!tree->left()->isEmpty())
      {
            tree = tree->left();
      }
```

```
    // but if not, the right child, sits atop the parent
        else if (!tree->right()->isEmpty())
              tree = tree->right();
    // otherwise, the parent is on the stack and ready to
    // return
        else return;
    } while (true);
}
```

The *hasMoreElements*() method is the same as for the preceding classes, but the *nextElement*() method is a little more complicated than the corresponding methods of the previous classes, as we must pop off the top tree and check the new top tree (if any) to determine whether it is the parent. If it is, and the tree popped off is the left child, we must call *pushToBtm*() on the right subtree. Thus, the method is as follows:

```
template <class DataType>
DataType& PostOrderEnumerator<DataType>::nextElement ()
{
    if (_stack->isEmpty() ) throw BinaryTreeEmptyTree();
    AbstractBinaryTree<DataType>* tree = _stack->pop();
// if the stack is empty after tree is popped,
// tree must be _tree, so we are done.
// Otherwise, check for left child or right child status.
    if (!_stack->isEmpty() )
    {
        AbstractBinaryTree<DataType>* parent = _stack->peek();
        if (parent != NULL)
        {
// if this is the left child of the parent, the right subtree
// (if any) must be returned before the parent.
            if (parent->left() == tree)
            {
                pushToBtm (parent->right());
            }
        }
    }
    return tree->rootData();
}
```

Once again, the reader should write a *postOrderEnumerator()* method for the *AbstractBinaryTree* class and verify that this enumerator works correctly and that it properly handles empty trees.

6.1.2.6   The display() and printtree() Methods

We can implement the *display()* method for the *AbstractBinaryTree* using an enumerator, as we have done for previous data structures. Which form of enumeration should we use for the *display()* method? There are arguments in favor of each of the three, but we have elected to use an inorder enumeration:

```
template<class DataType>
void AbstractBinaryTree<DataType>::display (ostream& os)
{
    bool first = true;
    Enumeration<DataType>* e = inOrderEnumerator();
    os<< "<";
    while (e->hasMoreElements())
    {
        if (!first) os << ", ";
        first = false;
        os<< e->nextElement();
    }
    os<< ">";
    delete e;
}
```

For convenience, we shall write one more method for *AbstractBinary-Tree*, which displays the actual tree structure of the binary tree. The right subtree of each tree will be displayed above and to the right of the tree; it's left subtree will be displayed below and to the right. Thus, the structure can be viewed as rotated 90° to the right. In order to indent properly, we must have a parameter establishing the indentation level. For the first call, this level should be 0. If we wished to conceal this complexity from the user, we could make the method below a protected method and write another for the caller to use. This is left as an exercise for the reader.

```
template<class DataType>
void AbstractBinaryTree<DataType>::printtree
                 (ostream& os, int level)
{
    if (isEmpty()) return;
    right()->printtree (os,level+1);
    for (int i = 0; i < level; i++) os << "   ";
    os<< " +--" << rootData() << endl;
    left()->printtree (os,level+1);
}
```

The reader should revise the *main*() function previously provided to use this method and display the tree structure rather than just the data.

6.2   The Binary Search Tree Data Structure

The binary search tree is a binary tree with the following additional properties if the tree is nonempty:

1. Its subtrees are themselves binary search trees;
2. The root value is greater than or equal to that of all nodes in the left subtree and less than that of all nodes in the right subtree, where "greater than" and "less than" are defined appropriately according to the type of data stored in the nodes.

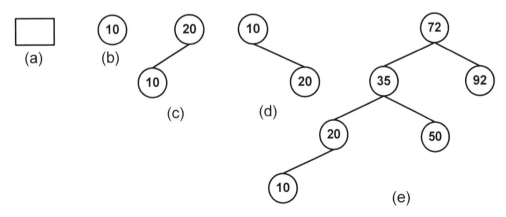

Figure 6.8:   Examples of a few types of binary search trees. Note that (a) is an empty tree.

In order to locate a particular element say 10 in the binary search tree (e) in Figure 6.5, we start the comparison from the root with the element 72. Since 10 is less than 72 our procedure to locate 10 starts from the left subtree of the root. After comparing with 35 and since 10 is less than 35 we continue to locate starting from the left subtree of the node with value 35. The process will continue until the element 10 is found. During the search process, if we end up with a leaf node then we can declare that the element is not found. As you can see from the above description each element in the tree is guiding the search process and tells which direction to follow the search based on the result of the comparison.

Does this not appear to be like a binary search? Recall in the binary search the result of the comparison dictates which half to process. In fact there is a close relationship between binary search and the binary search tree. The time complexity of a binary search on a n element sorted array is $O(\log_2 n)$. In order to locate an element in a binary search tree as explained above, we have to compare the element we are looking for with exactly one element from each level of the binary tree. The maximum number of levels in a binary search tree (or the height of the tree) with n nodes is n when the value in the root is greater (resp. lesser) than the value of its left child and the value of the left child is greater (resp. lesser) than the value of its left child and so on. This is illustrated in Figure 6.6.

The advantages of a binary search tree over a sorted array are that adding and removing elements are easier on a binary search tree. For example, if we have to add an element to a sorted array, first we have to find the appropriate position for which we can perform a binary search (as we did in the case of binary insertion sort in Chapter 3) and then move the existing elements from the point of insertion to the right. These operations would take $O(n)$ time on a n element sorted array. In the case of a binary search tree we will perform a search on the element to be inserted and when the search terminates at the leaf node we will replace the leaf node with a node containing the new element. This operation on a binary search tree does not involve moving data and has the same complexity as the search (or find) method. Note that the time complexity of the search method on the binary search tree is proportional to the height of the tree.

The binary search tree has a very close relationship with the binary search algorithm previously described, as we shall see.

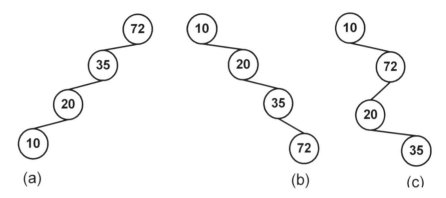

Figure 6.9:   Binary search tree showing the worst case height for storing four
elements. Note that the minimum height binary search tree for four
elements is 3.

6.2.1   Abstract Data Type

A minimal specification of an abstract data type for the binary search tree is as follows:

```
createEmpty()
    // creates an empty binary search tree
createNonempty (data)
    // create a binary search tree with data in the root
isEmpty()
    // returns true if tree is empty, but otherwise false
data ()
    // returns the data in the root of the tree
Height ()
    // returns the height (or depth) of the tree
Size ()
    // returns the number of nodes in the tree
find (q)
    // returns a node which matches q, or null if no match
insert (data)
    // inserts data into tree
delete (data)
    // removes data from tree
rangeSearch (low, high)
    // returns all node values between low and high, inclusive
```

6.2.2   Implementation of the Binary Search Tree

We shall implement the binary search tree abstract data type recursively in this section, as we did the binary tree. There are other ways to implement it, as we shall see.

6.2.2.1   Node Data Type

In implementing the binary search tree abstract data type, note that a binary search tree must make a three-way comparison on its nodes in order to satisfy its second property. Therefore, unlike the binary tree class previously implemented, the binary search tree class must store instances of some type which supports all of the comparison operators.

6.2.2.2   Exceptions

In accordance with our practice, we will create a family of exceptions associated with *BinarySearchTree*. Because of the obvious connection between binary search trees and binary trees, which we will explore in more depth in the course of implementing the binary search tree, we will add the binary search tree exceptions to the binary tree exception hierarchy.

Since the binary search tree will be implemented recursively, it will have left and right subtrees which are themselves binary search trees. However, we certainly cannot allow a user to obtain one of these subtrees and insert into it, as that might well destroy the second binary search tree property given above, that is, the property that the root value of a tree is less than or equal to the root value of its left subtree and greater than that of its right subtree. In the new class, we will wish to throw an exception if the user obtains a pointer to a subtree and attempts to modify it.

■   `class BinarySearchTreeChangedSubtree : public BinaryTreeException { };`

We will of course wish to use the *BinaryTreeEmptyTree* and *Binary-TreeMemory* exceptions as well. If we search for a node and do not find it, we will need to throw another exception:

■   `class BinarySearchTreeNotFound : public BinaryTreeException { };`

6.2.2.3   Abstract Base Class Definition

We can now make a first cut at a design of an abstract base class for the binary search tree. For convenience, we have added one more method, *contains*(), which allows us to determine whether a given object is present in the tree.

```
template<class DataType>
class AbstractBinarySearchTree
{
friend ostream& operator << (ostream& s,
    AbstractBinarySearchTree<DataType>&bt);
public:
    virtual ~AbstractBinarySearchTree ();
    virtualDataType& rootData () = NULL;
    virtual bool isEmpty() = NULL;
        // returns true if tree is empty, but otherwise returns
        // false
    virtual int Height () = NULL;
        // returns the height (or depth) of the tree
    virtual int Size ()= NULL;
        // returns the number of nodes in the tree
    virtualDataType find (DataType& q) = NULL;
        // returns a node which matches q,
        // or throws exception if no node matches
    virtual bool contains (const DataType& q) = NULL;
        // returns true if tree contains a node which matches q
    virtual void insert (DataType& data) = NULL;
        // inserts data while maintaining
        // binary search tree properties
    virtual void remove (DataType& data) = NULL;
        // removes the node matching data, if any,
        // while maintaining binary search tree properties
    virtual void makeEmpty ()= NULL;
        // empties tree by setting root to
        // null and removing subtrees
    virtual Enumeration<DataType>* inOrderEnumerator ();
        // Returns an inorder enumeration of the data
        // from all nodes contained in the tree
    virtual Enumeration<DataType>* postOrderEnumerator ();
        // Returns a postorder enumeration of the data
        // from all nodes contained in the tree
    virtual Enumeration<DataType>* preOrderEnumerator ();
```

```
        // Returns a preorder enumeration of the data
        // from all nodes contained in the tree
    virtual void printtree (ostream& os, int level);
        // display tree structure (rotated)
    virtual void rangeSearch (DataType& low, DataType& high);
        // outputs all node values in range low to high, inclusive
};
```

Relationship Between AbstractBinaryTree and AbstractBinarySearchTree

We can clearly see that there is a relationship between the *AbstractBinary-Tree* and the *AbstractBinarySearchTree*. Both have the methods *isEmpty()*, *Height()*, *Size()*, *makeEmpty()*, *printtree()*, *inOrderEnumerator()*, *postOrderEnumerator()*, and *preOrderEnumerator()*. It would be helpful if binary search trees could be enumerated by the existing *InOrderEnumerator*, *PostOrderEnumerator*, and *PreOrderEnumerator* classes. Such reuse requires that *AbstractBinaryTree* and *AbstractBinarySearchTree* be related in a hierarchy and that the parent class declare the enumeration methods, along with *left()*, *right()*, and *root()*, all of which are used by the enumerator classes.

The *left()*, and *right()* methods are not part of the binary search tree abstract data type, for the very good reason that they permit direct access to portions of the tree, which might permit changes which destroy the binary search tree properties, as described under **Exceptions**, above. For implementation reasons, however we will provide such functions in our implementation of the binary search tree, taking precautions to ensure that the subtree cannot be used to change the original tree. However, the *setroot()*, *setright()*, and *setleft()* methods of the *AbstractBinaryTree* interface are absolutely inappropriate in a binary search tree interface, as all of them have the potential to destroy the binary search tree properties, and we cannot reasonably implement them so as to avoid the problems. Thus, if they were part of the binary search tree interface, we would have to throw an exception or else produce no result. On the other hand, the *find()*, *insert()*, *remove()*, and *rangeSearch()* methods of the binary search tree interface are not appropriate for the binary tree interface, as a binary tree has no way of searching for a particular value except exhaustively.

Summarizing the above discussion, *AbstractBinaryTree* and *AbstractBinarySearchTree* have these methods in common: *isEmpty()*, *Height()*, *inOrderEnumerator()*, *postOrderEnumerator()*, *preOrderEnumerator()*, *Size()*, *makeEmpty()*, and *printtree()*.

They could usefully share these methods: *left()*, *right()*, and *root()*. *AbstractBinaryTree*, alone, has these methods: *setroot()*, *setright()*, and *setleft()*, and *AbstractBinarySearchTree*, alone, has these methods: *find()*, *insert()*, *remove()*, and *rangeSearch()*. Neither class' methods are a subset of the other's, though there is a large intersection.

The *AbstractBinaryTree* class should not be the parent of the *Abstract-BinarySearchTree* class, nor should the *AbstractBinarySearchTree* interface be the parent of the *AbstractBinaryTree*. Yet they are clearly related, and the only reasonable way to relate them is to make them siblings: the children of a parent class. We will call this parent interface *AbstractBinaryTreeAccess*, since it declares many of the accessor methods for binary trees and binary search trees. Thus, we will create a hierarchy of abstract classes:

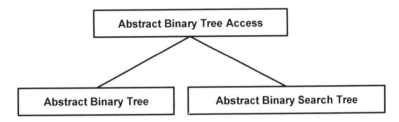

Figure 6.10:   Hierarchy of abstract classes for the binary tree data structure.

But now we have another problem: if *left()* is declared in *AbstractBina-ryTreeAccess*, then what is its return type? If its return type is *AbstractBina-ryTreeAccess*, both *BinaryTree* and *BinarySearchTree* can implement it, but most uses of *left()* in the *BinaryTree* class will require type casting, which is undesirable. If its return type is *AbstractBinaryTree*, the *Binary-SearchTree* class will not be able to implement *left()* in a reasonable way. Of course one could have avoided this organization altogether and have allow the classes *AbstractBinaryTree* and *AbstractBinarySearchTree* to have the class *AbstractBinaryTreeAccess* as one of its fields. But such an implementation would make the access to the methods in *AbstractBinaryTreeAccess* non intuitive and hence we have opted to proceed with the above implementation.

This suggests that there should be two methods to access the left subtree in the *AbstractBinaryTree* class: *left()*, which is of type *AbstractBinary-TreeAccess*, and *btleft()*, which is of type *AbstractBinaryTree*. The *AbstractBinarySearchTree* class will have only *left()*. The three existing enumerators can then be modified to use *AbstractBinaryTreeAccess* at every point instead of *AbstractBinaryTree*. This modification is strictly mechanical and left for the reader.

Three Binary Tree Abstract Classes

Thus, we have three abstract classes. First, *AbstractBinaryTreeAccess*:

```
template<class DataType>
class AbstractBinaryTreeAccess
{
public:
    virtual ~AbstractBinaryTreeAccess();
    virtual bool isEmpty() = NULL;
        // returns true if tree is empty,
        // but otherwise returns false
    virtual int Height ()= NULL;
        // returns the height (or depth) of the tree
    virtual int Size ()= NULL;
        // returns the number of nodes in the tree
    virtualDataType& rootData ()= NULL;
        // returns data from the root
    virtual AbstractBinaryTreeAccess<DataType>* left ()= NULL;
        // returns the left subtree
    virtual AbstractBinaryTreeAccess<DataType>* right ()= NULL;
        // returns the right subtree
    virtual Enumeration<DataType>* inOrderEnumerator ();
        // Returns an inorder enumeration of the data
        // from all nodes contained in the tree
    virtual Enumeration<DataType>* postOrderEnumerator ();
        // Returns a postorder enumeration of the data
        // from all nodes contained in the tree
    virtual Enumeration<DataType>* preOrderEnumerator ();
        // Returns a preorder enumeration of the data
        // from all nodes contained in the tree
    virtual void display (ostream& os);
    virtual void printtree (ostream& os, int level);
        // display tree structure (rotated)
};
```

The implementations of the non-virtual methods of the class are identical to the prior implementations of the identically named methods in the *AbstractBinary-Tree* class, with the exception of the name of the class.

The second class is the revised *AbstractBinaryTree* (which requires some modifications to *BinaryTree* itself):

```
template<class DataType>
class AbstractBinaryTree : public AbstractBinaryTreeAccess
<DataType>
{
public:
    virtual ~AbstractBinaryTree ();
    virtual AbstractBinaryTree<DataType>* btleft () = NULL;
        // returns the left subtree
    virtual AbstractBinaryTree<DataType>* btright () = NULL;
        // returns the right subtree
    virtual void setrootData (DataType& data) = NULL;
    virtual AbstractBinaryTree<DataType>* setleft
            (AbstractBinaryTree<DataType>* newleft) = NULL;
        // sets the left subtree to newleft;
        // return value: the former left subtree
    virtual AbstractBinaryTree<DataType>* setright
            (AbstractBinaryTree<DataType>* newright) = NULL;
        // sets the right subtree to newright;
        // return value: the former right subtree
};

// -------------------------------------------------------
template<class DataType>
AbstractBinaryTree<DataType>::~AbstractBinaryTree () { }
```

And finally, the revised *AbstractBinarySearchTree*:

```
template<class DataType>
class AbstractBinarySearchTree : public
AbstractBinaryTreeAccess<DataType>
{
public:
    virtual ~AbstractBinarySearchTree ();
    virtual bool contains (const DataType& q);
        // returns true if tree contains a node which matches q
    virtualDataType find (DataType& q) = NULL;
        // returns a node which matches q,
        // or throws an exception if no node matches
    virtual void insert (DataType& data) = NULL;
        // inserts data while maintaining
        // binary search tree properties
    virtual void remove (DataType& data) = NULL;
        // removes the node matching data, if any,
        // while maintaining binary search tree properties
    virtual void rangeSearch (DataType& low, DataType& high) = NULL;
        // outputs all node values in range low to high, inclusive
};
```

6.2.2.4   Class Definition

At long last, we are able to begin implementing the binary search tree abstract data type in a class called *BinarySearchTree*. Initially, we can see that we will want to provide methods to create both empty and non-empty trees.

Fields, Constructors, and Destructors

The observation above, that subtrees cannot be changed directly, suggests that *BinarySearchTree* should have a boolean field which indicates whether a given instance is a subtree or not. Therefore, the *BinarySearchTree* will have the same fields as the *BinaryTree*, plus a *_subtree* field. The user cannot create subtrees, as the public constructors always set this field to *false*.

As in the case of the *BinaryTree*, we will not allow a non-empty tree to have NULL subtrees, but will create empty subtrees when a non-empty tree is created. Since subclasses of *BinarySearchTree* will need to create subtrees in their own image, we will write a method, which can be overloaded, to create empty subtrees.

Finally, all of the reasoning which applied to the *BinaryTree* destructor applies even more strongly to the *BinarySearchTree* destructor: there is no reason to expect the user to dispose of the subtrees, so the instance being destroyed must dispose of them. Since the code of the destructor is identical to that of the *BinaryTree* destructor, it will not be presented here.

Thus, our class initially appears as follows:

```
template<class DataType>
class BinarySearchTree : public AbstractBinarySearchTree
<DataType>
{
protected:
    DataType* _rootData;
    BinarySearchTree<DataType>* _left;
    BinarySearchTree<DataType>* _right;
    bool _subtree;
public:
    BinarySearchTree ();
    BinarySearchTree (DataType& data);
    virtual ~BinarySearchTree ();
};
// ------------------------------------------------------------
template<class DataType>
BinarySearchTree<DataType>::BinarySearchTree ()
{
    _rootData = NULL;
    _left = NULL;
    _right = NULL;
    _subtree = false;
}
// ------------------------------------------------------------
template<class DataType>
BinarySearchTree<DataType>::BinarySearchTree (DataType& data)
```

```
{
    _subtree = false;
    _rootData = new DataType(data);
    if (_rootData == NULL) throw BinaryTreeMemory();
    _left = makeSubtree ();
    _right = makeSubtree ();
}
// ------------------------------------------------------------
template<class DataType>
BinarySearchTree<DataType>* BinarySearchTree<DataType>::make
Subtree()
{
    BinarySearchTree<DataType>* bst = new
BinarySearchTree<DataType> ();
    bst->_subtree = true;
    return bst;
}
```

Accessor Methods

Many of the accessor methods are quite straightforward and are presented below
without comment.

```
template<class DataType>
bool BinarySearchTree<DataType>::isEmpty()
{
    return (_rootData == NULL);
}
// ------------------------------------------------------------
template<class DataType>
DataType& BinarySearchTree<DataType>::rootData ()
{
    if (isEmpty()) throw BinaryTreeEmptyTree();
    return *_rootData;
}
// ------------------------------------------------------------
```

```
template<class DataType>
AbstractBinaryTreeAccess<DataType>*
        BinarySearchTree<DataType>::left ()
{ return _left; }
// ----------------------------------------------------------
template<class DataType>
AbstractBinaryTreeAccess<DataType>*
        BinarySearchTree<DataType>::right ()
{ return _right; }
// ----------------------------------------------------------
template<class DataType>
bool BinarySearchTree<DataType>::subtree() { return _subtree; }
```

The *Height*() and *Size*() methods are identical to those of the `BinaryTree` class:

```
template<class DataType>
int BinarySearchTree<DataType>::Height ()
{
    if (isEmpty()) return 0;
    return (1 + max (_left->Height(), _right->Height()));
}
// ----------------------------------------------------------
template<class DataType>
int BinarySearchTree<DataType>::Size ()
    // returns the number of nodes in the tree
{
    if (isEmpty())
        return 0;
    return (1 + _left->Size() + _right->Size());
}
```

Mutator Methods

Just as we had a *makeEmpty*() method in the `BinaryTree` class, we shall have one in the `BinarySearchTree` class. However, since we do not want the user to modify subtrees, this method will throw an exception if called on a subtree.

```
template<class DataType>
void BinarySearchTree<DataType>::makeEmpty ()
{
    if (_subtree)  throw BinarySearchTreeChangedSubtree();
    if (_rootData != NULL)
        delete _rootData;
    _rootData = NULL;
    if (_left != NULL)
        delete _left;
    _left = NULL;
    if (_right != NULL)
        delete _right;
    _right = NULL;
}
```

We will also find it convenient to copy one binary search tree to another, but this is a method that should not be made available to the user at all, and therefore should definitely be protected:

```
template<class DataType>
void BinarySearchTree<DataType>::copyTree
    (BinarySearchTree<DataType>* bst)
{
    _rootData = bst->_rootData;
    if (_left != NULL) _left->makeEmpty();
    _left = bst->_left;
    if (_right != NULL) _right->makeEmpty();
    _right = bst->_right;
}
```

Looking at the first statement in the copyTree() method it is clear that the new tree that is begin constructed is pointing to the same data (_rootData) for the tree bst that is passed. Hence once we have called *copyTree ()*, there will be two *Binary-SearchTree* instances (that on which *copyTree ()* was called and that which was passed as *bst*), with pointers to the same data, and left and right subtrees. If we want to delete one of them, we must set its pointers to NULL, or it will delete the data to which the other points. Setting its pointers to NULL takes three statements, so we will package those three up into one method, which must be protected since we certainly do not want the user arbitrarily setting the pointers:

```
template<class DataType>
void BinarySearchTree<DataType>::_makeNull ()
{
    _rootData = NULL;
    _left = NULL;
    _right = NULL;
}
```

The find() Method

The remaining three important methods, *find()*, *insert()*, and *remove()*, are entirely different from the methods of `BinaryTree`, and require some thought. The *find()* method is easily implemented by analogy with the binary search algorithm:

```
template<class DataType>
DataType BinarySearchTree<DataType>::find (DataType& q)
{
    BinarySearchTree<DataType>* bst = this;
    while (true)
    {
        if (bst->isEmpty()) throw BinarySearchTreeNotFound();
        if (*(bst->_rootData) < q)
            bst = bst->_right;
        else if (*(bst->_rootData) > q)
            bst = bst->_left;
        else
            return bst->rootData();
    }
}
```

The total number of comparisons in *find()* is equal to the height of the tree, which is, at worst, equal to the number of nodes in the tree. So, if the number of nodes is n, the complexity of *find()* is $O(n)$.

Consider the binary search tree shown in the figure below. The square boxes indicate the empty subtree or nodes wherein the _rootData, _left, and _right values are all set to NULL.

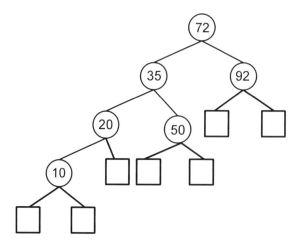

Figure 6.11:   A binary search tree with empty nodes shown in square boxes.

Now let us say that we are looking into finding the value of 45 in the binary search tree. Clearly, the value should be to the left of node that contains 50 and it is not there. The following figure shows the sequence of comparisons that are performed when finding the value of 45 in the binary search tree.

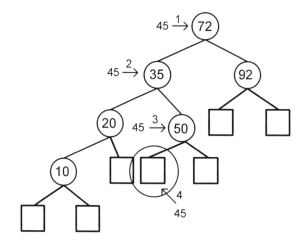

Figure 6.12:   Sequence of comparisons numbered on the top of the arrows that are performed to find the value of 45 in the binary search tree. The find method throws an exception in this case while the _find method will return the empty node shown in the circle where 45 should have been found.

Let us now consider *insert()* and *remove()*. The *insert()* method needs to identify a node matching *data*, if any exists, but if none exists, *insert()* needs to identify the nearest node, so that it can place *data* in the appropriate subtree. Similarly, *remove()* needs to identify a node matching *data*, if any exists, so that it can be removed. Code resembling that of *find()* could be placed in the other two methods, or we could create a protected method which all three could use. This greatly simplifies the *find ()* method previously given:

```
template<class DataType>
BinarySearchTree<DataType>* BinarySearchTree<DataType>::_find
        (DataType& data)
{
    BinarySearchTree<DataType>* bst = this;
    while (true)
    {
        if (bst->isEmpty())
            return bst;
        if (*(bst->_rootData) < data)
            bst = bst->_right;
        else if (*(bst->_rootData) > data)
            bst = bst->_left;
        else
            return bst;
    }
}
// ------------------------------------------------------------
template<class DataType>
DataType BinarySearchTree<DataType>::find (DataType& q)
{
    BinarySearchTree<DataType>* bst = _find (q);
    if (bst->isEmpty()) throw BinarySearchTreeNotFound();
    return bst->rootData();
}
```

We can now immediately implement the *contains()* method using *_find()*:

```
template<class DataType>
bool BinarySearchTree<DataType>::contains (const DataType& q)
{
    BinarySearchTree<DataType>* bst = _find (q);
    return !bst->isEmpty();
}
```

The insert() *method*

With *_find()*, we can readily implement *insert()*. If *_find()* returns an empty tree, then *data* belongs in that empty tree which will no longer be empty. If *_find()* returns a non-empty tree, then the root of that tree matches *data* on the comparison, and its value is to be overwritten by *data*.

```
template<class DataType>
void BinarySearchTree<DataType>::insert (DataType& data)
{
    if (_subtree) throw BinarySearchTreeChangedSubtree();
    BinarySearchTree<DataType>* bst = _find (data);
    if (bst->isEmpty())
    {
        bst->_rootData = new DataType (data);
        bst->_left = makeSubtree ();
        bst->_right = makeSubtree ();
    }
    else
    {
        delete bst->_rootData;
        bst->_root = new DataType (data);
    }
}
```

Now let us say that we would like to insert the value 45 into the binary search tree shown in Figure 6.12. Based on the above program segment the empty node in the shown inside the circle (Figure 6.12) will be returned. The _rootData of the returned empty node will be set to an object that contains 45 as shown in the following Figure.

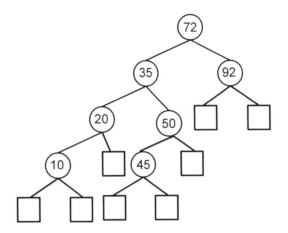

Figure 6.13:   A binary search after inserting a value of 45 into the tree that is shown
in Figure 6.12.

It should be evident that the complexity of *insert*() is also $O(n)$, since *insert*()
calls _*find*() which, like *find*() is $O(n)$, and everything else *insert*() does can be done
in constant time. To insert all *n* nodes of an n–node binary search tree would take
$n \times O(n)$ in the worst case, or $O(n^2)$ time.

The remove() *method*

The only important method remaining to be implemented is *remove*(). This method
too can be implemented by calling _*find*(), which returns a `BinarySearchTree`,
bst. There are four possibilities with regard to *bst* and these are illustrated with the
binary search tree show in Figure 6.14:

1. If *bst* is empty, then *data* was not present in the tree and *remove*() should throw an
    exception. For example, we are tried to remove node that has a value of 100, the
    remove operation will throw an exception.

2. If *bst* has empty subtrees, then it will become empty when its root value is removed;
    this is easily implemented. Consider that we remove the node that has a value of
    10. Both its left and right subtrees are empty (square boxes) and hence we can
    simply delete 10 (that is, delete _rootData on the node that contains the value 10).
    We next set the new _rootData value to NULL, delete the left and right subtrees
    (even though they are empty they are all objects and can be deleted) and set them
    to NULL.

3. If *bst* has a single non-empty subtree, that subtree can simply take the place of *bst*, though *bst*'s subtree flag must not be overwritten by the subtree's flag. If we want to remove node that has a value of 50 with can simply copy the contents of node 45. That is _rootData (resp. _left and _right) of node 50 will now be the _rootData (resp. _left and _right) of node 45.

4. The difficult case is where *bst* has two non-empty subtrees. In this case, we need to replace *bst* with a node that is greater than any node in the left subtree and less than any node in the right subtree. We can find such a node by starting with the right subtree and seeking down the left subtrees until we find a tree *t* that has an empty left subtree. The tree *t* that we will find is called the *inorder successor* of *bst*, since *t* will be immediately after *bst* in the inorder enumeration of the binary search tree. The root of that tree replaces *bst*'s root, and that tree's root is deleted, meaning that its own right subtree must replace it, or it must be made empty. For example, let us consider the case where remove is executed on the node with value 35. The value 35 will be replaced with value 45 (the smallest value in the right subtree of 35) and the remove operation will be performed on old node that contains 45. Once the second remove operation is performed, node 48 will become the left child of node 50. For the second remove operation we will follow the steps at outlined for case (3) above.

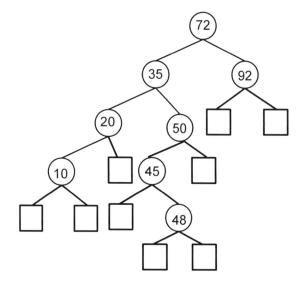

Figure 6.14: Binary search tree is used for explaining the remove operation.

```
template<class DataType>
void BinarySearchTree<DataType>::remove (DataType& data)
{
    if (_subtree) throw BinarySearchTreeChangedSubtree();
    BinarySearchTree<DataType>* bst;
    BinarySearchTree<DataType>* bst2;
    BinarySearchTree<DataType>* bst3;

    bst = _find (data);
    if (bst->isEmpty()) throw BinarySearchTreeNotFound();

    // dispose of the existing data; the pointer will be over
    // written delete bst->_rootData;

// ------------------------------------------------------------
    if (bst->_left->isEmpty())
    {
    // the left subtree exists, but the pointer will be overwritten,
    // so we must dispose of it
      delete bst->_left;
      bst2 = bst->_right; // save the pointer to the right subtree
      bst->copyTree (bst2); // copy the right subtree;
                      // this empties tree if right empty
      bst2->_makeNull ();    // prepare right subtree for deletion
      delete bst2;    // delete right subtree to avoid garbage
    }

// ------------------------------------------------------------
    else if (bst->_right->isEmpty())
    {
    // the right subtree exists, but the pointer will be overwritten,
    // so we must dispose of it
      delete bst->_right;
      bst2 = bst->_left;   // save the pointer to the left subtree
      bst->copyTree (bst2);    // copy the left subtree
      bst2->_makeNull (); // prepare left subtree for deletion
      delete bst2;         // delete left subtree to avoid garbage
```

```
        }

//  . . . . . . . . . . . . . . . . . . . . . . . . . . . . . . . . . . . . . . . . . . . . . . . . . . . .
    else        // both subtrees non-empty
    {
    // move to the right
      bst2 = bst->_right;
    // then move down to the left as far as possible
      while (!bst2->_left->isEmpty()) bst2 = bst2->_left;
    // overwrite the data pointer
      bst->_root = bst2->_rootData;

    // bst2's left child is known to be empty and
    // pointer will be overwritten
      delete bst2->_left;

    // now bst2's right child is copied into it
      if (bst2->_right->isEmpty())
      {
        delete bst2->_right;
        bst2->_makeNull();
      }
      else
      {
        bst3 = bst2->_right;
        bst2->copyTree(bst2->_right);
        bst3->_makeNull ();
        delete bst3;
      }
    }
  }
}
```

The complexity of *remove*() is once again $O(n)$, since it calls *_find*() and then, if necessary, seeks down the left subtrees of the deleted node's right subtree, requiring at most n steps. Every action in *remove*(), other than those two, can be done in constant time.

The reader should verify that *find*() and *remove*() work correctly, even on empty binary search trees.

Unfortunately, although the BinarySearchTree class does work correctly, it is not as efficient as it might be. If, for instance, nodes are added to an empty tree in the order A, B, C, D, E, F, G, then the tree will have height 7, although seven elements could be stored in a binary tree of height 3. More sophisticated binary search trees are able to maintain themselves at or close to the minimum height required for their size, as will be described in the next chapter.

The rangeSearch() *Method*

Our implementation of the *rangeSearch*() method merely outputs the nodes in the specified range. An implementation that would return the nodes is left as an exercise for the reader.

The *rangeSearch*() method can be implemented recursively: if the root value is less than the *low* value, then its left subtree can be completely ignored, and similarly the right subtree can be ignored if the root value is greater than the *high* value.

We have given a inorder listing of the nodes, but of course other orderings can be used:

```
template<class DataType>
void BinarySearchTree<DataType>::rangeSearch (DataType& low,
DataType& high)
{
    if (isEmpty()) return;
    if (*_rootData >= low)
    {
        _left->rangeSearch(low,high);
        if (*_rootData <= high)
        cout << *_rootData << " ";
    }
    if (*_rootData <= high)
    _right->rangeSearch(low,high);
}
```

The enumeration and display methods for the *BinarySearchTree* class are inherited from the *AbstractBinaryTree* class, and need not be reimplemented.

6.2.2.5 Testing the Class

The following *main()* function tests the *insert()* method. Writing a *main()* function to exercise the other methods is left as an exercise.

```
void main()
{
    BinarySearchTree<char> bst ('Q');
    cout<< bst << endl;
    bst.insert ('J');
    cout<< bst << endl;
    bst.insert ('A');
    cout<< bst << endl;
    bst.insert ('S');
    cout<< bst << endl;
    bst.insert ('B');
    cout<< bst << endl;
}
```

When the above code is tested, the output is:

```
<Q>
<J, Q>
<A, J, Q>
<A, B, J, Q>
<A, B, J, Q, S>
```

Although the nodes were added in the order Q, J, A, S, B, they are correctly printed in alphabetical order.

6.3 Sets

A set can be informally defined as a collection of distinct, distinguishable objects. A set is not ordered, so it may seem odd to consider this data type in a chapter devoted to binary search trees. It is however convenient in many cases to implement the set data type using a binary search tree, so the data type will be presented here.

6.3.1 Abstract Data Type

A minimal specification of an Abstract Data Type for the set is as follows:

```
CreateEmpty ()
    // creates an empty set
isEmpty ()
    // returns true if set is empty, but otherwise returns false
Size ()
    // returns the number of elements in the set, or its cardinality
contains (element)
    // returns true if element is in the set, but otherwise
    // returns false
add (element)
    // adds element to the set; if the set already contains
    // element, no effect
remove (element)
    // removes element from the set; if element was not in the
    // set, no effect
intersection (otherSet)
    // returns a new set containing those elements in both set
    // and otherSet
union (otherSet)
    // returns a new set containing those elements in set or
    // otherSet or both
difference (otherSet)
    // returns a new set containing those elements in set but
    // not in otherSet
equals (otherSet)
    // returns true if every element of set is in otherSet and
    // vice versa, otherwise false
isSubsetOf (otherSet)
    // returns true if every element of set is in otherSet but
    // perhaps not vice versa, otherwise false
```

6.3.2   Implementation of the Set Abstract Data Type

The operations intersection, union, and difference in the set abstract data type produce a problem in our normal construction of a hierarchy based on an abstract base class and concrete subclasses. If *intersection*() is declared in the abstract base class `AbstractSet`, what is its return type?

The return type should not be `AbstractSet`, for that return type would imply that we have created an instance of the class and returned it on the stack, but we cannot create an instance of `AbstractSet` because it is an abstract class. We might consider returning a reference to `AbstractSet`, but that would be a reference to an object created on the stack and returning it would be a serious error. We could also return a pointer to a newly created instance of a concrete subclass, but that requires the caller to delete the instance. For convenience in the implementation, we have instead implemented three methods corresponding to but not identical to the abstract data type methods. The methods, *makeIntersection*(), *makeUnion*(), and *makeDifference*(), alter the set on which they are called so that it itself becomes the corresponding set. This avoids the problem of disposing of a new instance.

6.3.2.1   Element data type

The elements of a set must support at least an equality test in order for us to determine whether a given element is present or not. Strictly speaking, no other comparison is required since sets are not ordered. However, as we shall see, a tree-based implementation of the set will require the ability to perform a three-way comparison, and a bitset implementation will require that the elements be assigned numbers. Thus, in this case the type of data we have may determine which type of set we can use.

6.3.2.2   Exceptions

There is basically only one error that can occur with respect to a general set: it may not fit into the available memory. Since a bitset-based implementation is limited to a very small universe of elements, it is possible that the caller might try to add an element which is outside the universe, or to form a union with a TreeSet containing elements outside the universe. We will declare a small family of exceptions:

```
class SetException : public Exception { };
class SetMemoryException : public SetException { };
class SetOutOfUniverseException : public SetException { };
```

6.3.2.3 Abstract Base Class

With the exception classes in hand, we can prepare an abstract base class based on the abstract data type. In addition to those operations required by the abstract data type, we shall include operations for enumerating the elements. These operations are not part of the abstract data type, which assumes that the elements are unordered, but we will find that it is convenient to order the elements in our implementation.

```
#include <iostream.h>
#include "Enumeration.h"

template <class DataType>
class AbstractSet
{
public:
    virtual bool isEmpty() const = NULL;
    // returns true if set is empty, but otherwise false
    virtual int Size () const = NULL;
    // returns the number of elements in the set
    virtual bool contains (const DataType& element)
                    const = NULL;
    // returns true if element is in the set, but false
    virtual void add (const DataType& element) = NULL;
    // adds element to the set; if set already contains
    // element, no effect
    virtual void remove (const DataType& element) = NULL;
    // removes element from the set; if element was not in the
    // set, no effect
    virtual bool equals (const AbstractSet<DataType>& otherSet)
                    const = NULL;
    // returns true if every element of set is in otherSet and
    // vice versa
    virtual bool isSubsetOf (const AbstractSet<DataType>&
                    otherSet) const = NULL;
    // returns true if every element of set is in otherSet
```

```
    virtualAbstractSet<DataType>& makeIntersection
            (const AbstractSet<DataType>& rightSet) = NULL;
    // returns elements that are in this set and rightSet
    virtualAbstractSet<DataType>& makeUnion
            (const AbstractSet<DataType>& rightSet) = NULL;
    // returns non-duplicate elements from this set and the
    // rightSet
    virtualAbstractSet<DataType>& makeDifference
            (const AbstractSet<DataType>& rightSet) = NULL;
        // returns elements in this set but not in rightSet
    virtual Enumeration<DataType>* enumerator () const = NULL;
    // returns an enumeration of the data contained in the set
    virtual void display (ostream& s) const = NULL;
        // display the nodes of the set
};
```

6.3.2.4   TreeSet Class

One way to implement the above interface is to create a *TreeSet* class, each instance
of which has an underlying binary search tree field in which it stores elements. We
can determine whether the set contains a given element by trying to find it in the
binary search tree; we can form a union by traversing the elements of the two sets
and adding all of their elements to a new binary search tree; and so on. We can even
perform the *display*() method by displaying the underlying binary search tree, and the
TreeSetEnumerator class we will need can have an underlying *PreOrderE-
numerator*.

Fields and Constructors

As noted, the *TreeSet* class will have an underlying binary search tree field. We will
find it convenient in implementing *makeIntersection*() and like to replace our underlying binary search tree, so we will make our instance field a pointer. Our constructor
creates the contained instance; our destructor deletes it but takes no responsibility for
the contained elements; the *BinarySearchTree* is responsible for deleting the
elements.

```
template<class DataType>
class TreeSet : public AbstractSet<DataType>
{
protected:
BinarySearchTree<DataType>* pbst;
public:
    TreeSet ();
    virtual ~TreeSet ();
};
// ----------------------------------------------------------
template<class DataType>
TreeSet<DataType>::TreeSet ()
{
    pbst = new BinarySearchTree<DataType>;
}
// ----------------------------------------------------------
template<class DataType>
TreeSet<DataType>::~TreeSet ()
{
    delete pbst;
}
```

Methods

The implementations of most of the methods of the *TreeSet* class are simple since they simply pass through to the BinarySearchTree, so we shall illustrate *add*() and leave *isEmpty*(), *Size*(), *contains*(), *remove*(), *enumerator*(), and *display*() to the reader:

```
template<class DataType>
void TreeSet<DataType>::add (const DataType& data)
{
    if (!pbst->contains (data))
        pbst->insert(data);
}
```

We should now consider how to implement *makeIntersection*(). In this case, we will want to replace the original *BinarySearchTree* containing our elements with a new one containing the intersection.

```
template<class DataType>
AbstractSet<DataType>&TreeSet<DataType>::makeIntersection
    (const AbstractSet<DataType>& rightSet)
{
    TreeSet<DataType>* result = new TreeSet<DataType>();

    Enumeration<DataType>* leftEnum = enumerator();

    while (leftEnum.hasMoreElements())
    {
        DataType& object = leftEnum.nextElement ();
        if (rightSet.contains (object))
            result->add(object);
    }
    delete leftEnum;

    return *result;
}
```

Implementation of the other methods is left to the reader as an exercise.

6.3.2.5   BitSet Class

The above *TreeSet* class is convenient in that it can store a potentially unlimited number of elements from a universe of indefinite size. However, this is not always the problem with which we are presented. Sometimes we have a very limited universe, perhaps just five or six simple elements. For instance, suppose we are writing a word processor and wish to give the user the option of putting borders around a paragraph. There are four borders: {top, bottom, left, right}. The user can select any subset of this set, but the overhead of a binary search tree seems unwarranted in this case.

How else can we form a set? One solution is to use the individual bits of an integer: if a bit is on (1), the corresponding element is in the set; if the bit is off (0), the corresponding element is not in the set. Such an implementation necessarily implies that the universe of elements can be placed in a specific, constant order. This does not imply that the order is in any way meaningful, just that it is constant. So, in the word processor example, we may simply declare that the order is top, bottom, left, right, even though left, right, top, bottom would be equally defensible. The small set could be formed of strings entered by the user, in which case we might sort them lexically, perhaps for convenience in searching them, but if searching is not necessary, then we can simply use them in the order of entry.

In any case, once we have the universe of elements in a specific, constant order, given any element we can find the corresponding bit and determine in constant time whether the element is present. Unfortunately there is no general method for finding the corresponding bit. However, we can restrict our *BitSet* to storing integers, and the caller will be responsible for translating each element to a bit number before adding it. We will declare a constant indicating the largest permissible bit number, as follows:

```
const int MAX_BIT_NUMBER = 31; // assumes four-byte integer
```

Our *BitSet* class would have the following constructors and fields:

```
class BitSet : public AbstractSet<int>
{
protected:
    int elements;
    BitSet (int startingElements);
public:
    BitSet ();
};
// ------------------------------------------------------------
BitSet::BitSet ()
{
    elements = 0;
}
// ------------------------------------------------------------
BitSet::BitSet (int startingElements)
{
    elements = startingElements;
}
```

Then the *add()* method is quite simple:

```
void BitSet::add (const int& bitNumber)
{
    if ( (bitNumber < 0) || (bitNumber > MAX_BIT_NUMBER) )
        throw SetOutOfUniverseException ()
    elements |= (1 << bitNumber); // note bitwise or, not logical or
}
```

It is easy to see how to form an intersection between two *BitSets*: just perform a logical *and* (&) on their *elements* fields. But how do we know whether we received a *BitSet* or some other kind of set? We can tell by trying to dynamic_cast the address of the other set to a pointer to *BitSet*. If the cast fails, the result will be a NULL pointer rather than an exception, and we will know we have some other kind of set.

```
AbstractSet<int>& BitSet::makeIntersection (const
AbstractSet<int>& otherSet)
{
    const BitSet* pOtherBitSet
            = dynamic_cast< const BitSet*> (&otherSet);
    BitSet* result = new BitSet(pOtherBitSet->elements);
    if (NULL != pOtherBitSet) // this _is_ a BitSet
    {
        result->elements = elements & pOtherBitSet->elements;
    }
    else
    {
        int newElements = 0;
        Enumeration<int>* otherEnum = otherset.enumerator();

        while (otherEnum.hasMoreElements())
        {
            int elem = otherEnum.nextElement ();
            if ( (elem < 0) || (elem > MAX_BIT_NUMBER) )
                throw SetOutOfUniverseException ()
            newElements |= (1 << elem);
```

```
        }
        delete otherEnum;

        result->elements &= newElements;
    }
    return *result;
}
```

The reset of the implementation is left as an exercise for the reader.

6.4   Performance Comparisons

We have presented two implementations of the SET operations, one using binary search tree (TreeSet) and the second BitSet using the bits represented by an integer (can be thought of as an array of Boolean values). Sets can also be represented using an array data structure wherein the elements can be kept sorted or unsorted. Operations that involve a single set such as *CreateEmpty*, *isEmpty*, *add*, *remove*, and *contains* can be completed very fast on the BitSet data structure provided the largest element in the set is not too large. An integer that is presented with 32 bits can store a maximum of 32 elements by assigning a bit position to an element in the set. When a bit position is set (equal to 1) then the corresponding set element is present in the set, otherwise absent. An *unsigned char* requires 8 bits and can be used to store a set that contains at most 8 elements. Consider a set that contains three elements such as $S = \{10, 14, 200\}$. The elements of the set can be stored in an array of type *unsigned char* and this will require a total of 24 bits of storage. For each element of the set S we can provide integer aliases – 10, 14, and 200 are given 0, 1, and 2, respectively as aliases. Now we can use an *unsigned char* and set bits 0, 1, and 2 to store the elements of the set. To determine the presence or absence of an element in a set, to add an element to the set, and to remove an element from a set, we now have to find the element's integer alias first and then check if the corresponding bit is set or unset. Thus the mechanism of storing and providing integer aliases does not have any added advantage for performing single set operations.

The operation *contains* can be implemented in $O(1)$ time on a BitSet representation and will require $O(h)$ time to search for the element on a TreeSet representation, where h is the height of the binary search tree used to present the TreeSet data structure. Note that in the worst-case the value of h is equal to n. If the elements of the set are stored in a sorted array, then the *contains* operation can be implemented using a binary search which would require $O(\log n)$ time, where n the number of elements in the set. In an unsorted array, we can perform a sequential search to implement the *contains* operations and this would require $O(n)$ time. The worst-case time complexities for the other single set operations are represented in the table below.

Consider two sets S_1 and S_2 of sizes n and m, respectively. In order to perform the intersection operation, we need to take each element from set S_1 and determine if it exists in set S_2. On a TreeSet data structure this operation would require the execution of *contains* operation for each element of S_1 on the TreeSet data structure that represents the set S_2. The total time complexity for this operation would be $O(n \times h)$, where h is the height of the binary search tree that stores S_2. Using the BitSet data structure the set *intersection* operation is a logical *and* operation and requires the examination of each bit. The maximum number of bits to be examined is equal to $maximum(n, m)$. Given two unsorted arrays to store the sets, the intersection operation will use a sequential search on the array that stores the elements of S_2 and this will require has a time-complexity of $O(n \times m)$. If sorted arrays are used to store the elements in the sets, then a binary search can be used thereby reducing the total time-complexity for the set intersection operation to $O(n \times \log m)$. We leave it to the reader to show that the set intersection operation using the sorted array representation can be completed in $O(n)$ time.

The following table summarizes the worst-case time complexities for the various set operations.

The qualitative assessment of the various structures used to store the set elements is presented in Figure 6.8.

6.5   *set* Adapters in STL

The adapters such as stack and queue studied earlier uses the vector or list sequence container. The vector or list sequence container maintains items in the order in which they are inserted in to the adapters and in a linear arrangement. Associative containers or more explicitly sorted associative containers keep items in a sorted order based on the key value of the items stored. The key for an item can either be the item itself or a field in a complex data class. For example, if the data class stores information about a student, then the social security number of the student can be the field that is used as a key.

SETs Implementations Worst-case Time Complexity Comparisons n is the number of elements in each set				
Operation	TreeSet	BitSet	Unsorted Array	Sorted Array
Create()	$O(n)$	$O(n)$	$O(n)$	$O(n\log n)$
isEmpty()	$O(1)$	$O(n)$	$O(1)$	$O(1)$
Size()	$O(1)$	$O(n)$	$O(1)$	$O(1)$
contains(element)	$O(h)$, where h is the height of the binary search tree	$O(1)$	$O(n)$	$O(\log n)$ using binary search.
add(element)	$O(h)$	$O(1)$	$O(1)$	$O(n)$
remove(element)	$O(h)$	$O(1)$	$O(n)$	$O(n)$
equal (S1, S2)()	$O(n\log h)$	$O(n)$	$O(n \times n)$	$O(n\log_2 n)$
isSubsetOf (S1, S2)	$O(n\log h)$	$O(n)$	$O(n \times n)$	$O(n)$
makeIntersection(S1, S2)	$O(n\log h)$	$O(n)$	$O(n \times n)$	$O(n)$
makeUnion(S1, S2)	$O(n\log h)$	$O(n)$	$O(n \times n)$	$O(n)$
makeDifference(S1, S2)	$O(n\log h)$	$O(n)$	$O(n \times n)$	$O(n)$

Figure 6.15: Comparison of worst-case execution times for different set operations using different set implementations. Note that h in the above table is the height of the binary search tree used to store the set elements.

Set Implementations Qualitative Assessment	
Implementation	Assessment
TreeSet	Excellent for single set operations in comparison with Sorted Array, if the height of the tree is smaller. This data structure is not efficient for operations involving two sets in comparison with sorted array.
BitSet	When the elements of the set are from a fixed domain this representation is the most optimal one.
Unsorted Array	Is the weakest of all the representations, but the addition operation can be efficiently implemented.
Sorted Array	Other than the addition of element operation, this implementation is the most efficient one for both single set and two set operations. It requires initial sorting of the elements in the set and hence the create operation takes more time.

Figure 6.16: Qualitative assessment of various set implementations.

The set adapter uses a sorted associative container by default to store the items. In fact, the associative container used by the set adapter is a binary search tree (more specifically, a red-black tree discussed in Chapter 7 whose height is always maintained at $O(\log n)$). The TreeSet and BitSet are examples of sorted associative containers. If we replace, the binary search tree used in the TreeSet implementation above with the red-black tree data structure, the essentially we have a set adapter implementation provided in the standard template library. Of course iterators and other methods have to be completed for the TreeSet implementation.

If the items to be stored in the set adapters are by themselves keys, then the standard template library provides two adapters: *set* and *multiset*. Unlike the set adapter, the multiset adapter allows duplicate items to be stored. In the case where key is part of a complex data, the STL provides the adapters *map* and *multimap*, where multimap unlike a map is used to store duplicate items. The adapters *map* and *multimap* are discussed in Chapter 10. Unlike the stack and queue adapters, the STL provides iterators for the set adapters. The set and multiset adapters have the three template parameters: first, the type of item to be stored; second, the specific relational operator that is used to order the keys in the sorted container that the adapter uses; and third, the type of storage allocator implemented (by default this will be *allocator* and need not be specified).

The following statement shows the creation a set *mySet*. The first element of the template corresponds to the data type of the set items and the second element of the template states that the items are kept ascending order in the set.

```
set<int, less<int>> mySet;
```

The equivalents of methods in the set adapter for add and remove are *insert* and *erase*, respectively. The insert method in the *set* adapter returns an object of type *pair* (which is part of the STL and is given in utility.h). A *pair* is an object that contains two other objects. The method prototype for the insert method for the *set* adapter is given below.

```
pair<iterator,bool> insert (const item& x);
```

The pair object that is returned by the insert method contains two useful fields, *first* that stores the iterator positioned at the item that is being inserted, and *second* which is either *true* or *false* according to whether the item in the parameter of insert was actually inserted into the set. For a set adapter, if the item that is to be inserted is already in the set, then the *second* is set to *false*, otherwise it is set to *true*. The iterator in the pair object is of type const_iterator belonging to the set object. For example, the pair object for the above mySet is defined and used in the insert method as follows:

```
pair<set<less, less<int>>::const_iterator, bool> p;
p = mySet.insert(42);
if (p.second)
    cout<< "Element is inserted" << endl;
else
    cout<< "Element is already in the set" << endl;
```

The *insert* method on a multiset does not return any value. The *erase* method has the following prototype.

```
int erase (const item& x);
```

The erase method returns the number of occurrences of item in the set (resp. multiset) with a key value of x. In the case of a set adapter the number of items is either 0 or 1 depending on whether the item is found or not found. For the multiset adapter the erase method returns the number of items matching the key x that was removed from the multiset.

Both set and multiset support iterators support *iterators*. This implies (as in the case of vector and list containers) that methods *begin*() and *end*() return the first element and element after the last element of the set, respectively. The iterator for the set adapters is bi-directional as in the case of list container. The operators "++" and "--" move the iterator forward and backward, respectively.

A number of set operations are defined in the standard template library. These set operations are defined in the header file algorithm.h. The *find* method takes a key and if the item with the matching key is found in the set it returns an iterator positioned at the item, otherwise it returns an iterator positioned at *end*(). The *find*() method in the STL is equivalent to the *contains*() method discussed in our TreeSet implementation. The *count*() takes as parameter a key and returns the number of items with the matching key. External methods, which are methods that are not members of the set adapter class, are also provided for performing set operations such as includes (isSubset), set_union, set_difference, and set_intersection. For example the set_union operation requires the beginning and ending iterators of the two sets on which the union is to be performed along with an output iterator as the last parameter. The elements in the set union are written at the position specified at the output iterator. The output iterator is a position defined in the output set. The standard template library provides a helper function called *inserter* which takes a set and an iterator (usually the beginning of the set) and returns an iterator that specifies the first element of the set.

In the following main method we illustrate the use of the set adapter.

```
#include <iostream.h>
#include <set>
#include <algorithm>
using namespace std;

int main ()
{
    set<int, less<int>> mySet;  //first set
    set<int, less<int>> yrSet;  //second set
```

```
set<int, less<int>> utSet;    //output set
pair<set<int, less<int>>::const_iterator, bool> p;

for (int i=0; i < 10; i++)
    p = mySet.insert(i*10);        // insert elements into
                                        the set mySet


p = mySet.insert(20);
if (p.second)
    cout<< "Element is inserted" << endl;
else
    cout<< "Element is already in the set" << endl;

if (mySet.find(60) != mySet.end())
    cout<< "Element 60 is in the set" << endl;
else
    cout<< "Element 60 is not in the set" << endl;

for (i=5; i < 12; i++)
    p = yrSet.insert(i*10);  //create a second set

set_union(mySet.begin(),mySet.end(),yrSet.begin(),yrSet.
             end(),inserter(utSet, utSet.begin()));

cout "<"
for (set<int, less<int>>::const_iterator ptr = utSet.begin();
     ptr != utSet.end(); ++ptr)
    cout<< *ptr << " ";
cout ">" << endl;
}
```

The above program will have the following output.

```
Element already in the set
Element 60 is in the set
<0 10 20 30 40 50 60 70 80 90 100 110>
```

The methods of the set adapter are presented below.

set< DataType, Compare>()	Default constructor. The key values of the elements stored in the set of type *DataType* and the *Compare* class allows the keys to be stored in that order. For example, if Compare is *less*<DataType>, then the keys are stored in the set in the ascending order.
set(constset<DataType, Compare>& set)	The copy constructor.
~set()	Destructor.
=	*set< DataType, Compare>&operator=(const set< DataType, Compare>& rhsSet)* Overloaded assignment operator. The contents of the set on the left hand side are replaced with the contents of the set on the right hand side of the assignment operator.
==	*bool operator==(const* *set< DataType, Compare>& rhsSet)* Return true if both the sets contain the same items in the same order, false otherwise.
<	*bool operator<(const* *set< DataType, Compare>& rhsSet)* Return true if first set is lexicographically less than the second set, false otherwise.
iterator begin()	Return the iterator positioned at the first element.
iterator end()	Return the iterator positioned immediately after the last element.
iterator& find(const DataType&key)	If the set contains the *key* return the iterator positioned at that element, otherwise return *end()*.
pair<const_iterator, bool> insert(*const DataType& key)*	If the set does not contain an element that matches *key*, insert a copy of the *key* and return a *pair* object whose first element is an iterator positioned at the new element and the second element is true. If the set contains the element that matches *key*, return a pair whose first element is an iterator positioned at the existing element and whose second element is false.
voiderase(iteratorpos)	Erase the element at *pos*.
int erase(constDataType& key)	Erase all elements that match *key* and return the number of elements that were erased. For the set adapter this value is either 0 or 1.
int max_Size()	Return the maximum number of items that the set can contain.
int Size()	Return the number of elements stored in the set.
bool empty()	Return true if the set does not contain any elements, false otherwise.

Figure 6.17: Methods of the set adapter in the STL. The multiset adapter in addition to the above methods has a method *int count(const DataType& key)* which returns the number of items matching *key*.

6.6   Exercises

6.1.   A binary tree data structure can be represented by an array-of-objects representation similar to the array implementation of a linked list. Each object contains *value*, *leftindex*, and *rightindex*. Using this representation of a binary tree rewrite the methods that relate to the binary tree class.

6.2.   Given a preorder (or a postorder) traversal and an inorder traversal of a binary tree a unique binary tree satisfying the traversals can be constructed. Given the following preorder and inorder traversals of a binary tree construct the binary tree.

>   Preorder: a, e, f, h, g, b, c, d.
>   Inorder: h, f, e, g, a, c, b, d.

6.3.   Write an algorithm to construct a unique binary tree given the preorder and inorder traversals.

6.4.   Show that, given only a preorder and a postorder traversal of a binary tree, a unique binary tree cannot necessarily be constructed.

6.5.   Show the contents of the stack during the inorder traversal of the binary search tree constructed as part of exercise 6.2.

6.6.   A preorder traversal of a binary tree can be performed iteratively without the use of a stack. The basic idea is to make the left pointer (resp. right pointer) of a node temporarily point to its parent when the left tree (resp. right tree) is traversed. This is useful when the algorithm has to go back to the parent after the left tree is processed. The "repair" operation is to make the temporary parent pointer point back to the left (resp. right) child. You may need to use additional temp pointers (three of them at most) to accomplish the task. Write a method to perform this preorder traversal of a binary tree.

6.7.   Given a binary tree data structure with n nodes and each node storing a unique integer in the range from 0 through n-1, write a method to construct the parent array P such that $p[i] = j$, where j is stored in the parent node of the node that stores the integer i.

6.8.   Devise a method to construct a binary tree given the parent array that is discussed in the previous exercise.

6.9.   An *elimination ordering* of a binary tree is defined using the following steps.

        i) $i = 0$

        ii)   T = input binary tree

        iii)   while T is not empty do

        iv)   All leaf nodes of T get an elimination order of i

        v) $i = i + 1$

        vi)   remove leaf nodes from T

        vii)   endwhile

    Write a method to assign elimination ordering numbers to all the nodes in the binary tree. Can this method be performed in $O(n)$ time, where n is the number of nodes in the binary tree?

6.10.   An *expression tree* for an arithmetic expression consisting of binary operators $(+, -, \star, /)$ is binary tree whose leaf nodes are operands and whose internal nodes are operators. Given an expression construct an expression tree and perform all the binary tree traversals on it.

6.11.   Given an expression tree with integer operands in the leaf nodes, write a method to evaluate the arithmetic expression corresponding to the expression tree. Note that an internal operator can be applied only if both the child nodes are operands. The operator after evaluation is replaced with the result of the operation to form an operand child.

6.12.   Two binary trees are said to be equivalent if and only if they have the same structure and same information in the corresponding nodes. When we say two trees are the "same", we mean that every branch in one tree corresponds to a branch in the *second* tree. Write a method that overloads the $==$ operator to verify that two trees are equivalent.

6.13.   In the pointer implementation of a binary tree with n nodes there are $n+1$ null links out of a total of $2n$ links. These null links can be used to point to other nodes. A null left (resp. right) pointer of a node x is made to point to the node that will be visited before (resp. after) x in an inorder traversal. A tree whose links have been assigned in this manner is called a "threaded binary tree". For the binary tree constructed as part of exercise 6.2 draw the threaded binary tree.

6.14.   Write a method that takes as input a binary tree and constructs a threaded binary tree.

6.15. Write a method to perform a non-recursive traversal of a threaded binary tree without the use of a stack or temporary pointers.

6.16. Assume that the output medium is a fixed grid of cells (for instance, it is a printer with a fixed-size font). You are to write a method to display a binary tree that stores single character in each of its nodes. The display should satisfy four basic rules of style:

    i) Nodes at the same level should be displayed on the same horizontal line in the same order.

    ii) Adjacent levels should be displayed adjacently.

    iii) The distance between two adjacent displayed levels should be the same throughout the display.

    iv) Parents should appear above and centered between their children.

In order to perform this task one may want to assign a temporary horizontal position to each node. If a parent is at a temporary position i, the left child is at position $i-1$ and the right child is at position $i+1$. The tree should be processed in post order and hence the leftmost node in the tree is assigned its final position before any other node is assigned.

6.17. Given a binary search tree, an inorder traversal gives a sorted list. Assume this sorted set of elements is stored in an array A. A *globally balanced binary search tree* has $A[mid]$ in the root of the tree and left (resp. right) subtree is the globally balanced binary search tree of the elements in the array $A[0..mid-1]$ (resp. $A[mid+1...n-1]$). Write a recursive method to construct a globally balanced binary search tree from the array A.

6.18. Write a non-recursive method to construct a globally balanced binary search tree.

6.19. A *rooted general tree* contains a root and each node in the tree can have zero or more children. A rooted general tree can be represented using the parent array described in exercise 6.7. A rooted binary tree can be converted to a binary tree as follows: the root of the general tree is the root of the binary tree, every leftmost child (denote it x) in the general tree becomes the left child (denote it lc) in the binary tree, and now if y and z are the siblings of x, then y becomes the right child of x and z becomes the right child of y in the binary tree. Now given a rooted general tree, write a program in C++ to convert it to a binary tree using the above method.

6.20. Let T_1 and T_2 be two binary search trees such that the elements in T_1 are strictly less than the elements in T_2. Let x be a value such that $T_1 < x < T_2$. Write a method join(T_1, T_2, x) that produces a binary search tree containing elements in T_1, T_2, and x. What is the time-complexity of your algorithm? What is the time-complexity of your algorithm if T_1 and T_2 are globally balanced?

6.21. Assuming that set elements are stored in sorted arrays, write an algorithm to and show that the operations involving two sets can be implemented in $O(n)$ time.

6.7   References for Further Reading

Argo, G., "Weighting without waiting: the weighted path length tree", *Computer Journal* vol. 34, pp. 444–449, 1991.

Bentley, J. L., and Friedman, J.H., "Algorithms and Data Structures for Range Searching", *ACM Comput. Surveys*, vol. 11, no. 4, Dec. 1979.

Berztiss, Alfs, "A taxonomy of binary tree traversals", *BIT* vol. 26, pp. 266–276, 1986.

Burkhard, W.A., "Nonrecusive tree traversal algorithms", *Computer Journal* vol. 18, pp. 227–230, 1975.

Chang, H., and Iyengar, S.S., "Effective algorithms to globally balance a binary search tree", *Communications of the ACM* vol. 27, pp. 695–702, 1984.

Culberson, J., "The Effect of updates in Binary Search Trees", *Proceedings of the 17th Annual Symposium on Theory of Computing*, pp. 205–212, 1985.

Day, A. C., "Balancing a Binary Tree", *Computing Journal* vol. 19, no. 4, pp. 360–61, Nov. 1976.

Devroye, L., "A note on the height of binary search trees", *Journal of the ACM* vol. 33, pp. 489–498, 1986.

Driscoll, J. R., and Lien, Y.E., "A Selective Traversal Algorithm for Binary Search Trees", *Communications of the ACM* vol. 2, no. 6, June 1978.

Eppinger, J.L., "An empirical study of insertion and deletion in binary search trees", *Communications of the ACM* vol. 26, pp. 663-669, 1983.

Lewis, H.R., and Denenberg, L., *Data Structures and Their Algorithms*, Harper-Collins, New York, 1991, 509 pages.

Morris, J., M., "Traversing binary trees simply and cheaply", *Information Processing Letters* vol. 9, pp. 197–200, 1979.

Neivergelt, J., "Binary Search Trees and File Organization", *Computing Surveys* vol. 6, no. 3, pp. 195–207, 1974.

Sedgewick, R., and Flajolet, P., An Introduction to Analysis of Algorithms, Addison-Wesley, Reading, Mass., 1996.

Wood, D., *Data Structures, Algorithms, and Performance*, Addison-Wesley, Reading, Mass., 1993, 594 pages.

7 Self-Modifying Search Trees

IN THE PREVIOUS chapter, we implemented binary search trees and optimum binary search trees. We saw that our "naïve" implementation of the binary search tree did not guarantee a minimum height tree. Indeed, if data happened to be inserted in sorted order (as might occur if we were copying data from one data structure to another), our naïve implementation would produce a *maximum* height tree! In the Figure 7.1 below, we see the trees produced with the seven values A, B, C, D, E, F, and G, when they are inserted in sorted order and when they are inserted in the order D, B, A, C, F, E, and G.

We also saw that our implementation of the optimal binary search tree would produce a tree with the minimum expected searching cost, but it required that (1) the values be in correct order already and (2) we know the access probabilities. Generally we do not know the access probabilities, and the advance sorting required is an additional step, which we may not wish to take.

In this chapter, we will see two types of binary search trees: the height-balanced trees, which keep their height close to minimum no matter the order in which nodes are inserted and the splay trees, which "mutate" toward an optimum binary search tree by trying to ensure that the nodes most frequently accessed, will be nearest the root. Additionally, we will present the 2–3 tree and B-tree, which are not binary trees, but are related to some of the height-balanced binary search trees.

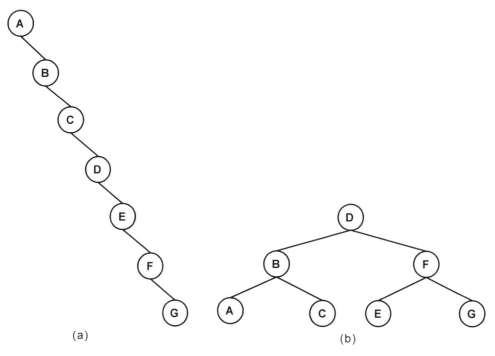

Figure 7.1:   The tree in (a) is produced when the 7 nodes A, B, C, D, E, F and G are inserted in sorted order. (b) is the tree produced when these 7 nodes are inserted in the order D, B, A, C, F, E and G.

7.1   Height-Balanced Binary Trees

As noted in the introductory remarks for this chapter, a height-balanced tree seeks to ensure that its height is near the minimum, no matter the order in which node values are inserted and deleted, without greatly increasing insertion and deletion cost.

It should be noted that a height-balanced tree does not attempt to keep its height exactly minimum since to do so might require a total restructuring of the tree (an $O(n)$ operation) after insertion. The diagrams below illustrate the degree of restructuring necessary to keep a tree at precisely minimum height. The tree in Figure 7.2 (a) is of minimum height for a tree with six nodes. The tree in Figure 7.2 (b) shows where B would have to be inserted into the tree in Figure 7.2 (a). The tree in Figure 7.2 (c) shows the minimum height binary tree containing the same node values as

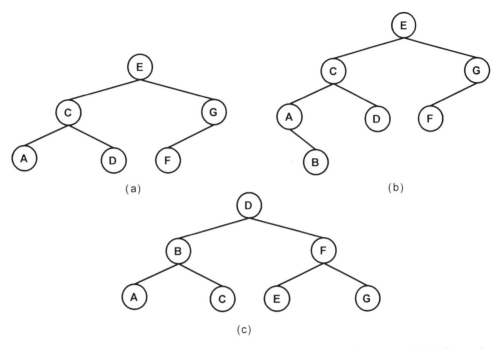

Figure 7.2:   The tree in (a) is of minimum height with 6 nodes, tree in (b) is formed
by inserting the node **B** in the tree in (a). Also, the tree in (c) is the
binary tree of minimum height for the same node values as in (b).

Figure 7.2 (b). Notice that every node value, except *A*, has been shifted to a new position. A restructuring like that from (b) to (c) would clearly be an $O(n)$ operation.

Thus, the best that we can hope for in a height-balanced tree is that the height
will be "close" to the minimum. Since the minimum height of an *n*-node binary search
tree is $\lceil log_2(n+1) \rceil$, we can hope that a height-balanced binary search tree will maintain
a height which is $O(log_2 n)$. If we ensure that the number of operations involved in
insertion and deletion is proportional to the height, then insertion and deletion will
remain $O(log_2 n)$ operations, as they are in the non–height-balanced trees.

All height-balanced trees rely upon rotations of trees to keep the heights of the
left and right subtrees balanced, so we shall create a parent class for all of them and
will add methods for rotations to that class. The class itself is a subclass of *BinarySearchTree* but has no additional fields. So the class initially is as follows:

```
template<class DataType>
class SelfModifyingBST : public BinarySearchTree<DataType>
{
protected:
    BinarySearchTree<DataType>* makeSubtree();
public:
    SelfModifyingBST ();
    SelfModifyingBST (DataType& data);
    virtual ~SelfModifyingBST ();
};
// -----------------------------------------------------------
template<class DataType>
SelfModifyingBST<DataType>::SelfModifyingBST()
    : BinarySearchTree<DataType> ()
{ }
// -----------------------------------------------------------
template<class DataType>
SelfModifyingBST<DataType>::SelfModifyingBST(DataType& data)
    : BinarySearchTree<DataType> (data)
{ }
// -----------------------------------------------------------
template<class DataType>
SelfModifyingBST<DataType>::~SelfModifyingBST() { }
// -----------------------------------------------------------
template<class DataType>
BinarySearchTree<DataType>* SelfModifyingBST<DataType>::
            makeSubtree()
{
    BinarySearchTree<DataType>* bst = new
                SelfModifyingBST<DataType> ();
    ((SelfModifyingBST<DataType>*)bst)->_subtree = true;
    return bst;
}
```

7.1.1 Rotations of Trees

Certain trees are to be closely related, even though the nodes have been rearranged. In the pair below, for instance, Figure 7.3 (a) can be produced from Figure 7.3 (b) by pivoting about the point indicated by the arrow. The reader should note that the ordering of any pair of nodes is unchanged: all nodes in subtree 2 are between nodes A and B in either tree, for instance.

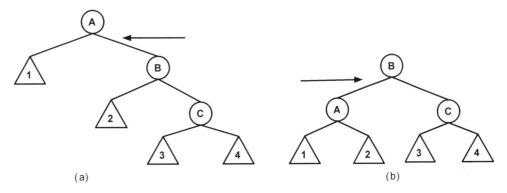

(a)   (b)

Figure 7.3: The structures (a) and (b) can be produced interchangeably from each other by pivoting about the point indicated by the arrow.

The above operation is called a single rotation since only one pair of nodes (A and B) has been rotated. The rotation producing Figure 7.3 (b) from Figure 7.3 (a) (a counter–clockwise rotation) will be called a "zag". The rotation producing Figure 7.3 (a) from Figure 7.3 (b) (a clockwise rotation) will be called a "zig".

Now, how would we perform the zag operation on a `BinarySearchTree` instance as described in the prior chapter? We will assume that the instance is that diagrammed in Figure 7.3 (a). The first point to notice is that the right-right grandchild (C) of the tree has moved up to the position of right child. What happened to the original right child (B)? Since the tree has a new left child, we can suppose that the B child became the new left child. The left subtree of the B child (labeled 2) became its right subtree (replacing the right–right grandchild which was adopted by the tree), and the left subtree of A (1) was adopted as the left subtree of the B child. The operations described so far produce the tree illustrated below:

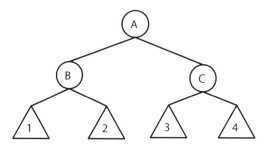

Figure 7.4:   The tree produced as a result of zag operation on Figure 7.3 (a). This tree is not a binary search tree as the nodes are not in order.

The tree is, unfortunately, not a binary search tree, since the nodes are not in order. However, this can be readily corrected by swapping the data values in the parent and left child, producing the correct tree. Based on the above discussion, the *zag ()* method in the *SelfModifyingBST* class is therefore as follows:

```
template<class DataType>
void SelfModifyingBST<DataType>::zag()
{
// nothing to rotate in an empty tree
   if (isEmpty()) return;
// if the right subtree is empty, no way to rotate its data
// to root
   if (_right->isEmpty()) return;
// so now we have something to rotate
   SelfModifyingBST<DataType>* rightchild =
       (SelfModifyingBST<DataType>*) _right;
// right-right grandchild becomes right child
   _right = rightchild->_right;
// former right child moves its left child to right
   rightchild->_right = rightchild->_left;
// former right child adopts left child
   rightchild->_left = _left;
// former right child is adopted as left child
   _left = rightchild;
// and interchange data with new left child,
// recreating search tree properties
   swap (_rootData, rightchild->_rootData);
}
```

This method must be declared "virtual" and it should be protected, as we would not want a caller to change the structure at will, otherwise it is possible for the tree to violate the conditions of the binary search tree. The corresponding *zig()* method is left for the reader.

Now we will consider the so-called double rotations. These are operations in which two rotations must be performed. For a simple example, consider what would be required to transform the tree in Figure 7.5 (a) to the tree in Figure 7.5 (b);

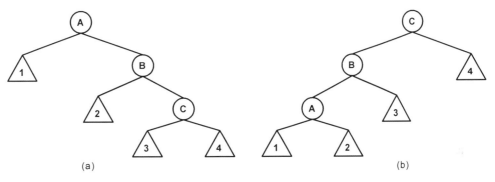

Figure 7.5:   Zagzag operation (double rotation) produces the tree in (b) using the
                  tree in (a).

This transformation can be achieved by zagging twice (the reader should draw the diagrams to demonstrate this). Since it is a very common operation, we will add a *zagzag()* method to perform it:

```
template<class DataType>
void SelfModifyingBST<DataType>::zagzag()
{
    zag();
    zag();
}
```

Similarly, we may add a *zigzig()* method which would transform Figure 7.5 (b) to Figure 7.5 (a). This is left for the reader. Finally, consider the diagrams below:

It should be clear that simply zagging and zigging with regard to the root of the tree in Figure 7.6 (a) does not produce Figure 7.6 (b). To produce Figure 7.6 (b)

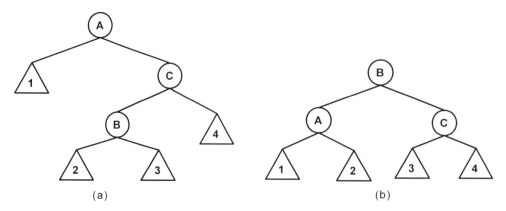

Figure 7.6:   Performing a zig operation on the tree with root **C** in (a) and a zag
              operation on the result produces the tree in (b).

from Figure 7.6 (a), we must perform a zig operation on the tree with root C, and a zag operation on the result. Since the zag is performed on the entire tree, we give it priority and call the entire operation a zagzig operation. Thus, what we need here is a *zagzig()* method:

```
template<class DataType>
void SelfModifyingBST<DataType>::zagzig()
{
 // if this instance is empty, _right will be NULL,
 //so we can't operate on it
    if (isEmpty()) return;
    ((SelfModifyingBST<DataType>*) _right)->zig();
    zag();
}
```

The previous rotations we have seen (zag, zig, zagzag, and zigzig) have been reversed by their mirror-image rotations. The mirror image of the zagzig rotation is the zigzag rotation which transforms Figure 7.7 (a) below to Figure 7.7 (b):

This clearly is *not* the reverse of the zagzig rotation. However, we do not need a reverse of the zagzig rotation in the trees described below. The *zigzag()* method is left for the reader.

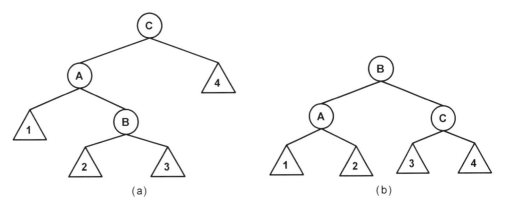

Figure 7.7:   Performing a zag operation on the tree with root **A** in (a) and a zig
operation on the result produces the tree in (b).

7.1.2   Red-Black Trees

The first height-balanced binary search tree which we will consider is called the Red–
Black Tree. The Red–Black tree is a binary search tree, which keeps itself balanced in
height by labeling each tree (or subtree) as either *red* or *black*, and restricting the red/
black relationships between parents and children.

Because it is a binary tree, the Red–Black tree naturally consists of a set of nodes,
partitioned into a node value and a left subtree and a right subtree; the subtrees of a
Red–Black tree are themselves Red–Black trees. Because it is a binary search tree, the
Red–Black tree maintains the property that all nodes in the left subtree have values
less than the node value, and all nodes in the right subtree have values greater than the
node value.

In order to keep it height-balanced, the Red–Black tree maintains the following
four invariants:

1.   An empty tree is black.
2.   An empty tree that becomes non–empty also becomes red.
3.   The *red condition*: a red tree never has a red subtree.
4.   The *black condition*: the number of black trees along a path from the root to a leaf
     (the black-height of the leaf) is the same along the path from the root to any other
     leaf.

In the diagrams below, nodes marked with a double circle are red, and all others
are black. Figure 7.8 (a) is a Red–Black tree, since it satisfies all the invariants and is,

moreover, a binary search tree. Figure 7.8 (b) is not a Red–Black tree since, although it maintains the invariants above, it is not a binary search tree. Figure 7.8 (c) is not a Red–Black tree since it violates the red condition. Finally, Figure 7.8 (d) is not a Red–Black tree since it violates the black condition.

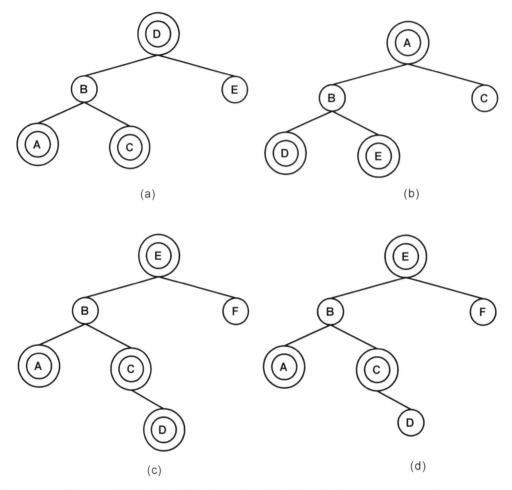

Figure 7.8: The tree (a) is a Red–Black tree but (b), (c) and (d) are not Red–Black trees.

7.1.2.1   Height of a Red-Black Tree

We can see that a Red–Black tree in which all subtrees are black would be a full tree, since every subtree which had one non-empty (therefore black) child would be forced to have a second non-empty child, and all leaves would be at the same depth because they have the same black-height. Viewed another way, if a Red–Black tree has black-height b, then the minimum number of nodes in the tree is 2^b-1, for that is the number it would have if every subtree were black.

Suppose we have an n-node Red–Black tree of black-height b. We know from the discussion above that $2^b-1 \leq n$, or $b \leq log_2(n+1)$. We know from the third invariant that a red tree cannot have a red subtree, so that, to have the maximum number of red subtrees, the red subtrees must alternate with black subtrees. Thus, the number of red subtrees along any path from root to leaf cannot exceed one more than the number of black subtrees along that path (both the root and the leaf might be red). Therefore, the height h of a Red–Black tree with black-height b is not more than $2b+1$; combining this with the inequality above, we have $b \leq h \leq 2b+1 \leq 2log_2(n+1) + 1$.

Clearly, the height of a Red–Black tree with n nodes is $O(log_2 n)$, and so searching in a Red–Black tree is of complexity $O(log_2 n)$. If insertion and deletion require numbers of operations proportional to the height (and we will see that they do), they too will be $O(log_2 n)$.

7.1.2.2 Operations on a Red-Black Tree

Because of the necessity of maintaining the red condition and black condition, insertion and deletion in a Red–Black tree are more complicated than insertion or deletion into the binary search tree described in the previous chapter.

Insertion

As can be observed in the diagrams below, insertion *may* be performed without disturbing the red condition, as in Figure 7.9 (a), but insertion may instead cause the red condition to fail, as in Figure 7.9 (b). Since a newly inserted node is always red, insertion will not cause the black condition to fail.

Let us consider how a violation produced by an insertion may be repaired. As is our habit, we will assume that operations will be performed recursively, so that we will consider the problem fully solved when we can repair the damage starting at the leaf, and repeating our steps until we reach the root.

Consider first the problem of insertion into an empty tree (or subtree). The tree was formerly black; now it is red and has two black (and empty) subtrees. Clearly, the black height formerly obtained by passing from the root to the former empty tree, and the black height passing from the root through the newly red tree and the new empty subtrees, are the same. The black height condition has been preserved. If our newly red

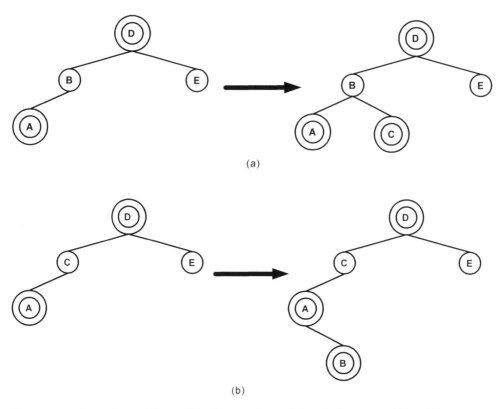

Figure 7.9:   Insertion without disturbing red condition is shown in (a) and the Insertion causing violation in red condition is shown in (b).

tree has no parent, or if its parent is black, the red condition is also preserved, and we are done. But if the newly red tree has a red parent, we have a red condition violation. Since such a violation may occur at any level in our recursive operation, we will consider the general cases.

Suppose first that the red parent of a red child itself has no parent, as illustrated in Figure 7.10 (a) below, and that there are no other violations anywhere in the tree, excepting the red condition violation shown. Then we can correct the problem by simply recoloring the red parent to black, as illustrated in Figure 7.10 (b) below. This certainly solves the red condition violation, and it does not cause a black condition violation, for *every* path from root to leaf simply increased in black-height by one.

Of course this is the easy case. The hard case occurs if the red parent does have a parent. In this case, we can be certain that the grandparent is black otherwise we would have two red condition violations, contrary to our assumption that there is only one

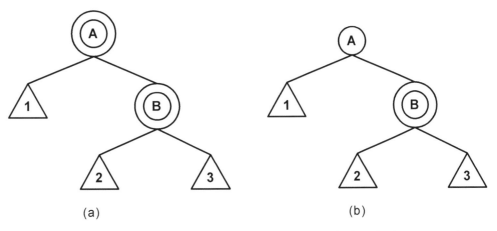

Figure 7.10: Red condition violation in (a) which is rectified in (b) by just recoloring the red parent to black.

violation in the whole tree. What, then, is the color of the sibling of the parent red
tree? If its sibling is red, as illustrated in diagram (a) below, then we can easily fix the
problem by recoloring the parent red tree and its sibling to black and the grandparent
to red, as illustrated in diagram (b). This cures the red condition violation at this level
without producing a black condition violation, but may produce a red condition violation in the tree rooted at the parent of the (newly red) grandparent. As noted before,
our problem is solved recursively, so this method will be applied again to deal with the
new red condition.

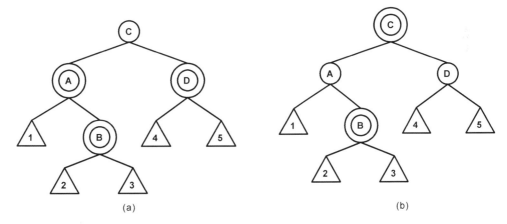

Figure 7.11: Red condition violation in (a) is rectified by simple re-coloring of the
parent node **A**, its sibling **D** and its grandparent **C**.

Now we consider the hardest case, where the sibling of the red parent is black, not red. This situation can arise two ways; the first is illustrated in the diagram below.

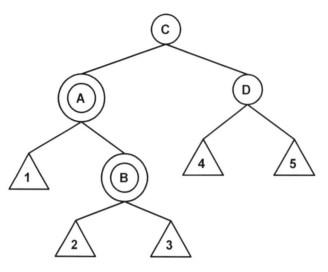

Figure 7.12: A red condition violation where the sibling of the red node **A** is not a red node but a black node (**D**) instead.

Here, simple recoloring is not the answer, as black heights in the right subtree of the tree rooted at C would be reduced by one, and those in left subtree would not, producing a black condition violation. It can be deduced that the subtrees labeled 1, 2, and 3 all have black roots, for otherwise we would have more red condition violations. So the tree rooted at C has two red descendants, rooted at A and B, and four black descendants, subtrees 1, 2, 3, and the tree rooted at D. If these six subtrees are rearranged as two red children and four black grandchildren, the red condition can be restored without causing a black condition violation. But we have already seen ways of rearranging children and grandchildren: the six rotations previously discussed. The diagram above suggests the sort of tree on which we would use a zigzag rotation, so we will give that a try. A zigzag rotation on the tree (as above, which does not interchange colors at all) produces the following tree:

The reader should verify that this tree satisfies both of the required conditions, and that it is still a binary search tree. This operation did not cause any violation to propagate upward, so the tree has no remaining problems.

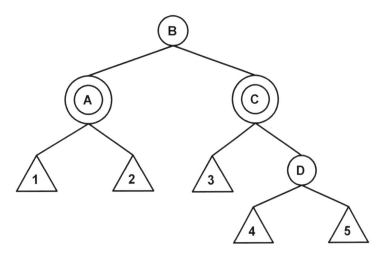

Figure 7.13:   Result of zigzag rotation on the tree in Figure 7.12.

Finally, the other way in which the sibling of the red parent may be black is that illustrated below:

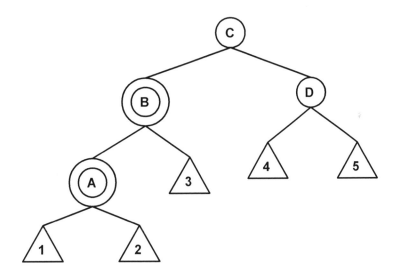

Figure 7.14:   A case of red condition violation where the sibling of the red node
              B is a black node **D**.

A simple zig operation will correct this situation, producing the same diagram as in the previous case.

The number of special cases to be considered in implementing insertion in a Red-Black tree is actually larger than demonstrated above, for each has a mirror image.

Deletion

Deletion *may* be performed without disturbing the black condition, as in Figure 7.15 (a) below, but may instead cause the black condition to fail, as in Figure 7.15 (b). (The squares are empty trees and are, of course, black). In our binary search tree implementation, we delete only nodes with no children or only one child; a node with two children is not deleted but acquires the node value of its inorder successor, which is then deleted. As a result, we shall see that deletion can never cause the red condition to fail.

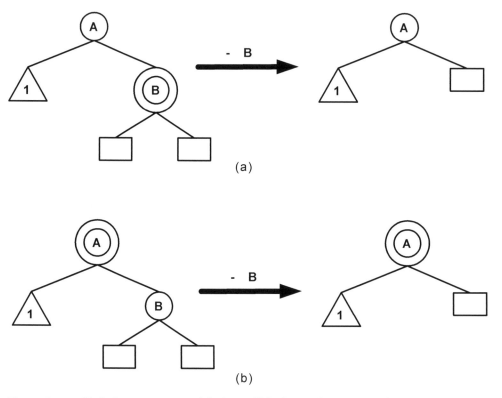

Figure 7.15: Deletion causes no violation of black condition in (a) but violation occurs in the case of (b).

As in the case of insertion, we will correct black condition violations recursively. Since the violation arises through deletion, we can view black condition violations as arising only when the leaves of one subtree come to have a black–height shorter by one than that of the leaves of the sibling subtree. Once again, we will consider all the possibilities.

First, if the offending subtree is red, we can readily correct the situation by coloring it black. This increases the black-height of the subtree by one, making it equal to the black-height of the sibling subtree, and solving the problem at once. We can therefore assume in the discussion below that the offending subtree is black.

Suppose that the parent of the affected subtree is red. Then the sibling tree is black as in Figure 7.16 (a) below (the affected subtree is indicated by an arrow). We can trade colors between the parent and sibling, as in Figure 7.16 (b) below.

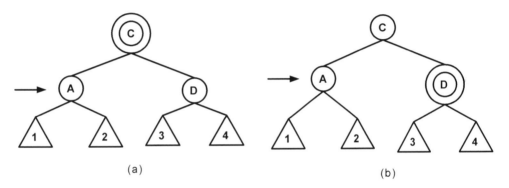

(a)   (b)

Figure 7.16:   A case where the parent of the affected subtree is red with its sibling being black as shown in (a). This violation is rectified by trading colors between the parent and sibling as shown in (b).

This corrects the black condition violation entirely (increasing black heights in the offending subtree without changing those in the sibling subtree), but at the cost of a possible red condition violation in the sibling subtree. If only one child of the sibling is red, we can correct the red condition violation as previously described with regard to insertion, without any violations propagating upward. If both children are red, we have a different problem.

In this case, subtrees 3 and 4 are both red. If we do a zag rotation on the root, we produce the following tree as shown in Figure 7.17, which contains a red condition violation because subtree 3 is red as is its parent rooted at C. We can now resolve the red condition violation as previously discussed. Though this may cause the tree rooted at D to become red, no red condition violation will be created since that tree was originally red before we began our operations to correct the black condition violation.

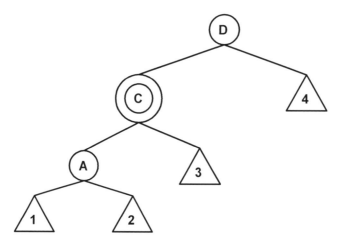

Figure 7.17:   Result of zag rotation on the root node **C** in Figure 7.16 (a) causing a red condition violation as **subtree 3** is red and its parent is rooted at **C**.

Suppose now that the parent of the affected subtree is black. The sibling subtree may be either red or black. If the sibling tree is black as in figure (a) below, we have a situation which can be corrected (at this level anyway) by making the sibling red. This corrects the black-height imbalance, and leaves the entire tree with a black-height one less than its sibling, which can be corrected recursively. We also have a possible red condition violation in the right subtree, but this is the same problem we had before, and can be corrected the same way.

Ah, but what happens if the root of the tree currently under consideration becomes red? Its own parent might also be red. Could we have a red condition violation propagating upward at the same time as the black condition violation? In fact, we cannot. If the root becomes red, we recolor it to black, solving the red condition violation and black condition simultaneously.

The final possibility is that the parent is black and the sibling is red, as illustrated below in Figure 7.18. Here, we can observe that the sibling tree (headed by D) must have non-empty black children, for its children must be black and they cannot be empty. If they were empty, then prior to deletion, the other subtree would have had to be empty or to be red with empty subtrees, in order to satisfy both red and black conditions. In the first case no deletion would have been possible and in the second a black condition violation would not have been produced.

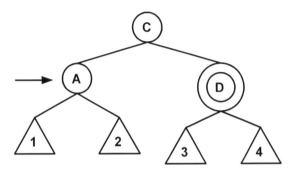

Figure 7.18:   A case where the parent node **C** is black. The red node **D** therefore must have non–empty black children (**which are subtrees 3 and 4**).

We can begin to resolve this situation by a zag operation. This produces the diagram below, as shown in Figure 7.19, in which the subtree rooted at A has a black height one less than its sibling subtree 3 (which has the same black height as subtree 4), while its parent is red and its sibling subtree 3 is black. We have already seen how to resolve a black condition violation in such a case (red parent and black sibling).

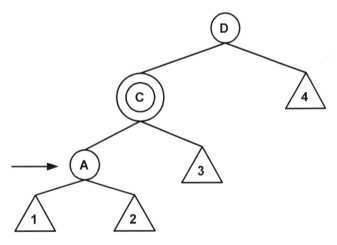

Figure 7.19:   Result of zag rotation on the tree in Figure 7.18 causing black condition violation.

We have now seen how to correct all possible black condition violations or red condition violations, and we can proceed to implement the Red-Black tree in C++.

7.1.2.3   Implementation of the Red-Black Tree

The Red-Black tree can be implemented as a subclass of the *SelfModifyingBST*, so that it inherits every method of the *BinarySearchTree*. It is clear that merely retrieving a node from a Red-Black tree, or enumerating or displaying it, cannot cause it to violate any of Red-Black invariants. Thus, all of the accessor methods of the *BinarySearchTree* can be used without change. The constructors and the mutator methods, *insert*() and *delete*(), on the other hand, must be overridden so as to ensure that the invariants are maintained.

Constants and Fields

A field must be added to the parent class to hold the color label. This may be of type int. Although, of course, we can simply use numbers like 0 and 1 to represent the colors, it is easier and more comprehensible to use named constants. We shall, therefore, place named constants, RED and BLACK, within the header file containing the *Red-BlackBST* class. We can begin our class declaration as follows:

```
const int RED = 0;
const int BLACK = 1;

class RedBlackBST : public SelfModifyingBST
{
protected:
    int _color;
};
```

Constructors and Destructors

The constructor methods are relatively simple to implement, simply ensuring that empty trees are black and non-empty trees are initially red. The *makeSubtree*() method must be overridden so that *RedBlackBST* instances always have children which are *RedBlackBST* instances. The destructor is trivial since no new pointer fields have been introduced.

```
template<class DataType>
RedBlackBST<DataType>::RedBlackBST()
    : SelfModifyingBST<DataType> ()
{
    _color = BLACK;
}
// -------------------------------------------------------------
template<class DataType>
RedBlackBST<DataType>::RedBlackBST (DataType& data)
    : SelfModifyingBST<DataType> (data)
{
    _color = RED;
}
// -------------------------------------------------------------
template<class DataType>
BinarySearchTree<DataType>* RedBlackBST<DataType>::makeSubtree()
{
    BinarySearchTree<DataType>* bst = new RedBlackBST<DataType> ();
    ((RedBlackBST<DataType>*)bst)->_subtree = true;
    return bst;
}
```

Accessor methods

Since the _left_ and _right_ fields are of type `BinarySearchTree`, they must be cast to `RedBlackBST` every time they are used. To avoid this inconvenience and the resulting obscure code, we shall have two simple methods which will handle the casting each time.

```
template<class DataType>
RedBlackBST<DataType>* RedBlackBST<DataType>::rbleft()
{
    return ((RedBlackBST<DataType>*)(left()));
}
// -------------------------------------------------------------
template<class DataType>
RedBlackBST<DataType>* RedBlackBST<DataType>::rbright()
{
    return ((RedBlackBST<DataType>*)(right()));
}
```

The new class should have a method to report the color of a tree, since the caller might want to know it even though the caller cannot change it:

```
template<class DataType>
int RedBlackBST<DataType>::color ()
{
    return _color;
}
```

As noted before, all of the accessor methods inherited from the *BinarySearchTree* are usable with the Red–Black tree. However, although the existing *printtree()* method will work, it will be helpful to write a new one which will display the color of each node. For purposes of clarity, the empty nodes are all omitted; they are, in any case, all black.

```
template<class DataType>
void RedBlackBST<DataType>::printtree (ostream& os, int level)
{
    if (isEmpty()) return;
    rbright()->printtree (os, level+1);
    for (int i = 0; i < level; i++)
        cout << "   ";
    cout << " +--" << rootData();
    if (color() == RED)
        cout << "(r)" << endl;
    else
        cout << "(b)" << endl;
    rbleft()->printtree (os, level+1);
}
```

The makeEmpty(), _makeNull(), and copyTree() methods

The virtual methods *makeEmpty()* and *_makeNull()* must perform the same actions as the corresponding methods in the *BinarySearchTree* class but also set the color to BLACK (since empty trees are always black). We will override the _makeNull() method, but simply call the prior method and add the new action. For the makeEmpty() method, we will find later that we need to be able to call it even on subtrees (though we do not want anyone else to be able to call it on subtrees!), so we will write a protected _makeEmpty() method which performs the actual actions, and a public makeEmpty() which overrides the inherited method but simply calls the _makeEmpty() method:

```cpp
template<class DataType>
void RedBlackBST<DataType>::_makeEmpty ()
{
    if (_rootData != NULL)
        delete _rootData;
    _rootData = NULL;
    if (_left != NULL)
        delete _left;
    _left = NULL;
    if (_right != NULL)
        delete _right;
    _right = NULL;
    _color = BLACK;
}
// ----------------------------------------------------------
template<class DataType>
void RedBlackBST<DataType>::makeEmpty ()
{
    if (_subtree) throw BinarySearchTreeChangedSubtree ();
    _makeEmpty();
}
// ----------------------------------------------------------
template<class DataType>
void RedBlackBST<DataType>::_makeNull ()
{
    BinarySearchTree<DataType>::_makeNull();
    _color = BLACK;
}
```

The `copyTree ()` method need not be overridden, for it copies the `_root-Data`, `_left`, and `_right`, but does not copy the `_color`. Since we do not wish to change the color of a tree when we copy another onto it, this is entirely acceptable.

Insertion

The `insert ()` method inherited from the `BinarySearchTree` class must be overridden to maintain the invariants listed above. We have written a protected helper method called `_insert ()` which does the actual insertion, since it is not necessary to check for errors repeatedly.

```
template<class DataType>
void RedBlackBST<DataType>::insert (DataType& data)
{
    if (_subtree) throw BinarySearchTreeChangedSubtree ();
    _insert (data);
}
```

The _insert() Method
The _insert() method is somewhat complex, and the code will be developed in stages below. The shell of the method is shown below, and the code that lies between the braces will be presented as it is described.

```
template<class DataType>
void RedBlackBST<DataType>::_insert (DataType& data)
{
}
```

If the tree (or subtree) into which we are inserting data is in fact empty, our task is, at least initially, simple. The tree was previously black and had no children. After the data is inserted, the tree is red and has two empty black children, which are leaves. This preserves the black condition, since the black-height for the two paths terminating in the new children is the same as the black-height of the path that terminated in the formerly empty tree, as previously discussed. However, while the insertion preserves the black condition, it does not necessarily preserve the red condition. If the parent happens to be red, the red condition will be immediately violated, but the parent must correct this problem. The code testing for an empty tree and for insertion into an empty tree is shown below:

```
// if we've reached an empty tree, insert the data
   if (isEmpty())
   {
       _rootData = new DataType(data);
       _color = RED;
       _left = makeSubtree ();
       _right = makeSubtree ();
       return;
   }
```

If the tree is not empty, we must decide where the data belongs. In the original *BinarySearchTree* class, we were able to use the _find () method to locate the proper position for insertion. In this case, we cannot use _find (), for we need the complete path from the root to the point of insertion. Thus, we must carry out the binary search within the _insert() method.

We begin by comparing the new *data* argument with the _rootData field in the current tree. If there is a match, *data* is merely replacing existing _rootData, so the insertion method is quite simple: replace the _rootData field without changing the color of the tree, as shown in this code fragment:

```
// check where the data goes relative to the current data;
// if it goes right here, we need not worry
// about red or black conditions
   if ((*_rootData) == data)
   {
       delete _rootData;
       _rootData = new DataType (data);
       return;
   }
```

If *data* does not merely replace the existing _rootData, we must recursively insert *data* into the appropriate subtree, either left or right. We must then correct the red condition if necessary (the black condition is unaffected, as demonstrated above). The insertion code itself is relatively simple:

```
// we must recursively insert the data in the correct tree
    if ((*_rootData) > data)
        rbleft()->_insert (data);
    else
        rbright()->_insert (data);
```

Finally, we must deal with the red condition, which may be violated after the insertion. It should be noted that, if the red condition was not violated prior to the insertion, it can be violated in only one part of the tree: the former leaf, now a non-empty red tree holding *data*, and its red parent. We have already discussed in general how this problem can be corrected; now we will implement the procedure in a method called *fixred ()*. Thus, we can complete the _insert *()* method by adding just one more line:

```
    fixred();
```

The fixred() method
As previously noted, if the red parent of a red child has no parent of its own (is not a subtree), the problem can be corrected by making the red parent black. We can therefore begin our *fixred ()* method as follows:

```
template<class DataType>
void RedBlackBST<DataType>::fixred ()
{
// an empty tree doesn't need to be fixed
    if (isEmpty()) return;

// symbolic names for left and right child, to simplify code
    RedBlackBST<DataType>* lft = rbleft();
    RedBlackBST<DataType>* rgt = rbright();

// if current instance is not a subtree, fix it immediately
    if (!subtree())
    {
        if (_color == RED)
        {
            if ((lft->color() == RED) || (rgt->color() == RED))
```

```
                {
                        _color = BLACK;
                }
        }
    }
}


// fix problems in a subtree
}
```

As previously diagrammed, a red condition violation in a subtree must be corrected by its grandparent, not its parent. Thus, in the *fixred*() method, we focus our attention on the parent (which we shall call tree "g" for grandparent) of the red parent (which we shall call tree "p") which has a red child (which we shall call tree "c"). Since the red condition is violated in only one place, and we know that tree p is a subtree and red, tree g must be black.

There are four configurations for trees g, p, and c since tree p may be either the left or the right child of tree g and tree c may be either the left or the right child of tree p. Each of these configurations calls for different handling, so the basic outline of the remainder of the *fixred*() method is as follows:

```
// test for red condition violation in the left child
    if (lft->color () == RED)
    {
// ----------------------------------------------------------
    // if the left child violates the red condition because
    // its left child is RED
        if (lft->rbleft()->color() == RED)
        {
// correct left-left violation
        }
// ----------------------------------------------------------
    // if the left child violates the red condition because
    // its right child is RED
        else if (lft->rbright()->color() == RED)
        {
// correct left-right violation
        }
    }
```

```
// test for red condition violation in the right child
   if (rgt->color () == RED)
   {
// ------------------------------------------------------------
   // if the right child violates the red condition because
   // its right child is RED
      if (rgt->rbright()->color() == RED)
      {
// correct right-right violation
      }
// ------------------------------------------------------------
   // if the right child violates the red condition because
   // its left child is RED
      else if (rgt->rbleft()->color() == RED)
      {
// correct right-left violation
      }
   }
```

We shall write the code for correcting left-left or left-right violations, leaving it to the reader to correct right-left or right-right violations.

To correct a red condition violation where p is the left child of g, we must first examine the right child of g, that is, p's sibling. If it is red, then as previously discussed, we can recolor g to red and p and its sibling to black. If p's sibling is black, however, we can perform a rotation, either zig (if c is p's left child) or zigzag (if c is p's right child). So the code to correct left-left or left-right violations is as follows:

```
// test for red condition violation in the left child
   if (lft->color () == RED)
   {
// ------------------------------------------------------------
   // if the left child violates the red condition because
   // its left child is RED
      if (lft->rbleft()->color() == RED)
      {
          if (rgt->color() == RED)
          {
```

```
                    _color = RED;
                    lft->_color = BLACK;
                    rgt->_color = BLACK;
             }
             else
                    zig();
       }
// -----------------------------------------------------------
   // if the left child violates the red condition because
   // its right child is RED
       else if (lft->rbright()->color() == RED)
         {
             if (rgt->color() == RED)
             {
                    _color = RED;
                    lft->_color = BLACK;
                    rgt->_color = BLACK;
             }
             else
                    zigzag();

         }
   }
```

Complexity of _insert()

The reader should observe that _insert() calls itself recursively for every ancestor of the subtree into which the insertion is to be made. Since the number of ancestors is no more than the height of the tree, which has been previously shown to be $O(log_2 n)$, the number of recursive calls to _insert() is $O(log_2 n)$. Further, all of the operations in _insert(), other than method calls, are of constant complexity, and *fixred()* is also of constant complexity. Thus, the total complexity of _insert() is $O(log_2 n)$.

7.1.2.4   Deletion

The `delete()` method inherited from the `BinarySearchTree` class must be overridden to maintain the invariants of the red-black tree. As will become evident, deletion preserves the red condition, but it may not preserve the black condition.

While a red condition violation can be readily detected by checking the children and grandchildren of a node, a black condition violation is much more difficult to detect, since we must check to see that every single path from root to leaves has equal length. This checking can be done recursively, but it would be a very time-consuming operation. Therefore, we will use a boolean *blackCondition* parameter in our deletion method. This parameter will be set true if the *blackCondition* remains satisfied, and set false otherwise.

As we did with insertion, we shall implement deletion recursively. Any violation of the black condition will be resolved at each level, if possible, backing up to the root. A violation of the black condition will occur in only one subtree, which can be detected by the parent of the subtree, and we will so implement deletion that a violation will always take the form of the affected subtree's being shorter than its sibling.

The remove() Method

We can begin implementation of deletion from a red-black tree by overriding the inherited *remove ()* method. This method can be called only on the root (which is not a subtree), since any method call on a subtree will throw an exception. Because we need a *blackCondition* parameter, this method must call a protected *_remove ()* method which accepts that parameter. What happens if the root (not a subtree) finds that the value of *blackCondition* is false on return from *_remove ()*? Clearly, if its subtrees do not have black condition violations, the root itself does not have a black condition violation. Therefore, the root can simply ignore the value of *blackCondition*. Thus, the *remove ()* method is as follows:

```
template<class DataType>
void RedBlackBST<DataType>::remove (DataType& data)
{
    bool blackCondition = true;
    if (_subtree) throw BinarySearchTreeChangedSubtree ();
    _remove (blackCondition, data);
}
```

The protected helper method *_remove()*, which does the actual deletion by calling itself recursively, is presented below.

The _remove() Method

The _remove() method will again be developed in stages. The shell of the method is shown below, and the code that lies between the braces will be presented as it is described.

```
template<class DataType>
void RedBlackBST<DataType>::_remove (bool& blackCondition,
DataType& data)
{
}
```

The _remove() method will be called recursively until either an empty subtree is reached (in which case the data to be deleted does not exist in the tree), or the data to be deleted is found. The first case, where an empty tree is reached, is simple, since we merely throw an exception:

```
if (isEmpty()) throw BinarySearchTreeNotFound();
```

If the tree is not empty, we must decide where the data might be found, using a binary search technique. We begin by comparing the new *data* argument with the _rootData field in the current tree. If *data* does not match the existing _rootData, we must recursively delete *data* from the appropriate subtree, either left or right, being careful to repair the black condition if necessary. This code is relatively simple, although we will need to write the *fixblackleft()* and *fixblackright()* methods later.

```
// check where the data goes relative to the current data
// we may need to recursively remove the data from a subtree
    if ((*_rootData) > data)
    {
        rbleft()->_remove (blackCondition, data);
        fixblackleft(blackCondition);
    }
    else if ((*_rootData) < data)
    {
        rbright()->_remove (blackCondition, data);
        fixblackright(blackCondition);
    }
```

```
        else
        {
// there is a match; remove subtree
        }
```

If there is a match, we must remove the data from the subtree. As in the *BinarySearchTree*, there are three possibilities: (1) the tree to be removed has no non-empty subtrees; (2) the tree to be removed has one non-empty subtree; (3) the tree to be removed has two non-empty subtrees.

The first case is the simplest. The tree is either red or black. If it is red, then it will become an empty black subtree and the black condition for its parent will not be affected. If the tree is black, then the black condition for its parent will be affected and it will simply report the problem and let its parent handle it:

```
// there is a match; delete subtree
    if ((_left->isEmpty()) && (_right->isEmpty()))
    {
        if (_color == BLACK)
            blackCondition = false;
        makeEmpty ();
    }
```

The second case arises when the tree to be removed (call it tree g) has only one non-empty subtree. Here, the non-empty subtree (call it tree p) can simply replace tree g. What colors are tree g and tree p? Since tree g satisfied the black condition previously, and its empty subtree is of necessity black, the non-empty subtree tree p cannot be black (if it were, there would be at least two black subtrees along a path from tree g to empty subtrees in tree p, and only one along a path from tree g to leaves in its empty subtree). Thus, tree p is red, and it must have empty subtrees, for its subtrees cannot be red and they cannot be non-empty black subtrees, for the same reason that tree p cannot be black. But then tree g must be black, since tree g satisfied the red condition prior to deletion.

Therefore, we can preserve the black condition in this case by simply replacing the node value of tree g with that of tree p.

```
else if ((!_left->isEmpty()) && (_right->isEmpty()))
{
    RedBlackBST<DataType>* oldleft = rbleft();
    delete _right;
    delete _rootData;
    copyTree (_left);
    oldleft->_makeNull();
    delete oldleft;
}
else if ((_left->isEmpty()) && (!_right->isEmpty()))
{
    RedBlackBST<DataType>* oldright = rbright();
    delete _left;
    delete _rootData;
    copyTree (_right);
    oldright->_makeNull();
    delete oldright;
}
```

Finally, if the tree to be removed has two non-empty subtrees, we replace its node value with that of its inorder successor. Then we remove its inorder successor, which has either no non-empty subtrees, or only one.

```
else
{
    RedBlackBST<DataType>* succ = rbright();
    while (!succ->_left->isEmpty())
        succ = succ->rbleft();
    delete _rootData;

    // can't replace succ->_rootData with NULL, since
    // following _remove call will fail.
    _rootData = new DataType(*(succ->_rootData));
    rbright()->_remove (blackCondition, *(succ->_rootData));
    fixblackright(blackCondition);
}
```

We must now write the *fixblackleft()* and *fixblackright()* methods. Since they are mirror-image methods, we have written only *fixblackleft()*, and left *fixblackright()* for the reader.

The fixblackleft() method

Since *fixblackleft()* is always called after a node is removed from a left subtree, we must test whether *blackCondition* is false; if it is true, then the removal caused no problems and we can just exit. We then check whether the left subtree (the offending subtree) is red; if it is, we can just color it black and return. So the *fixblackleft()* method is initially as follows:

```cpp
template<class DataType>
void RedBlackBST<DataType>::fixblackleft (bool& blackCondition)
{
    if (blackCondition) return;
    if (rbleft()->color() == RED)
    {
        rbleft()->_color = BLACK;
        blackCondition = true;
        return;
    }
// take care of case where left child is black
}
```

As previously discussed, the case where the parent is red and the sibling black can be corrected by trading their colors and then fixing any violations of the red condition. The code that follows performs these operations:

```cpp
// take care of case where left child is black
    if (color() == RED)
    {   // parent is red, so right child is black
        _color = BLACK;
        rbright()->_color = RED;

        // if both of right child's children are red
        // zag to put one over in the left child
        if ((rbright()->rbleft()->color() == RED) &&
                (rbright()->rbright()->color() == RED))
```

```
            zag();

      // at this point one or none of right child's children is red
      fixred();
      blackCondition = true;
      return;
   }   // parent is red
```

If the parent is black, then the sibling may be either red or black. If the sibling is black, then, as previously discussed, we can change its color and then zag (if necessary) and fix the red condition. Unlike the previous case, the black condition will *not* be repaired unless the parent managed to become red again during these operations:

```
// if we got here, parent is black
   if (rbright()->color() == BLACK)
   {
       rbright()->_color = RED;
       // if both of right child's children are red
       // zag to put one over in the left child
       if ((rbright()->rbleft()->color() == RED) &&
           (rbright()->rbright()->color() == RED))
                zag();

    // at this point one or none of right child's children is
   // red
       fixred();

// if parent became red, turning it black fixes everything
       if (_color == RED)
       {
           _color = BLACK;
           blackCondition = true;
       }
       return;
   } // right child is black
```

Finally, if the parent is black and the right child is already red, we can zag to move a red node over to the left, and then fix the black condition in the left child. This will correct the problem for the entire tree.

```
// if we got here, parent is black and right child is red
    zag();
    rbleft()->fixblackleft (blackCondition); // left child now red
```

Complexity of _remove()

The _remove () method recursively calls itself until it reaches the node to be deleted or an empty subtree. The maximum number of recursive calls to _remove () is, therefore, the height of the tree, which is $O(log_2 n)$. All of the operations in _remove () are of constant complexity except for the method calls, and fixblackleft () and fixblackright () are of constant complexity. Thus, _remove () is of complexity $O(log_2 n)$.

7.1.2.5   Testing the RedBlackBST class

For purposes of testing, we shall write four special accessor methods that will test for maintenance of the red and black conditions:

```
template<class DataType>
bool RedBlackBST<DataType>::isRedBlack ()
{
    return redcondition() && blackcondition();
}
// ------------------------------------------------------------
template<class DataType>
bool RedBlackBST<DataType>::redcondition ()
{
    if (isEmpty()) return true;
    if ((color() == RED) &&
        ((rbleft()->color() == RED) ||
         (rbright()->color() == RED)))
            return false;
```

```
        if ((!rbleft()->redcondition()) ||
            (!rbright()->redcondition()))
            return false;
        return true;
    }
    // ------------------------------------------------------------
    template<class DataType>
    bool RedBlackBST<DataType>::blackcondition ()
    {
        if (isEmpty()) return true;
        int bhl = rbleft()->blackheight();
        int bhr = rbright()->blackheight();
        if (bhl != bhr) return false;
        return (rbleft()->blackcondition())
            && (rbright()->blackcondition());
    }
    // ------------------------------------------------------------
    template<class DataType>
    int RedBlackBST<DataType>::blackheight ()
    {
        int add = 0;
        if (isEmpty()) return 0;
        if (color() == BLACK) { add = 1; }
        return rbleft()->blackheight() + add;
    }
```

Finally, we shall write a simple *main*() function, which inserts twenty-six nodes and then deletes them, testing for errors at each step:

```
void main()
{
char inserts[] = "ABCDEFGHIJKLMNOPQRSTUVWXYZ";
char deletes[] = "ZBXDVFTSHQKONMLPJIRGUEWCYA";
RedBlackBST<char> bst;
try
{
    for (int i = 0; i < 26; i++)
    {
```

```
            bst.insert (inserts[i]);
            cout << "+" << inserts[i] << ":" << bst.isRedBlack()
            << " ";
        }
        cout << endl;
        bst.printtree(cout, 0);

        for (int i = 0; i < 26; i++)
        {
            bst.remove (deletes[i]);
            cout << "-" << deletes[i] << ":" << bst.isRedBlack()
            << " ";
        }
        cout << endl;
        bst.printtree(cout, 0);
    }
    catch (Exception e) { cout << "Exception!" << endl; }
}
```

The resulting output, though not very attractive, shows that the Red–Black tree properties were maintained at all times, and also that the tree is relatively well-balanced, even though the nodes were inserted in sorted order.

```
+A:1 +B:1 +C:1 +D:1 +E:1 +F:1 +G:1 +H:1 +I:1 +J:1 +K:1 +L:1
+M:1 +N:1 +O:1 +P:1 +Q:1 +R:1 +S:1 +T:1 +U:1 +V:1 +W:1 +X:1
+Y:1 +Z:1
                        +--Z(r)
                +--Y(b)
            +--X(r)
                +--W(b)
        +--V(b)
            +--U(b)
    +--T(r)
            +--S(b)
        +--R(b)
            +--Q(b)
    +--P(b)
            +--O(b)
```

```
    +--N(b)
          +--M(b)
    +--L(r)
          +--K(b)
       +--J(b)
          +--I(b)
+--H(r)
       +--G(b)
    +--F(b)
       +--E(b)
    +--D(b)
          +--C(b)
       +--B(b)
          +--A(b)
-Z:1 -B:1 -X:1 -D:1 -V:1 -F:1 -T:1 -S:1 -H:1 -Q:1 -K:1 -O:1
-N:1 -M:1 -L:1 -P:1 -J:1 -I:1 -R:1 -G:1 -U:1 -E:1 -W:1 -C:1
-Y:1 -A:1
```

7.1.3 AVL Trees

The AVL tree (named for the mathematicians who first described it, Adel'son-Vel'skii and Landis) is a height-balanced binary search tree that maintains its height-balanced property by ensuring that its right and left subtrees do not differ in height by more than one.

Both subtrees of an AVL tree are also AVL trees, so they satisfy the same property. Because it is a binary tree, an AVL tree consists of a set of nodes, partitioned into a node value and the left and right subtrees. Because it is a binary search tree, an AVL tree must have the property that all nodes in the left subtree must have values less than the node value, and all nodes in the right subtree have values greater than the node value. The invariant for AVL trees is:

The difference in heights between the left subtree and the right subtree does not exceed one.

In the diagrams below, Figure 7.20 (a) is an AVL tree, since it satisfies the invariant and is also a binary search tree. Figure 7.20 (b) is not an AVL tree, since it is not a binary search tree, although it does satisfy the invariant. Finally, Figure 7.20 (c) is not an AVL tree, since it does not satisfy the invariant, even though it is a binary search tree.

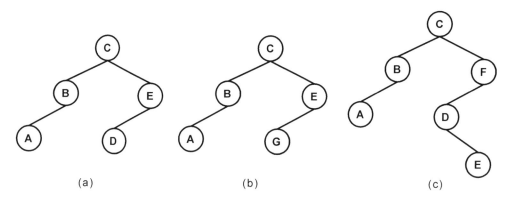

Figure 7.20:   The tree in (a) is an AVL tree while (b) and (c) are not AVL trees.

7.1.3.1   Height of an AVL Tree

In order to determine the maximum height of an n-node AVL tree, we shall first determine the minimum number of nodes that must be in an AVL tree of height h. We shall call this number M_h.

Consider the two subtrees of T, an AVL tree of height h. One obviously must have height h-1, but the other may have height h–2. If we want T to have the minimum number of nodes for its height, then each of its subtrees must have the minimum number of nodes for a tree of its height. In other words, the subtree of height h-1 must have M_{h-1} nodes, and the other subtree must have M_{h-2} nodes. T has exactly one node not contained in either of its subtrees; thus, $M_h = 1 + M_{h-1} + M_{h-2}$. Further, we can easily see that $M_1 = 1$ and $M_2 = 2$. The formula for M_h looks strikingly like that of the Fibonacci numbers, and indeed $M_h = F_{h+2} - 1$. Proof of this equality is left as an exercise.

We can therefore be certain that an AVL tree of height h has n nodes, where $n \geq F_{h+2}-1$. But we would like to have an expression for h in terms of n, not vice versa. In this case we take advantage of the fact that $F_k \approx \phi^k/\sqrt{5}$, where $\phi = (1+\sqrt{5})/2$. This indicates that $n \geq \phi^{h+2}/\sqrt{5}$, or $log_2 n \geq (h+2)log_2\phi - log_2\sqrt{5}$, so that $(log_2 n + log_2\sqrt{5})/log_2\phi - 2 \geq h$. Thus, $h < 1.44 log_2 n$.

Clearly, then, the height of an n-node AVL tree is $O(log_2 n)$.

7.1.3.2   Operations on an AVL Tree

Insertion and deletion in an AVL tree are more complicated than insertion and deletion in the binary search tree described in the previous chapter, since insertion can increase the height of a subtree, and deletion can decrease it. As may be observed in the diagrams below, where nodes have been added to the tree in Figure 7.21 (a), insertion may increase the height of a subtree, as in Figure 7.21 (b), or it may not, as in Figure 7.21 (c).

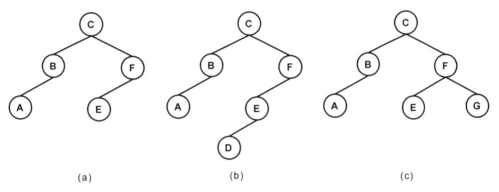

(a)   (b)   (c)

Figure 7.21: Inserting node **D** in (a) causing an increase in the height of subtree in (b). Inserting node **G** in (a) with no change in height of subtree in (c).

Similarly, deletion may cause the height of a subtree to decrease, as in Figure 7.22 (a) below, or it may not, as in Figure 7.22 (b) below, both derived from Figure 7.21(c) above by deletion of one node.

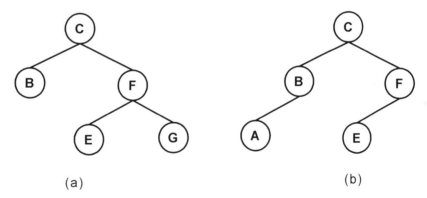

(a)   (b)

Figure 7.22: Deletion of node **A** in Figure 7.21 (c) decreases height of subtree in (a). Deletion of node **G** causes no change in height of subtree in (b).

For both insertion and deletion, we must move nodes between subtrees so as to restore the invariant, without thereby destroying the binary search tree properties. The implementations of the algorithms for insertion and deletion are, therefore, the difficult aspects of implementation of the AVL tree class. Because the AVL tree is defined recursively, we will implement insertion and deletion recursively. After insertion or deletion in a subtree, we will restore the height invariant within that subtree, then move back to the parent of the subtree and restore the height invariant within the parent, and so on until we reach the root.

The AVL tree can be implemented as a subclass of the BinarySearchTree, so that it inherits every method of the BinarySearchTree. It is clear that merely retrieving a node from an AVL tree, or enumerating or displaying it, cannot cause it to violate the height invariant. Thus, all of the accessor methods of the BinarySearchTree can be used without change. The constructors and the mutator methods, *insert*() and *delete*(), on the other hand, must be overridden so as to ensure that the height invariant is maintained.

Fields, Constructors, and Destructors

Initially, therefore, our AVL tree will be a subclass of the `SelfModifyingBST` class. How can our methods compute the difference in heights between the subtrees of a tree? There are several possibilities:

1. We could use the *height*() method to determine the heights, and simply compare them. This is, however, extraordinarily inefficient.
2. We could maintain a height field in the tree, initialized to 0 in an empty tree and updated with each insertion or deletion. This would certainly work, but it requires computation of the difference from the heights of the subtrees every time the difference is needed.
3. We could maintain the difference itself as a field in the tree, and update it with each insertion or deletion. This is the method used in the AVL tree.

Suppose we compute the difference as (right subtree height − left subtree height). Then a difference of 0 implies that the two subtrees are of equal height, a negative difference implies that the left subtree is of greater height than the right, and a positive difference implies that the right subtree is of greater height than the left. Given this formula, if we know the height of the left subtree, we can compute that of the right, and vice versa.

We can implement the third possibility given above by adding a _*diff* field to our trees. The constructors must initialize this field. Also, the *makeSubtree*() method must be overridden so that an AVL tree always has AVL subtrees, and the *makeEmpty*() method must be overridden to set the difference between subtrees to 0 in an empty tree. The destructor, as in the `RedBlackBST`, is trivial.

```
template<class DataType>
class AVLBST : public SelfModifyingBST<DataType>
{
protected:
    int _diff;
    virtual BinarySearchTree<DataType>* makeSubtree();
    virtual void _makeNull ();
    virtual void _makeEmpty ();
public:
    AVLBST ();
    AVLBST (DataType& data);
    virtual ~AVLBST ();
    virtual void makeEmpty ();
};
// ------------------------------------------------------------
template<class DataType>
AVLBST<DataType>::AVLBST () : SelfModifyingBST<DataType> ()
{
    _diff = 0;
}
// ------------------------------------------------------------
template<class DataType>
AVLBST<DataType>::AVLBST (DataType& data) :
SelfModifyingBST<DataType> (data)
{
    _diff = 0;
}
// ------------------------------------------------------------
template<class DataType>
BinarySearchTree<DataType>* AVLBST<DataType>::makeSubtree()
{
    AVLBST<DataType>* bst = new AVLBST<DataType> ();
    bst->_subtree = true;
    return bst;
}
// ------------------------------------------------------------
template<class DataType>
void AVLBST<DataType>::_makeEmpty ()
```

```
{
    if (_rootData != NULL)
        delete _rootData;
    _rootData = NULL;
    if (_left != NULL)
        delete _left;
  _left = NULL;
    if (_right != NULL)
        delete _right;
  _right = NULL;
  _diff = 0;
}
// ----------------------------------------------------------
template<class DataType>
void AVLBST<DataType>::makeEmpty ()
{
    if (_subtree) throw BinarySearchTreeChangedSubtree ();
    _makeEmpty();
}
// ----------------------------------------------------------
template<class DataType>
void AVLBST<DataType>::_makeNull ()
{
    SelfModifyingBST<DataType>::_makeNull();
    _diff = 0;
}
```

Accessor Methods

Obviously, a user of an AVL tree cannot be allowed to tamper with the _diff_ field, but
there is no reason that the difference cannot be reported to the user. So we will provide
an accessor method to report it:

```
template<class DataType>
int AVLBST<DataType>::difference () { return _diff; }
```

Since the AVLBST class is a subclass of the *BinarySearchTree* class, all of
the accessor methods inherited from the *BinarySearchTree* class are usable with

the AVL tree. However, it will be helpful to override the *printtree ()* method so that we can display the difference between subtrees for each tree:

```
template <class DataType>
void AVLBST<DataType>::printtree (ostream& os, int level)
{
    if (isEmpty()) return;
    right()->printtree (os, level+1);
    for (int i = 0; i < level; i++) cout << "   ";
    cout << " +--" << rootData() << "(" << _diff << ")" << endl;
    left()->printtree (os, level+1);
}
```

Since the *_left* and *_right* fields are of type *BinarySearchTree,* they must be cast to *AVLBST* every time they are used. To avoid this inconvenience and the resulting obscure code, we shall have two simple accessor methods to handle the casting each time:

```
template<class DataType>
AVLBST<DataType>* AVLBST<DataType>::avlleft ()
{
    return ((AVLBST<DataType>*) _left);
}
// ------------------------------------------------------------
template<class DataType>
AVLBST<DataType>* AVLBST<DataType>::avlright ()
{
    return ((AVLBST<DataType>*) _right);
}
```

7.1.3.3 Insertion

The *insert()* method inherited from the *BinarySearchTree* class must be over-ridden to maintain the AVL invariant. We will write a protected helper method, *_insert ()*, which can be called recursively to do the actual insertion. Thus, the *insert ()* method itself is quite simple:

```
template<class DataType>
void AVLBST<DataType>::insert (DataType& data)
{
    if (_subtree) throw BinarySearchTreeChangedSubtree ();
    _insert (data);
}
```

The _insert() method

The _insert () method is somewhat complex, since it is responsible for rebalancing the tree if one subtree becomes much greater in height than the other. The shell of the method is shown below, and the code that lies between the braces will be presented as it is developed.

```
template<class DataType>
void AVLBST<DataType>::_insert (DataType& data)
{
}
```

If the subtree into which we must insert data is in fact empty, our task is simple. We must insert the data and create two empty subtrees. The difference in height between the subtrees is obviously 0. So the code for this portion is as follows:

```
// if we've reached an empty tree, insert the data
    if (isEmpty())
    {
        _rootData = new DataType(data);
        _left = makeSubtree ();
        _right = makeSubtree ();
        _diff = 0;
        return;
    }
```

The tree into which insertion was made had a height of 0 and now has a height of 1. Thus, although it itself satisfies the AVL invariant, its parent or other ancestors may not. Since _insert() is called recursively, the affected ancestor will be responsible for rebalancing itself. We shall develop the code for this rebalancing operation later.

If the tree is not empty, we must decide where the data belongs. In the original *BinarySearchTree* class, we used the _*find()* method to locate the position for insertion. In this case, however, we may need to rebalance the ancestors of the tree where insertion is made, so we must carry out a binary search within the _*insert()* method.

We begin by comparing the new *data* argument with the _*rootData* field in the current tree. If there is a match, then *data* is merely replacing the existing _*rootData*, so the insertion method is simply to replace the _*rootData* field. This cannot affect the height of the tree.

```
// check where the data goes relative to the current data
// if it goes right here, we need not worry about heights
   if ((*_rootData) == data)
   {
       delete _rootData;
       _rootData = new DataType(data);
       return;
   }
```

If *data* does not merely replace the existing _*rootData*, we must recursively insert *data* into the appropriate subtree, either left or right, being careful to rebalance the tree if necessary.

There are essentially two possible results when *data* is inserted into a subtree: either the height of the subtree increases, or it does not. It is impossible for the height of the subtree to decrease on insertion. If the height of the subtree does not increase, it will not be necessary to rebalance any part of the tree.

So we need only consider the situation where the height of the subtree increases. The height of the subtree may increase in three circumstances: it was previously empty; or it was previously balanced (_*diff* was 0) and one subtree became longer, making it unbalanced (_*diff* is no longer 0), or it was previously unbalanced but became worse, as the longer subtree became even longer. In any case, if the left subtree becomes longer, we must decrease _*diff* by 1, but if the right subtree becomes longer, we must increase _*diff* by 1. The change to _*diff* may bring _*diff* to 0, indicating that the current tree is now balanced and has not increased in height, or may bring _*diff* to −1 or 1, indicating that the current tree is unbalanced but does not violate the AVL invariant. And then again, of course, it may bring _*diff* to −2 or 2, indicating that the AVL invariant is no longer satisfied.

```
// olddiff contains the _diff in the subtree before insertion
int olddiff;
// ------------------------------------------------------------
// we must recursively insert data
    if ((*_rootData) > data)
    {
        if (avlleft()->isEmpty())
        {
            avlleft()->_insert(data);
            _diff--;
        }
        else
        {
            olddiff = avlleft()->_diff;
            avlleft()->_insert(data);
// if avlleft()->_diff goes to 0, then the left subtree did
// not get longer, but instead just evened out its subtrees;
// otherwise, if avlleft()->_diff changed, then
// the left subtree got longer.
            if ((olddiff != avlleft()->_diff) &&
                (avlleft()->_diff != 0))
                _diff--;
        }
    }
// ------------------------------------------------------------
    else // (*_rootData) < data
    {
        if (avlright()->isEmpty())
        {
            avlright()->_insert(data);
            _diff++;
        }
        else
        {
            olddiff = avlright()->_diff;
```

```
        avlright()->_insert(data);
        if ((olddiff != avlright()->_diff) &&
            (avlright()->_diff != 0))
            _diff++;
    }
}
```

After insertion, we will invoke a method called *rebalance()* to ensure that the AVL invariant is restored in the current tree if it has been violated. So the final line of the *_insert()* method is simply this:

```
rebalance();
```

The reader will have noticed that the *rebalance()* method is called whether or not the AVL invariant is actually true in the current tree. Thus, the first action of the *rebalance()* method will be to return if the AVL invariant is not violated. Next we must consider the circumstances in which the invariant may have become untrue, given that it was true previously. Clearly, the given tree must have been unbalanced (*_diff* was 1 or −1) to start with, and the subtree, which was of greater height before, must have increased in height.

Left-Left Violation
One possible situation in which the AVL invariant will be violated is illustrated below. The height of each subtree is given to the right of its node value, and the *_diff* value (if relevant) is shown to the left. Before insertion, in Figure 7.23 (a), the subtree with node value B exceeds its sibling in height by one, but it is itself balanced in height. After insertion, in Figure 7.23 (b), its left subtree has increased in height by one. Now the subtree with node value B exceeds its sibling in height by two. This is called a left-left violation, since the left subtree of the current tree is of excessive length and the left subtree of that subtree is longer than its right subtree. A right–right violation is the mirror image of a left-left violation.

Suppose we were to zig the tree in diagram (b). Then we can recompute the heights of the various subtrees and find the following results:

The above operation can be performed by overriding the *zig()* method to change the *_diff* values. Since, as we shall see, *zig()* might be called in cases with somewhat different *_diff* values, we shall use the existing *_diff* values to compute new *_diff* values. We can assume that the *_diff* value of the current tree is negative (we certainly

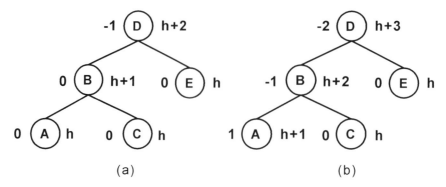

Figure 7.23: Left-Left violation occurring in (b) after insertion in (a).

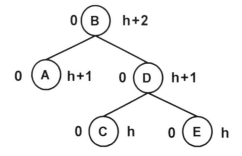

Figure 7.24: Result of zig operation on 7.23 (b).

would not want to perform *zig*() otherwise, since it would increase the difference in heights between the subtrees). We shall find that it makes a difference whether the *_diff* value for the left subtree is negative or not, so we shall consider the two possibilities separately.

So, let us consider a new Figure 7.25 (a) below. In this diagram, we assume that *gdiff* (the *_diff* field for tree *g*, the subtree with node value D) is negative, and *pdiff* (the *_diff* field for tree *p*, the subtree with node value B) is also negative. We have arbitrarily chosen the subtree with node value E as a reference point for the height. Its height is *h*, and all other heights are computed using *h* and the formula for the difference between subtrees.

In Figure 7.25 (b) above, we have performed a zig operation. We have also recomputed the heights. The height of tree *p* is $h+1$, rather than $h-gdiff+pdiff$, because $-2 <= gdiff <= -1$ and $pdiff <= -1$. Thus, $h-gdiff+pdiff-1 <= h-gdiff-2 <= h+2-2 = h$ and the right subtree of tree *p* is no shorter than the left. Also, $h-gdiff-1 <= h+2-1 =$

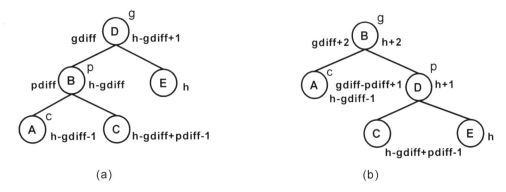

(a)   (b)

Figure 7.25:   The tree in (b) is a tree produced as a result of zig operation on (a).

$h+1$, so that the right subtree of tree g is no shorter than the left subtree. The `_diff` values have been computed by subtracting the computed height of the left subtree from that of the right subtree, in each case.

Now, let us consider the other possibility, where *pdiff* is non–negative. This possibility is diagrammed below, in Figure 7.26 (a). The value of *gdiff* is still negative.

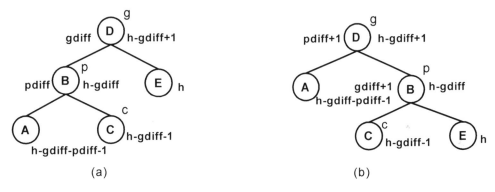

(a)   (b)

Figure 7.26:   The tree in (b) is produced as a result of zig operation on (a).

In Figure 7.26 (b) above, after the zig operation, the heights of trees p and g are recomputed. To recompute them, we note that *gdiff* $<= -1$, so that $h-gdiff-1 >= h$. Thus, tree c is at least equal in height to its new sibling, and tree p is of height $h-gdiff-1+1 = h-gdiff$. Since *pdiff* is non–negative, $h-gdiff-pdiff-1 < h-gdiff$. Thus, tree p is of greater height than its new sibling, and tree g is of height $h-gdiff+1$. The `_diff` values are again computed by subtracting the height of the left subtree from that of the right in each case.

Thus, the *zig ()* method for this class is as follows:

```
template<class DataType>
void AVLBST<DataType>::zig()
{
// nothing to rotate in an empty tree
   if (isEmpty()) return;
// if the left subtree is empty, no way to rotate its data to root
   if (_left->isEmpty()) return;
// so now we have something to rotate
   int gdiff = _diff;
   int pdiff = avlleft()->_diff;
// call the parent to do all the basic actions
   SelfModifyingBST<DataType>::zig();
// update the _diff fields for the parent and new right child
   if (pdiff < 0)
   {
        avlright()->_diff = gdiff-pdiff + 1;
        _diff = gdiff + 2;
   }
   else
   {
        _diff = 1 + pdiff;
        avlright()->_diff = 1 + gdiff;
   }
}
```

Since the left-left violation is corrected with a zig, it is no surprise that the right-right violation is corrected with a zag. However, all of the computations require modification as well. The *zag ()* method is left as an exercise for the reader.

Left-Right Violation

What shall we do about a left-right violation such as that illustrated below? Invoking *zig()* on it will not improve the situation; the reader can confirm that invoking *zig()* on a left-right violation will simply convert it to a right-left violation. What if we instead tried to repair this situation by invoking *zigzag ()* on it? A zag on tree *p* will convert this situation to a left–left violation. Certainly tree p itself must satisfy the AVL invariant (since we correct violations as soon as they occur, allowing them to propagate only upward, never downward), so $-1 <= c\text{->}\_diff <= 1$.

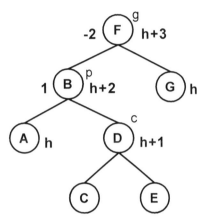

Figure 7.27:   A case of Left–Right violation.

If $c\text{->}\_diff = 1$, then the heights of the left and right subtrees of tree "c" are $h-1$ and h, respectively, and we get the situation below after invoking $zag()$ on tree "p". This is now a left–left violation which can be corrected by calling $zig()$.

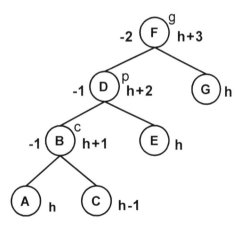

Figure 7.28:   A case of Left–Left violaion, which can be rectified by zig operation.

On the other hand, if $c._diff <= 0$, then the heights of the left and right subtrees of tree c are h and $h+c\text{->}\_diff$, respectively. After invoking $zag()$ on tree p, we get the situation below. This too is a left-left violation, but one that is slightly more complex, since the difference between subtrees of tree p may now be either -1 or -2.

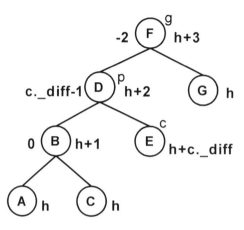

Figure 7.29:   A more complex case of Left–Left violation.

Still, when zig() is run, the result is a properly balanced tree, as shown at left. Note that, since $c\text{->}\_diff$ was either 0 or -1 originally, $p\text{->}\_diff$ will be either 0 or 1 after this operation, and the height of tree c will be either h or $h-1$. In either case, tree g is properly balanced.

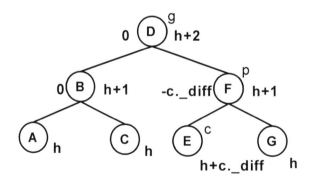

Figure 7.30:   A properly balanced tree produced from Figure 7.29 as a result of zig operation.

Since *zag()* and *zig()* are virtual methods, we can simply call *zigzag()* on a left-right violation, and the above rotations and computations will be automatically performed. Similarly, a right-left violation can be corrected by calling *zagzig()*.

The rebalance() method
Putting all of the above together, we can write a *rebalance()* method:

```
template<class DataType>
void AVLBST<DataType>::rebalance()
{
    if (_diff < -1)
    {
        if (avlleft()->_diff <= 0)
            zig (); // correct left-left violation
        else if (avlleft ()->_diff > 0)
            zigzag(); // correct left-right violation
    }
    else if (_diff > 1)
    {
        if (avlright ()->_diff >= 0)
            zag ();// correct right-right violation
        else if (avlright ()->_diff < 0)
            zagzig(); // correct right-left violation
    }
}
```

Complexity of _insert()

The *_insert()* method must call itself recursively until it reaches an empty tree; the maximum number of recursive calls is, therefore, equal to the height of the tree, which has been previously shown to be $O(log_2 n)$. The operations performed by this method, other than the recursive calls, are all of constant complexity. The *rebalance()* method is also of constant complexity. Thus, the complexity of the *_insert()* method is $O(log_2 n)$.

We have now completed the methods necessary to insert data into an AVL tree. The only remaining task is implementation of deletion, to which we now turn our attention.

7.1.3.4   Deletion

As in the case of insertion, we shall override the inherited *remove()* method, and use a protected method to do the actual deletion recursively. The *remove()* method is simple:

```
template<class DataType>
void AVLBST<DataType>::remove (DataType& data)
{
    if (_subtree) throw BinarySearchTreeChangedSubtree ();
    _remove (data);
}
```

The _remove() method

As before, we shall present the shell of the *_remove()* method and then develop it in stages. The shell is as follows:

```
template <class DataType>
void AVLBST<DataType>::_remove (DataType& data)
{
}
```

If the tree on which *_remove()* is invoked is empty, then the data to be deleted is not in the tree and we simply throw an exception:

```
        if (isEmpty()) throw BinarySearchTreeNotFound();
```

If the tree is not empty, we must decide where the data might be found, using a binary search technique. We begin by comparing the *data* argument with the *_rootData* field in the current tree. If *data* does not match the existing *_rootData*, we will recursively delete *data* from the appropriate subtree, being careful to rebalance the tree as necessary.

There are two cases in which the height of a subtree might change through deletion: either the subtree from which deletion was made became empty as a result of the deletion; or a subtree which was previously unbalanced (one of its subtrees having greater height than the other) became balanced, indicating that the subtree of greater height has been reduced in height. We must check for these two cases after the recursive call to *_remove()*:

```
// olddiff holds the old _diff from the affected subtree
int olddiff;
// check where the data goes relative to the current data
// we may need to recursively delete the data from a subtree
   if ((*_rootData) > data)
   {
      olddiff = avlleft()->_diff;
      avlleft()->_remove (data);
// check for change in height of left subtree
      if (((_left->isEmpty())||
// _left.isEmpty() would indicate that the data in _left
// was deleted and so it is now of height 0, previously of
// height 1. if the left subtree was previously unbalanced and
// became balanced,its longer subtree must have reduced in
// height and so the left subtree itself has also been
// reduced in height.
        ((avlleft()->_diff != olddiff) &&
                  (avlleft()->_diff == 0)))
      _diff++;
   }
   else if ((*_rootData) < data)
   {
      olddiff = avlright()->_diff;
      avlright()->_remove (data);
      if (((_right->isEmpty())||((avlright()->_diff != olddiff)
             && (avlright()->_diff == 0)))
        _diff--;
   }
   else
   {
// there is a match; delete subtree
   }
   rebalance();
```

If there is a match, we must delete the data from the current tree. There are three possibilities in this case: the current tree has an empty right subtree (the left subtree may or may not be empty), it has a non-empty right subtree but an empty left subtree, or both of its subtrees are non-empty.

If its right subtree is empty, its left subtree is empty or of height 1; in either case, we can copy the left subtree into the current tree, and be guaranteed that the current tree will be balanced. This operation is shown below:

```
// there is a match; delete from subtree
    if (_right->isEmpty())
    {
        AVLBST<DataType>* oldleft = avlleft();
        delete _right;
        delete _rootData;
        copyTree (_left);
        oldleft->_makeNull();
        delete oldleft;
        _diff = 0;
    }
```

If the current tree does have a non-empty right subtree, but its left subtree is empty, we can similarly replace it with its right subtree, which has height 1, and the resulting tree will be balanced.

```
    else if (_left->isEmpty())
    {
        AVLBST<DataType>* oldright = avlright();
        delete _left;
        delete _rootData;
        copyTree (_right);
        oldright->_makeNull();
        delete oldright;
        _diff = 0;
    }
```

Finally, if both subtrees are non-empty, we replace the current tree's node value with that of its inorder successor. Then we delete from its inorder successor, which certainly has an empty left subtree, and rebalance.

```
    else
        {
            // find inorder successor
            AVLBST<DataType>* succ = avlright();
            while (!succ->_left->isEmpty())
                  succ = succ->avlleft();
            delete _rootData;
            _rootData = new DataType(*(succ->_rootData));

            // save the old difference in the right subtree
            // so we can tell if it changed
            olddiff = avlright()->_diff;

            // delete the inorder successor
            avlright()->_remove (*(succ->_rootData));

            // check for change in height of right subtree
            if ((_right->isEmpty()) ||
            // we know that the right subtree was not empty;
            // if it is now empty, it has been reduced in
            // height if the right subtree was previously
            // unbalanced but is now balanced, it has been
            // reduced in height
                  ((avlright()->_diff != olddiff) &&
                        (avlright()->_diff == 0)))
                _diff--;

        } // two non-empty subtrees
```

Complexity of _remove()

Once again, the _remove() method calls itself recursively until it reaches an empty tree or the node to be deleted. Therefore, the maximum number of recursive calls is equal to the height of the tree, and is $O(log_2 n)$. All other operations of _remove() and rebalance(), which it calls, are of constant complexity. Thus, the complexity of the _remove() method is $O(log_2 n)$.

7.1.3.5 The *main*() function

We can now test the AVL tree by using the same main() method as we used for the red-black tree, the only change being in the class of the tree. The output from this function, while not very polished in appearance, shows that for the same input an AVL tree tends to be better balanced than a Red–Black tree.

```
+A +B +C +D +E +F +G +H +I +J +K +L +M +N +O +P +Q +R +S +T
+U +V +W +X +Y +Z
                    +--Z(0)
               +--Y(1)
           +--X(0)
                    +--W(0)
               +--V(0)
                    +--U(0)
      +--T(1)
                    +--S(0)
               +--R(0)
                    +--Q(0)
  +--P(0)
                    +--O(0)
               +--N(0)
                    +--M(0)
           +--L(0)
                    +--K(0)
               +--J(0)
                    +--I(0)
      +--H(0)
                    +--G(0)
               +--F(0)
                    +--E(0)
           +--D(0)
                    +--C(0)
               +--B(0)
                    +--A(0)
-Z -B -X -D -V -F -T -S -H -Q -K -O -N -M -L -P -J -I -R -G
-U -E -W -C -Y -A
```

7.2 The 2-3 Tree

A 2-3 tree is not a binary tree. Instead, a 2-3 tree is a finite set of nodes such that each node is either a 2-node (with a single value and two subtrees) or a 3-node (with two values and three subtrees). A 2-3 tree is empty (the number of nodes is zero), or its nodes satisfy the following properties:

1. Each 2-node has a single node value, and two 2-3 trees as subtrees, the left subtree and the middle subtree. All values in the left subtree are less than the node value and all values in the middle subtree are greater than the node value. Either both subtrees are non-empty, or else both subtrees are empty.
2. Each 3-node has two node values, the smaller node value and the larger node value, and three 2-3 trees as subtrees, the left, middle, and right subtrees. The smaller node value, not surprisingly, is less than the larger node value. All values in the left subtree are less than the smaller node value, all values in the middle subtree are greater than the smaller node value and less than the larger node value, and all values in the right subtree are greater than the larger node value. Either all subtrees are non-empty, or else all subtrees are empty.
3. All of the leaves (subtrees with no non-empty subtrees) are at the same depth.

It should be noted that a 2-3 tree, unlike a binary search tree, never has exactly one non-empty subtree. In the Figure 7.31 below, (a) and (b) are 2-3 trees, while (c) and (d) are not.

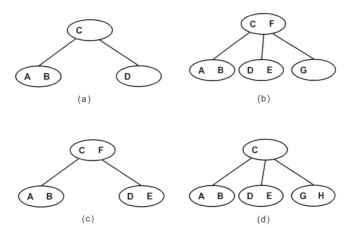

Figure 7.31: The tree in (a) and (b) are 2-3 trees while the trees in (c) and (d) are not 2-3 trees.

7.2.1   Overview of 2-3 Tree Operations

A 2–3 tree has the same operations as a binary search tree: searching, inserting, and deleting.

Searching

Searching is the simplest of the three operations. In a 2-node, searching is precisely the same as in a binary search tree, since there is only one node value and only two subtrees. In a 3-node, searching is similar, except that we compare the query with the smaller value; if the query is less, we search in the left subtree, and otherwise we compare the query with the larger value so as to decide between the middle and right subtrees.

Insertion

Insertion in a 2-3 tree is rather different from insertion in a binary search tree. In a binary search tree, insertion (other than insertion into a newly created, empty, tree) is accomplished by creating a new leaf, inserting the new value in the new leaf, and then perhaps performing rotations which might move the leaf to a new location. In a 2-3 tree, on the other hand, insertion is always made into an existing leaf.

Consider first a newly created, empty, 2-3 tree. By definition, the tree is a leaf since it has no children, and if we insert one value, we have a 2-node. So, after the first insertion, we can treat it as any other leaf which is a 2-node.

So, let us consider insertion into a leaf which is a 2-node. If we insert a second value, we can simply arrange the two node values correctly and no other changes need be made. Now the leaf is a 3-node. The process is diagrammed below.

Figure 7.32:   Inserting the node **A** into a 2 node tree.

Now we consider insertion into a leaf that is a 3-node. It already has two values and we cannot insert another value, as there is no place to put it. Instead, we arrange the three values in order, and split the node in two, with the smallest value going into the left new node, and the largest value going into the right new node (note that the new nodes are both 2-nodes). The middle value is passed back up to the parent, if the leaf has one. If the leaf has no parent, then it becomes a 2-node with the new nodes as its children and the middle value as its sole value. The process is diagrammed below.

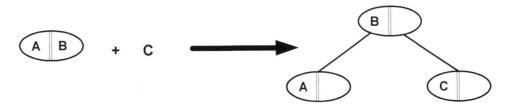

Figure 7.33:   Inserting the node **C** into a 3 node tree.

Now, what happens when the middle value is passed back up to a parent? If the parent is itself a 2-node, then it becomes a 3-node. There is no problem with resorting the subtrees, as they are in order and correctly arranged relative to the node values, as illustrated below.

Figure 7.34:   Inserting node **C** causing a split in the internal nodes.

On the other hand, if the parent is a 3-node, it will have to split just as the 3-node leaf had to split, but it has to be careful to split its subtrees correctly between the two new nodes. Again, it can pass its middle value to its parent, but if it has no parent, it itself must become a 2-node and adopt the two new nodes as its children. The splitting of an internal node is illustrated below.

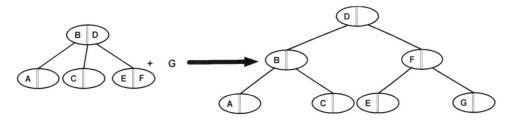

Figure 7.35:   Inserting node G causing a split in internal nodes.

The reader should note carefully that, since the new subtrees created by splitting remain siblings, or at least cousins, the height of a 2-3 tree never increases on insertion unless the root itself (the tree with no parent) splits. In that case, every leaf increases in depth by one, which is why the 2-3 tree remains height-balanced.

Deletion

Just as insertion always occurs in a leaf, deletion always occurs in a leaf of a 2-3 tree. Of course, the value to be deleted may be in an internal node, but we can readily handle this problem by replacing the value to be deleted with its inorder successor, and then deleting the inorder successor from the subtree from which it came. So our problem reduces to deleting a value from a leaf node.

If the leaf node is a 3-node, deletion is simple; it becomes a 2-node. If the leaf node is already a 2-node, however, it will become empty, which is impermissible if it has a parent. If it has a parent, then it has a sibling or two as well. The values contained in the parent and sibling(s) are redistributed so as to give the parent at least two children with at least one value per child, if possible. This means that there must be at least three values available between the parent and sibling(s), as there will be unless the parent and the only sibling are both 2-nodes already. One of the possibilities is illustrated below.

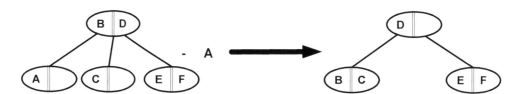

Figure 7.36:   Deletion of node **A** causing reorganization of a 3-node tree to a 2-node.

Suppose, however, that the parent and only sibling are in fact 2-nodes. Then we have only two values available. If the parent itself has no parent, then it combines with its sole non-empty child, discarding its children and becoming a 3-node leaf node. If the parent does have a parent, then it combines its own value and that of its non-empty child to produce a single child, so that it has no value and a single 3-node child. It then expects its own parent to give it a value. Now, suppose that an internal (non-leaf) subtree has become empty as described above. It will have a single non-empty child. Its parent will give it a non-empty value and a second non-empty child in a way similar to that described for leaves, with the added complication that all non–empty subtrees must be kept in proper relation to each other and to the node values.

If the parent of the internal subtree is a 3–node, there will be four, five, or six node values available, and five, six, or seven subtrees (respectively) to be distributed. There is no problem achieving such redistribution, and the parent will remain a proper 2–node or 3–node. One of the possibilities for such redistribution is shown as Figure 7.37 (a) on the following page.

If the parent of the internal node is a 2–node, but the sibling is a 3–node, we have three values and four subtrees, which we can redistribute as shown in Figure 7.37(b), following.

The problem arises, again, where the parent and only sibling are both 2–nodes. In that case we have two values and three subtrees. If the parent has no parent, we can combine its children into it, so that it becomes a 3–node. In this case, then, all leaves of the tree will be reduced in depth by 1, and the whole tree will be reduced in height by 1. This is illustrated in Figure 7.37 (c), following.

If the parent of the internal node has a parent, however, we are forced to combine its two children into one 3–node that include the parent's value, and we make the parent's value empty. Now the problem has been passed up to its parent, and we proceed backward until we reach one of the other cases described above.

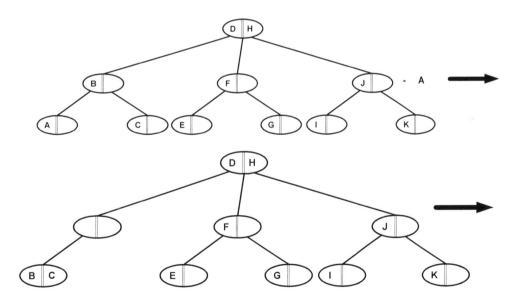

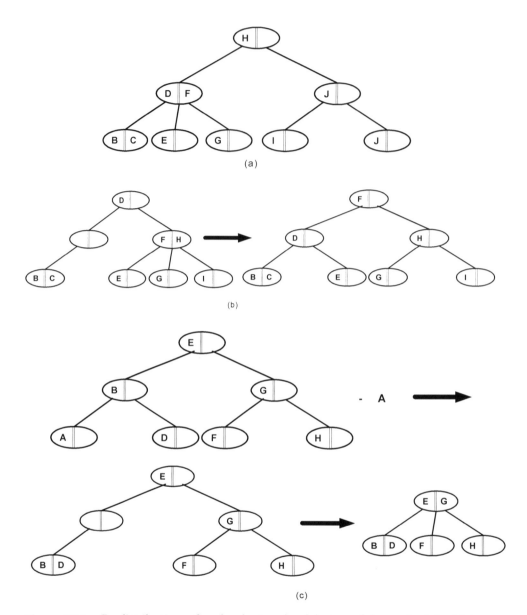

Figure 7.37: Redistribution of nodes during the deletion of the node **A** in (a) is
shown. Redistribution of nodes in a case where the parent is a 2-node
with its sibling being a 3-node. Deletion of node **A** causing restructuring is shown in (c).

7.2.2   Height of a 2-3 Tree

It is apparent that a 2-3 tree of height h has a minimum number of values when every node is a 2-node. But if every node is a 2-node, the 2-3 tree can be viewed as a full binary tree, and we know that the number of nodes in a full binary tree of height h is 2^h-1. On the other hand, the tree has a maximum number of values when every node is a 3-node. But if every node is a 3-node, the number of nodes is $(3^h-1)/2$, and the number of values is twice that, or 3^h-1. Thus, if a 2-3 tree of height h has n values, $2^h \leq n+1 \leq 3^h$, or $log_3(n+1) \leq h \leq log_2(n+1)$. Therefore h is certainly $O(log_2 n)$.

7.2.3   Abstract Data Type

A minimal specification of an abstract data type for the 2-3 tree is as follows:

```
CreateEmpty ()
    // creates an empty 2-3 tree
CreateNonempty (data)
    // creates a 2-3 tree with a 2-node in the root and data
    // as the smaller value
CreateNonempty (data1, data2)
    // creates a 2-3 tree with a 3-node in the root, data1 as
    // the smaller value, and data2 as the larger value
isEmpty ()
    // returns true if tree has no nodes, but otherwise returns
    // false
height ()
    // returns the height of the tree
size ()
    // returns the number of nodes in the tree
find (q)
    // returns a node value which matches q, or null if no
    // node value matches
insert (data)
```

```
    // inserts data into the tree while maintaining 2-3 tree
    // properties
remove (data)
    // removes data from the tree while maintaining 2-3 tree
    // properties
```

The reader may note that this abstract data type is essentially identical to that for the Binary Search Tree. Since both are search trees, this is no great surprise.

7.2.4   2-3 Tree Exceptions

As in the case of the binary search tree, we will wish to throw an exception if the user obtains a reference to a subtree and tries to modify it, since such modification might cause the tree to cease to be a search tree or a 2-3 tree. Also, we may run out of memory, or the user might seek to examine the data in an empty tree. As usual, we will create a family of exceptions associated with our 2-3 trees:

```
class Two3TreeException   : public Exception { };
class Two3TreeChangedSubtree   :  public Two3TreeException { };
class Two3TreeMemory           :  public Two3TreeException { };
class Two3TreeEmptyTree        :  public Two3TreeException { };
class Two3TreeNotFound         :  public Two3TreeException { };
```

7.2.5   2-3 Tree Abstract Base Class

It is clear that a 2-3 tree needs data, which have the same abilities as that inserted into binary search trees. Thus, we can require data inserted into a 2-3 tree to support the comparison operators. Using the Exception classes created in the previous subsection, we can write the abstract base class for the 2-3 tree:

```
template<class DataType>
class Abstract23Tree
{
friend ostream& operator <<(ostream& s,
                            Abstract23Tree<DataType>& bt);
public:
```

```
virtual ~Abstract23Tree();
virtual bool isEmpty () = NULL;
    // returns true if tree is empty, otherwise false
virtual bool isLeaf () = NULL;
    // returns true if tree is a leaf, otherwise false
virtual bool threeNode () = NULL;
    // returns true if tree is a 3-node, otherwise false
virtual int height ()= NULL;
    // returns the height of the tree
virtual int size ()= NULL;
    // returns the number of nodes in the tree
virtual bool subtree ()= NULL;
    // returns true if tree is subtree, otherwise false
virtualDataType& small ()= NULL;
    // returns smaller value from root,
    // or throws error if tree is empty
virtualDataType& large ()= NULL;
    // returns larger value from root,
    // or throws error if tree is empty or a 2-node
virtual Abstract23Tree<DataType>* left()= NULL;
    // returns leftmost subtree if tree is not empty;
    // throws error if the tree is empty
virtual Abstract23Tree<DataType>* middle()= NULL;
    // returns middle subtree if tree is not empty;
    // throws error if the tree is empty
virtual Abstract23Tree<DataType>* right()= NULL;
    // returns rightmost subtree if tree is not empty;
    // throws error if the tree is empty
virtualDataType find (DataType& q) = NULL;
    // returns a node value which matches q,
    // throws error if the tree is empty
virtual void insert (DataType& data) = NULL;
    // inserts data while maintaining 2-3 tree properties
virtual void remove (DataType& data) = NULL;
    // removes the value matching data, if any, while
```

```
        // maintaining 2-3 tree properties; throws exception
        // if value is missing
    virtual void makeEmpty ()= NULL;
        // empties tree by setting node values
        // to null and removing subtrees
    virtual void printtree (ostream& os, int level);
        // display tree structure (rotate)
    virtual Enumeration<DataType>* enumerator ();
        // returns an inorder enumeration of the data
    virtual void display (ostream& os);
};
// -----------------------------------------------------------
template<class DataType>
Abstract23Tree<DataType>::~Abstract23Tree() { }
```

We will want a *display()* method and a *printtree()* method similar to those of the binary search trees so that we can examine the structure of the tree, together with an ostream << operator. The *printtree()* method will have to make use of internal aspects of the implementation, but the other two can be implemented in the abstract base class. With the binary trees, we used the inorder enumerator to implement *display()*, and used `display()` to implement the `ostream` << operator; we will repeat that pattern here:

```
template<class DataType>
void Abstract23Tree<DataType>::display (ostream& os)
{
    bool first = true;
    Enumeration<DataType>* e = enumerator();
    os << "<";
    while (e->hasMoreElements())
    {
        if (!first) os << ", ";
        first = false;
        os << e->nextElement();
    }
    os << ">";
    delete e;
```

```
    }
    // ------------------------------------------------------------
    template<class DataType>
    ostream& operator << (ostream& s, Abstract23Tree<DataType>& bt)
    {
        bt.display(s);
        return s;
    }
```

The Enumerator

So now we have to write the enumerator. For simplicity, we shall do only an inorder enumerator. For a binary tree, an inorder enumeration can be obtained by one of the following: enumerating the left subtree, printing the root value, and enumerating the right subtree. With a 2-3 tree, however, we may have two node values and three subtrees, so we must enumerate the left subtree, return the _small_ value, enumerate the middle subtree, return the _large_ value, and finally enumerate the right subtree.

Recall that in the binary trees, we pushed left subtrees on a stack until we reached a subtree which had no left subtree. As we popped each tree from the stack, we returned its node value and pushed its right subtree on the stack. Unfortunately, we cannot do exactly the same procedure in a 2-3 tree, because we need to return the _small_ value of a node, then leave the node on the stack so that the middle and right subtrees are still available. However, let us consider again the steps we must follow:

1.   Enumerate the left subtree;
2.   Return the smaller value;
3.   Enumerate the middle subtree;
4.   Return the larger value (if this is a 3–node);
5.   Enumerate the right subtree (if this is a 3–node).

Steps (2) and (3) can be accomplished by pushing the middle subtree just before returning the smaller value, and steps (4) and (5) can be similarly accomplished. But how do we get from step 3 to step 4? We can, of course, push the current tree back on the stack just before the middle subtree in step 2, but how do we know, when we pop a tree off the stack, whether we should carry out step (2) or step (4)? One way would be to associate a boolean value with each tree on the stack, this value indicating whether step (2) has been performed yet, and that is what we shall do. For simplicity, we shall use two stacks, one for the tree and one for the boolean value, advancing and retreating in parallel.

The implementation of the inorder enumerator, along the lines described above, is set out below. Most of the implementation follows that of the binary tree inorder enumerator described in the previous chapter, except for *pushtobtmleft()* and *nextElement()*.

```cpp
template<class DataType>
class Two3TreeEnumerator : public Enumeration<DataType>
{
protected:
        // these two stacks advance in parallel
    StackLinked< Abstract23Tree<DataType>* >* _stackTree;
    StackLinked< bool >* _stackBool;
        // a value on this stack indicates whether
        // smaller value of corresponding tree has
        // been returned yet
    void pushToBtmLeft (Abstract23Tree<DataType>* tree);
public:
    Two3TreeEnumerator (Abstract23Tree<DataType>* t);
    virtual ~Two3TreeEnumerator ();
    virtual bool hasMoreElements ();
    virtual DataType& nextElement ();
};
// -----------------------------------------------------------
template<class DataType>
Two3TreeEnumerator<DataType>::Two3TreeEnumerator
    (Abstract23Tree<DataType>* t)
{
    _stackTree = new StackLinked< Abstract23Tree<DataType>* > ();
    _stackBool = new StackLinked< bool > ();
    if (t != NULL) pushToBtmLeft (t);
}
// -----------------------------------------------------------
template<class DataType>
Two3TreeEnumerator<DataType>::~Two3TreeEnumerator ()
```

```
{
    if (_stackTree != NULL) delete _stackTree;
    if (_stackBool != NULL) delete _stackBool;
}
// -----------------------------------------------------------
template<class DataType>
void Two3TreeEnumerator<DataType>::pushToBtmLeft
    (Abstract23Tree<DataType>* tree)
{
    // push left subtrees until reach the bottom;
    // when trees are first pushed, we know their
    // smaller values haven't been returned yet
    do
    {
        if (tree->isEmpty()) return;
        _stackTree->push (tree);
        _stackBool->push (false);
        tree = tree->left();
    } while (true);
}
// -----------------------------------------------------------
template<class DataType>
bool Two3TreeEnumerator<DataType>::hasMoreElements ()
{
    return (!_stackTree->isEmpty());
}
// -----------------------------------------------------------
template<class DataType>
DataType& Two3TreeEnumerator<DataType>::nextElement ()
{
    if (_stackTree->isEmpty() ) throw Two3TreeEmptyTree();
    Abstract23Tree<DataType>* tree = _stackTree->pop();
    bool smallDone = _stackBool->pop();
    if (!smallDone)         // smaller value not returned yet
    {
        if (tree->threeNode())
        // don't push a 2-node, as it has no larger value to return
```

```
        {
            _stackTree->push(tree);
            _stackBool->push(true); // <- true indicates
                                    //    smaller returned
        }
        pushToBtmLeft (tree->middle());
        return tree->small();
    }
    else // smaller value already returned
    {
        // since we got here, we know we have a 3-node
        pushToBtmLeft (tree->right());
        return tree->large();
    }
}
```

Now we can implement the *enumerator ()* method:

```
template<class DataType>
Enumeration<DataType>* Abstract23Tree<DataType>::enumerator()
{
    return new Two3TreeEnumerator<DataType> (this);
}
```

7.2.6   Implementation

We shall implement the Abstract23Tree interface in a class called Two3Tree. Initially, we need to consider how to represent 2-nodes and 3-nodes. Since a single node may change from a 2-node to a 3-node, and back again, in the course of insertions and deletions, it is clear that our instances must have space for a 3-node at all times. Also, as in other search trees, we cannot insert into a subtree, because this could destroy the ordering of the values.

The Two3Tree class therefore requires the following instance fields, corresponding to the two node values and the subtrees, and a flag for subtree status:

```
template<class DataType>
class Two3Tree : public virtual Abstract23Tree<DataType>
{
protected:
    DataType* _small;
    DataType* _large;
    Two3Tree<DataType>* _left;
    Two3Tree<DataType>* _middle;
    Two3Tree<DataType>* _right;
    bool _subtree;
};
```

7.2.6.1   Constructors and Destructor

In the binary tree, we had two constructors, one for an initially empty tree, and one for a tree with one value. In the 2-3 tree, we will have three constructors, for we can also create a tree with two values.

Since we never insert into empty nodes (other than the root of an entirely empty tree), we can save space by making all subtrees of leaves NULL. The tree will grow from the top down, as the root creates new children for itself. In this case, since there are five pointer fields, we will write a _makeNull() method to initialize all of them to NULL, so we can just set the ones that are needed. Thus, our constructors are as follows:

```
template<class DataType>
Two3Tree<DataType>::Two3Tree ()
// creates an empty 2-3 tree
{
    _makeNull();
    _subtree = false;
}
// -----------------------------------------------------------
template<class DataType>
Two3Tree<DataType>::Two3Tree (DataType& data)
// creates a 2-3 tree with one node value
{
    _makeNull();
```

```
        _small = new DataType (data);
        _subtree = false;
}
// ----------------------------------------------------------
template<class DataType>
Two3Tree<DataType>::Two3Tree (DataType& data1, DataType& data2)
// creates a 2-3 tree with two node values
{
    _makeNull();
    if (data1 < data2)
    {
        _small = new DataType (data1);
        _large = new DataType (data2);
    }
    else
    {
        _small = new DataType (data2);
        _large = new DataType (data1);
    }
    _subtree = false;
}
// ----------------------------------------------------------
template<class DataType>
void Two3Tree<DataType>::_makeNull ()
{
    _small = NULL;
    _large = NULL;
    _left = NULL;
    _middle = NULL;
    _right = NULL;
}
```

Although it is not a constructor, we will also show the *makeEmpty ()* method here, as it makes the affected instance "new". Because we may wish to apply this method on subtrees, we will write both a public *makeEmpty ()* method, which throws an exception if called on a subtree, and a protected *_makeEmpty ()* method, which does not.

```
template<class DataType>
void Two3Tree<DataType>::_makeEmpty()
{
    if (_small != NULL) delete _small;
    if (_large != NULL) delete _large;
    if (_left != NULL)  delete _left;
    if (_middle != NULL) delete _middle;
    if (_right != NULL) delete _right;


    _makeNull();
}
// ---------------------------------------------------------
template<class DataType>
void Two3Tree<DataType>::makeEmpty()
{
    if (subtree()) throw Two3TreeChangedSubtree();
    _makeEmpty();
}
```

We will also present the *copyTree()* method, which copies the data and subtree references from one tree to another (note that after this method is called, both trees point to the same subtrees and data):

```
template<class DataType>
void Two3Tree<DataType>::copyTree(Two3Tree<DataType>* fromtree)
{
// dispose of all the existing pointers
    _makeEmpty ();
    _small = fromtree->_small;
    _large = fromtree->_large;
    _left = fromtree->_left;
    _middle = fromtree->_middle;
    _right = fromtree->_right;
}
```

Finally, the destructor needs to delete any non–NULL pointers the instance might have. But this is precisely what _makeEmpty () does, so the destructor is quite simple, if not quite trivial:

```cpp
template<class DataType>
Two3Tree<DataType>::~Two3Tree ()
{
    _makeEmpty();
}
```

7.2.6.2 Accessor methods

The accessor methods are fairly obvious, and are generally implemented similarly to the corresponding methods of the binary trees.

```cpp
template<class DataType>
bool Two3Tree<DataType>::isEmpty () { return (_small == NULL); }
    // returns true if tree is empty, but otherwise returns false.
    // There is no need to check whether _large is NULL, as
    // we will never have a circumstance in which _small is
    // NULL and _large is not.
// ----------------------------------------------------------
template<class DataType>
bool Two3Tree<DataType>::isLeaf () { return (_left == NULL); }
// ----------------------------------------------------------
template<class DataType>
bool Two3Tree<DataType>::threeNode () { return (_large != NULL); }
// ----------------------------------------------------------
template<class DataType>
int Two3Tree<DataType>::height ()
    // returns the height of the tree
{
    if (_left == NULL) return 1;
// all subtrees are the same height, so we check only one
    else return 1 + _left->height();
}
// ----------------------------------------------------------
```

```
template <class DataType>
int Two3Tree<DataType>::size ()
    // returns the number of nodes in the tree
{
    int lsize = 0;
    int msize = 0;
    int rsize = 0;
    int thissize = 0;
    if (_small != NULL)
    {
        thissize++;
        if (_large != NULL) thissize++;
    }
    if (_left != NULL)
    {
        lsize = _left->size();
        msize = _middle->size(); // if left isn't NULL, middle isn't
        if (_right != NULL) rsize = _right->size();
    }
    return thissize + lsize + msize + rsize;
}
// ----------------------------------------------------------
template<class DataType>
bool Two3Tree<DataType>::subtree () { return _subtree; }
// ----------------------------------------------------------
template<class DataType>
DataType& Two3Tree<DataType>::small ()
{
    if (isEmpty()) throw Two3TreeEmptyTree ();
    return *_small;
}
// ----------------------------------------------------------
template<class DataType>
DataType& Two3Tree<DataType>::large ()
{
    if (_large == NULL) throw Two3TreeEmptyTree ();
    return *_large;
}
```

We previously indicated that we would allow the (empty) subtrees of a leaf to be represented by a NULL reference, rather than consuming memory with empty trees. However, the description of a 2–3 tree requires that a 2-node must have two subtrees and a 3-node must have three, even if they are empty. How can we accommodate this requirement? We shall create a single empty tree, which is a static field and which all non-empty leaves will return when asked for a child that is, in fact, null. Since this tree will be a subtree (its _subtree field will be true), it cannot be modified and so the fact that it is shared among all leaves will not produce a problem.

To create this empty tree, we will need a protected *static* method which creates a subtree (this corresponds to the `makeSubtree()` method of the binary search trees).

```
template<class DataType>
Two3Tree<DataType>* Two3Tree<DataType>::bottom =
Two3Tree::makeSubtree ();


template<class DataType>
Two3Tree<DataType>* Two3Tree<DataType>::makeSubtree ()
{
    Two3Tree<DataType>* sub = new Two3Tree<DataType> ();
    sub -> _subtree = true;
    return sub;
}
```

With this static field, we can implement *left*(), *middle*(), and *right*().

```
template<class DataType>
Abstract23Tree<DataType>* Two3Tree<DataType>::left()
    // returns leftmost subtree if tree is not empty;
    // returns null if the tree is empty
{
    if (isEmpty()) return NULL;
    if (_left == NULL) return bottom;
    return _left;
}
// ---------------------------------------------------------
template<class DataType>
Abstract23Tree<DataType>* Two3Tree<DataType>::middle()
    // returns middle subtree if tree is not empty;
```

```
        // returns null if the tree is empty
{

    if (isEmpty()) return NULL;
    if (_middle == NULL) return bottom;
    return _middle;
}
// --------------------------------------------------------
template<class DataType>
Abstract23Tree<DataType>* Two3Tree<DataType>::right()
    // returns rightmost subtree if tree is not empty;
    // returns null if the tree is empty
{

    if (isEmpty()) return NULL;
    if (_right == NULL) return bottom;
    return _right;
}
```

We can also implement the *printtree ()* method, previously deferred:

```
template<class DataType>
void Two3Tree<DataType>::printtree (ostream& os, int level)
    // display tree structure (rotated)
{

    if (isEmpty()) return;

    right()->printtree(os, level+1);

    if (_large != NULL)
    {
        for (int i = 0; i < level; i++)
            cout << " ";
        cout << (*_large) << "(" << level << ")" << endl;
    }

    middle()->printtree(os, level+1);

    for (int i = 0; i < level; i++)
```

```
            cout << " ";
        cout << (*_small) << "(" << level << ")" << endl;

        left()->printtree(os, level+1);
}
```

7.2.6.3 The *find*() method

The *find ()* method follows the procedure outlined previously, and is essentially similar to the *find ()* method of the binary search trees:

```
template<class DataType>
DataType Two3Tree<DataType>::find (DataType& q)
{
    if (isEmpty())
    throw Two3TreeNotFound();

// does it match a value in this node
    if ((*_small) == q)
    return *_small;
    if ((_large != NULL) && ((*_large) == q))
    return *_large;

// search a subtree in a two-node
    if ((*_small) > q)
    return _left->find (q);
    if (_large == NULL)  // then there's no right subtree
    return _middle->find (q);

// now we know there's a large value and a right subtree
    if ((*_large) > q) // _small is less and _large is more
        return _middle->find (q);
// so it must be in the far right
    return _right->find (q);
}
```

Complexity of find()

Every step in the *find ()* method can be done in constant time except the recursive invocations. The recursion moves down the tree one level at a time until it reaches a leaf, so the number of recursive invocations is equal to the height of the tree, which is $O(log_2 n)$. Thus, the complexity of the *find ()* method is $O(log_2 n)$.

7.2.6.4   The *insert*() method

The *insert ()* method again follows the procedure previously outlined, and does so recursively. One problem which must be handled in the *insert ()* method is that the root is different from other nodes: it has no parent to which it can pass its middle child. We therefore split insertion into two methods: the *insert ()* method itself, which can be called only on the root, and the *_insert ()* method which is recursively called. The *insert ()* method handles splitting of the root, and *_insert ()* handles splitting of any other node.

However, we have a problem: assuming that a node overflows and the middle value is passed back up to the parent, where do we store that value? And where do we store the new nodes that are formed from the node when it splits? We shall pass *_insert ()* a pointer, initially NULL, which it can point to new memory which it allocates and fills in with the middle value and node pointers if necessary. If this pointer comes back still NULL, we know that no middle value was passed up.

Our *insert ()* method, then, is as follows:

```
template<class DataType>
void Two3Tree<DataType>::insert (DataType& data)
{
    if (_subtree) throw Two3TreeChangedSubtree ();
    Two3Tree<DataType>* extra = NULL;

// _insert() will fill allocate space for extra
// and fill it with a middle value and two subtrees
// if the node needs to split
    _insert (data, extra);

// if a middle value was passed up, the tree needs to grow upward
```

```
   // -- but we already know the necessary root value and subtrees
      if (extra != NULL)
      {
   // dispose of all the subtrees - but not their pointers,
   // which have been adopted by extra or its subtrees
         if (_left != NULL)
         {
            _left->_makeNull();
            delete _left;
         }
if (_middle != NULL)
         {
            _middle->_makeNull();
         delete _middle;
         }
         if (_right != NULL)
         {
         _right->_makeNull();
         delete _right;
         }
         copyTree(extra);
         extra->_makeNull();
         delete extra;
      }
}
```

The _insert () method is more complicated, so we will develop it in stages.
The shell of the method is as follows:

```
template<class DataType>
void Two3Tree<DataType>::_insert (DataType& data,
Two3Tree<DataType>*& extra)
{
}
```

If the node is empty (this can only happen at the root), then our task is simple. We just store the new value in the _*small* position and return:

```
if (isEmpty())
{
    _small = new DataType (data);
    return;
}
```

If the node is not empty, however, we need to compare the *data* value with both the _*small* value and the _*large* value, bearing in mind, however, that the _*large* value will not be present in a 2-node. If the _*large* value is not present, the *data* must go to its left, since it cannot go to the right. The easy cases here occur when the *data* value matches an existing value:

```
if ((*_small) == data)
{
    delete _small;
    _small = new DataType (data);
    return;
}
if ((_large != NULL) && ((*_large) == data))
{
    delete _large;
    _large = new DataType (data);
    return;
}
```

Now we have two possibilities: the current node is a leaf, in which case we must insert here, or it is not a leaf, in which case we must insert recursively into a subtree, and handle a value passed back up, if necessary. We will take the first possibility first.

If the current node is a leaf, but is a 2-node, we can certainly insert the data and have only to decide whether it belongs in the _*small* position or in the _*large* position. If the current node is a 3-node, then we must find the middle of the three available values (_small, _large, and data), move it to extra, and create two new nodes for the remaining two values. Fortunately, we need not deal with subtrees; since this is a leaf, they are all NULL.

For simplicity in this and the following section of code, we will write a helper method to carry out the task of moving a value to extra and creating two new nodes. We will pass in the root value for extra, followed by the root value for its left subtree, together with the subtrees for its left subtree, followed by the root value and subtrees for its middle subtree. Thus, our helper method is as follows:

```
template<class DataType>
Two3Tree<DataType>* Two3Tree<DataType>::constructTree
  (DataType* rootval, // _small value in tree
  DataType* leftval, // _small value for new left subtree
  Two3Tree<DataType>* leftleft, // left subtree for new left
  Two3Tree<DataType>* leftmid, // middle subtree for new left
  DataType* midval, // _small value for new middle
  Two3Tree<DataType>* midleft, // left subtree for new middle
  Two3Tree<DataType>* midmid) // middle subtree for new mid
{
   Two3Tree<DataType>* tree = new Two3Tree<DataType> ();
   tree->_small = rootval;
   tree->_left = new Two3Tree<DataType> ();
   tree->_left->_small = leftval;
   tree->_left->_left = leftleft;
   tree->_left->_middle = leftmid;
   tree->_left->_subtree = true;
   tree->_middle = new Two3Tree<DataType> ();
   tree->_middle->_small = midval;
   tree->_middle->_left = midleft;
   tree->_middle->_middle = midmid;
   tree->_middle->_subtree = true;
   return tree;
}
```

Now we can finally present the code for inserting a value into a leaf:

```
// if _left is NULL, we have a leaf, and if we got here, we know
// the data wasn't already here, so we need to insert, and we
// may have to split the node
   if (_left == NULL)
   {

   // if _large is null, this is a 2-node and we have room
      for the data
         if (_large == NULL)
         {
            if ((*_small) > data) // _small is greater than data
            {
                  _large = _small;
                  _small = new DataType (data);
            }
            else _large = new DataType (data);
            return;
         } // if (_large == null) - i.e., two node

   // if _large is not null, we have to split the node
      else
         {
            if ((*_small) > data) // _small is greater than data
            {
                  extra = constructTree (_small,
                         // _small becomes the middle
                            new DataType (data), NULL, NULL,
                         // new left subtree with data
                            _large, NULL, NULL);
                         // new middle with former large
            }
            else if ((*_large) > data) // data is the middle value
            {
                  extra = constructTree (new DataType (data),
                         // data becomes the middle
                  _small, NULL, NULL,
```

```
                              // new left subtree with small
                _large, NULL, NULL);
                              // new middle subtree with large
          }
          else // data is the largest value
          {
                extra = constructTree (_large,
          _small, NULL, NULL,
                new DataType (data), NULL, NULL);
          }


      _makeNull(); // we're going to be deleted in any case
      return;
   } // if (_large != null)
} // if (_left == null) // i.e., leaf
```

The reader should confirm that the value passed up to the parent is correct in each case, and that all allocated memory is properly deleted.

The second possibility is that the node is not a leaf. In that case, we will have to insert the data recursively, in a fashion similar to the binary search trees. However, we have the possibility that we will receive a value and subtrees from *extra*. This value and these subtrees arise from one of the existing subtrees, so that we know exactly how the value compares with the existing *_small* and *_large*: if it came from the left subtree, it is less than both; if it came from the middle subtree, it falls between them; if it came from the right subtree, it is greater than both. Thus, we can immediately determine where to place it and the new subtrees. After placing the values, we must dispose of *extra* so that the parent of the current node will not attempt to reference it.

Once again, we must handle the possibility of overflow, and this time we must be careful to assign the subtrees correctly. It should be noted that we will have exactly three values (*_small*, *_large*, and *extra->_small*) and four subtrees (two of the original three, and two replacing a single original subtree), and that we know the ordering of these seven items. Thus, we can fill in *extra* with little trouble. The code for inserting into a non-leaf is therefore:

```
// if we got to here, this is a non-leaf
// if _left is not null, we need to insert recursively, then
   handle
// extra if something is passed back up

 else {
// we may have two extra trees
        Two3Tree<DataType>* oldextra;
// ----------------------------------------------------------
// if we inserted in the left subtree, extra will contain a value
// and two trees left of our _small value
        if ((*_small) > data)
        {
            _left->_insert (data, extra);
            if (extra != NULL) // a value was passed back up
            {
        delete _left;    // certainly don't need _left anymore

    // if _large is NULL, we have room for the two trees and
    // one value
                if (_large == NULL)
                {
                    _large = _small;
                    _right = _middle;
                    _small = extra->_small;
                    _left = extra->_left;
                    _middle = extra->_middle;
                // we've handled extra, so don't pass it up
                    extra->_makeNull();
                    delete extra;
                    extra = NULL;
                }

    // _large is not NULL, so we have to split
                else
                {
                    oldextra = extra;
```

```
                    extra = constructTree (_small,
                    oldextra->_small, oldextra->_left, oldex-
                    tra->_middle,
                          _large, _middle, _right);
                    oldextra->_makeNull();
                    delete oldextra;
                    _makeNull();// prepare to be destroyed
               }
            }
          } // small > data


// ----------------------------------------------------------
// if we inserted in the middle subtree, extra will contain a
// value and two trees between our values
          else if ((_large == NULL) || ((*_large) > data))
          {
               _middle->_insert (data, extra);
               if (extra != NULL) // a value was passed back up
               {
                    delete _middle; // certainly don't need _middle
                                    // anymore

     // if _large is NULL, we have room for the two trees and
     // one value
                    if (_large == NULL)
                    {
                         _large = extra->_small;
                         _middle = extra->_left;
                         _right = extra->_middle;
                         extra->_makeNull();
                         delete extra;
                         extra = NULL;
                    }

     // _large is not NULL, so we have to split
```

```
                else
                {
                    oldextra = extra;
                    extra = constructTree (oldextra->_small,
                        _small, _left, oldextra->_left,
                        _large, oldextra->_middle, _right);
                    oldextra->_makeNull();
                    delete oldextra;
                    _makeNull();// prepare to be destroyed
                }
            }
        }    // belongs in middle


        else // belongs in right
        {
            _right->_insert (data, extra);

            if (extra != NULL) // certainly need to split
            {
                delete _right;
                oldextra = extra;
                extra = constructTree (_large,
                    _small, _left, _middle,
                    oldextra->_small, oldextra->_left, old-
                    extra->_middle);
                oldextra->_makeNull();
                delete oldextra;
                _makeNull(); // prepare to be destroyed
            }
        } // belongs in right
    }    // insert in non-leaf
```

At length, having placed the *data* value where it belongs, we are finally able to return to the caller:

Complexity of insert()

Every step in the *insert()* method can be done in constant time except the recursive invocations of *_insert()*. The recursion moves down the tree one level at a time until it reaches a leaf, so the number of recursive invocations is equal to the height of the tree, which is $O(log_2 n)$. Thus, the complexity of the *insert()* method is $O(log_2 n)$.

7.2.6.5   The *remove*() method

As in the case of the *remove()* methods of the binary search trees, we have implemented deletion recursively, using a public *remove()* method which can be called only on the root node, and a protected *_remove()* method which is called recursively.

If, after deletion, a node finds itself with one subtree and no node values, it normally relies upon its parent to combine it with other subtrees so as to bring it back to a 2-node or 3-node. However, the root has no parent, and has to handle this problem by itself. Thus, the *remove()* method will handle the problem for the root, and the *_remove()* method will handle it for all other nodes. In the case of the root, handling the problem consists of simply copying the one and only subtree into the root, since the subtree is guaranteed to be a proper 2-3 tree.

The reader will recall that we want to delete only from a leaf. This implies that, if we need to delete from an internal node, we must replace the value to be deleted with its inorder successor, and then delete the inorder successor. To accomplish this, we will pass *_remove()* a reference to a subtree; as long as the value to be deleted has not been found, this reference is NULL, but once we find the value, we will pass a reference to the node containing it.

Therefore the *remove*() method is as follows:

```
template<class DataType>
void Two3Tree<DataType>::remove (DataType& data)
{
    if (_subtree) throw Two3TreeChangedSubtree();
    // _remove returns false if data not found
    if (!_remove (data, NULL))
```

```
                    throw Two3TreeNotFound();
    // if tree is now empty, but _left has a valid tree,
    // then all other values have been deleted,
    // so move _left into the root and delete _left
    if ((isEmpty()) && (_left != NULL))
    {
        Two3Tree<DataType>* oldleft = _left;
    // null-out _left so it doesn't get deleted by copyTree
        _left = NULL;
        copyTree (oldleft);
        oldleft->_makeNull();
        delete oldleft;
    }
}
```

As with the _insert () method, we will develop the _remove () method in stages. The shell of the method is as follows:

```
template<class DataType>
bool Two3Tree<DataType>::_remove
    (DataType& data, Two3Tree<DataType>* tradewith)
{
}
```

Deletion from a leaf is the base case of the recursive method. When a leaf is reached, we need to replace the value to be deleted with its inorder successor, which must be the _small value in the leaf, and then delete the successor from the leaf. No rearrangement of subtrees is necessary, since the subtrees are NULL. This case is, therefore, as follows:

```
// if this is a leaf, replace the value to be deleted (if
// any) with its successor, and delete the successor
    if (_left == NULL)   // i.e., a leaf
    {
        if ((*_small) == data)
            // the value to delete is in _small
        {
            delete _small;
```

```
            _small = _large;
            _large = NULL;
            return true;
        }
        else if ((_large != NULL) && ((*_large) == data))
            // the value to delete is in _large
        {
            delete _large;
            _large = NULL;
            return true;
        }
        else if (tradewith != NULL)
            // the value to delete is somewhere above
        {
            if (*(tradewith->_small) == data)
            {
                delete tradewith->_small;
                tradewith->_small = _small;
            }
            else
            {
                delete tradewith->_large;
                tradewith->_large = _small;
            }
            _small = _large;
            _large = NULL;
            return true;
        }
        return false; // if we got here, it's nowhere in the tree
    }
```

If the current node is not a leaf, then we need only make a recursive call to _remove(), and then correct the situation if a subtree finds itself with a left subtree and no node value.

If the value to be deleted is in the left subtree, it certainly doesn't match any value in this node, so we just make the recursive call using the *tradewith* parameter passed in.

If the left subtree becomes empty, we fill it with a value from the middle subtree or else merge the left and middle subtree. So the code for deleting from the left subtree is as follows:

```
// now we know we're looking at a non-leaf
   bool result; // variable to hold result reported by leaf
// deletion from the left subtree
   if ((*_small) > data)
   {

       result = _left->_remove (data, tradewith);
   // since this is not a leaf, we know that _left should not
   // be empty
       if (_left->isEmpty())
       {
       // we will certainly move the _small value
       // and _middle's _left to _left
           _left->_small = _small;
           _left->_middle = _middle->_left;
               // now _left is a good 2-node

       // if _middle._large is NULL, then _middle is a 2-node
       // and must be merged with _left
           if (_middle->_large == NULL)
           {
               _left->_large = _middle->_small;
               _left->_right = _middle->_middle;
               _small = _large; // note that _large might
                                 // be NULL already

               _middle->_makeNull();
               delete _middle;

               _middle = _right;
               _large = NULL;
               _right = NULL;
```

```
              } // middle is a 2-node
// otherwise, _middle is a 3-node and can spare a value
        else
        {
                _small = _middle->_small;
                _middle->_left = _middle->_middle;
                _middle->_small = _middle->_large;
                _middle->_middle = _middle->_right;
                _middle->_large = NULL;
                _middle->_right = NULL;
        } // middle is a 3-node
    } // left comes back empty
} // deleting from left
```

Deletion from the middle subtree may occur either because the _small value needs to be deleted or because the value to be deleted is in the middle subtree. However, the only difference is that, if the _small value is to be deleted, we must pass a reference to the current tree instead of the tradewith parameter previously passed in. If the middle subtree becomes empty, we merge it with the left subtree, or take a value from the left subtree, since the right subtree is not guaranteed to exist. The code for deletion from the middle subtree is, therefore:

```
else if ((_large == NULL) || ((*_large) > data))
    // data is between _small and _large
{
    if ((*_small) == data) tradewith = this;

// since this is not a leaf, we know that
// _middle should not be empty
    result = _middle->_remove (data, tradewith);
    if (_middle->isEmpty())
    {
    // if _left._large is null, then _left is a 2-node
    // and must be merged with _middle
        if (_left->_large == NULL)
        {
                _left->_large = _small;
```

```
                              _left->_right = _middle->_left;
                              _small = _large; // note that _large might
                         be null already

                              _middle->_makeNull();
                         delete _middle;

                              _middle = _right;
                              _large = NULL;
                              _right = NULL;
                    }
          // otherwise, _left is a 3-node and can spare an element
               else
               {
                         _middle->_middle = _middle->_left;
                         _middle->_small = _small;
                         _middle->_left = _left->_right;
                         _small = _left->_large;
                         _left->_large = NULL;
                         _left->_right = NULL;
               }
          }
     }
```

Additionally, deletion from the right subtree can occur either because we are deleting the *_large* value or because the value to be deleted is in the right subtree. Again, we pass either a reference to the current subtree or the *tradewith* parameter passed in. If the right subtree becomes empty, we merge it with the middle subtree or else fill it with a value from the middle subtree.

```
     else // _large is less than or equal to data
     {
          if ((*_large) == data) tradewith = this;
     // since this is not a leaf, we know that _right should
     // not be empty
          result = _right->_remove (data, tradewith);
```

```
            if (_right->isEmpty())
            {// if _middle->_large is null, then _middle is a 2-node
             // and must be merged with _right
                if (_middle->_large == NULL)
                {
                    _middle->_large = _large;
                    _middle->_right = _right->_left;
                    _right->_makeNull();
                    delete _right;
                    _large = NULL;
                    _right = NULL;
                }
            // otherwise, _middle is a 3-node and can spare an element
                else {
                    _right->_middle = _right->_left;
                    _right->_small = _large;
                    _right->_left = _middle->_right;
                    _large = _middle->_large;
                    _middle->_large = NULL;
                    _middle->_right = NULL;
                }
            }
        }
```

Finally, whatever value was returned from the recursive call is passed back to the caller.

```
    return result;
```

Complexity of remove()

Every step in the *remove()* method can be done in constant time except the recursive invocations of *_remove()*. The recursion moves down the tree one level at a time until it reaches a leaf, so the number of recursive invocations is equal to the height of the tree, which is $O(log_2 n)$. Thus, the complexity of the *remove()* method is $O(log_2 n)$.

7.2.6.6   The *main*() function

The worst possible case for a (non-height-balanced) binary search tree is insertion of the nodes in order. So in the *main*() test function for the *Two3 Tree* class, we will insert the nodes in order, to see what happens:

```
void main()
{
    char inserts[] = "ABCDEFGHIJKLMNOPQRSTUVWXYZ";
    char deletes[] = "KBXKV";
    Two3Tree<char> bst;
    for (int i = 0; i < 26; i++)
    {
        bst.insert (inserts[i]);
        cout << "+" << inserts[i] << " ";
    }
    cout << endl;
    bst.printtree(cout, 0);
    for (int i = 0; i < 5; i++)
    {
        cout << "-" << deletes[i] << " ";
        try
        {
            bst.remove (deletes[i]);
        }
        catch (Exception e) { cout << "Exception!" << endl; }
    }
    cout << endl;
    bst.printtree(cout, 0);
}
```

The output from this method is as follows:

```
+A +B +C +D +E +F +G +H +I +J +K +L +M +N +O +P +Q +R +S +T
+U +V +W +X +Y +Z
        Z(3)
        Y(3)
    X(2)
        W(3)
    V(2)
        U(3)
  T(1)
        S(3)
    R(2)
        Q(3)
P(0)
        O(3)
    N(2)
        M(3)
  L(1)
        K(3)
    J(2)
        I(3)
H(0)
        G(3)
    F(2)
        E(3)
  D(1)
        C(3)
    B(2)
        A(3)
-K -B -X -K Exception!
-V
        Z(3)
    Y(2)
        W(3)
        U(3)
  T(1)
        S(3)
    R(2)
```

```
                    Q(3)
        P(0)
                  O(3)
              N(2)
                M(3)
            L(2)
                J(3)
                I(3)
          H(1)
                G(3)
            F(2)
                E(3)
            D(2)
                C(3)
                A(3)
```

The number of nodes inserted was 26, but the height was only four. Four nodes were deleted ("K" was deleted twice to show that the exception produces no problem), leaving 22 nodes.

7.2.7   The B-Tree

The 2-3 tree is actually a special case of a more general data structure, the B-tree. The B-tree is not a binary tree (as we have seen with the 2-3 tree) and satisfies the following properties:

1. A B-tree has a maximum number of node values which is called MAX.
2. Every B-tree has between MAX/2 and MAX (inclusive) node values, except the root, which may fewer than MAX/2 values.
3. The number of subtrees belonging to each non-leaf B-tree is one more than the number of node values.
4. The node values of a B-tree are in sorted order.
5. Suppose the values in a non-leaf B-tree are numbered left to right from 0 to n, and the subtrees of the B-tree are numbered left to right from 0 to $n+1$. Then node value i is greater than every value in subtree i, and less than every value in subtree $i+1$.
6. Every leaf in a B-tree lies at the same depth.

The 2-3 tree previously developed is a B-tree with MAX of 2. In the 2-3 tree, we had separately named larger and smaller values. Implementation of the general B-tree would require an array of MAX values and MAX+1 subtrees. The development of the B-tree is left as a project for the reader.

7.3 Splay Trees

The height-balanced trees previously presented attempt to reduce the average number of accesses required in a search for an element by avoiding the worst case of a very deep and unbalanced tree. An entirely different approach to reducing the average number of accesses is to cause the tree to "mutate" toward an optimum tree, that is, one in which the elements most likely to be accessed are also those closest to the top of the tree.

This is the approach taken by the splay trees. In such trees, an element may be moved to the root of the tree (also called as *splaying*) when it is accessed in any way, although splay trees may differ in the probability that an element will be moved on a given access. In the splay tree presented here, every element is moved to the root each time it is accessed. In any splay tree, therefore, the elements most frequently accessed tend to be close to the root, while those infrequently accessed tend to end up near the leaves.

A splay tree need not be height-balanced at all; indeed, it may be grossly unbalanced. Because it need not be height-balanced, there is no need for the additional fields used by the height-balanced trees. It has no additional fields at all. It relies solely on the process of moving an element to the root while searching, inserting, or deleting. The move-to-root algorithm will be developed as part of the *find*() method.

The splay tree will be implemented as a subclass of the `SelfModifyingBST`, as it has the same fields and the same interface.

7.3.1 Constructors and Destructor

Because the splay tree has no additional fields, it is necessary only to implement the constructors and destructor, and also to reimplement the `makeSubtree()` method so that the subtrees of a splay tree are also splay trees. The methods are quite simple:

```
template<class DataType>
class SplayBST : public SelfModifyingBST<DataType>
{
protected:
    virtual BinarySearchTree<DataType>* makeSubtree ();
public:
    SplayBST ();
    SplayBST (DataType& data);
    ~SplayBST();
};
// ---------------------------------------------------------
template<class DataType>
SplayBST<DataType>::SplayBST ()
    : SelfModifyingBST <DataType> () { }
// ---------------------------------------------------------
template<class DataType>
SplayBST<DataType>::SplayBST (DataType& data)
    : SelfModifyingBST <DataType> (data) { }
// ---------------------------------------------------------
template<class DataType>
SplayBST<DataType>::~SplayBST () { }
// ---------------------------------------------------------
template<class DataType>
BinarySearchTree<DataType>* SplayBST<DataType>::makeSubtree()
{
    SplayBST<DataType>* bst = new SplayBST<DataType> ();
    bst->_subtree = true;
    return bst;
}
```

7.3.2   Accessor methods

As we did with the height balanced trees, we will simplify our code by adding methods which automatically typecast the left and right subtrees to splay trees. These methods, *spLeft ()* and *spRight ()*, are again quite simple, and only *spLeft ()* is shown below:

```
template<class DataType>
SplayBST<DataType>* SplayBST<DataType>::spLeft ()
{
    return (SplayBST<DataType>*) _left;
}
```

Most of the accessor methods can be used unchanged, but we will need to reimplement the *find ()* method so that some element will be moved to the root after a search.

7.3.3   Searching

Whenever we search for an element, either that element (if present in the tree) or the last element examined (if not) will move to the root, if it was not already there. The algorithm for moving an element to the root involves three cases, together with their mirror images. In two cases, we reduce the depth of the element by two, by moving the element to its grandparent and rearranging the subtrees of the grandparent to maintain the search tree properties. There are two cases since a left-left (or right-right) grandchild is treated differently from a left-right (or right-left) grandchild. In the third case, we reduce the depth of the element by one, by moving the element to its parent and, again, rearranging the subtrees.

When we move the left-left grandchild's value to its grandparent, the subtree with the grandparent's value becomes the right-right grandchild, as illustrated below. The reader will recognize this as a zigzig operation. The right-right case is the mirror image of this, and requires a zagzag operation. The depth of the affected element has been reduced by 2.

When we move the left-right grandchild's value to its grandparent, the subtree with the grandparent's value becomes the right child, while the left child remains unchanged, as illustrated below. This is, of course, the zigzag operation. Again, the right-left case is the mirror image of this, and the depth of the affected element (B) is reduced by 2.

The transformations above always reduce the depth of the affected element by two. But what if the depth was initially odd? Clearly, repeated applications of the above transformations will not bring the element to the root.

We therefore need to handle the case where the depth must be reduced by exactly 1. But this is easy; it is a simple rotation (zag or zig) such as ones we have seen before.

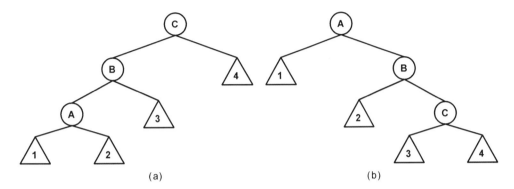

Figure 7.38:   Zigzig operation producing (b) from (a). Similarly zagzag operation produces (a) from (b).

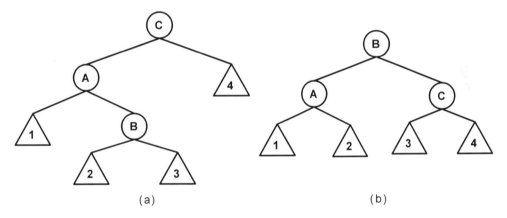

Figure 7.39:   Zigzag operation produces (b) from (a).

As usual, we shall implement our algorithm recursively. In previous trees, we have decided which child is affected, then called the method on the child. Here, however, we must treat the left-left grandchild differently from the left-right grandchild; it is not enough to know that the left child is affected. Therefore, we will decide in the recursive procedure whether the left or right subtree is affected, then whether the child itself, or the left or right grandchild through that child, is affected. Thus, we have six possible cases, in addition to the case where the search ends in the current subtree itself.

In previous trees, we have had a protected recursive method to handle insertion and deletion; here we will have one to handle the search. Thus, we will have the *find()* method required by the interface, and a recursive *_find()* method to move the correct element to the root. This *_find()* method will move either the required element itself,

or the element which was in the subtree in which the search terminated. Once _find()
has moved an element to the root, we have only to check whether the element in the
root is, in fact, the required element; if so, we return it, and otherwise we return null.
Thus, the find() method itself is as follows:

```
template<class DataType>
DataType SplayBST<DataType>::find (DataType& q)
{
    if (isEmpty()) throw BinarySearchTreeNotFound();
    _find (q);
    if ((*_rootData) == q) return rootData();
    throw BinarySearchTreeNotFound();
}
```

The implementation of the _find() method is the key to the splay tree. This
method is recursive, and it has three base cases: the search ends in the current tree, or in
the left child (but not a child of the left child), or in the right child (but not in a child
of the right child).

In the first base case, no action is required and we simply return from the method.
In the other two base cases, we will move the affected child's value to the current subtree using *zig* () or *zag* (), as appropriate.

If we have not reached a base case, we determine the correct grandchild, call
the method recursively on that grandchild, and then move the grandchild's value to
the current subtree using *zigzig*() (for a left-left grandchild), *zigzag* () (for a left-right
grandchild), *zagzig* () (for a right-left grandchild), or *zagzag* () (for a right-right grandchild). Thus, the value in the subtree where the search ends will move backward to the
root, and the tree will be rearranged along the way.

The code for the _find() method is as follows:

```
template<class DataType>
void SplayBST<DataType>::_find (DataType& q)
{
    if ((*_rootData) == q) return;
// -----------------------------------------------------------
    if ((*_rootData) < q)
    {   // go right
```

```
            if (spRight()->isEmpty()) return;

            if (*(spRight()->_rootData) == q)
                zag();
            else if (*(spRight()->_rootData) < q)
            {    // go right-right
                if (spRight()->_right->isEmpty())
                    zag();
        else

                {
                    spRight()->spRight()->_find(q);
                    zagzag();
                }
            }    // go right-right
            else
            {    // go right-left
                if (spRight()->_left->isEmpty())
                    zag();
                else
                {
                    spRight()->spLeft()->_find(q);
                    zagzig();
                }
            }    // go right-left
    }    // go right
// -------------------------------------------------------
    else
    {    // go left
        if (spLeft()->isEmpty()) return;

        if (*(spLeft()->_rootData) == q)
            zig();

    else if (*(spLeft()->_rootData) < q)
        {    // go left-right
            if (spLeft()->_right->isEmpty())
                zig();
```

```
      else
            {
                  spLeft()->spRight()->_find(q);
                  zigzag();
            }
      }   // go left-right
      else
      {   // go left-left
            if (spLeft()->_left->isEmpty())
      zig();
            else
            {
                  spLeft()->spLeft()->_find(q);
                  zigzig();
            }
      }   // go left-left
   } // go left
}
```

7.3.4   Insertion

In previous trees, the insertion code has been more difficult than the searching code. In this case, the insertion code is relatively simple. We call _find() to guarantee that the desired element, if present in the tree, is in the root. If it is not present, the element below which it would be inserted is in the root. Thus, if the desired element was not present, we can insert it into the root and move the existing element to a new subtree either to the left or to the right. The insertion method is, therefore, not recursive. It is as follows:

```
template<class DataType>
void SplayBST<DataType>::insert (DataType& data)
{
   if (_subtree)
        throw BinarySearchTreeChangedSubtree();

   // if the tree is empty, just insert the data
```

```
    if (isEmpty())
    {
        _rootData = new DataType (data);
        _left = makeSubtree();
        _right = makeSubtree();
        return;
    }

    // if the tree is not empty, call _find() to move
    // the correct element to the root
    _find (data);

    // now check whether the desired element was
    // in the tree to start with

    // if the desired element was in the tree to start
    // with, just replace it and return the old value
    if ((*_rootData) == data)
    {
        delete _rootData;
        _rootData = new DataType (data);
        return;
    }

    // otherwise, the desired element is not in the tree
    // so we need to move the value from the root either
    // to left or right, and therefore we need a new tree
    SplayBST<DataType>* newtree = (SplayBST<DataType>*) make-
    Subtree();
    newtree->copyTree (this);
    _rootData = new DataType(data);

    // if the data to be inserted needs to go to the right,
    // we need to move the old root to the left and then
    // decide whether the old right subtree should belong
    // to the current tree or to the new left subtree
    if (*(newtree->_rootData) < data)
```

```
    {
        _left = newtree;


        // the same tree is the right subtree of the root and the
        // right subtree of the root's left child. Since there are
        // no values between the value inserted and the value
           splayed
        // to the root during the find, the root's left child
        // should have an empty right subtree.
        spLeft()->_right = (SplayBST<DataType>*) makeSubtree();
    }
    // otherwise, we similarly handle the right subtree
    else
    {
        _right = newtree;


        // the root and the root's right child have the same left
        // subtree, and the root's right child should have an
        // empty left subtree.
        spRight()->_left = (SplayBST<DataType>*) makeSubtree();
    }
}
```

7.3.5   Deletion

In the case of the splay tree, remarkably, the deletion code is actually shorter and simpler than the insertion code. The deletion method uses _find() to bring the desired element to the root, and then deletes it if it is present. When we do delete, there are two cases:

1. The right subtree is empty. In this case we copy the left subtree into the current tree.
2. The right subtree is not empty. In this case we splay the right subtree to bring the inorder successor to its root. We can achieve this splay by searching the right subtree for the data that was already deleted. The right subtree is then guaranteed to have no left subtree of its own (because the inorder successor has to be the smallest value in the right subtree), so we can attach the left subtree of the current tree to the right subtree and copy the right subtree into the current subtree.

```
template<class DataType>
void SplayBST<DataType>::remove (DataType& data)
    // removes the node matching data, if any, while maintaining
    // binary search tree properties; throws error if data is
       missing
{
    if (_subtree) throw BinarySearchTreeChangedSubtree();
    if (isEmpty()) throw BinarySearchTreeNotFound();


// bring the data (if present) to the root
    _find (data);


// check whether we actually have the data in the root
// if the data is in the root, remove it
    if ((*_rootData) == data)
    {
        delete _rootData;
// if we have an empty subtree, we can just replace the current
// tree with the left subtree (all the remaining nodes)
        if (_right->isEmpty())
        {
            SplayBST<DataType>* oldleft = spLeft();
            delete _right;
            copyTree (oldleft);
            oldleft->_makeNull();
            delete oldleft;
        }
// if we have a non-empty right subtree, we can locate the
// inorder successor of data by searching the right subtree
// for data. That causes the inorder successor to move to
// the root of the right subtree
        else
        {
            spRight()->_find(data);
```

```
        // the right subtree has no left subtree, so we attach
        // our own left subtree to it
                SplayBST<DataType>* oldright = spRight();
                delete oldright->_left;
                oldright->_left = _left;
        // then we copy the right subtree on top of the current
        // tree, preserving all nodes except the one to be deleted
                copyTree (oldright);
                oldright->_makeNull();
                delete oldright;
            }
        }
// if we do not have the data in the root, throw error
    else throw BinarySearchTreeNotFound();
}
```

The following main() function, essentially identical to that used to demonstrate the Two3Tree class, produces an output which graphically demonstrates that, first, the splay tree makes no effort to balance itself, but also becomes considerably more balanced as it is accessed:

```
void main()
{
char inserts[] = "ABCDEFGHIJKLMNOPQRSTUVWXYZ";
char deletes[] = "KBXKV";
SplayBST<char> bst;
    for (int i = 0; i < 26; i++)
    {
        bst.insert (inserts[i]);
        cout << "+" << inserts[i] << " ";
    }
    cout << endl;
    bst.printtree(cout, 0);
    cout << "===============Now delete===========" << endl;
    for (int i = 0; i < 5; i++)
    {
        cout << "-" << deletes[i] << " ";
```

```
        try
            { bst.remove (deletes[i]);}
        catch (Exception e) { cout << "Exception!" << endl; }
    }
    cout << endl; bst.printtree(cout, 0);
}
```

Here we have the output:

```
+A +B +C +D +E +F +G +H +I +J +K +L +M +N +O +P +Q +R +S +T
+U +V +W +X +Y +Z
  +--Z
   +--Y
    +--X
     +--W
      +--V
       +--U
        +--T
         +--S
          +--R
           +--Q
            +--P
             +--O
              +--N
               +--M
                +--L
                 +--K
                  +--J
                   +--I
                    +--H
                     +--G
                      +--F
                       +--E
                        +--D
                         +--C
                          +--B
                           +--A
======================Now delete=================
```

```
-K -B -X -K Exception!
-V
    +--Z
  +--Y
+--W
    +--U
      +--T
    +--S
        +--R
      +--Q
        +--P
      +--O
        +--N
      +--M
  +--L
+--J
    +--I
  +--H
      +--G
    +--F
      +--E
    +--D
  +--C
    +--A
```

7.4 Performance Comparisons

All data structures expect the splay trees discussed in this chapter have logarithmic worse-case execution times for all operations: insert, remove, and find. The worst-case execution time for all operations on a splay tree is proportional to the height of the tree which in the worst case would be $O(n)$, where n is the number of nodes in the tree. The 2-3 tree has a worst case height of $O(log_2 n)$ when every node is a 2-node.

The red-black tree requires one additional bit per node to keep track of the color of the node that is used for balancing the tree after insertion and deletion. The AVL tree requires two bits (to represent –1, 0, +1) for keeping the balance information. The

Self Adjusting Trees Worst-case Time Complexity Comparisons				
Operation	Red-Black Trees	AVL-Trees	2-3 Trees	Splay Trees
Find(element)	$O(\log_2 n)$	$O(\log_2 n)$	$O(\log_2 n)$	$O(h)$, h is the height of the splay tree
Insert(element)	$O(\log_2 n)$	$O(\log_2 n)$	$O(\log_2 n)$	$O(n)$
Delete(element)	$O(\log_2 n)$	$O(\log_2 n)$	$O(\log_2 n)$	$O(n)$
RangeSearch(x,y)	$O(p)$	$O(p)$	$O(p)$	$O(p)$

Figure 7.40: Comparison of worst-case execution times for different implementations of the self-adjusting trees. Note that p is the number of elements that satisfies the *rangesearch* query.

number of cases that need to be checked during update operations on a red-black tree is significantly higher than that of the AVL tree. The 2-3 tree data structure requires additional pointers and two comparisons are made at every level even if every node is a 2-node.

The 2-3 data structure and its variant the B-tree can be stored on disk and retrieved at the time of processing. Many operating systems store instructions and data in fixed sized memory blocks on disk called *pages*. A given program occupies several hundreds of pages. During the execution of a program, the operating system requests a set of relevant pages from disk and stores it in the main memory for execution. A B-tree data structure can be used to store millions of records such as one pertaining to all social security recipients. Due to main memory size limitations all the million records cannot be brought to main memory for searching. Records pertaining to each node are stored in a single page (preferably) or in a set of pages. Initially the page(s) corresponding to the root node is brought to the main memory and searched. If there is successful match, the page that corresponds to the appropriate child node is brought next, and so on. In this manner, not all the records have to be in main memory before the searching can take place. Due to this reason the B-tree is the most effective data structure for storing large number of records. The qualitative assessment of the various self adjusting structures is presented in Figure 7.41.

Self Adjusting Trees Qualitative Assessment	
Implementation	Assessment
Red-Black Trees	Logarithmic worst-case execution times; smallest additional storage for balance information; many cases to deal with during balancing.
AVL Trees	Logarithmic worst-case execution times; two bits per node of additional information; fewer cases to deal with during balancing.
2-3 Trees	Execution times ranges from $O(\log_3 n)$ to $O(\log_2 n)$; additional storage required (2 for data and 3 for pointers); requires two comparisons at each level; excellent for storing large volumes of data that is organized for searching on disk.
Splay Trees	Easy to implement; improves the worst-case height of the binary search tree with increases in the number of operations performed on the tree.

Figure 7.41: Qualitative assessment of different self-adjusting trees.

7.5 Exercises

7.1. Fully implement the SelfModifyingBST base class, including the `zigzig()` and `zigzag()` methods, which were not presented in the text.

7.2. Let S be a sequence of integers, 10, 15, 5, 3, 25, 12, 11, 30, 2, 6. Draw the binary search tree produced by inserting the elements in S into an initially empty tree. Draw another binary search tree, which is produced by inserting the elements in S into an initially empty tree, but as each element is inserted, the node into which it was inserted is rotated, so that that node becomes the root of the tree.

7.3. A "right comb" is a binary search tree such that (1) every right child except a leaf has two children and (2) every left child is a leaf. A "left comb" can be similarly defined. Show that any binary search tree may be transformed into a left or right comb using only zig() and zag() operations. Write a method to perform this transformation.

7.4. In a red-black tree, where a red condition violation has occurred and the red parent of the red child has a black sibling, why does the zigzag() method inherited from the Self-ModifyingBST class correct the situation, even though it does not change the colors of the nodes?

7.5.   Develop a method to determine whether it is possible to assign colors to the nodes of a given binary search tree such that the red and black conditions are satisfied.

7.6.   Suppose that a node x is inserted into a red-black tree using the insertion algorithm previously described and then immediately deleted using the delete algorithm. Is the resulting red-black tree equivalent to the initial red-black tree? In other words, does it have the same tree structure and the same elements in corresponding nodes? Justify your answer.

7.7.   Beginning with an empty red-black tree, show the tree at each step of inserting successively the elements 25, 11, 2, 14, 12, 30, 6, and then deleting successively 11, 6, 2, 12, 14, 25, 30.

7.8.   Write a method for the join(T_1, T_2, x) operation described in problem 6.20, assuming that T_1, T_2, and the resulting tree are all red-black trees.

7.9.   Prove that M_h, the minimum number of nodes for an AVL tree with height h, is equal to $F_{h+2}-1$, where F_h is the h-th Fibonacci number.

7.10.   Prove that every AVL tree can be colored as a red-black tree.

7.11.   Repeat problem 7.7, beginning with an AVL tree instead of a red-black tree.

7.12.   Write a method for the join(T_1, T_2, x) operation described in problem 6.20, assuming that T_1, T_2, and the resulting tree are all AVL trees.

7.13.   Is it possible to modify the implementation of the AVL tree such that it uses a single bit (indicating whether a height violation exists in a tree) rather than an integer to maintain height information? If so, how?

7.14.   Write a method which, given a set of n numbers, constructs the "worst" possible AVL tree, i.e., the AVL tree with the maximum height for that set.

7.15.   Repeat problem 7.7, beginning with a 2-3 tree instead of a red-black tree.

7.16.   Write a method for the join(T_1, T_2, x) operation described in problem 6.20, assuming that T_1, T_2, and the resulting tree are all 2-3 trees.

7.17.   Consider a variation of a 2-3 tree in which elements are kept only in leaf nodes. Each leaf has exactly one element, and the remaining nodes are 2-nodes or 3-nodes. Each such nodes keeps only a "small" value, which is the largest key value in its left subtree, and a "large" value, which is the largest key value in its middle subtree. Define a class called External23Tree to implement this version of the 2-3 tree, implementing the find(), insert(), and remove() methods.

7.18.   Write a constructor for the Two3Tree class, which accepts a sorted array of keys and constructs a 2-3 tree containing those keys without inserting each key separately.

7.19.   Generalize the 2-3 tree to a 2-3-4 tree, where each internal node may be a 2-node, a 3-node, or a 4-node. What would be the advantage of this new structure over the 2-3 tree? What would be the disadvantages?

7.20.   Implement the B-tree in a C++ class.

7.21.   Repeat problem 7.7, beginning with a splay tree instead of a red-black tree.

7.22.   In the splay tree, each node to be splayed is brought all the way to the root of the tree. In a half-splay tree, the node to be splayed is brought only to a position that is halfway between its original height and the root. Implement a half-splay tree class.

7.6   References for Further Reading

Adel'son-Vel'skii, G.M. and Landis, E.M., "An algorithm for the organization of information", *Soviet Mathematics* vol. 3, pp. 1259–1263, 1962.

Allen, B. and Munro, I., "Self-organizing search trees", *Journal of the ACM* vol. 25, pp. 526–535, 1978.

Baer, J. L., and Schwab, B., "Comparison of Tree-Balancing Algorithms", *Communications of the ACM* vol. 20, no. 5, May 1977.

Bayer, R. and McCreight E., "Organization and maintenance of large ordered indexes", *Acta Informatica* vol. 1, pp. 173–189, 1972.

Bayer, R., "Symmetric binary B-trees: Data structures and maintenance algorithms", *Acta Informatica* vol. 1, pp. 290–306, 1972.

Bitner, J.R., "Heuristics that dynamically organize data structures", *SIAM Journal of Computing* vol. 8 , pp. 82–110, 1979.

Brown, M., "A Storage Scheme for Height-Balanced Trees", *Inform. Process. Lett.* vol. 7, no. 5, pp. 231–32, Aug. 1978.

Bruno, J., and Coffman, E.G., "Nearly Optimal Binary-Search Trees", *Proc. IFIP Congr.* vol. 71, pp. 99–103, 1972.

Foster, C. C., "A Generalization of AVL Trees", *Communications of the ACM* vol. 16, no. 8, Aug. 1973.

Garey, M. R., "Optimal Binary Search Trees with Restricted Maximal Depth", *SIAM Journal of Computing* vol. 2, pp. 101–110, 1974.

Hu, T. C., and Tucker, A.C., "Optimum Computer Search Trees", *SIAM J. Appl. Math.* vol. 21, pp. 514–532, 1971.

Karlton, P. L., Fuller, S.H., Scroggs, R.E., and Kachler, E.B., "Performance of Height-Balanced Trees", *Communications of the ACM* vol. 19, no. 1, pp. 23–28, Jan. 1976.

Luccio, F., and Pagli, L., "On the Height of Height-Balanced Trees", *IEEE Trans. Comput.* vol. c-25, no. l, Jan. 1976.

Miller, R., Pippenger, N., Rosenberg, A., and Snyder, L., "Optimal 2-3 Trees", *IBM Research Report RC* 6505, Thomas J. Watson Research Center, Yorktown Heights, N.Y., 1977.

Raiha, and Zweben, S.H., "An Optimal Insertion Algorithm for One-Sided Height-Balanced Binary Search Trees," *Communications of the ACM* vol. 22, no. 9, Sept. 1979.

Rivest, R. "On Self-Organizing Sequential Search Heuristics", *Communications of the ACM* vol. 19, no. 2, Feb. 1976.

Rosenberg, A., and Snyder, L., "Minimal Comparison 2-3 Trees," *SIAM Journal of Computing* pp. 465–80, Nov. 1978.

Sleator, D. D. and Tarjan R.E., "Self-adjusting binary search trees", *Journal of the ACM* vol. 32, pp. 652–686, 1985.

8   Priority Structures

P RIORITY STRUCTURES ALLOW retrieval, insertion, and deletion of records based on priorities of records in an efficient manner. This is useful when, for instance, the records are used to schedule jobs for action, where the jobs with the highest priority are acted on first and those with lesser priority must wait for a chance. Determining the record with the highest priority (resp., lowest priority) can be performed in $O(1)$ time on *priority trees*, while insertion of records with priorities and deletion of a record with highest or lowest priority can be performed in $O(\log n)$ time, where n is the number of records the priority tree stores. Of course these operations can be performed in the same time bounds on balanced search trees, but unlike the pointer based implementation of binary trees, priority trees can be implemented using arrays without any additional storage.

In this section, we will study several implementations of priority structures including standard *heap*, *min–max heap*, and *deap*; all implemented using arrays. The balanced search trees (that stores x-values) can be combined with priorities to form the *priority search trees* (that stores y-values) which can answer queries such as

Given x_1, x_2, and y_1 find all the records that contain (x,y) pair of values such that
$x_1 \le x \le x_2$ and $y < y_1$.

We call this a 1.5 *dimensional range query* and it has several applications including memory management and higher dimensional range searching.

The abstract data type for a priority tree contains only a few operations:

```
createEmpty ()
    // creates an empty priority tree
isEmpty()
    // returns true if tree is empty, but otherwise returns
    // false
size ()
    // returns the number of nodes in the tree
max ()
    // returns the record with the highest priority
deleteMax ()
    // deletes the record with the highest priority and
    // returns it to the caller
insert (record)
    // inserts record into the tree
halfRangeSearch (value)
    // returns all records having higher priority than value,
    // without removing them from tree
```

The above is a maximum priority tree; a minimum priority tree would have *min* and *deleteMin* operations instead of *max* and *deleteMax*. As noted above, we could implement this abstract data type using a binary search tree, but a binary search tree requires excessive overhead for such a limited (though useful!) functionality. We will therefore implement the abstract data type using other data structures, beginning with the standard heap.

8.1   Standard Heaps

A heap is a data structure that satisfies the following two properties:

a) structural: It is a complete binary tree.
b) ordering: In a maximum heap (resp. minimum heap) the value stored at a node in the tree is greater (resp. smaller) than the values stored at the nodes in its subtrees.

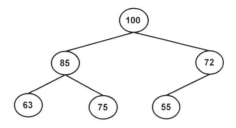

Figure 8.1:   Example of a maximum heap.

8.1.1   Implementing a Heap with an Array

The heap data structure could be implemented by extending the binary tree class that is presented in the earlier chapters. However, a simple implementation that takes advantage of the structural property is an array. The above tree can be stored in an array as follows:

0	1	2	3	4	5
100	85	72	63	75	55

The reader will notice that the array is created by processing the tree from the root level by level moving from left to right and copying the elements into the array. Assuming the array is 0-based, for the element at position i in the array, its left child (in the binary tree representation) is at position $2i+1$ and its right child is at position $2i+2$. The parent of an element at position i is at position $\lfloor (i-1)/2 \rfloor$. If we searched for an element, we would need to compare, in the worst case, with all the elements in the heap. However, in a maximum heap, the largest element can be determined in constant time as it is at position 0 of the array.

8.1.2   Inserting Into a Heap

We are now ready to discuss techniques for insertion into a heap data structure implemented as an array. Consider the case of inserting an element 150 into the heap. First we place this element as the last element in the array.

0	1	2	3	4	5	6
100	85	72	63	75	55	150

The new binary tree representation is as follows:

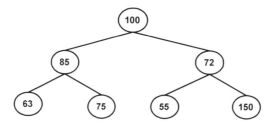

Figure 8.2: Heap structure after the insertion of the node **150**.

The position of this new element, i, is 6. We want it to "reheap up" to a position such that all nodes in its subtrees are less than it, and its parent (if any) is greater than it. We will compare this with the element stored in its parent, that is, with 72. Note that $heap[\lfloor (i-1)/2 \rfloor] = heap[\lfloor (6-1)/2 \rfloor] = heap[2] = 72$ for $i=6$. We will compare $heap[i]$ and $heap[\lfloor (i-1)/2 \rfloor]$ and, if $heap[i]$ is larger (which it is), then we will swap $heap[\lfloor (i-1)/2 \rfloor]$ with $heap[i]$. The result is shown below.

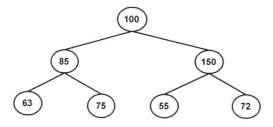

Figure 8.3: Heap structure after one reheap up operation.

The above structure still does not satisfy the ordering property as $100 < 150$, hence we will continue the above comparison with the new value of i being $\lfloor (i-1)/2 \rfloor$, or 2. Upon completion of this operation, the tree will be as follows:

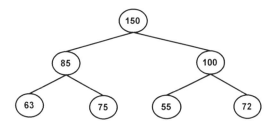

Figure 8.4:   Standard heap structure got after completion of reheap up operation.

In short, the insertion algorithm adds the new element as the new last element of the heap and performs a reheap up process. During a step in the reheap up process, this new element is compared with the value in its parent and moved to the child position if the value of the parent is less than the new element. This comparison continues until either there are no more down movements or the root of the tree is reached. After no more down movements, the new value is inserted into the empty spot. Figure 8.5 illustrates the changes to the maximum heap when a new element with the value 90 is inserted into the heap.

The complete algorithm for insertion into a maximum tree is presented below. The algorithm for insertion into a minimum tree is similar except that the sense of the comparison between the current element and its parent is reversed.

```
ALGORITHM INSERT (HEAP , ELEMENT)
1.Heap.length ← Heap.length + 1
2.currentPos ← Heap.length
3.while(currentPos > 0) and
               (Heap[⌊(currentPos-1)/2⌋] < element)
4.   Heap[currentPos] ← Heap[⌊(currentPos-1)/2⌋]
5.   currentPos ⌊(currentPos-1)/2⌋
6.endwhile
7.Heap[currentPos] ←element
```

From the preceding example it can be seen that the number of comparisons that has to be made in the worst case before an element is inserted in the right place is equal to the height of the complete binary tree. For a complete binary tree which stores *n* nodes, that height is O(*log n*).

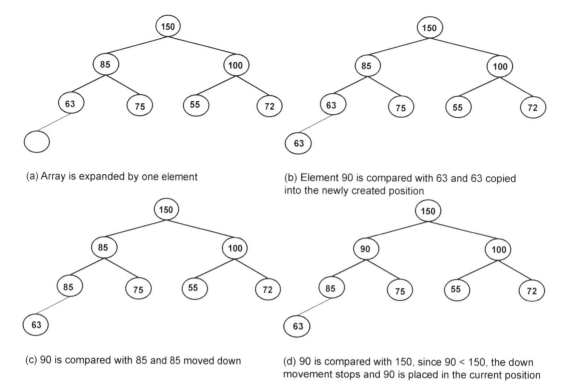

(a) Array is expanded by one element

(b) Element 90 is compared with 63 and 63 copied into the newly created position

(c) 90 is compared with 85 and 85 moved down

(d) 90 is compared with 150, since 90 < 150, the down movement stops and 90 is placed in the current position

Figure 8.5: Changes to the maximum heap as the new element 90 is inserted.

8.1.3   Deletion of the Maximum (Minimum) Element

The only element that can be deleted from a maximum heap (resp. minimum heap) is the largest (resp. smallest) element, which is stored at the root node at heap position 0. The basic idea behind deletion is to replace the element in position 0 with the one in position $n-1$, i.e., the last element in the array. If we delete the maximum element from the tree in the Figure 8.4, the tree would appear as follows:

Unfortunately, the element in position 0 no longer satisfies the ordering property, so we will let it "reheap down" the tree until it is in a position such that all elements in the subtrees of the node have values less than 72. In order to perform this, we will compare 72 with the values in both its children. If it is less than the value of one of its children, then we will swap it with that child. If it is less than both children, we will swap it with the larger of its children. This process of reheap down will stop until we find that the values in both children are less than or equal to 72.

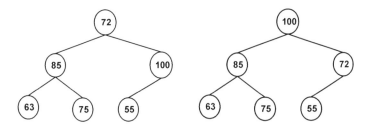

Figure 8.6:   Deleting the maximum element 150 from the heap in Figure 8.4. The
node with containing element 72 is placed at the root and the tree in the
right is after the "reheap down" operation.

The following algorithm, called *Heapify*, performs the reheap down operation in
a maximum heap, given an index position i.

```
ALGORITHM HEAPIFY (HEAP, I)
1.   lcPos ← 2I+1
2.   rcPos ← 2I+2
3.   largestPos ←I
4.   if (lcPos <= Heap.length-1) and (Heap[lcPos] > Heap[i])
5.        largestPos ← lcPos
6.   endif
7.   if (rightChildPos <= Heap.length) and (Heap[rcPos] >
8.        Heap[largestPos])largestPos ← rcPos
9.. if (largestPos != I)
10.       swap (Heap[I], Heap[largestPos])
11.       Heapify (Heap, largestPos)
12. endif
```

Given the above algorithm, the algorithm for the deletion of the maximum element is given below.

```
ALGORITHM DELETE (HEAP)
1.Output Heap[0]
2.Heap[0] ← Heap[Heap.length-1]
3.Heap.length ← Heap.length - 1
4.Heapify (Heap, 0)
```

Since we make at most two comparisons at every level in the course of deletion, the worst case number of comparisons for the delete algorithm is twice the height of the complete binary tree minus 1, which is $O(log\ n)$ for an n node heap data structure.

8.1.4   Implementation of the Heap Data Structure

With this preliminary understanding of the heap data structure, we can begin to implement it in C++. As was noted in the discussion of heaps in general, insertion and deletion in a maximum heap are identical to insertion and deletion in a minimum heap, except for the sense of the comparison of the element in question with its parent or children. This suggests that we should have an abstract Heap class that contains almost all of the functionality of the heap, and that the Heap class should have two subclasses, MinimumHeap and MaximumHeap, and a method for this comparison that is overridden in the subclasses.

8.1.4.1   Heap Data Elements

The question arises as to what sort of data can be stored in our new Heap class. Normally priorities are numeric, but clearly, we want to use complex objects, not simple integers, and we must be able to compare them so as to determine which of two elements is the larger. In other words, we need to use a data type that supports all comparison operations.

8.1.4.2   Heap Exceptions

As is our habit, we will create a family of exceptions for the Heap class:

```
class HeapException : public Exception { };
```

Since we intend to implement the heap using an array, we must also consider what happens if the user attempts to insert data into a full Heap . This would produce a heap overflow, and we will signal this with an exception:

```
class HeapOverflow : public HeapException { };
```

What happens if the user attempts to delete the maximum (minimum) element from an empty heap? This would produce an underflow, which we must signal by throwing an exception:

```
class HeapUnderflow : public HeapException { };
```

Finally, there is always the possibility of a memory error, which we must signal with an exception:

```
class HeapMemory : public HeapException { };
```

8.1.4.3   Heap Interface

We have already determined that we will need three related classes: *Heap* , *MinimumHeap*, and *MaximumHeap*. These classes share a large part of their code and the C++ implementation we will present reflects this. Thus, we will have not one but three abstract base classes: *AbstractHeap*, *AbstractMinimumHeap*, and *AbstractMaximumHeap*.

The *AbstractHeap* class includes all of the functionality of the priority tree abstract data type except *min*() and *deleteMin*(), which are replaced by *root*() and *deleteRoot*(), and *createEmpty*(), which will be implemented by a constructor in the class. It also has methods to report whether the heap is full and its maximum size.

```
template <class DataType>
class AbstractHeap
{
friend ostream& operator << (ostream& s,
                       AbstractHeap<DataType>& h);
public:
    virtual ~AbstractHeap ();
    virtual bool isEmpty() = NULL;
// returns true if tree is empty, but otherwise returns false
    virtual bool isFull() = NULL;
// returns true if tree is full, but otherwise returns false
    virtual int size () = NULL;
// returns the number of elements in the heap
    virtual int maxsize () = NULL;
// returns the maximum number of elements the heap can hold
```

```
    virtual void insert (DataType& record) = NULL;
// inserts record into the heap
    virtual DataType& root () = NULL;
// returns value in root, which is min or max depending on heap
    virtual void deleteRoot () = NULL;
// deletes value in root
    virtual Vector<DataType> halfRangeSearch
                        (DataType& value) = NULL;
// returns all records having higher priority
// than value, without removing them from heap
    virtual Enumeration<DataType>* enumerator () = NULL;
    virtual void display (ostream& os);
};
// ----------------------------------------------------------
template <class DataType>
void AbstractHeap<DataType>::display (ostream& os){
    bool first = true;
    Enumeration<DataType>* e = enumerator();
    os << "<";
    while (e->hasMoreElements()){
        if (!first) os << ", ";
        first = false;
        os << e->nextElement();
    }
    os << ">";
    delete e;
}
// ----------------------------------------------------------
template <class DataType>
AbstractHeap<DataType>::~AbstractHeap () { }
template <class DataType>
ostream& operator << (ostream& s, AbstractHeap<DataType>& h)
{
    h.display(s);
    return s;
}
```

The maximum heap and minimum heap base classes simply add the necessary access methods for their respective types:

```
template <class DataType>
class AbstractMaximumHeap : virtual public AbstractHeap
<DataType>
{
public:
    virtual ~AbstractMaximumHeap ();
    virtual DataType& max () = NULL;
        // returns value in root, which is maximum in heap
    virtual void deleteMax () = NULL;
        // deletes maximum value
    virtual Vector<DataType> halfRangeSearchGreater
                        (DataType& value) = NULL;
        // returns all records having greater priority
        // than value, without removing them from heap
};
```

```
template <class DataType>
class AbstractMinimumHeap : virtual public AbstractHeap <DataType>
{
public:
    virtual ~AbstractMinimumHeap ();
    virtual DataType& min () = NULL;
        // returns value in root, which is minimum in heap
    virtual void deleteMin () = NULL;
        // deletes minimum value
    virtual Vector<DataType> halfRangeSearchLesser
                        (DataType& value) = NULL;
        // returns all records having lesser priority
        // than value, without removing them from heap
};
```

8.1.4.4   Implementation

We will begin by implementing the *Heap* class itself.

Fields, Constructors, and Destructors

Since the heap will be implemented using an array, we will need an array field and a constructor that fixes the size of the array. Since insertion takes place at the current end of the array, we will need an integer field to hold the position of the current end of the array. This field doubles as the number of elements in the array, so we can call it *_size*. Initially, of course, it is 0. Finally, we also need a field for the maximum size of the array (though we could avoid this by using an *ArrayClass* object instead of an array). The constructor and destructor should be obvious to the reader. We provide only the basic constructor in this development; as the class includes a pointer field, it obviously must have a copy constructor and an overloaded assignment operator, which are left for the reader.

So our *Heap* class will initially appear as follows:

```
template <class DataType>
class Heap : virtual public AbstractHeap<DataType>
{
protected:
    DataType* _array;
    int _size;
    int _maxsize;
public:
    Heap (int maxsize);
    virtual ~Heap ();
};
// ------------------------------------------------------------
template<class DataType>
Heap<DataType>::Heap (int maxsize)
{
    _array = new DataType[maxsize];
    if (_array == NULL) throw HeapMemory ();
    _size = 0;
    _maxsize = maxsize;
}
```

```
// --------------------------------------------------------------
template<class DataType>
Heap<DataType>::~Heap ()
{
    if (_array != NULL) delete[] _array;
    _size = 0;
    _maxsize = 0;
    _array = NULL;
}
```

The Accessor Methods

The accessor methods of the Heap class are simple to implement:

```
template <class DataType>
int Heap<DataType>::size () { return _size; }
// ----------------------------------------------------------
template <class DataType>
int Heap<DataType>::maxsize () { return _maxsize; }
// ----------------------------------------------------------
template <class DataType>
bool Heap<DataType>::isEmpty() { return (size() == 0); }
// ----------------------------------------------------------
template <class DataType>
bool Heap<DataType>::isFull() { return (size() == maxsize());
}
// ----------------------------------------------------------
template <class DataType>
DataType& Heap<DataType>::root ()
{
    if (isEmpty()) throw HeapUnderflow();
    return _array[0];
}
```

We already know that we will need to access the position of the parent of a given node and the left and right children of a given node. For convenience, we will write protected helper methods to compute all of these:

```
template <class DataType>
int Heap<DataType>::parent (int pos) { return (pos-1)/2; }
// -------------------------------------------------------
template <class DataType>
int Heap<DataType>::leftChild (int pos) { return 2*pos+1; }
// -------------------------------------------------------
template <class DataType>
int Heap<DataType>::rightChild (int pos) { return 2*pos+2; }
```

The insert() Method

The *insert()* method will not be implemented; it must be overridden by a subclass. However, we will write a protected method called *_insert()*. This method follows the insertion algorithm previously given, but must be passed a boolean flag, indicating whether the inserted data will move upward if it is **greater than** its parent. This makes it easy to write the *insert()* method for a minimum heap, by passing false to the *_insert()* method, and for a maximum heap, by passing true to the *_insert()* method.

```
template <class DataType>
void Heap<DataType>::_insert (DataType& record, bool upIfMore)
{
    if (isFull()) throw HeapOverflow();
// save position of end of array
    int pos = _size;
    int par = parent(_size);
// expand array to make room for record
    _size++;
// reheap record up
    while ((pos > 0) && ((_array[par] < record) == upIfMore))
    {
        _array[pos] = _array[par];
        pos = par;
        par = parent(pos);
    }
    _array[pos] = record;
}
```

The deleteRoot() Method

Finally, we must consider the implementation of *deleteRoot*(), and for that we will need to add a method for *heapify*(). The *deleteRoot*() method itself would be quite simple to implement; the code would look something like this:

```
void deleteRoot ()
{
    if (isEmpty()) throw HeapUnderflow();
    _size--;
    if (size > 0)
        _array[0] = _array[_size];
    heapify (0);
}
```

However, we do not know (in the `Heap` class) whether a node should reheap down if it is greater than its child, or if it is less than its child. That decision depends on whether the heap in question is a min-heap or a max-heap. In other words, the `deleteRoot ()` method must be deferred to the descendants of the `Heap` class. However, we can implement `heapify ()`, provided that it has a flag as `_insert ()` did. This flag is called `downIfLess`, but it has the same value as `upIfMore` did in `_insert ()`: true in a maxheap, false in a min-heap. It closely follows the algorithm previously given:

```
template <class DataType>
void Heap<DataType>::heapify (int pos, bool downIfLess)
{
    int left = leftChild(pos);
    int right = rightChild(pos);
    int top = pos;
    if ((left < _size) &&
    ((_array[top] < _array[left]) == downIfLess))
            top = left;
    if ((right < _size) &&
    ((_array[top] < _array[right]) == downIfLess))
            top = right;
    if (top != pos)
    {
        swap (_array[pos], _array[top]);
        heapify (top, downIfLess);
    }
}
```

The halfRangeSearch() method

In a maximum (minimum) heap, the half range search returns all records greater than (less than) a specified value, without deleting them from the heap.

In implementing the *halfRangeSearch*() method, we can take advantage of the fact that the heap can be treated as a binary tree, allowing us to use recursive methods on it. Since each node of the heap is greater than (less than) its children, we can stop the recursion when a node is less than (greater than) the specified value.

Since we will return a Vector, the first iteration of the method must be responsible for creating the Vector and the subsequent iterations must be passed that Vector. Therefore, we must have the public method declared in the base class, which must be implemented in the concrete subclasses, and a protected recursive method that actually collects the records. The recursive method must have parameters indicating (1) the current position at which record collection must begin, (2) the value with which the records should be compared, (3) the Vector into which results are inserted, and (4) a boolean flag indicating whether to add a given record to the Vector if it is *more* than the specified value. Thus, the recursive method is as follows:

```
template <class DataType>
void Heap<DataType>::_halfRangeSearch
(int pos, DataType& value, Vector<DataType>&outVector, bool
addIfMore)
{
// if we've exhausted the heap, take no action
    if (pos >= _size) return;

// if specified value belongs higher in heap than the value
// in current position, take no action
    if ((value < _array[pos]) != addIfMore) return;

// otherwise, value in current position must go in
// heap and its children must be checked
    outVector.add (_array[pos]);
    _halfRangeSearch (leftChild(pos), value, outVector, addIfMore);
    _halfRangeSearch (rightChild(pos), value, outVector,
                      addIfMore);
}
```

The Enumerator

Finally, we will need an *Enumeration* subclass to enumerate the heap. Given that the elements of the heap are already stored in an array, the most obvious way to enumerate the heap is simply to return the elements of the array, in order. We could add methods to the heap to return elements by number; such methods could be public and thus available to any user of the *Heap* class, or they could be protected with the enumerator class being a friend of the *Heap* class. But if the enumerator class is a friend of the *Heap* class, then it can access the array directly. For simplicity, therefore, we will simply access the array directly. The implementation should be fairly obvious to the reader by now, as should the process of adding the *HeapEnumerator* as a friend of the *Heap* class.

```
template <class DataType>
class HeapEnumerator : virtual public Enumeration<DataType>
{
    Heap<DataType>* _heap;
    int pos;
public:
    HeapEnumerator (Heap<DataType>* h);
    virtual ~HeapEnumerator ();
    virtual bool hasMoreElements();
    virtual DataType& nextElement();
};
// ----------------------------------------------------------
template <class DataType>
HeapEnumerator<DataType>::HeapEnumerator (Heap<DataType>* h)
{
    _heap = h;
    pos = 0;
}
// ----------------------------------------------------------
template <class DataType>
HeapEnumerator<DataType>::~HeapEnumerator () { }
```

```
template <class DataType>
bool HeapEnumerator<DataType>::hasMoreElements ()
{
    return ((_heap != NULL) && (pos < _heap->_size));
}
// ------------------------------------------------------------
template <class DataType>
DataType& HeapEnumerator<DataType>::nextElement ()
{
    if (!hasMoreElements()) throw HeapOverflow ();
    pos++;
    return _heap->_array[pos-1];
}
```

The MaximumHeap and MinimumHeap Classes

This completes the implementation of the *Heap* class. It is an abstract class, but not a pure abstract class, as it has quite significant amounts of code in it. We have now to implement *MaximumHeap* and *MinimumHeap*, which are not abstract. They derive from *AbstractMaximumHeap* (or *AbstractMinimumHeap*) and *Heap*, in one of the few instances of multiple inheritance in this text. Because *Abstract-MaximumHeap* (or *AbstractMinimumHeap*) is pure abstract, this will not produce conflicts. The implementation of *MaximumHeap* is self-explanatory, given the above *Heap* class. The implementation of *MinimumHeap* closely follows that of *MaximumHeap*, and is left for the reader.

```
template <class DataType>
class MaximumHeap :
    virtual public Heap<DataType>, AbstractMaximumHeap<DataType>
{
public:
    MaximumHeap (int maxsize);
    virtual ~MaximumHeap ();
    virtual void deleteMax ();
    virtual void deleteRoot ();
    virtual Vector<DataType> halfRangeSearch (DataType& value);
    virtual Vector<DataType> halfRangeSearchGreater
                              (DataType& value);
```

```
        virtual void insert (DataType& record);
        virtual DataType& max ();
    };
    // ----------------------------------------------------------
    template <class DataType>
    MaximumHeap<DataType>::MaximumHeap (int maxsize)
        : Heap<DataType>(maxsize) { }
    // ----------------------------------------------------------
    template <class DataType>
    MaximumHeap<DataType>::~MaximumHeap () { }
    // ----------------------------------------------------------
    template <class DataType>
    DataType& MaximumHeap<DataType>::max () { return root(); }
    // ----------------------------------------------------------
    template <class DataType>
    Vector<DataType> MaximumHeap<DataType>::halfRangeSearch
    (DataType& value)
    {
        Vector<DataType> vector;
        _halfRangeSearch (0, value, vector, true);
        return vector;
    }
    // ----------------------------------------------------------
    template <class DataType>
    Vector<DataType> MaximumHeap<DataType>::halfRangeSearchGreater
                                    (DataType& value)
    {
        Vector<DataType> vector;
        _halfRangeSearch (0, value, vector, true);
        return vector;
    }
    // ----------------------------------------------------------
    template <class DataType>
    void MaximumHeap<DataType>::insert (DataType& record)
    {
        _insert (record, true);
    }
```

```
template <class DataType>
void MaximumHeap<DataType>::deleteRoot ()
{
    if (isEmpty()) throw HeapUnderflow();
    _size--;
    if (size > 0)
        _array[0] = _array[_size];
    heapify (0, true);
}
// -----------------------------------------------------------
template <class DataType>
void MaximumHeap<DataType>::deleteMax ()
{
    deleteRoot ();
}
```

Testing the Class

We can now test our implementations of the maximum heap with the following *main()* function:

```
void main ()
{
    int MAXVAL = 64;
    MaximumHeap<int> maxheap (MAXVAL);
    for (int i = 0; i < MAXVAL/2; i++)
    {
        maxheap.insert (i);
        maxheap.insert (MAXVAL-1-i);
    }
    cout << "The heap: " << endl << maxheap << endl;
    cout << "The values (in order): " << endl;
    while (!maxheap.isEmpty())
    {
        cout << maxheap.max() << " ";
        maxheap.deleteMax();
    }
    cout << endl;
}
```

The output from this function demonstrates that the class is operating correctly:

```
The heap:
<63, 62, 61, 60, 59, 58, 57, 56, 55, 54, 53, 52, 51, 50, 49,
48, 47, 46, 45, 44, 43, 42, 41, 40, 39, 38, 37, 36, 35, 34,
33, 32, 16, 8, 17, 4, 18, 9, 19, 2, 20, 10, 21, 5, 22, 11,
23, 1, 24, 12, 25, 6, 26, 13, 27, 3, 28, 14, 29, 7, 30, 15,
31, 0>
The values (in order):
63 62 61 60 59 58 57 56 55 54 53 52 51 50 49 48 47 46 45 44
43 42 41 40 39 38 37 36 35 34 33 32 31 30 29 28 27 26 25 24
23 22 21 20 19 18 17 16 15 14 13 12 11 10 9 8 7 6 5 4 3 2 1 0
```

8.1.5   Sorting with a Heap

From both the insertion and deletion methods described it is clear that the heap can be used to sort a set of elements. If we have an n-element set, then by repeated insertion a minimum heap can be created in $O(n \log n)$ time. We could then delete each minimum element in turn, obtaining the elements in sorted order. Since deletion takes $O(\log n)$ time, n deletions would give us the sorted set in $O(n \log n)$ time. The above technique is called a *heap sort*.

As discussed before, given n elements it takes $O(n \log n)$ time to construct the heap by repeatedly calling the Insert algorithm. Another way to build a heap is to place all the elements in an array and call the Heapify algorithm for all elements in the array except the leaf nodes. The leaf nodes are in positions $\lfloor Heap.length\,/2 \rfloor$ through $Heap.length$ in the array Heap. Thus it is sufficient to call Heapify for positions 0 through $\lfloor Heap.length\,/2 \rfloor - 1$. The following algorithm builds a heap with n elements in $O(n)$ time.

```
ALGORITHM FASTHEAP (HEAP)
1.  for i = ⌊Heap.length/2⌋ – 1 down to 0
2.        Heapify (Heap, i)
3.  endfor
```

If we call Heapify for a node at height h, then it takes $O(h)$ time to heapify. The total cost of FastHeap is then given by

$$\sum_{h=0}^{\lfloor \log n \rfloor} (\textit{number of nodes at height h}) \times O(h)$$

Since there are at most $\left\lceil \dfrac{n}{2^{h+1}} \right\rceil$ nodes at height h in a complete binary tree (Chapter 6), we have the total cost as

$$\sum_{h=0}^{\lfloor \log n \rfloor} \left\lceil \frac{n}{2^{h+1}} \right\rceil \times O(n) = O\left(n \times \sum_{h=0}^{\lfloor \log n \rfloor} \frac{h}{2^h} \right)$$

Note that $\displaystyle\sum_{k=0}^{\infty} kx^k = \frac{x}{(1-x)^2}$ and $\displaystyle\sum_{h=0}^{\infty} h \times (1/2)^h = \frac{1/2}{(1-1/2)^2} = 2$. Hence, we have

$$O\left(n \times \sum_{h=0}^{\lfloor \log n \rfloor} \frac{h}{2^h} \right) = O(n).$$

Thus, the total cost of building the heap is $O(n)$. Of course, the deletion of each minimum element must still be performed, so the total cost of heap sort is $O(n \log n)$. We will show in chapter 9, this complexity is the best we can achieve for comparison based sorting methods.

8.1.5.1   Implementation of Heap Sort

Heap sort can be performed using an array of objects and the `MinimumHeap` class, if we add the following constructor to the `MinimumHeap` class[1]:

---

[1] You *did* implement `MinimumHeap`, didn't you?

```
template <class DataType>
MinimumHeap<DataType>::MinimumHeap
    (int maxsize, int size, DataType* array)
    : Heap<DataType>(maxsize)
{
    for (int i = 0; i < size; i++)
        _array[i] = array[i];
    _size = size;
    for (int i = _size/2 - 1; i >= 0; i--)
        heapify (i, false);
}
```

We can now easily sort an array. In the demonstration method below, the reader should note that the actual sorting takes three lines. All the rest of the method is devoted to creating the array and printing it before and after sorting. The reader should also note that, although we have used integers, there is no reason, other than convenience, not to have used String objects; the heap would have sorted them equally well.

```
void main ()
{
    const int MAXVAL = 64;
    int array[MAXVAL];
    int i;
    int j;
// ----------------- Preliminaries - create an array out of order
    for (i = 0, j = 0; i < MAXVAL/2; i++, j+=2)
    {
        array[j] = i;
        array[j+1] = MAXVAL-1-i;
    }
// print the array
    cout << "The array:" << endl;
    for (i = 0; i < MAXVAL; i++)
        cout << array[i] << " ";
    cout << endl;
// ----------------- Sorting starts here -------------------
    MinimumHeap<int> minheap (MAXVAL, MAXVAL, array);
```

```
        cout << "The heap: " << endl << minheap << endl;
// pull the elements out, one at a time
    i = 0;
    while (!minheap.isEmpty())
    {
        array[i] = minheap.min();
        i = i+1;
        minheap.deleteMin();
    }
// ----------------- Sorting ends here --------------------

// print the elements to show the order
    cout << "The values (in order): " << endl;
    for (i = 0; i < MAXVAL; i++)
        cout << array[i] << " ";
    cout << endl;
}
```

The output of the above main program is given below.

```
The array (Out of Order):
0 63 1 62 2 61 3 60 4 59 5 58 6 57 7 56 8 55 9 54 10 53 11 52
12 51 13 50 14 49 15 48 16 47 17 46 18 45 19 44 20 43 21 42
22 41 23 40 24 39 25 38 26 37 27 36 28 35 29 34 30 33 31 32


The heap (After Heapify Operation):
<0, 2, 1, 4, 5, 6, 3, 8, 9, 10, 11, 12, 13, 14, 7, 16, 17, 18,
19, 20, 21, 22, 23, 24, 25, 26, 27, 28, 29, 30, 15, 32, 56, 47,
60, 46, 55, 45, 62, 44, 54, 43, 59, 42, 53, 41, 63, 40, 52, 39,
58, 38, 51, 37, 61, 36, 50, 35, 57, 34, 49, 33, 31, 48>

After Sorting.....

The array values (in order):
0 1 2 3 4 5 6 7 8 9 10 11 12 13 14 15 16 17 18 19 20 21 22 23
24 25 26 27 28 29 30 31 32 33 34 35 36 37 38 39 40 41 42 43
44 45 46 47 48 49 50 51 52 53 54 55 56 57 58 59 60 61 62 63
```

8.2 Double Ended Priority Trees

An *n*-node minimum heap data structure described earlier performs deletion of the minimum element and insertion of an element in $O(log\ n)$ time. The largest element of a minimum heap can be anywhere in the heap, hence its deletion will require that the entire heap be reorganized. In this section, we will present two data structures called min-max heaps and Deaps. They perform insertion, deletion of the minimum element, and deletion of the maximum element, all in $O(log\ n)$ time, and reporting of the minimum and the maximum element in constant time.

8.2.1 Interface Definition

Since we have two structures that perform the same functions, their implementations should be related. As we shall see, the two structures are so different that it is impractical for one to be a descendant of the other. Therefore, we should have an abstract class, related to the Heap class, which declares methods to report and delete both the minimum element and the maximum element. Since we already have the abstract base classes AbstractMinimumHeap and AbstractMaximumHeap, we will make our new class a descendant of both:

```
template <class DataType>
class AbstractDoubleEndedHeap :
    virtual public AbstractMinimumHeap<DataType>,
        AbstractMaximumHeap<DataType>
{
public:
        virtual ~AbstractDoubleEndedHeap ();
};
// -------------------------------------------------------
template <class DataType>
AbstractDoubleEndedHeap<DataType>::~AbstractDoubleEndedHeap
() { }
```

In the development of various classes seen so far we have several instances of multiple inheritances and also have diamond inheritances. The following figure depicts all the classes developed in this chapter along with their inheritances.

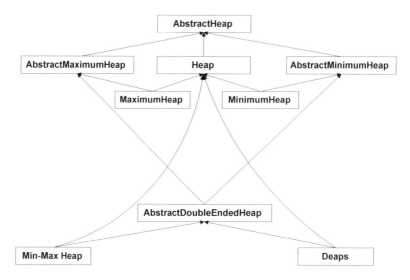

Figure 8.7: Classes developed for the priority search trees showing the various inheritances.

8.2.2   Min-Max Heap

A min-max heap is a complete binary tree. The root of the tree is said to be at level 1. A node at an odd (resp., even) level is called a minimum (resp., maximum) node. If a node x is a minimum node (resp., maximum) node then all elements in its subtrees have values larger (resp., smaller) than x. The following example illustrates a min-max heap.

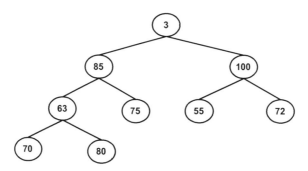

Figure 8.8: Example of a min-max heap data structure.

If a heap is a min-max heap, then the minimum element is at position 0, and the maximum element is the maximum of the elements at positions 1 and 2 if the root has two children, at position 1 if it has one child, and otherwise at position 0.

8.2.2.1   Insertion into a Min-Max Heap

The insert method for a min-max heap is similar to the reheap up technique described for the standard heap, with a slight modification that cuts down the number of comparisons by half. The new element, x, is inserted at the end of the array and then compared with its parent p, which may be on a minimum level or on a maximum level.

Suppose that p is on a minimum level; then x is on a maximum level. If $p.value > x.value$, then $p.value$ takes the position of $x.value$ in the Heap. Now x is on a minimum level and p is on a maximum level. Clearly, the value of x must be smaller than the values of all nodes in the maximum levels in the path from p to the root of the tree, because p was smaller than the values at nodes in all the maximum levels. Hence in this case we need to compare x only with the minimum nodes in the reheap up procedure. If, on the other hand, $p.value < x.value$, then since we assumed that p is on a minimum level, we need to compare x with only the maximum nodes in the path from p to the root of the tree in the reheap up technique. The case when p is at the maximum level can be handled similarly. The following algorithm performs the insertion of a new element into the min-max heap.

```
ALGORITHM INSERT (HEAP , ELEMENT)
1.  Heap.length ← Heap.length + 1
2.  if Heap is empty
3.        Heap[Heap.length] ← element
4.        Stop
5.  endif
6.  parent ←⌊(Heap.length-1)/2⌋
7.  if⌊log₂(parent+1)⌋ is even   //add 1 so we don't compute log₂0
                                 //parent is on a minimum level
8.        if (element < Heap[parent])
9.            Heap[Heap.length] ← Heap[parent]
10.           ReheapUpMin (Heap , parent, element)
11.       else
12.           ReheapUpMax (Heap , Heap.length, element)
13.       endif
14. else                        //parent is on a maximum level
15.           if element > Heap[parent]
16.           Heap[Heap.length] ← Heap[parent]
```

```
17.                  ReheapUpMax (Heap , parent, element)
18.       else
19.                  ReheapUpMin (Heap , Heap.length, element)
20.       endif
21. endif
```

The algorithms for ReheapUpMin and the ReheapUpMax are presented below.

```
ALGORITHM ReheapUpMin (HEAP , POSITION, ELEMENT)
1.  grandParent ⌊(position - 3)/4⌋
2.  while (grandParent >= 0)
3.       if element < Heap[grandParent]
4.            Heap[position] ← Heap[grandParent]
5.            position ← grandParent
6.            grandParent ⌊(position - 3)/4⌋
7.       else
8.            grandParent ← 0
9.       endif
10. endwhile
11. Heap[position] ← element
```

The ReheapUpMax algorithm is similar to the ReheapUpMin algorithm except that the operator "<" is replaced with a ">" operator in line 3 of the algorithm ReheapUpMin.

8.2.2.2 Deletion from a Min-Max Heap

Now let us focus on the deletion of the smallest element in the min-max heap. The deletion of the largest element is similar to deleting the smallest element and is left as an exercise. Consider the min-max heap previously displayed. After deleting the minimum element from the min-max heap, the value from the last position is placed in the position of the deleted minimum and a modified reheap down procedure (Heapify) is executed. The shape of the tree above is shown below after deleting the element 3.

In order to reorganize the above tree the value of the root should be the smallest among all values in the tree. Since it is not the case, we can swap 80 with the least of its grandchildren, namely 55, and the resultant tree will be a min-max heap and it is shown below.

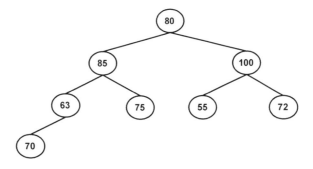

Figure 8.9:   After deleting the minimum element **3** from the min-max heap in
Figure 8.6.

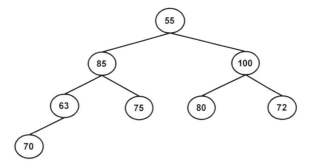

Figure 8.10:   Standard min-max heap got from Figure 8.7 by reheap down operation.

In general, if x is the new element that is moved to the root, we have to consider the following cases:

a) If the root has no children then x remains the root of the min-max heap.

b) Otherwise, let k be the index of the node with the smallest value among the children and grandchildren of the root. We have the following possibility:

i) if $x <$ Heap[k], then x is inserted into the root.

ii) if $x >$ Heap[k] and k is a child of the root, then Heap[k] is moved to the root and x is placed at position k. This will preserve the min-max property since Heap[k] is a maximum node.

iii) if $x >$ Heap[k] and k is a grandchild of the root, then Heap[k] is placed in the root and x is placed in the min-max heap tree rooted at node k, so that min-max heap must itself be heapified.

The complete algorithm for the deletion of the minimum element in a min-max heap is presented next.

The HeapifyMin algorithm is similar in nature to the Heapify algorithm presented for the standard heap.

```
ALGORITHM HEAPIFYMIN (HEAP , I)
1.  lcPos ← 2I+1
2.  rcPos ← 2I+2
3.  sPos ←I
4.  sPos ← BoundedCompareMin (Heap, lcPos, sPos)
5.  sPos ← BoundedCompareMin (Heap, rcPos, sPos)
6.  sPos ← BoundedCompareMin (Heap,2*lcPos+1,sPos)
7.  sPos ← BoundedCompareMin (Heap,2*lcPos+2,sPos)
8.  sPos ← BoundedCompareMin (Heap,2*rcPos+1,sPos)
9.  sPos ← BoundedCompareMin (Heap,2*rcPos+2,sPos)
10. if (sPos!= I)
11.          swap (Heap[sPos], Heap[I])
12.          if (sPos != lcPos) and (sPos != rcPos)
13.              HeapifyMin (Heap, sPos)
14.      endif
15. endif
```

```
SUBROUTINE BOUNDEDCOMPAREMIN (HEAP , K, I)
1,  if (k <= Heap.length) and (Heap[I] > Heap[k])
2.       return k
3.  else
4.       returnI
5.  endif
```

Given the above algorithm, the algorithm for the deletion of the minimum element is given below.

```
ALGORITHM DELETEMIN (HEAP )
1.  Output Heap[0]
2.  Heap[0] = Heap[Heap.length]
3.  Heap.length = Heap.length − 1
4.  HeapifyMin (Heap, 0)
```

8.2.2.3   Implementation of the Min-Max Heap Data Structure

We can now begin the implementation of the min-max heap data structure in C++. As a preliminary, we can see that this data structure is in many ways very similar to a standard heap. It is array-based. It can store the same types of data: objects of a class supporting comparisons. It has the same possibilities for errors: overflow and under-flow must be detected. Furthermore, it has all of the functionality of a minimum heap together with all of the functionality of a maximum heap. These similarities suggest that we need only implement the min-max heap as a subclass of the Heap class and the AbstractDoubleEndedHeap.

Thus, our new class will initially be as follows (the definition of the trivial destructor is omitted):

```
template <class DataType>
class MinMaxHeap :
    virtual public Heap<DataType>,
        AbstractDoubleEndedHeap<DataType>
{
public:
    MinMaxHeap (int maxsize);
    virtual ~MinMaxHeap ();
};
// -------------------------------------------------------
template <class DataType>
MinMaxHeap<DataType>::MinMaxHeap (int maxsize)
    : Heap<DataType> (maxsize) { }
```

As in the case of the minimum heap, the root of the min-max heap is the minimum. Since we must implement a *max()* method and a *deleteMax()* method, for consistency we will implement *root()* and *deleteRoot()* by calling the more complex *min()* and *deleteMin()*.

```
template <class DataType>
void MinMaxHeap<DataType>::deleteRoot () { deleteMin (); }
// -------------------------------------------------------
template <class DataType>
DataType& MinMaxHeap<DataType>::root () { return min (); }
```

The implementation of *min()* is of course quite simple:

```
template <class DataType>
DataType& MinMaxHeap<DataType>::min ()
{
    if (isEmpty()) throw HeapUnderflow();
    return _array[0];
}
```

So now we must implement *max()*, *insert()*, *deleteMin()*, and *deleteMax()*. In the implementation of *max()*, the simplest of the four, we must consider four cases: the tree is empty; the tree has only one node, which must be the maximum; the tree has two nodes, of which the second must be the maximum; or the tree has more than two nodes, and the second or third must be the maximum. Based on this discussion, the implementation of *max()* is as follows:

```
template <class DataType>
DataType& MinMaxHeap<DataType>::max ()
{
    if (isEmpty()) throw HeapUnderflow();
    if (_size == 1) return _array[0];
    if (_size == 2) return _array[1];
    if (_array[2] > _array[1])
        return _array[2];
    else
        return _array[1];
}
```

The deleteMin() and deleteMax() Methods

We shall now implement *deleteMin()* and *deleteMax()*. The algorithm previously given indicates that the *deleteMin()* method will need two helper methods, *heapifyMin()* and *boundedCompareMin()*. In considering *deleteMax()*, we would expect that it would require *heapifyMax()* and *boundedCompareMax()*— or does it?

Given our implementation of Node, this line from the BoundedCompareMin algorithm

■   `if(k <= Heap.length) and (Heap[i] > Heap[k])`

in a C++ method would translate to something like

■   `if ((k < _size) && (_array[i] > _array[j]))`

and reversing the sense of the test in the algorithm could be accomplished in the C++ method by adding an argument with the desired result of the comparison between _array[i] and _array[j], either true (if _array[i] should be more) or false (otherwise), so that deleteMin() and deleteMax() could share the method.

Thus, the comparebounded() method is as follows:

```
// curr is the index currently chosen as the result of
// a series of comparisons. test is returned if it should
// be chosen instead on the basis of the comparison, whereas
// curr is returned if it should be chosen again.
// returnIfMore is true if the returned index should
// point to a larger value, false if it should
// point to a smaller value
template <class DataType>
int MinMaxHeap<DataType>::compareBounded
    (int test, int curr, bool returnIfMore)
{
    if ((test < _size) &&
        ((_array[test] > _array[curr]) == returnIfMore))
// test has the desired relation with curr
        return test;
// test does not exist or curr has desired relation with test
    else return curr;
}
```

Now we can implement *deleteMin()* and *heapifyMin()* as indicated by the algorithms previously given:

```
template <class DataType>
void MinMaxHeap<DataType>::deleteMin ()
{
    if (isEmpty()) throw HeapUnderflow();
    _size--;
    _array[0] = _array[_size];
    if (_size > 1) heapifyMin (0);
}
// ----------------------------------------------------------
template <class DataType>
void MinMaxHeap<DataType>::heapifyMin (int position)
{
    int lPos = leftChild (position);
    int rPos = rightChild (position);
    int sPos = position;
// find smallest among positions, 2 children and
// 4 grandchildren
    sPos = compareBounded (lPos, position, false);
    sPos = compareBounded (rPos, sPos, false);
    sPos = compareBounded (leftChild(lPos), sPos, false);
    sPos = compareBounded (rightChild(lPos), sPos, false);
    sPos = compareBounded (leftChild(rPos), sPos, false);
    sPos = compareBounded (rightChild(rPos), sPos, false);
// if position is already smallest, no action required
    if (sPos == position) return;
// swap position with smallest pos
    swap (_array[position], _array[sPos]);
// if smallest pos was a child, no further action required
    if ((sPos == lPos) || (sPos == rPos)) return;
// otherwise, a grandchild heap may need heapifying
    heapifyMin (sPos);
}
```

Now, let us consider *heapifyMax*() and its differences from *heapifyMin*(). Clearly, it will need a similar sequence of comparisons to determine the largest among the root of a tree, its children, and its grandchildren. It will need to swap values if the root is not the largest, and it will have to call itself recursively if the root swapped values with a grandchild.

Thus, the same reasoning which suggests only one *comparebounded*() method also suggests only one *heapify*() method for the `MinMaxHeap`. This method too would receive an argument with a boolean flag for the desired relation: the root must have that relation with its children and grandchildren, and if it does not, a swap must be made. Instead of "smallpos," we shall use the variable name "extreme" since the object of *heapifyMin*() is to find the smallest extreme among the seven candidates and the object of *heapifyMax*() is to find the largest extreme. Given this reasoning, we can remove the `heapifyMin ()` method we just created and add the *heapify*() method as follows:

```
template <class DataType>
void MinMaxHeap<DataType>::heapify (int position,
                                     bool keepIfMore)
{
    int lPos = leftChild(position);
    int rPos = rightChild(position);
    int extreme = position;
// find the extreme among position, 2 children, 4 grandchildren
    extreme = compareBounded (lPos, position, keepIfMore);
    extreme = compareBounded (rPos, extreme, keepIfMore);
    extreme = compareBounded
        (leftChild(lPos), extreme, keepIfMore);
    extreme = compareBounded
        (rightChild(lPos), extreme, keepIfMore);
    extreme = compareBounded
        (leftChild(rPos), extreme, keepIfMore);
    extreme = compareBounded
        (rightChild(rPos), extreme, keepIfMore);
// if position is already the extreme, no action required
    if (extreme == position) return;
```

```
// swap position with extreme pos
    swap (_array[position], _array[extreme]);
// if extreme pos was a child, no further action required
    if ((extreme == lPos) || (extreme == rPos)) return;
// otherwise, a grandchild heap may need heapifying
    heapify (extreme, keepIfMore);
}
```

Now we can implement *heapifyMin*() and *heapifyMax*() quite simply:

```
template <class DataType>
void MinMaxHeap<DataType>::heapifyMax (int position)
{
    heapify (position, true);
}
// ------------------------------------------------------------
template <class DataType>
void MinMaxHeap<DataType>::heapifyMin (int position)
{
    heapify (position, false);
}
```

The *deleteMin*() method is now complete, and we must implement *deleteMax*(). This method is more difficult than *deleteMin*(), because it has the same four cases as *max*(): an empty heap, a 1–element heap, a 2–element heap, and a larger heap.

```
template <class DataType>
void MinMaxHeap<DataType>::deleteMax ()
{
    if (isEmpty()) throw HeapUnderflow();

// 1-element heap? if only one element, it's the maximum.
// 2-element heap? if only two nodes, second is maximum.
    if (_size < 3)
    {
```

```
        _size--;
        return;
    }


// heap of more than 2 elements - max is larger of root's children
    int maxpos;
    if (_array[2] > _array[1])
        maxpos = 2;
    else
        maxpos = 1;
// move last value to root of larger max heap
    _size--;
    _array[maxpos] = _array[_size];
// fix max heap
    heapifyMax (maxpos);
}
```

The insert() Method

The only method from the Heap class remaining to be implemented is *insert()*. The algorithm described for insertion requires two supporting algorithms, ReheapUpMin and ReheapUpMax. As in the case of HeapifyMin and HeapifyMax, we can see that the only difference between the two algorithms is the sense of the comparison, so that they can be implemented through a single method. To avoid obscurity in the code, we will in fact have three methods, *reheapUpMin()*, *reheapUpMax()*, and *reheapUp()*, having the same relationship among them as among *heapifyMin()*, *heapifyMax()*, and *heapify()*.

One complication in translating the algorithm to a programming language arises from the fact that mathematics is far more precise than are computers. We sometimes need to accommodate this discrepancy in precision when writing computer programs, as here. Specifically, in the algorithm, $\lfloor \log_2(\text{parent}+1) \rfloor$ will always equal $\log_2(\text{parent}+1)$ if parent+1 is a power of 2. We can compute $\log_2(\text{parent}+1)$ as log(parent+1)/log(2). Unfortunately, because of the limitations of precision in C++, floor(log(parent+1)/log(2)) may not be equal to log (parent+1)/log(2) when parent+1 is a power of 2. If log(parent+1)/log(2) happens to be slightly larger than mathematics would require, the floor function will return the correct number. But if it happens to be very slightly smaller, the floor function will return a number one less than the correct number –

which will change what should be a min level into a max level, or vice versa, producing incorrect behavior. A quick solution is to add a very small constant to the computed log (parent+1)/ log (2) before finding the floor. For clarity, we will show the constant named EPSILON[2] just before the method. In fact, it should be at the beginning of the header file.

```
const double EPSILON = 1e-10; // precision adjuster for log

template <class DataType>
void MinMaxHeap<DataType>::insert (DataType& record)
// inserts record into the heap
{
    if (isFull()) throw HeapOverflow();

// handle the case of an empty heap separately
// so we don't have a negative parent and try
// to compute log of zero
    if (isEmpty())
    {
        _array[0] = record;
        _size = 1;
        return;
    }

// now we know we have a heap with at least one node
    int par = parent(_size);
// compute log (par+1) so we don't compute log 0 - log is in math.h
    float flog2parent = (log (par+1)/ log (2)) + EPSILON;
    int log2parent = (int) (flog2parent);

    _size++;
```

---

2 The STL in its header file *limits* has a class named *numeric_limits* in which there is a method *epsilon()* that returns the epsilon value for a particular templated data type. To get the epsilon value for an integer we write *numeric_limits<int>::epsilon()*. The other useful methods are *min()* and *max()* that return the minimum and maximum value of the templated data type.

```
// if the parent is on a minimum level
   if (log2parent % 2 == 0)
   {
        // if the record is less than its parent, it replaces it
        if (record < _array[par])
        {
             _array [_size-1] = _array[par];
             reheapUpMin (par, record);
        }
        // but if it is more than its parent, it doesn't
        else
        {
             reheapUpMax (_size-1, record);
        }
   }
// if the parent is on a maximum level
   else {
        // if the record is more than its parent, it replaces it
        if (record > _array[par])
        {
             _array [_size-1] = _array[par];
             reheapUpMax (par, record);
        }
        // but if it is less, it doesn't
        else
        {
             reheapUpMin (_size-1, record);
        }
   }
}
```

Although we have been using integer division in C++ as a simple substitute for the floor function, we cannot do so in computing $\lfloor (position-3)/4 \rfloor$ as the result is incorrect when *position* is less than 3. Therefore, we have used *floor()* in the *reheapUp()* method implemented below. The same result can also be obtained, without a function call and without casting, by computing $(position+1)/4-1$, but this computation does not match that of the algorithm.

```cpp
template <class DataType>
void MinMaxHeap<DataType>::reheapUp
    (int position, DataType& record, bool keepIfMore)
{
    int grandParent = floor((position -3)/4.0);
    while (grandParent >= 0)
    {
        if ((record > _array[grandParent]) == keepIfMore)
        {
            _array[position] = _array[grandParent];
            position = grandParent;
            grandParent = floor((position -3)/4.0);
        }
        else { break; }
    }
    _array[position] = record;
}
// ------------------------------------------------------------
template <class DataType>
void MinMaxHeap<DataType>::reheapUpMax (int position,
DataType& record)
{
    reheapUp (position, record, true);
}
// ------------------------------------------------------------
template <class DataType>
void MinMaxHeap<DataType>::reheapUpMin (int position,
DataType& record)
{
    reheapUp (position, record, false);
}
```

The halfRangeSearch() method

The *halfRangeSearch*() method implemented in the `MinHeap` or `MaxHeap` class obviously will not be acceptable in the `MinMaxHeap` class, since the children of a minimum node are maximum nodes, and vice versa. Instead, we have to have separate methods for *halfRangeSearchLesser*() and *halfRangeSearchGreater*(). Worse, we cannot eliminate the subtree under a given node just because the node itself should not be added to the vector. For instance, if the node is on a minimum level, and is smaller than the specified value, then nodes on minimum levels below it might be larger than the specified value. Thus, we must check the children of each node, whether or not the node itself was added.

Since we have taken the position that *min*() and *root*() have the same effect, we will also take the position that *halfRangeSearchLesser*() and *halfRangeSearch*() have the same effect:

```
template <class DataType>
Vector<DataType> MinMaxHeap<DataType>::halfRangeSearch
(DataType& value)
{
    return halfRangeSearchLesser (value);
}
// ----------------------------------------------------------
template <class DataType>
Vector<DataType> MinMaxHeap<DataType>::halfRangeSearchLesser
(DataType& value)
{
    Vector<DataType> vector;
    _halfRangeSearch (0, value, vector, false);
    return vector;
}
// ----------------------------------------------------------
template <class DataType>
Vector<DataType> MinMaxHeap<DataType>::halfRangeSearchGreater
(DataType& value)
{
    Vector<DataType> vector;
    _halfRangeSearch (0, value, vector, true);
    return vector;
}
// ----------------------------------------------------------
```

```
template <class DataType>
void MinMaxHeap<DataType>::_halfRangeSearch
   (int pos, DataType& value, Vector<DataType>& vector, bool
   addIfMore)
{
// if we've exhausted the heap, take no action
   if (pos >= _size) return;

   if ((value < _array[pos]) == addIfMore)
       vector.add (_array[pos]);

   _halfRangeSearch (leftChild(pos), value, vector, addIfMore);
   _halfRangeSearch (rightChild(pos), value, vector, addIfMore);
}
```

Testing the Class

The implementation of the *MinMaxHeap* class is now complete. The reader should test it with a *main()* function. One simple way to test it is to modify the *main()* function for the *Heap* class so that *maxheap* is a *MinMaxHeap* instead of a *MaximumHeap*. The function needs no other modification.

8.2.3   Deaps

The deap is another doubly ended queue that can perform insert, delete minimum, and delete maximum in $O(log\ n)$ time on a *n*-element deap data structure. A deap is a complete data structure, which is either empty or satisfies the following properties:

1. The root contains no element.
2. The left subtree is a minimum heap data structure
3. The right subtree is a maximum heap data structure
4. If the right subtree is not empty, then let *i* be any node in the left (minimum) subtree. Let *j* be the corresponding node in the right (maximum) subtree. If such a *j* does not exists, then let *j* be the node in the right subtree that corresponds to the parent of *i*. The key value in node *i* is less than or equal to that in node *j*. The nodes *i* and *j* are called *partners*.

The following example illustrates the deap data structure.

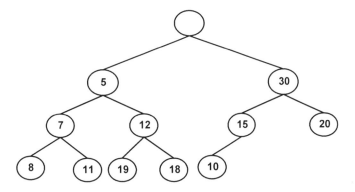

Figure 8.11   Example of a deap data structure.

As with the case of standard heap and min-max heap the deap data structure can be stored in an array since it is a complete binary tree. The array representation of the deap given above is as follows:

0	1	2	3	4	5	6	7	8	9	10	11
	5	30	7	12	15	20	8	11	19	18	10

From the definition of the deap data structure, it is clear that the maximum and the minimum element can be determined in constant time.

The element j described in property 4 is computed as follows: $j = i + 2^{\lfloor \log_2(i+1) \rfloor - 1}$ if element j exists, otherwise j is set to $\lfloor (j-1)/2 \rfloor$. In the example above, for the value 8 (at index $i=7$) the j partner is at index 11 and contains the value 10. For the value 7 (at position $i=3$) the j partner is at index 5 and contains the value 15. For the value 11 at index i=8 the j partner is evaluated to be 12, and since index 12 does not exist, the j partner is at index 5, containing the value 15.

8.2.3.1   Insertion into a Deap

We will now illustrate how to insert an element into the deap data structure. Let us insert a new element 6 into the deap in the above figure, by placing it in the last position of the array. The modified figure is shown below.

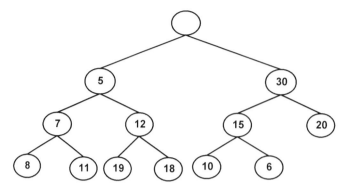

Figure 8.12: Inserting the element **6** into the deap in Figure 8.9.

In the above figure properties 1–3 are satisfied but, as we will show, property 4 is violated. The node with element 6 is in the maximum heap. How do we know this? We will now show the mechanics required to arrive at this conclusion.

The number of levels in a tree with n nodes is $\lfloor \log n \rfloor + 1$. The node at index k in the deap array is at level $\lfloor \log (k + 1) + 1 \rfloor$ in the deap data structure. The maximum number of nodes in a tree with l levels is $2^l - 1$. The last index position in the deap array will be $2^l - 2$. The nodes at the lth level are in indices $2^{l-1} - 2 + 1, \ldots, 2^{l-1} - 2 + 2^{l-1}$. Those in indices $2^{l-1} - 2 + 1, \ldots, 2^{l-1} - 2 + 2^{l-1}/2$ belong to the minimum heap and those in indices $2^{(l-1)} - 2 + 2^{l-1}/2 + 1, \ldots, 2^{l-1} - 2 + 2^{l-1}/2 + 2^{l-1}/2$ belong to the maximum heap. We can now say that a node at index k belongs to the minimum heap if $k \leq 2^{\lfloor \log(k+1) \rfloor} + 2^{\lfloor \log(k+1) \rfloor - 1} - 2 = 2^{\lfloor \log(k+1) \rfloor} \times 3 / 2 - 2$.

The value 6 is at index $k=12$ and $2^{\lfloor \log(k+1) \rfloor} + 2^{\lfloor \log(k+1) \rfloor - 1} - 2 = 10$, so since $12 > 10$, this element is at the maximum side of the deap. We have to compare with the partner node i (the minimum partner since element 6 is in the max heap). Note that i is at index $k - 2^{\lfloor \log(k+1) \rfloor - 1} = 8$ and the value at that position is 11. Since 11 is greater than 6, we swap them and the resulting tree is as follows:

The reader should note that the minimum partner was guaranteed to be less than the parent of the new node in the maximum heap by property 4, which was true before the insertion (the parent was previously its partner). It is, therefore, in the right position in the maximum heap after the swap. We now have to perform the reheap–up operation starting from 6 on the minimum heap rooted at element 5. The resulting tree is given below.

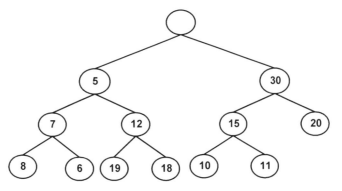

Figure 8.13:   Swapping between the **nodes 6 and 11** in Figure 8.10 done to restore the standard Deap structure.

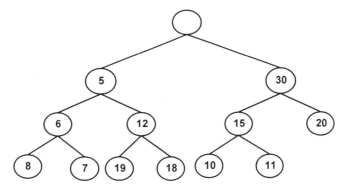

Figure 8.14:   Standard deap structure got by performing reheap up operation on the deap structure in Figure 8.11.

A similar approach can be adopted if the insert operation inserts the node in the minimum heap. In such a case we need to compare the value of the element inserted in the minimum heap with the maximum partner and swap if necessary to enforce property 4. After the swap we have to perform the reheap up operation on the maximum heap. If insertion on the minimum heap or the maximum heap does preserve property 4, so that no swap is necessary, the reheap up operation is still performed on the heap into which the insertion was made.

From the above discussion it can be seen that the insert operation takes $O(log\ n)$ time for the reheap up operation. The complete algorithm for insertion is presented below.

```
ALGORITHM INSERTIONINTODEAP (DEAP, MAXELEMENTS, x)
1.  if Deap is not full
2.      maxElements = maxElements + 1;
3.      if maxElements belongs to maximum Heap of the Deap
4.          i = maxElements - 2^(⌊log maxElements⌋-1);
5.          if x < Deap[i]
6.              Deap[maxElements] = Deap[i];
7.              ReheapUpMin (Deap, maxElements, x)
8.          else
9.              ReheapUpMax (Deap, maxElements, x)
10.         endif
11.     else
12.         j = (maxElements + 2^(log maxElements-1))/2
13.         if j > maxElements thenj = j/2;
14.         if x > Deap[j]
15.             Deap[maxElements] = Deap[j];
16.             ReheapUpMax (Deap, maxElements, x)
17.         else
18.             ReheapUpMin (Deap, maxElements, x)
19.         endif
20.     endif
21. endif
```

8.2.3.2   Deletion from a Deap

We will now present an approach to delete from the deap data structure. We will explain by deletion of the minimum element and the same approach can be adopted for the deletion of the maximum element. Let t be the value in the last element of the deap data structure as given in the figure. In the example, $t = 11$. Reduce the number of elements by one. Move the value t to the position $Deap[1]$, the minimum element position. Perform a reheap down operation on the minimum heap. Let i be the index where the value t finally rests and j be the index of its maximum partner.

By the deap properties, we know that $Deap[i].child.value > Deap[i].value > Deap[i].parent.value$ and $Deap[j].parent.value > Deap[j].value > Deap[j].child.value$. Further, $Deap[j].value > Deap[i].parent.value$ since $Deap[i].parent.value$ was previously in index i but was displaced in the reheap down operation. Now let us compare

Deap[i].value (that is, *t*) with *Deap[j].value* (call it *z*). If $t \leq z$, then we are done because all deap properties are satisfied. If $t > z$, then the two values must swapped. By the inequalities above, we can see that *Deap[i].child.value>z >Deap[i].parent.value*, so that after the swap the minimum heap will be a correct heap. But what about the maximum heap? Certainly *t>Deap[j].child. value*, so that *t* belongs no lower in the maximum heap, but it might belong higher in the heap. In other words, we need to reheap it back up through the maximum heap.

The deap after the deletion of the element 5 is given below.

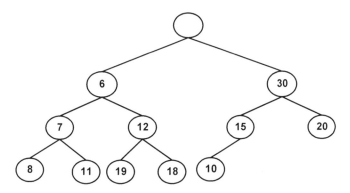

Figure 8.15:   Deap produced as a result of deletion of element **5** from the Figure 8.12.

The following algorithm deletes the minimum element from the deap data structure.

```
ALGORITHM DELETEMIN (DEAP)
1.  Output Deap[1]
2.  Deap[1] ← Deap[maxElements]
3.  t ← Deap[1]
4.  maxElements ← maxElements - 1
5.  HeapifyMin (Deap, 1)
6.  i ← index of value t in Deap
7.  j ← maximum partner of i
8.  if (Deap[i] > Deap[j])
9.       swap Deap[i] and Deap[j]
10.      reheapUpMax (Deap, j, Deap[j])
11. endif
```

8.2.3.3 Implementation of the Deap Data Structure

We now begin the implementation of the deap data structure in C++. As in the case of the min-max heap, it is clear that the deap is quite similar to the standard heap, so much so that it is reasonable to implement the deap as a subclass of the *Heap* and *AbstractDoubleEndedHeap* classes. One quirk that we must bear in mind, however, is that the deap always has one node: the empty root. We must compensate for the empty node by increasing the size by one in the constructor and changing the *size()* and *maxsize()* methods.

Note that, as with the min-max heap, we have a problem with the precision of computation. We will again declare the constant, *EPSILON*, to be used later as a precision adjuster.

Thus, the Deap class will initially be as follows:

```cpp
const double EPSILON = 1e-10; // precision adjuster for log


template <class DataType>
class Deap :
    virtual public Heap<DataType>, AbstractDoubleEndedHeap
    <DataType>
public:
    Deap (int maxsize);
    virtual ~Deap ();
    virtual int size ();
    virtual int maxsize ();
};
// -------------------------------------------------------------
template <class DataType>
Deap<DataType>::Deap (int maxsize)
    : Heap<DataType> (maxsize+1) { _size = 1; }
// -------------------------------------------------------------
template <class DataType>
Deap<DataType>::~Deap () { }
// -------------------------------------------------------------
template <class DataType>
int Deap<DataType>::size () { return _size - 1; }
// -------------------------------------------------------------
template <class DataType>
int Deap<DataType>::maxsize () { return _maxsize - 1; }
```

In the case of the deap, unlike the other structures we have seen in this chapter, the root is in fact empty. As we did with the min-max heap, we will implement *root ()* by returning the minimum and *deleteRoot ()* by deleting the minimum. This is consistent with the behavior of the min-max heap. So the implementations of these two methods are as follows:

```
template <class DataType>
DataType& Deap<DataType>::root () { return min(); }
// ------------------------------------------------------------
template <class DataType>
void Deap<DataType>::deleteRoot () { deleteMin (); }
```

The implementations of *min ()* and *max ()* are quite simple, based on the preceding discussion of the structure of a deap:

```
template <class DataType>
DataType& Deap<DataType>::min ()
{
    if (isEmpty()) throw HeapUnderflow();
    return _array[1];
}
// ------------------------------------------------------------
template <class DataType>
DataType& Deap<DataType>:: max ()
{
    if (isEmpty()) throw HeapUnderflow();
    if (size() == 1) return _array[1];
    return _array[2];
}
```

The insert() Method

We can see that there are several complex computations to be performed in the implementation of insertion (and deletion). We will particularly want a simple method for computing $2^{\lfloor \log (k+1) \rfloor}$, as we will need to make this computation several times. The result of this computation is, in fact, the largest power of two which is not greater than k+1, so we shall call the method *largest2power()*, and implement it as in the following code.

```
template <class DataType>
int Deap<DataType>::largest2power (int k)
{
    int log2 = log (k+1)/log(2) + EPSILON; // log (base 2) of k+1
 return (int) (pow (2, log2));
}
```

We must be able to determine whether a particular node is in the minimum heap or the maximum heap, and we must be able to find its partner in the other heap. Rather than strew these computations about the class, we will locate them in just three methods: *inMinHeap()*, which reports whether a node is in the minimum heap or not, *minPartner()*, which finds the partner in the minimum heap of a node in the maximum heap, and *maxPartner()*, which does the reverse for a node in the minimum heap. The implementation of these methods is straightforwardly based on the discussion above:

```
template <class DataType>
bool Deap<DataType>::inMinHeap(int index)
{
    return (index <= (3*largest2power(index))/2 - 2);
}
// ---------------------------------------------------------
template <class DataType>
int Deap<DataType>::minPartner(int index)
{
    return index - largest2power(index)/2;
}
// ---------------------------------------------------------
template <class DataType>
int Deap<DataType>::maxPartner(int index)
{
    int partner = index + largest2power(index)/2;
    if (partner < _size)
        return partner;
    return (partner-1)/2;
}
```

We can now implement the *insert()* method based on the algorithm previously presented:

```cpp
template <class DataType>
void Deap<DataType>::insert(DataType& record)
{
    if (isFull()) throw HeapOverflow();
    if (isEmpty())
    {
        _array[1] = record;
        _size = 2;
        return;
    }

    int pos = _size;
    int partner;
    _size++;
    if (!inMinHeap(pos)) // if node goes in max heap
    {
        partner = minPartner(pos);
        if (record < _array[partner])
        {
            _array[pos] = _array[partner];
            reheapUpMin (partner, record);
        }
        else
            reheapUpMax (pos, record);
    }
    else            // if node goes in min heap
    {
        partner = maxPartner(pos);
        if (record > _array[partner])
        {
            _array[pos] = _array[partner];
            reheapUpMax (partner, record);
        }
        else
            reheapUpMin (pos, record);
    }
}
```

Now we must implement *reheapUpMin()* and *reheapUpMax()*. It should be evident that these two methods are identical except for the sense of the comparison and the number of the node where reheaping up operation stops, which is 1 for the minimum heap and 2 for the maximum heap. We need not concern ourselves with the second difference, as the parent of the node where bubbling up stops is node 0 in either case. Thus, as in the case of the min-max heap, we can write three related methods:

```cpp
template <class DataType>
void Deap<DataType>::reheapUpMin (int position, DataType&
record)
{
    reheapUp (position, record, false);
}
// -----------------------------------------------------------
template <class DataType>
void Deap<DataType>::reheapUpMax (int position, DataType&
record)
{
    reheapUp (position, record, true);
}
// -----------------------------------------------------------
template <class DataType>
void Deap<DataType>::reheapUp
    (int position, DataType& record, bool keepIfMore)
{
    int par = parent (position);
    while ((par > 0) &&
    ((record > _array[par]) == keepIfMore))
    {
        _array[position] = _array[par];
        position = par;
        par = parent (position);

    }
    _array[position] = record;
}
```

We have now completed the implementation of insertion into the deap.

The deleteMin() and deleteMax() Methods

Now we must implement the *deleteMin()* and *deleteMax()* methods. Clearly, we need both a *heapifyMin()* and a *heapifyMax()*, which we will implement as part of a group of three, just as we implemented three reheap up methods above. We will also need to know the index where the "heapified" value comes to rest, so these methods must return that index. Thus, we can implement the heapify methods as follows:

```
template <class DataType>
int Deap<DataType>::heapifyMin (int pos)
{
    return heapify (pos, false);
}
// ----------------------------------------------------------
template <class DataType>
int Deap<DataType>::heapifyMax (int pos)
{
    return heapify (pos, true);
}
// ----------------------------------------------------------
template <class DataType>
int Deap<DataType>::heapify (int pos, bool keepIfMore)
{
    int left = leftChild (pos);
    int right = rightChild (pos);
    int highest = pos;
    if ((left < _size) &&((_array[left] > _array[pos]) ==
    keepIfMore))
            highest = left;
    if ((right < _size) &&
        ((_array[right] > _array[highest]) == keepIfMore))
        highest = right;
    if (highest == pos) return pos;
    swap (_array[pos], _array[highest]);
    return heapify (highest, keepIfMore);
}
```

Given these methods, the reheap up methods, and the utility method *maxPart-ner()*, we can readily implement *deleteMin()* based on the algorithm above:

```
template <class DataType>
void Deap<DataType>::deleteMin()
{
    if (isEmpty()) throw HeapUnderflow();
    _size--;
    _array[1] = _array[_size];
    if (isEmpty()) return;
    int pos = heapifyMin (1);
    int partner = maxPartner (pos);
    if (partner == 0) return;
    if (_array[pos] > _array[partner])
    {
        // record stores the value which may be reheaped up;
        // we can't use _array[pos] itself as it will be changed
        Object record = _array[pos];
        swap (_array[partner],_array[pos]);
        reheapUpMax (partner, record);
    }
}
```

The *deleteMax()* method is quite similar, although we must be careful about the possibility that there are fewer than three nodes in the deap. The implementation of *deleteMax()* is left as an exercise for the reader.

The halfRangeSearch() method

As in the case of the *MinMaxHeap*, we must implement *halfRangeSearch()* a little differently from the standard heap. We will take the position that *halfRangeSearch()* is equivalent to *halfRangeSearchLesser()*. The implementations of *halfRangeSearchLesser()* and *halfRangeSearchGreater()* are a little tricky, and will be explained separately.

Consider *halfRangeSearchLesser()*. The obvious implementation would involve working our way through the min-heap portion of the deap, stopping the recursion when an element is greater than the specified value, just as we would work through a normal min-heap. But what if the specified value is larger than some elements of the max-heap portion of the deap, as well? Do we need to work our way through the max-heap portion as well? Fortunately, we do not. If an element of the min-heap is out of range (it is too large), then its max-partner and elements of its sub-tree are out of range also. Furthermore, the elements of its max-partner's subtree are the max-partners of elements of its own subtree, so that we do not need to separately test any elements of its max-partner's subtree. Thus, we can just test the max-partner and add it if necessary, immediately after testing an element of the min-heap portion of the deap. The only other problem is that an element and its parent might have the same max-partner, but we can check for this; an element has the same max-partner as its parent if its max-partner's index is less than its own. Thus, *halfRangeSearch-Lesser ()* is as implemented as follows:

```
template <class DataType>
void Deap<DataType>::_halfRangeSearchLesser
        (int pos, DataType& value, Vector<DataType>& vector)
{
// if we've exhausted the heap, take no action
    if (pos >= _size) return;

    if (_array[pos] < value)
    {
        vector.add (_array[pos]);
        int maxP = maxPartner (pos);
        if ((maxP > pos) && (_array[maxP] < value))
            vector.add (_array[maxP]);
        _halfRangeSearchLesser (leftChild(pos), value, vector);
        _halfRangeSearchLesser (rightChild(pos), value, vector);
    }
}
// -----------------------------------------------------------
template <class DataType>
Vector<DataType> Deap<DataType>::halfRangeSearchLesser
    (DataType& value)
{
    Vector<DataType> vector;
    int pos = 1;
    _halfRangeSearchLesser (1, value, vector);
    return vector;
}
```

Having written the *halfRangeSearchLesser()* method, we might be tempted to simply reverse it in order to write the *halfRangeSearchGreater()* method. But there is a problem: an element of the min-heap is not necessarily the min-partner of an element of the max-heap. Consider the deap depicted below:

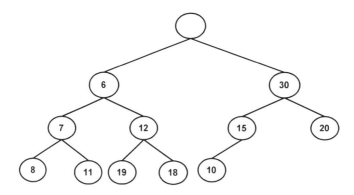

Figure 8.16: An example of a deap.

The max-partner of the element at position 8 (value 11) is the element at position 5 (value 15), but the min-partner of the element at position 5 is the element at position 3 (value 7). Thus, simply testing the min-partner is not enough, as that procedure would miss the elements at positions 8, 9, and 10 of this deap. However, we can see that an element of the min-heap is not a min-partner of its max-partner if and only if its max-partner lacks a corresponding child. If an element of the max heap is in range, we must check whether its min-partner is in range, then test each of its children recursively; if a child is missing, we must check the element that would be the min-partner of that child. Thus, the *halfRangeSearchGreater()* method is implemented as follows:

```
template <class DataType>
void Deap<DataType>::_halfRangeSearchGreater
        (int pos, DataType& value, Vector<DataType>& vector)
{
// if we've exhausted the heap, take no action
    if (pos >= _size) return;

// if this element is in range, its min-partner and subtree
// might be
```

```
        if (_array[pos] > value)
        {
            vector.add (_array[pos]);

        // check the min-partner; it is guaranteed to exist
            int minP = minPartner (pos);
       if (_array[minP] > value)
       vector.add (_array[minP]);

        // if the left child exists, call recursively
            int left = leftChild (pos);
            if (left < _size)
                _halfRangeSearchGreater (left, value, vector);

    // otherwise, check what would be the min-partner of
    // the left child (though this may not exist either)
        else
        {
           minP = minPartner (left);
           if ((minP < _size) && (_array[minP] > value))
             vector.add (_array[minP]);
        }

        // do the same thing for the right child
            int right = rightChild (pos);
            if (right < _size)
              _halfRangeSearchGreater (right, value, vector);
        else
        {
           minP = minPartner (right);
           if ((minP < _size) && (_array[minP] > value))
             vector.add (_array[minP]);
        }
    }
}
// ----------------------------------------------------------
```

```
template <class DataType>
Vector<DataType> Deap<DataType>::halfRangeSearchGreater
    (DataType& value)
{
    Vector<DataType> vector;
    // handle the special case of a one-element tree
    if (size() == 1)
    {
        if (_array[1] > value) vector.add (_array[1]);
    }
    else
        _halfRangeSearchGreater (2, value, vector);
    return vector;
}
```

The Enumerator

The enumerator for ordinary heaps works for deaps, roughly speaking. However, the element at position 0 may not be initialized and is displayed as garbage. This can be corrected if the Object instance has a default constructor that initializes or it can be corrected by making a slight modification to the constructor of the *HeapEnumerator* class and overriding the *enumerator()* method in the *Deap* class. These changes are left as an exercise for the reader.

8.3   Performance Comparison

We will now compare the different implementations of the priority search queue data structures. As mentioned in the introduction a balanced binary search tree can perform all the operations of a priority search tree, but requires additional space that is needed for all the pointers. The array implementations of the priority queues are simple and space efficient in comparison with the pointer based implementation. Certain operations such as *change* that changes the value stored in the priority queue can be implemented only by using a deletion followed by an addition on a balanced binary search tree, while direct ReheapUp and ReheapDown operations can be used to implement it on array based priority queues. Figure 8.17 presents a summary of the of the worse-case execution times for the various implementations of the priority queues. The minimum element (resp. maximum element) in a binary search tree is the leftmost element (resp. rightmost) and can be obtained by traversing from the root of the tree.

Priory Queue Implementations Worst-case Time Complexity Comparisons				
Operation	Min Heap/Max Heap	Min-Max Heap	Deaps	Balanced Binary Search Trees
Create()	$O(n)$	$O(n)$	$O(n)$	$O(1)$
isEmpty()	$O(1)$	$O(1)$	$O(1)$	$O(1)$
Size()	$O(1)$	$O(1)$	$O(1)$	$O(n)$
Max()	$O(n)/O(1)$	$O(1)$	$O(1)$	$O(1)$, if we use additional pointer to point to the max node otherwise, it is $O(\log_2 n)$.
Min()	$O(1)/O(n)$	$O(1)$	$O(1)$	$O(1)$, if we use additional pointer to point to the min node otherwise, it is $O(\log_2 n)$.
Insert(record)	$O(\log_2 n)$	$O(\log_2 n)$	$O(\log_2 n)$	$O(\log_2 n)$
deleteMax() *deleteMin()*	$O(\log_2 n)$	$O(\log_2 n)$	$O(\log_2 n)$	$O(\log_2 n)$
halfRangeSearch (value)	$O(p)$	$O(p)$	$O(p)$	$O(p)$

Figure 8.17:   Comparison of worst-case execution times for different implementations of the priority queues. Note that p is the number of elements that satisfies the *halfrangesearch* query.

The qualitative assessment of the different implementations of the priority queues is presented in Figure 8.18.

Priory Queue Implementations Qualitative Assessment	
Implementation	Assessment
Standard Heap	Easy to implement; logarithmic worst case for all operations; can be only minimum heap or maximum heap.
Min-Max Heap	It is both a minimum and maximum heap; number of comparisons for operations are half the number required for standard heap.
Deaps	Same as for min-max heap; requires additional space for null root.
Balanced Binary Search tree	Logarithmic worst case for all operations; can delete an arbitrary element; requires additional space for pointers.

Figure 8.18:   Qualitative assessment of different priority queue implementations.

8.4   The Priority Queue Adapter in STL

The priority_queue adapter in the standard template library implements the standard heap data structure discussed previously. One can either define a min or max heap depending on the value of the comparator specified during the time of object creation. All operations specified for the queue adapter can be applied for the priority_queue adapter except the front and back operations are not allowed. This is reasonable since a heap data structure does not support front and back operations. The equivalents of min (resp. max), insert, and deleteMin (resp. deleteMax) operations on a min heap (resp. max heap) data structure for a priority_queue adapter are top, push, and pop, respectively. The methods of the priority_queue adapter are exactly same as the ones presented for the stack adapter.

In the following example we are using a priority_queue adapter that uses the deque container. Note that the comparator greater in the template for priority indicates that the heap formed is a max heap. Replacing the keyword greater with less would create a min heap data structure.

```cpp
#include <iostream> // for i/o functions
#include <deque>
#include <queue>

using namespace std;

void main ()
{
    int MAXVAL = 64;
    priority_queue<int, deque<int>, greater<int>>
              maxheap (MAXVAL);
    for (int i = 0; i < MAXVAL/2; i++)
    {
        maxheap.push (i);
        maxheap.push (MAXVAL-1-i);
    }
    cout << "The values (in order): " << endl;
    while (!maxheap.isEmpty())
    {
        cout << maxheap.top () << " ";
        maxheap.pop ();
    }
    cout << endl;
}
```

The output from this function demonstrates that the class is operating correctly:

```
The values (in order):
63 62 61 60 59 58 57 56 55 54 53 52 51 50 49 48 47 46 45 44
43 42 41 40 39 38 37 36 35 34 33 32 31 30 29 28 27 26 25 24
23 22 21 20 19 18 17 16 15 14 13 12 11 10 9 8 7 6 5 4 3 2 1 0
```

8.5   Applications

The data structures presented in this chapter can be used to perform certain operations quite efficiently.

8.5.1   Huffman Compression

Huffman compression is a type of data compression that is used to save storage space. Huffman compression takes a data file and creates a compressed file whose size is as small as possible. This compressed file can then be uncompressed to get the original file. Consider the following text T, a string containing 32 characters:

"HUFFMAN COMPRESSION IS LOSSLESS!"

If we assume that all characters are represented using the same number of bits as in ASCII (American Standard Code for Information Interchange) then the number of bits needed to store the above text is $32 \times 7 = 224$ (7 bits for each character in ASCII encoding). In the above text T, the number of different characters is 16 and four bits is sufficient to represent each character uniquely. Hence the number of bits needed to store the above text is reduced to 128.

We call the assignment of bit patterns to characters based on ASCII or on other forms *encodings*. An encoding such that no character has a bit pattern which is also a prefix bit pattern for some other character is called a **prefix conditioned** encoding. For example, if we assign a bit pattern of 1011 to the character A and 101101 to character B, then this encoding is not prefix conditioned. Prefix conditioned encodings help in faster reconstruction of the text after it has been compressed.

Huffman compression takes a given text and determines prefix-conditioned encodings that minimize the total number of bits required to encode the text. More formally, if f_s is the frequency of a character s in the text T (the number of times the symbol s occurs in the text T) and B_s is the number of bits assigned to the symbol s in the encoding, then the goal of Huffman is to minimize $\sum f_s \times B_s$, where s ranges over the set of all symbols in the text T.

The Huffman algorithm constructs a binary tree with symbols in the text T as leaf nodes and internal nodes with null symbols. Each edge of the binary tree is assigned a 0 bit if it is a left edge and a 1 bit if it is a right edge. Now the bit string assigned to a symbol is formed by concatenating the bits in edges in the path from root to the leaf node that contains the symbol. The encoding of this type is prefix conditioned (proof of this fact is left as an exercise). The frequency of occurrence of each symbol in the text above is given below.

A	C	E	F	H	I	L	M	N	O	P	R	S	U	"	!
1	1	2	2	1	2	2	2	2	3	1	1	7	1	3	1

The binary tree for the Huffman encoding is constructed using the following algorithm.

```
Algorithm HuffmanTree (T)      // T is the text
1.  Create a binary tree corresponding to each symbol of T;
    each node contains as data the symbol and its frequency.
2.  Place these trees in a minimum Heap data structure ordered
    by frequency
3.  while the number of elements in the Heap is greater than 1
4.        Delete two elements from the heap and call them as K1
          and K2.
5.        Create a new node K3 and assign the left childto
          pointto K1 and the right childto pointto K2.
6.        The Symbol field in K3 is null and the frequency field
          of K3 is the sum of the   frequencies in K1 and K2.
7.        Insert the node K3 in the minimum Heap .
8.  endwhile
```

At the end of the execution of this algorithm, the last binary tree remaining in the heap is the Huffman tree.

The number of Heap operations that are performed bounds the complexity of the above algorithm. If we have n symbols, the initial Heap can be constructed in $O(n)$ time. Also, there are at most $O(n)$ insertions inside the while loop since a binary tree with n leaf nodes has at most $O(n)$ internal nodes. The number of deletions is also bounded by $O(n)$. Since each deletion and insertion takes $O(\log n)$ on a minimum heap, the total complexity of the above algorithm is $O(n \log n)$.

The C++ method for the above algorithm requires that we declare a *BinaryTree* subclass for the nodes to be placed in the heap. This subclass must, of course, support comparisons (which the *BinaryTree* class itself does not). Its data field will need to be an instance of a class, which has two data fields, one for the frequency and the other for the symbol. We will express frequency as number of occurrences rather than proportion. The data field class will have public fields, since we will use it only through the *BinaryTree* subclass. We must write an ostream << method for the data field class so that the BinaryTree subclass can print itself. The data field class is as follows:

```cpp
class HuffmanNode
{
friend ostream& operator<< (ostream& os, HuffmanNode& hn);
public:
    int frequency;
    char letter;
    HuffmanNode (const HuffmanNode& node);
    HuffmanNode (int freq);
    HuffmanNode (int freq, char ltr);
};
// ----------------------------------------------------------
HuffmanNode::HuffmanNode (const HuffmanNode& node)
{
    frequency = node.frequency;
    letter = node.letter;
}
// ----------------------------------------------------------
HuffmanNode::HuffmanNode (int freq)
{
    letter = 0;
    frequency = freq;
}
// ----------------------------------------------------------
HuffmanNode::HuffmanNode (int freq, char ltr)
{
    frequency = freq;
    letter = ltr;
}
// ----------------------------------------------------------
ostream& operator<< (ostream& os, HuffmanNode& hn)
{
    os << hn.letter << "(" << hn.frequency << ")";
    return os;
}
```

For the binary tree itself, we need several different constructors to handle the various situations in which a tree would be created: the initial trees are created with frequencies and letters, and trees created by combination will have frequencies (but not letters) and subtrees. Also, the *BinaryTree* has pointer fields, indicating a need for a copy constructor and assignment operator. Finally, we need a suite of comparison operators.

```
class HuffmanTree : public BinaryTree<HuffmanNode>
{
public:
    HuffmanTree ();
    HuffmanTree (HuffmanTree& left, HuffmanTree& right);
    HuffmanTree (int freq, char ltr);
    HuffmanTree (const HuffmanTree& ht);
    virtual ~HuffmanTree ();
    int frequency ();
    void operator= (const HuffmanTree& ht);
    bool operator< (HuffmanTree& ht);
    bool operator> (HuffmanTree& ht);
    bool operator== (HuffmanTree& ht);
};
// ------------------------------------------------------------
HuffmanTree::HuffmanTree() : BinaryTree<HuffmanNode> () { }
// ------------------------------------------------------------
HuffmanTree::HuffmanTree
    (HuffmanTree& left, HuffmanTree& right)
    : BinaryTree<HuffmanNode> ()
{
_rootData = new HuffmanNode (left.frequency()
                            + right.frequency());
 if (_rootData == NULL) throw BinaryTreeMemory();
 _left = new HuffmanTree(left);
 _right = new HuffmanTree(right);
}
// ------------------------------------------------------------
HuffmanTree::HuffmanTree(int freq, char ltr)
    : BinaryTree<HuffmanNode> ()
{
```

```
 _rootData = new HuffmanNode (freq, ltr);
 if (_rootData == NULL) throw BinaryTreeMemory();
 _left = new HuffmanTree();
 _right = new HuffmanTree();
}
// ------------------------------------------------------------
HuffmanTree::HuffmanTree(const HuffmanTree& ht)
    : BinaryTree<HuffmanNode> ()
{
    if (ht._rootData != NULL)
    {
        _rootData = new HuffmanNode (*ht._rootData);
        _left = new HuffmanTree (* ((HuffmanTree*) ht._left));
        _right = new HuffmanTree (* ((HuffmanTree*) ht._right));
    }
}
// ------------------------------------------------------------
HuffmanTree::~HuffmanTree() { }
// ------------------------------------------------------------
int HuffmanTree::frequency () { return _rootData->frequency;
}
// ------------------------------------------------------------
bool HuffmanTree::operator< (HuffmanTree& ht)
{ return _rootData->frequency < ht._rootData->frequency; }
// ------------------------------------------------------------
bool HuffmanTree::operator> (HuffmanTree& ht)
{ return _rootData->frequency > ht._rootData->frequency; }
// ------------------------------------------------------------
bool HuffmanTree::operator== (HuffmanTree& ht)
{ return _rootData->frequency == ht._rootData->frequency; }
// ------------------------------------------------------------
void HuffmanTree::operator= (const HuffmanTree& ht)
{
// delete all existing data; we will overwrite fields
    if (!isEmpty())
    {
```

```
            delete _rootData;
            delete _left;
            delete _right;
    }
// if ht is empty, make this tree empty too
    if (ht._rootData == NULL)
    {
        _rootData = NULL;
        _left = NULL;
        _right = NULL;
    }
// otherwise, copy each part of ht
    else // ht is not empty
    {
        _rootData = new HuffmanNode (*ht._rootData);
        _left = new HuffmanTree (* ((HuffmanTree*) ht._left));
        _right = new HuffmanTree (* ((HuffmanTree*) ht._right));
    }
}
```

Once these classes are created, the method closely follows the above algorithm.

```
HuffmanTree huffmanTree (char* T)
{
    ArrayClass<int> freq (256,0);

    int len = strlen (T);
    int i;

    for (i = 0; i < len; i++) freq[T[i]]++;
    MinimumHeap<HuffmanTree> mh(len);

    for (i = 0; i < 256; i++)
    {
    if (freq[i] > 0)
        {
            HuffmanTree ht (freq[i], (char) i);
            mh.insert (ht);
```

```
            }
      }
      while (mh.size() > 1)
      {
            HuffmanTree ht1 = mh.min();
            mh.deleteMin();
            HuffmanTree ht2 = mh.min();
            mh.deleteMin();
            HuffmanTree ht3 (ht1, ht2);
            mh.insert (ht3);
      }
      return mh.min();
}
```

The Huffman tree for the symbols in the text "HUFFMAN COMPRESSION IS LOSSLESS!" is given below.

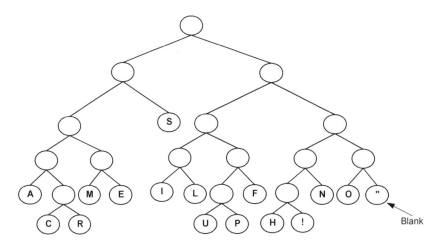

Figure 8.19:   Huffman Tree for the given text, which is to be compressed.

The following table gives the bit strings assigned to each symbol after the Huffman tree is traversed from the root to the leaf node containing the symbol and concatenating the bits in the edges.

A	0000	U	10100
C	00010	P	10101
R	00011	F	1011
M	0010	H	11000
E	0011	!	11001
S	01	N	1101
I	1000	O	1110
L	1001	(blank)	1111

Figure 8.20:   Bit strings assigned to each symbol of the given text, which is to be compressed after the Huffman tree is traversed from the root to the leaf node containing the symbol and concatenating the bits into edges.

Based on the frequencies of each symbol given for each symbol and the length of the bit string assigned to them, it can be verified that the total number of bits need to represent the text T is 120 which is less than 128 when we assigned four bits to each symbol – not a great improvement, but then this is only a short string. Apart from the encodings for the text, the compression technique also maintains a dictionary that helps us map the bit strings to the symbols. The dictionary for the Huffman compression is the binary tree above stored in some succinct form. The size of a compressed file is the sum of the size of the dictionary and the number of bits to encode the text. Hence it is important that the binary tree is stored in an efficient manner that reduces the number of bits required to store it. Determining this form is left as an exercise.

In order to determine the sequence of characters from the bit string, we scan the sequence of bits one by one. At the beginning of the scanning process, we start from the root of the binary tree and when a bit is encountered we take the right branch and a left branch when a 0 bit is encountered. If we reach a leaf node, then the symbol in the leaf node is output and we start from the root again till all the bits in the sequence are processed.

8.6   Exercises

8.1.   Let S be a sequence of key values, 18, 7, 21, 42, 6, 2, 4, and 15.

   a) Beginning with an empty minimum heap, draw the heap after each key value is inserted into the heap.
   b) Draw the heap after deleting the minimum element, and then after deleting the minimum element again.

8.2.   Let minHeap be a minimum heap data structure containing n elements, implemented using an array of elements, and let minHeap[i] be the element at position i in min-Heap. Write a method change(i, newValue) that changes the value of the element minHeap[i] to contain the new value and appropriately modifies the minHeap data structure so that it remains a minimum heap. What is the complexity of the change() method?

8.3.   Write a method delete(i) to delete the element in position i of the minimum heap data structure, implemented as an array. The resulting heap should remain a minimum heap. What is the time complexity of your method?

8.4.   The binary tree data structure discussed in chapter 6 can also be used to represent the minimum heap data structure. Write such an implementation of the minimum heap data structure.

8.5.   If the minimum heap is implemented using an array, the array must be of fixed size n. To avoid overflow as elements are inserted, we can instead implement the minimum heap using a vector. Write such an implementation.

8.6.   Consider the elements given in problem 8.1. Beginning with an empty min-max heap, draw the heap after each element is inserted.

8.7.   Draw the min-max heap constructed in problem 8.6 after performing deleteMin(), and after then performing deleteMax().

8.8.   Provide a vector implementation of the min-max heap that allows the heap to grow or shrink as elements are inserted or deleted, respectively.

8.9.   Write an enumeration class for the min-max heap.

8.10.   Given n elements, is it possible to construct a min-max heap in O(n) time, as the build-Heap() procedure constructed a heap in O(n) time?

8.11. Consider the elements given in problem 8.1. Beginning with an empty deap, draw the deap after each element is inserted.

8.12. Draw the deap constructed in problem 8.6 after performing deleteMin(), and after then performing deleteMax().

8.13. Provide a vector implementation of the deap that allows the deap to grow or shrink as elements are inserted or deleted, respectively.

8.14. Write an enumeration class for the deap.

8.15. Given n elements, is it possible to construct a deap in O(n) time, as the buildHeap() procedure constructed a heap in O(n) time?

8.16. Implement the operations of a double ended priority queue data structure on a balanced binary search tree data structure.

8.17. For the following string construct a Huffman tree and determine the codes for each of the symbols.

"PRIORITY SEARCH TREES ARE USEFUL"

8.18. Write a method which, given a Huffman tree, traverses the tree and returns the bit strings assigned to each symbol, as discussed in the text.

8.7 References for Further Reading

Bentley, J.L., "Programming pearls: Thanks, heaps", *Communications of the ACM*, vol. 28, pp. 245–250, 1985.

Cormen, T., Leiserson, C. and Rivest, R., *Introduction to Algorithms*, McGraw-Hill, NY: 1992.

Fredman, M.L., and Tarjan, R.E., "Fibonacci Heaps and their uses in improved network optimization algorithms", *Journal of the ACM*, vol. 34, pp. 596–615, 1987.

Frieze, A., "On the Random Construction of Heaps", *Information Processing Letters*, vol. 27, pp. 103, 1998.

Gallager, R.G., "Variations on a theme of Huffman", *IEEE Transactions on Information Theory*, vol. IT-24, pp. 668–674, 1978.

Gonnet, G.H., and Munro, I., "Heaps on Heaps", *SIAM Journal of Computing*, vol. 15, pp. 964–97, 1986.

Horowitz, E., Sahni, S., and Mehta, D., and Freeman, W.H., *Fundamentals of Data Structures in C++*, New York, NY, 1994.

Huffman, David A., "A method for the construction of minimum-redundancy codes", *Proceedings of the Institute of Radio Engineers*, vol. 40, pp. 1098–1101, 1952 (also in Davisson & Gray).

Jonassen, A., and Dahl, O., "Analysis of an Algorithm for Priority Queue Administration", *BIT.* vol. 15, pp. 409–22, 1975.

Lelewer, D., and Hirschberg, D., "Data Compression", *Computing Surveys*, vol. 19, no. 3, pp. 261–296, 1987.

McCreight, E., "Priority Search Trees", *SIAM Journal on Computing*, vol. 14, no. 2, pp. 257–276, 1985.

McDiarmid, C.J.H., and Reed, B.A., "Building Heaps Fast", *Journal of Algorithms* vol. 10, pp. 351–365, 1989.

Tarjan, R., "Data Structures and Network Algorithms," Monograph, *SIAM Journal of Computing*, Philadelphia, PA, 1983.

Williams, J.W. J., "Algorithm 232: Heapsort", *Communications of the ACM*, vol. 7, pp. 347–348, 1964.

Wood, D., *Data Structures, Algorithms and Performance*, Addison-Wesley, Reading, MA: 1993, 594 pages.

CHAPTER

9 Sorting

S ORTING IS A process of arranging items in some order. If the items to be sorted can be said to be "less than", "greater than", or "equal to" each other, then the items can be arranged in an ascending or descending order. In programming environments, sorting of integers, real numbers or strings is a common problem. In his classic book on Sorting and Searching, Knuth writes "I believe that virtually every important aspect of programming arises somewhere in the context of sorting and searching." We have studied various sorting techniques in the previous chapters. In this chapter we will compare and contrast each of the sorting techniques. We will also develop several sorting techniques that assume the data elements to be sorted do not fit in the main memory entirely. Such sorting techniques are referred to as *external sorting*.

Sorting has several applications. A sorted set of items is easier to browse than the one that is unsorted. For example, a set of book titles, index terms found in the back of a book, or a list of student names in a class is easier to browse when arranged in alphabetical order. We saw in an earlier chapter that if we have two sorted lists, we can merge them with one pass on both the lists. Previously we described a method called binary search that efficiently finds a member in a sorted set of items. Now, let us formally define the sorting process.

Let $K_1, K_2, \ldots, K_n$ be a set of n keys to be sorted. The goal of sorting is to determine a permutation $p(1), p(2), \ldots, p(n)$ of integers $1, 2, \ldots, n$ which puts the keys in non-decreasing order: $K_{p(1)} \leq K_{p(2)} \leq \ldots \leq K_{p(n)}$. The sorting is called *stable* if we further require that records with equal keys retain their original relative order, i.e., if $K_{p(i)} = K_{p(j)}$ and $i < j$ then $p(i) < p(j)$. It is desirable for a sorting algorithm to be stable for the following reasons. Consider a set of records containing two fields each, say age and salary. Let us say that the goal is to sort the records on both fields; first on age and second on salary. If we have two or more records that have the same salary but different age values, then the desirable sorting technique will be *stable* sorting.

A sorting procedure is called *inplace* if we do not require any extra working storage. This is especially useful when large amounts of data need to be sorted. Clearly, an *inplace sorting* method would avoid the cost of extra storage and associated data manipulations.

The sorting is called *physically unchanged* if the keys are never moved during the sorting process and an auxiliary array is used to store the permutation of the sorted positions. Sorting techniques that are physically unchanged simply store the rank of each record in the auxiliary array. Such techniques are useful as they eliminate large data movements, which result from moving large records from one position in the list to be sorted to another position. The auxiliary array is known as an *index*, and we will discuss indexing methods in the following sections.

Apart from the above classification of sorting techniques, the sorting methods can also be classified as *internal* in which all keys to be sorted are kept in main memory and *external* when there are more keys to be sorted than that can be held in main memory.

9.1   Internal Sorting Methods

In earlier chapters we have studied different sorting techniques. These sorting techniques can be broadly classified as those involving counting, insertion, exchanges, merging and distribution. Sorting by merging using Merge sort is discussed in Chapter 3. Radix sort discussed in Chapter 5 is an example of sorting by distribution. We will discuss the other classifications in the next subsections.

9.1.1   Sorting by Counting

Sorting techniques that involve counting determine the rank of each key K_i in the set of all keys. The rank of a key K_i in a set of keys is the number of keys K_j that are less than or equal to K_i where $i \neq j$. A simple algorithm is to iterate over all the keys and *count* for each key the number of other keys with value less than or equal to it. Since a key need not be compared to itself, the number of comparisons is at most $n^2 - n$. This can be improved by making the observation that any two keys are compared twice in the above estimate but one comparison is sufficient.

```
Algorithm CompareAndCount (K₀, K₁, …, Kₙ₋₁)    // Kᵢ's are keys
that are to be sorted.
1.  Rank ← CreateArray(n) // Output: Rank, an array of size n
    such that Rank[j] = rank of Kⱼ
2.  for i = 0 to n-1 Do Rank[i] ← 0
3.  for i ← n-1 downto 1
4.      for j ← i-1 downto 0
5.          if Kᵢ<Kⱼ
6.              Rank[j] ← Rank[j] + 1
7.          else
8.              Rank[i] ← Rank[i] + 1
9.          endif
10.     endfor
11. endfor
```

The following table illustrates the above algorithm as applied to the keys 35, 25, 36, 45, 34, 22, 11, 12, and 30:

Key

35	25	36	45	34	22	11	12	30

	Rank[0]	Rank[1]	Rank[2]	Rank[3]	Rank[4]	Rank[5]	Rank[6]	Rank[7]	Rank[8]
Iteration 0	1	0	1	1	1	0	0	0	4
Iteration 1	2	1	2	2	2	1	0	1	4
Iteration 2	3	2	3	3	3	2	0	1	4
…									
Iteration n-1	6	3	7	8	5	2	0	1	4

Figure 9.1: Sequence of steps involved in sorting by counting.

This sorting technique is one example of what we called earlier as "physically unchanged." The sorting is done implicitly and of course, we could then linearly scan the array containing the ranks and obtain the sorted order of keys, if we wanted to. As we noted earlier, the time-complexity of the algorithm is $O(n^2)$ and the method requires a working storage of size n for storing the ranks.

Implementation

The implementation of *CompareAndCount* in C++ is a simple translation of the algorithm:

```
template <class DataType>
ArrayClass<int> compareAndCount (ArrayClass<DataType>& K)
{
    ArrayClass<int> rank (K.size(), 0);
    for (int i = K.size()-1; i > 0; i--)
        for (int j = i-1; j >= 0; j--)
        {
            if (K[i] < K[j])
                rank[j]++;
            else
                rank[i]++;
        }
    return rank;
}
```

9.1.2   Sorting by Insertion

Sorting by insertion works by taking a sorted list (which contains only a single element to begin with) and successively inserting each new element into the already sorted list by finding its position in the sorted list. That is we assume that keys K_0, K_2, ...,K_{i-1} have been already sorted. Now, to process key K_i we find a slot q in positions 0, 2, ...,$i-1$ to insert K_i such that all keys K_1,...K_i are sorted. After we find the slot q, we have to move the keys in positions $q...i-1$ by one position to make room for the new DataType. This form of sorting is often likened to the process of putting a bridge hand in order by picking up the cards one at a time and inserting each card in its proper position *relative to those already in the hand*.

9.1.2.1 Straight Insertion Sort

The following algorithm performs straight insertion sort. The elements are already in an unsorted 0-based array. We examine each in turn, moving from left to right. As each element K_i is examined, we move it to its correct slot by comparing it with the elements to its left – which are guaranteed to be in order already. As we make comparisons, we move from right to left. After each comparison, we may find that the element K_j with which we compared K_i belongs after K_i, in which case we shift K_j one position to the right, leaving a "gap" behind it (in its former position). Alternatively, we may find that K_j belongs before K_i, in which case we can place K_i immediately after K_j, in the gap left by another element that was moved. Once K_i is placed, we have finished that iteration of the algorithm. The reader should examine the algorithm to verify that the cases where K_i belongs in the far left position (it is the smallest in the array), or K_i is in the correct position to start with, are properly handled.

```
ALGORITHM STRAIGHTINSERTIONSORT (LIST)
1.  for i=1 to List.Size-1
2.        InsertElement ← list[i]
3.        j ← i-1
4.        while (j ≥ 0) and (InsertElement < list[j])
5.             list[j+1] ← list[j]
6.             j ← j -1
7.        endwhile
8.        list[j+1] ← InsertElement
9.  endfor
```

The table below illustrates the straight insertion sort operation on an array containing 35, 25, 36, 45, 34, 22, 11, 12, and 30. The elements of the array are shown as they appear at the end of any given step, and the part of the array that is considered to be in order at the end of that step is to the left of the heavy black line.

The while loop is performed at most i times for each value of i=1 to n–1. Thus the worst case time complexity of the StraightInsertionSort algorithm is $O(\sum_{i=1}^{n-1} i) = O(n^2)$.

	0	1	2	3	4	5	6	7	8
Unsorted	35	25	36	45	34	22	11	12	30
i = 1	25	35	36	45	34	22	11	12	30
i = 2	25	35	36	45	34	22	11	12	30
i = 3	25	35	36	45	34	22	11	12	30
i = 4, j = 3	25	35	36	45	45	22	11	12	30
i = 4, j = 2	25	35	36	36	45	22	11	12	30
i = 4, j = 1	25	35	35	36	45	22	11	12	30
i = 4	25	34	35	36	45	22	11	12	30
i = 5, j = 4	25	34	35	36	22	45	11	12	30
...									
i = 5, j = 1	25	22	34	35	36	45	11	12	30
i = 5, j = 0	22	25	34	35	36	45	11	12	30
...									
i = 8	11	12	22	25	30	34	35	36	45

Figure 9.2: Sequence of steps involved in straight insertion sort.

On the other hand, consider the best case time complexity: if the list is already in order, then the while loop will be performed just once for each value of $i=1$ to $n-1$, as each element is compared with its left neighbor and found to be in the correct position. In the best case, then, the complexity is $O(n)$. Although our analysis tells us that this algorithm is not as efficient in the worst case as some of the others we have studied in previous chapters, it may well have a practical use in an application where the data to be sorted is expected to be nearly in order to start with.

Implementation

The implementation of *StraightInsertionSort* in C++ is a simple translation of the algorithm:

```
template <class DataType>
void insertionSort (ArrayClass<DataType>& list)
{
    int i;
    int j;
    DataType insertElement;

    for (i = 1; i < list.size(); i++)
    {
        insertElement = list[i];
        j = i - 1;
        while ((j >= 0) && (insertElement < list[j]))
        {
            list[j+1] = list[j];
            j--;
        }
        list[j+1] = insertElement;
    }
}
```

9.1.2.2 Binary Insertion Sort

The above straight insertion sort algorithm incurs a cost of $O(n^2)$ in comparisons and another $O(n^2)$ in data movements. The number of comparisons can be improved if we use binary search to locate the position at which the new element has to be inserted. After the insertion the elements have to be moved to the left or right to create space for the new element. This approach improves the total number of comparisons to $O(n\log n)$, but the total number of data movements remains $O(n^2)$. Knuth names this sorting technique *binary insertion sort* and says that this is the first published discussion of computer sorting due to John Mauchly in 1946. We studied the binary insertion sort in Chapter 3, when we discussed Vectors. In case of the Vector data structure elements could be inserted at any position in the Vector without explicit movement of data to the left or right. This movement was performed by the vector implementation method we provided.

The binary search trees discussed in Chapters 6 and 7 can be used for sorting. Each element of the list to be sorted is inserted one at a time into a binary search tree. For an *n* element list and a unbalanced binary search tree, it will take a total of $O(n^2)$

time. After the binary search tree is constructed, we can perform an inorder traversal to get the sorted list. The inorder traversal takes $O(n)$ time. Since in this case the tree is unbalanced, there are no data movements. We can reduce the total time to $O(nlogn)$ if we use a balanced binary search tree such as an AVL or Red-Black tree (Chapter 7). This is because each insertion takes $O(logn)$ time for a total for $O(nlogn)$ and the inorder traversal in $O(n)$ time will give the sorted list. The total data movements in the worst case would be $O(nlog\ n)$ for the balanced binary search structures since they may have to perform movements to rebalance the tree after every insertion.

9.1.2.3   Shellsort

Shellsort is an improved version of insertion sort discovered by Donald Shell in 1959. It is also sometimes called the *diminishing increment* sort. Shellsort tries to take a list of items to be sorted and make it "nearly sorted" so that a final sorting by insertion can complete the work. Shellsort has the potential to yield worst-case running time better than $O(n^2)$.

Shellsort works by exchanging keys that are far apart in an array. It arranges the array such that every k^{th} item forms a sorted subarray for a decreasing sequence of values of k. For instance, if k is 5, every fifth key forms a sorted subarray. Finally, when k is 1, we will have a sorted array. Shellsort's efficiency lies in the fact that insertion sort works best on nearly sorted arrays. Shellsort breaks the array of elements into subarrays. Each subarray is sorted using an insertion sort. Another group of subarray is chosen and sorted and so on. During each iteration, Shellsort breaks the array into subarrays such that each element in it is a fixed distance apart from its "neighbors". For example, if the number of elements is a power of 2, say, $n=2^t$, then one way to carry out Shellsort is as follows. First, break the array into $n/2$ subarrays of two elements each, and perform insertion sort on the two-element subarrays. Here, each element in the subarray will have distance $n/2$ (in the original array) from its neighbors. In the second iteration, Shellsort would have $n/4$ subarrays of four elements each, with the elements in the subarrays $n/4$ positions apart. An insertion sort is performed again for each of the subarrays. The third iteration will have $n/8$ subarrays, and so on and the last will have one array (the entire array) and the usual insertion sort will be performed on the entire array. The key observation here is that by now the array has been nearly sorted and insertion sort should work well. The sequence of distance increments between array elements in this case is $2^{t-1}, 2^{t-2}, \ldots, 1$. In general, however, it does not have to be that way. Any sequence that ends with the final increment being 1 would work. But obviously, as we should expect, some sequences are better than others. In fact, the power of 2 sequence turns out to be not so efficient. A better choice is using the increment sequence based on division by three, for example, $\ldots, 200, 66, 22, 7, 2, 1$. A mathematical analysis is beyond the scope of this book and a detailed analysis for the *division by three* approach yields an average case of $O(n^{1.5})$.

We now provide the algorithm for Shellsort below. The input is an array A of elements and a sequence of increments $t_{p-1}, t_{p-2}, \ldots, t_0 = 1$ (the increments are in decreasing order of size). The output is the sorted array A in nondecreasing order.

```
ALGORITHM SHELLSORT (A, P)
1.  for s ← 0 to P.size-1
2.        t ← t_s
3.        for i ← t to A.size-1
                              // insertion sort on subarray
4.              item ← A[i]
5.              j ← i-t;
6.              while j ≥ 0 and A[j] > item
7.                    A[j+t] ← A[j]
8.                    j ← j-t
9.              endwhile
10.             A[j+t] ← item
11.       endfor
12. endfor
```

The following example shows the working of the Shellsort algorithm for an array of 18 elements using the division-by-3 increment sequence viz., 6, 2, 1.

The efficiency of Shellsort comes from the fact that sorting with one increment will not undo any of the work done previously when a different increment was used.

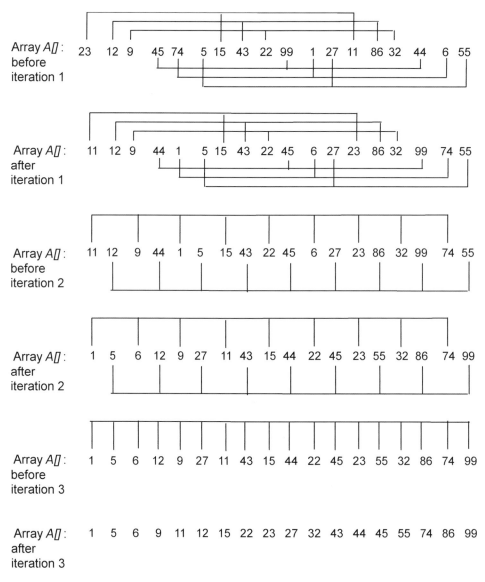

Figure 9.3: Sequence of steps involved in shell sort.

Implementation

The implementation of *ShellSort* in C++ is again simple:

```cpp
template <class DataType>
void shellSort (ArrayClass<DataType>& list)
{
    for (int inc = 0; inc < incs.size(); inc++)
    {
        int dist;
        int j;
        dist = incs[inc];
        for (int i = dist; i < list.size(); i++)
        {
            DataType item = list[i];
            j = i - dist;
            while ((j >= 0) && (list[j] > item))
            {
                list[j+dist] = list[j];
                j = j - dist;
            }
            list[j+dist] = item;
        } // end for-loop part of insertion sort
    } // end for-loop on reducing increments
}
```

9.1.3   Sorting by Exchanges

Algorithms that sort by exchanges in a given step exchange two elements that are out of order. We will study two sorting algorithms, the *bubble* sort and the *quicksort*, that use exchanges to perform sorting.

9.1.3.1   Bubble Sort

In bubble sort the elements of an array are processed from the first position such that whenever two adjacent elements are out of order they are interchanged. During the first phase adjacent elements are compared until all elements in the array are processed.

Note that, if the largest element is anywhere but the last position (the top) of the array, it is necessarily out of order when compared with any adjacent element. Thus, the largest element will be exchanged with adjacent elements until it "bubbles up" to the top of the array. In the second phase, we again start from the first element and make the comparisons and interchanges until we compare with the last-but-one element. After the second phase the second largest element will be in the correct position. In n-1 phases the array will be sorted and the worst case number of comparisons is $O(n^2)$. The following algorithm performs bubble sort on an array of elements.

```
Algorithm BubbleSort (List)
1.  for i = 0 to List.Size - 1
2.      for j = 0 to List.Size - i -2
3.          if List[j] > List[j+1]
4.              Swap (List[j],List[j+1])
5.          endif
6.      endfor
7.  endfor
```

	0	1	2	3	4	5	6	7	8
Unsorted	35	25	36	45	34	22	11	12	30
i = 0; j = 0	25	35	36	45	34	22	11	12	30
i = 0; j = 1	25	35	36	45	34	22	11	12	30
i = 0; j = 2	25	35	36	45	34	22	11	12	30
i = 0, j = 3	25	35	36	34	45	22	11	12	30
i = 0, j = 4	25	35	36	34	22	45	11	12	30
i = 0, j = 5	25	35	36	34	22	11	45	12	30
i = 0, j = 6	25	35	36	34	22	11	12	45	30
i = 0, j = 7	25	35	36	34	22	11	12	30	45
...									
i = 6, j = 0	11	12	22	25	30	34	35	36	45

Figure 9.4: Sequence of steps involved in bubble sort.

Implementation

We can implement the BubbleSort algorithm by simply translating the algorithm into the C++ language:

```
template <class DataType>
void bubbleSort (ArrayClass<DataType>& list)
{
    for (int i = 0; i < list.size(); i++)
        for (int j = 0; j < list.size() - i -1; j++)
            if (list[j] > list[j+1])
                swap (list[j],list[j+1]);
}
```

It is easy to observe from the above BubbleSort algorithm that whenever no swaps are performed during any iteration of the j loop, then the array A is sorted. Thus the algorithm can terminate immediately, giving the best case complexity of $O(n)$. The above implementation can be improved by noting this condition. Another way to improve the above implementation that reduces the number of swaps is to find the position of the largest element in positions 0 through $n-i$ during the ith phase. Let this position be k. Instead of swapping each time, after the j loop completes, we simply swap elements $A[n-i]$ and $A[k]$, reducing the total number of data movements from $O(n^2)$ to $O(n)$.

9.1.3.2   Quicksort

In this section we will present another algorithm that is dubbed the "Quicksort" algorithm and is due to C. A. R. Hoare (Comp. J. 5 (1962) 10-15). This algorithm uses sorting by exchanges to sort a given set of elements. We will see that the worst-case time complexity of quicksort is the same as insertion sort, but quicksort on the average has a time complexity of $O(n\log n)$. The basic idea behind quicksort can be summarized in the following steps:

1. **Pivot Value Choice**: Given an array A containing n keys, let the first key value in the array be called the pivot value. (Any element in the array can be chosen to be the pivot value. Later you will see that choosing the median of the set elements is the best choice.)
2. **Partition Step**: Perform exchanges of key values in the array A such that key values that are less than or equal to the pivot value are to the left of it in the array

and the keys that are greater than the pivot value are to its right in A. Note that after the partition step the key that is the pivot value will be in the correct position in the array A.

3. **Recursive Step**: Perform quicksort on the elements that are left of the pivot value and perform quicksort on the elements that are to the right of the pivot value.

The key ingredient in the quicksort procedure is the partition step. To perform this step we will choose two indices i and j which are initially set to 0 and $n-1$, respectively. Let the pivot value be $A[0]$. Next we keep incrementing the index i until we find an element $A[i]$ such that $A[i] > pivot\_value$. We also have to make sure that i is less than $n-1$ during the process of incrementing. Similarly, we decrement j until we find the first

A = {10, 11, 3, 4, 12, 14, 6, 5, 20, 9}

A[0]	A[1]	A[2]	A[3]	A[4]	A[5]	A[6]	A[7]	A[8]	A[9]
10	11	3	4	12	14	6	5	20	9
Pivot	i								j

10	9	3	4	12	14	6	5	20	11
Pivot		i						j	

10	9	3	4	12	14	6	5	20	11
Pivot			i				j		

10	9	3	4	12	14	6	5	20	11
Pivot				i			j		

10	9	3	4	5	14	6	12	20	11
Pivot					i	j			

10	9	3	4	5	6	14	12	20	11
Pivot					j	i			

6	9	3	4	5	10	14	12	20	11
Pivot					j	i			
↑					↑				

Figure 9.5: Sequence of steps involved in sorting by the partition step of quick sort.

element $A[j]$ such that $A[j] <= $ *pivot_value*. After the process of finding desired i and j we have to check if $i < j$ and swap $A[i]$ and $A[j]$. We will continue this process until $i > j$ and at which point we will place the *pivot_value* in position $A[j]$. We will illustrate the above partition method as follows. Let A be an array containing 10 elements.

After completing the above partition, the value 10 is in the right position in the array. Now we have to recursively execute quicksort for two sub-arrays $A[0]...A[4]$ and $A[6]...A[9]$.

Let us analyze the complexity of quicksort. The partition step takes at most $O(n)$, where n is the number of the elements in the array on which the partition has to be performed. If the two sub-arrays to be sorted are of size at most $n/2$ each, then the time-complexity of the quicksort algorithm is given by the following recurrence relation:

$$T(n) = 2T(n/2) + n{-}1 = O(n\log n).$$

It is entirely possible that the after each partition of an array of size n, we are left with sub-arrays of sizes 1 and $n{-}2$. The recurrence relation for this would be:

$$T(n) = T(1) + T(n{-}2) + 1 = O(n^2).$$

Thus Quicksort in the worst case is same as the insertion sort, and hence not really quick! However, we shall soon see that Quicksort in the average case has a time complexity of $O(n\log n)$. The complete Quicksort algorithm is presented below.

```
ALGORITHM QUICKSORT (A, LEFT, RIGHT)
1.  if (left < right)
                                //Pivot Value Choice Step
2.        pivot ← A[left]
                                //Partition Step
3.        i ← left
4.        j ← right + 1
5.        do
6.            do
7.                i ← i + 1
8.            while (i < A.size) and (A[i] < pivot)
9.            do
10.               j ← j - 1
11.           while (A[j] > pivot)
```

```
12.              if (i < j) then swap (A[i], A[j])
13.         while (i < j)
14.         swap (A[left], A[j])
                                    //Recursive Step
15.         quicksort (A, left, j-1)
16.         quicksort (A, j+1, right)
17. endif
```

Implementation

As is the case with the preceding sorting algorithms, quicksort is readily implemented in C++:

```cpp
template <class DataType>
void quicksort (ArrayClass<DataType>& list, int left, int
right)
{
    if (left < right)
    {
                                // Pivot Value Choice Step
        DataType pivot = list[left];
                                // Partition Step
        int i = left;
        int j = right + 1;
        do
        {
            do
                i = i + 1;
            while ((i < list.size()) && (list[i] < pivot));
            do
                j = j - 1;
            while (list[j] > pivot);
            if (i < j)
                swap (list[i], list[j]);
        } while (i < j);
```

```
        swap (list[left], list[j]);
                              // Recursive Step
        quicksort (list, left, j-1);
        quicksort (list, j+1, right);
    }
  }
```

In the above algorithm the first element of the list A is chosen to be the pivot value. If the list A is unsorted, this is acceptable. If the list is in fact sorted, or nearly so, this choice degrades the performance of Quicksort. A better choice would be the median of the first, middle, and the last element of the list A, as this protects against a truly unfortunate choice of pivot. In the next section we will show that although the behavior of Quicksort appears to be bad in the worse-case analysis, in theory (and in practice as well), it works extremely well on an average.

Average Case Analysis of Quicksort:

In Quicksort, the pivot controls how the input data is partitioned and the size of the partitions determine the running time of the algorithm. To determine the average-case complexity of the algorithm, we have to assume that the pivot is chosen uniformly randomly. In other words, we assume that the pivot is as likely to be indexed at position x of the array as it is at position y of the array for $x \neq y$. The average-case time complexity of the algorithm is hence determined by obtaining the run-time complexity of the algorithm for each position of the pivot i varying from 1 to the size of the array, say n, and then finding the average of them all. Diagramatically, we illustrate it below:

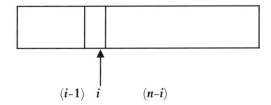

$(i-1)$ i $(n-i)$

Let the average-case time-complexity of the Quicksort algorithm be denoted by $T(n)$ for input size n. It has been shown that experimentally Quicksort's run-time grows as $O(n \log n)$, where the logarithmic base is 2. We will prove here formally that is indeed the case.

We know that each pivot operation involves rearranging the data so that items on the left(right) of the pivot position is less(greater) than pivot value. The time taken to do this is at most kn for some constant $k \geq 1$. The recursive calls take an average-case time of $T(i-1) + T(n-i)$. Hence we can write the following expression for the average-case runtime as

$$T(n) = kn + \frac{1}{n} \sum_{i=1}^{n} T(i-1) + T(n-i)$$

It can be observed that in the summation in the expression above, the term $T(i)$, $0 <= i <= (n-1)$, occurs twice. Hence we can write,

$$T(n) = kn + \frac{1}{n} \sum_{i=1}^{n} 2T(i-1)$$

We can rewrite this as,

$$nT(n) = kn^2 + 2\sum_{i=1}^{n} T(i-1), k \geq 1 \quad \textbf{(1)}$$

We extend the recurrence to $(n+1)$ as

$$(n+1)T(n+1) = k(n+1)^2 + 2\sum_{i=1}^{n+1} T(i-1), k \geq 1 \quad \textbf{(2)}$$

Subtracting equation **(1)** from equation **(2)**, we get

$$(n+1)T(n+1) - nT(n) = k(2n+1) + 2T(n), \text{ or equivalently}$$

$$T(n+1) = \frac{k(2n+1)}{n+1} + \frac{(n+2)}{(n+1)} T(n) \quad \textbf{(3)}$$

We assume that $T(0)=0$, and $T(1)=1$. From equation **(1)** we can write,

$$T(2) = 2k + T(0) + T(1) = 2k + 1 \quad \textbf{(4)}$$

We will prove that $T(n) = O(n \log n)$ by induction on n. In other words, we will prove that
$T(n) \leq cn \log n$, where $n \geq 2$, and c is a constant. We will also assume that $c=2k$ to make things work.

Base Case: $T(2)=2k+1$ from **(4)**. Also $T(2) \leq 2k \star 2 \log(2) = 4k$. Since $(2k+1) \leq 4k$, for $k>1$, the base case holds.

Induction Step: Let $T(n) \le cn \log n$, for $2 \le n < m$, for some integer m. We will show that

$T(m) \le cm \log m$. Using equation **(3)** we can write,

$$T(m) = \frac{k(2m-1)}{m} + \frac{(m-3)T(m-1)}{m}$$

By induction hypothesis, we know that $T(m-1) \le c(m-1)\log(m-1)$. Hence

$$T(m) \le \frac{k(2m-1)}{m} + \frac{(m-3)}{m}c(m-1)\log(m-1)$$

Substituting for k, we get

$$T(m) = \frac{c(2m-1)}{2m} + \frac{(m-3)}{m}c(m-1)\log(m-1)$$

It is easy to see that $\frac{2m-1}{2m} < 1$ and $\frac{m-3}{m} < 1$. Hence we can write

$T(m) \le cl_1 + cl_2(m-1)\log(m-1)$, where $l_1, l_2 < 1$.

Since $l_2(m-1)\log(m-1) < (m-1)\log m$, for $m > 2$, and $l_1 < \log m$, for $m > 2$, we can write $cl_1 + cl_2(m-1)\log(m-1) < c(\log m + (m-1)\log m = cm \log m$. Thus we have proved that the average-case time-complexity of Quicksort is indeed $O(n\log n)$.

9.1.4   Sorting by Selection

The above algorithms for sorting by exchanges can be inefficient when the number of items to be exchanged is large, as is often the case. Where exchanges are expensive, we might prefer to use an algorithm which sorts by selection, that is, which finds the correct position for an element and places it directly in that position, reducing the total amount of data movement per element.

9.1.4.1   Straight Selection Sort

A straightforward mechanism to perform sorting consists of $n-1$ phases. In the first phase, the largest element in the set of n elements is selected and placed in the $n-1$th position. In the ith phase, the largest element in positions $A[0]\ldots A[i-1]$ is selected and placed in the ith position of the array. The following algorithm performs sorting by selection. Clearly, the total number of comparisons is $O(n^2)$ and the number of data movements is $O(n)$.

```
Algorithm SelectionSort (A)
1.  for i ← A.Size-1 downto 1
                        //  find largest element in subarray
2.       maxindex ← 0
3.       for j ← 0 to i
4.           if A[j] > A[maxindex]
5.               maxindex ← j
6.           endif
7.       endfor
                //  place largest element in its proper place
8.       Swap (A[i],A[maxindex])
9,  endfor
```

Figure 9.6 illustrates the sequence of swaps that are part of the selection sort algorithm.

	0	1	2	3	4	5	6	7	8
Unsorted	35	25	36	45	34	22	11	12	30
i = 8; j = 8; MI = 3	35	25	36	30	34	22	11	12	45
i = 7; j = 7; MI = 2	35	25	12	30	34	22	11	36	45
i = 6; j = 6; MI = 0	11	25	12	30	34	22	35	36	45
i = 5, j = 5; MI = 4	11	25	12	30	22	34	35	36	45
i = 4, j = 4; MI = 3	11	25	12	22	30	34	35	36	45
i = 3, j = 3; MI = 1	11	22	12	25	30	34	35	36	45
i = 2, j = 2; MI = 1	11	12	22	25	30	34	35	36	45
i = 1, j = 1; MI = 1	11	12	22	25	30	34	35	36	35

Figure 9.6: Sequence of steps involved in Selection Sort. The notation MI stands for maxindex.

9.1.4.2   Heap Sort

In Chapter 8, we will study the heap data structure. A heap data structure for n elements can be constructed in $O(n)$ time. Given a minimum heap data structure deletion can be performed in $O(logn)$ time. A sequence of n deletions can be performed in $O(nlogn)$ time, which is the time required to sort. This algorithm is a sort by selection since we find the minimum element repeatedly.

9.2   Lower Bound for Sorting

In this section we will determine the minimum number of comparisons needed to sort a given set of n elements. Clearly, if we use radix sorting (Chapter 5) then this number is *zero*. Thus the lower bound for the number of comparisons that we will determine will apply only to sorting algorithms that are comparison-based.

We have seen algorithms whose time complexity is dominated by the number of comparisons and others whose complexity is dominated by the number of data movements. For example, in straight selection sort the total number of comparisons is $O(n^2)$ and the total number of data movements is $O(n)$. In the case of binary insertion sort, the total number of comparisons is $O(nlogn)$ and the total number of data movements is $O(n^2)$. Our goal is to show that there does not exist a comparison-based sorting algorithm that can sort n elements in less than $O(nlogn)$ time.

We introduce the notion of a decision tree. A decision tree is a binary tree. Each internal node x contains two indices $i:j$ which denotes the comparison between keys K_i and K_j. The left subtree of x represents subsequent comparisons that will be made if $K_i < K_j$, and the right subtree represents comparisons that will be made when $K_i > K_j$. Each leaf node of the binary tree contains a permutation $p(1), p(2), ..., p(n)$ of $\{1,2,...,n\}$, denoting the fact that the ordering $K_{p(1)} < K_{p(2)} < ... < K_{P(n)}$ has been established. A path from the root of the tree to this leaf node establishes the relationships between the keys shown above. A decision tree for three keys is shown in the following figure.

The number of possible permutations of n keys is $n!$ Thus there are $n!$ leaf nodes in the decision tree for n keys. We have seen in Chapter 6, the number of levels in a binary tree containing $n!$ leaf nodes is at least $log(n!)$. The most efficient sorting algorithm will use the minimum number of comparisons, that is, it will choose the shortest path from the root to a leaf node which is $log(n!)$ and this is $O(nlogn)$. This leads us to conclude that it is impossible to design a sorting algorithm that is comparison based which takes less than $O(nlogn)$ time.

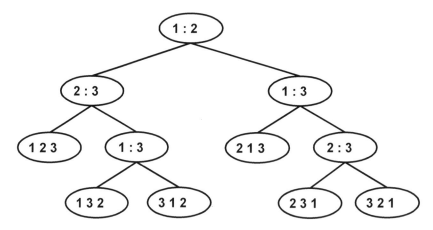

Figure 9.7: Decision tree for 3 keys.

9.3 Adaptive Sorting

The key question is: can we improve the performance of comparison based sorting if the list to be sorted is "somewhat sorted"? First, we have to present a more concrete definition of "somewhat sorted." We say that two elements K_i and K_j at positions i and j in the array A are out-of-order if $K_i > K_j$ and $1 \leq i < j \leq n$. We will say that an array A is *p-sorted*, for some $p \geq 0$, if and only if for all pairs of keys in positions i and j that are out-of-order, we have $j-i \leq p$. For example, if we look into a 2-sorted array, the pairs of elements that are out-of-order are no more than two index positions apart. The p-sortedness gives the estimation of how nearly an array is sorted. Note that a 0-sorted array is a sorted array. All the comparison based algorithms that we have seen so far will require O(n*log*n) to sort an n-element array, even if that array is p-sorted.

We will now present an adaptive algorithm with complexity of O(n*log* p) to sort an n-element array. Since the value of *p* can be at most n, the complexity of the adaptive sorting algorithm is O(n*log*n). Of course when *p* is small, we have a linear time sorting algorithm! The algorithm does not determine the value of *p* in advance, but it adapts itself. The algorithm is a variant of merge sort with a different splitting strategy. In each recursive step of the adaptive sorting algorithm, the list A is split into two lists, one consisting of elements in the odd positions of the array A and the other containing elements in the even positions. After the split step, instead of recursively calling the algorithm (as in the pure merge sort algorithm), we will determine if both the sublists are sorted. If the sublists are sorted then we will merge them; otherwise, we will recursively call the adaptive algorithm for the list that is not sorted. The final step as in the case of the merge sort we merge the sorted lists.

It can be shown that if array A is p-sorted for some $p > 0$, then the sublists containing elements in odd and even positions in A are $\lfloor p/2 \rfloor$-sorted. With this observation, it can be seen that the depth of the recursion is bounded by $\lceil \log p \rceil$, hence the complexity of the adaptive sorting algorithm is $O(\log p)$.

9.3.1   Implementation

The implementation of the adaptiveSort algorithm described above closely follows that of the mergeSort algorithm. We have added a helper method, *isSorted()*.

```
template <class DataType>
bool isSorted (ArrayClass<DataType>* list)
{
    if (list->size() < 2) return true;
    DataType* prev = & ((*list) [0]);
    for (int i = 1; i < list->size(); i++)
    if (*prev > (*list)[i]) return false;
    return true;
}
// ------------------------------------------------------------
template <class DataType>
void adaptiveSort (ArrayClass<DataType>& list)
{
    if (list.size() < 2) return;

    // split step
    ArrayClass<DataType>* evens =
        new ArrayClass<DataType> (ceil (list.size() / 2.0));
    ArrayClass<DataType>* odds =
        new ArrayClass<DataType> (floor (list.size() / 2.0));

    int lim = list.size() / 2;
    for (int i = 0, i2 = 0; i < lim; i++, i2++)
    {
```

```
            (*evens) [i] = list[i2];
            i2++;
            (*odds) [i] = list[i2];
    }
    if (list.size() % 2 > 0)
            (*evens) [evens->size() - 1] = list[list.size() - 1];

    // recursive step
    if (!isSorted (evens)) adaptiveSort (*evens);
    if (!isSorted (odds)) adaptiveSort (*odds);
    list = merge (*evens, *odds);

    delete evens;
    delete odds;
}
```

9.4   Comparison of Internal Sorting Methods

In all of the sorting algorithms we have seen so far, there is no one algorithm that can be considered the "best". The choice of sorting algorithm to use usually depends on the application and the type of data. The worst-case, the best-case and the average-case time complexities of algorithms have to be taken into account in deciding the particular sorting method to use, as must space complexity, at least in some cases. The following table summarizes the properties of the sorting algorithms we have seen thus far.

We will now make some general comments based on empirical observations. Selection sort, bubble sort, and insertion are all $O(n^2)$ time algorithms and they are slow for large problems. In the average case quicksort is among the fastest known sorting algorithms. It has been observed that the quicksort's worst-case input occurs rarely in practice and that the hidden constants for mergesort are higher than for quicksort; hence, quicksort can be considered better than mergesort in some sense. In terms of storage, mergesort needs a working space equal to the size of the array to be sorted. Lastly, although radix sort is $O(n)$, it is not a general-purpose sorting algorithm because of its unreasonably large storage requirements. Furthermore, it is one of the few sorting algorithms that do not use comparisons and hence the lower bound is not applicable in this case.

Algorithm	Worst case complexity	Average case complexity	Stable	Inplace
Bubble sort	n^2	n^2	yes	yes
Selection sort	n^2	n^2	no	yes
Straight insertion sort	n^2	n^2	yes	yes
Binary insertion sort	n^2	n^2	no	yes
Merge sort	$n \log n$	$n \log n$	no	no
Quicksort	n^2	$n \log n$	no	yes
Heap sort	$n \log n$	$n \log n$	no	no
Shell sort	n^2	$n^{1.5}$	no	yes
Adaptive sort	$n \log n$	$n \log p$	no	yes
Radix sort	n	n	yes	yes

Figure 9.8: Properties of various sorting algorithms.

9.5 External Sorting Methods

We know there are various kinds of limits that a program is subject at various stages of its life cycle. Some of these limits are based on hardware and the rest are usually based on software. Some of the hardware limits a program's performance can be subject to are listed below:

1. Number of registers, caches, and physical memory (RAM)
2. Processor speed (measured in terms of number of floating-point operations or integer operations per second) and also in terms of clock frequency.
3. Memory to processor bandwidth (measured in megabits per second)
4. Disk space.
5. Disk to memory transfer rate (measured in megabytes per second)

From the perspective of software, usually the limits are imposed by the operating system and programming tools such as compilers. If we assume that we are only interested performance of algorithmic implementations and data structures, then the limits imposed by the Operating System typically involve, resource limits such as,

1. Amount of physical memory (RAM) available to a process (viz., program in execution)
2. Number of processes/threads a program can start,
3. Number of files a program can open or close,
4. Size of disk space a program can use for writing, and
5. Maximum size for a single file in a file-system.
6. Amount of swap space.

Limits imposed by programming tools such as compilers are those that are in place during compile time and link time. Compile-time limits *can* include such resources as

1. Maximum number of variables declared,
2. Maximum size of an array, and
3. Maximum number of functions declared in a class

Link-time limits typically place limits on the size of the overall process that can reside in main memory including the sizes of the libraries that are linked dynamically or statically to the compiled program. Other link-time options are operating system specific and are usually included by the developer during linking time. In many instances, a program may never actually test any of these limits. But when it does, the manner in which the limits are overridden, depends on the choice of programming language, the hardware and the operating system. It is also true that an application developer may not really try to overcome the limits but really work within the confines of the limits, but perhaps more intelligently, as in the case of many of the hardware or operating system limits. Among all of these resource parameters, from the perspectives of both successful execution of a program and good run-time performance, nothing stands out as much as the physical memory available to a program.

9.5.1   Physical Memory and 32-bit versus 64-bit systems

Special attention needs to be paid to the physical memory needed by a program during its runtime. Sometimes, it is easy to find out memory requirements by looking over the code, and cataloging all of the statically declared storage. Sometimes, it is not so easy to find out how much physical memory is needed, especially when storage is dynamically allocated. The maximum amount of physical memory that a computer system can support depends on the hardware architecture. A 32-bit CPU usually supports a 32-bit instruction set, 32- bits of physical memory addressability, 32-bit registers, 32 bit operands, and 32-bit basic operations. Likewise, a 64-bit CPU is based on 64 bit long architectural components. A system based on 32-bit architecture has a little over 4GB of physical memory address space whereas one based on the 64-bit architecture has several hundreds of petabytes of address space. For programs to benefit from the astronomical increase in memory addressing capabilities, apart from the hardware, the operating system, the programming language tools that the programs use such as compilers, interpreters, and libraries would all have to be 64-bit enabled or compatible.

The above description of 32-bit and 64-bit systems is somewhat limited in scope. We know computers are usually designed to operate on data of fixed size. The early computers had everything defined in terms of this fixed size, sometimes also known as *word length*. Computers were described as 8-bit, 16-bit or 32-bit with the understanding that the longer the word length is the faster the machine is. To a large extent, this naming convention continues even today. However, what is complicating the matter is that computers of today operate on various sized chunks on different parts of the system. It is not uncommon for a computer system today to operate on 32-bit integers, 64-bit floating point numbers, and 128-bit memory bus. Hence, contemporary classification is best based on:

1. Size of integer operands in arithmetic computations.
2. The size of physical addresses generated by memory hardware.

In other words, if the above two sizes are 32 bits then we can call the system a 32-bit system, on the other hand, if they are of size 64 then we can call it a 64-bit system. It is possible to have the size of the physical address to be 32 and the size of integer operands to be 64. Such as system is also referred as a 64-bit system.

Computers of few decades ago, had only few hundred kilobytes of memory, compared to the computers of today which have anywhere from a few hundreds of megabytes of memory (in personal computers) to several tens of gigabytes of memory (symmetric multiprocessors also known as SMPs) to terabytes of memory (clusters of SMPs). In contrast, the disk storage (sometimes known as secondary memory) in personal computers usually start at 20 to 30 GB. Main memory access speeds are typically in nano seconds whereas disk access speeds are in milliseconds and hence the difference is in the order of a million times. While the disk access speed is improving steadily, (with faster disk spin rates, better software protocols, and bigger disk caches), this huge difference is not being bridged rapidly. Current disk data transfer rates (from disk to memory) are in the order of 10 to 100 MB per second for sustained data transfer and much less for short bursts of data transfer. Programs that need to access large amounts of data for applications in banking, insurance, and science strive to keep all of the data in memory whenever possible; because the run-time penalty in accessing data in disk is excruciatingly high (up to a million times).

9.5.1.1 Virtual memory address space

Usually, the actual physical memory available in a machine is well short of the maximum address space dictated by the architecture. For instance, in a 32-bit system, it is fairly common to have memory sizes in the order of 256 MB to 1 GB. Often 64-bit hardware architecture can support both a 64-bit and 32-bit Operating System kernels. Secondly, even when a 64-bit operating system is being run on a piece of hardware, it is possible for it to support a 32-bit process with limited *virtualmemory* addressing capabilities. *Virtual Memory* mechanism allows a process to access the memory needed by it by mapping all memory addressed within the process space to "pages" in disk. A virtual memory manager uses a page table that keeps track of the pages that will be accessed by the process during its execution. A page belonging to the process is placed in the main memory from disk and the page table keeps the address in main memory where it is placed. When an instruction on a page is executed, the virtual memory manager checks the page table to find the address of the page in main memory. If the page is in main memory it proceeds with the execution, otherwise it brings the page from disk, places the page in the main memory (swapping out other pages, if necessary), updates the page table, and executes the instruction.

Since disk sizes are much more than physical memory sizes, it is hence possible for a process to address memory much bigger than what is really available. The Virtual Memory Manager is usually implemented in hardware and hence the physical addresses are generated quickly. While the virtual memory mechanism allows a process to address memory beyond the physical memory available, it is still capped by the virtual memory address space. For instance, in a 32-bit system, the virtual memory address space is usually limited to roughly 4 GB ($\sim 2^{32}$). If a process deals with data sizes larger than the available physical memory, then one can expect a certain portion of the data to be resident in the disk. Clearly, it is not desirable to keep any data on disk because of excessive paging times that can be a big drag on the run-time performance of the program. *External memory algorithms* (programs) or *External algorithms* (programs) are defined as those whose *data* cannot all fit in main memory. In the definition, the term *data* is loosely used to include the memory footprint of the entire process (includes program text, libraries, data accessed by the process etc.).

Segmentation

Any program that needs to access large data may have to go through several hurdles before it can make full use of available memory. Windows operating systems are not 64-bit enabled as of the writing of this book. The various flavors of UNIX operating systems such as Solaris, AIX, HP-UX, IRIX, and Tru64 are. We will use the example of IBM systems running AIX operating system as an example throughout. The first hurdle is the limit imposed by the administrator of the system (in UNIX, it is given by the *ulimit* command), and the second is due to the policy of most operating systems that allocate memory in *segments* (a segment contains a set of pages of fixed size) to a process. The size of a segment varies between operating systems (even within different flavors of UNIX system, for instance). For example, IBM's operating system AIX version 4.3.x allocates memory in 256 MB segments. Hence, a process running in AIX 4.3.x, gets a default 256 MB segment and no more even if the physical memory available is 2 GB.

The segments play a huge role in deciding how much real memory a process can actually get. In a 32-bit system having 4 GB of main memory, the physical address space is divided into 16 segments of 256 MB each. Not all of the segments can be used for a process address space. In fact, the kernel of the operating system may get one segment, the texts of all processes may get a segment (called the *text segment*), shared libraries may get a segment, the process private information such as user data, user stack, and heap may get one segment, and so on. As a result, the address space available for a process may be significantly less than the actual physical memory available. This is the third hurdle which sets a hard-limit to the maximum space that can be used by a process. Again, in the case of AIX version 4.3.x, a 32-bit process can only address up to 2 GB of memory. This is a hard limit and it is insurmountable. Since AIX 4.3.x, does support 64-bit processes, any process requiring access to more than 2 GB data would have to be run as a 64-bit process.

Let us put all these thoughts in perspective by looking at hypothetical 32-bit process running on a hypothetical 64-bit system. Let us say that the system has 4 GB of main memory. It is usually easy to scale the first *user limit* hurdle namely, the *ulimit*. (Actually, *ulimit* sets not only memory limits but other limits such as file sizes, heap sizes, as well). In general, the user can change that by running the *ulimit* command and setting a new value. This will work as long as the virtual address space needed is less than the segment limit. To climb the second hurdle, namely the segment limit, the user may have to use a link time option. (In the case of AIX again, the option is *bmaxdata* that can take the per process virtual memory address space up to 2 GB). The third hurdle can only be overcome by switching the process to a 64-bit process.

If a process expects to use 1 GB of memory while in fact, only 512 MB of physical memory is available then the process needs to overcome the segment limit. Furthermore, several hundreds of megabytes of data that the process expects to use would be paged in disks. If a process needs 5 GB of memory in a 64-bit system having 4 GB of main memory, then it would have to be run as a 64-bit process expecting a lot of data to be paged in disks.

This rather elaborate prelude to discussing external memory algorithms is founded on the following thoughts. First of all, external memory algorithms have to be avoided at all costs if performance is a criterion. We mentioned earlier that both hard disk prices and RAM prices have fallen dramatically, but the decrease in price of RAM has made it possible for machines to be equipped with 1 GB of RAM for anywhere between $10 and $20 today. In early days of computing, the cost of RAM was either too prohibitive or machines were not usually designed to be equipped with high amounts of memory, and most importantly architectural limits that forced algorithm designers to study and implement external memory algorithms. In other words, the study of external memory algorithms was considered a space–time tradeoff wherein more time in execution was considered in return for less memory (mainly a result of architectural constraints). However, in contemporary situations, designers of algorithms and tools which need a large memory layout that are used in the industry, in research settings and in high-performance computing scenarios, rarely look to using the space–time tradeoff. Because the cost of time penalty is extremely high (up to a factor of a million times) and there is simply no good reason any more considering the low prices for memory and the availability of 64-bit systems which have largely facilitated the transformation in thinking. To a large extent, it is true that applications still continue to use external memory algorithms such as sorting, but it is mainly in legacy applications and/or due to the fact that knowledge needs to be tapped into making new applications (possibly 64-bit) work with existing 32-bit applications. Finally, as one can expect, just as clusters of high-performance machines are available supporting main memory in the order of terabytes, we are faced with astronomical explosion in data sizes as well, in the order of petabytes and more. This perpetuates the need to continue to study external memory algorithms but with a clear understanding the bar needs to be high for having to go that route.

9.5.2 External Sorting

The previous section essentially motivates the need for external memory algorithms as much as it discourages using them when you can afford the cost of extra memory or a move to an appropriate architecture for application development. Certainly, while there are potentially many applications that use a large memory layout, sorting algorithms play a central role in understanding how to design external memory algorithms. There are two approaches to sort data externally. One that requires little work on the programmer's part and the other requires significant programmer effort.

9.5.2.1 Modifying internal-sorting algorithms for external sorting

Let us consider the example of a file of database records of size 200 MB that needs to be sorted in a 32-bit system that has only 128 MB of main memory. It is really not a problem, because a good internal sorting algorithm can be adapted to this situation by declaring large enough data structures to support access to the large amounts of data. Sure, there will be a huge paging overhead and the runtime performance will be poor but we know that the performance problem can be avoided by equipping the system with adequate memory, say 512 MB. But if we want to leverage virtual memory support to complete the work, we must make sure that (i) we select internal sorting algorithms which have a good locality-of-reference characteristic that is the pages that are required to be processed are located closely in the virtual memory, and (ii) the virtual memory implementation itself is good. There is not much we can do about the second property because it is a function of the operating system being used. Hence, the choice of the internal-sorting algorithm plays a crucial role. The rationale for choosing an internal sorting algorithm with good locality-of-reference is simple. Anytime, it is known that paging to disks would be involved, we must make sure that disk I/O is minimized. Clearly, sorting algorithms with good locality-of-reference characteristic would keep disk I/O low. Quicksort has a good locality-of-reference, at least in the initial phases of it; on the other hand, radix sort is not a good choice. If the data to be sorted exceeds the 32-bit system virtual memory limits (typically 2 GB), then external sorting can be done with 64-bit operating system support. Let us consider the example of sorting, say 5 GB of database records. Based on our discussion earlier, the sorting effort using internal sorting methods would stipulate that the internal sorting programs themselves be 64-bit enabled and that we have access to a 64-bit system. On the other hand, if there is no access to a 64-bit system then the database can be split into smaller chunks each of which fitting within the virtual memory of a 32-bit system followed by applying new sorting strategies. This approach is detailed in the next section.

9.5.2.2   External sorting algorithms

Most external sorting algorithms are based on splitting the data into manageable chunks of data that can fit into main memory, applying a suitable internal sorting algorithm to sort the chunks one at a time, and then performing a series of merges on increasingly larger chunks. The simplest kind of one such algorithm is called the *two-way mergesort*. We will see an example to illustrate the method.

Two-Way Mergesort

Let us consider a hypothetical machine that has just enough memory to hold 300 records each of certain fixed size. Let us say there is a total of 9600 records that needs to be sorted. We first split the set of 9600 records into 32 groups of 300 records each.

Step 1: Move each group into memory and sort the records using say Quicksort. After this step there are 32 groups of sorted data in files. Let the sorted groups be labeled $G_1, G_2, \ldots, G_{32}$.

Step 2: Each sorted group is known as a *run*. Consider the two groups G_1 and G_2 and move 100 records from each group to two *input buffers* in memory. Since the memory can hold 300 records, the remaining memory for 100 records is used as an *output buffer* to hold the result of the merge operations. Perform a standard merging of the two sorted groups and store the result in the output buffer. Anytime the output buffer gets full, it is written out to the disk and when either of the input buffers becomes empty, another 100 blocks is read into it from the same group until there is no more data left in the group in the disk. Merge continues to move forward until all of the records in the groups are merged into a larger run. This operation is repeated for other pairs of groups G_3 and G_4, G_5 and G_6, ..., and G_{31} and G_{32}. After this step, the number of runs in disk is reduced to 16 and each run has 600 records.

Step3: Repeat Step 2 for the new runs in the disk by moving 100 records at a time from the runs, merging them and writing them out to disk. After every execution of step 2 the number of records in the runs doubles, while the number of runs keeps halving. The last iteration is when there are two runs with 4800 records each and it is merged into a sorted list of 9600 records, written out to the disk 100 records at a time from the output buffer. This completes the external sorting process.

Example 6.1

Let S = {12, 4, 5, 9, 20, 32, 16, 78, 65, 44, 6, 18, 29, 53, 98, 78, 54, 91} be the given set of integers to be sorted. Hypothetically assume the size of each run to be 2 (easy for demonstration). After initial sorting of each run the groups are as follows:

(4, 12), (5, 9), (20, 32), (16, 78), (44, 65), (6, 18), (29, 53), (78, 98), (54, 91)

After we merge consecutive groups the runs are of size 4 are given below:

(4, 5, 9, 12), (16, 20, 32, 78), (6, 18, 44, 65), (29, 53, 78, 98), (54, 91)

The next iteration yields the following runs:

(4, 5, 9, 12, 16, 20, 32, 78), (6, 18, 29, 44, 53, 65, 78, 98), (54, 91)

We now have three runs and in two iterations we obtain the following sorted list.

(4, 5, 6, 9, 12, 16, 18, 20, 29, 32, 44, 53, 54, 65, 78, 78, 91, 98)

In the above example, we have not specified the size of the main memory. Assuming that the main memory can hold 8 keys, it will be a good exercise to show the keys that will be in main memory and the those that will written to disk at each iteration.

Analysis of Two-Way Mergesort

In the analysis, we will compute both the cost of I/O and CPU time via order estimates. We will denote the cost of reading (or writing) n records into (from) the memory from (into) disk by $I(n)$ time units. The cost of sorting n records is denoted by $sort(n)$ time units and the cost of merging two runs of aggregate size n by $merge(n)$ time units. Step 1 of the example will take

$32 \times I(300) + 32 \times I(300) + 32 \times sort(300) = 64 \times I(300) + 32 \times sort(300)$ time units.

Notice that the first two items of the sum arise from the cost of I/O reads and writes respectively. The first iteration of Step 2 will take

$96 \times I(100) + 96 \times I(100) + 16 \times merge(600) = 192 \times I(100) + 16 \times merge(600)$ time units.

The second iteration of step 2 takes

$192 \times I(100) + 8 \times merge(1200)$ time units.

The third iteration would take

$192 \times I(100) + 4 \times merge(2400)$ time units.

The fourth iteration would take

$192 \times I(100) + 2 \times merge(4800)$ time units.

And the last iteration would take

$192 \times I(100) + merge(9600)$ time units.

We now make simplifying assumptions based on the fact that the merge algorithm has a linear-time complexity in the number of aggregate records merged and that the I/O cost is linear in the number of records read or written. Hence we assume that $merge(n)+merge(m)=merge(n+m)$ and $I(n)+I(m)=I(n+m)$. Based on these assumptions, the total cost of the two-way mergesort algorithm is

$I(9600)+5\times I(9600)+32\times sort(300)+5\times merge(9600)$ time units.

Notice that the above formula is a simplification based on adding all the quantities calculated above. It can also be observed that the numbers 9600 and 5 in the formula above refer to the total number of records, and $log_2(9600/300)$ respectively.

General Analysis

Let us say that there are n records to be externally sorted using the two-way merge sort and that the list of records is split initially into groups of size (the initial *run length*) m each. Then there are a total of (n/m) groups initially. Based on the last observation in the example above, we can readily write that the time-complexity is

$I(n)+I(n)\times log_2(n/m)+(n/m)sort(m)+log_2(n/m)\times merge(n)$ time units.

We know that $sort(m)$ is $O(m\ log\ m)$ and $merge(n)$ is $O(n)$. Hence the time-complexity of two-way mergesort can be written in the big-oh notation as

$(1+log_2(n/m))\times I(n)+(n/m)O(m\ log\ m)+log_2(n/m)\times O(n)$.

The first term is the cost of I/O and the next two terms are the compute costs. Since the I/O costs are substantially higher than the compute costs, the overall time-complexity can be minimized by keeping $log_2(n/m)$ small from a fixed n. This implies the number of iterations or passes be kept small or we could keep the run length high. This is a crucial observation that we make here to improve external sorting even further. If you keep run length high, then the number of passes would be small, on the other hand, you could keep the number of passes small by using a *multiway merge*, in other words by keeping more than two runs in memory during the merge step. These two different techniques give raise the two improved algorithms that we will discuss below. We will study an algorithm called *replacement selection* that strives to keep the run length high, and an algorithm called the *multiway merge* that keeps the number of passes small.

Multiway Merging Algorithm

The intuition behind the design of the multiway merging algorithm is based on minimizing the I/O cost in the merge phases by keeping the number of passes small. The merging operation looks only at the leading values of each of the runs. Hence the values at the end of the runs are not involved early on leading to inefficient use of scarce memory. By bringing many runs into memory, each shorter than what may be possible in the case of the two-way mergesort, more efficient use of memory can be achieved. The multiway algorithm is similar to the two-way mergesort. It starts by first dividing the data into several groups and producing sorted runs for all groups using internal sorting methods. This step is the same as Step 1 in the two-way mergesort. In the second step, namely, the merge phase, k, $(k > 2)$, runs are brought into memory and merges are performed just like before. It is fairly straightforward to see that the I/O cost becomes a function of $log_k(n/m) \times I(R)$. Hence the multiway mergesort cuts down the I/O cost by a factor $log_2 k$.

Replacement Selection Algorithm

In replacement selection algorithm, the idea is to produce large runs in the initial phase. To achieve this objective, a clever variant of heap-sort is used. This variant is the key to improving the running time of the external sort algorithm. Let us first describe how replacement selection works by means of an example. Recall that in a min-heap, is a binary tree in which the key values at a parent is less than each of its children. As a specific example, let us consider the following min-heap shown in Figure 9.8 with keys a the nodes and a stream of keys <48,12,34,28> arriving in the order right to left.

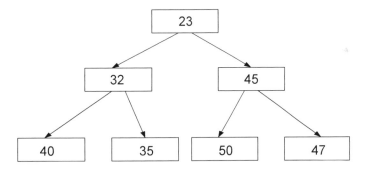

Figure 9.9:   A min–heap structure with keys stored at the nodes.

When a new key value (actually a record with the key value) arrives, the following rules are used to manipulate the heap when comparing the incoming key value with the key at the root.

1. If the incoming key is bigger than the root key then output the root key value to the buffer containing the current run and place the incoming key value at the root.
2. If the incoming key value is less than or equal to the root key then output the root key value to the buffer containing the current run, and place then
    a. place the key value in the last position of the heap at the root, and
    b. place the incoming key value in a separate buffer for generating the next run.
3. In either case, perform the percolate down operation to reorder the heap.

We will now look at the stream of incoming keys <48,12,34,28> and apply the above algorithmic rules above. First incoming key is 28, which is bigger than the one at the root. Hence key 23 will be added to the output run buffer, 28 will be placed at the root followed by a percolate-down operation. Since the children are already bigger than the new root, the heap looks as shown in Figure 9.9.

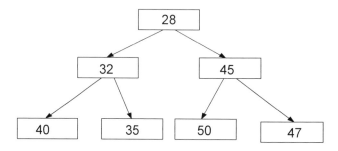

Figure 9.10:   The minimum heap after processing the record with key value 28.

Next, we look at the incoming key 34 and compare it with root value 28. Key 28 will go the output buffer; key 34 gets placed at the root, which percolates down to form the following modified heap.

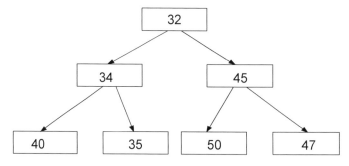

Figure 9.11:   The minimum heap after processing the record with key value 34.

Next, we consider the incoming key 12 which is less than the root value. First, key 32 goes to the output run. Then the last key value 47 is placed at the root and a percolate down operation takes place to result in the following new heap. Key 12 will not be considered in the current run any more and but will be considered for the next run.

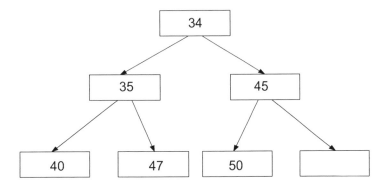

Figure 9.12:   The minimum heap after processing the record with key value 12.

Finally, we consider the incoming key 48 which is bigger than the root value. First, the root value 34 is placed in the output run. Then key 48 is placed at the root to perform the trickle down operation. The reader is invited to complete this operation to obtain the modified heap.

The way the external sort algorithm, based on replacement selection, works is as follows. Given n records, and available memory to hold m records and two memory buffers (one for input and the other for output) of size equal to the operating system block size, where $m << n$, we first load the memory with m records and build a min-heap with them. Then, records are loaded into the input buffer and streamed one at a time into the min-heap, applying the replacement selection algorithm we just described. Periodically, when the output buffer gets full, it is written out to the disk. A run is said to be complete when the heap is emptied. At this time, a new run generation is started. The process is repeated until all the records in the disk processed generating possibly many runs.

The interesting question is why this run generation is better than previous discussed run generation techniques. First of all, it is clear that the replacement selection algorithm generates runs of size at least m, since in the worst-case the min-heap gets emptied out into the output buffer and no new records are added. But you can expect that runs can be size considerably larger than *m* by considering the fact that there is a good chance that initial key values in early runs are likely to be big. This has the effect of producing runs longer in the early phases of run generation. During the late phases the runs are likely to be of size close to *m*. It turns out that the expected length of a run, on an average, is 2*m*. This can be proved by a beautiful argument based on the analogy of a snowplow clearing snow on a circular track. The reader is referred to Knuth's Searching and Sorting Volume 3, for a detailed explanation of the snowplow argument. This expected value depends on the assumption that the records are uniformly distributed and not skewed in any way.

Finally, a hybrid external sorting can be achieved by combining multiway merge with replacement selection. Experiments suggest that multiway merge with replacement selection performs the best.

9.6   Exercises

9.1.   Given the following set of Integers show the rank of each element at each iteration of the CompareAndCount method used in sorting by counting. The elements are 10, 5, 30, 6, 40, and 8.

9.2.   Modify the CompareAndCount method so that it can sort a list of integers with duplicates.

9.3.   Modify the straight insertion sort such that the insertions occur at the end of the array. That is, the last element of the array is assumed to be a sorted list containing a single element. The last but one element is inserted into the sorted list containing one element and so on.

9.4.   What is the total number of data movements in an insertion sort and why?

9.5.   Let there be an unknown number of integers to be sorted. We will use a Vector data structure to store the integer as they are read in. Suppose, as we read in the integer into the Vector we keep the vector sorted using the straight insertion sort, then what is the total number of data movements. Write a method similar to the straight insertion sort to take advantage of the Vector data structure.

9.6.   Show all the steps necessary to sort the following set of integers using shell sort. The elements are 10, 5, 30, 6, 40, 8, 50, 9, 60, and 11.

9.7.   What is the total number of data movements in shell sort and why?

9.8.   Swapping on two integers can be performed without the using of a temporary variable by using several assignment statements involving addition and subtraction. Show these steps to perform swapping of two integers.

9.9.   If there are no swaps during a single outer loop iteration of the Bubble Sort, then the list is sorted. Modify the BubbleSort method to take advantage of this observation.

9.10.   Rewrite the BubbleSort method that reduces the total number of data movements to $O(n)$.

9.11.   Given the following set of integers show the partition steps for each of the partitions (left and right partition) until the positions of each of the elements are fixed. The elements to be sorted are 10, 15, 3, 4, 20, 30, 40, 14, 18, 19, and 1.

9.12.   Rewrite the partition step so that it uses the middle element of the partition to be the pivot element.

9.13.   The running time of quicksort can be improved by calling insertion sort when the partition to be sorted is less than k elements. Rewrite the Quicksort method to take advantage of this observation. Derive the time complexity of your algorithm.

9.14.   Yet another way to improve quicksort is use the medium of the first element, middle element, and the last element of the partition as the pivot element. Rewrite the quicksort to incorporate this observation and perform a empirical evaluation with the Quicksort method given in this chapter.

9.15.   A *Tournament-Selection* is a sorting algorithm that is based on selection. In this sorting method, the sequence of n elements to be sorted is divided into bins each containing at most n/k elements. A single round of competition consists of the following steps. Let B[i][j] correspond to the jth element of the ith bin. Each of the bin is treated like a stack data structure. Let D be an array that represents a complete binary tree containing n/k leaves. The adjacent leaves from left to right are compared and the smaller of the leaves is moved to the parent. This process is continued until the smallest element reaches the root of the complete binary tree. The empty spaces are filled with numbers from the appropriate bin. The root node at the end of the first round will contain the smallest element. After n rounds the elements sequence can be printed in sorted order. Write a method to perform Tournament-Selection sorting.

9.16.   Given four elements draw the decision tree.

9.17.   Give a sequence of integers that is 1-sorted, but not 0-sorted. Why is this list not 0-sorted? Generalize the example to show that there are sequences that are $(p+1)$-sorted but not p-sorted, for all $p \geq 0$.

9.18.   Write a function to declare a static array of type *int* of different sizes that can pass compilation without errors on different 32-bit hardware, operating system platforms. Use a constant value named SIZE in your declarations.

    (a) In the same function, initialize the static array by using a while loop. Then determine the size of largest static arrays that can pass the execution phase without errors.

    (b) How do the answers for questions above, relate to available physical memory?

9.19.   In most flavors of Unix operating system, there is a file called *limits.h*. It is usually found in /usr/bin/include. Study the contents of the file, and write a few page research notes on what the *limits* describe. Furthermore, compare the contents of the *limits.h* in at least two flavors of Unix operating system. Also, run the command *ulimit* and note the output.

9.20.   In most flavors of Unix operating system, there is a standard utility called *qsort*, which as the name implies, is an implementation of the standard *quicksort* algorithm. Write a suitable C or C++ program, to use the *qsort* utility (on a 32-bit system) to sort increasingly larger sizes of integer arrays and plot a graph using the run-time against the size of the array. Push the size of the integer array beyond available physical memory and note the results. Explain your observations.

9.21.   Repeat Exercise 3 for a 64-bit system with more than 2 GB of RAM. Notice that you need to obtain a *qsort* utility that is 64-bit enabled. (In some systems, it may go by the name of *qsort* 64. Compiling and linking 64-bit programs need to be done by referring to system manuals.) Push the size of the array to be sorted such that the total size exceeds 2 GB but remains within available physical memory. Compare the results of this question with what you found in question 3. Also note the run-time when the array size exceeds physical memory available.

9.22.   Implement the two-way mergesort on a 32-bit system and plot the size of data with respect to the run-time. Compare the performance of the implementation with respect to results in Exercise 9.20, especially when the size exceeds available physical memory. This is likely to yield interesting insights because you are comparing two-way mergesort without virtual memory support that uses *quicksort* to build the initial runs against *quicksort* with virtual memory support.

9.23. Try to get access to a symmetric multiprocessor (SMP) system with at least 4 processors and implement an efficient two-way mergesort algorithm that uses threads to improve the I/O and computation time.

9.7 **References for Further Reading**

Boothroyd, J., "Sort of a Section of the Elements of an Array by Determining the Rank of Each Element: Algorithm 25", *Comput. J.* vol.10, Nov. 1967.

V.E. Castro, and D.E. Wood, "A Survey of Adaptive Sorting Algorithms", ACM Computing Surveys, Vol. 24, No. 4, pp.441–476, 1992.

Cook, C. R., and Kim, D.J., "Best Sorting Algorithm for Nearly Sorted Lists", *Communications of ACM* vol. 23, no.11, Nov. 1980.

Darlington, J., "A synthesis of several sorting algorithms", *Acta Informatica* vol. 11 , pp. 1–30, 1978.

Dobosiewicz, W., "An Efficient Variation of Bubble Sort", *Inform. Process. Lett.* vol. 11, no.1, pp. 5–6.1980.

Dromey, R. G., "Exploiting partial order with quicksort", *Software Practice and Experience* vol. 14, pp. 509–518, 1984.

Estivill-Castro, V., and Wood, D., "A survey of adaptive sorting algorithms", *Computing Surveys* vol. 24, 1992.

Flores I., *Computer Sorting*, Englewood Cliffs, NJ: Prentice-Hall, 1969.

Hoare, Charles A.R., "Algorithm 63: Quicksort", *Communications of the ACM* vol. 4, pp. 321, 1961.

Hoare, Charles A. R., "Quicksort", *Computer Journal* vol. 2, pp.10–15, 1962.

Incerpi, J., and Sedgewick, R., "Practical variations of Shellsort", *Information Processing Letters* vol. 26 ,pp. 37–43, 1987/88.

Knuth D., E., *The Art of Computer Programming, Vol. 3 : Sorting and Searching*, Reading, MA: Addison-Wesley 1975.

Loeser, R., "Some Performance Tests of 'Quicksort' and Descendants", *Communications of ACM* vol. 17, no. 3, Mar. 1974.

Lorin, H., *Sorting and Sort Systems*, Addison-Wesley, Reading, Mass., 1975.

Martin, W., "Sorting", *Computing Surveys* vol. 3, no. 4, pp. 147, 1971.

Mehlhorn, K., *Data Structures and Algorithms, Vol I : Sorting and Searching*, Berlin: Springer, 1984.

Moret, B.M.E., "Decision trees and algorithms", *Computing Surveys* vol. 14, pp. 593–623, 1982.

Sedgewick, R., "Data Movement in Odd-Even Merging", *SIAM Journal of Computing* vol. 7, no. 3, Aug. 1978.

Sedgewick, R. "The Analysis of Quicksort Programs" *Acta Informatica* vol. 7, pp. 327–55, 1977.

J. S. Vitter. "External Memory Algorithms and Data Structures: Dealing with Massive Data", ACM Computing Surveys, Vol. 33, No. 2, pp. 209–271, 2001.

L. Xiao, X. Zhang, and S. Kubricht. "Improving Memory Performance of Sorting Algorithms", ACM Journal on Experimental Algorithmics, vol. 5, August 2000.

CHAPTER

10 Hashing

LET US CONSIDER the scenario of a grocery shopper who walks into a grocery store looking to buy a box of cereal among possibly other things. One way for the shopper to get to the aisle that holds the cereal boxes would be to start from a certain point in the grocery store, and scan aisle by aisle until the desired aisle is reached. In algorithmic search terminology, this process is akin to a linear search. Since we have studied binary search, one may wonder, if binary search could be applied to the grocery store scenario to help the grocery shopper. A little reflection would reveal that for binary search to work, somehow, the aisle labeling need to be ordered, perhaps lexicographically, but then it is not clear if there would be a label called "cereal" at all. The reason for this is that the store perhaps decided to keep cereals under the aisle labeled "breakfast foods". Secondly, even if the naming of the labels worked out correctly, the shopper really could not "jump" to a certain aisle. Hence it appears that the binary search is infeasible for the grocery shopper. Certainly, scanning the grocery store aisle-by-aisle is a feasible approach but perhaps not as fast as we would desire it to be. Since searching is a major problem of interest, a related question is not how fast you could perform the search but rather how faster you could not do. This can be otherwise stated as the problem of finding lower bounds.

10.1 Lower Bound on Searching

We have seen that nontrivial lower bounds can be obtained by using simpler models of computation. One of the useful and simple models of computation is the *comparison* model wherein **only** comparisons between data elements are allowed. No complicated algebraic or arithmetic operations are permitted. Let us look at the searching problem based on our discussions above in both unordered and ordered lists.

Searching in Unordered List

In an unordered list L, let us suppose there are n elements. The problem is to determine whether the list L has an element x. We will prove that the lower bound is n comparisons for this problem, under the assumption that only comparisons are allowed. We will use the *adversary* model in conjunction with induction for this problem to obtain the lower bound. In the *adversary* model, for every possible algorithmic strategy, the *adversary* will place x in the nth position and initially present the first n-1 elements to the algorithm. If the list L contains exactly one element, it is clear that a minimum of one comparison is needed. Hence the lower bound is met. Assume that the lower bound holds for list of size at most n-1. Now consider a list of size n. Given an element x to be searched, the adversary will make up a list L of size n such that x is in L (but this fact is unknown to the search algorithm). The adversary will present the list of $(n$-1$)$ elements to the algorithm hiding x itself. Clearly, by induction hypothesis, a minimum of n-1 comparisons will be needed for the algorithm to declare that x cannot be found and one more comparison is needed to find that x is indeed in the list. Hence we have shown that the lower bound for searching in unordered list is n comparisons using the restrictive comparison model.

Searching in Ordered List

Given an ordered list of n values and a key value, again, the question is whether the key is in the list or not. We will obtain a lower bound of $O(\log_2 n)$ comparisons by using a *decision tree* model for this problem. Since the list is ordered, we can assume that the list is stored in an array whose index can be used for searching. Any algorithm for solving the problem has to work in the following manner.

At the very beginning, it uses the input key value to compute an index to the array and does one comparison. The result of this falls into one of three categories: (1) if the comparison is a success, then the algorithm halts, (2) if the value in the array is less than the key value, then it computes a new index, (3) if the value in the array is more than the key value, then it computes a new index. This approach would have to be repeated by the algorithm until the algorithm either halts with a success message or a failure message.

If you consider each comparison as a node in a tree, the results of *less than* and *greater than* in steps (2), and (3) can be considered to be the branches of this node. Furthermore, an iterated version of the comparison approach, results in a model of a binary tree that we call a *binary decision tree* (see also Chapter 9 on information dealing with lower bound for sorting). Each internal node of the tree corresponds to a comparison operation involving the key with an item in the list. Any algorithm that solves the problem could potentially take either branch down an internal node. It is also clear that the binary tree has to have at least n nodes corresponding to each item in the list. In other words, there is not a single item in the list that the decision tree could afford to miss, lest the algorithm will fail to work correctly. We also know that any binary tree having n nodes has a minimum height of $\lceil \log_2 (n+1) \rceil$ (see Chapter 6). The height of the decision tree corresponds to the number of comparisons starting from the root of the tree and following a specific search path to a leaf (see Chapter 9). Hence the minimum number of comparisons needed is $O(\log_2 n)$.

10.2   Hashing Introduced

In the case of ordered lists, we know that binary search works well and results in an $O(\log n)$ algorithm which is really an upper bound on the running time. Hence in this case, both the upper and lower bounds are the same and hence the algorithm is termed *optimal*.

Returning to the grocery shopper problem and considering the lower bounds we obtained above, it looks like there is no hope for our grocery shopper. Clearly, binary search could not be performed that gives an optimal algorithm for searching. On the other hand, linear search seems to take too long even though it is also optimal.

However, things are not so bleak because an out-of-the-box approach for the grocery shopper would be to ask for help from a store clerk and go straight to the desired aisle. Hypothetically, if you assume that, in this case, no effort was spent looking for the aisle or walking down to the desired aisle, then the situation is similar to the use of a *look-up* function (the look-up function is the store clerk) that provides an instant answer. For the look-up technique to succeed and be better than linear-search, it is important that the *look-up* be quick. Otherwise, the grocery shopper might be better off scanning the store aisle-by-aisle. (Consider the scenario that the store clerk does not know the answer and tries to page someone else overhead to help the shopper. Despite the best intentions of the clerk, we all know how long it takes for help to arrive!)

In the context of searching, essentially, this type of approach allows you to search for a certain item in constant time. It would indeed be a wonderful new search method, if you could achieve this in computer algorithms. It turns out there does exist a method, quite similar to the quick look-up function technique, known by the name *hashing*. The look-up function is known as the *hashing* (or *hash*) *function*. In hashing, the list of items can be stored in an array or in a database. The data store can be as complicated as that of a large enterprise with several departments and thousands of employees or can be simple as in the case of a dictionary of, say, English words, or a list of grocery times.

The trick in hashing is to let the key by itself tell us where it is to be stored and then when we have to retrieve it we again let the key tell us where to find it.

There are two parts to organizing information in this manner. The first part is to find a means to store the data efficiently (*insert* operation), and the second is to retrieve the data (*find* operation) efficiently. Optionally, there could be *delete* and other operations as well. We want to achieve either constant time or near constant-time for *insert* and *find* operations. Notice that the existence of hashing functions does not in any way violate our lower bounds because they do not use the comparison operation model to look for keys. Hence the lower bounds are not applicable to hash functions.

Example 10.1

Let us first consider a simple example as an illustration of the basic principles of the hashing technique. Suppose we have 50 records whose keys are distinct and in the range 1 to 50. As a concrete example, let us say that these are customer records numbered uniquely from 1 thru 50. Then we can use an array A indexed from 1 to 50 and place the record with key i in array location $A[i]$. When we have to search for a record whose key is, say, j all we need to do is obtain the record $A[j]$. This is a constant time operation as we know from Chapter 2.

In Figure 10.1, we show the mechanics of hashing. Basically, a hashing function $H(X)$ computes the index Y into an array *Table* (*Hash Table*) in which item X can be stored and retrieved.

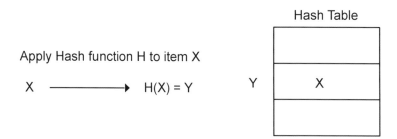

Figure 10.1: Hash Table – Function H that is applied to a key X to obtain an index position Y of the hash table.

Let us now try to think what we can do if, in Example 10.1, the keys of the records are *not* integers in the range 1 to 50 but instead, character strings. A little thought would reveal that we can use a similar approach as above, provided we could somehow map the character strings to integers. There can be so many ways of mapping strings to numbers but we would like the mapping to result in integers in a certain range that can be indexed into an array. We will see that the choice of the hash function is crucial to correct and efficient working of this technique.

Mathematically, a hash function $H: K \rightarrow I$ takes a set of key values K and maps it to a set of non–negative integers I.

Example 10.2

Let us now consider a set of keys $K = \{1,2,3,5,100,1000\}$. By using the obvious mapping function $H(x) = x$, and using an array location *Table*(x) to store the record with key value x, we can observe that the record with key value equal to 1 will be stored in *Table*(1), and the record with key value equal to 2 will be stored in *Table*(2) etc. In particular, the record with key value equal to 100 will be stored in *Table*(100), and the record with key value equal to 1000 will be stored in *Table*(1000). Hence, as we expected the hash function H is easy to compute, and in constant–time we are able to both store and search for a record with a certain key value.

However, there is one serious deficiency. With this hash function we would have to declare an array of size 1000 to store merely 6 records. This results in a waste of memory and if the range of keys spans even larger numbers then the size of the array *Table* needs to be even bigger, despite having to store perhaps only a small number of items.

Example 10.3

Let us consider a different hash function H' that maps the keys to (*key value mod* 13). The *mod* function takes a key value and calculates the remainder upon dividing the input number by the divisor. We can now calculate the hashed values for the keys in Example above to be $H'(1)=1$, $H'(2)=2$, $H'(3)=3$, $H'(5)=5$, $H'(100)=9$, and $H'(1000)=12$.

Now H' requires only a store of size 13 as opposed to H that required 1000 and hence is superior in terms of memory performance and equal in terms of both storing and retrieval performance of data items. Let us move to a new example with a different set of data.

Example 10.4

Let the set of keys be $K=\{1,6,9,10,11,15,2,100\}$. For this data set, we know that the function H would use a table of size 100. Let us compute H' for K. The hashed values are $H'(1)=1$, $H'(2)=2$,$H'(6)=6$, $H'(9)=9$, $H'(10)=10$, $H'(11)=11$, $H'(15)=2$, and $H'(100)=9$.

In Example 10.4, the hash function H' causes two pairs of keys to map to the same array locations. In particular, both keys 2 and 15 map to location 2 of the data store and keys 9, and 100 map to location 9 of the data store. This phenomenon is called a *collision* that essentially puts a new twist in the way we have been looking at hash functions. The reason is, you simply cannot store two or more records in the same location. Hence the collision needs to be resolved by relocating the collision–causing records to separate locations that can be found when needed. Furthermore, note that H' provides exactly 13 locations, alternatively called *slots* or *buckets* to store the records at. As a result, any time you have more than 13 records there will be collisions. The immediate question of how exactly to handle collisions will be addressed later in more detail. But this scenario brings up the issue that not all hash functions are the same. They behave differently, and have different performance characteristics. Hence, the choice of a hash function has to be made carefully.

Example 10.5

Consider the following keywords in a programming language: **while**, **do**, **until**, **for**, **if**, **then**, and **else**. Each keyword can be converted into an integer by adding the ASCII values corresponding to each letter in the keyword. For example the integer value corresponding to the keyword **do** is $100 + 111 = 211$. After computing the integer value for each of the keyword we can apply the hash function to determine the location in the table where it is to be stored.

We will now discuss the essential elements of a good hash function.

A hash function should be fast to compute: We have seen that for quick look-ups or quick inserts in constant-time a hash function should be computable easily. We will see that there are different hashing schemes that satisfy this property.

A hash function should spread the data uniformly in the hash table: If the keys are not known well in advance or arrive in unpredictable order, then it is difficult to guess the size of the hash table. Regardless of the size of the table, collisions can happen. Hence what we want to avoid is too many key values getting mapped to the same address thereby not using the available free space effectively. Overcrowding can cause skewed performance and increase retrieval time. To ensure uniform spreading of hashed values, the hash function should use all of the information in the key values.

10.3   Hash Functions

We know that a hash function must satisfy some basic properties for it to be useful. These properties imply that the collisions be kept at a minimum. Furthermore, the size of the hash table may also affect the ability of the hash function to distribute the keys uniformly throughout the table. We shall now describe five commonly used hash functions and discuss the applicability of the properties.

Division Modulo

We have seen this scheme first in Example 10.4 and again in Example 10.5. The idea here is to treat a key k as an integer and to let $H(k) = k \bmod m$, that is, the hash value of a key is the remainder when it is divided by the size, m, of the hash table. It is clear that the hash values are in the range $0,1,2,...,m-1$. The choice of m is very important. For instance, the table size, should not be a power of 2, since $k \bmod m$ will then be just the $\log m$ low-order bits of k, independent of the rest of k. For example, if k is an 8-bit number and $m = 32 = 2^5$, then $k \bmod m$ is the five least significant bits of k. Obviously, such a hash function will not spread the keys uniformly since it does not take into account all of the bits of the key. Such biases will result in frequent collisions. As a rule of thumb, division modulo m provides a good hash function if m is prime. In practice it has been found that one can choose m such that it does not have prime divisors less than 20.

Mid-Square Method

The mid-square hash function is simple. The function h is computed by first squaring the key under question and selecting an appropriate number of bits from the middle of the square. It can be intuitively seen how selecting from the middle of the square would involve bits from the whole key. The mid-square function is commonly used in symbol table applications such as in compilers. The symbol table is a central storage of all information in a program such as *identifiers, type* names, *function* names etc. The number of bits r selected from the square will determine the size of the hash table which is equal to 2^r. We will illustrate the mid-square hash function by means of an example.

Example 10.6

Let the English alphabet 'A', 'B', 'C',..., 'Z' be represented by numbers 1 through 26. A string from this alphabet can be represented by concatenating the numeric representations. For instance, the string "DEED" will have the numeric representation 4554. Squaring this we get 20738916 and the binary representation for the square is 1001110001110011011000100. If we decide to select the middle 9 bits of the square then we get 001110011 which would give the hash value, $h(DEED) = 115$ in a table of size 512.

Folding

Folding is a hashing technique computed by first dividing the key to be hashed into several parts and adding the parts together for the hash value. In general, the sizes of the individual parts should be the same except perhaps the last one. The addition can be performed in two ways. The first method called the *shift folding* works by shifting all of the parts so that the least significant bits (digits) are lined up corresponding to the other parts and then adding the parts together. The second method called the *boundary folding* works by first reversing the bits (digits) of every other part and then performing the shift folding. Again, this type of hashing can be expected to produce different hash values for different keys owing to its dependence on all the bits of the key.

Example 10.7

Let $p = 79502412349672$ be the key to be hashed. We divide p into $p_1 = 795$, $p_2 = 024$, $p_3 = 123$, $p_4 = 496$, and $p_5 = 72$. Using shift folding the hash value is $h(p) = 795+024+123+496+72 = 1510$. Using the boundary folding technique we reverse the digits of p_2 and p_4 and use the shift folding approach. Hence the hash value in this case is $795+420+123+694+72 = 2104$.

Digit Selection

This technique is especially appropriate when all of the keys are fixed and do not change over time. The idea is to consider each key as a string of bits and select certain bits (digits) from the representation based on a set of pre-decided bit (digit) positions. For instance, let $p = 2479583572$ be a key. Based on the knowledge of the characteristics of the keys to be hashed, let us say, we will take the 3rd, 6th, and 9th positions from left to right. This would give us a hash value of 787. It is clear how critical it is to have a good knowledge of the keys in the key space to be able to use this technique effectively. Otherwise, there will be frequent collisions and searches will take more time than other hashing techniques.

Multiplication

Instead of modulo operation, which is implemented by division, we can use multiplication to hash keys. The idea is use a positive real constant fraction to multiply the key (converted into an integer value) and truncate the number obtained by multiplying the fractional part of the result with the size of the table. In other words if *key* is an integer key, *c* is a positive real constant fraction, and *n* the size of the hash table, then the multiplicative hash function is $H(key) = trunc(n \times frac(c \times key))$.

It is clear that the hash function so defined will produce integers in the range 0 to *n*-1. The multiplicative method tends to scatter the keys more or less uniformly for applications such as the management of symbol tables in compilers. The *golden ratio* $\phi = (\sqrt{5} - 1)/2 \approx 0.618034$ is a commonly used value for the constant *c*. This method has the advantage over the division modulo method, in that the table size can be any number; it does not have to be prime.

Example 10.8

Let us consider hashing the word "DEED" in Example 10.4. Using the same integer representation for DEED we need to hash 4554 into a table of size, say 100. We will use the constant $c = \phi$. Then the hash value is

$$h(4554) = trunc(100 \times frac(4554 \times 0.618034)) = 52$$

10.4   Hash Table Abstract Data Type

As noted in the introduction to this chapter, the essential operations on a hash table are *insert()*, *remove(item)*, and *find(item)* (in addition, of course, to *create()*). Another operation which is obviously necessary is *isempty()*, which reports, as one would expect, whether the hash table is empty. We will also have the operations *size()* and *capacity()* which would report the number of items that are stored in the hash table and the size of the hash table, respectively. The operation *hash(item)* is used by operations *insert()*, *remove(item)*, and *find(item)* and it returns an index position of the hash table wherein the item can be either found or inserted at. The operations *insert(item)* and *remove(item)* should also handle collisions. Since there are several collision handling schemes, the implementation of the operations would be dependent on the specific collision-resolution mechanisms.

The specification of an abstract data type for a hash table class is given below.

```
create ()
    // creates an empty hash table
isempty ()
    // returns true if there are no elements in the hash
    // table, otherwise false
size ()
    //returns the number of items stored in the hash table
capacity ()
    // returns the maximum number of items that can be stored
    // on the hash table
insert (item)
    //inserts a new item into the hash table
remove (item)
    // removes the item from the hash table
find (item)
    // returns the items if found on the hash table,
    // otherwise returns NULL
hash (item)
    // computes the hash value for the item based on the hash
    // function and returns an integer that is the
    // index position in the hash table
```

10.5   Array implementation of Hash Table

We can now proceed with the implementation of the hash table abstract data type in C++.

10.5.1   Node Data Type

The node data type in our implementation assumes that the hash function can be applied either on it or on a field it contains. One may assume that the node data type contains a field named "key" on which the hash function can be applied. The node should support the equality test operation that will be used as part of the *find*() operation. Our implementation below does expect that the node data type supports the assignment operator, that is, that one data object can be assigned to another without error.

10.5.2   Exceptions

If the hash function is not properly designed, it is possible for the hash function to return a index value that is out of bounds of the hash table. The *HashTableOutOfBounds* exception will be thrown in this case. The *find*() operation may fail to find the element that is stored in the hash table resulting in the *HashTableElementNotFound* exception. It is also possible, during initialization, that a hash table with the desired size may not be created. Then, the *HashTableMemory* exception will be thrown.

Therefore, we shall create a small family of exceptions to go with our `HashTable` class:

```
class HashTableException       : public Exception { };
class HashTableOutOfBounds     : public HashTableException { };
class HashTableElementNotFound : public HashTableException { };
class HashTableMemory          : public HashTableException { };
```

10.5.3   Abstract Base Class Definition

Given the specification of the abstract data type for a hash table, we can prepare an abstract base class for the hash table class, or classes, which we will write. As usual, we have added an enumeration function, even though this is not actually part of the abstract data type. The interface is given below:

```
#include <iostream.h>
#include "Exception.h"
#include "Enumeration.h"

class HashTableException        : public Exception { };
class HashTableOutOfBounds      : public HashTableException { };
class HashTableElementNotFound  : public HashTableException { };
class HashTableMemory           : public HashTableException { };

template <class DataType>
class AbstractHashTable {
friend ostream& operator<< (ostream& s,
                    const AbstractHashTable<DataType>& HT);
protected:
    virtual int hash (const DataType& data) = NULL;
        // determines the hash value for the data.
public:
    virtual ~AbstractHashTable ();
    virtual DataType find (const DataType& q) = NULL;
    // returns the element which matches q,
    // or throws an exception if no element matches
    virtual void insert (const DataType& data) = NULL;
    // inserts data while maintaining using the hash function
    virtual void remove (const DataType& data) = NULL;
    // removes the element matching data, if any.
    virtual bool collision(int pos) = NULL;
    // returns true if there is no element in the
    // table at position pos, but otherwise returns false
    virual isEmpty() = NULL;
    // returns true is there are no elements in the table,
    // otherwise returns false;
    virtual int capacity () = NULL;
    // returns the size of the hash table.
    virtual int size() = NULL;
    // returns the number of elements stored in the table
    virtual DataType& operator [] (int k) = NULL;
```

```
    // returns the object that is stored in position k
    // of the hash table
    virtual void display (ostream& s);
    // display the nodes of the linked list
    virtual Enumeration<DataType>* enumerator ();
    // returns an enumeration of the data in the list
};
```

Enumeration of Items

The enumeration of the hash table is used for listing the items stored in it. The enumeration of the hash table will list the items stored in the increasing order of their hash values. That is, items in the table will be listed from lower to higher index positions. The *nextElement()* method returns the object stored in the next non-empty index position. There may be some index positions in the hash table without any items in them. Let the last item that the method *nextElement()* returns be at an index position j. The immediate call to the method *hasMoreElements()* method will return *true* if the there exists an index position k containing an non-empty item such that $k > j$, otherwise it will return *false*.

   The enumeration class HTEnumerator for the hash table class is presented below. The HTEnumerator class has two fields: a pointer to the object (belonging to AbstractHashTable<DataType> class) and an integer variable that keeps track of index position to be processed next by the method *nextElement()*. The constructor for HTEnumerator is made protected for reasons explained previously for the linked list enumerator class.

```
template <class DataType>
class HTEnumerator : public Enumeration<DataType>
{
friend AbstractHashTable<DataType>;
protected:
    AbstractHashTable<DataType>* _HT;
    HTEnumerator (AbstractHashTable<DataType>* HT);
    int _currentIndex;
// address in the table for the element to be returned next
```

```
public:
    virtual bool hasMoreElements ();
    virtual DataType& nextElement ();
};
// --------------------------------------------------------
template <class DataType>
HTEnumerator<DataType>::HTEnumerator (
                            AbstractHashTable<DataType>* HT)
{
    _HT = HT;
    _currentIndex = 0;
}
// --------------------------------------------------------
template <class DataType>
bool HTEnumerator<DataType>::hasMoreElements ()
{
    return ((_HT != NULL) && (!_HT->isEmpty() &&
    (_currentIndex < _HT->size())));
}
// --------------------------------------------------------
template <class DataType>
DataType& HTEnumerator<DataType>::nextElement ()
{
    int temp;
    if ((_HT == NULL) || (_HT->isEmpty())
                    || (_currentIndex == _HT->Capacity()))
        throw LinkedListBounds();
    temp = _currentIndex;
    while (*_HT[currentIndex] == NULL) &&
          (_currentIndex < _HT->Capacity())
        _currentIndex++;

    return *_HT[temp];
}
```

The *display()* method and *ostream* << operator for the *AbstractHashTable* are simple to write:

```
template <class DataType>
void AbstractHashTable<DataType>::display (ostream& os){
    bool first = true;
    Enumeration<DataType>* e = enumerator();
    os << "<";
    while (e->hasMoreElements())
    {
        if (!first) os << ", ";
        first = false;
        os << e->nextElement();
    }
    os << ">";
    delete e;
}
// ---------------------------------------------------------
template <class DataType>
ostream& operator<< (ostream& os,
                 AbstractHashTable <DataType>& s)
{
    s.display (os);
    return os;
}
```

The implementation of an enumeration method for the hash table involves creating an instance of the *hashTableEnumerator* class. A pointer to the hash table is passed to the non-empty constructor of the hashTableEnumerator which stores this information in order to access the hash table. The '*this*' pointer that is passed to the *hashTableEnumerator* is of type *AbstractHashTable<DataType>* in the enumeration method presented below.

```
// part of the implementation of the class AbstractHashTable
template <class DataType>
Enumeration<DataType>* AbstractHashTable <DataType>::
                                 enumerator () {
// Returns an enumeration of the data contained in the hash table
    return new HTEnumerator <DataType> (this);
}
```

We can now write an ostream $<<$ operator function which uses display(). This function must be a friend of the *AbstractHashTable* class.

```cpp
template <class DataType>
ostream& operator << (ostream& s, const
                            AbstractHashTable<DataType>& HT){
    HT.display(s);
    return s;
}
```

10.5.4   The Hash Function

The hash function returns an integer value that represents a position in the hash table. For example, the division modulo method discussed previously will take an integer key value and returns modulo of that key with the size of the hash table. Note that in our implementation, the modulo arithmetic is applicable only to those objects that are integers. For all other object types, appropriate conversion to an integer value has to be done. The hash function is presented below.

```cpp
template <class DataType>
int HashTable<DataType>::hash (const DataType& data)
{
    return (data % size());
}
```

10.5.5   Class Definition

The above interface can be implemented using the built-in C++ array, or the *Array-Class*, *Vector*, or *LinkedList* classes developed in the preceding chapters, although the implementation will be different in each case. We will implement the hash table using the *ArrayClass* to store the items in the table.

Our *ArrayClass* implementation of the *AbstractHashTable* will be a subclass of *AbstractHashTable* and will be called *ArrayHashTable*, so that the implementation is revealed in the name. The class *ArrayHashTable* could have been inherited from the *ArrayClass* and in such a case it would have exposed all the operations on *ArrayClass* that are not required for the ArrayHashTable class. Hence, we have intentionally chosen to use a field of *ArrayClass* within the *ArrayHashTable* implementation.

Fields, Constructors, and Destructor

We will make use of an integer field called *_size* that stores the number of items stored in the hash table. The maximum size of the hash table (since it is implemented using the *ArrayClass*) can be obtained by invoking the *size*() method on the *ArrayClass* object. Our *ArrayHashTable* class will be initially as follows:

```
template <class DataType>
class ArrayHashTable : public AbstractHashTable<DataType>
// ----------------------------------------------------------
{
protected:
    ArrayClass<DataType>* Table;
    // determines the hash value for the data.
    int _size;
public:
    ArrayHashTable ();
    ArrayHashTable (int n);
    ArrayHashTable (const ArrayHashTable<DataType>& HT);
    virtual ~ ArrayHashTable ();
};
// ----------------------------------------------------------
template <class DataType>
ArrayHashTable<DataType>:: ArrayHashTable ()
{
    Table = NULL;
    _size = 0;
}
// ----------------------------------------------------------
template <class DataType>
ArrayHashTable<DataType>:: ArrayHashTable (int n)
{
```

```
    try
    {
        Table = new ArrayClass<DataType>(n);
        for (int i = 0; i < n; i++)
            (*Table)[i] = NULL;
        _size = 0;
    }
    catch (ArrayMemoryException e)
    {
        Table = NULL;
        throw HashTableMemory();
    }
}
// ------------------------------------------------------------
template <class DataType>
ArrayHashTable<DataType>::~ ArrayHashTable ()
{
    if (Table != NULL)
        delete Table;
    _size = 0;
}
```

Accessor Methods

Given that the number of objects which can be stored in the *ArrayClass* used in the *ArrayHashTable* is limited, we need a few methods: the `capacity()` method to report the size of the hash table, the *size()* method to return the number of items stored in the hash table, and the corresponding *isEmpty()* method which reports true if there are no items stored in the hash table. We have also included a method called *collsion (int Pos)* that returns true if there is an item stored in position *Pos* of the hash table. The implementations of these methods are presented below. The *find(key)* returns the object stored in location *hash(key)*.

```
template <class DataType>
bool ArrayHashTable<DataType>::collision (int Pos)
{
    return ((*Table)[Pos]==NULL);
}
// -----------------------------------------------------------
template <class DataType>
int ArrayHashTable<DataType>::capacity ()
    // returns the size of the hash table
{
    if (Table == NULL) return 0;
    return ((*Table).size());
}
// -----------------------------------------------------------
template <class DataType>
int ArrayHashTable<DataType>::size ()
// returns the number of items stored in the hash table
{
    return (_size);
}
// -----------------------------------------------------------
template <class DataType>
int ArrayHashTable<DataType>::isEmpty()
// returns true if the number of items stored in the hash
// table is 0, false otherwise
{
    return (_size == 0);
}
//------------------------------------------------------------
template <class DataType>
DataType ArrayHashTable<DataType>::find(const DataType& key)
// returns the item stored in location hash(key)
{
    return ((*Table)[hash(key)]);
}
```

For the class *ArrayHashTable* we have included the overloaded '[]' operator. Note that the overloaded '[]' operator is provided for the *ArrayClass* and it is used on the Table object as presented below:

```
template <class DataType>
DataType& ArrayHashTable<DataType>::operator [] (int k)
{
    if ((k < 0) || (k >= capacity())) throw HashTableBounds();
    return (*Table)[k];
}
```

The insert() Method

When a new object is to be added through the *insert()* method, the new object is placed at the position that is obtained by computing the hash function on the new object. If the hash function returns a position that is outside the range of the hash table the *HashTableBounds()* exception is thrown. The *insert()* method below does not handle collisions. The implementation of the *insert()* method is as follows:

```
template <class DataType>
void HashTable<DataType>::insert (const DataType& data)
{
    int k;

    k = hash(data);
    if ((k < 0) || (k >= capacity())) throw HashTableBounds();
    if ((*Table)[k] == NULL) //no collisions
        _size++;
    (*Table)[k] = *(new Object(data));
}
```

The remove() Method

The implementation of the `remove ()` method is simple. It involves computing the hash value of the item to be deleted, checking if the hash value is within the bounds of the table, making the table at the valid position null, and returning the element that is removed.

```
template <class DataType>
DataType ArrayHashTable<DataType>::remove
                                     (const DataType& data)
{
    int k;
    DataType temp;
    k = hash(data);
    if ((k < 0) || (k >= size())) throw HashTableBounds();
    temp = (*Table)[k];
    (*Table)[k] = NULL;
    _size--;
    return temp;

}
```

10.5.6 Testing the Class

We shall write a very simple *main*() function to test the *ArrayHashTable* class. Our *main*() function will insert five items on the hash table and remove them again.

```
void main()
{
  ArrayHashTable<int> myTable(10);

  myTable.insert(102);
  myTable.insert(105);
  myTable.insert(22);
  myTable.insert (47);

  cout << myTable << endl;

  cout << myTable.find(102) << endl; //102 would be found
  myTable.remove(22);
  cout << myTable.find(102) << endl; //102 will not be found since
  //102 and 22 hash to the same value using the division method
  cout << myTable << endl;
}
```

The result shows the correct working of the `ArrayHashTable` class:

```
Size = 10, No. Elements = 3
[(0,0),(1,0),(2,22),(3,0),(4,0),(5,105),(6,0),(7,47),(8,0),(9,0)]


The element is found in the Hash Table
22


Sorry!!! Element is not found in the Hash Table


Size = 10, No. Elements = 2
[(0,0),(1,0),(2,0),(3,0),(4,0),(5,105),(6,0),(7,47),(8,0),(9,0)]
```

10.6   Collision Resolution Techniques

We know that two or more keys can get mapped to the same hash value resulting in a collision. Although the hash functions described earlier are good they cannot prevent collisions from occurring. When collisions occur we could either try to keep the data within the table or change the structure of the table to be able to place in the same locality more than one key. The first approach is called the *open addressing* scheme and the second is called the *chaining* scheme.

10.6.1   Open Addressing Scheme

When we try to insert a new key in a hash table, if the hash value indicates a location that is already occupied, we try to probe for some other empty or open location to place it. It is conceivable that we may not be able to find an open location at the first probe and hence a sequence of probes may be necessary. Such a sequence is called the *probe sequence*. Hash table operations such as *delete* and *find* should be able to reproduce the probe sequence so they can work correctly. We will see three techniques in open addressing scheme that differ in the manner of probing for an empty location. These are *linear probing*, *quadratic probing*, and *double hashing*. Also, for all the open addressing schemes, it is assumed that at each location k in the hash table we have a value *count* that keep tracks of the number of items stored in the hash table with the same hash value of k. The use of this *count* variable will be presented in the discussion on linear probing.

10.6.1.1 Linear Probing

In linear probing, the hash table is searched linearly to find the closest unfilled position from the location where collision occurred. In other words, if T is the hash table and $T(h(key))$ is occupied then probes are made at $T(h(key)+1)$, $T(h(key)+2)$ and so on until an unfilled location is found. Figure 10.2 illustrates linear probing using the division modulo hash function $h(k)=k\ mod\ 47$.

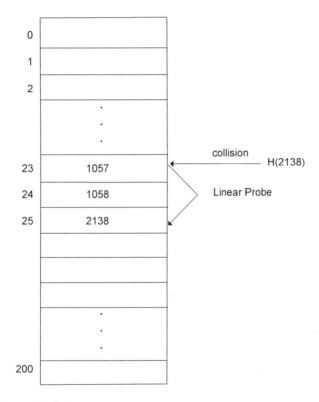

Figure 10.2:   Linear Probing

Find Operation

In linear probing, one of three things can happen while searching for a *key*.

1. The probing sequence wraps around to the initial hash value. In this case the table is full and does not contain the key.
2. At position $h(key)$ if the *count* value is 0, then the table does not contain the key.
3. At some location $(h(key)+j)\ mod\ m$, we have $T(h(key)+j)=key$, where $j \geq 0$. In this case the *key* is found in the table.

Deletion Operation

Deletion of a key follows a lookup and decrementing the count at location $h(key)$ if the key is found, and setting the location $h(key)$ to "NULL". The variable *count* is useful in the following way. Assume that two elements x_1 and x_2 hash to the same location k and one of the elements say x_1 be stored in location k and the other at location say l after a linear probe. The count at location k will be 2. Upon deletion of x_1 the count at location k will be set to 1. For a subsequent lookups of keys with hash value of k, if count at location k is 0, then immediately we can say that the item is not found, otherwise we have to follow the probe sequence as presented in the *find* operation above. Clearly, without the *count* information, every lookup will involve following the probe sequence and this in the worst case would be searching the entire hash table thereby making the hash table approach cost prohibitive.

One of the main problems with linear probing is that elements in the table cluster together. To see this, let us say that there are r number of records (in a larger collection of records) whose keys all map to the same initial hash address. Then these r records will get placed in a chain of (mostly, but not necessarily consecutive) locations in the hash table due to linear probing. It is also clear that search for a record in this chain might take up to r probes. Instead of just one such group of records having this property, there can be several such groups of records each within itself hashing to the same address but hashing to a different address across groups. This phenomenon of collision causing records to occupy consecutive storage locations is called *primary clustering*. As a result, parts of the table can be dense and the rest sparse causing long searches and hence costing efficiency.

10.6.1.2   Quadratic Probing

In quadratic probing, as the name suggests, instead of probing locations linearly we probe quadratically. That is, starting with the original hash value $T(h(key))$, we probe $T(h(key)+1^2)$, $T(h(key)+2^2)$, $T(h(key)+3^2)$, etc. Figure 10.3 demonstrates this type of hashing for the same example in Figure 10.2.

The probing sequence wraps around the hash table in quadratic probing as well. It is clear that quadratic probing eliminates the primary clustering associated with linear probing. However, collision causing records follow the same probe sequence. This phenomenon is called *secondary clustering*.

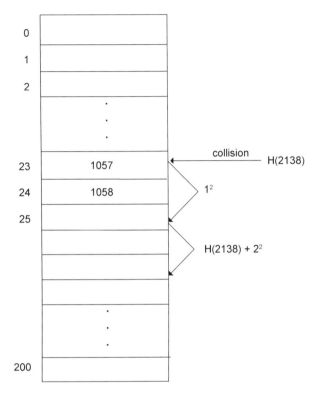

Figure 10.3: Quadratic probing with $h(k) = k \bmod 47$.

10.6.1.3 Double Hashing

In double hashing, when collision occurs, the key is rehashed using a second hashing function. The second hashing function's hashed value is used as an increment to compute the probe sequence. For instance, if the hashed value from the second function turns out to be 7, from a collision at location 10, then we can consider the next probe at location 17 *mod tablesize* and the next at 24 *mod tablesize* etc.

The choice of the second hash function needs to be made wisely. If h_1 is the original hash function and h_2 is the rehash function then the following guidelines must be true of these functions.

1. $h_2 \neq h_1$, and
2. $h_2\,(key) \neq 0$.

The first condition is needed to avoid clustering and the second condition is needed for a non-zero step size. Unlike the two previous open addressing schemes the probes, after a collision in the case of double hashing, are dependent on the key itself. Hence it virtually eliminates any type of clustering. The rehash function is used to determine the number of locations where the *insert* operation must be Tried starting from the location where the collision occurred. For instance, if the rehash function applied to a key resulted in a number 5 then an insert attempt must be made at the 5th location from where the collision occurred.

Example 10.9

Let us consider the primary hash function to be $h_1(k) = k \bmod 59$ and rehash function to be $h_2(k) = 11 - (k \bmod 11)$. Let the hash table size be 59 (indexed by 0, 1, 2, 3,…, 58). Given a key $k = 75$, we have $h_1(k) = 16$. Given another key $k = 134$ to be inserted into the hash table, we have $h_1(134) = 16$ causing a collision. Using the rehash function the probe sequence should take steps of size $h_2(134) = 11 - (134 \bmod 11) = 9$. Hence the probe sequence will be 16, 25, 34, 43, 52, 2, 11, 20, 29, 38, 47, etc. In a table of size 59, let locations 16 and 25 be occupied by entries and location 34 be empty. If a new key 134 is to be inserted we will first consider location 16 and then $(16+9) = 25$ next. Since both the locations are occupied, we will consider the next location 34 as given in the probe sequence. Since location 34 is empty the item 134 will be inserted in it.

10.6.1.4   Chaining Strategies

One of the major drawbacks with open addressing schemes is that as the number of keys grows the hash table has to be resized and all keys have to be rehashed. Secondly, in open address schemes the keys and records are scattered all over the hash table. A new strategy called *Chaining* presents an excellent alternative. In chaining, the idea is to keep the elements that map to the same address together in the form of linked lists. There are two approaches in the chaining strategies. One is called *separate chaining* and the other is called *coalesced chaining*. The coalesced chaining is a simple variation of the separate chaining method.

Separate Chaining

In the *separate chaining* approach collisions are resolved by keeping the *overflow* entries in linked lists. This also allows for the table to grow dynamically avoiding recalculation of hashed entries when the table becomes full. See Figure 10.4 for an illustration of separate chaining scheme.

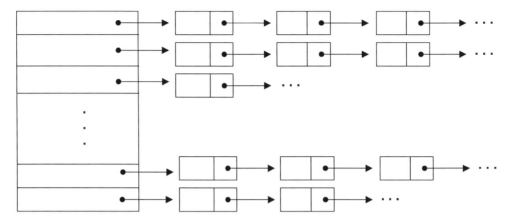

Figure 10.4:   Separate Chaining

One of the major advantages of separate chaining is in deleting a hashed entry. We can use the straightforward algorithm for deletion in a linked list. The principal disadvantages are the extra memory used by pointers and a possible slower execution at run-time due to the use of dynamic storage allocation needed for maintaining linked lists.

Coalesced Chaining

In separate chaining, searching for a key involves at least two probes. We first find the index of the head of the linked list (by applying the hash function to the key being searched for) and then follow the pointer to the first element of the linked list. One easy way to increase storage efficiency is to store the first element in the head itself. If the sizes of the records are too large and if the hash table is not full then there is a lot of wasted space due to empty records at the head of the linked lists. This is an improvement especially if the size of each record is not too big. Because if the sizes of the records are too large and if the hash table is not full then there is a lot of wasted space due to empty records at the head of the linked lists. A logical extension to this idea is to use the empty locations of the hash table to store the linked lists.

In separate chaining, we know that each key in a chain has the same hash value as any other key in the chain. However, in the case of coalesced chaining it is possible that a chain may have keys with different hash values. Let us see how such a scenario can happen. It is clear when a chain C is formed the keys are stored in locations in the hash table itself and hence it is possible a key k_1 may be stored in a location l different from its hash value. Suppose a new key k_2 gets hashed to location l directly. Then it is clear there is a collision which needs to be resolved. But whatever be the collision resolving mechanism, we have to have a pointer from location l to the actual location p where k_2 will be stored. Clearly, the chain C now has keys k_1 and k_2 with different hash values.

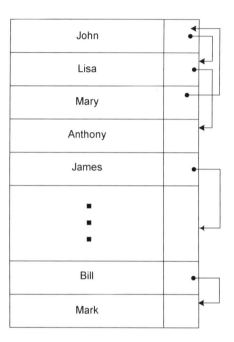

Figure 10.5: Coalesced Hashing

   Collisions such as above can be resolved by sequential probing. Although a chain can contain keys with multiple hash values, all keys with same hash value will be present in one chain. As a result, the search operation can be implemented in a straightforward manner. In coalesced chaining, the chains tend to be longer and in general, a probe does not necessarily begin from the start of a chain. In terms of performance it has been determined that coalesced chaining is storage efficient but with a higher average access time than separate chaining.

10.7   Quantitative Analysis of Hashing Schemes: Efficiency

We have so far seen several hashing techniques and discussed mutual advantages and disadvantages in an intuitive manner. Some of the hashing schemes can be compared using analytical means in terms of a parameter called the *load factor*. The *load factor* α is defined as the ratio of the number of items in the table at a given time to the size of the table T. That is,

$$\alpha \;=\; \frac{\text{Current number of keys in the table}}{\text{Size of Table (T)}}$$

The efficiency of any hashing scheme depends on the search time for a key. As the table fills, α increases. As α increases the chances of a collision increases and therefore the efficiency decreases. Analytical estimates for the average number of probes needed for a successful search (P_s) and the average number of probes needed for an unsuccessful search (P_U) can be derived in terms of the load factor (see Knuth[3]). The actual mathematical derivations of these analytical estimates are beyond the scope of this text.

	Linear Probing	Quadratic Probing	Double Hashing	Separate Chaining
P_S	$\dfrac{1}{2}\left(1+\left(\dfrac{1}{1-\alpha}\right)\right)$	$1-\log_e(1-\alpha)-\dfrac{\alpha}{2}$	$\dfrac{1}{\alpha}\log_e\left(\dfrac{1}{1-\alpha}\right)$	$1+0.5\times\alpha$
P_U	$\dfrac{1}{2}\left(1+\left(\dfrac{1}{(1-\alpha)^2}\right)\right)$	$\dfrac{1}{1-\alpha}-\alpha-\log_e(1-\alpha)$	$\dfrac{1}{1-\alpha}$	$\alpha+e^{-\alpha}$

Figure 10.6:   Formulae for computing the average number of probes for successful and unsuccessful searches (Knuth [3]).

The following table in Figure 10.7 shows the average number of probes for various α values.

α	Linear Probing		Quadratic Probing		Double Hashing		Separate Chaining	
	P_S	P_U	P_S	P_U	P_S	P_U	P_S	P_U
0.05	1.03	1.05	1.03	1.05	1.03	1.05	1.03	1.00
0.1	1.06	1.12	1.06	1.12	1.05	1.11	1.05	1.00
0.15	1.09	1.19	1.09	1.19	1.08	1.18	1.08	1.01
0.2	1.13	1.28	1.12	1.27	1.12	1.25	1.10	1.02
0.25	1.17	1.39	1.16	1.37	1.15	1.33	1.13	1.03
0.3	1.21	1.52	1.21	1.49	1.19	1.43	1.15	1.04
0.35	1.27	1.68	1.26	1.62	1.23	1.54	1.18	1.05
0.4	1.33	1.89	1.31	1.78	1.28	1.67	1.20	1.07
0.45	1.41	2.15	1.37	1.97	1.33	1.82	1.23	1.09
0.5	1.50	2.50	1.44	2.19	1.39	2.00	1.25	1.11
0.55	1.61	2.97	1.52	2.47	1.45	2.22	1.28	1.13
0.6	1.75	3.63	1.62	2.82	1.53	2.50	1.30	1.15
0.65	1.93	4.58	1.72	3.26	1.62	2.86	1.33	1.17
0.7	2.17	6.06	1.85	3.84	1.72	3.33	1.35	1.20
0.75	2.50	8.50	2.01	4.64	1.85	4.00	1.38	1.22
0.8	3.00	13.00	2.21	5.81	2.01	5.00	1.40	1.25
0.85	3.83	22.72	2.47	7.71	2.23	6.67	1.43	1.28
0.9	5.50	50.50	2.85	11.40	2.56	10.00	1.45	1.31
0.95	10.50	200.50	3.52	22.05	3.15	20.00	1.48	1.34

Figure 10.7: Average number of probes for successful and unsuccessful searches for various hashing techniques obtained using the formulae in Figure 10.6.

For instance, for a typical load factor $\alpha = 0.7$, the average number of probes for successful and unsuccessful searches using the linear-probing technique are 2.16 and 5.6, respectively. For the same load factor, the average number of probes for successful and unsuccessful searches using double hashing is 1.56 and 3.33, respectively. For the separate-chaining technique with $\alpha = 0.7$ the values of P_S and P_U are 1.35 and 1.2, respectively. Hence for $\alpha = 0.7$, separate chaining technique performs the best and double hashing performs better than linear-probing. Separate chaining is superior to double hashing for high values of α as the Table in Figure 10.7 demonstrates.

10.8   Dynamic Hashing

All of the hashing schemes we have studied thus far use storage declared statically at compile time. In other words, the size of a hash table has to be a fixed number and hence such hash schemes are known as *static*. There are two drawbacks with this approach. One when the hash table becomes near-full, (i.e., the load-factor is high) collisions increase and therefore, insertion and search times start to increase as well. Secondly, when the hash table becomes full, and more items need to be inserted, the table needs to be resized and all of the keys need to be rehashed. This can be quite costly. Notice that we cannot easily address these problems, by guessing the correct size of a hash table. Because, if we guessed too small, then this will cause frequent overflows, on the other hand, if we guessed too large, then this will result in wasted memory. *Dynamic* hashing schemes effectively deal with the problems of costly reorganization of hash tables and incorrect sizes of hash tables. The reader is also referred to the excellent survey by Enbody and Hu [4].

10.8.1   Tries

As the name implies, a Trie (pronounced "try") is a type of tree data structure that supports fast retrieval times. It adapts to growth as a result of insertions and shrinking due to deletions. To see how tries work, let us suppose that the keys are represented using its binary representation. This is not an unrealistic assumption, because, even if keys are not in binary, there are simple ways to convert any sequence of characters into a binary representation. In a Trie, the keys will be stored at the leaves (also known as *buckets*) of the Trie. The buckets, in general, can hold more than one record. However, we will assume, for the sake of simplicity, that each bucket holds exactly one record unless otherwise stated. The branching of the Trie will be dependent only on a portion of the binary representation of the keys and not on the whole. As an example, consider the following keys and their binary representations. Of course the binary representations are chosen arbitrarily in the figure below; one may concatenate the binary equivalent of the ASCII value for each letter in the key to get the binary representation.

Keys	Binary Representation
April	0010
March	0100
October	1000
February	0001

Figure 10.8: Example keys and their binary representations

Let us now go through the steps of building a Trie for the above keys by inserting them one at a time. We start with the root and an empty bucket attached to it. When we insert the first key *April* we take the most significant bit namely 0, of its binary representation. In general, the scanning on each of the keys is done left to right namely, from the most significant to the least significant bit. Then we branch to the left if the bit scanned is 0 and right if the scanned bit is 1. In the case of *April*, we first branch to the left resulting in the following Trie.

Figure 10.9: Trie after inserting April

In general, if a key *k* is encountered as we traverse the binary tree to insert another key *l*, then two children (one each for keys *k* and *l*) are added to the node corresponding to key *k* in the binary representation. This is illustrated below, when we insert *March*.

Next we look to insert *March* in the Trie which has a representation of 0100. Looking at the first bit 0 we branch to the left again. Since we already have a bucket with *April* in it, we will split the node using the second bit of the two keys *April*, and *March*, namely, 0 and 1. Then, the Trie will look as shown below in Figure 10.10.

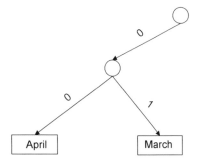

Figure 10.10: Trie after inserting *April*, and *March*

After the key *March* is inserted into the Trie, we insert keys *February* and *October*. The insertion of *October* requires branching to the right at the root of the tree and the insertion of *February* requires splitting the bucket containing *April* into two, using the third bit, as shown in the following figures.

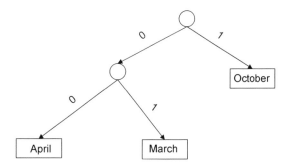

Figure 10.11: Trie after inserting *April*, *March*, and *October*

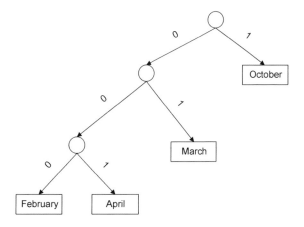

Figure 10.12: Trie after inserting *April*, *March*, *October*, and *February*

It is clear from the way the Trie is constructed, that leaf buckets are split as needed thereby expanding the structure. Analogously, when deletion occurs, buckets may be collapsed shrinking the structure. Furthermore, searching a Trie can be accomplished by proceeding from the root of the tree and branching to the left or right recursively and looking at each bit of the key from left to right. Given an arbitrary set of keys, it is possible that the Trie may be skewed or imbalanced thereby making the search complexity $O(n)$ where n is the number of bits in the binary representation. The reader is advised to find the similarity and differences between the Trie data structure and the *Huffman* tree that was developed in Chapter 8.

The Trie structure can be simplified and made search-efficient by applying one of two techniques, (1) the *directory* method, and (2) the *directoryless* method.

10.8.2 Directory Method

The *directory* method is also known by the terminology *extendible hashing*. Let us now consider Figure 10.12. In this Figure, the number of levels of the Trie is 3 and hence the worst-case search time is 3 units. To avoid having to traverse the Trie to look for a specific record, it is prudent to use a hash function with a directory and hence replace the Trie altogether. A directory can be thought of as an array in which each location would point to the bucket that holds the relevant record. The directory is indexed by the the bits of the keys which are produced by the hash function. The hash function needs to produce the same number of bits for each key so as to be used as the index of an array. In Figure 10.13, we will show how the Trie in Figure 10.12 can be *collapsed* into a directory.

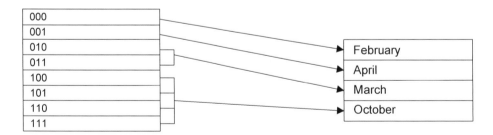

Figure 10.13:   Directory method

Insertion into the directory-based scheme involves, first hashing to get to an index in the table, following the pointer, if any, and splitting the node. For instance, let us say that there is a new record with a key value *December* and a hashed value of 1011 to be inserted. Following the index with a value of 101 leads to the bucket containing the key *October*. This bucket would be split as shown in Figure 10.14.

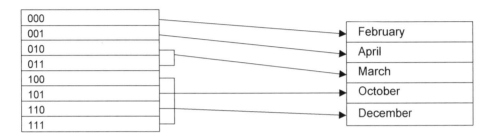

Figure 10.14:   Directory method shown after adding December

Furthermore, insertion can involve going from 2^{k-1} locations in the array to 2^k locations when the number of bits needed for resolution goes from (k-1) to k bits. An instance of this can be readily seen in the directories corresponding to the Tries in Figures 10.11 and 10.12. This involves doubling the directory size even if all of the extra storage is not required immediately.

Some points may be noted with regard to the directory method. Although all of the strings that have the format 1*xxx* point to the key, *October*, we know that only *October* is present in the data set. These results in wasted storage because of the fact that the array or table needed should be of size 2^k, where k is the number of bits used in the index, when in fact, the number of actual keys may be far less. This happens particularly in the case of skewed Tries which are a result of hash functions that map the keys non-uniformly. Secondly, the pointers use additional storage and hence require at least two accesses to reach the desired record. To alleviate some of the problems with the directory-based approach, we consider the *directoryless* approach.

10.8.3   Directoryless Method

In this technique, the basic ideas are to (1) avoid using the pointers and (2) use contiguous (possibly logical) space for storing the keys. To avoid using the pointers, we treat each hashed value as a bucket rather than a directory entry. Contiguous space for storing the keys makes it possible to add just one more bucket when needed and not allocate double the storage. The directoryless method is a bit more complicated than the directory method. It is governed by the splitting policy and how overflows are handled. Since we have assumed that the bucket size is 1, splitting is done whenever a bucket overflows. The directoryless method is best explained by means of an example.

Example 10.10

Let us look at the following set of keys in Figure 10.15 to be used in the directoryless scheme.

Keys	Binary Representation
April	0010
March	0100
October	1000
November	1100
August	0110
January	1110
May	1111
February	0111

Figure 10.15: Keys and their hash values

The first four keys when hashed into a directoryless table have the following configuration.

April	March	October	November
00	01	10	11

The next key to be inserted is *August* and it collides with *March* and hence causes an overflow. To handle the overflow, a new bucket is created to hold the key *August* and a pointer from bucket 01 to this new bucket is set. Secondly, we will use the splitting policy that allows an extra bucket to be inserted at the end of the list whenever an overflow occurs. Furthermore, the split will occur at buckets starting from left to right sequentially. This helps smooth out the expansion of the list by not splitting the bucket necessarily where the overflow occurs. This results in the following new configuration.

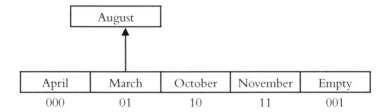

The next key to be inserted is *January* with a hash value of 1110 which collides with the bucket 11. This would be inserted as an overflow bucket at the bucket 11. Also, according to the split policy, bucket 01 splits now to result in the extra bucket 011. The key *August* will move into this one. This is illustrated in the diagram below.

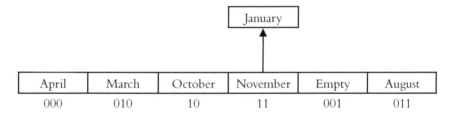

We next insert *May* with hash value 1111. This collides with bucket *November* again and hence forms an overflow bucket attached to it. Furthermore, bucket 10 splits now as illustrated below.

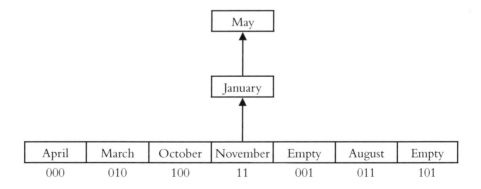

Finally, we insert key *February* with hash value 0111. This collides with bucket *August* forming an overflow bucket. Also, bucket 11 splits forming a new bucket 111 and as a result keys *January* and *May* migrate to this new bucket as shown below.

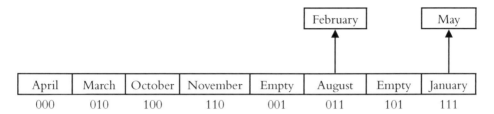

The last diagram completes the example showing how the splitting and over-flow are handled in several scenarios. Evidently, the implementation of this has to be done carefully. One measure of performance of dynamic hashing schemes is the space utilization defined as $U = S\,B/R$, where S is number of buckets used, B is the size of bucket, and R is the number of records to be stored. Evidently, we would like to have the utilization as high as possible. Analysis of several researchers has shown that the space utilization for splitting without overflow (directory method) results in a space utilization of 69%, assuming uniform key distribution. Overflow buckets allow the uti-lization ratio to be higher when split. We have thus learnt that both static and dynamic hash schemes provide an efficient way for storing and retrieval of records. Let us now study an important class of functions called the *perfect hashing* functions.

10.9   Perfect Hashing Functions

We know that collisions cause retrieval and search times to take more than constant time, but they are not easily avoidable. However, for fixed data sets in which no new insertions or deletions are made we can find suitable hashing functions that cause no collision. Such hashing functions are defined to be *perfect*. It should come as no surprise that such functions do exist. Because once the data set is static, we could analyze the properties of the data set to arrive at suitable hash functions that are collision-free. Of course, it is a different matter altogether how to systematically find such functions.

For a static data set, a perfect hashing function is not difficult to find because we can always choose a sufficiently large size table to map the keys into uniquely. To give a rather pathological example of such a hash function, let us say, there is a fixed set of *n* identifiers each of size at most *k* characters. Let us say that the characters come from a population of size s. We can assign numbers $1,2,3,\ldots,s$ to each of the characters respectively. Let $a(x)$ be such a mapping that assigns a character x to a number in the range $<1,2,3,\ldots,s>$. Given an identifier I, we can then construct a hash function $H(I) = p_1^{a(I(1))}$ $p_2^{a(I(2))}\ldots p_s^{a(I(s))}$ where $I(j)$ represents the jth character in the identifier I and $p_1,p_2,p_3,\ldots p_s$ are the first s prime numbers. Evidently, this will result in huge hash indexes and hence totally impractical. However, due to the uniqueness of prime decomposition, such a hash function will be collision free. The clear problems are (1) slow computation of hash values, and (2) huge table sizes.

A *minimal perfect hash* function for a static set of data of size n is a perfect hash function such that the hash table is of size n. The notion of a minimal hash function is important in keeping the table sizes as small as they can possibly be. Example static data sets include list of keywords in standard programming languages. Compilers use minimal perfect hashing schemes to map the keywords to tables just large enough to hold all the keywords. In the lexical analysis phase of a compiling a program, a compiler can retrieve a token in the program, and hash it into the keyword table to check if a token is a keyword.

Finding minimal perfect hash functions can be time-consuming and hence one can instead look for *non-minimal perfect* hash functions where the table size is close to (but clearly, larger than) the size of the dataset. The compromise is between spending a lot of time to find a minimal perfect hash function and hence increasing run-time efficiency versus spending minimal time to find a near-minimal perfect hash function and hence losing perhaps a bit in run-time efficiency. Another type of compromise might be in generating a *near-perfect* hash function. A near-perfect hash function does not possess the *perfectness* property, and may or may not have the minimality property but can be quickly generated resulting table sizes smaller than non-minimal perfect hash functions.

GPERF [2] is a freely available minimal perfect hash function generator, written by Douglas Schmidt, that can generate a near-perfect hash function, or minimal perfect hash function, or non-minimal perfect hash function in C or C++ , given a static set of identifiers. This has been used in academic compiler environments and in GNU C/C++ compilers.

Example 10.11

The following example of a minimal perfect hash function is adapted from Cichelli [1], used for the static dataset of 36 keywords or reserved words of the programming language Pascal. Pascal is a block-structured programming language used mainly in academia during the period 1975-1990.

Keywords of Pascal: DO, END, ELSE, CASE, DOWNTO, GOTO, TO, OTH-
ERWISE, TYPE, WHILE, CONST, DIV, AND, SET, OR, OF, MOD, FILE, RECORD,
PACKED, NOT, THEN, PROCEDURE, WITH, REPEAT, VAR, IN, ARRAY, IF,
NIL, FOR, BEGIN, UNTIL, LABEL, FUNCTION, PROGRAM.

The associated values for each alphabet are as follows: A = 11, B = 15, C = 1,
D = 0, E = 0, F = 15, G = 3, H = 15, I = 13, J = 0 , K = 0, L = 15, M = 15, N = 13,
O = 0, P = 15, Q = 0, R = 14, S = 6, T = 6, U = 14, V = 10, W = 6, X = 0, Y = 13,
Z = 0.

The minimal perfect hash function of a keyword as given by Cichelli is defined
as being equal to

key length + associated value of first character + associated value of last character.

For instance, for the keyword "WHILE", the hash value = 5 + value of "W" +
value of "E" = 5 + 6 + 0 = 11. The reader is urged to verify that the above function is
indeed a minimal perfect hashing function.

As a final thought on hash functions, it is important to know that hashed values
are difficult to sort. The hash functions that spread the data out uniformly and the
equally fair collision resolving techniques make it difficult to find order in the hashed
table. Hence alternatives to hashing would have to be looked into if data needs to be
sorted or even a partial ordering of data items is needed.

10.10   Hashing with STL's map and multimap Containers

A map container has all the features of a set container and it allows elements to be
accessed using a key. The data type for the key can be different from that of the elements stored in the map. For example, information on students can be stored with student identifier (a string) as the key and other data on the students as the corresponding
value. The value can be retrieved from the map container by specifying the associated
key. As in the case of set container, the map container does not allow duplicate elements to be stored. The multimap container allows multiple values to be stored for the
same key value. The map and multimap containers are implemented in the standard
template library using the red-black tree data structure.

In the following we will describe how a map container can be used and then we
will proceed to learn how a multimap can be used to implement a hash table. Note
that the return value of the hash function will be the key to the multimap container.
The following statement creates a map container called stocks. Each stock (that are

publicly traded in the stock market) has a unique symbol (a char★) and has a current price (a float).

■ ```
map<char*, float, less<char*>> stocks;
```

The first component in the template for map object above indicates the data type for the key, the second component the data type for the values, and the third component less<char ★> is used to make sure that the keys are kept in the ascending order.

Given a stock symbol which is the key we should be able to retrieve its current price. In order to demonstrate this, let us first add a set of individual stocks to the stocks container. The insert method on the map container takes a pair object as its argument (discussed in Chapter 6). The following statement creates a pair object with the name oneStock. The two values for the pair object are name of the stock and its current price.

■ ```
pair<char*, float> oneStock ("AMZN", 35.12);
```

The statement to insert the pair object into the map containers is written as:

■ ```
oneStock.insert (oneStock);
```

The elements in a map can be accessed using the array style [] operator. For example, to access the price of the stock with the symbol "AMZN" one can write as follows:

```
cout << oneStock["AMZN"] << endl; // 35.12 will be output
oneStock["AMZN"] = 40.50; //AMZN has a new price of 40.50
```

Iterator, find, erase, size, and other methods that are available for the set container are also available for the map container. The multimap container is similar to the map container except that more than one value can be associated with a particular key. Note that the array style [] operator cannot be applied on a multimap object. The count method on the multimap object with the key value as a parameter returns the number of values containing the key value. All the values for a key can be extracted by first performing a lookup using the find method which returns an iterator and iterating on it.

One may view the multimap as a hash table with the hash function generating the key. The multimap container can be thought of using chaining as a mechanism to resolve collisions. This concept is illustrated in the code segment given below.
```

```cpp
#include <iostream.h>
#include <set>
#include <algorithm>
using namespace std;

int main ()
{
    multimap<char*, float, less<char*>> hashStocks;
    multimap<char*, float, less<char*>>:: iterator k;
    pair<char*, float> p1 ("AMZN", 35.12);
    pair<char*, float> p2 ("AMZN", 40.50);
    pair<char*, float> p3 ("AMZN", 28.10);
    pair<char*, float> p4 ("INTL", 35.12);
    pair<char*, float> p5 ("MSFT", 30.12);
    pair<char*, float> p6 ("MSFT", 26.66);

    hashStocks.insert(p1);
    hashStocks.insert(p2);
    hashStocks.insert(p3);
    hashStocks.insert(p4);
    hashStocks.insert(p5);
    hashStocks.insert(p6);

    cout << "Number of values for AMZN is " << hashStocks.
    cout("AMZN");
    cout << endl;

    k = hashStocks.find("AMZN");

    while (k != hashStocks.end())
    {
        cout << (*k).first << " has a value of "
                        << (*k).second << endl;
        k++; //overloaded ++ that moves the iterator the next
            // element in the chain.
    }
}
```

The above program will have the following output.

```
Number of values for AMZN is 3
AMZN has a value of 35.12
AMZN has a value of 40.50
AMZN has a value of 28.10
```

The methods for the map adapter are exactly the same as for the set adapter and it also has the overloaded array style [] operator. The multimap adapter is exactly the same as the set adapter and in addition provides the *count* method as described above.

10.11   Exercises

10.1.   Given the following 10 keywords of Pascal DO, END, ELSE, CASE, DOWNTO, GOTO, TO, OTHERWISE, TYPE, WHILE, associated values for each of the alphabets as given in Example 10.11, and the hash functions as shown below, compute the hash values for each keyword.

(a) (sum of associated values for each letter in the keyword) *mod* 11
(b) (length of keyword + sum of associated values for each letter in the keyword) mod 11

10.2.   For problem 10.1, to resolve collisions use the following methods and illustrate by means of relevant diagrams:

(a) linear probing
(b) quadratic probing, and
(c) separate chaining.

10.3.   Find a smallest prime number *m* such that the following keys are hashed without collisions using the hash function $h(K) = K$ mod *m*.

$\{12, 22, 41, 48, 56, 85, 140, 209\}$

10.4.   Assume there exists a C++ method *int* hash (*const char* *key, *int* hashvalue) that takes a key and obtains a hashvalue, write methods for insertion, deletion, and searching using the following hash techniques:

(a) linear probing
(b) quadratic probing, and
(c) separate chaining

10.5.   A variation of double hashing is called *linear-quotienthashing* and it uses the remainder and the quotient given by the modulus *m*. The hash function is $h_1(K) = K$ mod *m* and $h_2(K) = ((K$ div *m*) mod (*m*-1)) + 1 is the increment. Implement double hashing and linear-quotient hashing and compare their performance for 100, 200, 300, and 1000 lookups and inserts randomly mixed together.

10.6.   Write a C++ program to implement the hashing with separate chaining method. You need to write your program in such a way that each element of the hash table is a linked list. Use the AVL-trees instead of linked list and compare both the implementations with large number of inserts and searches.

10.7.   Discuss the pros and cons of static hashing versus dynamic hashing schemes.

10.8.   Assume there exists a C++ method *int* hash (*constchar* ★key, *int* hashvalue) that takes a key and obtains a hashvalue, write methods for insertion, deletion, and searching using the directory-based dynamic hashing.

10.9.   For the following list of frequently occurring words in English use GPERF to obtain a minimal perfect hash function.

{*I, it, the, that, at, are, a, is, to, this, as, he, and, have, in, not, be, but, his, had, or, on, was, of, her, by, you, with, which, for, from.*}

10.10.   Compile the list of keywords in C++, and use GPERF to obtain a minimal perfect hash function.

10.11.   In the separate chaining method, overflows are handled by linked lists which only support sequential search. Discuss an implementation where the overflows handled by binary search trees. Write C++ methods to perform the operations of deletion, insertion and search. Analyze the asymptotic complexity of the search method.

10.12.   Write an efficient C++ function to sort a table that is hashed by a minimal perfect hash function. Obtain its time-complexity.

10.13.   Commercial database servers such as Oracle, and DB2 use hashing in creating objects called *clusters*. Clusters play a role in keeping data together for efficient retrieval. Choose one commercial database and write a short report explaining the role of hash functions in that database.

10.12   **References for Further Reading**

R.J. Cichelli. "Minimal Perfect Hash Functions Made Simple", Communications of the ACM, vol. 21, no. 1, pp.17–19–1980.

D.C. Schmidt. "GPERF: A perfect hash function generator", http:/www.cs.wustl.edu/~schmidt/

D.E. Knuth, "The Art of Computer Programming, vol. 1: Searching and Sorting. Addison-Wesley, 1973.

R.J. Enbody, and H.C. Du, "Dynamic Hashing Schemes", ACM Computing Surveys, vol. 20, No. 2, pp. 85–113, 1988.

P.K. Pearson, "Fast Hashing of Variable Length Text Strings", Communications of the ACM, vol. 33, No.6, pp. 677–680, 1990.

11   Graphs

W E SAW IN the earlier chapters that entities are modeled as "nodes" and that they are connected by "links" to establish the desired relationship amongst them. For example, nodes in a singly linked list are connected using the next link (pointer), and the desired relationships that this establishes are "before" and "after." The binary tree data structure establishes the relationships of "parent", "children", "siblings", "grandparent", and "grand children." *Graphs* are used to represent very general relationships between entities. Graphs can be created to model relationships that are established in linked lists and binary trees as well as many others.

A graph consists of a set of vertices and a set of edges connecting pairs of vertices. The vertices themselves may be complex objects; if the vertices represented cities, they might have names, populations, and locations by latitude and longitude. The edges may also be complex objects; in particular, an edge may have a numeric weight representing some measure of the cost of traversing the edge. This might be distance, if the edges represent highways, or ticket cost, if they represent air routes. If the edges have such weights, then the graph is a *weighted graph*, but otherwise it is an *unweighted graph*.

Just as city streets may be one-way or two-way, edges may be either *directed* or *undirected*. An undirected edge may be traversed in either direction, and the vertices joined by it are said to be *neighbors*. A directed edge can be traversed in only one direction, from the starting vertex to the ending vertex; the ending vertex is a neighbor of the starting vertex, but not vice versa. If the edges are directed, then the graph is a *directed graph*, but otherwise it is an *undirected graph*.

As seen from the above example, graphs can model many real-life entities and relationships. Such modeling has allowed algorithmic researchers to determine algorithms for many real-life problems. For example, using the graph modeling above for cities and distances between them, we have efficient algorithms to determine the shortest distance between two cities. Computer communication networks are modeled as graphs. Many optimization problems for computer communication networks require algorithms on graph structures. These include finding the shortest path to route a packet from source to destination, determining how error–resilient a network is to node and link failures, finding nodes to place information that is quickly accessible to all other nodes in the network, and many others.

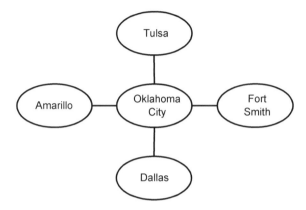

Figure 11.1: Example of a graph modeling cities and highways between them.

In this chapter, we will define terms and terminology associated with graphs. We will study the adjacency matrix and adjacency list representation of the graph, and define the abstract base Graph class that provides us with the interface to access elements of the graph in a uniform way without regard to what the underlying storage for the graph is. We will examine two commonly used approaches to traverse the nodes of the graph and present applications of these traversal mechanisms, and also study two classical optimization problems; the shortest path problems and the minimum spanning tree problem. As part of implementing an algorithm to compute the minimum spanning tree, we will also introduce a new data structure called the union-find data structure.

11.1 Terminology

A graph $G = (V, E)$ consists of a set of *vertices* $V = \{v_1, v_2, \ldots,\}$, and a set of edges $E = \{e_1, e_2, \ldots\}$ such that each edge e_i is identified with an ordered or unordered pair (v, v) of vertices. Edges of the kind (v_i, v_i) are called *self-loops*. If a graph has two edges between any two nodes, they are called *parallel edges*. A graph is a *simple graph* if it does not have any self-loops or parallel edges. A graph is said to be *undirected* if the edges are considered to have unordered vertices (Figure 11.2 (a)) and it is called *directed* (Figure 11.2 (b)) if the edges have ordered pairs of vertices. The first member of the ordered pair of the vertices will be referred to as the *source* (or *tail*) vertex and the second member as the *destination* (or *head*) vertex. An edge with an ordered pair of vertices is called an *arc*.

For each vertex in the undirected graph the *degree* of the vertex is the number of edges that contain the vertex. In a directed graph, the *outdegree* and *indegree* of a vertex are the number of edges in which the vertex is a source and destination, respectively. In an undirected graph, it can be easily seen that the sum of the degrees of the vertices is equal to twice the number of edges in the graph. More interestingly, it can be shown that the number of vertices of odd degree in an undirected graph is always even.

A graph $G' = (V', E')$ is a *subgraph* of $G = (V, E)$ if and only if $V' \subseteq V$ and $E' \subseteq E$. A *path* is a sequence of edges with the property that two edges adjacent in the sequence have a vertex in common. For example, $(v_0, v_1), (v_1, v_2), (v_2, v_3), \ldots (v_{k-1}, v_k)$ is a path (example, Figure 11.2 (c)) and the *length* of a path is the number of edges in the path. A path is *simple* if no two edges in the path are the same. A simple path is a *cycle* if the last vertex in the path is the same as the first vertex in the path. For example, in the path above if $v_k = v_0$, then the path is a cycle. A *directed path* (example, Figure 11.2 (d)) is a sequence of arcs $A_0, A_1, \ldots, A_k$ such that for any two arcs A_i and A_{i+1}, the destination vertex of A_i is the source vertex in A_{i+1}. A directed path is a directed cycle if the destination vertex of the last node in the path is the same the source vertex of the first node in the path.

Two vertices are *connected* in the graph (resp. directed graph) if and only if there is a simple path (resp. simple directed path) between them in the graph (resp. directed graph). A graph (resp. directed graph) is *connected* (resp. *strongly connected* (Figure 11.2 (g))) if and only if every pair of vertices is connected. A subgraph S is called a *connected component* (Figure 11.2 (f)) (resp. *strongly connected component* (Figure 11.2(g))) if and only if it is connected. A graph with no cycles is called an *acyclic* graph. A connected graph is a *tree* if it contains no cycles. Any graph is a *forest of trees* if in each of its connected components is a *tree*. A subgraph $T = (V, E')$ is called a *spanning tree* (Figure 11.2 (h)) of the connected graph $G = (V, E)$ if and only if T is a tree.

11.2   Representations of Graphs

A graph is said to be *sparse* if the number of edges in the graph is of $O(n)$, where n is the number of vertices in the graph, or otherwise it is called *dense*. In a *complete* graph (where, for every pair of vertices in the graph, there is an edge), the number of edges is $O(n^2)$. In the following discussion, n will represent the number of vertices and m the number of edges in the graph. There are two ways a graph can be stored: adjacency matrix and adjacency lists.

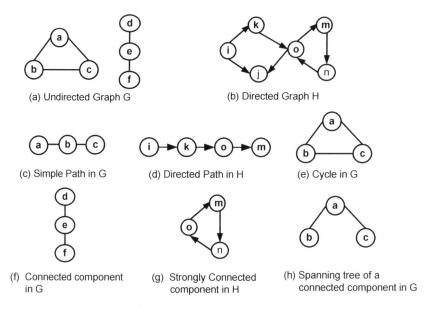

Figure 11.2: Various terminologies associated with graphs.

The graph G can be stored in matrix A, called the adjacency matrix. Each element A[i][j] of the matrix semantically refers to the edge between vertex i and vertex j. If A[i][j] = 1 we will say that there is an edge between vertices i and j; otherwise A[i][j] will be 0. Given an n-vertex graph, the space needed to store the graph using the adjacency matrix is $O(n^2)$. The storage requirement using an adjacency matrix is not dependent on the number of edges of the graph; it depends solely on the number of vertices. The relationship between the graph and its adjacency matrix is shown below.

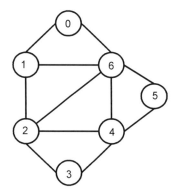

Figure 11.3: A graph with seven vertices.

	0	1	2	3	4	5	6
0	1	1	0	0	0	0	1
1	1	1	1	0	0	0	1
2	0	1	1	1	1	0	1
3	0	0	1	1	1	0	0
4	0	0	1	1	1	1	1
5	0	0	0	0	1	1	1
6	1	1	1	0	1	1	1

Figure 11.4:   The adjacency matrix for the graph in Figure 11.3.

Note that if $A[i][i] = 1$, for all $0 \leq i \leq 6$, each vertex is considered to be connected to itself. The adjacency matrix is symmetric and hence $A[i][j] = A[j][i]$; since edges have no directions, vertex i is connected to vertex j and vice versa. If the graph is a directed graph, the matrix need not be symmetric as there might be an arc from i to j but not vice versa. We can assign weights to the edges of the graph. For example, the weight on the edge from vertex i to vertex j could correspond either to the distance between vertices i and j or to some other cost factor. In this case the matrix A will have elements whose values represent either distance or cost.

We will now present a data structure called the adjacency list that can be used to store a graph and whose size is a function of the number of vertices and edges. An adjacency list requires $O(n+m)$ storage. The number of edges in the graph can be at most $O(n^2)$ when there is an edge from every vertex to every other vertex, but the number of edges might be as little as zero. If the graph is dense, the space requirements for adjacency matrix and adjacency list would be the same since m would be $O(n^2)$. But if the graph is sparse, that is, if the number of edges m is $O(n)$ then an adjacency list is the obvious choice. Of course, the comparison above is based on the Big-Oh notation.

Let us study this more carefully. Consider the un-weighted graph. The adjacency matrix can be matrix of Booleans; true representing presence of an edge, false otherwise. The number of bits required for the adjacency representation is n^2. In the adjacency list representation as shown below in Figure 11.6, we first need an array containing n pointers. Assuming the size of each pointer is 32 bits (at least majority of the current computers are 32 bit machines). The total number of bits required for the array is 32*n*. For each edge (u, v) in the graph, we have two nodes in the adjacency list; one in the linked list of u and the other in the linked list of v (see Figure 11.6). Each node has two elements: node number and a pointer to the next element. A node number can be represented using at most 32 bits (or least log*n* bits).and the pointer takes at most 32 bits and hence each node requires at most 64 bits. Hence the total number of bits consumed by the adjacency list representation is $64n + 2\times64m$. If the graph is dense, the number of bits required by the adjacency list representation is significantly higher.

The adjacency list is an array of linked lists. Each element *i* of the array corresponds to a vertex *i* of the graph. Each array index *i* contains a reference to a linked list that has elements corresponding to the edges connecting vertex *i* to its neighbors in the graph. The graph and its adjacency lists are shown below.

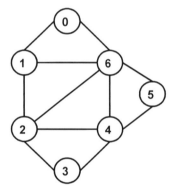

Figure 11.5:   A graph with seven vertices.

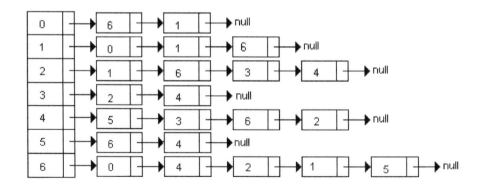

Figure 11.6:   The corresponding adjacency list representation.

Clearly, in an undirected graph, each edge of the graph appears in the adjacency list twice, one for each end, while in a directed graph each edge appears only once, in the linked list for the vertex at which it begins. In either case, the storage requirements are O($n+m$).

11.3   Abstract Data Type

In considering the abstract data type of a graph, we must bear in mind the fact that there are really four different types of graphs: weighted directed, unweighted directed, weighted undirected, unweighted undirected. However, they have a great deal in common, so we may write a basic graph abstract data type which all must satisfy:

```
create (n)
    // creates a graph with n vertices and no edges
vertexCount ()
    // returns the number of vertices
edgeCount ()
    // returns the number of edges
hasEdge (start, end)
    // returns true if the edge (start, end) exists in the
    // graph, otherwise false
neighbors (v)
    // returns the neighbors of vertex v
vertexInfo (v)
    // returns any data stored with the vertex v
edgeWeight (start, end)
    // returns the weight of the edge (start, end) if the edge
    // exists, otherwise returns 0;
    // in an unweighted graph, returns 1 if the edge exists
edgeInfo (start, end)
    // returns any data stored with the edge (start, end)
addEdge (start, end)
    // adds the edge (start, end) to the graph
deleteEdge (start, end)
    // deletes the edge (start, end)
```

11.4   The Graph Classes

We have seen that graphs may be represented two different ways: adjacency matrix and adjacency list. The implementations will be dramatically different, and yet there is clearly a close relationship between them. It would be helpful if they supported the same methods and could be used in the same code; to produce this result, an abstract base class is essential.

11.4.1   Node Data Type

We desire maximum flexibility in our new graph classes, so we must consider what data is to be stored for the vertices themselves. The graph classes themselves make no use of the data stored in the vertices; as far as they are concerned, a vertex might be referenced by number and have no associated data. However, the user may wish to store data for each vertex, so we will provide for that in our template. Again, the graph classes have no interest in the edge data, other than the beginning and ending vertices, and perhaps the weight, but the user might wish to associate data with an edge (e.g., if edges represent highways, we may wish to give each highway an associated name), so we will provide for that also in our template.

11.4.2   Exceptions

The graph classes will not concern themselves with the data stored with a vertex or an edge, so we need no exceptions with regard to that data. The weighted graph classes will not concern themselves with the weights of edges, as they have no way of knowing a priori what weights are appropriate, so we need no exceptions with regard to the weights. Therefore, the only possible errors would be an attempt to create a graph with a negative number of vertices, an attempt to access a vertex outside of the available set, an attempt to create an edge of which one end is not part of the available set, an attempt to change an edge which does not exist, or an attempt to add an edge which already exists. Additionally, of course, we might always run out of memory. Our family of graph exceptions is then as follows:

```
class GraphException : public Exception { };
class GraphDuplicateEdge : public GraphException { };
class GraphEdgeOutOfBounds : public GraphException { };
class GraphMemory : public GraphException { };
class GraphNegativeCount : public GraphException { };
class GraphNonExistentEdge : public GraphException { };
class GraphVertexOutOfBounds : public GraphException { };
```

11.4.3   Abstract Base Classes

Armed with the above abstract data type and the exceptions, we can now write the abstract base classes for the graph class family we will construct. First, there is the base class from which all graph classes must descend. The reader should note, below, that a graph has two classes in its template: *VertexObject* and *EdgeObject*. The user of the class is therefore forced to declare types for both vertices and objects, even if the application does not require any data to be stored with them. This is simply a side effect of the "template" structure, and can be handled by simply declaring *VertexObject* and *EdgeObject* both to be *int*.

```
template <class VertexObject, class EdgeObject>
class AbstractGraph
{
public:
    virtual ~AbstractGraph ();
    virtual int vertexCount () = NULL;
        // returns the number of vertices
    virtual int edgeCount () = NULL;
        // returns the number of edges
    virtual bool hasEdge (int start, int end) = NULL;
        // returns true if the edge (start, end) exists in the
        // graph, otherwise false
    virtual VertexObject& vertexInfo (int v) = NULL;
        // returns any data stored with the vertex v
    virtual double edgeWeight (int start, int end) = NULL;
        // returns the weight of the edge (start, end) if the
        // edge exists, otherwise returns 0;
```

```
        // in an unweighted graph, returns 1 if the edge exists
    virtual EdgeObject& edgeInfo (int start, int end) = NULL;
        // returns any data stored with the edge (start, end)
    virtual Vector<int> neighbors (int v) = NULL;
        // returns the neighbors of vertex v
    virtual void setVertexInfo
            (int v, VertexObject& info) = NULL;
        // sets the data stored with the vertex v
    virtual void setEdgeInfo
            (int start, int end, EdgeObject& info) = NULL;
        // sets the data stored with the edge (start, end)
    virtual void deleteEdge (int start, int end) = NULL;
        // deletes the edge (start, end)
};
// -----------------------------------------------------------
template <class VertexObject, class EdgeObject>
AbstractGraph<VertexObject,EdgeObject>::~AbstractGraph () { }
```

The abstract base class above does not provide a method to add edges. It is clear that weighted and unweighted graphs will differ in the type of data they store with respect to their edges, and that the weighted graph must require the user to add an edge with a weight, which the unweighted graph will not. This means that the weighted and unweighted graphs must differ in the signatures of their methods to add edges.

From the description above of the adjacency matrix and adjacency list structures, the reader may have noted that an undirected edge (*a,b*) is stored as if it were two directed edges, (*a,b*) and (*b,a*). Therefore, even an undirected class has the ability to store directed edges, although we do not wish to make that ability available to the user.

In other words, from the point of view of implementation, the four types of graph differ only in the methods they offer to add edges. Therefore, we need two abstract classes descended from that above, each providing different methods for adding edges:

```
template <class VertexObject, class EdgeObject>
class AbstractWeightedGraph :
    virtual public AbstractGraph<VertexObject, EdgeObject> {
public:
    virtual ~AbstractWeightedGraph ();
    virtual void addEdge
        (int start, int end, double weight) = NULL;
    virtual void addEdge (int start, int end,
        double weight, EdgeObject& info) = NULL;
};
// ---------------------------------------------------------
template <class VertexObject, class EdgeObject>
AbstractWeightedGraph<VertexObject,EdgeObject>::
    ~AbstractWeightedGraph () { }
// ---------------------------------------------------------
template <class VertexObject, class EdgeObject>
class AbstractUnweightedGraph :
    virtual public AbstractGraph<VertexObject, EdgeObject> {
public:
    virtual ~AbstractUnweightedGraph ();
    virtual void addEdge (int start, int end) = NULL;
    virtual void addEdge (int start, int end,
        EdgeObject& info) = NULL;
};
// ---------------------------------------------------------
template <class VertexObject, class EdgeObject>
AbstractUnweightedGraph<VertexObject,EdgeObject>::
    ~AbstractUnweightedGraph () { }
```

Displaying a Graph

We can write the display() method as we have for our other data structures and write
an ostream operator that calls the display() method.

```
template <class VertexObject, class EdgeObject>
AbstractWeightedGraph<VertexObject,EdgeObject>::
                    display(ostream& os)
{
  bool first = true;
  os << "Vertices: [";
  for (int i = 0; i < vertexCount(); i++) {
      if (first) first = false;
      else os << ", ";
      os << "(" << i << ") " << vertexInfo(i);
  }
  os << "]; Edges: [";
  first = true;
  for (int i = 0; i < vertexCount(); i++) {
      for (int j = 0; j < vertexCount(); j++)
      if (hasEdge(i,j))
      {
          if (first) first = false;
          else os << ", ";
          os << "(" << i << "," << j << ") " << edgeInfo(i,j);
      }
  }
  os << "]";
}
// ----------------------------------------------------------
template <class VertexObject, class EdgeObject>
ostream& operator<< (ostream& os,
  AbstractGraph<VertexObject,EdgeObject>& g)
{
  g.display(os);
  return os;
}
```

11.4.4   Class Definition for Adjacency Matrix Representation

We can now begin our definition of the class, which will represent a graph using an adjacency matrix representation.

Fields, Constructors, and Destructor

We know that an n-vertex graph will require an $n \times n$ matrix to represent the edges. What about edge data and vertex data? We must store vertex data separately, in its own array, but we could store edge data in the same $n \times n$ matrix. Should we? For efficiency's sake, we might not want to, as a given application might make no use of the edge data. In this discussion, we will use two $n \times n$ matrices, and will leave it as an exercise for the reader to handle the second matrix efficiently. Our class, initially, is as follows:

```
template <class VertexObject, class EdgeObject>
class GraphMatrix :
    virtual public AbstractGraph<VertexObject, EdgeObject>
{
protected:
    ArrayClass<VertexObject>* vertexData;
    Matrix<double>* edges;
    Matrix<EdgeObject>* edgeData;
public:
    GraphMatrix (int n);
    virtual ~GraphMatrix ();
};
// ----------------------------------------------------------
template <class VertexObject, class EdgeObject>
GraphMatrix <VertexObject, EdgeObject>::GraphMatrix (int n)
{
    vertexData = new ArrayClass<VertexObject> (n);
    edges = new Matrix<double> (n,n,0.0);
    edgeData = new Matrix<EdgeObject> (n,n);
}
// ----------------------------------------------------------
template <class VertexObject, class EdgeObject>
GraphMatrix <VertexObject, EdgeObject>::~GraphMatrix ()
{
    if (vertexData != NULL) delete vertexData;
    if (edges != NULL) delete edges;
    if (edgeData != NULL) delete edgeData;
}
```

Accessor Methods

The method for reporting the number of vertices is quite simple.

```
template <class VertexObject, class EdgeObject>
int GraphMatrix <VertexObject, EdgeObject>::vertexCount()
{
    return vertexData->size();
}
```

The method for reporting the number of edges will require us to actually count them, by iterating through the matrix (alternatively, we could have kept a count of edges, but this is left to the reader). We assume that edges with weight 0 do not exist (the reader may wish to modify the code to use another value):

```
template <class VertexObject, class EdgeObject>
int GraphMatrix <VertexObject, EdgeObject>::edgeCount()
{
    int count = 0;
    for (int i = 0; i < edges->rows(); i++)
    {
        for (int j = 0; j < edges->rows(); j++)
            if ((*edges)[i][j] != 0.0) count++;
    }
    return count;
}
```

The method for reporting the data stored for a vertex is also simple (note that there is no automatic initialization of data, so if no data has been stored, the result is random). If the user requests data that is "out of bounds", we must throw an exception to signal the problem.

```
template <class VertexObject, class EdgeObject>
VertexObject& GraphMatrix <VertexObject,
                            EdgeObject>::vertexInfo(int v) {
    if ((v < 0) || (v >= vertexCount()))
        throw GraphVertexOutOfBounds();
    return (*vertexData)[v];
}
```

The methods for reporting whether an edge exists, and determining the edge weight and the data associated with an edge, are straightforward:

```
template <class VertexObject, class EdgeObject>
bool GraphMatrix <VertexObject, EdgeObject>::
                                    hasEdge (int start, int end)
{
    if ((start < 0) || (start >= vertexCount())
        || (end < 0) || (end >= vertexCount()))
            throw GraphEdgeOutOfBounds();
    return ((*edges)[start][end] != 0.0);
}
// ----------------------------------------------------------
template <class VertexObject, class EdgeObject>
EdgeObject& GraphMatrix <VertexObject, EdgeObject>::
                                    edgeInfo (int start, int end)
{
    if ((start < 0) || (start >= vertexCount())
        || (end < 0) || (end >= vertexCount())
        || (!hasEdge(start,end)))
            throw GraphEdgeOutOfBounds();
    return (*edgeData)[start][end];
}
// ----------------------------------------------------------
template <class VertexObject, class EdgeObject>
double GraphMatrix <VertexObject, EdgeObject>::
                                    edgeWeight (int start, int end)
{
    if ((start < 0) || (start >= vertexCount())
        || (end < 0) || (end >= vertexCount()))
            throw GraphEdgeOutOfBounds();
    return (*edges)[start][end];
}
```

For our last accessor method, we would like to return a list of neighbors of a particular vertex. This will simply be a vector of integers, representing the numbers of the vertices in the graph. If the user needs the actual data for the neighbors, the *vertexInfo*() method can supply it.

```
template <class VertexObject, class EdgeObject>
Vector<int> GraphMatrix <VertexObject, EdgeObject>::
                         neighbors (int v)
{
    Vector<int> result;
    if ((v < 0) ||(v >= vertexCount())) return result;
    for (int i = 0; i < vertexCount(); i++)
        if ((*edges)[v][i] != 0.0) result.add (i);
    return result;
}
```

Mutator Methods

One mutator method declared in the *Graph* base class can be readily implemented: it is *setVertexInfo ()*, which is sufficiently simple that it can be left to the reader's imagination. However, the other two mutator methods are more difficult: they are *setEdgeInfo ()* and *deleteEdge ()*. If we are implementing a directed graph, then *deleteEdge (1,2)* will delete the edge from vertex 1 to vertex 2, but the edge from vertex 2 to vertex 1 will be unaffected. However, if we are implementing an undirected graph, the edge from vertex 2 to vertex 1 will also be deleted. Similarly, *setEdgeInfo ()* will affect only the edge in one direction in a directed graph, but the edges in both directions in an undirected graph. We therefore need to implement these two methods, along with the *addEdge ()* methods, in subclasses.

However, the basic operation of deleting one (directed) edge will be common to all subclasses, so we will implement it as a protected method of the *GraphMatrix* class:

```
template <class VertexObject, class EdgeObject>
void GraphMatrix <VertexObject, EdgeObject>::_deleteEdge
            (int start, int end)
{
    if ((start < 0) || (start >= vertexCount())
        || (end < 0) || (end >= vertexCount())
        || (!hasEdge(start,end)))
            throw GraphEdgeOutOfBounds();
    (*edges)[start][end] = 0.0;
}
```

Subclasses

We have said that graphs may be directed or undirected, weighted or unweighted. This means that we have four different possible types of graph: undirected and unweighted, directed and unweighted, undirected and weighted, and directed and weighted. We can design four subclasses of *GraphMatrix*, implementing the four types of graph. As they are all fairly straightforward, we present only the undirected and unweighted graph and the directed and weighted graph. The reader can implement the other two.

```
template <class VertexObject, class EdgeObject>
class WeightedDirectedGraphMatrix :
    public GraphMatrix <VertexObject, EdgeObject>,
    virtual public AbstractWeightedGraph<VertexObject,EdgeObject>
{
public:
    WeightedDirectedGraphMatrix (int n);
    virtual ~WeightedDirectedGraphMatrix ();
    virtual void setEdgeInfo
            (int start, int end, EdgeObject& info);
        // sets the data stored with the edge (start, end)
    virtual void deleteEdge (int start, int end);
    virtual void addEdge (int start, int end, double weight);
    virtual void addEdge
        (int start, int end, double weight, EdgeObject& info);
};
// -----------------------------------------------------------
template <class VertexObject, class EdgeObject>
WeightedDirectedGraphMatrix <VertexObject, EdgeObject>::
    WeightedDirectedGraphMatrix (int n)
    : GraphMatrix<VertexObject,EdgeObject> (n) { }
// -----------------------------------------------------------
template <class VertexObject, class EdgeObject>
WeightedDirectedGraphMatrix <VertexObject, EdgeObject>::
    ~WeightedDirectedGraphMatrix () { }
// -----------------------------------------------------------
template <class VertexObject, class EdgeObject>
void WeightedDirectedGraphMatrix <VertexObject, EdgeObject>::
        deleteEdge (int start, int end)
{
```

```
        _deleteEdge (start, end);
}
// ----------------------------------------------------------
template <class VertexObject, class EdgeObject>
void WeightedDirectedGraphMatrix <VertexObject, EdgeObject>::
        addEdge (int start, int end, double weight)
{
    if ((start < 0) || (start >= vertexCount())
        || (end < 0) || (end >= vertexCount()))
            throw GraphEdgeOutOfBounds();
    if (hasEdge(start,end)) throw GraphDuplicateEdge();
    (*edges)[start][end] = weight;
}
// ----------------------------------------------------------
template <class VertexObject, class EdgeObject>
void WeightedDirectedGraphMatrix <VertexObject, EdgeObject>::
    addEdge(int start,int end,double weight,EdgeObject& info)
{
    if ((start < 0) || (start >= vertexCount())
        || (end < 0) || (end >= vertexCount()))
            throw GraphEdgeOutOfBounds();
    if (hasEdge(start,end)) throw GraphDuplicateEdge();
    (*edges)[start][end] = weight;
    (*edgeData)[start][end] = info;
}
// ----------------------------------------------------------
template <class VertexObject, class EdgeObject>
void WeightedDirectedGraphMatrix <VertexObject, EdgeObject>::
        setEdgeInfo (int start, int end, EdgeObject& info)
{
    if ((start < 0) || (start >= vertexCount())
        || (end < 0) || (end >= vertexCount())
        || (!hasEdge(start,end)))
            throw GraphEdgeOutOfBounds();
    (*edgeData)[start][end] = info;
}
```

```
class UnweightedUndirectedGraphMatrix :
    public GraphMatrix <VertexObject, EdgeObject>,
    virtual public AbstractUnweightedGraph<VertexObject,
    EdgeObject>
{
public:
    UnweightedUndirectedGraphMatrix (int n);
    virtual ~UnweightedUndirectedGraphMatrix ();
    virtual int edgeCount();
    virtual void deleteEdge (int start, int end);
    virtual void addEdge (int start, int end);
    virtual void addEdge
        (int start, int end, EdgeObject& info);
};
// -----------------------------------------------------------
template <class VertexObject, class EdgeObject>
UnweightedUndirectedGraphMatrix <VertexObject, EdgeObject>::
    UnweightedUndirectedGraphMatrix (int n)
    : GraphMatrix<VertexObject,EdgeObject> (n) { }
// -----------------------------------------------------------
template <class VertexObject, class EdgeObject>
UnweightedUndirectedGraphMatrix <VertexObject, EdgeObject>::
    ~UnweightedUndirectedGraphMatrix () { }
// -----------------------------------------------------------
template <class VertexObject, class EdgeObject>
void UnweightedUndirectedGraphMatrix <VertexObject,
    EdgeObject>::deleteEdge (int start, int end)
{
    _deleteEdge (start, end);
    _deleteEdge (end, start);
}
// -----------------------------------------------------------
template <class VertexObject, class EdgeObject>
void UnweightedUndirectedGraphMatrix <VertexObject,
    EdgeObject>::addEdge (int start, int end)
```

```
{
    if ((start < 0) || (start >= vertexCount())
        || (end < 0) || (end >= vertexCount()))
            throw GraphEdgeOutOfBounds();
    if (hasEdge(start,end)) throw GraphDuplicateEdge();
    (*edges)[start][end] = 1;
    (*edges)[end][start] = 1;
}
// ----------------------------------------------------------
template <class VertexObject, class EdgeObject>
void UnweightedUndirectedGraphMatrix <VertexObject,
  EdgeObject>::addEdge (int start, int end, EdgeObject& info)
{
    if ((start < 0) || (start >= vertexCount())
        || (end < 0) || (end >= vertexCount()))
            throw GraphEdgeOutOfBounds();
    if (hasEdge(start,end)) throw GraphDuplicateEdge();
    (*edges)[start][end] = 1;
    (*edgeData)[start][end] = info;

    (*edges)[end][start] = 1;
    (*edgeData)[end][start] = info;
}
// ----------------------------------------------------------
template <class VertexObject, class EdgeObject>
int UnweightedUndirectedGraphMatrix <VertexObject,
    EdgeObject>::edgeCount()
{
    return GraphMatrix<VertexObject,EdgeObject>::edgeCount() /2;
}
// ----------------------------------------------------------
```

```
template <class VertexObject, class EdgeObject>
void UnweightedUndirectedGraphMatrix <VertexObject,
EdgeObject>::
        setEdgeInfo (int start, int end, EdgeObject& info)
{
    if ((start < 0) || (start >= vertexCount())
        || (end < 0) || (end >= vertexCount())
        || (!hasEdge(start,end)))
            throw GraphEdgeOutOfBounds();
    (*edgeData)[start][end] = info;
    (*edgeData)[end][start] = info;
}
```

11.4.5 Class Definition for Adjacency List Representation

Now we will implement the adjacency list representation of a graph, again basing our class *GraphList* on the *AbstractGraph* class.

Fields, Constructors, and Destructor

Since we are implementing an adjacency list, the *GraphList* class will need an array of linked lists. What sort of data is stored in the linked lists? Clearly we will need the end points of each edge, its weight (if the graph is weighted), and any other data associated with it. To collect all this data together, we need a helper class (EdgeContainer) and subclass (WeightedEdgeContainer) as follows:

```
template <class EdgeObject>
class EdgeContainer
{
public:
    int start;
    int end;
    EdgeObject info;
    EdgeContainer (int st, int en);
    EdgeContainer (int st, int en, EdgeObject& inf);
    virtual ~EdgeContainer () { }
};
```

```cpp
// ------------------------------------------------------------
template <class EdgeObject>
EdgeContainer<EdgeObject>::EdgeContainer (int st, int en)
{
    start = st;
    end = en;
}
// ------------------------------------------------------------
template <class EdgeObject>
EdgeContainer<EdgeObject>::EdgeContainer
    (int st, int en, EdgeObject& inf)
{
    start = st;
    end = en;
    info = inf;
}
// ------------------------------------------------------------
template <class EdgeObject>
class WeightedEdgeContainer : public EdgeContainer<EdgeObject>
{
public:
    double weight;
    WeightedEdgeContainer (int st, int en, double w);
    WeightedEdgeContainer (int st, int en, double w,
    EdgeObject& inf);
    virtual ~WeightedEdgeContainer () { }
};
// ------------------------------------------------------------
template <class EdgeObject>
WeightedEdgeContainer<EdgeObject>::WeightedEdgeContainer
    (int st, int en, double w)
        : EdgeContainer<EdgeObject> (st, en)
{
    weight = w;
}
// ------------------------------------------------------------
```

```
template <class EdgeObject>
WeightedEdgeContainer<EdgeObject>::WeightedEdgeContainer
    (int st, int en, double w, EdgeObject& inf)
        : EdgeContainer<EdgeObject> (st, en, inf)
{
    weight = w;
}
```

For our weighted subclasses of the *GraphList* class, to be developed, we will use *WeightedEdgeContainer* objects to represent edges; for unweighted subclasses, we will use *EdgeContainer* objects. This implies that the linked lists must contain pointers to *EdgeContainer* objects, not the objects themselves, so that we can achieve polymorphism through pointers.

We will also need an array of *VertexObjects*. So our adjacency list graph class initially looks like this:

```
template <class VertexObject, class EdgeObject>
class GraphList :
    virtual public AbstractGraph<VertexObject, EdgeObject>
{
protected:
    ArrayClass<VertexObject>* vertexData;
    ArrayClass< LinkedList< EdgeContainer<EdgeObject>* > >*
    edgeData;
public:
    GraphList (int n);
    virtual ~GraphList ();
};
// --------------------------------------------------------
template <class VertexObject, class EdgeObject>
GraphList <VertexObject, EdgeObject>::GraphList (int n)
{
    vertexData = new ArrayClass<VertexObject> (n);
    edgeData = new
        ArrayClass<LinkedList<EdgeContainer<EdgeObject>*>>(n);
}
```

```
// ------------------------------------------------------------
template <class VertexObject, class EdgeObject>
GraphList <VertexObject, EdgeObject>::~GraphList ()
{
    if (vertexData != NULL) delete vertexData;
    if (edgeData != NULL) delete edgeData;
}
```

Accessor Methods

The method for reporting the number of vertices is the same as that in *GraphMatrix*.

```
template <class VertexObject, class EdgeObject>
int GraphList <VertexObject, EdgeObject>::vertexCount()
{
    return vertexData->size();
}
```

The method for reporting the number of edges will require us to actually count them by iterating through the linked lists.

```
template <class VertexObject, class EdgeObject>
int GraphList <VertexObject, EdgeObject>::edgeCount()
{
    int count = 0;
    AbstractLinkedList< EdgeContainer<EdgeObject>* >* list;
    for (int i = 0; i < edgeData->size(); i++)
    {
        list = &((*edgeData)[i]);
        while ((list != NULL) && (!list->isEmpty()))
        {
            count++;
            list = list->next();
        }
    }
    return count;
}
```

The method for reporting the data stored for a vertex is the same as that for the *GraphMatrix* class, and is not repeated here.

The methods for reporting whether an edge exists and determining the edge weight and the data associated with an edge, all require us to iterate through a linked list until we find the required edge. Rather than repeat this code, we will write a small-protected method that either both locates and returns a pointer to the linked list holding a particular edge or NULL if the edge does not exist:

```cpp
template <class VertexObject, class EdgeObject>
AbstractLinkedList< EdgeContainer<EdgeObject>* >*
    GraphList <VertexObject, EdgeObject>::findEdge (int start,
            int end) {
    if ((start < 0) || (start >= vertexCount())
        || (end < 0) || (end >= vertexCount()))
            throw GraphEdgeOutOfBounds();

    AbstractLinkedList< EdgeContainer<EdgeObject>* >* list;
    list = &((*edgeData)[start]);
    while ((list != NULL) && (!list->isEmpty())) {
        if (list->info()->end == end) return list;
        list = list->next();
    }
    return NULL;
}
```

The *findEdge ()* method makes our *hasEdge ()* and *edgeInfo ()* methods very simple:

```cpp
template <class VertexObject, class EdgeObject>
bool GraphList <VertexObject, EdgeObject>::hasEdge
    (int start, int end)
{
    return (findEdge (start, end) != NULL);
}
// --------------------------------------------------------
```

```
template <class VertexObject, class EdgeObject>
EdgeObject& GraphList <VertexObject, EdgeObject>::edgeInfo
    (int start, int end)
{
    AbstractLinkedList< EdgeContainer<EdgeObject>* >* list =
            findEdge (start, end);
    if (list == NULL) throw GraphNonExistentEdge ();
    return list->info()->info;
}
```

Now, what about the *edgeWeight ()* method? This method was implemented in the *GraphMatrix* class, not its subclasses, since in that class we always had a value available to be used as the weight for an edge. This is not the case with the *GraphList* class, where a weight is available for an edge only if the linked lists contain data of type *WeightedEdgeContainer*. We could write an *edgeWeight ()* method which tests whether the instance on which it is called is weighted or not, but this runs contrary to the object oriented ideal. Therefore, we will not implement this method here, but rather defer it to the subclasses.

For our last accessor method, we will return a list of neighbors of a particular vertex, obtained by iterating through the linked list for that vertex.

```
template <class VertexObject, class EdgeObject>
Vector<int> GraphList <VertexObject, EdgeObject>::neighbors
                                          (int v)
{
    Vector<int> result;
    if ((v < 0) || (v >= vertexCount()))
            throw GraphVertexOutOfBounds () ;
    AbstractLinkedList< EdgeContainer<EdgeObject>* >*
        list = &((*edgeData)[v]);
    while ((list != NULL) && (!list->isEmpty())) {
        result.add (list->info()->end);
        list = list->next();
    }
    return result;
}
```

Mutator Methods

The *setVertexInfo()* method declared in the *Graph* base class can be read-ily implemented. However, the other two mutator methods, *setEdgeInfo()* and *deleteEdge()*, must be implemented by subclasses, as previously discussed with respect to the *GraphMatrix* class. However, the basic operation of deleting one (directed) edge will be common to all subclasses, so we will implement it as a protected method of the *GraphList* class:

```
template <class VertexObject, class EdgeObject>
void GraphList <VertexObject, EdgeObject>::_deleteEdge
          (int start, int end)
{
    AbstractLinkedList< EdgeContainer<EdgeObject>* >*
        list = findEdge (start, end);
    if (list == NULL)  throw GraphEdgeOutOfBounds();
    list->remove();
}
```

Subclasses

Once again we have four different possible types of graph: undirected and unweighted, directed and unweighted, undirected and weighted, and directed and weighted. We can design four subclasses of *GraphList*, implementing the four types of graph. As they are all fairly straightforward, we present only the directed and weighted graph. The reader can implement the others.

```
template <class VertexObject, class EdgeObject>
class WeightedDirectedGraphList :
    public GraphList <VertexObject, EdgeObject>,
    virtual public
        AbstractWeightedGraph<VertexObject,EdgeObject> {
public:
    WeightedDirectedGraphList (int n);
    virtual ~WeightedDirectedGraphList ();
    virtual double edgeWeight (int start, int end);
    virtual void setEdgeInfo
            (int start, int end, EdgeObject& info);
    virtual void deleteEdge (int start, int end);
```

```
    virtual void addEdge (int start, int end, double weight);
    virtual void addEdge
       (int start, int end, double weight, EdgeObject& info);
};
// ------------------------------------------------------------
template <class VertexObject, class EdgeObject>
WeightedDirectedGraphList <VertexObject, EdgeObject>::
    WeightedDirectedGraphList (int n)
     : GraphList<VertexObject,EdgeObject> (n) { }
// ------------------------------------------------------------
template <class VertexObject, class EdgeObject>
WeightedDirectedGraphList <VertexObject, EdgeObject>::
    ~WeightedDirectedGraphList () { }
// ------------------------------------------------------------
template <class VertexObject, class EdgeObject>
double WeightedDirectedGraphList <VertexObject, EdgeObject>::
       edgeWeight (int start, int end)
{
    AbstractLinkedList< EdgeContainer<EdgeObject>* >*
       list = findEdge (start, end);
    if (list == NULL) throw GraphEdgeOutOfBounds();
    WeightedEdgeContainer<EdgeObject>* wec =
       (WeightedEdgeContainer<EdgeObject>*) (list->info());
    return wec->weight;
}
// ------------------------------------------------------------
template <class VertexObject, class EdgeObject>
void WeightedDirectedGraphList <VertexObject, EdgeObject>::
       deleteEdge (int start, int end)
{
    _deleteEdge (start, end);
}
// ------------------------------------------------------------
template <class VertexObject, class EdgeObject>
void WeightedDirectedGraphList <VertexObject, EdgeObject>::
       addEdge (int start, int end, double weight)
{
```

```
        if ((start < 0) || (start >= vertexCount())
            || (end < 0) || (end >= vertexCount()))
                throw GraphEdgeOutOfBounds();
        if (hasEdge(start,end)) throw GraphDuplicateEdge();
        WeightedEdgeContainer<EdgeObject>* wec = new
            WeightedEdgeContainer<EdgeObject> (start, end, weight);
        (*edgeData)[start].add (wec);
    }
    // ------------------------------------------------------------
    template <class VertexObject, class EdgeObject>
    void WeightedDirectedGraphList <VertexObject, EdgeObject>::
      addEdge (int start, int end, double weight, EdgeObject& info)
    {
        if ((start < 0) || (start >= vertexCount())
            || (end < 0) || (end >= vertexCount()))
                throw GraphEdgeOutOfBounds();
        if (hasEdge(start,end)) throw GraphDuplicateEdge();
        WeightedEdgeContainer<EdgeObject>* wec =
            new WeightedEdgeContainer<EdgeObject>
                (start, end, weight, info);
        (*edgeData)[start].add (wec);
    }
    // ------------------------------------------------------------
    template <class VertexObject, class EdgeObject>
    void WeightedDirectedGraphList <VertexObject,EdgeObject>::
            setEdgeInfo(int start, int end, EdgeObject& info)
    {
        AbstractLinkedList< EdgeContainer<EdgeObject>* >* list =
        findEdge (start, end);
        if (list == NULL) throw GraphEdgeOutOfBounds();
        WeightedEdgeContainer<EdgeObject>* wec =
            (WeightedEdgeContainer<EdgeObject>*) (list->info());
        wec->info = info;
    }
```

11.4.6   Performance Comparison

The comparison between the adjacency matrix and adjacency list representation of a graph in terms of the worst-case time-complexity for various operations is shown in Figure 7. The complexities are presented for a graph with n vertices and m edges. To determine the number of edges in the graph based on the adjacency matrix presentation we need to examine the number of non-empty cells. Since the total number of cells in an n vertex graph is n^2, it takes $O(n^2)$ to determine the number of edges. In order to determine the neighbors of a node v in an adjacency matrix representation we have to process the row v and print out the column indices corresponding to non empty cells. This operation requires $O(n)$ time. To add (delete) an edge using the adjacency matrix representation, the corresponding cell position is made non-empty (empty); to check for the presence of an edge, the corresponding call position is checked for non-emptiness. Since each cell can be accessed in $O(1)$ time, these operations require $O(1)$ time.

In the adjacency list representation the number of edges can be determined by traversing each linked list in the array of linked lists and counting the number of nodes. The number of edges in a connected undirected graph is always half the number total number of nodes. The complexity of this operation is proportional to the size of the adjacency list data structure that is $O(n+m)$. To add, delete, and determine the presence of an edge, the linked lists of the nodes corresponding to the end vertices of the edge have to be traversed. The complexity of this operation is proportional to the maximum of the sizes of the linked list corresponding to the linked lists of the end vertices of the edge; this can be as high as n and as small as 0. We leave it as an exercise to determine the complexities for addition and deletion of vertices. Note that in case a vertex is deleted all edges that have this vertex as the end vertex should also be deleted.

As observed earlier, the adjacency list presentation is highly space efficient and very desirable for sparse graphs (when the number of edges if small when is m is $O(n)$). When the graph is dense (number of edges is large), the adjacency matrix representation is more space efficient. Also note that the choice of representation is also based on the number of operations performed on the graph. If an algorithm repeatedly adds and removes edges, the adjacency matrix is a far superior data structure as evidenced from the worst-case execution time given in Figure 11.7. We summarize the qualitative assessment of the two graph representations in Figure 11.8

Graph Implementations Worst-case Time Complexity Comparisons		
Operation	Adjacency Matrix	Adjacency List
Create(n)	$O(n^2)$	$O(n)$
VertexCount()	$O(1)$	$O(1)$
EdgeCount()	$O(1)$, if a integer variable to used to keep track, otherwise $O(n^2)$	$O(1)$, if a integer variable to used to keep track, otherwise $O(n+m)$
HasEdge(start, end)	$O(1)$	$O(p)$; p is the number of neighbors of the vertex.
Neighbors(vertex)	$O(n)$	$O(p)$; p is the number of neighbors of the vertex.
AddEdge(start, end)	$O(1)$	$O(\mathbf{max}(p_1, p_2))$; p_1 and p_2 are the number of neighbors of *start* vertex and *end* vertex, respectively.
DeleteEdge(start, end)	$O(1)$	$O(\mathbf{max}(p_1, p_2))$; p_1 and p_2 are the number of neighbors of *start* vertex and *end* vertex, respectively.

Figure 11.7: Comparison of worst-case execution times for two representations of an undirected graph.

Graph Implementations Qualitative Assessment	
Implementation	Assessment
Adjacency Matrix	Easy to implement; Good for dense graphs
Adjacency List	Optimal space requirements; perfect space consumption for sparse graphs; requires extra space for pointers as required for linked lists.

Figure 11.8: Qualitative assessment of graph implementations.

11.5   Graph Traversals and Applications

We explained in the example of a binary tree that the nodes of the tree can be visited (or processed) in several different ways. The process of visiting the nodes of a data structure in any particular order is called a *traversal* (we have also referred to this as *enumeration* in prior chapters, but *traversal* is the more usual term with regard to graphs). In this section, we are interested in examining two traversal mechanisms on graphs: depth first search and breadth first search traversal. The idea of the depth first search traversal is to start from an arbitrary vertex in the graph and keep traversing successive unvisited neighbors. If we end up at a vertex where there are no unvisited vertices, we backtrack to a previous vertex, look for at least one unvisited neighbor of this vertex and continue the depth first search. In the figure below the depth first search is started from vertex 0 and the order in which the vertices are visited is shown next to each vertex. We examined depth first search when we tried to solve the maze problem in the discussion Stacks and Queues. We will show that depth first search is very useful in solving a number of problems on graphs.

The breadth first search does the opposite of depth first search in that it visits all the neighbors of a particular vertex before it visits subsequent unvisited neighbors. The order in which the vertices are visited during the breadth first search starting from vertex 0 is shown in the figure below. We will use a queue data structure to perform the breadth first search. We will show that the breadth first search tree is useful in determining the single source shortest path tree of unweighted graphs.

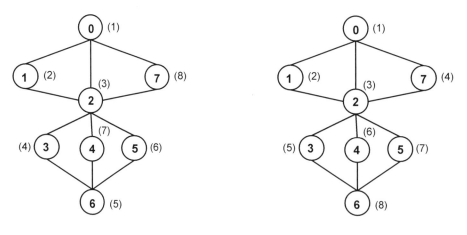

Depth First Search   **Breadth First Search**

Figure 11.9:   Graphs showing the order in which vertices are visited during a depth first and breadth first search.

11.5.1 Depth-First Search

Using the Graph class, we will now present an interesting algorithm called the depth-first search of a graph. The input to this algorithm is the adjacency list of the graph. The algorithm runs in time $O(n+m)$ and this is said to be *linear* in the size of the input. The algorithm, set forth below, keeps track through an array Booleans of whether a given vertex has been visited, and keeps track through a number called the depth first search number of when the vertex was visited. The depth first search number is incremented on each call to the recursive procedure called DFS.

```
ALGORITHM DEPTH-FIRST-SEARCH (G, v, VISITED, SEARCHNUM)
1.  Visited ← createNewArray (G.VertexCount)
         //Visited holds one boolean for each vertex
2.  Fill Visited with false
3.  SearchNum ← createNewArray (G.VertexCount)
         //SearchNum holds one number per vertex
4.  Fill SearchNum with 1
5.  DFS (G, v, Visited, SearchNum, 1)


PROCEDURE DFS (G, v, VISITED, SEARCHNUM, DEPTH)
    //Recursive procedure to carry out search
1.  Visited [v] ← true // Flag current vertex as visited
2.  SearchNum [v] ← Depth // and set depth first search number
3.  for each neighbor u of v in G
    //Iterate through neighbors of current vertex
4.       if Visited [u] = false
    //Make recursive call on unvisited vertices
5.           DFS (G, u, Visited, SearchNum, Depth + 1)
6.       endif
7.  endfor
```

Clearly, if a graph is connected a single call to $DFS(v)$ from any arbitrary vertex will visit all the vertices in the graph. The figure below shows one possible way to number the vertices of the previously presented graph, using depth first search numbers. The numbers in parentheses are the depth first search numbers.

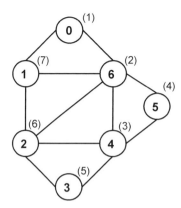

Figure 11.10:   Numbering of vertices based on recursive call to the Depth First
                    Search method.

Since the depth-first search algorithm does not concern itself with weights of
edges or with directions of edges, just with neighbors of vertices, we can place the
method implementing the algorithm in the *GraphList* class.

The following methods of the *GraphList* class implement the above algorithm by visiting the vertices in a depth-first manner and assigning a depth-first search
number for each vertex. The *dfs ()* method is a protected helper method. The *depthFirstSearch ()* returns an array whose size is equal to the number of vertices
in the graph. Each element *i* of the array will contain the depth-first search number
that is assigned to vertex *i* in the graph. This method differs from the algorithm given
in that it does not maintain a Visited array, but instead relies on the search number array
(DFSNumbers) to indicate whether a vertex has been visited, since an unvisited vertex
will have a number of 0 and a visited vertex will not.

```
template <class VertexObject, class EdgeObject>
ArrayClass<int> GraphList <VertexObject, EdgeObject>::
        depthFirstSearch (int vertex)
{
    ArrayClass<int> DFSNumbers(vertexCount(), 0);
    dfs (vertex, DFSNumbers, 1);
        // DFSNumbers is an array of DFS Numbers
    return DFSNumbers;
}
```

```
template <class VertexObject, class EdgeObject>
void GraphList <VertexObject, EdgeObject>::dfs
    (int vertex, ArrayClass<int>&DFSNumbers, int depth){
    DFSNumbers [vertex] = depth;
    //Assign the DFS number of vertex
    Vector<int> nbors = neighbors(vertex);
    for (int i = 0; i < nbors.size(); i++){
        if (DFSNumbers [nbors[i]] == 0)
            dfs (nbors[i], DFSNumbers, depth + 1);
    }
}
```

We can test this method with a *main()* function that creates an graph object based on that diagrammed above, then runs the *depthFirstSearch()* method on it. Since we did not implement the `UnweightedUndirectedGraphList` class, but left it for the reader, we must add each edge twice to produce the equivalent of an undirected graph.

```
void main ()
{
        WeightedDirectedGraphList<int,int> g (7);
        g.addEdge (0,1,1);      g.addEdge (1,0,1);
        g.addEdge (0,6,1);      g.addEdge (6,0,1);
        g.addEdge (1,6,1);      g.addEdge (6,1,1);
        g.addEdge (6,5,1);      g.addEdge (5,6,1);
        g.addEdge (2,6,1);      g.addEdge (6,2,1);
        g.addEdge (1,2,1);      g.addEdge (2,1,1);
        g.addEdge (6,4,1);      g.addEdge (4,6,1);
        g.addEdge (4,5,1);      g.addEdge (5,4,1);
        g.addEdge (2,3,1);      g.addEdge (3,2,1);
        g.addEdge (4,3,1);      g.addEdge (3,4,1);
        ArrayClass<int> dfs = g.depthFirstSearch(0);
        for (int i = 0; i < dfs.size(); i++)
            cout << dfs[i] << " ";
        cout << endl;
}
```

The output of this method is as follows:

■   0 6 4 5 3 2 1

The above output is the depth first search number of each vertex. This indicates that the search proceeded from 0 to 6 to 4 to 5, then from 4 again to 3 to 2 to 1. Note that it was necessary to back track from 5 to 4, because both neighbors of 5 had already been visited. The graph with depth-first search numbers appears above, in the example. The result would have been different if we had added the edges in a different order, and the reader is encouraged to try rearranging the *addEdge ()* calls to produce other depth-first search numberings.

11.5.2   Non-Recursive Depth First Search

In the previous section we presented a recursive algorithm for performing the depth first search of a graph. We will now show how this algorithm can be implemented non-recursively using a stack and a loop. This is in effect a "disguised" recursive algorithm since we are using our own stack instead of the system stack, but can be more efficient since we push only and exactly as much data as needed. Recall that the depth first search algorithm first marks all the vertices as "unvisited" and second invokes the recursive depth first search method passing an arbitrarily chosen vertex. The recursive depth first search method marks the vertex as "visited" and then processes each neighbor of the vertex in a sequence. If a neighbor is "unvisited," it recursively invokes the depth first search method, passing that neighbor node as a parameter.

The non-recursive implementation uses a stack to store the "unvisited" neighbors, and the depth first search method executes until the stack is empty. The basic algorithmic structure is presented below.

```
ALGORITHM DEPTH-FIRST-SEARCH (G, v, VISITED)
// G is the graph, u is the starting vertex,
// Visited is an array with one Boolean per node in G
1.   Visited ← createNewArray (G.NodeCount)
2.   Fill Visited with false
3.   S ← createNewStack()
4.   S.push (u)
```

```
5.   Visited[u] ←true
6.   while (S is not empty)
7.        v ← S.pop() // v is a node of G
8.        for each neighbor w of v
9.             if (Visited[w] = false)
10.                  Visited[w] ←true
11.                  S.push(w)
12.            endif
13.        endfor
14. endwhile
```

In the following figures, we show how the depth first search proceeds along with the operations on the stack.

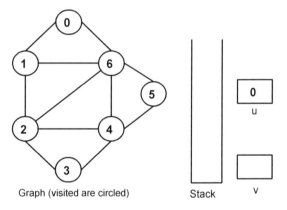

Graph (visited are circled)   Stack   v

Figure 11.11:   Non-recursive Depth First Search beginning with vertex 0. Initially no vertices are visited and the stack is empty.

Our search begins with vertex 0. Initially, no vertices are visited and the stack is empty.

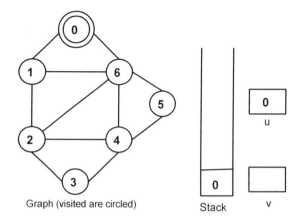

Figure 11.12: Vertex 0 is pushed on the stack and marked as visited.

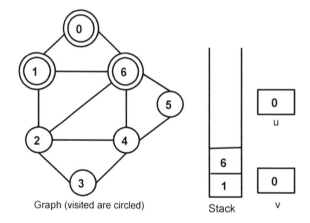

Figure 11.13: Vertex 0 has been popped off the stack and placed in the variable v. Vertices 1 and 6, which are the neighbors of vertex 0, have been marked as visited and pushed on the stack.

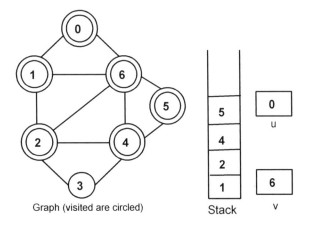

Graph (visited are circled)   Stack   v

Figure 11.14:   Vertex 6 has been popped off the stack and placed in the variable v.
Vertices 2, 4, and 5, which are the neighbors of vertex 6, have been
marked as visited and pushed on the stack.

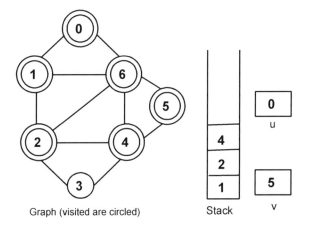

Graph (visited are circled)   Stack   v

Figure 11.15:   Vertex 5 has been popped off the stack and placed in the variable v.
The neighbors of vertex 5, vertices 4 and 6, are both marked as visited,
so they are not pushed on the stack.

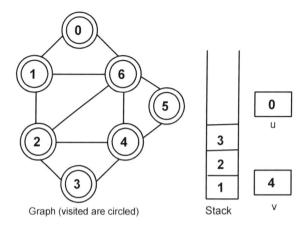

Figure 11.16: Vertex 4 has been popped off and placed in variable v. Vertex 3, the only neighbor of vertex 4 not already visited, has been marked as visited and pushed on the stack.

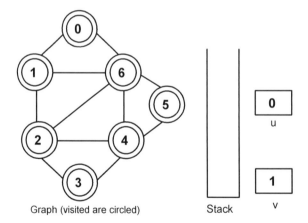

Figure 11.17: Now that every vertex has been visited, the remaining vertices, 3, 2, and 1, will be popped off in that order, and no further vertices will be pushed.

Once the stack is empty, the algorithm will terminate. In the implementation of this algorithm, we shall maintain a search number array, rather than a Visited array. This is similar to our implementation of the recursive *depthFirstSearch()* method previously presented. Again, the *depthFirstSearch()* method is part of the GraphList class. It should be noted that we make no effort to check stack exceptions. This is permissible in this case since we know that the stack, if created at all, is large enough to hold all of the vertices simultaneously, so that it will never overflow, and we check whether it is empty before popping from it, so that it will never underflow.

```
template <class VertexObject, class EdgeObject>
ArrayClass<int> GraphList <VertexObject, EdgeObject>::
    depthFirstSearch (int vertex)
{
    int v;                      // node popped from stack
    int w;                      // neighbor of node v
    int depth = 1;              // depth-first-search number
    Vector<int> nbors;          // array of neighbors for node v
    ArrayClass<int>DFSNumbers(vertexCount(), 0);
    StackArray<int> s (vertexCount());
    DFSNumbers[vertex] = depth;
    s.push (vertex);
    while (!s.isEmpty())
    {
        v = s.pop();
        nbors = neighbors(v);
        for (int i = 0; i < nbors.size(); i++)
        {
            w = nbors[i];
            if (DFSNumbers[w] == 0)
            {
                depth = depth + 1;
                DFSNumbers[w] = depth;
                s.push (w);
            }
        }
    }
    return DFSNumbers;
}
```

When we substitute this method for the *depthFirstSearch*() method implemented in the previous section and run the same *main*() function to test it, we find that the output is a little different because all of the neighbors of a vertex are examined before the method is recursively called on any, unlike the previous implementation. Nevertheless, all vertices are visited, this time in the order 0 to 6 to 1 to 2 to 3 to 4 to 5 as shown by the output below.

■   0 6 1 4 2 5 3

11.5.3   Applications of Depth First Search

There are a number of applications of depth-first search in computer science.

Connectivity of a graph

Consider a connected graph G = (V, E). It is easy to see that a single call to Depth-FirstSearch (in the recursive implementation) will visit all the vertices of G. If not all the vertices of G are visited during a single call to DFS from the recursive Depth-First-Search algorithm then the graph is not connected. Thus depth first search can be used to determine connectivity of a graph. A computer network should be testing for connectivity since it ensures a path between every pair of nodes in the network. A disconnected network due to link or node failures will be unable to route messages between certain pairs of nodes. The following method returns true if the given graph is connected and false otherwise:

```
template <class VertexObject, class EdgeObject>
bool GraphList<VertexObject,EdgeObject>::connected () {
    bool bConnected = true;
// call depthFirstSearch below and this will initialize the
// DFS Numbers of all vertices equal to 0 and once
// DFS terminates, all nodes will have a DFSSearch number
// if the graph is connected, otherwise some nodes with have
// a DFSNumber of 0. This will indicate that the graph is
// not connected.
    ArrayClass<int> ai = depthFirstSearch (0);
// Array of DFS Numbers
    for (int i = 0; i < vertexCount() && bConnected; i++)
```

```
    {
        if (ai[i] == 0) bConnected = false;
    }
    return bConnected;
}
```

Connected Components

The depth first search algorithm can be used to determine the connected components (subgraphs) of a given graph G. Each connected component is given an identifier that is the same as the identity of the smallest vertex it contains. Every vertex in a connected component *i* is assigned the value *i* to indicate that it belongs to connected component *i*. The basic idea behind the algorithm is as follows. Whenever the DepthFirstSearch method is called from the main method of the recursive implementation of the depth first search, a new component is obtained. We maintain an array *Component* such that *Component*[*i*] will indicate the component to which the vertex to *i* belongs. The algorithm Connected-Components is presented below.

```
ALGORITHM CONNECTED-COMPONENTS (G)
1.  Visited ← createNewArray (G.VertexCount)
2.  Fill Visited with false
3.  Component ← createNewArray (G.VertexCount)
4.  for v = 0 to G.VertexCount-1
5.    if (Visited[v] is false)
6.       ComponentNumber ← v
7.       CONNECTED-RECURSE (G,v,Visited,Component,ComponentNumber)
8.    endif
9.  endfor


PROCEDURE CONNECTED-RECURSE (G, v, VISITED, COMPONENT, COMPONENTNUMBER)
1.  Visited [v] ←true // Flag current vertex as visited
2.  Component[v] ← ComponentNumber
3.  for each neighbor u of v in G
    // Iterate through neighbors of current vertex
4.     if Visited [u] = false
    // Make recursive call on unvisited vertices
5.        CONNECTED-RECURSE (G,u,Visited,Component,ComponentNumber)
6.     endif
7.  endfor
```

The following figure shows a graph G with three connected components. The numbers in the parenthesis indicate the connected component number assigned to each vertex.

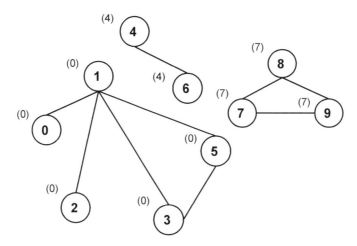

Figure 11.18: A graph with 3 connected components. The numbers in parenthesis indicate the connected component number assigned to each vertex.

The methods below (belonging to the *GraphList* class) implement the Connected-Components algorithm described above.

```
template <class VertexObject, class EdgeObject>
ArrayClass<int> GraphList <VertexObject,
dgeObject>::connectedComponents ()
{
    ArrayClass<bool> visited (vertexCount(), false);
    ArrayClass<int> components (vertexCount(), 0);
    int componentNumber = 0;
    for (int v=0; v < vertexCount(); v++)
    {
        if (!visited[v])
        {
            componentNumber = v;
```

```
                        _connectedComponents (v, visited, components,
                            componentNumber);
            }
        }
    return components;
}
// --------------------------------------------------------
template <class VertexObject, class EdgeObject>
void GraphList <VertexObject, EdgeObject>::_connectedComponents
    (int v, ArrayClass<bool>& visited,
    ArrayClass<int>& components, int componentNumber)
{
    visited [v] = true;
    components[v] = componentNumber;
    Vector<int> nbor = neighbors (v);
    for (int i = 0; i < nbor.size(); i++)
    {
        if (!visited [nbor[i]])
        _connectedComponents (nbor[i], visited, components,
                componentNumber);
    }
}
```

Strongly Connected Components

Given a directed graph $G = (V, A)$ a *strongly connected component* $H = (V', A')$ is a maximal subgraph of G such that for every pair of vertices u and v in V' there exists a directed path in H. For the directed graph shown below, the vertices in each strongly connected component are grouped to form *strong vertices* of a strongly connected components graph (SCC). There is a directed edge between two strong vertices X and Y in the SCC graph if and only if there is a vertex u of G in X and a vertex v of G in Y with (u, v) as a directed arc in A. Of course, it is possible to have multiple arcs for a pair of strong vertices, but in the SCC graph we will replace multiple arcs by a single arc. The SCC graph for the given graph G is shown below. It can be clearly seen that the SCC graph is an acyclic graph (a graph without a directed cycle).

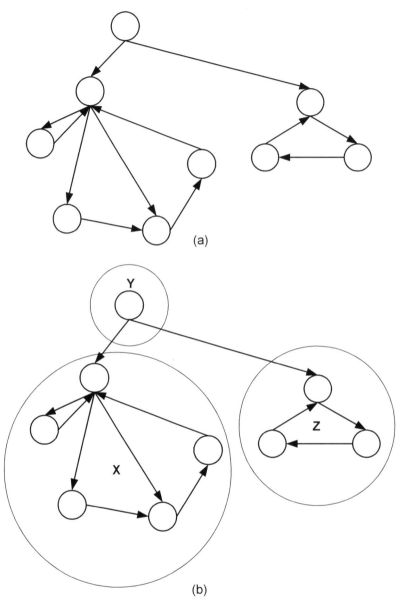

Figure 11.19: The graph in (a) is a directed graph and the graph in (b) is the corresponding graph with strongly connected components grouped into
strong vertices X,Y, and Z.

In order to determine the strongly connected components of a directed graph G, we need to define G^T (pronounced "G transpose") as the graph that contains all the vertices of G, with each arc (u, v) in G replaced by the arc (v, u). A transpose of matrix can be easily computed in $O(n^2)$ time, where n is the number nodes in the graph G. That is, the graph G^T is the graph G with all the arcs in G reversed. Given G we can construct G^T in time equal to the size of the representations of G and G^T.

The algorithm Strongly-Connected-Components determine the strongly connected components of a given directed graph G. First a depth first search is performed on G to determine the *DFSNumber* for each vertex. In this method, a vertex u is said to be a "neighbor" of v if and only if there is a directed arc from u to v in G. After G^T is constructed a second depth first search is performed but the vertices of G^T are processed in the decreasing sequence of *DFSNumber* in the main loop of the Connected-Components algorithm. The connected components obtained after the second depth first search forms the strongly connected components.

The sorting of the vertices based on *DFSNumber* can be performed in linear time using the simple bucket sort, since the largest *DFSNumber* is the number of vertices minus one. Since we will be performing two depth first searches, the time complexity of the Strongly-Connected-Components algorithm is $O(n+m)$ if we are using an adjacency representation of the input graph; otherwise, it is $O(n^2)$ for the adjacency matrix representation.

```
ALGORITHM STRONGLY-CONNECTED-COMPONENTS (G)
1.   Visited ← createNewArray (G.VertexCount)
2.   Fill Visited with false
3.   Component ← createNewArray (G.VertexCount)
4.   DFSNumber ← createNewArray (G.VertexCount)
5.   Fill DFSNumber with 0
6.   for v = 0 to G.VertexCount-1
7.        if(Visited[v] is false)
8.             ComponentNumber ← v
9.             STRONG-RECURSE (G, v, Visited, DFSNumber,
                    0, Component, ComponentNumber)
10.       endif
11. endfor
12. Compute Gᵀ
13. for v = G.VertexCount-1 down to 0
```

```
14.        SortedDFSNumber[DFSNumber [v]] ← v
15. endfor
// SortedDFSNumberkeeps track of vertices in sorted order of
// the DFSNumber of each vertex of the graph
16. Fill DFSNumber with 0
17. for v = G.VertexCount-1 down to 0
18.       if (Visited[SortedDFSNumber [v]] is false)
19.          ComponentNumber = SortedDFSNumber[v]
20.          STRONG-RECURSE (Gᵀ, SortedDFSNumber[v],
                Visited, DFSNumber, 0, Component, ComponentNumber)
21.       endif
22. endfor
// The above steps perform a depth first search of the graph Gᵀ by
// considering the vertices in decreasing order of DFSNumber
```

```
PROCEDURE STRONG-RECURSE (G,v,VISITED,DFSNumber,DEPTH,COMPONENT,COMPONENTNUMBER)
// Recursive procedure to carry out search
1.   Visited [v] ←true // Flag current vertex as visited
2.   Component[v] ← ComponentNumber
// Assign a component number to vertex v
3.   DFSNumber [v] ← Depth // and set depth first search number
4.   for each neighbor u of v in G
5.       if Visited [u] = false
6.             STRONG-RECURSE (G, u, Visited, DFSNumber,
                    Depth+1, Component, ComponentNumber)
7.       endif
8.   endfor
```

Implementation of this algorithm is left as an exercise for the reader.

Topological Sort

We come across directed acyclic graphs frequently in our lives. Consider the directed graph that models courses and prerequisites for each course. The vertices represent courses and there is an arc from vertex u to vertex v if and only if the course that corresponds to u is a prerequisite for the course that corresponds to v. We fervently hope that the directed graph that models the courses and their prerequisites is acyclic, for otherwise, there is no hope for graduation. Our problem is to give some sequence of these courses such that courses later in the sequence can be taken by satisfying all the prerequisite requirements that are listed earlier in the sequence. The algorithm to provide us with this sequence is called *topological sorting*. The following diagram illustrates a directed acyclic graph and the topological sorted order of the vertices of the graph.

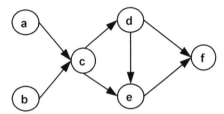

Figure 11.20:   This is a directed acyclic graph with a topological sorted order being a, b, c, d, e and f. Another topological sorted order for the same graph would be b, a, c, d, e, and f.

The basic idea behind the topological sorting algorithm is as follows. Every acyclic graph has at least one vertex u with indegree 0. In the example, this implies the course that vertex u models does not have any prerequisite requirements and hence can be added to the sequence at any position. We begin by adding the vertex u with indegree 0 to the sequence and removing it from the graph. For each arc (u,v) the indegree of vertex v is reduced by one. The remaining graph is still acyclic and hence has at least one vertex with an indegree of 0. The process of removing continues until all the vertices have been removed and added to the sequence.

The indegree of each vertex is determined as follows. The indegree of each vertex is set to 0 initially. Now, a depth first search traversal is performed on the graph. During the process of traversal, for each arc (u,v) processed the indegree of vertex v is incremented by one. The initializing of the indegree of each vertex can be completed in time that is equal to the time complexity of depth first search. The following algorithm Topological-Sort has time complexity of $O(n+m)$ plus time complexity to determine the indegree of each vertex using depth first search.

```
ALGORITHM TOPOLOGICAL-SORT (G)
1.  Compute the indegree of each vertex in G using Depth-
    First-Search Algorithm
2.  for (v=0; v < VertexCount; v++)
3.       if indegree[v] = 0
4.             Q.enqueue(v)    //Queue Q maintains the sequence
5.       endif
6.  endfor
7.  while(Q is not empty)
8.       u = Q.dequeue()          //vertex u has a indegree of 0
9.       output u
10.      for all arcs (u, v)
               //for all arcs (u,v) reduce the indegree of v
11.            indegree[v] = indegree[v] - 1
12.            if indegree[v] = 0
13.                  Q.enqueue(v)
14.            endif
15.      endfor
16. endwhile
```

Implementation of this algorithm is left as an exercise for the reader. Yet another way to implement topological sort is use a *postvisit(v)* number for each vertex *v* in the graph. The postvisit numbering of the vertices is obtained by performing the depth first search and numbering each vertex (number the vertices from high to low) after the recursive call. By numbering the vertices in descending order, each vertex that is visited before a particular neighbor will have a lower number than that of its neighbor. The vertices listed in the postvisit order (low to high) will be the topological sorted order. The complexity of topological sort using postvisit numbering is the same as the complexity of depth first search, which is $O(n+m)$.

11.5.4 Breadth First Search

Breadth first search is yet another traversal on graphs. Unlike the depth first search, all the unvisited neighbors of a given vertex are visited first. The breadth first search mechanism can be used to implement the branch-and-bound algorithmic technique presented in Chapter 2. Let us revisit the knapsack problem mentioned in Chapter 2. Let us assume that a vertex *v* corresponds to a set of items that do not violate the size constraint and *profit(v)* is the profit from the set of items. A vertex *u* is a neighbor of the vertex *v*, if the set of items that corresponds to *u* is obtained by either the addition or deletion of a single item from the items that corresponds to *v*. A neighbor *u* of *v* is promising if the *profit(u)* ≥ *profit(v)*. All promising neighbors are visited in the breadth first search process and it is invoked first on the "most" promising vertex the one whose profit value is the largest so far. It is important to note that the input graph that is used as part of the branch-and-bound algorithmic strategy for the knapsack problem is constructed dynamically as the breadth first search is carried out.

We will now show how to perform a breadth first search of an undirected graph that is given as an input. As in the case of depth first search, all vertices in the graph are initially marked as "unvisited." The breadth first search starts from an arbitrary vertex *x*. This vertex is added to a queue and marked as "visited". The breadth first search then processes this queue until it becomes empty. A vertex is removed from the queue, and all neighbors of this vertex that are marked as "unvisited" are marked as "visited" and added to the queue. We can number each vertex as to when it was visited by keeping an integer variable, *BFSnum*, and an array of integers, *BFSnums[]*, with as many elements as the graph has vertices. Initially, *BFSnum* is 0 and *BFSnums[i]* is 0 for every *i*. Whenever we add a vertex *x* to the queue, we increment *BFSnum*, and we set *BFSnums[x]* equal to *BFSnum*. Thus, *BFSnums[x]* is the breadth first search number for vertex *x*.

The algorithm described above is set out below:

```
Algorithm Breadth-First-Search (G, u)
// G is the graph to be searched and u is the starting vertex
1.   Q ← createQueue()
2.   Visited ← createNewArray (G.NodeCount) and fill with false
3.   BFSnums ← createNewArray (G.NodeCount) and fill with 0
4.   BFSnum← 0
5.   Q.enqueue(u)
6.   Visited [u] ←true
7.   while (Q is not empty)
8.         v = Q.dequeue();
9.         BFSnum← BFSnum + 1
10.        BFSnums[v] ←BFSnum
12.        for each neighbor w of v
12.              if (Visited [w] = false)
13.                    Visited [w] ←true
14.                    Q.enqueue(w)
15.              endif
16.        endfor
17. endwhile
```

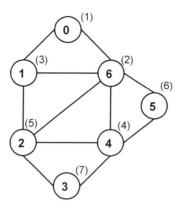

Figure 11.21: The graph shows one possible breadth first search numbering, where the search started with vertex 0.

Below, we provide an implementation of the breadth-first search algorithm, a method to be added to the GraphList class previously presented. As with the depth-first search method, we have omitted the Visited array, relying on the search number array to indicate whether a vertex has been visited, since an unvisited vertex will have a number of 0 and a visited node will not.

```
template <class VertexObject, class EdgeObject>
ArrayClass<int> GraphList <VertexObject,EdgeObject>::
        breadthFirstSearch (int u)
{
    int v; // node popped from the queue
    int w; // neighbor node of v
    Vector<int> nbors; // neighbors array of v
    int BFSnum = 1;
// breadth-first-search counter starts at 1 (value for u)
    QueueArray<int> Q = (vertexCount());
    ArrayClass<int> BFSnums (vertexCount(), 0);
    BFSnums[u] = 1;
    Q.enqueue (u);
    while (!Q.isEmpty()) {
        v = Q.dequeue();
        nbors = neighbors(v);
        for (int i = 0; i < nbors.size(); i++)
```

```
        {
            w = nbors[i];
            if (BFSnums [w] == 0)
            {
                BFSnum = BFSnum + 1;
                BFSnums [w] = BFSnum;
                Q.enqueue (w);
            }
        }
    }
    return BFSnums;
}
```

We can test this method by simply substituting the lines

```
ArrayClass<int> bfs = g.breadthFirstSearch(0);
for (int i = 0; i < bfs.size(); i++)
    cout << bfs[i] << " ";
```

for the lines

```
ArrayClass<int> dfs = g.depthFirstSearch(0);
for (int i = 0; i < dfs.size(); i++)
    cout << dfs[i] << " ";
```

in the *main*() function which we used to test the *depthFirstSearch*() method. The result is:

```
1 3 5 7 4 6 2
```

We can see that the ordering is different, but all vertices were visited, this time in the order 0 to 6 to 1 to 4 to 2 to 5 to 3. This is the ordering in the diagram above, illustrating the breadth-first search numbering.

11.5.5   Applications of Breadth First Search

The breadth first search is useful in determining the shortest path from a given vertex to all the vertices of an unweighted graph. The *length* of a path between two vertices is the number of edges in the path. The *distance* or the *shortest distance* between vertex u and vertex v in the graph is a minimum length of a path from u to v among all paths from u to v. A tree T with root r is a single source shortest path tree if and only if for any two nodes (u, v) such that one is the ancestor of the other, the shortest path is obtained by following the parent links in the tree.

The breadth first search can be used to determine the single source shortest path tree as follows. Let us maintain an array called *parent* with size equal to the number of vertices in the graph. The *parent[i]* will give the parent of a node *i* in the single source shortest path tree. The following algorithm Single-Source-Shortest-Path-Tree-UnWeighted performs a breadth first search and creates the parent array. Once the array is created the shortest path from the root r of the tree to any vertex v in the graph can be determined by following v, parent[v], parent[parent[v]], …, r. Assume that the input graph for the algorithm is connected.

```
Algorithm Single-Source-Shortest-Path-Tree-UnWeighted (G, u)
// G is the graph to be searched and u is the root vertex
1.   Parent ← createNewArray (G.NodeCount)
2.   Parent[u] ← -1
3.   Q ← createQueue()
4.   Visited ← createNewArray (G.NodeCount) and fill with false
5.   BFSnums ← createNewArray (G.NodeCount) and fill with 0
6.   BFSnum← 0
7.   Q.enqueue (u)
8.   Visited (u) ←true
9.   while (Q is not empty)
10.      v = Q.dequeue ();
11.      BFSnum← BFSnum + 1
12.      BFSnums (v) ←BFSnum
13.      for each neighbor w of v
14.          if (Visited (w) = false)
15.              Parent[w] ← v
16.              Visited (w) ←true
17.              Q.enqueue (w)
18.          endif
19.      endfor
20. endwhile
```

The following diagram shows a unweighted graph and the single source shortest path tree for the graph, with vertex $u=0$.

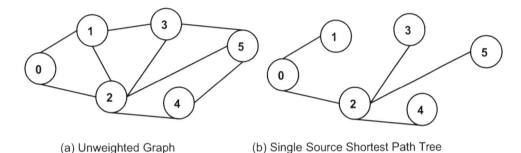

(a) Unweighted Graph   (b) Single Source Shortest Path Tree

Figure 11.22:   Example of an unweighted graph and a single source shortest path tree.

11.6   Shortest Path Problems

Given a weighted directed graph $G=(V,E)$, the weight of a directed path $P = (v_0, v_1)$, $(v_1, v_2), (v_2, v_3), \dots (v_{k-1}, v_k)$ (denoted $w(P)$) is the sum of the weights of the arcs in the path P. The shortest minimum weighted path (or shortest path in short) from a vertex u to a vertex v is a path from u to v whose weight is the minimum among all paths from u to v. Previously, using breadth first search, we showed that the shortest path from one vertex to all the other vertices can be determined in $O(n+m)$ time provided the edge weights are all equal to 1. In this section, we will present a simple algorithm that computes the shortest distance and the paths between every pair of vertices in the graph. This problem will be termed as the *all-pair shortest path*.

In all–pair shortest path problem, the shortest distances can be stored in a matrix SD, such that SD[i][j] corresponds to the shortest distance from vertex i to vertex j. How can we store the actual shortest path? Before we can answer this question, we have to convince ourselves that any subpath of a shortest path is also a shortest path. That is, if the shortest path from u to v contains vertices $u, i_1, i_2, \dots, i_k, v$ such that the arcs $L = \{(u, i_1), (i_1, i_2), \dots (i_{k-1}, i_k), (i_k, v)\}$ are arcs in the graph, then the shortest path from i_p to i_q, for $1 \le p \le q \le k$ is $(i_p, i_{p+1}), \dots, (i_{q-1}, i_q)$. Given this property we can now imagine that the shortest path from u to v forms a tree with root u and leaf v. Each node in the tree has a parent. In order to determine the shortest path from node u to v, we first determine the parent of v, and its parent, and so on until we reach u. The parent information for the case of the all–pair shortest path problem can be kept in a matrix $parent$ such that parent[i][j] gives the parent vertex k of vertex j in the shortest path from i to j. Knowing this, we next determine parent[i][k] which is the parent of vertex k in the shortest path from i to k. By continuing this process, we can list all the vertices in the shortest path from any two given vertices. For the case of single source shortest path problem, we just need one array to keep track of the parent information similar to the one we used in the single source shortest path problem for the unweighted case.

Our next goal is to compute the parent matrix for the all-pair shortest path problem. The algorithm that discussed in the next section is due to R. W. Floyd. It is a great example of dynamic programming, discussed in Section 2.7.3.

11.6.1   Undirected Graphs - All-Pair Shortest Path Problem

The following figure shows the adjacency matrix for a weighted graph. Note that if there are no direct edges connecting two vertices i and j, then M[i][j] is set to a large number, in this case 99.

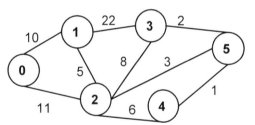

Edge Weighted Graph

Adjacency Matrix

	0	1	2	3	4	5
0	0	10	11	99	99	99
1	10	0	5	22	99	99
2	11	5	0	8	6	3
3	99	22	8	0	99	2
4	99	99	6	99	0	1
5	99	99	3	2	1	0

Figure 11.23:   This shows the adjacency matrix for a weighted graph. If there are no direct edges connecting two vertices I and j, then M[i][j] is set to a large number, say, 99.

Using the adjacency matrix of a weighted undirected graph G, we can solve the all-pairs shortest distance problem. The algorithm iteratively fills in a matrix D of shortest distances, where D[i][j] is the shortest distance between vertex i and vertex j. Initially, D[i][j] = M[i][j] for all $i \neq j$, and each diagonal element of D is set to 0. Thus, D contains only distances between adjacent vertices, that is, distances along paths that have no intermediate vertices.

The algorithm performs n iterations over the matrix D. On the kth iteration, for each pair of vertices i and j, the algorithm compares the current best distance between vertices i and j with the best distance which can be obtained by passing through vertex k on the path from i to j, and places the better of the two distances in D[i][j]. After the first iteration, then, D contains the best distances along paths with at most one intermediate vertex (that vertex being numbered 1). After k iterations, it contains the best distances along paths with at most k intermediate vertices, all numbered 1 through k. Thus, assuming that k-1 iterations have completed, the shortest distance after the kth iteration is computed as follows:

$$D[i,j] \leftarrow \min \{D[i,j], D[i,k]+D[k,j]\}$$

After the kth iteration, D[i][j] will have the shortest distance from vertex i to vertex j along a path which does not go through any vertex that is numbered higher than k. Clearly, then, after n iterations D[i][j] will have the shortest distance from vertex i to vertex j that does not go through any vertex numbered higher than n, and this will be the shortest distance in the given input graph (there being no higher numbered vertices).

For the graph given in the above figure, the successive computation of matrix D is shown below.

Note that the matrix is the same for values k = 3, 4, and 5. This is because, as the reader can see from the graph, there is no shortest path that goes through vertices numbered higher than 3. The program given below takes as input the distance matrix D and returns the shortest distance matrix.

k = 0

	0	1	2	3	4	5
0	0	10	11	99	99	99
1	10	0	5	22	99	99
2	11	5	0	8	6	3
3	99	22	8	0	99	2
4	99	99	6	99	0	1
5	99	99	3	2	1	0

k = 1

	0	1	2	3	4	5
0	0	10	11	32	99	99
1	10	0	5	22	99	99
2	11	5	0	8	6	3
3	32	22	8	0	99	2
4	99	99	6	99	0	1
5	99	99	3	2	1	0

k = 2

	0	1	2	3	4	5
0	0	10	11	19	17	14
1	10	0	5	13	11	8
2	11	5	0	8	6	3
3	19	13	8	0	14	2
4	17	11	6	14	0	1
5	14	8	3	2	1	0

k = 3

	0	1	2	3	4	5
0	0	10	11	19	17	14
1	10	0	5	13	11	8
2	11	5	0	8	6	3
3	19	13	8	0	14	2
4	17	11	6	14	0	1
5	14	8	3	2	1	0

k = 4

	0	1	2	3	4	5
0	0	10	11	19	17	14
1	10	0	5	13	11	8
2	11	5	0	8	6	3
3	19	13	8	0	14	2
4	17	11	6	14	0	1
5	14	8	3	2	1	0

k = 5

	0	1	2	3	4	5
0	0	10	11	16	15	14
1	10	0	5	10	9	8
2	11	5	0	5	4	3
3	16	10	5	0	3	2
4	15	9	4	3	0	1
5	14	8	3	2	1	0

Figure 11.24: The successive computations of adjacency matrix for weighted graph in Figure 10.20 at different values of k ranging from 0 to 5 is shown.

```
template <class Object>
Matrix<Object> allPair (Matrix<Object>& D)
{
    Matrix<Object> result = D;
    int i, j, k;
    for (k = 0; k < result.length(); k++)
        for (i = 0; i < result.length(); i++)
          for (j = 0; j < result.length(); j++)
            if (result [i][j] > (result [i][k]+ result [k][j]))
              result [i][j] = result [i][k] + result [k][j];
    return result;
}
```

11.6.2   Dijkstra's Shortest Path Algorithm

We will present Dijkstra's shortest path algorithm, which determines the shortest path from one source vertex to all the other vertices in a weighted graph. This is an example of a greedy algorithm, discussed in Section 2.9.1. Consider the graph shown below, where the vertices represent cities and the weights on edges represent distance between cities.

Edge Weighted Graph

Adjacency Matrix

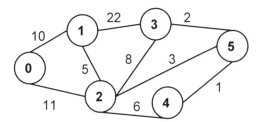

	0	1	2	3	4	5
0	0	10	11	99	99	99
1	10	0	5	22	99	99
2	11	5	0	8	6	3
3	99	22	8	0	99	2
4	99	99	6	99	0	1
5	99	99	3	2	1	0

Figure 11.25:   This shows the adjacency matrix for a weighted graph. If there are no direct edges connecting two vertices I and j, then M[i][j] is set to a large number, say, 99.

How would we find the shortest path from node 0 to every other node in the above graph? In 1968, Dijkstra presented a novel algorithm for this problem, which we will present next.

Algorithm Description

Let s be the source vertex. Set S={s}. Let $D[i,j]$ be the distance between vertex i and vertex j such that they are directly connected by an edge. If there is no edge (i,j) in the graph then $D[i,j]$ is set to infinity. Let $SD[i]$ be the shortest path from s to vertex i found so far. Initially, $SD[i] = D[s,i]$ for all i.

The crux of the algorithm is as follows. From s find the vertex x to which it has the shortest distance. Initially this will be one of the neighbors x to whom it has an edge having weight w which is the minimum of weights for all edges to its neighbors. Set $SD[x] = w$ and S = S∪{x}. The set S presents the set of vertices for which the shortest distances from s has been determined. Execute the following two steps until S contains all the vertices in the graph.

1. For each neighbor y of x with $y \notin$ S, check whether a path from s to y, passing through x, is shorter than the shortest path from s to y found so far. That is, for each y which is a neighbor of x, if $SD[y]$ (the current known shortest distance) is greater than $SD[x] + D[x,y]$, then $SD[y]$ is set to $SD[x] + D[x,y]$.
2. In the next step, among all vertices that are not in S, we determine a vertex x such that $SD[x]$ is the smallest. Set S = S∪{x} and go to Step 1.

At the end of the above execution the array SD contains the shortest distance from vertex s to every other vertex in the graph.

The number of times Step 1 and Step 2 are executed is exactly $n-1$, since during every execution of the above steps a vertex is added to S and the above steps are executed until all the vertices are added to S.

During the first iteration of the above steps, Step 2 takes $n-2$ comparisons to determine the x with minimum $SD[x]$ value. The second iteration takes $n-3$ comparisons and the ith iteration takes $n-i-1$ comparisons to determine the x with minimum $SD[x]$ value. Thus the total number of comparisons during $n-1$ iterations of step 2 is $O(n^2)$.

In Step 1, edges (x,y) are processed and since there can be at most $O(m)$ edges, the total complexity of the Dijkstra's algorithm is $O(n^2+m)$. But m can be at most $O(n^2)$ (when the graph is dense), so the total time complexity is $O(n^2)$.

The algorithm described above, as presented below, uses a minHeap to efficiently perform steps one and two.

```
ALGORITHM DIJKSTRA (V, s)
// V is the set of vertices, s is the source vertex
1.  Compute D array
// D contains distances from s to each vertex
2.  Compute SD array
// SD contains current shortest distance from s to each vetex
3.  Remove s from the set V
4.  for each vertex p∈\s// remove vertex s from set V
5.        Insert a vertex containing SD[p] and vertex number p
          as a vertex in the MinHeap
          pointer[p] points to the corresponding vertex in
          the Minheap
    // The MinHeap is based on the SD[p] values.
6.  endfor
7.  while the MinHeap is not empty
8.        x ← deleteMin (MinHeap)      // x is a vertex number
9.        for each neighbor y of x in the graph with w=D[x,y]
10.           if (SD[y] > (SD[x] + w))
11.               perform a change operation on pointer[y]
                  vetex in the MinHeap, where SD[y] value is
                  changed to SD[x]+w;
    // The array SD contains the shortest distance from s to
    // every other vertex in the graph.
12.           endif
13.       endfor
14. endwhile
```

In Figure 11.26 we illustrate the execution of Dijkstra's algorithm on the graph shown in Figure 11.25. The choice of x that results from deleteMin operation is also shown.

Steps	Distance from s as a result of choosing x
0. Initially, s=x={0}	0 1 2 3 4 5 0 10 11 99 99 99
1. x={1}	0 1 2 3 4 5 0 10 11 32 99 99
2. x={2}	0 1 2 3 4 5 0 10 11 19 17 14
3. x={5}	0 1 2 3 4 5 0 10 11 16 15 14
4. x={4}	0 1 2 3 4 5 0 10 11 16 15 14
5. x={3}	0 1 2 3 4 5 0 10 11 16 15 14

Figure 11.26: Each iteration of the Dijkstra's algorithm on the graph in Figure 11.26 is shown. Vertices that have been selected are shaded and the values that have been modified as a result of the choice of x are also shaded.

11.7   Minimum Spanning Tree

A minimum spanning tree of a weighted graph G is a spanning tree T of the graph with the sum of the weights of the edges of the tree T being a minimum compared to all spanning tree of the graph G. Our main goal is to construct a minimum spanning tree of a given weighted graph. Before we proceed to discuss the algorithm, we need a data structure that speeds up the implementation of the algorithm. This algorithm is called the disjoint union-find data structure which we will discuss next.

11.7.1   Disjoint Union-Find Data structure

The disjoint union-find problem deals with sets and their representation. Let the elements of the set be integers $0, 1, \ldots, n$. Each element i, $0<=i<=n$ will initially belong to the singleton set $S_i = \{i\}$. The two operations that are performed on the sets are:

Union (S_i, S_j) (Disjoint set union): Here elements of the set S_j are copied into the set S_i, and S_j ceases to exist. The new S_i now consists of elements from the old S_i and S_j. For example, if $S_1 = \{1,3,7\}$ and $S_5 = \{5, 6\}$ then Union$(S_1, S_5) = \{1,3,7,5,6\}$.

Find (i): Find the set containing the element i. For example, given S_1 and S_5 as in above (before the Union operation), Find(6) will return the set numbered 5.

A linked list representation of the sets will enable us to perform the above two operations. Each element will be represented as a linked list with (initially) a single node. The linked lists will be stored in an array. The *Union*(S_i, S_j) operation can be implemented by traversing the linked list headed by S_j to its last node, then pointing the *_next* field to the list headed by S_i. The reader will note that this means that multiple lists may all point to the same node.

As an example, we shall use nine integers, 0 through 8. Initially, each element is contained in a list having a single node (pointers to null are depicted as broken arrows):

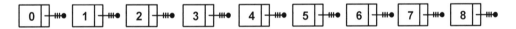

Figure 11.27:   Initial state when each element from 0 to 8 is contained in a list having a single node.

We shall perform this sequence of operations: Union (1,2), Union (5,6), and Union (7,8), producing this result:

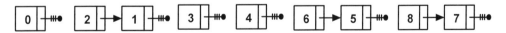

Figure 11.28:   This is as a result of Union (1, 2), Union (5, 6) and Union (7, 8) on Figure 11.27.

The current sets are $S_0=\{0\}$, $S_1=\{1,2\}$, $S_3=\{3\}$, $S_4=\{4\}$, $S_5=\{5,6\}$, and $S_7=\{7,8\}$. Sets S_2, S_6, and S_8 can be identified as no longer valid, since the _next pointers for those three lists are non-null.

After execution of Union (1,3) and Union (5,7), the sets take this form:

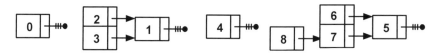

Figure 11.29:   This is as a result of Union $(1, 3)$ and Union $(5, 7)$ on Figure 11.28.

It is to be noted that Union $(5, 7)$ = Union (Find(5), Find(7)) = Union (Find(6), Find(8)).

Finally, Union (1,5) will produce the following result:

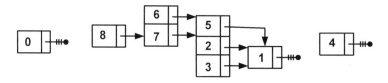

Figure 11.30:   This is as a result of Union $(1, 5)$ on Figure 11.29.

At this point, there are only three surviving sets: $S_0=\{0\}$, $S_1=\{1,2,3,5,6,7,8\}$, and $S_4=\{4\}$.

11.7.1.1 Class Definition

We can use the *LinkedList* class to produce a *DisjointUnionFind* class, using the above ideas. Linked lists will represent the sets themselves. What sort of data will the sets contain? The *DisjointUnionFind* set does not concern itself with that, so the data stored in the linked lists will simply be *Object*s. Our definitions of the sets S_i says it contains only integers, but this can be naturally extended to Objects.

To avoid overcomplicating this example, we will not declare a family of exceptions, but will silently handle them. The declaration of the family of exceptions and modification of the methods to use the exceptions are left as an exercise.

Fields, Constructors, and Destructors

Since linked lists represent the sets, we will need an array of linked lists. The constructors will need to create the array of linked lists for the sets, where the user specifies an array of elements for the values to be stored in the linked lists.

We already know that we will point the _next field of one linked list in the array to another linked list in the array, as diagrammed above. This necessarily implies that we cannot simply delete the linked lists, as the recursive deletion would attempt to delete linked lists out of the middle of the array. Our destructor must therefore begin by setting all the _next fields to NULL, and then delete the array of linked lists.

The initial declaration of the *DisjointUnionFind* class, then, is as follows:

```
template <class DataType>
class DisjointUnionFind
{
protected:
    ArrayClass<LinkedList <DataType>>* _sets;
public:
    DisjointUnionFind (DataType* ao, int count);
    virtual ~DisjointUnionFind ();
};
// -----------------------------------------------------------
template <class DataType>
DisjointUnionFind<DataType>::DisjointUnionFind
                (DataType* ao, int count)
{
    _sets = new ArrayClass<LinkedList <DataType>> (count);
    for (int i = 0; i < count; i++) (*_sets)[i].add(ao[i]);
}
// -----------------------------------------------------------
template <class DataType>
DisjointUnionFind<DataType>::~DisjointUnionFind ()
{
    if (_sets != NULL) {
        for (int i = 0; i < _sets->size(); i++)
            (*_sets)[i].setNext (NULL);
        delete _sets;
    }
}
```

Accessor Methods

We would like to be able to report the total number of elements in all sets, and the total number of distinct sets. We would also like to be able to report elements by number. The first and third of these methods are easily implemented:

```
template <class DataType>
int DisjointUnionFind<Object>::numElements ()
{
    return _sets->size();
}
// -----------------------------------------------------------
template <class DataType>
DataType& DisjointUnionFind<Object>::element (int index)
{
    return (*_sets)[index].info();
}
```

The second of the methods is a little more difficult. There are *_sets->size()* elements, but the only way to count the distinct sets is to count the number of linked lists with *next()* of NULL. Such lists represent the last element of a distinct set. The *numSets()* method is implemented in accordance with this discussion:

```
template <class DataType>
int DisjointUnionFind<Object>::numSets ()
{
    int count = 0;
    for (int i = 0; i < _sets->size(); i++)
        if ((*_sets)[i].next() == NULL) count++;
    return count;
}
```

Thus, in the last diagram above, repeated here for reference, count will be incremented for elements 0, 1, and 4, but not for the others. Thus, *numSets()* will return 3 for this case.

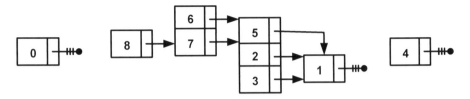

Figure 11.31:   Figure 11.30 repeated again for reference.

The find() *Method*

The *find()* method must return the index of the last element of the set containing the given element. Finding the linked list containing the last element is easy; we just follow the linked list of the given element until we reach a node with *next()* of NULL. Returning the index is more difficult, as we must locate that linked list in our array.

Since we are silently disregarding errors, how do we handle an element out of bounds? Such an element could be regarded as belonging to its own set, so we will just return the element index we were given.

```
template <class DataType>
int DisjointUnionFind<Object>::find (int element)
{
    if ((element >= 0) && (element < _sets->size()))
    {
      AbstractLinkedList<DataType>* LL = &((*_sets)[element]);
      while (LL->next() != NULL) { LL = LL->next(); }
        for (int i = 0; i < _sets->size(); i++)
            if (&((*_sets)[i]) == LL) return i;
    }
    return element;
}
```

The reader may wish to implement a version of *find()* which accepts an *Object* for the element and returns the last *Object* in the set.

The Union() *Method*

The Union() method[1] will accept the indices of two elements and join the sets to which they belong. This can be accomplished, as previously noted, by finding the last node of the linked list representing each element and then attaching one list to the other:

```
template <class DataType>
void DisjointUnionFind<DataType>::Union (int e1, int e2)
{
// silently ignore errors
    if ((e1 < 0) || (e1 >= _sets->size()) ||
        (e2 < 0) || (e2 >= _sets->size()))
            return;

// find the last nodes of each linked list
    int set1 = find (e1);
    int set2 = find (e2);

// do nothing if already in same set
    if (set1 == set2) return;

// attach set1 to set2; set1 is the surviving set
    (*_sets)[set2].setNext (&((*_sets)[set1]));
}
```

Enumeration of Disjoint Union Find Structure

We shall not implement an enumerator of the elements, as the user can easily use *numElements()* and *element()* to enumerate them. However, it would be helpful to provide an enumerator of the elements in a given set, and also an enumerator of the distinct sets. So we will provide two enumerators and will have to create two *Enumeration* subclasses. Finding the distinct sets requires only checking the linked lists, so we will just pass the *_sets* field to the *Enumeration* subclass responsible for distinct sets. Enumerating the elements will require the use of the *find()* method, so we must pass both the *this* pointer and the index of the required element.

---

1 The method name is *Union()*, not *union()* because *union* is a reserved word.

```
public Enumeration elementsOfSet (int element)
{
    return new DUFEnumElements <Object> (this, element);
}
// -------------------------------------------------------
public Enumeration distinctSets ()
{
    return new DUFEnumSets <Object> (_sets);
}
```

Enumerating the Distinct Sets

Enumerating distinct sets is actually fairly simple; we return the indices of only those vertices for which the linked list has *next*() of NULL. We will have a *next* field to indicate the next vertex which has not yet been returned or skipped over because its linked list does not have *next*() of null. So the DUFEnumSets class initially will be as follows:

```
template <class DataType>
class DUFEnumSets : public Enumeration<DataType>
{
protected:
    ArrayClass < LinkedList<DataType>>* _sets;
    int next;
public:
    DUFEnumSets (ArrayClass < LinkedList<DataType>>* sets);
    virtual ~DUFEnumSets () { };
};
// -------------------------------------------------------
template <class Object>
DUFEnumSets<Object>::DUFEnumSets
    (ArrayClass < LinkedList<DataType>>* sets)
{
    _sets = sets;
    next = 0;
}
```

The *hasMoreElements*() method advances *next* until it points to an element for which the linked list has *next*() of NULL, or until the sets are exhausted.

```cpp
template <class DataType>
bool DUFEnumSets<DataType>::hasMoreElements()
{
    if (_sets == NULL) return false;
    while (next < _sets->size())
    {
        if ((*_sets)[next].next() == NULL) return true;
        next++;
    }
    return false;
}
```

The `nextElement ()` method must advance `next` to a disjoint set, if it does not already index one, then must advance `next`, then must return the previous value of `next`, if `next` is in range. But `hasMoreElements ()` already contains the code to advance `next`, so we will just call it for that purpose.

```cpp
template <class DataType>
DataType& DUFEnumSets<Object>::nextElement()
{
// advance next to a disjoint set
    if (!hasMoreElements()) throw EnumerationException();
// get the index of the element - which is guaranteed
// to belong to a distinct set.
    int temp = next;
// advance so hasMoreElements will not look at this element
// again next++;
// return the element from the disjoint set
    return (*_sets)[temp].info();
}
```

Enumerating Elements of a Set

Enumerating the elements of a set containing a given element requires us to find all elements for which the last element of the linked list is the same as that of the given element. We can implement this along the same lines as the *DUFEnumSets* class, with a *next* field and a *hasMoreElements ()* method which is responsible for advancing the *next* field. We will also need a field that contains the value for the last element of the linked list for the given element, so we don't have to find it again each time. Implementation of the *DUFEnumElements* class is left as an exercise for the reader.

11.7.2 Kruskal's Algorithm

We will next show how the disjoint union-find data structure can be used to construct a minimum spanning tree of an edge-weighted undirected graph. The following illustrates a graph G and two spanning trees for it.

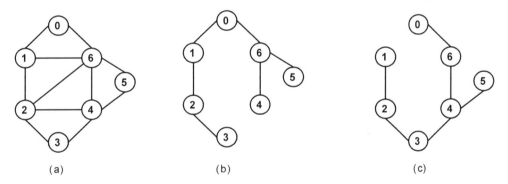

Figure 11.32: The graph G is shown in (a) and (b) and (c) are two spanning trees for (a).

If the edges of the graph are weighted, we can assign a weight to a spanning tree by adding the weights on the edges of the tree. Now the Minimum Spanning Tree problem is one of finding a spanning tree with a minimum total weight compared to all other spanning trees. In the following we present an algorithm due to Kruskal that finds a minimum spanning tree of a given weighted graph.

```
ALGORITHM MINIMUM-SPANNING-TREE (G, S)
// G is the graph S is the set of edges sorted on edge
// weights
1.   T ← create () // T will be the minimum spanning tree
2.   while S is not empty
3.       Remove first edge (u, v) from S
4.       Add (u, v) to T if it does not form a cycle in T
5.   endwhile
6.   return T
```

The key step in the Kruskal's algorithm that requires the use of disjoint union-find algorithm is detecting whether the new edge to be added to the tree forms a cycle. To implement this, initially we place each vertex u of the graph in a singleton set $S_u = \{u\}$. As an edge (u, v) is added to the tree T, we perform $Union(Find(u), Find(v))$. Before adding an edge (u, v), however, we test whether if $Find(u)$ is equal to $Find(v)$; if they are equal, adding the edge would produce a cycle.

Why is $Find(u) \neq Find(v)$ a sufficient condition to avoid a cycle? Initially each vertex is in a tree by itself, forming a forest of (disconnected) trees. Adding an edge (u, v) to T corresponds to finding the tree containing vertex u and the tree containing vertex v, and combining them. If both the vertices u and v already belong to the same tree, then adding the edge (u, v) will create a cycle in the tree; but if they already belong to the same tree, the sets to which they belong were, at some point, joined by means of the Union operation, so $Find(u)$ will be equal to $Find(v)$.

Example

Below are a weighted graph G and the sorted set of edges S. The edges are listed as (edge; weight).

Note that each edge appears only once even though the edges are undirected. We can achieve this result by scanning through the edges and adding an edge to the set only when the beginning vertex is less than the ending vertex.

The execution sequence for finding the minimum spanning tree using the disjoint union-find algorithm on the graph above is shown below.

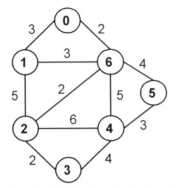

$$S = \{ (0, 6; 2), (2, 3; 2), (2, 6; 2), (4, 5; 3), (1, 6; 3),$$
$$(0, 1; 3), (5, 6; 4), (3, 4; 4), (1, 2; 5), (4, 6; 5), (2, 4; 6) \}$$

Figure 11.33:   A weighted graph with sorted set of edges S.

Figure 11.34:   Initial state when all the vertices belong to separate trees.

Initially, above, all vertices belong to separate trees. We will add the edge $(0, 6; 2)$, since adding it does not create a cycle in any tree in the forest of trees.

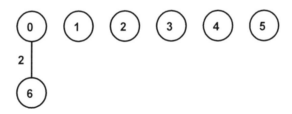

Figure 11.35:   Adding the edge $(0, 6; 2)$ without creating any cycle.

We can then add $(2, 3; 2)$ and $(2, 6; 2)$ without creating a cycle:

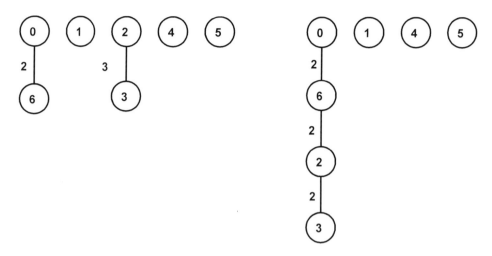

Figure 11.36: Adding the edges $(2, 3; 2)$ and $(2, 6; 2)$ without creating a cycle.

We can similarly add $(4, 5; 3)$ and $(1, 6; 3)$ without creating a cycle:

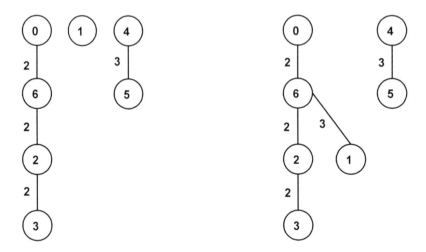

Figure 11.37: Adding the edges $(4, 5; 3)$ and $(1, 6; 3)$ without creating a cycle.

At this point, we have deleted five edges from set S, so set S is now { $(0, 1; 3)$, $(5, 6; 4)$, $(3, 4; 4)$, $(1, 2; 5)$, $(4, 6; 5)$, $(2, 4; 6)$ }. The next edge to be added is $(0, 1; 3)$. Unfortunately, adding edge $(0, 1; 3)$ will produce a cycle, as shown below. Therefore, edge $(0, 1; 3)$ is simply deleted from S, but not added to T.

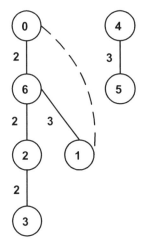

Figure 11.38: If edge $(0, 1; 3)$ is added it will produce a cycle as shown above. So this edge is deleted from S.

We now add the next remaining edge from S, $(5, 6; 4)$, producing the result below:

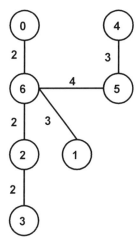

Figure 11.39: Adding the edge $(5, 6; 4)$ produces the spanning tree.

Since we now have a connected graph, no more edges can be added; any edge will produce a cycle. We have found the minimum spanning tree, with a weight of 16.

Implementation

Since finding the minimum spanning tree of a graph is obviously a graph operation, it might seem logical to add a method to the *AbstractGraph* class. However, such a method will be useful only in a weighted graph, and further should be used with an adjacency list. This suggests that the *WeightedDirectedGraphList* class should implement the method for finding the minimum spanning tree.

The *minimumSpanningTree*() method

The Minimum-Spanning-Tree algorithm took a set of sorted edges as input, but a method in the WeightedDirectedGraphList class obviously cannot expect the edges to be ordered and must sort the edges based on edge weights. In developing the *MinimumSpanningTree*() method, there are a number of different sorting algorithms which we could use, but for purposes of illustration here, we shall use a simple insertion sort. In a truly practical implementation, we would, of course, use a more efficient sorting method.

```
template <class VertexObject, class EdgeObject>
GraphList<VertexObject, EdgeObject>*
    WeightedDirectedGraphList<VertexObject,EdgeObject>::
        minimumSpanningTree ()
{
    int eCount = edgeCount();
        // so we don't have to keep finding edgeCount()
// ....................................................
// create the minimum spanning tree to be returned
// ....................................................
    WeightedDirectedGraphList<VertexObject, EdgeObject>* T =
        new WeightedDirectedGraphList<VertexObject,
            EdgeObject>(vertexCount());

// add the vertex data, if any
    for (int i = 0; i < vertexCount(); i++)
    {
        T->setVertexInfo (i, vertexInfo(i));
    }
```

```
    // create an array of edges, sorted by weight
    // .................................................
        WeightedEdgeContainer<EdgeObject>** edges =
        new WeightedEdgeContainer<EdgeObject>* [eCount];

    // initially, insert all edges into array, unsorted
        int curr = 0;
        for (int i = 0; i < edgeData->size(); i++) {
          if (!(*edgeData)[i].isEmpty()) {
            AbstractLinkedList< EdgeContainer<EdgeObject>* >*
                ll = &((*edgeData)[i]);
            while ((ll != NULL) && (!ll->isEmpty())){
                edges[curr] = (WeightedEdgeContainer<EdgeObject>*)
                                            ll->info();
            ...ll = ll->next();
            ...curr++;
            }
          }
        }
    // sort the edges by weight
        WeightedEdgeContainer<EdgeObject>* temp;
        for (int i = 1; i < eCount; i++) {
          int j = i;
          temp = edges[j];
          while ((j >=1) && (edges[j-1]->weight > temp->weight))
          {
            edges[j] = edges[j-1];
            j--;
          }
          edges[j] = temp;
        }
    // Add edges to T, using disjoint union find to check for
    // cycles
    // .................................................
        // elements of the set are the vertices
        int* pai = new int[vertexCount()];
        for (int i = 0; i < vertexCount(); i++) pai[i] = i;
        DisjointUnionFind<int> DUF (pai, vertexCount());
        delete pai;
```

```
    for (int i = 0; i < eCount; i++)
    {
        // check for cycles
        if (DUF.find(edges[i]->start) !=
                            DUF.find(edges[i]->end))
        {
// put vertices together in a set if they are joined by an edge
            DUF.Union (edges[i]->start, edges[i]->end);
// add the edge to the minimum spanning tree
            T->addEdge (edges[i]->start, edges[i]->end,
                    edges[i]->weight, edges[i]->info);
        }
    }
    delete edges;
    return T;
}
```

The following is a main function that calls the minimum spanning tree method. The input graph is initialized in the main function below.

```
#include "DisjointUnionFind.h"
#include "GraphList.h"

void main ()
{
        WeightedDirectedGraphList<int,int> g (7);

        g.addEdge (0,1,3);      g.addEdge (1,0,3);
        g.addEdge (0,6,2);      g.addEdge (6,0,2);

        g.addEdge (1,2,5);      g.addEdge (2,1,5);
        g.addEdge (1,6,3);      g.addEdge (6,1,3);

        g.addEdge (6,5,4);      g.addEdge (5,6,4);
        g.addEdge (6,4,5);      g.addEdge (4,6,5);

        g.addEdge (2,6,2);      g.addEdge (6,2,2);
```

```
                g.addEdge (2,4,6);      g.addEdge (4,2,6);
                g.addEdge (2,3,2);      g.addEdge (3,2,2);


                g.addEdge (4,5,3);      g.addEdge (5,4,3);
                g.addEdge (4,3,4);      g.addEdge (3,4,4);



                GraphList<int,int> * mst = g.minimumSpanningTree();


                cout << mst << endl;


                cout << endl;
        }
```

The output of the above main function is as follows:

```
T is Vertices: [(0), (1), (2), (3), (4), (5), (6)];
Edges: [(0,6) 2, (1,6) 3, (2,3) 2, (2,6) 2, (4,5) 3, (5,6) 4]
```

After the sorted array of edges is prepared, the actual creation of the minimum spanning tree is actually quite simple, requiring just a few lines of code — a tribute to the powers of object-oriented programming, since the three simple calls to *DUF.find()* or *DUF.union()* mask the extensive work involved in working with an array of linked lists.

11.8   Exercises

11.1. For the graph given below write down the adjacency matrix and adjacency list representations.

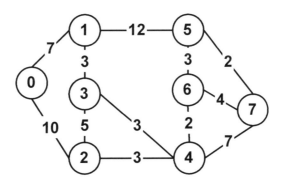

11.2. For the graph in Exercise 10.1 construct and perform the following:

   a) Construct a Depth first search tree starting from vertex 0.
   b) Construct a Breadth first search tree starting from vertex 0.
   c) Construct the Single source shortest path tree starting from vertex 0.
   d) Show all intermediate steps in the execution of the Dijkstra's shortest path algorithm.
   e) Construct a minimum spanning tree.

11.3. Write a constructor for the WeightedDirectedGraphMatrix class that accepts an instance of the WeightedDirectedGraphList class and constructs a corresponding instance.

11.4. Similarly, write a constructor for WeightedDirectedGraphList class that accepts an instance of the WeightedDirectedGraphMatrix class.

11.5. Write subclasses of the GraphMatrix class which implement the following graph data structures:

   a) Unweighted directed graph;
   b) Weighted undirected graph.

11.6. Write subclasses of the GraphMatrix class which implement the following graph data structures:

   a) Unweighted undirected graph;
   b) Unweighted directed graph;
   c) Weighted undirected graph.

11.7. What would be the worst-case time complexity for addition and deletion of a vertex in adjacency matrix and adjacency list representation of a graph?

11.8. Implement methods to add and remove a single vertex for the GraphMatrix class.

11.9. Implement the algorithm presented above for detecting strongly connected components.

11.10. Implement the algorithm presented in the textbook for performing a topological sort.

11.11. A spanning tree of a graph can be constructed using depth first search by keeping a parent array such that *parent*[*v*] of a vertex *v* is a node *u* that was visited during the invocation of the depth first search on u. Write a method to construct a spanning tree of a connected graph G.

11.12. Write a method to perform topological sort using the *postvisit* numbering mechanism presented in the textbook.

11.13. Prove that a connected directed graph G is acyclic if and only if the DFS() method previously presented does not encounter any node that has already been visited.

11.14. A connected undirected graph is "biconnected" if the graph cannot be made disconnected by the removal of any single vertex. If a graph is not biconnected, then a vertex is called an "articulation point" if the removal of that vertex causes the graph to become disconnected. Develop an algorithm which uses depth-first search to find all articulation points in a connected undirected graph, and runs in O(n + m) time.

11.15. Write a method to perform breadth-first search and assign breadth-first-search numbers to the nodes, for the adjacency-list implementation of graphs.

11.16. Implement the single source shortest path algorithm for the unweighted undirected graph presented in this chapter. Store the shortest path using the parent array discussed in the text. Write a method to list the nodes from the source S to a given node v along the shortest path.

11.17. An undirected graph $G = (V, E)$ if V can be partitioned into two disjoint sets V_1 and V_2 such that every edge in E joins a vertex in V_1 with a vertex in V_2. Develop an algorithm which determines whether an undirected graph is bipartite, and runs in O(n + m) time.

11.18. Write a method to implement the Dijkstra's shortest path algorithm, assuming that the graph is represented using the adjacency list structure. Make use to the heap class presented in Chapter 9.

11.19. The Dijkstra's shortest path algorithm will not work correctly if the graph contains negative-weight edges. Find a graph on which this algorithm fails.

11.20. The "diameter" of a tree is the maximum distance between any two vertices. Write an algorithm for finding a spanning tree of minimum diameter, given a connected, undirected graph.

11.21. Prim's algorithm for constructing a minimum spanning tree starts from an arbitrary root vertex r and grows until the tree spans all vertices in V. At each step, a minimum weighted edge connecting a vertex in A (the current tree) to a vertex in V-A is added to the tree. For the graph in Figure 10.31 and in Exercise 10.1, show the sequence of trees that will result during the execution of the Prim's algorithm.

11.22. Implement the Prim's algorithm, assuming an adjacency list representation of a graph. Note that the Dijkstra's shortest path algorithm can be easily modified to construct the minimum spanning tree.

11.23. Given a graph in which all edge weights are distinct, show that there exists a unique minimum spanning tree.

11.24. Prove or disprove that a single-source shortest path tree is also a minimum spanning tree.

11.9   References for Further Reading

Dijkstra, E.W., "A note on two problems in connexion with graphs", *Numische Mathematik* vol. 1, 1959.

Dijkstra, E.W., "Some theorems on spanning subtrees of a graph", Indagationes *Mathematicae* vol. 28, pp. 196-199, 1960.

Even, S., *Graph Algorithms*, Computer Science Press, Potomac, Md,, 1978.

R.W. Floyd, "Algorithm 97: shortest path," Comm. ACM 5:6, p.345, 1962.

Garsia, A. M., and Wachs, M.L., "A New Algorithm for Minimum Cost Binary Trees", *SIAM Journal of Computing* vol. 6, no. 4, Dec. 1977.

Goodman, S. E., and Hedetniemi, S.T., *Introduction to the Design and Analysis of Algorithms*, McGraw-Hill, New York, 1977.

Harary, F., *Graph Theory*, Addison-Wesley, Boston, 1969.

Hwang, F. K., and Lins,S. "A Simple Algorithm for Merging Two Disjoint Linearly Ordered Sets", *SIAM Journal of Computing* vol. 1, pp. 31-39, 1972.

Kruskal, J.B., "On the shortest spanning tree of a graph and the traveling salesman problem", *Proceedings of the American Mathematical Society* vol. 7, pp. 48-50, 1956.

Kruskal, J.R., Jr., "On the shortest path spanning subtree of a graph and the traveling salesman problem", *Proceedings of the AMS*, vol. 7, no.1, pp. 48-50, 1956.

Maurer, H.A., and Ottmann,T. "Tree Structures for Set Manipulation Problems", in *Mathematical Foundations of Computer Science*, J. Gruska (ed.), Springer-Verlag, New York, 1977.

Moret, B and Shapiro, H., "An Empirical Assessment of Algorithms for constructing a Minimum Spanning Tree", *DIMACS Series in Discrete Mathematics*, vol. 15, pp. 99-117, 1994.

Tarjan, R. and Leeuwen, J., "Worst case Analysis of Set Union Algorithms", *Journal of the ACM*, vol. 31, no. 2, pp. 245-281, 1984.

Tarjan, R.E., "Depth-first search and linear graph algorithms", *SIAM Journal on Computing* vol. 1, no. 2, pp. 146-160, 1972.

Van Leeuwen, J. and Tarjan, R.E., "Worst-case analysis of set-union algorithms", *Journal of the ACM* 1986.

Warren, H. S. "A Modification of Warshall's Algorithm for the Transitive Closure of Binary Relations", *Communications of the ACM* vol. 18, no. 4, Apr. 1975.

Index

Made in the USA
Coppell, TX
22 July 2021

59297057R00453